Books by Eric F. Goldman

THE TRAGEDY OF LYNDON JOHNSON

THE CRUCIAL DECADE

RENDEZVOUS WITH DESTINY

THE WORLD'S HISTORY (*co-author*)

JOHN BACH MCMASTER, AMERICAN HISTORIAN

HISTORIOGRAPHY AND URBANIZATION (*editor*)

CHARLES F. BONAPARTE, PATRICIAN REFORMER

THE TRAGEDY OF LYNDON JOHNSON

The Tragedy of
Lyndon Johnson

by Eric F. Goldman

 1969 *Alfred A. Knopf, New York*

Published February 10, 1969
First and Second Printings Before Publication
Third Printing, May 1969

FOREWORD

Soon after the assassination of President Kennedy, President Johnson asked me to undertake an assignment. A little later I was given the title of Special Consultant to the President and a White House office, and I continued to work as a member of the White House staff until my resignation in the fall of 1966, a period totaling two years and about nine months.

During the early stage of this association, I had no thought of writing a book about my experiences or the Johnson Presidency. The intention took shape gradually. The LBJ Presidency as a human story was proving intensely interesting to me. Moreover, only the most cloddish person could work in the atmosphere of the White House without a considerable heightening of his sense of responsibility to his nation. More and more, the Johnson Presidency appeared to me not only an intriguing tale but the center of things being done and said—some by the President and some by his critics—which were thoroughly disturbing. In many respects Lyndon Johnson was about as American in make-up as any man we have had in the White House. Much of the response to him had the same authentic ring—and neither was particularly glorious. A person who worked in the vortex during the period might conceivably contribute something to an understanding of the United States of the 1960's—and thereby, in some small measure, to an improvement in the national condition—by writing about the LBJ years with whatever insight he could command. At about the midway point of my service in the White House, I decided that I would undertake a book after I left the staff.

My first plan was to write a relatively brief volume, placing within a historical framework certain points about Lyndon Johnson and his Administration that seemed to me significant and helpful. But as I went ahead with the actual writing I became convinced that brevity would bring lack of balance. Enlarging the task carried my work on the book into the year 1968 with its spectacular rapid-fire of political events—the challenge of Senator McCarthy, the withdrawal of President Johnson, the murder of

Senator Kennedy and the onrushing election itself. None of these affected the substance of the manuscript. From the beginning, it had been written from a point of view and with a purpose largely removed from such eventualities. In particular the new developments did not alter my interpretation of Lyndon Johnson; they seemed to me to confirm it. Yet they did cause me—out of considerations of taste and perspective—to go over the manuscript in the light of recent circumstances.

The volume that emerges is, in a basic respect, history. It treats most of the main events of the LBJ Presidency during 1963–1966, when I was in Washington, and it connects this period with the remaining two years of the Johnson Administration. Yet the book is as much in the tradition of the memoir as of history. In many instances, the allocation of space and of emphasis are determined not by the relative significance of occurrences but by my own interests and firsthand knowledge.

The volume rests on the kinds of sources, printed, manuscript and oral, to which a historian naturally turns, and of course on the knowledge resulting from my service in the White House. Although many of the facts come from within the Johnson circle and the interpretations are heavily influenced by my own period in the White House, this is not an "insider's book," at least in the meaning often given to the phrase. I was not an LBJ "insider" in the sense that I was an intimate of President Johnson, or was regularly called upon by him to help determine domestic and foreign policies of great moment. I simply worked in the White House, was part of its life and its atmosphere, dealt with the President and First Lady when the task called for it and sometimes saw them on social occasions, knew and functioned with the people around them, and inevitably heard a great deal of what was going on in connection with matters big and small.

This is not an "insider" book in another, quite different and quite deliberate sense. People have long argued whether public figures, by virtue of that fact, have surrendered their private lives; they have also differed over what may be revealed with propriety concerning men or events still involved with important and intense national problems. The reader and I will understand each other much better if I state my views, whatever their validity, on these two points.

It is my opinion that public figures do surrender their private selves insofar as their personal lives significantly affect what they do in their public capacities; beyond that, they should be granted as much privacy as anyone else. Consequently, I have excluded all personal material which in my judgment does not directly bear on an attempt to increase the reader's understanding of Lyndon Johnson the President, his Administration and their relationship to the public.

Concerning the second point, I think that a writer on contemporary affairs, who happens to have been in a position of special knowledge, should particularly bear in mind the responsibilities of citizenship in a free society. He should avoid the "revelation" that serves no important purpose of illumination but mainly titillates and sensationalizes. Nothing appears in this book which was placed there for the purpose of catching a headline, and a good many incontestable and perhaps significant facts that are borderline cases have been omitted on the basis of the same criterion. The restriction has been applied with particular severity in the realm of foreign affairs, which in the 1960's affect the security and repute of all of us and directly involve the lives of other people's sons.

Of course, essential to any good history or memoir is the venerable triad of rules: to respect the facts enough to keep burrowing for them, especially when they confound your preconceptions; to care enough about your subject to express judgments clearly, vigorously and, if necessary, in a way that may antagonize; and withal, to exercise restraint on yourself so that what you call history or memoir is not an emanation of your own prejudices and self-interests but a work which makes an honest and sustained effort to deserve that fine old adjective, *fair*.

When I began writing this book, I was bothered by that word. President Johnson had made publicly plain his dim view of me, and certainly he would not have been my choice for a fishing trip. In the numerous telephone calls from the mass media which followed my resignation and in subsequent conversations with friends and others I kept sensing the licking of chops—this would be a book to "get" LBJ. My discomfiture was the greater because the manuscript was being written during widespread revulsion from Lyndon Johnson, an emotion that was especially intense in my natural circles. I wondered how much genuine objectivity I could bring to the manuscript.

Yet the more I proceeded with the book, the less I felt the difficulty. I came to believe that President Johnson, the people with whom he was associated and the events that swirled around him presented the same problem of objectivity as any work of historical interpretation—about the same and really not much more. Some of the most opinionated, biased, ideology-ridden and ego-lashed histories have been written by eighteenth-century authors concerning ancient times, nineteenth-century writers on the eighteenth century, twentieth-century writers about anything. It seemed to me a question of how much you want to use history or memoir to flay your own devils and advance your own causes, and the degree to which you resist the abundant opportunities. I have tried to stand firm guard, and I leave to the reader the judgment of the extent to which I may have been successful.

Each statement of fact or quotation in this book is supported by detailed documentation. I plan to place my notes in a library where, after an appropriate interval, they will be open to all serious students of the era.

No doubt the reader of the present volume will be annoyed, as I am embarrassed, by the frequent references to participants or sources of information only as an "old friend of President Johnson's," "a White House aide," etc. Naturally I would prefer to name the man. But in these instances the person was close to President Johnson and spoke or wrote to me, or showed me a document, with the explicit or implicit understanding of anonymity. Even when no such understanding existed, I am sure that identification of most of these people would disturb their relationships with Lyndon Johnson, and I do not care to do that. Many individuals outside the immediate LBJ circle were also of major assistance, by providing information or in a variety of other ways. Again, to mention some of them could create unfortunate situations; yet to include a partial list would be invidious. The customary acknowledgments for the use of copyrighted material appear on the copyright page, and at the end of the volume I have expressed my appreciation to the people who granted me permission to quote from various types of their unpublished writings. Apart from these mentions, I am omitting public thanks to a far larger group who were exceedingly generous in their gifts to this book. They and I know what they did, and I have conveyed my appreciation privately.

One particular acknowledgment, happily, I can speak out—to President and Mrs. Johnson, who gave me an opportunity to contribute what I could to the national life. I went to Washington an individual whose personal experiences had brought him the strong sense that the United States, with its bedrock credo that ordinary men and women have a right to peace, material comfort, self-respect, and a touch of joy in living, is a very special nation, "the last best hope of earth," as the best of us once said, worth any song that anyone cares to sing to it and equally deserving of the most persistent effort and the most relentless criticism to make it what it could be. Whatever the abrasions of my period in Washington, I left the White House with that sense not diminished but deepened. The American credo has gone through many periods of debilitating trauma, and none more so than during the LBJ years. Yet again and again it has reasserted itself in powerful catalytic form within the national mind and conscience. This book has been written with a continuing excitement in the sheer decency of the achievements of the American credo and with the abiding conviction that it will sweep on performing its wondrous and warming works, beyond Presidents who do not fulfill their promise, even beyond the falterings of the rest of us.

E.F.G.

Princeton, N. J.
November 12, 1968

CONTENTS

THE TRAGEDY OF LYNDON JOHNSON

CHAPTER 1

Call from
the White House

On my way home for dinner one night in December of 1963, I ran into a friend and stopped off with him for a drink at the Nassau Inn in Princeton. Mostly we talked about the latest developments in Washington; it was just ten days after the assassination of President Kennedy. The bartender answered the phone, asked, "Mr. Goldman? Mr. Goldman?" and handed the instrument over to me. "It's your home—they say it's urgent."

The call did have a certain urgency. A White House operator, it seems, had telephoned to alert me that I was about to be called by the President.

I hurried the five blocks home. Amid a confusion of clicking and operators, the voice came on, heavy and tired but outgoing and warm. After a few pleasantries President Johnson went speedily to the point. He didn't believe he had ever met me—no, Mr. President, I have not had that privilege—he wanted to talk with me, and could I manage to come down to Washington very soon?

It was a cluttered week for me but people have a way of making the time to go talk with the President of the United States very soon. The appointment was arranged for two days hence, Wednesday, December 4, 1963, at 11:30 A.M. And with that, while I was thanking the President for the invitation, the connection broke. I made no effort to restore it. I too had been reading about the endless LBJ telephoning, which no doubt overwhelmed even the White House switchboard.

Intriguing as the call might be, it did not come entirely as a surprise. In the course of teaching modern American history at Princeton University, I had met Richard H. Nelson, of Norfolk, Virginia, a sharp-minded, energetic young man with an offbeat sense of humor and a full quotient of his generation's puzzlement about what to do with their lives. Graduating from Princeton in

1961, Nelson went to work in Washington as an assistant to Bill D. Moyers, then the No. 2 man in the Peace Corps and a key figure in the circle of Vice-President Lyndon Johnson. About eighteen months later, through the entanglements of the LBJ entourage, Nelson was assigned to the Vice-President's office, serving as a youthful jack-of-all-trades. At Princeton I had taught Nelson only in a large lecture course and did not know him well. Our chief personal contact had been a conversation in which we discovered a mutual enthusiasm for H. L. Mencken's comic sense and his mastery of the American language, however inane some of the things Mencken could say. But one day Nelson had spoken generously about me to the Vice-President, and Mr. Johnson had expressed a desire to meet me. Shortly before the assassination of President Kennedy, Nelson phoned and we agreed to arrange an appointment in the near future. Now, through a grisly quirk, the meeting was to be not with Vice-President but with President Johnson.

Traveling down to Washington, I had other reasons to reflect on the accidents of life. Obviously the appointment might lead to some kind of work for the President. If it did, I—who had been as little connected with government as anybody in the United States—would be entering Washington in the strange and rarefied air at the top. My activities outside the university had been oriented toward the writing world; unlike many professors, I had never been associated in any way with government at the federal, state or local level. I was a Democrat but not a particularly partisan one, and I wrote and voted as an independent liberal. My one political stint came in 1962 when the liberal Republican Senator Jacob K. Javits of New York read an article of mine on the G.O.P. in *Holiday* magazine and asked me to help with advisory work and speech writing during his re-election campaign against a relatively conservative Democrat. Except for an occasional research trip, I had not visited Washington since boyhood. As a matter of fact, I was so little Washington-wise that I proceeded to make a reservation for my night's stay before the appointment with President Johnson in a hotel which was near the White House but which turned out to be a relic of the Woodrow Wilson era. I slept fitfully, amid half-dreams of the wise things I was going to say to the President and of animal life marching across the bed.

Next morning, the guard at the Northwest Gate of the White House greeted me knowingly and directed me to the Press Lobby in the West Wing, where Nelson, making his way through reporters sprawled in chairs, came forward to meet me. He seemed bone-tired and harassed; I was getting my first impression of the pressure-cooker chaos of the Johnson White House.

Nelson took me through the Press Lobby, then to the right to the long rectangular "Sherman Adams office," so called because it was the staff command room in the Eisenhower days. As I learned later, the office was one of the few areas taken over in this early period by the Johnson men, who had been given the word not to appear to be elbowing out Kennedy staff members. Desks, tables and people crowded the room. Nelson introduced me to his boss, Walter W. Jenkins, who sat at a heaped desk at the far end, interrupting our conversation several times for lengthy low-voiced talks on the phone with the President. At this first meeting, Jenkins, except for his frenzied busyness, seemed like nothing so much as a small-town clerk; he appeared utterly incongruous in the role of a top-ranking aide to the most important leader in the world.

Nelson and I made our way down the hall to the Cabinet Room, which is separated from the Oval Office of the President only by a small area for the personal secretaries. The schedule was running late, and additional people kept being sandwiched in for a word with President Johnson. One of these impromptu visitors brought a sudden aura of the LBJ world. The veteran Texas Congressman Wright Patman emerged from the President's office and I remembered reading that when the youthful Lyndon Johnson left for his first term in the House of Representatives, his father had advised him, "If you don't know how to vote, watch my friend Wright Patman."

While we were waiting, Nelson and I sat in the Cabinet Room chatting somewhat stiffly. In the Johnson White House, it was clear, staff members did not make mistakes lightly. Friendly as he was to me, Nelson did not entirely escape the air of a fight manager wondering nervously whether his man was really going to live up to his billing. At one point he looked at me with a fidgety grin. "I guess you have some things ready to say?"

"Yes, I do. But I'm not at all sure they're appropriate. Do you have any idea why the President wants to see me?"

"I think he just wants to meet you, to talk with you."

When my turn came and Nelson took me into the Oval Office, I was struck by the atmosphere. President Johnson had begun using the room the day after the funeral of President Kennedy. Now, eight days later, it was as if one man had been removed from the office and another had not really occupied it.

The elaborately carved oak desk made from timber of H.M.S.

Resolute, the tiny water colors painted by Mrs. Kennedy for her husband, the copies of the carriage lamps that hung in Boston's Old North Church to signal Paul Revere—these and other things so associated in the mind of the newspaper reader with JFK were all gone. They were replaced by few personal LBJ objects, little more than a photograph of his daughters, another of President Kennedy and himself, and a small bust of Franklin Roosevelt. As President Johnson and I exchanged amenities, my eye must have gone to a rocking chair that very much suggested the other man. "Had it brought over from my house," President Johnson said hastily. "Very comfortable" (and so it was, a skillfully padded rocker designed for Vice-President Johnson by the White House physician, Dr. Janet G. Travell, at about the same time she prepared the famous chair for President Kennedy). In a curious way, the most personal note in the room came from some smoothed-over scars in the floor near the door leading to the Rose Garden. Later I discovered that these were neither JFK nor LBJ; the markings had been made by the spikes on the golf shoes of President Eisenhower when he headed with his clubs for the White House grass.

President Johnson appeared extremely tired, but he did not stint the outgoing words and gestures. This was a man, just as the press had been saying, who made the extra effort to please, whatever the occasion. As Nelson moved to a side chair, the President smilingly motioned me to the position which would soon be so familiar in photographs: LBJ in his rocker, the visitor on a short sofa placed at a right angle.

He did not take the lead in the conversation, and I suddenly had a feeling I might be in his office only because he wanted to please an able young aide. Nevertheless, there was a point I wanted to make, and I decided to make it. I did not know why he had asked to see me, I said to the President, but I certainly had no desire to waste his time with polite conversation. With his permission, I would like to express a particular thought to him, one that I would state as a historian and which might be of some help to him in thinking about the general context of his Administration.

President Johnson looked at me sharply, removed his thin plastic-rimmed glasses and nodded a go-ahead.

I plunged in. Historically speaking, every so often the United States has gone through a period of serious division in public opinion, not so much over specific policies but as a result of general attitudes. Americans lined up on opposite sides with conviction and emotion. Such was the case in the years after World

War II, and in this particular period the clash was the more serious because there were two areas of conflict, one in foreign and one in domestic policy.

In foreign policy, the conflict came from the Cold War. Generally speaking, it was marked by the split between those who accepted coexistence with the Communist powers and those who did not. In the domestic field, the division resulted from the decades of reform which had taken place in the United States, and the current civil rights agitation was only the climactic part of this development. Here the basic issue was between those who were ready to go along with the economic and social democratization of the United States and those who were not.

Whenever such a conflict had developed in the past, sooner or later a strong President appeared and found a set of policies and a tone which substantially bridged the divide in public opinion.

I stopped, embarrassed at talking so much. President Johnson was jiggling his glasses from one hand and his eyes had narrowed into hard slits. I wondered whether these were signs of impatience or of interest. "But Mr. President," I said, "I don't want to subject you to a history lecture."

"Go on," he replied with a quick grin. "I can use a history lecture."

Bill Moyers had entered the office, and after we were introduced, sat to one side, saying little, intent and tight-faced.

I went on. Faced with such situations, past Presidents had drawn the country together by calling upon the doctrine of the national interest. They advocated policies and pushed legislation which represented what a variety of significant groups had come to agree upon, or substantially to agree upon, or could be persuaded to agree upon. These Chief Executives were careful to preserve a relatively nonpartisan and nonideological tone and to emphasize the Office of the Presidency as "the steward" of the needs and aspirations of the general population, to use a phrase of President Theodore Roosevelt, who had brought the country out of the divisiveness of the 1890's.

It was important to do this, I added, because a too-sharply divided nation was an immobilized nation, incapable of carrying out a coherent foreign policy or of meeting the demands of the domestic scene. A President who effectively identified himself with the national interest was in a position to lead away from the stale, obstructive emotions associated with past divisions— in the 1960's, away from the doctrinaire liberalism and conservatism carried over from the 1930's—toward the kind of attitudes that met changed circumstances. In the 1960's, in foreign affairs, this could mean leadership from Cold War to post-Cold War think-ing. At home, the President could clean up what the millions knew to be essential unfinished business, such as action directed toward educational needs, the legitimate restiveness of the Negro, and the dangerously mounting costs of medical care. Moreover, in both the domestic and foreign areas this approach, by taking care of what obviously should be done in the present, would clear the air for fresh thinking about the hopes and possibilities of the future.

Now I was sure that President Johnson was listening beyond the requirements of politeness. His long face was fixed on me and he would interject an occasional "Yes." But I was more un-comfortable than ever at talking so much and I hurried to my conclusion.

In recent years Presidents Eisenhower and Kennedy, each in his different way, had performed something of this role. Yet there was still a long way to go. President Johnson, by virtue of the circumstances surrounding his taking office and what I under-stood to be his natural bent, was in a peculiarly good position to complete the process for the 1960's. It could be a proud historic function of the Johnson Administration if, in its first phase, it were to join the select group of Presidencies which have moved the country solidly ahead and opened avenues to the future by providing a consensus leadership. Later it could push forward, as some other consensus Administrations had done, to a different role.

The President made no direct comment on what I had said, and we drifted into general conversation. As I became more com-fortable talking to him, I was also more aware of Lyndon Johnson the human being. Television, strange instrument, has its favorites, whom it somehow shows at their best, but it also has its stepchil-dren, and television had certainly done nothing for this man. It caught little of the sheer physical force emanating from him, the handsomeness, in its own way, of the strong-featured, weathered face, the nuances that came in looks, gestures and intonations of the drawl.

At one point in our rambling talk, President Johnson asked me to send him my suggestions concerning how he ought to handle presidential press conferences. Later he inquired what major con-cerns I thought would be coming up. I replied that our cities, now heading for such disarray, appeared certain to be a prime prob-lem. I added that the suburbs in the metropolitan regions seemed to be producing a new type of American—restless, educated, public-spirited and realistic—who would be particularly helpful to him in any nonideological effort to bring about genuine solutions.

President Johnson nodded agreement but his mind was obviously elsewhere. "The cities, yes," he murmured. "They are something I am going to have to learn a lot about."

More conversation and I glanced at my watch. I had been taking forty-five minutes of the President's time. I rose to leave but he motioned me to sit down again and leaned back in his rocker, looking off toward the garden outside.

"You know how I came to be in this room," he said. "I don't know how long I will be here. As long as I am the President, I have one resolve. Before I leave, I am determined to do things that will make opportunities better for ordinary Americans, and peace in the world more secure. But I badly need help—I badly need it. And I especially need the help of the best minds in the country."

For perhaps a minute he went on in the same vein, several times using the phrase "best minds"—a favorite of his, as I was to learn.

Now President Johnson was on his feet, pacing slowly around the office and ticking off details. It was important, he declared, to form a group of these best minds to suggest goals and specific programs for the Administration. Would I undertake to form such a group?

As I said, "Of course, Mr. President," he scarcely paused. There was no money to pay the men—his hand went up in a gesture of fending off any such idea—and it was essential, absolutely essential, that the whole procedure be carried out in total secrecy. Again and again he stressed secrecy.

After a few more words it was clearly time to go. The President's good-bye was warm with flattery. As Moyers and Nelson introduced me to the secretaries outside, Moyers, with remarks about "very interesting, very important," took over. The next step, he said, was for me to lunch with Walter Jenkins, Nelson and himself. He disappeared momentarily and Nelson and I headed toward the basement of the West Wing, where the White House Mess is located (this glistening clean, incredibly efficient restaurant is called the Mess because the Navy, to its unsung glory, operates it). "Dick," I asked as we walked along, "did you expect anything like that?"

"No, I certainly did not. You can't tell what is going to happen once you get in there with him. He makes decisions fast."

Around a corner table in the Mess, with the Filipino waiters performing their discreet, impassive service, Jenkins, Moyers, Nelson and I worked out details. That morning Walter Jenkins may have seemed like an incongruous small-town clerk; now it was abundantly clear that he, of all the President's aides, was the chief of staff. He spoke with the confidence of a man who was sure he understood what was on the President's mind and who had wide authority to act for him. It was equally clear that, in his quiet way, Walter Jenkins was highly intelligent, decisive and dedicated.

We agreed that I would begin work immediately on a suggested group of the "best minds." Jenkins, joined by Moyers, stressed that they should represent the West and South as well as the North and East. The next move would be for Jenkins' office to determine whether there was any reason—security or otherwise— why a particular individual should not be picked. Then I would get in touch with the men chosen and begin work with them as individuals. In a short while the group would be brought to Washington for a meeting with the President and a one- or two-day working session. Throughout the conversation, Jenkins reiterated the importance of keeping every aspect of the operation confidential and we were all soon referring to the group as the "quiet brain trust."

Late that afternoon, as I boarded the train for Princeton, all kinds of questions were churning through my mind. What did President Johnson really know about me and my work, apart from young Nelson's enthusiasm? Could it be—as I later discovered to be true—that some of the President's senior aides had read my writings and liked them? Had the President planned—provided that I passed muster when he met me—to ask me to undertake the organization of the group, or did he act on impulse? Was he seriously interested in the "best minds," or was this merely a move he felt politically wise in view of President Kennedy's appeal to the intellectual community? If so, what was the reason for the fetish about secrecy, and did he actually believe that the group would remain unknown?

Questions there might be but meanwhile, for better or for worse, until something did us part, I was a Johnson man, with a presidential instruction that could prove of high moment or end up a quixotic nothing.

CHAPTER 2

JFK, with a Difference

Several days later I went back to Washington, planning to confer with Walter Jenkins about a preliminary list for the brain trust and to return to Princeton that evening. But I did not return that evening; in any real sense, I never returned during the two years and nine months that I was part of the Johnson White House. Once in that vortex, I found it impossible to do much of anything else or to get away from Washington except for brief trips. There were always more and more White House tasks, many of them having little or no connection with the brain trust, which I was asked to do or which seemed very much in need of doing.

By coincidence, at this time I was on leave from my university duties to finish a book about a 1911 lynching of a Negro which had occurred in a decidedly Northern community, Coatesville, Pennsylvania, a one-time Quaker center thirty-eight miles west of Philadelphia. I had been drawn to the episode, a particularly revealing one, by a growing conviction that the Negro question was being discussed too much in terms of the South and that it was equally, and perhaps more critically, involved with the Northern social structure. As the focus of the race problem shifted North during the period of my White House work, my mind often went back to this manuscript and I wished I had been able to finish it. But now my life was far removed from historical writing.

Continuing to maintain my home in Princeton, I took an apartment in Washington, partially meeting the added expense by the government per diem I was now receiving. My first work space was the less cluttered end of a table in Walter Jenkins' office, amid more of his long low-voiced phone conversations with President Johnson, the rushing in and out of aides who sought a moment of Jenkins, and the appearance of people for conferences who— when I read my Washington *Post* the next morning—turned out to be new high-level appointees. After a few weeks Jenkins, who was as much in need of space as I was of peace, arranged an office for me in the adjoining Executive Office Building, which was used for the White House overflow.

Back in the 1890's a number of architecture critics lavished glowing adjectives on the Executive Office Building, with its French Renaissance redolence and its outbursts of mansards, cupolas, balusters, newels and lacelike iron balconies. In 1958 President Harry Truman expressed one of his more accepted aesthetic dicta when he demurred at letting EOB be torn down because "it's the greatest monstrosity in America." Whether the building was monstrosity or masterpiece, going to work in it was an experience.

Originally constructed between 1871 and 1888 to house the old combined State, War and Navy Department, it had gone through fourteen changes in name and as many different uses. Its "Indian Treaty Room" on the fourth floor, a large area with a slab of verd marble from the excavation of Pompeii over its entry, a brightly tiled floor, sculptured lighting fixtures and a balustraded balcony made from Mexican onyx, had been the scene of the signing of the post-World War II treaties with Bulgaria, Hungary, Italy and Rumania, of emergency meetings on an enormous variety of national problems, of years of presidential press conferences—in fact, of all kinds of events except the signing of Indian treaties, a name which apparently was the fancy of some newspaperman. The second-floor office which had been assigned to me was part of a suite occupied during World War I by Secretary of the Navy Josephus Daniels and his Assistant Secretary, Franklin D. Roosevelt; in the 1920's by General of the Armies John J. Pershing when he served as Army Chief of Staff and while he was writing his memoirs; and in 1929–30 by President Herbert Hoover after a fire damaged the White House. The remnants of ripped-out heavy communication lines in my office were a memento of the most recent occupant of the suite, Vice-President Lyndon Johnson, and it was from here that President Johnson took over during the weekend when John Kennedy was buried.

As I came to know the White House itself, just across a narrow, closed, carefully guarded street, I was struck by the duality of its atmosphere. More than any building in America, the White House has an aura of ageless, impersonal continuity, of a serene monument that stands while Presidents come and go. Its immutable personality is accentuated by the famous reminders all around you of transient occupants, whether the bronze inkstand inscribed "T. Jefferson, 1804" or the fireplace in the Diplomatic

Reception Room before which Franklin Roosevelt delivered his Fireside Chats. On the other hand, no building more quickly takes on the added tone of the particular situation represented by the particular man who for a time occupies its central Oval Office.

Shortly after the assassination of President Kennedy, shrewd old Congressman Clarence Cannon had made a prediction: "Everything will be Kennedy for a while. Then people will forget." The congressman had history to support him. Up to 1963, of the seven American Presidents who were assassinated or who died from natural causes while in office, two were major figures. Lincoln, although the subject of a great deal of immediate sentimentality, did not become the unassailable Abraham Lincoln of the schoolbooks until two decades after his murder. Franklin Roosevelt, idolized and reviled while alive, went on being idolized and reviled, with the proportions only partially changed. In 1968, twenty-three years after FDR's death, Washington still had no building in his honor.

But history, in addition to repeating itself, has a way of spinning off into strikingly different patterns. Congressman Cannon was wrong. In the early weeks of the Johnson Administration the newspapers were beginning to use the words "the Kennedy legend," and the phrase was entirely appropriate. Alone among American Chief Executives, President Kennedy was passing from life to apotheosis with no interval of critical evaluation.

By some measurements, the brief thirty-five months of the Kennedy Presidency had scarcely been a conspicuous success. The term began with the Cuban Bay of Pigs, and then the Administration had made little progress in finding a stable non-Communist formula for South Vietnam. Three weeks before the assassination at Dallas, a military coup in Saigon was accompanied by the murder of the South Vietnamese President, Ngo Dinh Diem. Arthur M. Schlesinger, Jr., recalls seeing President Kennedy "somber and shaken. I had not seen him so depressed since the Bay of Pigs. No doubt he realized that Vietnam was his great failure in foreign policy. . . ." In domestic affairs, at the end of the Kennedy Administration its big four legislative proposals—civil rights, tax reduction, Medicare and federal aid to education—were all still without congressional approval.

President Kennedy's caution in handling civil rights had brought widespread criticism. Administration actions at the time of the steel price rise—and the President's quotation of his father's opinion that businessmen were "sonsofbitches"—had angered a considerable segment of the conservative community. The JFK youthful following, at first so enthusiastic, had become restive.

In its last issue before the assassination, *Time* magazine, having surveyed the colleges, generalized: "Campus disenchantment with President Kennedy now spreads far and wide." In the month before Dallas, the Kennedy general-approval rating in the polls, at one time as high as 83 per cent, was down to 59 per cent. An inner group of JFK men who met to plan for the 1964 election had additional worries. President Kennedy had just visited Philadelphia, the kind of big Northern city he had to carry heavily in order to win, and been given the poorest reception since he entered the White House.

By some measurements, John Kennedy had been no shining leader—but there were other ways of remembering the murdered President. For millions of Americans, the brutal assassination was muting faults and questionings and bringing to the fore the distinctions of the Administration. People forgot the Bay of Pigs and remembered the courage and intelligence of the eyeball-to-eyeball victory over Khrushchev in the missile crisis. They brushed aside Vietnam and recalled the relaxation the Administration seemed to have brought in East-West tensions, the Nuclear Test Ban Treaty it had negotiated, its mounting effort to move beyond weary Cold War dogmas. The key domestic legislation might remain unpassed; it had the ring of the times, and it was JFK and his men who had conceived the measures. If the President had been leery in civil rights, he had also moved far and fast enough to enrage the South—so much so, many were sure, that his pro-Negro stand had contributed to the atmosphere which brought about his murder. The youthful, who so easily become restless with anyone in power, remembered now that John Kennedy had been theirs, born to the twentieth century, close to their attitudes and manner. Young or old, people were thinking not so much about government policies as about John Kennedy the human being and the human beings around him, and a hundred engaging memories crowded back.

The emotions were magnified by a unique setting. Seven previous Presidents may have died in office, three by assassination, but no other President had been cut down in the appealing vigor of his mid-forties. None had been buried to four days of haunting television, or left behind a large, talented, copiously endowed family with intense ambitions for the memory of their departed leader and for themselves.

None had been succeeded by a man so well structured to encourage the legend of his predecessor. For years Lyndon Johnson had been a power in national politics, for six years the most potent Senate Majority Leader in American history. But he had functioned largely behind congressional doors, and the country had little real impression of him; what Americans vaguely knew, and what they were being told by the news media, roused little enthusiasm.

Throughout the post-World War II period, the American public, whatever its temporary moods, had shown a marked tendency to move down the general path of liberalism in domestic affairs, and in foreign affairs to seek the knowledgeability, moderation and flexibility which would make coexistence with Communism possible. In 1963 people sized up their new President and they wondered. Lyndon Johnson's real instincts in domestic affairs? Probably those of a wheeler-dealer out of the Southern Democratic tradition who believed few things very strongly, and who in the case of his genuine convictions tended toward a conservatism modified merely by a sense of where the votes lay. That particularly worrisome area, foreign affairs? Did the new President know much about foreign affairs? Did he really much care?

And Lyndon Johnson was from Texas, that state which had so special an ability to provoke snickers and outrage from the other forty-nine states. To millions, Texas was an outsized collection of Boasters, boomsters, millionaire ignoramuses, violence worshippers and fanatic right-wing enemies of the United Nations, social security, free lunches for poor children, and other decencies which Western civilization had managed to construct over the decades. Now Lyndon Johnson, a Texan of the Texans, was succeeding a President who had been gunned down in that most Texan of cities, Dallas.

All of this played its part in heightening the Kennedy legend but it was probably not the heart of the story. Public figures establish their place in the popular mind not so much by what they are but by a conjunction between what they are and what is sought. To an extraordinary extent, the memory of John Kennedy represented one of these conjunctions of history. He was the almost perfect man for an emerging era.

In 1893 the Wisconsin historian Frederick Jackson Turner pointed out that, for all practical purposes, the frontier was closed. The period of the frontier American was over; the day of the town and city man was at hand. No one Turner appeared in the 1960's to proclaim the coming of still another epoch but the fact of a new era was plain. The leadership of the town or the merely urban American was waning. More than one half of the population of the United States now lived in the sprawling metropolitan areas. Here the poor of the central cities might remain the city poor. But in the upper-income city neighborhoods, and particularly in the suburbs, a new and influential type was emerging, the Metroamerican.

Relative to the rest of the country, this Metroamerican was youthful, educated, affluent, more likely to have some minority blood in his veins. His mind had been shaped by an environment which had been good to him. It was no less formed by an American scene of aggravating big organizations, brassy media and grinding social dislocations, and by a world situation of wars and threats of still worse wars. His thinking and his attitudes were a tangle of ambivalence. The Metroamerican was avidly on the make, economically and socially, but he shied away from the appearance of sheer moneymaking or sheer caste and preferred the manner of public-spiritedness and cultivation. He had ideals but was skeptical of other people's—and even, a bit, of his own. He was liberal but without ideology; tolerant but intolerant of do-goodism; flexible, pragmatic and a devotee of the ironic edge.

The Metroamericans, Republicans as well as Democrats, had voted heavily for John Kennedy in 1960. During his Presidency they did their share of grousing, but when he was killed what he meant to them came back with tremendous force. In the glow of their memories, almost everything about JFK seemed just right— whether the fact that he was a minority boy who made it to the White House, his cool liberalism, his throw-away wit or his cultivation of the graces. The criticisms they themselves had expressed now turned into ways by which they felt identified with him. Had they complained that much of the Kennedy family money was made in decidedly uninhibited operations, that JFK politics could be rough-handed, that the Administration was not long on achievement, that the Kennedys were acting extraordinarily patrician for people just fifty years from Grandfather Pat Kennedy's brogue and corner saloon? Exactly—that was their kind of America, the America they lived in and which, like John Kennedy, they intended to conquer. As for national achievement, the point was not a lot of blunderbuss action but the sophisticated, informed approach, and in time the right actions would follow. Jackie Kennedy—and what Metroamerican did not want to be told his wife resembled Jackie?—had put it right when she said of her husband that he was an "idealist without illusions," "an activist who does not worship action."

Metroamericans were abundantly numerous, articulate and powerful, and they were especially important in determining national attitudes because of their dominance in the world of books, magazines, radio and television. Without Metroamericans, the Kennedy legend would have been potent; with them, it was a pervasive factor in American life.

Lyndon Johnson was now President of the United States and the most powerful man in the world. But he was the President, and the most powerful man in the world, with a heavy shadow over his White House.

If the shadow affected the whole public view of the new Administration, it also fell across the day-by-day operations of the White House. In the strongest possible terms President Johnson urged the entire Kennedy staff, up and down the line, to stay on. Not only was his own group sparse; he needed the JFK people because of their knowledge of what had been going on and he needed them no less out of obvious considerations of good taste and politics. On their part, the Kennedyites could hardly say no to the plea of a man hurtled into the responsibilities of the Presidency. During the early period of the new Administration virtually all the JFK people remained and functioned amid the smaller number of new faces. This White House was a sharply divided house. There were "Kennedy men" and "Johnson men," and in a number of cases they worked in awkward, wary apartness.

Most JFK people, particularly at the higher level, found the situation emotionally tearing. Almost all Presidents evoke intense loyalty from their aides; a few, something quite beyond. These men had not only admired John Kennedy as President but had been entranced by him as a human being and had found a good deal of the excitement and of the meaning in their own lives through their feeling of closeness to him. They were bereft, almost numbed, at the abrupt and bloody end to their idyll. Kenneth O'Donnell, the JFK Appointments Secretary and roving politico, customarily so self-possessed, said, "Every day I get up, I hope to feel better. But I don't, not yet. All I can think of is that I was lucky to have known the guy at all." Daniel P. Moynihan—"Pat" Moynihan, the brilliant Assistant Secretary of Labor who was a part of the JFK circle—sat in my apartment, tears in his eyes. With his touch of Irish grandiloquence, he exclaimed, "Nothing, nothing at all will ever be the same for me, for any of us who knew what it was like."

Hardest hit of all was Theodore Sorensen, the chief JFK aide and a man whose sense of himself had been so entwined with John Kennedy that, as White House people said, he not only wrote to the President's rhythm but thought, talked and waiked like him. Soon after I arrived in Washington I went to see Sorensen to talk over ways of tying in the work of the new brain trust with previous projects. Sorensen was an utterly drained man. He made an effort but obviously could not bring himself to do much retracing of tracks that now seemed so bleak. I left soon.

Some of the Kennedy group were not only bereft but bitter and vicious, patently frustrated by their waning power and glory. The Constitution of the United States may provide that if the President dies in office, the Vice-President will succeed him; to JFK men of this type, Lyndon Johnson was a usurper, and an ignoble one at that. They snickered and sniped, half performed their tasks, engaged in petty sabotage, busily plotted for the day when a Kennedy and they could take back the White House.

They found it unthinkable that a true Kennedy man would work for Lyndon Johnson beyond the amenities of the transition period. McGeorge Bundy, the White House Special Assistant for National Security Affairs, had been a Kennedyite of the Kennedyites, but by background and inclination he also had something of the British career man's attitude that the undersecretaries go on regardless of changes at the top. From the earliest LBJ days, Bundy was clearly establishing a long-term, if not radiant, working relationship with the new President, and more than a few forked tongues in Kennedy Washington hissed at "that turncoat Bundy."

Many Johnson aides also had strong feelings. John Kennedy and Lyndon Johnson had both gone after the Democratic presidential nomination in 1960 with few holds barred, and it was the Johnson men who had to take defeat. Then they went through the three dismal years of the Vice-Presidency, with their chief thrashing about in "this lousy job," and he and they listening to persistent reports of Kennedy people laughing at "Uncle Cornpone," of Kennedy parties brightened with the question, "Say, whatever happened to Lyndon?" and of gay plannings how best to dump Lyndon Johnson from the 1964 ticket. Their special anathema was Attorney General Robert F. Kennedy; they felt sure that he had opposed Lyndon Johnson as the vice-presidential candidate in 1960 and had persistently tried to undermine his activities as Vice-President. Nor did they forget that after John Kennedy had won the nomination in 1960, he gave his brother a cigarette case inscribed, "When I'm through, how about you?" and they did not believe the words were simply a family joke.

Apart from this festering background, there were firmly held convictions in the present. To most LBJ men, JFK and his group were a band of clever, opportunistic sophomores who had taken on a man's job and settled for a patina of style. Robert Kennedy as an enlightened public leader? A one-time supporter of Senator Joseph R. McCarthy, they snorted; then an Attorney General who could manhandle civil liberties; always a gut politician, Boston-style, and a practitioner of self-righteous ruthlessness and self-aggrandizement. For RFK they had their own dinner-party remarks: "The perfect model of the liberal fascist," "Rover Boy, without birth control," "For God and country—in that order, after the Kennedys."

Each faction had its anecdotes, which may or may not have been true, and which it told with scathing disdain. Each also had its undeniable, unpleasant facts, which it generalized unfairly into a total characterization. In such an atmosphere, anything could be misinterpreted, by either group.

On the evening of his return from Dallas, the new President, arriving at his EOB office, asked an aide to get him two pieces of presidential stationery. The assistant went to the nearby room of a Kennedy aide, who handed over the sheets with eyes flashing. "The body not cold yet—and he's grabbing for the President's stationery." Lyndon Johnson wanted the paper so that his first letters as President of the United States would be handwritten notes to Caroline and John Kennedy, Jr.

The LBJ aide who had gone for the stationery added a comment when he told me the incident: "You see, we're just one big happy family."

To put any man in the Oval Office under these circumstances would have had its consequences. To put Lyndon Johnson there was to loose a phenomenon.

At the age of fifteen Lyndon Johnson heard that four Johnson City boys were heading West in a jalopy. They said he was too young for the trip. He insisted on going, and taking his turns at the wheel, drove the longest stretches and the fastest speeds. At the age of twenty-two Lyndon Johnson was the debating coach at the Sam Houston High School. He tutored, lashed and wheedled his team to the state finals, sat in agony while the judges conferred and when the vote went 2 to 1 against Houston High, "I got sick to my stomach." In his fifties Lyndon Johnson discovered bowling. He studied the stance of the players, fired a series of questions about technique, threw the ball with enormous force, knocked down seven pins. A friend said, "Pretty good for the first time," and Lyndon Johnson glared at him. In the next frame, he adjusted his position carefully, took meticulous aim, knocked down all ten pins; thereafter he merely tolerated a spare. As President of the United States, Lyndon Johnson did not lose his pride, his vanity, his cascading competitiveness. For years he had dreamed of being President of the United States. He had never doubted that he could be a great one. The more he heard of the "great John Kennedy," the more he was driven to be "the greatest of them all, the whole bunch of them," as he remarked.

In scores of other ways, little and big, the power of the Kennedy legend was showing its goading effects on the new President. The more Lyndon Johnson heard the cultivated Kennedy from Harvard compared with his boorish Texas self, the more he held himself back on occasion, at other times deliberately exaggerated Lyndon Johnson from Johnson City, drawl, boisterousness, banality and all. The more he heard of the hold of the Kennedy legend on the public, the more he determined to win the election of 1964 by a roaring landslide that would make the 119,000-vote victory of 1960 seem like a pathetic peep. Above all, the more he was pressed in upon by JFK, the more eager he was to place the LBJ stamp on the Administration, just as fast—and maybe a bit faster—than circumstances and the amenities would permit.

The problems were mountainous. In the twentieth century, when the Oval Office has been the center of so much power and pressure, four men have gone through the overnight transition from Vice-President to President: Theodore Roosevelt in 1901, Calvin Coolidge in 1923, Harry Truman in 1945 and Lyndon Johnson. In the easygoing 1920's Calvin Coolidge simply minced ahead with small thoughts and small decisions. Theodore Roosevelt and Harry Truman, taking action on real and formidable issues, at least had almost full terms to make their impressions on the public before they faced a presidential election. Lyndon Johnson was allotted a little more than eleven months—the shortest span in American history for a former Vice-President seeking to win the Presidency in his own right. Onrushing were complex and critically important documents for a modern Administration. The 1964 State of the Union address had to be delivered when Congress reconvened, and Congress was scheduled to open forty-seven days after the assassination. The Budget Message could be delayed, at the most, several weeks beyond the State of the Union address.

"When you have something to do," declared Lyndon Johnson, "don't sit there. Do it, and do it fast." His congressional office had always been hard-driving. Mrs. Johnson, watching the sharply heightened pace in the White House, was moved to one of her soft-mannered observations about her husband. "Lyndon," she said, "acts as if there is never going to be a tomorrow."

The new President worked what we were all soon calling the "two-shift day." He was up at six-thirty or seven and, still in his bedroom, went over the schedule with an aide. This first shift often ended about two o'clock when he left the Oval Office, perhaps for a walk or a swim before lunch. Then he put on pajamas for a nap, usually on a couch in the small sitting room adjoining his office. By four o'clock he was showered and freshly clothed. "It's like starting a new day," he said, and so it was. The new day would end at midnight or at one or two o'clock in the morning, the LBJ principle being that you stayed up working until you were too tired to do any more. And sometimes the two-shift day turned into an unbroken fourteen or sixteen hours.

One night Mrs. Johnson, falling asleep while her locomotive husband still plunged ahead in the Oval Office, tacked a note to his pillow with some firm words about not omitting that nap in the afternoon. Mrs. Johnson was a White House figure of no small influence; the President made an effort to follow the firm words, sometimes did. At about this time President Johnson sent John McCone, head of the Central Intelligence Agency, to brief Dwight Eisenhower on world affairs and to seek his general counsel. The former President replied in writing and added a page on the subject of health. As another veteran of a heart attack, he commented, he knew well how hard it was to lead a regular life in the White House. But he had listened to the doctors, tried to follow a sensible schedule and remain relaxed, and he very much hoped the new President would do the same. Generally, Lyndon Johnson had the highest regard for Dwight Eisenhower's advice; he did not relax.

Shortly after the Johnson Administration began, the digit imperialists of Bell Telephone scored their greatest triumph. The White House number changed from NAtional 8-1414 to 456-1414 (the fifth change since 1878, when the "Executive Mansion" was assigned its first number, a magisterial 1 for a hallway booth outside the President's office), and if the digits added their alleged efficiency, it was certainly needed. President Johnson was annoyed by all the talk about his telephonitis. He used the instrument, he insisted, just about as much as any other busy man. The President was so addicted to the phone that he simply did not realize how much he lived by it. Often he awoke reaching for the receiver, and on many an evening he went to sleep just having hung up. Even his limousine had three instruments. One guest came away bedazzled by the LBJ telephone techniques; he swore that the President was able to talk on all three at once while carrying on a conversation in the car, not to speak of occasionally telling the driver how to beat the traffic.

The presidential tempo pounded up and down the White House. If Lyndon Johnson drove himself, his top aides regularly worked a twelve-to-fourteen-hour day, left the office half expecting a return summons on the two-way auto radio, reached home wondering when the special telephone directly connected to the White House would ring. If the President was perpetually on the phone, all true Johnson men, it seemed, had long since developed three arms, two for living and one for telephoning. The White House Mess, which had imperturbably watched so many Administrations come and go, was shaken. An LBJ aide had his first bites of food, the mobile white phone would be brought over to his table and he was off, to return ten, twenty or sixty minutes later for a final gulping or not to return at all. One day I sat down to eat with a key assistant, and the Filipino waiter, taking the order, asked him, "Do you think you would like it now or maybe?"

The White House corridors were witnessing the emergence of the LBJ trot. For some Johnson men, physique presented its difficulties. In Jack Valenti, small and wiry, and Bill Moyers, young and slim, the LBJ trot reached its perfection. It was a forward movement—the face intent, the hand full of papers—which was controlled enough to avoid bowling over people and headlong enough to register total commitment.

The long, furious hours of the President himself were devoted to everything in the White House, minuscule as well as monumental in significance. Lyndon Johnson went over guest lists for social functions name by name; he checked the equipment for White House cars; he would go walking around the building poking into things. Once when a secretary had left her desk stacked high, she returned the next morning to find a note: "Neatness counts too. J." Day and night the President intervened in matters big and small that were supposedly in the hands of subordinates.

All of this produced an enormous amount of work. It also combined with the double layer of LBJ and JFK men ("I don't know who the hell to call," a nabob accustomed to dealing with the White House growled. "It's like Noah's Ark. There's two of everybody") to create some of the most monumental confusion in all the none-too-tidy administrative history of the White House. One sparkling winter morning I received three red-tagged "Rush" memos in my inter-office mail. The first two discussed a particular anti-poverty project and based their main points on two lengthy office conferences which had been held the day before, with no knowledge on the part of either group that the other one was meeting. The third concerned a different matter but, in a casual aside, mentioned that the anti-poverty project had been vetoed three days before.

A little later I fell into conversation with a veteran administrative staff member. (The White House has a number of administrative civil service employees who do not change with elections.) With the asperity of too many years and too much familiarity, he offered a description of each of the White house atmospheres since World War II: "Under Truman it was like a small town around here—as friendly and as nasty. With Eisenhower it was cold and sleepy. Under Kennedy it was half the Irish third ward and half as frisky as I guess a Harvard cocktail party is. Now my friends say it's a Texas county courthouse moved North. I don't know about that, but I'll tell you one thing"—his sigh was heartfelt—"it's one hell of a whirl."

Whirl it may have been, but behind it all was a plan. However pell-mell some of Lyndon Johnson's habits, there was nothing careless or hectic about his approach to any important matter. "I'd rather be slow and right," he remarked with his most emphatic drawl, "than smart and dead." He liked to go at the big considerations "feelin', smellin', knowin'," trying out the alternatives on the largest army of outside advisers since the FDR days and on people as different as the doggedly conservative Robert Anderson, the Eisenhower Secretary of the Treasury, and the spirited liberal Abe Fortas. From these disparate sources came not a blueprint— LBJ's mind does not work in symmetrical patterns—but a kind of jelling of judgment.

Not unnaturally, the plan started with the problem of the John Kennedy legend. Lyndon Johnson had mixed feelings toward his predecessor. He was not only goaded but irritated by the tremendous waves of JFK sentiment which washed back on him so forcibly; he grinned appreciatively at the remark of his friend Harry Truman that it was fine to honor a dead President but he hoped the emotion would not reach the point of renaming "every pup and kitten." Lyndon Johnson had been put off by some of John Kennedy's "airs." Generally, he thought him ineffectual as a senator and no illustrious Chief Executive, certainly not in a class with Franklin Roosevelt and Harry Truman. He could readily do without a number of the JFK entourage, most especially those "overbred smart alecks who live in Georgetown and think in Harvard."

But the new President, like most people who had dealt directly with John Kennedy, had rather liked him as a human being. He was profoundly shocked by the murder, and emotional as he was, lived uncomfortably with the awareness of the youthful widow and the two small children. More than most of his aides, Lyndon Johnson had controlled his bitterness at the loss of the nomination in 1960 and at the Kennedyite attitude toward him while he was Vice-President. An old pro, he knew the necessity of rolling with defeat, and he was keenly aware that if some JFK men had sniped at him while he was Vice-President, John Kennedy himself—who was sensitive to his awkward position—never did.

The new President saw strong points in his predecessor's career. As a senator, he had proved himself "something more than a playboy politician" by backing the compromise provision which made passage of the 1957 civil rights bill passable at a time when the JFK political situation did not make this the expedient move ("If they want to look for that courage they talk about, they ought to look there"). As President, John Kennedy was notable for "a lot of the damn smart men he surrounded himself with in the Cabinet and on the staff," for the legislative program he devised "even if he did not know how to pass it," and for some "necessary toughness" in foreign policy.

Whatever President Johnson's complex of feelings, he saw only one possible way of handling the JFK-LBJ situation. After all, the country had voted for a presidential candidate, not for the other name on the ballot, and he was now rightly expected to carry on the main lines of his predecessor's program. After all, the Kennedy legend was a fact, with its refraction of strongly favorable light on the policies associated with John Kennedy, and Lyndon Johnson had not made his way from Johnson City to the White House by an indifference toward facts.

Consequently, the LBJ plan assumed that for a while the essential guide to action would be the demands of the transition period. He must make plain his respect for the memory of John Kennedy, which he deeply felt, and adopt another attitude which did not come so easily, humility. A world and a nation wondering whether he would carry out the JFK policies, foreign and domestic, must be swiftly and thoroughly convinced. He had to work away at getting rid of the tag of the wheeler-dealer with mossback tendencies and present himself as the broadly liberal leader, attuned to the politics of modernity. To help create this picture, special attention would be given to winning the confidence and affection of groups which had long been stand-offish toward Lyndon Johnson: labor, Negroes, intellectuals and those whose minds generally fell into the Northeastern pattern of thinking.

The main effort would go to domestic affairs. While taking every opportunity to dramatize his interest and his competence in foreign affairs, the new President hoped that he could hold world relations largely in their existing situation, and above all, that he could avoid crises. Calling upon the emotions generated by the assassination, using to the hilt his special relationship to Congress, he would attempt to get the House and Senate to enact quickly the major legislation proposed by the Kennedy Administration. At the same time, that other prime activity would go ahead—putting an LBJ stamp on the Administration.

The nature of the LBJ stamp was strongly influenced by a conviction of the new President. The JFK campaign of 1960 had been deeply affected by a belief that the 1960's was a period when the American people were ready to break away from Eisenhower-type lethargy. John Kennedy had campaigned on the slogan of getting the nation moving again. When he won, he sent the progressive legislation to Congress, but Congress balked at much of it. In the later stage of the Kennedy Administration many of its leaders concluded that in fact the country was not in the mood for significant change. This reading, President Johnson was convinced, had been inaccurate. The country was ready—but there are ways and ways of seeking to translate such a mood into legislation.

Ever since his days in the House of Representatives, Lyndon Johnson had been increasingly persuaded that the liberal advocates of economic and social reform made a fundamental error. Once when he was Senate Majority Leader, he expressed this attitude vigorously in a memorandum to Arthur Krock, then chief of the Washington Bureau of the *New York Times*. "The basic mistake the present-day 'liberals' have made is to equate liberalism with spending the public's money. They have fallen into a trap set by the Republican party. . . . As a result, the public has gained the impression . . . that a 'liberal' is a man who wants to reach into the hip pocket of the American public and extract as much money from the wallet as possible." The costs of liberal legislation, he stressed, should be balanced by constant attention to legitimate demands for economy and by an attitude that the liberal really appreciated the value of a dollar. The failure to do this, he was sure, was a fundamental reason why liberal legislation aroused so much antagonism in the business community.

The failure to do this was also a reason why liberals frequently left Lyndon Johnson cold. The Johnsons may have entered the White House a wealthy family—the fortune was estimated at from $4–$14 million by friends or foes—but this money was not viewed in any parvenu spirit of we've got it, let's spend it, or with any patrician attitude that the money is there, let's assume it. The Johnson fortune was middle-class money, avidly made and covetously retained. Long-time Johnson employees remembered wryly how hard the congressman had always been on the subject of a raise. Now the White House staff was learning how careful the President and First Lady were with a dollar, public or private. One of the stories visitors to the Oval Office heard frequently was about the early days of Lyndon and Lady Bird Johnson's marriage when he made $267 a month and, by God, they had put $18.75 a month, and sometimes more, into government bonds. On official trips as First Lady, Mrs. Johnson usually rode in commercial planes, and the reason was only partly to please the airlines. As her husband said, "A buck is a buck, in the family or over there in the Treasury Building."

The continuance of JFK, the colorations of LBJ—the eerie last days of November 1963 gave way to a more normal December, December settled into January. But always the White House moved to the drumbeat of action, action, action.

Some of the action was a muting process. Lyndon Johnson kept trying to present himself as the grave, dignified President, humbly walking in the footsteps of John Kennedy. The shiny-silk senatorial suits were replaced by subdued herringbone; the drawl was usually low and somber. Riding back to the Dallas airport on the day of the assassination, the new President had been accompanied by an aide, Mrs. Elizabeth S. Carpenter, who came out of her daze long enough to realize that he would have to make a statement to the press when he landed in Washington. She scribbled a few words: "This is a sad time for all people. We have suffered a loss that cannot be weighed. I will do my best. That is all I can do. I ask for your help—and God's." Lyndon Johnson used these words for his first presidential message. He liked the tone and tried to continue it. In urging the major Kennedy aides to remain on the staff, he kept saying, "I need you more than President Kennedy did," and "I'm the only President you've got." He helped see to it that the expressions were widely quoted.

Other actions consisted of decisions which could have been minor but which were to prove anything but minor as the Administration went on. Scandals involving hundreds of thousands of dollars, vending machines and call girls were breaking around

Robert G. Baker, thirty-six, the short, fox-faced whiz-bang from Pickens, South Carolina, he of the blue fedora and the overcoat lined with lavender silk, who had been Senate Majority Leader Johnson's prized assistant and who had just hastily resigned as Secretary to the Senate majority. Influential LBJ advisers urged President Johnson to repudiate Baker promptly and thoroughly with a statement to the effect that he had trusted and been fond of this bright young man and was sorry he had turned bad. Lyndon Johnson decided against the advice and said nothing.

The new President also had to determine the disposition of the Johnson family property, including the core holding, the multi-million-dollar radio-television station KTBC in Austin and its affiliated operations. Here again some intimates urged prompt and total disassociation, and they were persistent. They argued that since KTBC enjoyed a monopoly in the Austin area, and since radio and television were regulated by a federal agency, any continued connection of the Johnson family with the station would prove a fertile source of criticism. But the President had an especially influential adviser in this matter. Mrs. Johnson had purchased KTBC largely with funds from her inheritance and had personally built the station from a ramshackle enterprise to a flourishing property. Her mind was on the facts that the Johnsons would go on being the Johnsons after the White House days and that she had two daughters; she did not want to dispose of KTBC. President Johnson put most of the family holdings, including the station, in a trust, and they could be taken back once he left office.

More and more, often planned and controlled, often simply irrepressible, the LBJ touches were coming. Partly they were manner; more basically they were a determination to get his plan rolling. President Johnson was moving to win over to himself both the liberal coalition, so attached to the JFK memory, and the conservative business community, which JFK could never really claim.

Shortly before Dallas, President Kennedy had made an announcement of great emotional significance to liberals. The celebrated physicist J. Robert Oppenheimer, his security clearance revoked by the Eisenhower Administration, was to be given partial vindication by being awarded the government-sponsored Fermi Prize—and by receiving it from the hand of the President himself. Conservatives stirred angrily. Liberals asked, Would President Johnson go through with the personal presentation?

He did, and handsomely, standing in the Cabinet Room flanked by his Secretaries of State and Defense and pointedly paying tribute to Oppenheimer's "high standards of achievement" not only in producing the atomic bomb at Los Alamos but "since the war." All of us grieve, he went on, that President Kennedy could not present the award, but he personally felt "great pleasure and pride" in substituting on this occasion. Then, a Johnson ad lib: "Behind every great man there must be two great women—a great mother and a great wife." Calling Mrs. Oppenheimer forward for applause, President Johnson said, "You may have observed she got hold of the check."

Liberal intellectuals winced at Motherhood and hail-fellow humor about wives and money. But they did not overlook Oppenheimer's remarks in accepting the prize: "It is just possible, Mr. President, that it has taken some charity and some courage for you to make this award today. That would seem to me to be a good augury for all our futures."

For the liberals, a moment of vindication; for the business-minded, a thrust toward governmental economies. Within a few days of the Oppenheimer award, President Johnson sent a memorandum to the heads of federal departments and agencies which began: "I have pledged that the Executive Branch will be administered with the utmost thrift and frugality." That seemed to be par for the course; all Presidents, especially at the beginning of their terms, are for thrift and frugality. But the next words in the memo were ones that no aide had concocted. They were authentic LBJ, a phrase used by him for many years: "The Government will get a dollar's worth for a dollar spent." As the words were repeated in conversation and speeches, and as they were accompanied by action, it became clear that Lyndon Johnson actually meant to do something about spending.

Well over half the budget of the United States was absorbed by military costs. The President and Secretary of Defense Robert S. McNamara went into frequent huddles and out came the order: twenty-six defense installations in fourteen states were to be shut down or curtailed, and seven overseas bases were to be closed. Secretary McNamara added, "We have just scratched the surface."

Shortly after the order, the banker Edwin P. Neilan, president of the United States Chamber of Commerce, visited President Johnson. Emerging from the talk, he told the television cameras what a fine thing the closing of the military installations was and how many businessmen "approved of the way Mr. Johnson has taken over his job." Of course the president of the Chamber of Commerce was a Republican, and reporters wanted to know what all this meant in terms of 1964. "I don't always vote a straight ticket," said Edwin Neilan.

Hour after hour, interspersing the visitors between anything, Lyndon Johnson saw people, particularly people who meant something in that business world or that liberal coalition. He saw them individually, in small groups, in full-blown receptions—on the one day of December 4, at White House affairs for both the ninety-nine-man Business Council and thirty-five members of the executive council of the AFL-CIO. The receptions, at times televised, showed the dignified and humble successor to John Kennedy, and something else too. For the first time, the national audience was seeing Lyndon Johnson as a virtuoso in handshaking. He revealed himself equally adept at shaking one person's hand with both of his, shaking two people's hands at the same time, shaking a hand while patting an elbow or a shoulder, and using the handshake to move someone along in a reception line. Watching the fervor that LBJ managed to get into any of the varieties, the awed television critic of the *New York Times* was reminded of the great passing quarterback of the pro football New York Giants. "The President," Jack Gould wrote, "can only be described as the Y. A. Tittle of handshakers; he does not let go until the last minute."

Above all, President Johnson was pressuring Congress, in the name of JFK ("President Kennedy fought hard for this legislation. No topic was closer to his heart") and in the manner of LBJ.

Much of this intense effort was given to laying the groundwork for later passage of major Kennedy bills. But President Johnson was also pushing for immediate action on other legislation. By mid-December, bills were trickling through, most notably three Kennedy-sponsored measures connected with education: the Higher Education Facilities Act, substantially increasing the funds for colleges and universities and for loans to students; the Vocational Education Act, for the first time making federal money available to construct vocational schools; and amendments to the Manpower Development and Training Act, expanding federal aid in this field.

In speaking of the bills, President Johnson repeatedly gave the credit for them to his predecessor. But there were constant flashes of LBJ. The laws were signed at crowded, jostling gatherings in the White House, and the ancient pen ceremony achieved new dimensions. In the case of the Higher Education Facilities Act, the President, husbanding his signature, went through the first forty pens without using up "Lyndon B. Johnson," and Jack Valenti hurried off for more. For the three bills, he managed a record one hundred and sixty-nine pens.

Former Senate Majority Leader Johnson did not neglect praise and joviality for congressmen, or an occasional spur. At the signing of the amendments to the Manpower Development and Training Act, he singled out for lavish tribute Senator Joseph S. Clark of Pennsylvania, who had been a sharp critic of the LBJ leadership in the Senate. He gave Clark a pen with a warm "You're the *y* in Lyndon." Then, turning to Speaker John W. McCormack, he observed with a chuckle, "A bill a day keeps the President away."

The rough one lay just ahead. During the immediate post-assassination period, opposition tactics were noticeably softened in Congress but not in the case of the House Republican Leader Charles A. Halleck, who was the chief figure in a coalition of Republicans and Southern Democrats. The sixty-three-year-old warhorse from Jasper County, Indiana, dedicated to political ideas just left of King George III, was going after JFK-LBJ legislation relentlessly. Halleck picked as his prime target the foreign aid bill which President Kennedy had sent to the Hill. His technique of obstruction was shrewd. Instead of opposing the bill or seeking to cut its appropriation, he called for an amendment forbidding the United States Export-Import Bank to finance a $250 million wheat sale to the Soviets. This, he knew, was unacceptable to the White House. Yet it had great appeal to Red-hunting congressmen and to Republicans and Southern Democrats who, by voting for it, could give Lyndon Johnson his comeuppance without voting against the martyred John Kennedy's foreign aid measure. Moreover, Halleck could count on the facts that this Congress had already been in continuous session longer than any peacetime Congress in American history and that Christmas was at hand. By droves the House members were departing for home, for vacations or for junkets, leaving the pro-Administration forces depleted.

Speaker McCormack advised President Johnson to let Congress adjourn for Christmas and to worry about Russian wheat when the House reconvened. Lyndon Johnson would have none of this. To him the Halleck amendment was a direct challenge, both to his leadership of Congress and to his freedom of action in the field of foreign affairs, where he was so anxious to present himself as a man of mastery. He made it plain that the only deviation he would accept was a "compromise," which took the scarcely compromising form of neither authorizing nor forbidding the financing of the wheat sale but of leaving the decision to the discretion of the President.

In an action unusual in the annals of the White House, President Johnson then sent a memorandum to the Democratic leadership in the House of Representatives which amounted to giving them the choice of going all-out for this compromise or of not caring about their country. "What has happened . . . is that a new President has suddenly been thrust into office. This is an event of tremendous magnitude to other nations. The countries of the free world are watching anxiously to determine . . . whether the new President is so strong . . . [that the Communist nations] will have to come to terms with him or so weak that they can start hacking away at the free world with impunity. Against this background, it is not difficult to imagine the reaction of the rest of the world if the first disagreement between Congress and the new President results in a restriction upon the powers of the President." On the basis of this argument, President Johnson declared support of his position a matter of fundamental Democratic party policy. He virtually ordered the Democratic House leadership to keep Congress in session, to join with the White House in bringing back pro-Administration House members who had left Washington, and to get the foreign aid bill, with his version of the amendment, passed forthwith.

Tempers flared. A White House aide snapped to a reporter that the whole affair was "an attempt by the Midwest isolationist wing of the Republican party, headed by Halleck, to seize control of the party and impose its will on the foreign policy of the United States." Representative Halleck let it be known that he deemed the House of Representatives to be an independent body. On December 20 the House wrangled all night into the dawn. Lyndon Johnson, getting a few scattered hours sleep, directed the strategy of keeping Congress in session and of delaying the vote while the faithful were being summoned back to the capital. The final possibility for delay was December 24, when the vote in the House would surely come.

The phone calls went out from the President's office, the House leadership and from Walter Jenkins' office, the President himself speaking to certain of the more important or more difficult congressmen. An unusual storm had hit the nation. Heavy snow was falling in much of the country, even in the Deep South, and highways from Mississippi to Florida were glazed with ice. Chartered planes, flying around the storms, kept ferreting out usable landing fields and rounding up congressmen. One two-engine jet hedge-hopped from Brookley Air Base in Alabama to the Clovis Airport in New Mexico, arriving in Washington at a triumphant 2:30 A.M. with six congressmen. Some returnees were not so lucky. Two Michigan Democrats, John Lesinski and Harold M. Ryan, raced for a commercial flight leaving Detroit, were waved off from landings at Washington, Baltimore and Philadelphia, and ended the trip back home in Detroit.

House Majority Leader Carl B. Albert of Oklahoma was getting in a little fishing in Canada. He was confronted by a Mountie, the horse pushing upstream. "Is your name Carl Albert? The President of the United States is trying to reach you." The White House operators had trouble finding Representative John F. Shelley of California; even his family could not track him down. The White House switchboard, which never gives up, turned to the San Francisco chief of police and found that Shelley, recently elected mayor of San Francisco, was sitting talking with the chief.

J. J. Pickle, a devoted acolyte of the President, had also just been elected—as representative from Lyndon Johnson's former congressional district—in a special election held because the President had just appointed another old friend, Representative Homer Thornberry, to a federal judgeship. Representative-elect Pickle had a problem. Under Texas law the certification of a congressman cannot be made until seven days after the election, which would be the day of the House vote on the Halleck amendment, December 24. Furthermore, the certification must be performed by the secretary of state of Texas in the presence of the governor of Texas. At 12:00 A.M. on December 24 the representative-elect, the secretary of state and the governor assembled in Austin, and a few minutes later Representative Pickle and his wife were off to a 3:30 A.M. arrival in Washington.

"Get me Tic Forrester," the President phoned Walter Jenkins' office. "I want to talk to him. Now, you find him." The voice trailed off in the years of congressional camaraderie. "Little biddy fellow —no bigger than a tic." But the secretary to the Honorable Elijah J. Forrester, representative from Leesburg, Georgia, said she was sorry. The congressman had started home for the Christmas holiday the day before, he was driving, and she did not know how to locate him. Oh yes, she could describe his car, she had the number of the license plate, and by now he had no doubt crossed into Georgia.

The White House switchboard reached the director of the Georgia State Patrol, Major L. E. Floyd, and the major snapped to it. "I will send our helicopters out and phone you shortly." Within fifteen minutes the call came. "Our helicopter has intercepted the congressman and we have him on it. The helicopter has a two-way radio and we can patch that into your telephone." Then Major Floyd paused and his voice boomed. "You can tell the President of the United States, suh, that the Georgia State Patrol stands behind him to a man."

Meanwhile the President of the United States had an idea. The official mourning period for President Kennedy ended on December 22. Why not a White House party on December 23 for all the representatives, senators, Supreme Court justices and Cabinet members who were still in town, to salve the feelings of congressmen and to help ensure that pro-Administration House members stayed in Washington one more night? President Johnson had his idea about noon; the guests were to arrive at five o'clock. The stunned social organization of the White House rallied in a state of higher frenzy. The invitation to the representatives, in an improvisation of etiquette, was announced on the floor of the House at two thirty-five in the afternoon. The last of the black mourning crepe was still being replaced as the first arrivals made their way into the White House, stomping off the six-inch snow.

Guests agreed that the Christmas decorations, the casual profusion of holly, the giant Southern kissing ball of boxwood, the mistletoe hanging from the gold chandelier in the State Dining Room, had never seemed more cheerful and homey. As the party reached its height, President Johnson picked up a chair delicately upholstered with gold damask, carried it to the middle of the room and climbed up on it. "Your attention, please," he called out.

The startled guests clustered around. LBJ, his eyes sunk from weariness, was at his most pleasant and conciliatory. The United States "is composed of many nationalities, many religions and many regions. Yet it is one nation." The battle over the wheat amendment was a sharp one—he glanced at Representative Halleck—but "we're all Americans first" and "we can disagree without being disagreeable. You only have one President, you only have one Congress, you only have one judiciary." He was sorry that the Christmas recess of the representatives had been disrupted, but then, with a laugh, "members of Congress have better working hours and conditions than I do, at least most of the time." He wanted to thank the congressmen who had "labored through the vineyard and ploughed through the snow" to cast their votes and to come to the White House party. He hoped they would always feel welcome, as they certainly were this evening, in "your house." With that, Lyndon Johnson was down off the gold damask chair, dispensing eggnog, fruitcake and hail-fellowship.

He had a special word for Minority Leader Halleck. The President took him aside and said he wanted to apologize. He was sorry if "anybody here has made any ugly remarks about you." Minority Leader Halleck smiled, as a persimmon greets the sun.

Four women reporters were putting on their coats when a social aide came up to them. The President, it seemed, would like to have a photograph of each of them with himself and Mrs. Johnson. The photographs taken, the reporters again prepared to leave. "Hey, want to see the swimming pool?" Lyndon Johnson called after them. Off they went, LBJ conducting a forty-five-minute tour of the White House, pointing out the "beautiful paintings" of the Virgin Islands on the swimming pool walls which Joseph Kennedy had given to his son, leading them into the Oval Office and fingering the bust of Franklin Roosevelt ("Look at that chin—that's what I love about him"), expressing his admiration for Dwight Eisenhower ("He sat right there at that desk for two hours, writing on those yellow tablets, giving me ideas for my first speech to Congress, and I used a lot of them"), taking the women into the Cabinet Room as he declared there ought to be more women in government and that "if a man can't get along with Congress, he can't get along with the world."

Next morning, in an unprecedented 7:00 A.M. Christmas Eve session, the House stood behind President Johnson on the Halleck amendment. The vote was a strict party one (only two Republicans voted with the Administration, one of them Congressman John V. Lindsay, whom Halleck considered no Republican at all). The White House cracking of the party whip and the recall of the pro-Administration representatives had obviously made the difference. Beyond that, the LBJ conciliation, glad-handing and pressure? How much did they matter? In what ways did they matter? The questions trailed off into the Christmas season. The Johnson Christmas at the Texas ranch—"seventy-four relatives and a turkey," said the President—was filled with more references to "our beloved President John F. Kennedy." It was also filled with more bursts of the emerging Lyndon B. Johnson.

The explosive urge of the President to be his own man was expressed for me in a small personal incident. Try as I did, I could not keep my work for President Johnson entirely secret, particularly since I was contacting people in his name all over the country. On January 2 the Washington *Post* broke a front-page story stating that Arthur Schlesinger, Jr., planned to resign from the White House staff and that I would be appointed to his position. President Johnson was agitated; Walter Jenkins was agitated. At first I thought the disturbance came from the publication of the fact that I was working for the President, and I emphasized the efforts I had made to keep my activities out of the papers. But that was not the point, at least for the moment.

Jenkins' mild voice rose as he told me, "You are not the Johnson Arthur Schlesinger. Nobody is going to be the Johnson Schlesinger. Nobody is going to be the Johnson anything of Kennedy. *This is a different Administration.*"

CHAPTER 3

Old Jim, Economy and the Consensus

*T*he State of the Union address was scheduled to be delivered on January 8, 1964, the Budget Message to follow on January 21. To President Johnson, they were one package. The State of the Union address, the prime document, would announce the overall budget figure and indicate broadly how it was to be spent; the Budget Message provided the fiscal details. Together they would express the new Administration's commitment to the Kennedy foreign policy, call for the passage of the Kennedy domestic legislation, and add a Johnsonian emphasis on economy and at least one identifiable LBJ program.

Theodore Sorensen, a wan figure obviously carrying on only through the transition, was in charge of the drafting of the State of the Union message and President Johnson made two things clear to him from the beginning. He had sat through too many soporific presidential speeches to Congress, and he winced at the memory of the first State of the Union message of that other Vice-President become President, Harry Truman, who droned through twenty-five thousand words, the longest such document in American history. The LBJ speech was to be short—not more than three thousand words. Domestic affairs were to be given priority—in order of placement in the address and in emphasis—the first such stress in a State of the Union message since World War II.

Because the speech was largely an appeal for the Kennedy legislative programs, much of it was preordained. The real question concerned the way in which it would express LBJ as well as JFK, and it was primarily this aspect which set President Johnson off on one of his periods of arduous brain picking. At breakfast, lunch and dinner, through a telephone net thrown far and wide, he talked, talked, talked the possibilities.

At the time, I was far along in my choices for the brain trust, and I set aside that work momentarily to join the general White

House concentration on the State of the Union message. I telephoned a number of people, some of whom were the same as the proposed brain trusters. In this list I made no effort at regional balance, and I was interested less in specialized expertise than in a seasoned understanding of the national scene. I also kept in mind that the address would basically concern domestic affairs.

Among others, the group included the writer Bruce Catton and John Fischer, editor of *Harper's* magazine; the academics Fedele F. Fauri, professor of public welfare administration at the University of Michigan, William C. Friday, president of the University of North Carolina, David Riesman, the Harvard sociologist, Clinton Rossiter, professor of American institutions at Cornell, and Arthur M. Ross, the industrial relations expert at the University of California in Berkeley; and the scientist-businessman Edwin H. Land. I asked each person I called to write me a letter concerning two points: What should be the general theme of the State of the Union message? What specific new programs, particularly in domestic affairs, should it recommend? And of course, acting on the President's instruction, I emphasized that my request was to be considered rigidly confidential.

At my insistence on secrecy I could sense the smiles of a number of these knowledgeable people. Of course, of course, they replied, and the tone of their voices made it unnecessary for them to add, Do you really expect the project to remain confidential for long? In any event, what is the point in making it such a mystery?

Another response was still more general, so much so that I felt impelled to report it to President Johnson despite its awkward nature. A large percentage expressed surprise that Lyndon Johnson would be interested in the suggestions of intellectuals. In some instances, the remarks went beyond surprise to an outright questioning of the President's sincerity. One man, a Negro scholar long active in public affairs, stated bluntly that he thought LBJ was simply trying to spread the word for vote-getting purposes that he, as well as John Kennedy, cared what academics and writers thought. I later noted that this scholar, though he said he would write me, did not do so.

The others all responded, and within the severe forty-eight-hour deadline I had to impose because of the imminence of the final drafting of the State of the Union message. Throughout my work in the White House I had this experience over and over again. Whether out of pleasure at being called by someone representing the President, or out of feeling for their country, or from some combination of the two, in instance after instance extremely busy men and women put aside their work and did what was asked, speedily, uncomplainingly, and in most cases, with great care.

This particular group showed striking near-unanimity in their suggestions concerning the general theme of the address for domestic affairs. Almost all urged that it be a call for aggressive, wide-ranging action, and most—without knowing President Johnson's estimate of the national mood—believed the country was ready for such moves. Clinton Rossiter wrote: "There is so damned much to be done simply to keep us afloat." David Riesman: "We stand at a point unlike any in our history, with everything prepared and clarified and in suspension. . . . Ten or five years ago the agenda was not clear; the needs and crises were masked or vaguely defined. Today they are visible, inescapable." Bruce Catton: "One of the most encouraging developments of the last few weeks has been a general feeling that the new President will really get things done. We had a long time of preparation in which magnificent expression was given to a number of basic ideas, but nothing much resulted in the way of a concrete program. It seems to me right now there is in the air a touch of the feeling that was abroad during the first few months of the New Deal Administration when concrete programs were being presented and put into effect. I think the country is in the mood to applaud any indication that this man can, through his leadership and his political skill, stir Congress into movement once more."

As to specific recommendations in domestic affairs, the group showed as much concurrence. Of course the details of the proposals varied but they added up to the program: Get ahead with the major Kennedy bills already sent to Congress and add a sweeping legislative attack on poverty. Calling for concentration on the poor in a nation enjoying unprecedented affluence might seem like asking for a psychological contradiction. But during the period immediately before Dallas, a remarkable agreement had been forming among thoughtful Americans that just such an effort was needed. It was produced by the prosperity itself, which made sensitive men uncomfortable that a nation so wealthy did so little about its millions living in squalor; by the economic studies indicating a drastic slowdown in the rate at which the economy was taking Americans out of the slums; by the fear of what hard-core poverty could mean in an increasingly technological society; and above all by the mounting Negro unrest, which was so plainly connected with the low income of black America. Two widely read books, John Kenneth Galbraith's *The Affluent Society* and Michael Harrington's *The Other America,* had expressed and broadened this trend of thinking. At the time of the assassination, the Kennedy Administration had been planning an anti-poverty program to present to Congress in 1964, though its form had not taken full shape. Anti-poverty was in the air.

The emphasis on the poor by the people I had telephoned was summarized by the comments of Edwin Land, the inventor of the Polaroid camera and president of the flourishing Polaroid Corporation, a man of an unusual mixture of scientific gifts, business acumen and a feel for the American society. Despite the enormous social achievements of the United States, Land wrote, it was urgent to recognize that the country contained millions who "were the by-products of the American dream rather than the product. . . . Those of us who should feel responsible are for the most part completely preoccupied with the exciting, brilliant, and effective segment of American life. The rest of our population is as far away as the occupants of some distant land. As our country grows and prospers, this second part of American life must always be a burden to the conscience and the health of the nation."

All of this I duly digested for President Johnson and sent to him, together with the suggested draft of the State of the Union message which he had requested from a number of us on the White House staff. One result was a conference which brought me my first real sense of the man who, throughout the Johnson Administration, was probably the single greatest influence on the President.

I had first met Abe Fortas when he walked into Walter Jenkins' office, a small, dark figure in his well-preserved fifties with a deliberate air that was relieved by a certain courtliness and a twinkle that occasionally flashed across his face. He conducted his business—settling a high-level appointment—with the manner of a man who thoroughly knew his way around the power centers of the United States. The son of a cabinetmaker who had migrated from England to Memphis, Tennessee, helping to pay for his education by clerking in a shoe store and playing the violin at dances, Fortas had gone on to make a superb record at Yale Law School and then to success in the tangled upper echelons of the New Deal. After World War II he left the government to become the driving force in Arnold, Fortas & Porter, a Washington law firm with a roster of blue-chip corporate clients and a formidable reputation for being able to steer them through Washington's anti-trust, tax and regulatory maze. Fortas moved easily in the world of big business; at various times he himself, in addition to his law practice, was an officer of one major firm and a director of several others. He and his wife—another lawyer, a tax expert at

Arnold, Fortas & Porter—lived in a luxurious yellow brick home in the fashionable Dumbarton Oaks section of Washington and rode to work in a Rolls Royce.

In the New Deal days, Secretary of the Interior Harold L. Ickes had introduced Congressman Lyndon Johnson and the bright young man of Interior, Abe Fortas. They got along well and worked together enthusiastically on a project to dam the lower Colorado River, which flowed across the LBJ district. Their acquaintance blossomed in 1948 when Representative Lyndon Johnson won a Texas senatorial primary by a rickety 87 votes. He was about to be removed from the ballot because of a court order obtained by his opponent on the plea of voting irregularities, but was reinstated by Fortas' legal intervention. The two men were on their way to a historic relationship reminiscent, despite important variations, of the Wilson–Colonel House or the FDR–Harry Hopkins liaison.

The first call Lyndon Johnson made after the shots at Dallas was to Fortas. The lawyer was at the airport when *Air Force One* landed, and from then on he was frequently at the White House or on the other end of the presidential phone. The relationship had its tensions. Fortas too was proud and impatient, and at times he could be imperious, cryptic or cold. The lawyer turned down at least two important posts urged by President Johnson and eventually took the only one that would leave him independent, a seat on the Supreme Court. But the tensions never affected the larger reality: Abe Fortas was the President's confidant, legal sharpshooter, personal ambassador and jack-of-all-advisers. The White House knew him as the man Lyndon Johnson would turn to when the problem was especially important or knotty, and as the only adviser he treated with a respect not untouched by awe. A real Washington power broker, Washington said of Fortas, a shrewd, tough operator who knew exactly what he was doing. But then, except for his strongest enemies, people added, Of course the man has another side.

There was an air of the enigma about Fortas, as if he knew all about power and money and half wished he did not know so much. "I wouldn't be surprised," one of his law clerks remarked, "if I were to find out that Abe Fortas leads a secret life as a published poet in South America." The Dumbarton Oaks home was not merely sumptuous; it was filled with art that expressed subtle taste. If Fortas was a wheeler and dealer, he was also a contributor of articles to the journal *Psychiatry* and an accomplished violinist who delighted in a Sunday afternoon playing chamber music with friends who might include Isaac Stern or Rudolf Serkin. "Abe Fortas—I'm a violinist," he would introduce himself at White

House social functions, in a way that was part pixie, part some
world of his own. Arnold, Fortas & Porter, in addition to serving
its Daddy Warbucks clients, was a kind of organized Clarence
Darrow, ready to defend the liberal in trouble, the poor man, the
outcast floundering against the norms, without regard to whether
the client could pay a fee. Fortas' own persistent activities of this
type were climaxed in 1962 when the Supreme Court asked him
to take the case of Clarence Earl Gideon, prisoner number 003826
in the Florida State Prison at Raiford, Florida.

Gideon was a fifty-one-year-old pauper who had been in and
out of prisons most of his life, a frail, wrinkled figure with a voice
and hands that trembled, but he was also a man with a cause. In
laborious penciled printing, on lined paper provided by the prison,
Gideon spelled out his passion to the Supreme Court of the United
States. He had been indicted for breaking into the Bay Harbor
Poolroom in Panama City, Florida, had asked for a lawyer to
defend him, the judge had denied his request, and he was con-
victed. Under the Constitution of the United States, Clarence Earl
Gideon declared, he, destitute or not, had a right to a lawyer.
Fortas, in an intensively prepared and beautifully argued brief,
won—and won unanimously—a landmark Supreme Court decision that all states must assure legal counsel to any citizen indicted for a felony. The Fortas fee: nothing.

President Johnson, asked about his close relationship to Fortas,
once replied, "He's as smart as they come, he has a heart, but he's
no damn knee-jerk liberal." This was Johnsonese for the fact that
Fortas is an exceptionally able example of a certain type of post-
New Deal liberal: aroused by injustice but with little sentimental
reformism; not anti-business, in fact having considerable empathy
for it; a devotee, in business or reform, of the practical move deftly
played. The President's remark did not encompass one of Fortas's
most salient characteristics, a pronounced intellectualism and
the kind of intellectualism that keeps pushing toward the frontiers
of thinking about public affairs. The United States, Fortas believed,
had not had much genuinely "creative" thinking in public affairs
for a number of years. This resulted from the general affluence of
the nation, the carry-over effects of the Joseph McCarthy era,
the heightened emphasis on science and the "Keynesian plateau."

Fortas' intellectual restlessness was plain when a group of us
—Fortas and LBJ staff men—gathered in the Cabinet Room for an
evening session (the White House has remarkably few places suit-
able for a conference, and the Cabinet Room, with its long table
and big comfortable chairs, was often used for this purpose). Part

of the time was given to another going over of the list for the brain trust. Fortas consistently threw his weight behind the man "who sounds like his mind is roused."

Most of the session concerned the State of the Union address, and here too he responded to the adventurous. He was attracted by a point David Riesman had made in his letter to me which moved directly into the politically explosive area of relations with Red China: "One possible theme for the message concerns freedom for goods and ideas around the world. As the confident new Executive of a hopefully confident country, President Johnson is in a wonderful position to declare that we have nothing to fear from the exchanges of goods or ideas and from the free flow of goods and ideas both domestically and abroad. He could announce, for example, that he is prepared to deal without fear or favor with everybody and anybody (as Roger Hilsman already suggested vis-à-vis Mainland China) and that he proposed to throw overboard by Executive action wherever possible all barriers to travel and exchange of persons. He could continue the fight already begun concerning the sale of wheat to the Soviet Union and its satellites, and argue for a general principle of openness which I think would have a startling effect all over the world. . . ."

It was approaches like this, Fortas commented, that we must concentrate on, even if the State of the Union address was not the right vehicle.

The conversation turned to whether the speech could be rescued from its usual laundry-list quality and given an arresting theme. I suggested that the domestic legislation we all had in mind amounted to an effort to stop the development of a "spectator society" in the United States, to a program for bringing millions more of the population to some feeling that they were "participants" in America both in the economic and noneconomic meanings of the word. Fortas took up the thought, playing with it brilliantly.

Encouraged by this reaction, I went on to the substance of what was on my mind, the desirability of getting under way a degree of decentralization in the United States which would revitalize and rehumanize the lower governments that deal most directly with human needs. My thought was centered on the metropolitan areas. The existing governmental structure of the United States, I argued, made it impossible to cope with some of the most serious metropolitan problems. Needed—and urgently needed—was a "Metropolitan Authority," a new governmental instrumentality inserted between Washington and state and local governments which would take the definition of its function from the fact that so many Americans now lived in areas that cut across state and local lines.

I thought the proposal was going pretty far at this stage and brought it up at the meeting as a catalytic. It was not going too far for sympathetic consideration by Fortas. The next day he incorporated essential steps toward it in a proposed section for the State of the Union address.

The Fortas draft did not go into the message. President Johnson responded to it with interest but it was a casualty of his drive for brevity and, still more, of his caution against taking on too much at the beginning. However, the theme of attention to governmental structure below the federal level lingered on in the early years of the Administration. Without the Vietnam War—and with Abe Fortas—it might have become a major concern.

One subject we scarcely mentioned at the meeting was an anti-poverty program. No one needed to talk about it. From the first plannings for the State of the Union message, President Johnson had seized upon anti-poverty.

The Kennedy Administration may have begun work on legislation of this type but it had said little publicly; anti-poverty could be presented as an LBJ program. An influential segment of public opinion was ready for it. And there was the most important fact— an attack on poverty was Lyndon Johnson's kind of legislation.

Was he sincere in his enthusiastic adoption of the program? The answer has to be that he was sincere and he was insincere. In any simple sense, the concept of sincerity does not have too much relevance to political leadership in a large, heterogeneous and socially volatile democracy. A President who believes that a particular program is vital to the welfare of the nation and who does not advocate it is patently insincere. A President who, out of political expediency, sponsors action which he is convinced is harmful to the country is obviously insincere. But few issues come to the Oval Office in this cut-and-dried form. Instead, they reach the President freighted with entirely legitimate pros and cons, with sensible arguments over whether to act now or later, with equally defensible, or at least equally inevitable, considerations of the effect of this particular move on other efforts which the President deems important, as well as on that matter which he considers of paramount significance—the degree of respect and affection with which the country views him.

Little that is morally definitive, which clearly establishes or denies sincerity, can be derived even from this presidential yearning to be supported, loved and re-elected. American history has long since demonstrated that a President who does not believe himself and his leadership virtually indispensable does not turn out to be much of a President. The men generally recognized as great Chief Executives all were determined to be re-elected and the most modern of them, Franklin Roosevelt, did not conceive of his contribution to the nation being finished short of four terms. About all that can be realistically said on the subject of sincerity and political leadership in a democracy like the United States is that a President is being true to himself when, with due regard to the balance of political forces in the country, concerned with timing but not enslaved by it, he moves within the broad purview of his own personal attitudes.

For President Johnson, anti-poverty recognized the political situation, was suitably timed and bespoke Lyndon Johnson. It was a key part of the President's make-up that he viewed himself with great emotional intensity as a son of poverty. In fact, he was the product of a middle-class or, depending on the definition, a lower-middle-class family. Among the four hundred or so inhabitants of Johnson City, Texas, few were rich or poor; the white frame Johnson house, with its own few acres, was just about average. The father, Sam Ealy Johnson, Jr., was a sometime farmer, a dabbler in real estate, mostly a politician serving in the Texas Legislature and then in an appointive post on the State Railroad Commission. With his Stetson hat, high stiff collar and four-in-hand tie, "Mr. Sam" was a great talker, a town figure, and not concerned too much with being a provider. But he kept the house going for his wife and five children, with an occasional plunge into debt. Lyndon Johnson went to college into the Depression years—which was scarcely customary for the impoverished—and if he did it by borrowing money from the Blanco Bank, his family was the kind the Blanco Bank would approve for a loan. A friend of President Johnson's, the University of Texas historian Walter Prescott Webb, used to tell him that he did not know what real poverty is; he should go into West Texas and see it. But Lyndon Johnson had no ear for such talk.

He remembered boyhood days of shoe shining to make spending money; the jalopy trip to the West Coast after high school to find a high-paying job and the doors that did not open; his decision against going to college and the eighteen months with pick-and-shovel on Route 290 between Johnson City and Hye, in scorching heat and numbing cold, until one night he came home raw-handed and exhausted, dropped down on his bed and said to his mother, "Will you please help me get to college?" The President's sense of poverty was increased by the atmosphere of the region around Johnson City, which was not the lush Texas of thousand-acre ranches and oil derricks but an area of small ranches, small farmers and a rapidly increasing number of tenant farmers, most of them scrounging a living from brush-covered hills and caliche soil. As with all of us, what mattered about Lyndon Johnson was not only what he was but what he thought he was. With a feeling akin to passion, he identified himself with those who had known the pain of battling poverty.

President Johnson's readiness for an anti-poverty program also came from an ideological bent. In the days of his boyhood, Texas politics were intensely personal, the one man beating his way up and down the huge districts and gathering to himself a following. Issues were often secondary. Even the usual regional splits within a state were not much evident; candidates tended to run remarkably the same in East, Central or West Texas. But personalized Texas politics did not escape the great divide in American life in the early twentieth century between those who went along with business interests and those who wanted legislation favoring low-income groups. In its own way, Texas had its Populism, its Progressive movement, its class ferocities—and Texas had James E. Ferguson.

In 1914, at the age of forty-three, a lawyer, owner of a bank, an abstract company and a large breeding ranch, Ferguson, without consulting anyone except his dutiful wife, suddenly announced: "Whereas, I, James E. Ferguson, am as well qualified to be Governor of Texas as any damn man in it; and, Whereas, I am against prohibition and always will be; and, Whereas, I am in favor of a square deal for tenant farmers; Therefore Be It Resolved that I will be elected." Running against a seasoned and well-financed campaigner, without the backing of any powerful group or a single prominent citizen, "Farmer Jim," spindly, suspender-snapping and tobacco-chewing, with a voice like an unhappy marsh frog, headed for the country districts. The tenant farmers rallied to his promise to get a law passed limiting the landlord's share of crops. The Texas Liquor Dealers' Association poured in campaign funds when he announced he would veto any bill concerning liquor. On inauguration day Governor Ferguson looked out at the sea of sunburned faces, intoned, "If you love me as I love you/No knife can cut our love in two," and began a rule which he described as "not just one damn thing after another but one damn thing all the time."

Despite his many unfulfilled promises Ferguson did, amid a continual uproar, bend Texas legislation toward the lower-income groups. But in his second term, ample evidence was produced that he had "loaned" himself most of the money in his bank and that the breweries had "loaned" him another $156,000, neither of which he had made any move to repay. The Texas Legislature, hostile for good and for not so noble reasons, impeached the governor and voted to ban him from ever holding office in Texas again. Promptly he offered as a candidate Mrs. Miriam Amanda ("Ma") Ferguson, who was elected governor in 1924 and in 1932, with "Pa" setting up an office next door and "lending a hand." "Two governors for the price of one," declared "Pa," now beginning to be affectionately known to hundreds of thousands of Texans as "Old Jim."

It was wild politics, in many ways mountebank and corrupt. But "Fergusonism," as Texans called it, represented something different from traditional Southern demagoguery, which had specialized in hypocritical ranting against corporations and a cover-up of its do-nothing nature by the baiting of Negroes. Fergusonism was not anti-business; Old Jim could even occasionally announce that he was "the businessman's candidate." It was not racist per se. It found its emotional outlet in apostrophes to Texas and to the man who worked with his hands. It was strongly against prohibition and the Ku Klux Klan, in considerable measure because of its annoyance with crabbed restrictions on private life. Fergusonism was a freewheeling, loose-scrupled boondocks liberalism, a type in which the leader burst up from the soil filled with a lust for attention, power and money, and joining that with a confused sympathy for the bottom groups, worked with anybody or anything at hand to advance himself and the plain folks, especially the plain folks of his native countryside. It was a Texas phenomenon, but it was not confined to that state. Huey Long, with greater ruthlessness and corruption, practiced similar politics in Louisiana.

During Lyndon Johnson's formative years, the prime political division in Texas was between "Ferguson men" and "anti-Ferguson men." Sam Johnson pushed for bills benefiting the lower-income groups, and he and his neighbors, Clarence W. Martin and A. W. Moursund, Sr. (father of a close friend of President Johnson's and chief trustee of the Johnson family trust), were the most ardent Ferguson men in the area. Sam Johnson, Martin and Moursund stumped every town and hollow in their counties for Ferguson tickets, and when the impeachment came, it was Martin who served as chief counsel for the defense. Young Lyndon grew up to Fergusonism; it was as natural a part of his life as a dish of boiled beef and turnip greens.

In 1931, when Lyndon Johnson left Houston High School for his first job in Washington, as secretary to Congressman Richard M. Kleberg, he soon made an arrangement with the Senate page office to notify him whenever Senator Huey Long was about to make a speech. "I would go over there," President Johnson recalled, "perch in the gallery and listen to every word he said. And I heard 'em all." Oh yes, he knew the criticisms of Huey Long. "But I never heard him make a speech that I didn't think was calculated to do some good for some people who needed some speeches made for them."

Long, the President went on, was years ahead of most politicians in fighting for ordinary people. "He thought that every man had a right to a job, and that was before the Full Employment Act. He thought that every boy and girl ought to have a chance to have all the education they could take, and that was before the GI Bill of Rights. He thought that the old folks ought to have social security and old-age pensions. I remember when he just scared the dickens out of Mr. Roosevelt and went on nationwide radio talking for old folks' pensions. And out of that probably came our social security system." The President added with an emphatic snap of his head, "He hated poverty with all of his soul and spoke against it until his voice was hoarse."

So anti-poverty went into the 1964 State of the Union message, first in emphasis, and it was expressed in language which made the program, whatever plans the Kennedy Administration may have had, an LBJ measure. "This Administration," declared Lyndon Johnson like a trumpet call at the Alamo, "today, here and now, declares unconditional war on poverty in America. . . . It will not be a short or easy struggle, no single weapon or strategy will suffice, but we shall not rest until that war is won. . . . [We] must pursue poverty, pursue it wherever it exists-—in city slums and small towns, in sharecropper shacks or in migrant-worker camps, on Indian reservations, among whites as well as Negroes, among the young as well as the aged, in the boom towns and in the depressed areas."

Most Johnsonian of all was the core of the message. Social legislation plus economy—the blend was heavily emphasized near the start of the speech, and the President touched on it at every opportunity. The new budget, he proudly announced, would represent a decrease of $500 million from the previous year. "It will cut our deficit in half. . . . It will be, in proportion to our national output, the smallest budget since 1951. It will call for a substantial reduction in Federal employment, a feat accomplished only once before in the last ten years. . . . But it is not a stand-still budget . . . By insisting on a dollar's worth for a dollar spent, I am able to recommend in this reduced budget the most Federal support in history for education, for health, for retraining the unemployed, and for helping the economically and the physically handicapped."

The theme was Johnsonian and the manner was Johnsonian too. The LBJ formal-address style, carefully discussed and worked over, was now set. President Kennedy had talked to Congress in a rush of words, finger jabbing out, gestures sudden, often tram-pling on his own applause lines. President Johnson spoke slowly, deliberately. His text bore cues planned with his aide Jack Valenti, "Pause," "Look Right," "Look Left," and he paused, looked right and looked left. Every facet was perfectly controlled: the drawl not suppressed but not too pronounced, the tone dignified but with ups and downs for emphasis, the key phrases delivered in an everyman's anapest, guaranteeing the applause.

At the end of the State of the Union message President John-son walked down the aisle smiling broadly. A senator shook his hand in congratulation. "Yeah," the President said. "I got applause eighty times."

Though reporters were becoming aware of an asset of Lyndon Johnson's—a fantastic memory—they could not believe that he was able to keep count of applause while making a carefully delivered speech. They checked their notes. He had been ap-plauded seventy-nine or eighty times, depending on how you reckoned one instance when the applause stopped, then started up again after a few words.

Meanwhile the details of the Budget Message were being hammered out against one persistent presidential question: Can't the item be reduced? Kermit Gordon, a former Williams College economist and the Kennedy holdover as Director of the Budget, a wry, supple personality, was moving along in stride. One morn-ing he announced cheerily, "The President is only calling me now during office hours—eight to eight." Gordon was the first hurdle. An agency or department head would meet with him or one of his staff, and the cutting in appropriations would occur. In important cases, the item came up again with the President, who, eyeglasses down on his nose, scrutinized it like a bull he was considering for his ranch.

One department head, his funds sharply reduced, growled to

Gordon, "If you had named the Apostles, there would have been ten instead of twelve."

The Budget Director smiled. "Yes, and Mr. Johnson would have reduced the figure to eight."

At the same time the President was busy using the cuts to help prod passage of the tax-reduction bill, one of the big four of JFK legislation. The measure had been bottled up in the Senate Finance Committee by its chairman, the unreconstructable conservative Senator Harry F. Byrd of Virginia, whom no new-fangled economics could convince that taxes should be lowered when expenditures were mounting. During one White House budget discussion, Walter M. Heller, chairman of the Council of Economic Advisers, argued that a $101.5 billion budget was thoroughly defensible in terms of 1964 needs. President Johnson laughed. "*I* can defend 101.5 billion dollars—*you* take on Senator Byrd." If the demand for economy was not at least appeased, "forget about a tax cut. You won't pee one drop."

Senators Byrd and Johnson had gotten along well in the Senate; they were both pros. Nor did Senator Byrd forget that in 1952, when his daughter died, he turned around at the funeral in Westwood, Virginia, and saw Lyndon Johnson, the only senator who had come. Now, as the Budget Message neared completion, President Johnson invited Senator Byrd to the White House for a drink and a confidential look at the document.

The senator spoke forcefully about his opposition to tax reduction while the federal deficit was so high. He was against the tax measure and would so vote. The President spoke forcefully about how much he respected the senator's principles. The senator also looked at the substantial cuts in the budget with a broad smile and expressed his pleasure at the general attitude of the President toward government expenditures. Late that night Lyndon Johnson translated the conversation in a phone call to an aide: "Harry is going to let the tax bill out of committee."

The day before the Budget Message formally went to Congress, President Johnson decided to make its economy point in a way that the newspapers would play up—"to show a little garter," as he liked to say. He invited Director of the Budget Gordon and his chief aides to the Cabinet Room for the signing of the document.

The President had glowing words for their cost cutting. "When you go home, you tell Molly and the babies that your President specifically decorated you today for a job well done." He had thoughts about the world. "We are a relatively small number as the make-up of the whole world goes. We are outnumbered 17 to 1. But fate has smiled upon us, and our forefathers left us with a great system. There are only six nations in the world that have a per capita income of more than $80 a month and we lead all of the rest. That doesn't mean, because we are compassionate, we have to be wasteful. We can take the money we save on waste and spend it on compassion and doing things for people that need it."

LBJ had a joke, or maybe not a joke. As he wrote his signature and gave out pens, he said that he understood the manufacturer was going to give them free to the White House.

At one point his voice turned indignant. "I want to ask you to ride herd . . . even on the White House itself, to see where we can eliminate any unnecessary expense. Someone told me that the light bill in the White House ran several thousand dollars a month. I challenged Mr. Valenti over there and my maid this morning when I left to turn out all the lights on those chandeliers when there is no one in the House. . . . I don't know how much we saved today. I want a bill for the last three months to see if we are making any headway. . . . A stitch in time saves nine. You don't accumulate anything unless you save in small amounts."

Turn out the lights in the White House—there were those in the White House, including me, who thought this intolerably corny. There were those outside who felt the same way. A distinguished academic authority on the American government wrote me to urge that at least the exterior should be reilluminated. "The White House," he declared, "is a national monument. . . . As the Presidency is figuratively a 'clear beacon of national purpose,' so the beautiful mansion associated with it should be literally a beacon. It is my impression that thousands of Americans have been disappointed as they walked or drove by a darkened White House." I agreed, and it occurred to me that the 175th anniversary of the Office of the Presidency, the year 1964, offered a tactful opportunity to turn on again the floodlights at the front of the building. After all, George Washington's inaugural in New York City had been celebrated by turning on everything that would light.

The distinguished authority on American government and the professor of history from Princeton happened to be wrong in their facts. We promptly foundered on President Johnson's attention to White House details and his limitless knowledge of Congress. When I mentioned the possibility of relighting the front of the White House to the veteran LBJ aide Horace Busby, he replied in his soft way that he did not think the suggestion would be "well received" by the President. Lyndon Johnson, it seems, had already covered that territory. One day he had pointed out to Busby that the White House was *not* a national monument and that Congress had explicitly refrained from declaring it one.* What's more, there were no floodlights out front which he had turned off and could turn on, and the President had taken Busby tramping around the lawn to prove it.

Aside from its corniness, some of us thought that turning out the lights would backfire on President Johnson, and it was true that for days it was a sure subject for derision. But Lyndon Johnson understood the feelings of the middle class and the business community about economy. During the campaign of 1964, he had a number of us on the White House staff serving as hosts for the endless groups of business leaders he invited to luncheons, and I experienced more than a few conversations like the one with a Midwestern telephone executive. The subject of turning out the lights came up, as it often did, and the telephone executive rubbed his chin. "Well, you know, that was a good thing the President did. The example—that's what counts. We've got to practice economy in all ways."

The businessmen and the liberal coalition were moving with the Administration. The President was particularly pleased to be able to read at one sitting the comments of Roy Wilkins, head of the National Association for the Advancement of Colored People, and of Henry Ford II. "Quite simply," Wilkins said, "a very fine State of the Union message indeed." Henry Ford rambled on happily, "I don't know, I guess it's just chemistry. Mr. Johnson is a realist, a practical man. His problems are vast, more important than mine, but he approaches them the same way I deal with mine. So I feel rapport with him—and I trust him."

The symphony of approval contained one discordant note. President Johnson had been talking about his budget to White House correspondents almost from the day he took office. At his first press conference, on December 7, he pointed out that President Kennedy's budget had been $98.8 billion and that an additional $3.5 billion was needed for built-in increases and new programs, leaving the distinct impression that his own budget would be $102–$103 billion. A little later White House aides spread the story that the budget would be about $100 billion, and then the President himself let it be known that the sum could not be below $98 billion and would be somewhere between $98 and $100 billion. The figure actually given to Congress was $97.9 billion, and this was soon triumphantly lowered to $97.4 billion. White House

* *The President was referring to an obscure 1962 action of the House Committee on Government Operations, when the committee voted down a bill to make the White House a national monument on the ground that it was inappropriate to declare a place so active a "monument."*

reporters are accustomed to a little hanky-panky about the budget. In modern times Presidents have often talked of their grim budgetary problems and then, magically, solved them. The newsmen were not accustomed to a President who engaged in deliberate confusion that was obviously calculated to heighten an impression of devotion to economy and skill in achieving it.

The day after the final budget figure was made public, I ran into a White House correspondent for one of the major newspapers. He was a testy man. "That boss of yours, why don't you tell him to look to his credibility."

It was the first time I heard Lyndon Johnson and "credibility" linked.

In the draft of the State of the Union message I had given to the President, I included a passage based on the point I had made in my first conversation with him. The section stated: "Today, in a very real sense, we are all liberals, we are all conservatives— and we are all moving toward a new American consensus." It went on to urge action based on this "emerging consensus" and efforts to keep the consensus alive and effective, "for . . . the State of this Union will be good enough only when there is a genuine sense of union among the people of these States." The State of the Union message, as the President finally delivered it, edged toward the consensus philosophy with an appeal not to "fritter and fumble away our opportunity in needless, senseless quarrels. . . . If we can achieve these goals by forging in this country a greater sense of union, then, and only then, can we take full satisfaction in the State of the Union."

In mid-January, between the State of the Union and the Budget messages, Bill Moyers telephoned me in the course of a Johnsonian second shift, about one-thirty in the morning. Moyers said that he had been talking with President Johnson, and a book of mine on recent American history, *The Crucial Decade*, had come up. The President was interested in the fact that I had made assessments of the roles of Presidents Truman and Eisenhower, that is, how their general approaches to national problems did and did not fit their eras. President Johnson wanted me to make such an assessment for him, indicating how the consensus role I had been urging might fit into "the big pattern" in his case.

I had a sense of what the President was groping for. He had come to the White House remarkably equipped with political experience and insights, but quite unprepared by anything that could be called a political philosophy. Commentators, casting about for some statement, kept turning to a 1958 essay Horace Busby had drafted for him, "My Political Philosophy," published in the *Texas Quarterly* and then in *Reader's Digest*. "At the heart of my own beliefs is a rebellion against . . . classifying, labeling, and filing Americans under headings . . . ," the article stated. "I bridle at the very casualness with which we ask each other, 'What is your political philosophy?' . . . I am . . . a free man, an American, a United States senator, and a Democrat, in that order, and there, for me, the classifying stops." That was fine for a United States senator, particularly for one from a state where the more you were classified, the more likely you were to be classified out of office. It was also fine for a Southern Democrat eager for national office and knowing that he could achieve it only by being vague enough to hold his Southern base while acquiring support in the North. It was not enough—and LBJ was acutely aware of this— for a President of the United States in the 1960's.

Following Moyers' call I worked out a more detailed form of the consensus approach, and placed it within a sharply abbreviated historical background. Only too conscious of Lyndon Johnson's Senate record of seriously weakening bills by compromise, of his present eagerness to please conservative business groups, and of the fact that consensus can easily be defined to mean a mere something-for-everybody or a consolidation of the status quo, I not only described the nature of the consensus which I thought was forming in the 1960's but added some emphatic negatives:

1. The consensus is not made up equally of liberalism and of conservatism. The consensus is a new form of liberalism, liberalism as consensus. The central points and the emotional aura of the consensus are thoroughly liberal.

2. The arrival at some degree of consensus does not mean that the tasks of liberalism are completed or anywhere near completed. . . . [To indicate in a way that might catch the President's eye the continual lifting of sights that was inherent in the American tradition I brought in the evocative phrase of James Madison, "the Great Republic," and the sentences of Thomas Wolfe, "I think the true discovery of America is before us. I think the true fulfillment of our spirit, of our people, of our mighty and immortal land, is yet to come."]

3. To put this consensus most effectively to work, of course compromise is required—but not compromise in the sense that you give up anything substantial in which you believe. It is compromise which, by giving up nonessentials, moves you forward toward where you want to go.

The response to this memo was enthusiastic. In private conversation, then more and more frequently in public, President

Johnson spoke of his intention to associate his Administration with the idea of "a broad national consensus which can end obstruction and paralysis and can liberate the energies of the nation for the work of the future."

Before long, James MacGregor Burns, professor of political science at Williams College, was asked to write an article on the Johnson political philosophy for *Life*. The President was hesitant about granting an interview because Burns had written a highly favorable biography of John Kennedy. I was eager for the President to have the benefit of talking with men of the Burns type, and when my opinion was asked I was fortunately able to tip the scales by pointing out a fact which I had come upon in Washington. However laudatory the Kennedy biography, Burns had angered important Kennedyites by a final sentence in which, they believed, he had questioned the depth of JFK's convictions.

As the time for the Burns interview approached, I was asked for a memo with suggestions of what President Johnson might discuss. Again, among other points I emphasized the consensus concept, and I included a kind of shorthand of its background in American history. The President spoke to Burns with no real reference to notes, occasionally shuffling a pile of papers that largely concerned a different matter. What he said was another revelation of his extraordinary memory and an indication of his now total acceptance of the consensus definition for the first phase of his Presidency.

THE MEMO TO THE PRESIDENT	BURNS, REPORTING HIS INTERVIEW WITH THE PRESIDENT, IN *Life*
In the twentieth century, each of the periods of creative Presidential leadership has been building to the present special need for, and potentialities of, consensus leadership.	[The] key is Johnson's craving for consensus. . . . His enemies put this yearning down as sheer political greed; others ascribe it only to the normal love of politicians for votes writ large. But to the President this is more than a matter of electioneering. It is a matter of Leadership. And he has definite ideas as to the special possibilities for his own political leadership.
Theodore Roosevelt and Wilson In a broad sense, these Administrations got under way the ideas and the practice of: 1. The President as the one leader of the whole nation in a moral,	As the President sees it, Theodore Roosevelt and Woodrow Wilson fashioned wide backing for the concept of the President as the one moral, economic and social leader of

The Memo to the President	Burns, reporting his Interview with the President, in *Life*

economic and social sense as well as politically—the "steward" of the nation, to use T.R.'s phrase.

2. Considerable responsibility of the federal government for general social and economic welfare.

New Deal

Continued the previous and added:
1. Idea of some degree of planning.
2. More attention to and aid for the outcast groups, primarily labor and the minorities.

Truman Years

Continued the previous and added:
The ideas of strong Presidential leadership and of help for the disadvantaged applied in the field of foreign affairs.

Kennedy Years

Continued the previous and added:
The drive for qualitative as well as quantitative reforms, so that ordinary men could enjoy a richer life as well as have adequate food, clothing and housing.

All of these changes in domestic and foreign affairs (of course generally called liberalism) kept developing decade after decade in the twentieth century and naturally piled up opposition and resentment (of course generally going under the name of conservatism).

After World War II, the split between liberalism and conservatism seemed to be deepening. At times we appeared less a nation than two blocs, snapping and snarling at each other.

In domestic affairs, the liberal emphasized economic and social opportunities brought about largely by

the whole nation. In T.R.'s famous phrase, the President is "steward" of the whole nation; and the national government assumes considerable responsibility for general social and economic welfare.

The New Deal reaffirmed this idea in the 1930's; it also stressed some degree of planning and it gave special attention to "outcast groups"— especially labor and ethnic minorities. Harry Truman, exerting strong presidential leadership through the Marshall Plan and the Point Four Program, extended to foreign affairs the idea of help for the disadvantaged. It was in this new tradition that John Kennedy drove for qualitative as well as quantitative reforms.

All these developments, under the strong presidents of this century, were vitally necessary for a better society, Johnson feels; but they produced tension and strain in the nation. It has appalled him when this country at times seemed less a nation than two blocs snapping and snarling at each other.

One bloc has generally been called "liberal," says this hater of labels, and the other has gone by the description "conservative." According to the President, however, the line between liberals and conservatives is blurring. Increasingly, the conservatives see that the federal government must play a major part in

The Memo to the President	Burns, reporting his Interview with the President, in *Life*
actions of the federal government. The conservative stressed economy and the freedom of the individual from governmental restraints, particularly from restraints imposed by the federal government.	expanding individual opportunity and that the nation must take a path of genuine internationalism to avert a world catastrophe. Similarly, the President believes, liberals increasingly are coming to understand the conservatives' fear of overcentralization and heavy federal spending, have tried to strengthen state and local government, and have seen value in the conservatives' insistence that hardheadedness, as well as idealism, has its place in foreign policy. . . .
In foreign affairs, the liberal called for a sympathetic understanding that the world is in a revolution of rising expectations. The conservative argued that, no matter what the world expected, a tough-minded concern for American security is the core of wisdom.	
But in very recent years, the line between liberalism and conservatism, instead of hardening, has been steadily blurring. More and more the conservative accepts the doctrine that the federal government must play an important role in expanding opportunity and that the road away from catastrophe is the path of genuine internationalism. Increasingly the liberal has understood the conservatives' worries over centralization and over the size of the federal budget; has sought to revitalize state and local government; and has responded to the conservative insistence that in dealing with the world, hardheadedness too has its virtues.	
Today, in a very real sense, almost all of us are liberals, almost all of us are conservatives—and we are all moving toward a new American consensus.	Today President Johnson contends that, in a very real sense, almost all of us are liberals, almost all of us are conservatives—and we are all moving toward a new American consensus.

I watched the adoption of the consensus philosophy with pleasure. I thought it good for the nation at this stage; I was happy that President Johnson agreed. I was excited by the thought that the United States, through a not always neglectful Providence, might have stumbled upon a leader who, in a combination of Old Jim, chamber of commerce instincts and a drive for greatness, could move us a long way toward the aspirations of James Madison and Thomas Wolfe. Of course I had my jabs of concern. It was not possible to hear Lyndon Johnson talking consensus without visions of a relentless pursuit of that last possible vote down that farthest creek bottom.

I was excited, a bit bothered, and I plunged ahead in an atmosphere where somehow it was always unexpectedly one-thirty in the morning.

CHAPTER 4

Prime Minister Johnson

L yndon Johnson admired a number of modern American Presidents. He responded to the hyperactive White House of Theodore Roosevelt, to the bantam-cock ways of Harry Truman, to what he considered the prudent good sense of Dwight Eisenhower. Franklin Roosevelt was a hero to him; he kept saying so and he meant it. Of the more important twentieth-century Chief Executives, he did not cotton at all to only one, President Wilson, whom he considered an insufferable prig. There was irony in this. For it was Woodrow Wilson who made his academic reputation arguing that the President should be, as much as the American system permitted, a Prime Minister, and it was Lyndon Johnson who, more than any other President including Woodrow Wilson, was proceeding to function in that manner.

Once the State of the Union address and the Budget Message were over and the new President headed into the long drive, his deeper attitude emerged. However incongruous in some respects it may be to speak of President Johnson as a Prime Minister, much is lost by ignoring the similarities, at least in the early years of his Administration. Like the head of a parliamentary government, he thought of himself as a leader who had risen, and properly so, from the ranks of Congress, and as a man who retained close ties to it. For thirty-two years Congress had been his "home," he would say publicly and privately; his feeling for its ways was "deep in the marrow of my bones." He believed that a Chief Executive should never stint on time or energy in attempting to remain in rapport with the congressional powers and that it was a main function—often he acted as if it were the prime function—of a President to keep all possible members of his own party in the House and Senate and detachable men from the other party behind his policies. While recognizing the need at times to appeal over the head of Congress to the general public, he did not like to do this, and for a strong President, he resorted to the practice relatively little. Instinctively he thought it better to move the House and Senate by working from within rather than by prodding from without. At bottom he took his greatest sense of achievement not from an executive action but from a measure that the Administration had been able to steer through Congress. "The thing that counts," he remarked, "is getting those bills through. They really do things, because they have the stamp of the country on them."

Lyndon Johnson believed that the President should be the leader of Congress, and in early 1964 he was leading. A legitimate argument has arisen over how much the new President was responsible for the swiftly accelerating pace of congressional action. The Kennedy Administration had prepared a legislative program which was suited to the era and had brought it a long way toward passage. As the JFK bills tumbled through under LBJ, Senate Republican Leader Everett McK. Dirksen and House Democratic Leader Carl B. Albert agreed, in Dirksen's words, that "this program was on its way before November 22, 1963. Its time had come." The assassination itself, by muting partisan differences and throwing a glow around everything associated with JFK, made the passage of the legislation easier. It is also true that after the congressional elections of 1966, which added a sizable number of anti-LBJ men in the House and Senate, President Johnson's control of Congress faltered. Yet whatever the reasons, the inescapable fact is that during the first period of his Presidency he exercised an extraordinary and unprecedented mastery over the House and Senate.

In early 1964 the new President was giving so much attention to Congress and achieving such striking results that Washington revived a phrase from his Senate days. The city was full of talk of the "Johnson treatment" in dealing with the House and Senate, and an awed mystique was growing up about his techniques. Actually, there was no great mystery about the Johnson treatment. It was based on certain quite comprehensible facts.

Americans have always had two sharply divergent attitudes toward the democratic process. One group, centered among the upper-educated, and particularly among the upper-educated of the Northeastern states, has tended to view congressmen as a necessary evil, the source of little that is distinguished in the national life and an almost constant drag on enlightened efforts in domestic and foreign affairs. This tradition has put its main faith in the President and in the relatively nonpolitical career people of the federal government.

The other group, spread through the rank and file and especially numerous in the South and West, has made the elected official almost synonymous with democracy, and regarded the congressman as the most democratic of all the elected officials. These Americans have been skeptical of the career man as a person who does not understand the needs and hopes of ordinary people, and they have been quite ready to take sides against a President, elected though he may be, when he clashed with representatives and senators, who were chosen by a process closer to home. It was no coincidence that during the upsurge of the civil service movement at the turn of the century, some of its sharpest enemies were men like William Jennings Bryan, who spoke for the most populistic strain of public sentiment. Nor is it surprising that opinion of this type has shown a persistent tendency to want to apply the elective process even to offices like judgeships, for which professional competence, not the ability to win an election, is the obvious criterion.

Lyndon Johnson grew up in an area and in a home guided by these attitudes. State legislator Sam Johnson used to say, "Our feeling in this part of the country is that if you want somebody who will really speak for the folks, make him come back and face the voters." Lyndon Johnson had spent almost all of his mature life running for office and was proud, belligerently proud, of the fact. He wanted no japeries about politicians and elections in his speeches, as I soon learned. "Public service" and "schoolteaching," the President often remarked, were the best ways to spend a life, and what he really meant by public service was elective office. He genuinely esteemed many career people and worked with them rather easily. But his greatest sense of rapport went to the man who had stood up before a constituency and won a majority. This respect for the role of Congress—Mrs. Johnson once called it a "fierce respect"—showed itself plainly in his dealings with members of the House and Senate, and it was the foundation of his ability to get along with them and to sway them.

Lyndon Johnson had taken the trouble to be intricately informed about Congress. He "knew the deck," to use the phrase of the New Deal's highly successful congressional liaison man, Thomas G. Corcoran. He knew where every wire of power ran, whose influence was waxing or waning, the rules and habits of the committees, what each had done three years before and wanted to do next year, the skeletons and the hopes in scores of closets. Observers spoke of his consummate sense of "timing" in dealing with the House and Senate. It came not only from the facts he had learned but from the moods he sensed. As he once ruminated about the Senate, "It's like a dangerous animal that you're trying to make work for you. Push him a little bit, and he'll go. Push him a little bit harder, and he may go or he may balk and turn on you. You've got to sense just how much he'll take and what kind of mood he's in each day, and if you lose your feel for him, he's going to turn around and go wild."

Feeling thoroughly at home with the House and Senate as institutions, President Johnson also respected and liked an enormous number of individual congressmen; he liked the congressional type and the way of life. Give Franklin Roosevelt an evening off and he was likely to call for a movie of sophisticated comedy and watch it with friends ranging from David Dubinsky to the British ambassador. For Harry Truman, it might be a quiet evening with Bess or a game of poker with buddies from the old days; for Dwight Eisenhower, a bridge session with corporation executives; for John Kennedy, some reading or a gay dinner party with guests from the Social Register and the sophisticate set. Once in his Senate days Lyndon Johnson went with an aide to a Broadway musical; in ten minutes he was out of his seat heading for a phone to talk over the state of a bill with another senator. LBJ did not enjoy musicals, concerts, books, cards, dinner parties as dinner parties, or conversation as conversation. He liked dancing on occasion, especially if there were attractive women present, and good food, of which he could eat little since his heart attack. Most of all he liked politics, politicians and political talk. Lyndon Johnson with an evening off was more than likely to surround himself with political friends, largely from Congress. As he slowly stirred his Cutty Sark, the talk would meander on, how we did this in 1939 and that in 1947 and especially what we're going to do next week. His humor was the politician's humor, aided by unusual gifts for mimicry—the knee-slapping phrase about old George, the garter-snapping gossip, the we-fellows-all-know stories of the campaigns.

A favorite of the President's concerned Representative Magnus Johnson from Värmland, Sweden, via Kimball, Minnesota, who— so Lyndon Johnson would declaim in a splendid Swedish accent— rose in the House to declare, "What we have to do is to take the bull by the tail and look the situation in the face." Given the right company, he would lean back and tell the story of "little Juan," who was found crying on a curbstone in Austin. Asked why, little Juan said, "Because my father didn't come to see me."

"But your father has been dead for six years."

"Yes, but last Tuesday he came back to vote for Lyndon Johnson and he didn't come to see me."

Responding to congressmen as human beings, President Johnson understood them as human beings. He never forgot that like the rest of us, they need to feel that they are men of importance. He telephoned members of the House and Senate sometimes because he wanted to talk to them, sometimes because he wanted them to be able to remark casually, "Now, when the President called me this morning . . ." Chief Executives customarily send influential congressmen staff-written notes on their birthdays. Lyndon Johnson phoned them, and was likely to add, "I just read that wonderful speech of yours in the *Congressional Record*." Since Washington knew that President Johnson was a devotee of the *Congressional Record*—actually a White House messenger was at the Government Printing Office early each morning and by seven A.M. an aide was culling the *Record* for items to send to the Oval Office—the congressman was ready to assume that the President had really read the speech, and was not averse to believing that he thought it wonderful.

LBJ kept saying to House and Senate members, "Our house is your house," and scarcely forty-eight hours went by when he did not invite some of them to the White House, singly or in selected groups for a business session during the day, at night in larger groups for a social "howdy." He courted in depth as well as in breadth. He kept in mind his first days in Washington as secretary to Representative Kleberg, who was much more interested in having a good time than in the chores of a congressman, when Lyndon Johnson was the representative for all practical purposes. At the height of one LBJ congressional drive, astonished assistants in the office of each representative and senator, as well as staff members of all congressional committees—some thirteen hundred in all—received invitations to a social function arranged for them on the South Lawn of the White House. They sipped punch, nibbled at a delicious buffet, got in their observations to the President or Mrs. Johnson, and ambled about to the selections of the Navy steel band and the scarlet-coated Marine musicians.

Congressmen have wives and wives have new dresses waiting for the right occasion and friends, not to speak of enemies, to impress. President Johnson strained the White House facilities including wives in every possible activity. When calling a representative or a senator on business, he often included the wife in the invitation. While the President had his talk, Mrs. Johnson would be escorting Mrs. Congressman through rooms of the White House rarely seen even by state guests.

Congressmen, like the rest of us, not only need to feel important; perhaps more than the rest of us, they need to feel that they are recognized as men of principle. Since most human beings are to some degree and in some sense people of principle, in discussing legislation with a congressman LBJ sought to say the thing which caught up the best in the man or at least expressed that combination of ideals, prejudices, self-interest and reflex actions which the man called principles. The President concentrated on this and spoke with all stops pulled out. He could flatter in geysers because he had learned that the extravagant compliment may make others wince but rarely the person to whom it is directed.

One of the illusions I took to Washington was that there is a limit to the effectiveness of flattery, at least in the case of sophisticated men, even when uttered by a President of the United States. I was soon disabused. A month after I arrived I lunched with an eminent gentleman—a worldly one in this or any other civilization—who that morning had been asked by President Johnson to do something which he did not want to do and should not have done in view of his opinions and commitments. Now he was going to do it, and the reason was clear. During our lunch, he could not resist letting me know, in a backhanded way, what the President had said to him, and it was obvious that Lyndon Johnson had laid it on not only with a trowel but in dump-truck proportions.

So President Johnson knew how much congressmen are like the rest of us and he knew, with an instinct developed over the long years of politicking, the essential difference: congressmen want to run for office, once again, and to win. LBJ responded to this urge and to its accompanying considerations. The decades of congressional life, the national campaigns, the photographic memory, the voracious interest in political situations all counted. He had studied not only Congress but the circumstances surrounding congressmen. Especially in the case of men from the South and Midwest—he was not so well informed about the big cities of the North and Far West—he had a surgical knowledge of states and districts, the political strengths and weaknesses of individual congressmen, their supporters and opponents back home, their allegiances, apprehensions and ambitions. One day I ran into a freshmen representative, whom I had known in a different milieu, as he emerged from the Oval Office. The congressman had a numbed look. "It was like talking to my campaign manager—only I wish he knew that much."

In dealing with men who were inveterate candidates, President Johnson avoided asking them either to commit political suicide or to vote against their "principles." Since he rarely sponsored bills lacking a spectrum of support, only congressmen on the extremes of either side were likely to be totally out of sympathy with the measure. He believed wholeheartedly—even if the holy overtones rang strangely—in his favorite quotation, from Isaiah 1:18: "Come now, and let us reason together, saith the Lord." He assumed that there was usually more in common than in conflict between his position and that of the man in the other chair, and patiently, pragmatically, he set about widening the area of agreement. The fact that he had customarily expended the effort ahead of time to build support from relevant pressure groups often eased the path of the congressman in coming over to his side.

President Johnson resented the repeated statements that when persuasion failed, he resorted to "arm twisting." Of course he twisted arms. The puckish theologian Reinhold Niebuhr soon pointed out that what follows Isaiah 1:18 is Isaiah 1:19-20: "If ye be willing and obedient, ye shall eat the good of the land: But if ye refuse and rebel, ye shall be devoured with the sword: for the mouth of the Lord hath spoken." But there are two varieties of the arm-twisting procedure, and Lyndon Johnson's resentment came in part from the fact that they were often thrown together in discussing him.

One type is simply a part of the persuasion process, in which the President more or less directly offers something which, politically speaking, makes it more advantageous or at least equally advantageous for the congressman to go along rather than hold out. Certainly a Chief Executive has plenty to offer—ranging from a photograph with himself for the hometown paper to White House support for a multimillion-dollar works project in the district or state. The other kind of arm twisting is sheer force—embarrassing, bullying, threatening a man into compliance—and if these fail, the use of political reprisals to make the congressman more amenable on the next occasion. The congressionally active Presidents of the twentieth century all used both types of arm twisting. The difference in the case of Lyndon Johnson was that he employed them much more systematically, with a dogged reluctance to accept a no. More than a few times Isaiah was joined by Samson, towering to all his six-foot-three of physical vigor. At the climax of an LBJ persuasion the President might well be out of his chair, peering intently into the other man's eyes, literally grasping a lapel, a shoulder or an arm.

The arm twisting had a greater effect because of its background. Like all good politicians, Lyndon Johnson had taken the trouble to accumulate political debts. In his case, his long-time power in

Congress and his years in the top echelon of the Democratic party had placed in his hands a tremendous number of IOU's, probably more than any modern President could rely upon. The bills callable ranged all the way from an act like his sincere sentimental journey to the funeral of Senator Byrd's daughter to the fact that as Senate Majority Leader he had—with scarcely concealed intent to collect later—arranged a seat on a major committee for each freshman senator. In the Senate days the political banking operation had been conducted not only indefatigably but with considerable subtlety. In particular, LBJ avoided what he called "winning little victories at the expense of a big one." Many times he did not push an abrasive minor point when he had the votes, or gave another man credit for some small achievement he himself had largely brought about. "After all," LBJ said, "you need a friend down the line."

Later the friend might think the interest high but here too Lyndon Johnson, now President, had soothing balm. As he remarked to one congressman, all the while tightening the twist, "That's the way it goes. Often at this desk I don't do what I really want to do. I do what I have to do. You go through the same thing, and you and I understand."

And all along President Johnson kept ready his ultimate weapon, one that was thoroughly natural to him—unadorned, emotional patriotism. Such an appeal had not come easily to the stiff-backed Woodrow Wilson, to the precinct-minded Harry Truman, to the ironical John Kennedy. Theodore and Franklin Roosevelt turned to it more frequently, but the very sophistication of these Presidents blunted its effect. Lyndon Johnson, with his broad streak of simple patriotism, often sentimental in his thinking and evangelical in tone, could use it with a sincerity and effusion of statement that made many a man leave his office having agreed to cast a vote he had been sure he never would.

The appeal to America and the arm twisting, the knowledge of the deck and the genuine rapport with congressmen—all of these came together, wondrously integrated, in the virtuoso congressional performances of LBJ as he moved into the full swing of his Presidency.

Of the big four of Kennedy legislation—civil rights, federal aid to education, Medicare and tax reduction—the first two in priority in the new President's mind were civil rights and the tax cut. Passage of the pro-Negro legislation was essential to answer the civil rights agitation; it was no less needed to spread an impression of Lyndon Johnson as a liberal, broadly national leader. Tax reduction was obvious good politics in an election year, and the President had accepted the arguments of Kermit Gordon and Walter Heller that it was also good economics because it would stimulate investment and consumer spending and keep the boom going.

Shortly before President Kennedy's death, a civil rights bill had been worked out which included key demands of the Negro leaders: the establishment of a national Fair Employment Practices Commission, a public-accommodations clause guaranteeing the right of access to hotels, restaurants and similar public facilities, and a provision permitting the Department of Justice to intervene in civil rights cases. This measure was almost certain to pass the House of Representatives. The task of the new President was to remove the "almost" and then see to it that the bill hurdled its big obstacle, the inevitable Southern filibuster in the Senate.

When President Johnson took office, the tax cut had already been approved by the House. Again the difficulty was the Senate but in a different form. The understanding between the President and Senator Byrd ensured that the bill would be reported out of the Senate Finance Committee and that it would not be unduly delayed on the floor. The danger was that the measure might well be amended in ways that the Administration considered harmful or downright dangerous to the economy.

On the morning of January 23, 1964, the threat took concrete form. The Finance Committee was about to approve the tax bill when Minority Leader Everett Dirksen, also a member of the committee, suddenly jammed through an amendment which cut a whopping additional $445 million in taxes by abolishing excises on furs, jewelry, cosmetics and other "luxuries." Lawrence F. O'Brien, the Kennedy holdover as the chief White House congressional liaison man, was alarmed. The Dirksen amendment would probably provoke others, and the floodgates would open.

O'Brien hurriedly phoned the White House, reaching President Johnson in the middle of lunch, and that was the end of the meal. One after another the President telephoned members of the Senate Finance Committee and practiced every form of arm twisting known to political osteopathy. That afternoon the Dirksen amendment was removed by a nine-to-eight vote, with Senator Byrd backing the White House, and the committee reported the bill to the Senate without significant change. Now LBJ sent word to his Senate leadership. He wanted no important amendments passed during the debate. Senator Byrd, avoiding the sponsorship of a measure with which he disagreed, turned over the floor generalship for the bill to the second-ranking Democrat on the Finance Committee, Huey Long's son, Senator Russell B. Long.

Promptly everyone's special interest began to show. Russell Long might be the floor leader; he was also from oil-producing Louisiana, and he tried to cut $30 million from the proposed $80 million increase in taxes on oil companies. Senator John O. Pastore, the stalwart Democrat representing Rhode Island, a center of the manufacture of costume jewelry, revived Republican Leader Dirksen's effort to remove the tax on "luxury" items and pleaded soulfully not to vote against "beauty." Senator Bourke B. Hickenlooper of Iowa, where ball-point pens are a considerable industry, suddenly discovered that taxing ball-point pens is erroneous fiscal policy.

Various ideas of tax reform, coupled with the White House insistence on no significant changes, produced all kinds of strange situations. Senator Eugene J. McCarthy of Minnesota proposed a "working girl's" amendment—counting an unmarried woman over thirty-five as the head of a household—only to be told by Floor Leader Long, somewhat to McCarthy's bewilderment, that his amendment would help couples "who live in sin." Senator Hubert H. Humphrey urged a $365 tax credit for each child in college, was phoned by the White House and voted against his own amendment. Nathan M. Pusey, president of Harvard University, found himself playing the role of a lobbyist, and an effective one at that. Some tax "reformers" had been urging the removal of the special tax benefit for individuals who regularly make large contributions to educational and charitable institutions, and that idea was now revived. President Pusey hurried to rally his troops. It was his efforts which probably tipped the scales against the amendment.

Senator Byrd, living up to the spirit as well as the letter of his understanding with President Johnson, left no doubt that he opposed the tax-cut legislation but kept on using his enormous influence to see to it that the bill was not significantly changed. The gale of telephone calls from Lyndon Johnson continued—a gale so sustained that the White House heard worried talk. "We don't want him to be one of the boys, just another senator," a political-minded aide fretted. "We only want to use those calls for maximum impact." Whatever the impact, the presidential effort and the alliance with Senator Byrd worked. Final congressional approval of the measure, virtually intact, came at 12:30 P.M. on February 26.

Six hours later President Johnson walked into the floodlit East Room of the White House to sign the bill and to make a television appearance hailing it. He was smiling broadly, and little wonder.

After languishing in Congress for thirteen months, the first of the JFK big four bills was now law, ninety-six days after he became Chief Executive.

Lyndon Johnson seemed much more at ease than in the earlier days of his Administration. He was using for the first time the Teleprompter, a device which has tripped many a skilled speaker, but this day he was having no trouble with anything. He read smoothly and genially, altered words effectively, once making what was to be a favorite change, substituting "this land" for "the nation."

He worked in the LBJ touches. Emphasizing that the bill had been passed "with the support of both Republicans and Democrats" and that it would benefit corporations as well as small taxpayers, he appealed, "Let us unite, let us close ranks." He had warm words not only for floor leader Long but for Senator Byrd—no doubt the only bill-signing ceremony at which a President has lauded a congressman who voted against the legislation.

President Johnson held back three of the pens piled in front of him. At the close of the occasion he and Mrs. Johnson left immediately for 3017 N Street, N.W., where Mrs. Kennedy was temporarily living. There he presented the pens to Mrs. Kennedy, Caroline and John.

On February 17, nine days before the signing of the tax measure, the Clerk of the House of Representatives came down the aisle of the Senate chamber with the House-approved civil rights bill. Immediately Senate Majority Leader Mike J. Mansfield of Montana was on his feet. "Mr. President, I request that House Bill 7152 be read for the first time." The Senate Clerk read the bill's title. "Mr. President," said Mansfield, "I object to the second reading of the bill today."

Thus, with due complexity, began weeks of some of the most complicated parliamentary maneuvering the Senate has ever known. The pro-civil rights Senate leadership sought to keep the bill out of the Committee on the Judiciary, whose chairman, Senator James O. Eastland of Mississippi, was not in the habit of permitting the committee to report out pro-Negro bills; to speed up action on the measure; and ultimately to find a way to impose cloture on debate and bring the bill to a vote. The opposition leader was the able and widely respected Democrat from Georgia, Richard B. Russell ("A real man," Lyndon Johnson said of Russell; the Negro leader Whitney M. Young, Jr., commented, "I'll take him to many a Northern liberal. He believes what he says and knows how to act on it"). A master of Senate procedure, Senator Russell had helped one civil rights bill after another to oblivion by skillful foot dragging. Now he had a target date, July 13, when the Republican National Convention would assemble. If he could keep the measure from being passed until then, Russell believed, the White House would drop it. No Democratic President running for re-election would tolerate the spectacle of Democrats deadlocked over civil rights in the Senate of the United States.

This time, however, the senator was fighting a powerful and rapidly mounting tide of public opinion. The summer before the assassination, well over two hundred thousand men and women— 10 to 15 percent white—had joined in the March on Washington, which made a hero out of Martin Luther King, Jr., and drove his cry, "I have a dream . . ." into the national folklore. In the opening period of the Johnson Presidency, the March on Washington echoed in endless demonstrations, and a different note—one making civil rights legislation seem still more urgent—had begun to sound. White Americans were reading more and more about the Black Muslim cult and its New York leader, Malcolm X, who was preaching bitter contempt for any Negro leadership that sought integration with the white world and was more than hinting, Fight fire with fire.

Senator Russell was also up against a President who had made a decision. Talking about the civil rights bill with a friend, President Johnson recalled a conversation with his fellow Texan, FDR's first Vice-President, John Nance Garner. "He was a great poker player, and he told me once that there comes a time in every game when a man has to put in all his stack. Well, I'm shoving in all my stack on this civil rights bill." The President made his position plain to the Senate leadership: he was for the measure just as it had passed the House, including the thorny public-accommodations provision. Any rumors that he was ready to accept significant amendment of that section were flatly wrong. Privately he stated his opinion that public accommodations was the section on which the Negro community had centered its emotions. Therefore it was not sensible to compromise it even if he himself were inclined that way, which he was not.

President Johnson made it equally clear to the Senate leadership that he was ready to make the necessary strong moves to defeat the Russell strategy of delay. If necessary, he was prepared to sacrifice all other legislative action in the Senate and keep the debate on civil rights going. He further intimated that if need be, he would summon Congress back in special session after the nominating conventions and hold it in Washington until the opposition let the measure come to a vote.

Lyndon Johnson also did not neglect leadership by restraint. Acting on his dictum that the Senate should be pushed but not too hard, he kept in his hands overall control of the strategy for the bill and maintained the full power of the White House behind it. However, he left the day-by-day management largely to the Senate leadership.

Majority Leader Mansfield managed to route the measure around Senator Eastland and bring it to floor action. Senator Russell succeeded in gaining more time by entangling the Senate in a dizzying debate over whether a motion to debate the bill was debatable. But by March the parliamentary maneuvers had run out. The legislation headed into an old-fashioned Southern filibuster, which the civil rights forces could end only by mustering the sixty-seven votes needed to impose cloture.

Senator Russell had a band of eighteen Southern senators whom he deployed in three platoons of six each, a fresh platoon each day. They talked on and on—about the "amalgamation and mongrelization of the races," the source of the grits that people in Minnesota eat, the living habits of Hungarian immigrants, sometimes about the bill itself, calling it, to use the phrase of Senator Russell Long, "a mixed breed of unconstitutionality and the NAACP."

President Johnson and his lieutenants were ready too; for the first time the anti-filibuster forces were as well organized as the talkers. After consultation with the Oval Office, Majority Leader Mansfield named Senator Hubert Humphrey floor manager for the measure. Humphrey, in co-operation with Senator Thomas H. Kuchel of California, a Republican civil rights leader, designated one senator to take charge of each major part of the bill, and these men kept watch over every parliamentary and public relations aspect of their particular sections. Relays of Justice Department experts were on hand to help with technical problems. To harass the filibuster, frequent quorum calls were necessary. Humphrey, a twinkle in his eye, named a group of senators to serve as "military police." They kept elaborate charts of the engagements of their colleagues and discussed with them whether keeping a date was really important. Each morning the "military police" or their aides were on the telephone to make sure that pro-civil rights senators who had said they would be on the floor actually appeared.

Meanwhile LBJ added fillips of another kind of pressure. Carefully avoiding too much appearance of an appeal over the head of Congress and insisting upon his full confidence in the workings of the Senate, he built occasional fires around the Hill. He had varied remarks for a variety of audiences. At a Swarthmore College convocation, he dwelt on the demands of history, ending a definition of twentieth-century freedom by asking, "Is freedom betrayed when in 1964 we redeem in full the pledge made a century ago by the Emancipation Proclamation?" To the leadership of the Southern Baptist Convention assembled in the Rose Garden of the White House, he was the simple man of faith: "I am not a theologian. I am not a philosopher. . . . But in more than three decades of public life, I have seen firsthand how basic spiritual beliefs and deeds can shatter barriers of politics and bigotry." It was the "responsibility" of the Southern Baptist leadership to aid in this process.

For an audience of business executives, President Johnson used the most Johnsonian way to make the point. Ad-libbing, he spoke of the family cook, Mrs. Zephyr B. Wright, "one of the great ladies that I have known. . . . She has been with us twenty years, she is a college graduate, but when she comes from Texas to Washington she never knows where she can get a cup of coffee. She never knows when she can go to a bathroom. She has to take three or four hours out to go across to the other side of the tracks to locate the place where she can sit down and buy a meal. You wouldn't want that to happen to your wife or your mother or to your sister, but somehow or other you take it for granted when it happens to someone way off there."

As the talk in the Senate went on, attention centered on one man who was saying very little at all—Minority Leader Everett Dirksen. If cloture were to be invoked, it could be done only with Republican aid, and only Dirksen could deliver a sufficient number of Republican senators. If enough Republicans were going to vote for cloture, amendments would have to be adopted, and only Dirksen could get Republican approval of amendments which did not gut the bill.

The relationship between President Johnson and Senate Minority Leader Dirksen is a fascinating and important part of the history of the Johnson Administration. The men were like two veterans of the ring, with no special fondness for each other but showing thorough respect for a fellow pro, recognizing that the other man was doing his job even if it included bloodying your face, circling warily for advantage while they went about their mutual business. As for the reality behind all the maneuvering, Dirksen was about as deceptive a personality as sleight-of-hand Washington could present. A county-fair conservative in his basic instincts, a rampant partisan, delighting in stratagems and oozing mellifluousness, he easily appeared a political con man out of the

McKinley era. Yet there were other, important sides to Everett Dirksen of which President Johnson was fully aware.

The senator was too good and too intelligent a Republican to want his party to take responsibility for the defeat of a civil rights bill in the existing national atmosphere. He was too much the Senate man, too fascinated by the role in which he found himself, not to want to play legislative kingmaker. He was also—especially now that the years and the ailments were settling on him—too responsible an American to help create the kind of situation that could result from failure to pass a strong civil rights bill. President Kennedy used to say of Dirksen, and President Johnson agreed, that "most of the time old Ev is a good man when the chips are down."

There was something inside the man which made him retreat into self-caricature. Shortly after Dirksen had been instrumental in putting through a major Administration bill, I saw him at a White House social affair and felt moved to go up to him and congratulate him on his role. The senator straightened up, his tangled gray mane went back, the words came out pure syrup. "Nothing, nothing at all to my credit. I simply glimpsed duty and followed its inexorable path."

Now President Johnson had the Senate Minority Leader over for a few "good long talks." In the Senate the courting of Dirksen was furious. At one point Majority Leader Mansfield turned to him and said, "I appeal to the distinguished Minority Leader, whose patriotism has always taken precedence over his partisanship, to join with me—and I know he will—in finding the Senate's best possible contribution at this time to the resolution of this grave national issue." Senator Russell, taking the tack that Dirksen of course would oppose the bill, declared, "I cannot refrain, even if it does harm to the Senator from Illinois, from expressing to him my great admiration for his political courage. It gives one hope for the future of the Republic to see a man who has convictions and the courage to sustain them even though it may endanger his seat in the Senate."

Everett Dirksen himself was magisterial. "I trust that the time will never come in my public career when the waters of partisanship will flow so swift and so deep as to obscure my estimate of the national interest. I trust I can disenthrall myself from all bias, from all prejudice, from all irrelevancies, from all immaterial matters, and see clearly and cleanly what the issue is and then render an independent judgment. Already some amendments have occurred to me. I shall try to shape them. I shall try to put them in form. If I think they have merit, I shall offer them."

By April the senator was sufficiently disenthralled from all evil impulses to begin to find merit in a number of amendments. He was holding frequent conferences with Justice Department officials and with pro-civil rights senators. The amendments were being shaped—ones that the White House did not object to and which would make the measure palatable for the Republican senators needed to vote cloture.

The filibuster lumbered on, to a Senate record of fifty-seven days. Daily the Southerners showed less heart; their speeches sounded more and more like obeisance to ritualism. When cloture was clamped down, it established two additional landmarks in Senate history. It was the first use of cloture by the Senate for the purpose of passing a civil rights bill. It soon led to the first pro-Negro legislation of modern times approved by the Senate without significant amendment.

On July 2, 1964—two hundred and twenty-three days after he became President—Lyndon Johnson again entered the East Room, for the signing of the second of the big four of Kennedy legislation. This time his smile was one huge glow.

CHAPTER 5

LBJ
Takes Over

*F*oreign affairs, President Johnson kept on hoping, would remain quiet, and for the most part the world had been co-operating. But as the tax-reduction and civil rights bills moved through Congress, noisy trouble if not crisis came from, of all places, tiny Panama.

There a military junta had taken over under President Robert F. Chiari, whose party faced an election in May. A perfect issue was at hand. Sixty-one years before, President Theodore Roosevelt, in one of his more rambunctious moments, had virtually seized the ten-mile-wide Canal Zone strip and then given Panama a treaty providing an initial sum of $10 million and a fee of $250,000 a year. The annual amount had never been raised and the United States exercised the rights of sovereignty over the Zone, offering an ideal target for a rising Panamanian nationalism and a small Communist movement. The situation was exacerbated by the fact that the area was administered by some twenty-seven thousand "Zonians," a near-hereditary caste of American bureaucrats. They lived in conspicuous comfort next door to the misery of Panama City and conducted themselves with nineteenth-century colonial hauteur, including an insistence as to just how and where American flags were to be flown.

In January 1964, a flag incident led to full-scale rioting during which twenty people, including three Americans, were killed and hundreds injured. Fearful that the nationalist sentiment would defeat him in the election, Chiari moved to outdo it. He broke off diplomatic relations with the United States and demanded "complete revision" of the Panama Canal treaty.

President Johnson told an aide, "Get me the President of Panama—what's his name—on the phone."

"Mr. President," the assistant ventured to say, "you can't do that. It isn't protocol. You just can't do things like that."

"Why in hell can't I? Come on now, get him on the phone."

The President of the United States told the President of Panama that he understood—he too had an election coming. But of course Chiari had to see to it that the disorder ended and then the United States would send some first-rate men to work out the difficulties. Chiari agreed that the violence should stop but insisted that revision of the treaty was the prerequisite for American-Panamanian amity. The President refused to accept such a prerequisite. He had no intention of taking terms from Panama, which, as he remarked later, is no bigger than St. Louis. What's more, "they were killing. . . . You can't say, 'I'll give you a blank check,' when there is a pistol pointed at your head." Apart from his own attitude, he had very much in mind November 1964 and what the Republicans might do with any diplomacy that could be called knuckling under to a banana republic.

The conversation ended inconclusively. That same day violence broke out again in Panama City and a mob attacked the American embassy. President Johnson dispatched his new appointee for Latin American affairs, Thomas C. Mann, a fellow Texan and former ambassador to Mexico, to Panama City. Negotiators from the Organization of American States joined in the efforts for an agreement. With that the President turned back to domestic and political affairs, spending several hours of the next day in an unhurried talk with James A. Farley, Franklin Roosevelt's architect of the great 1932 and 1936 victories.

The American-Panama conferences bumped along, soon centering around a tangled debate whether the United States would agree to "negotiate" a new treaty—the word President Chiari felt he needed to satisfy Panamanian nationalism—or to "discuss" the negotiation of a new treaty, the formula President Johnson felt was necessary to avoid a Republican uproar. By March 15 OAS negotiators felt that they had the concurrence of Mann and of the Panamanian government to name ambassadors for "discussions and negotiations." At 6:45 P.M. the OAS released this settlement to the press.

But President Johnson, although he was leaning enough toward the compromise to give Mann the impression that it was acceptable to him, was still not certain. Characteristically keeping a line to the Hill, that evening he summoned congressional leaders to the White House. Senate Majority Leader Mike Mansfield, Majority Whip Hubert Humphrey, J. William Fulbright, chairman of the Senate Foreign Relations Committee, and Wayne Morse, chairman of the Latin American Subcommittee, all favored going along with the OAS formula. The old-style Senator Richard Russell, present as chairman of the Armed Services Committee, and the Republican leaders in the House and Senate, Representative Halleck and Senator Dirksen, were strongly against it.

"Hell, Mr. President," Dirksen said, "if we give an inch we will be saying to every little country in the world that the way to get something out of us is to break off relations, attack our embassy and make demands on us." If President Johnson accepted the OAS formula, Dirksen and Russell agreed, it would stamp him as "weak" in foreign affairs and that reputation would dog him for the rest of his time in the White House.

Lyndon Johnson was not about to ignore powerhouse senators like Dirksen and Russell, and he was growing irritated at what he considered the grandstanding of the Panamanian government. As the evening went on, he was particularly annoyed by reports that Panamanian radio stations were broadcasting the OAS announcement in a way which made it sound like a total Panamanian victory. And by now a quite different element, of special emotional power, was becoming more and more important in the presidential reaction. By coincidence, the first serious foreign difficulty of the Johnson Administration was grinding on its most sensitive nerve.

To ardent JFK men, the Latin American policy of the Kennedy Administration epitomized the glory of the New Frontier years. They were enormously proud of the Alliance for Progress and believed that its promise of large-scale American government aid and its tone of understanding and sympathy for drastic social reform presaged an era in which the United States would move with, not against, the twentieth-century wave of economic and social change. Some of the most articulate of the New Frontiersmen had been especially articulate about Latin America and especially active in Latin American affairs. They were indignant at President Johnson's appointment of Thomas Mann, whom they called a "reactionary" and who, in fact, had little enthusiasm for the Alliance for Progress. A lean-faced, tough-talking man, he was given to remarks like "These people need the application of a little muscle and common sense," which made him sound even more conservative than he was. What he actually favored was something of the Alliance for Progress approach accompanied by more skepticism toward the leaders of Latin American change and financed to a greater extent by American private investment than by government expenditures.

As Vice-President, Lyndon Johnson had been largely silent about Latin American affairs, as he was concerning most policies. But he had developed the conviction that what John Kennedy was doing in the area, or permitting to be done, was a thoroughgoing mess. That was precisely why he had appointed Thomas Mann and given him not only the title of Assistant Secretary of State for Inter-American Affairs but—to make sure that no one misunderstood Mann's closeness to the President—the designation of White House Special Assistant as well. And that was a major reason why the Panamanian episode, with its call-up in his mind of irresponsible Latin American leaders being encouraged to push petty purposes in the name of reform, was producing a decidedly stiff presidential back.

Now, at about eleven o'clock, President Johnson left the meeting with the congressional leaders and instructed the Press Secretary to issue a statement contradicting the OAS announcement. There was no agreement, the White House news officer told the reporters.

The next day the President went to the Hall of the Americas of the Pan American Union for an address commemorating the third anniversary of the Alliance for Progress. He remained ceremonial for most of the speech, then suddenly said, "Let me depart for a moment from my main theme," and departed with a crash. In the dispute between Panama and the United States, "our own position is clear. . . . We don't ask Panama to make any precommitments before we meet, and we intend to make none. . . . I do not believe that there has been a genuine meeting of the minds between the two Presidents of the countries involved." That was enough to startle the Latin American diplomats, but Lyndon Johnson was not done. "Press reports indicate that the Government of Panama feels that the language which has been under consideration for many days commits the United States to a rewriting and to a revision of the 1903 Treaty. We have made no such commitment. . . ."

The diplomats went away muttering irritably about the use of an Alliance for Progress ceremony for such talk. In Europe and Asia the Johnson policy toward Panama was producing an acrid press because it was interpreted as a colossus riding roughshod over the sensitivities of a small and powerless nation. Besides, Lyndon Johnson had now taken his stance of toughness before Congress and the public, and he wanted to get Panama out of his hair. He decided it was time for him to soften—and to help soften Chiari. He let it be known in Latin American circles that he was thinking of ordering a study of a new canal which might, or might not, pass through Panama. He found something different to say publicly.

Six days after the repudiation of the OAS statement, President Johnson ambled into the office of the Press Secretary during a routine news briefing. "Is it all right with you folks," he grinned, "if I monitor your press conference?" He proceeded to read a statement he was sending to Juan Bautista de Lavalle of Peru, chairman of the Council of the OAS. It was full of warm words about the long friendship of the United States and Panama, stated that "the claims of the Government of Panama, and of the majority of the Panamanian people, do not spring from malice or hatred of America . . . [but] are based on a deeply felt sense of the honest and fair needs of Panama," and offered a formula that was face-saving for both sides. The United States was not promising to "negotiate" a new treaty but it was also not saying it was ready only to "discuss" whether a new treaty should be negotiated. It was prepared to "review" any issue that the Panamanian government wished to raise. On April 3, diplomatic relations were restored and an accord was signed to get the review under way. (The agreement led, once the elections in both countries were over, to a new treaty, giving Panama a greater role in the management of the Canal and more financial return, and it set in motion a plan gradually to integrate the Zonians into Panamanian life.)

Many New Frontiersmen were outraged by the episode. The appointment of Mann, they declared, had presaged just what was happening—a ruinous hardline-ism toward the crucial Latin American area, which President Kennedy had been swinging into a whole new relationship to the United States. They were sure that John Kennedy would never have engaged in such personal diplomacy, never paid so much attention to old-style senators, never spoken in a way so abrasive to Latin America. Above all, they asserted, Lyndon Johnson, in his hardening and in his softening, was using this first conspicuous trouble in international affairs to put the LBJ stamp on foreign policy.

Lyndon Johnson would scarcely have disagreed with the last point.

When the President entered the Press Office to read his statement concerning Panama, the Press Secretary was no longer Pierre Salinger. Two days before, with polite words for Lyndon Johnson and unconcealed nostalgia for John Kennedy, Salinger had abruptly resigned and gone off to California to run for United States senator. In his place was that unmistakable Johnsonian, George E. Reedy, a huge, rumpled newspaperman who, along with

Abe Fortas and other LBJ intimates, had met *Air Force One* when it returned from Dallas. Throughout the White House circle, the JFK men were leaving or were being converted to LBJ men, and the LBJ people were coming in.

In the Cabinet, Attorney General Robert Kennedy continued to be the special case. He no longer moved about in a glaze of shock, but he was plainly uncomfortable and restless. He walked through the White House halls, his manner nervous, staring straight ahead, so indrawn he sometimes neglected to say hello to men he knew well. All Washington was aware that he and his supporters were building a Kennedy faction, "the government-in-exile," as people said with warmth or venom. Kennedyites met at Mrs. Kennedy's home and in other Georgetown houses for stratagems and plannings, in an atmosphere of "It just isn't fair," to use the characterization of the New York *Herald Tribune* reporter, Douglas Kiker. Robert Kennedy made no bones about his bitterness. He and his circle thought he had every right to the vice-presidential nomination on the 1964 Johnson ticket. If that failed, he would resign and establish an independent political base.

The high feelings touched all relationships. The Kennedy in-law, R. Sargent Shriver, Jr., had been so close to the family that he did a large part of the planning for the funeral of President Kennedy. But Shriver, a man of mercantile background and with an amiable personality, lacked the fierce sense of faction. He sought to mollify Robert Kennedy's emotions, suggesting that he might usefully work with the new Administration. Shriver found he was "walking into a buzz saw" and stopped his urging. A little later President Johnson let it be known that he was giving consideration to Shriver as his vice-presidential nominee and Shriver made no move to end the talk. RFK and many of his group responded furiously. A coolness developed between the brothers-in-law which never entirely disappeared.

Lyndon Johnson kept telling the reporters how splendidly everyone was pitching in to help the new President and then, with his intimates, he would talk the politician's credo. When he had been licked for the nomination and was agonizing through that "God-awful job," the Vice-Presidency, he did not "whimper," he was not "disloyal," and he had made no effort to build a rival organization. He had kept his mouth shut, inconspicuously trying to further John Kennedy's purposes. Most of the Kennedy group were not acting like "big boys." They would learn how to act that way—or else.

As for Robert Kennedy, President Johnson's opinion was stark and unchangeable. "That upstart's come too far and too fast. He skipped the grades where you learn the rules of life. He never liked me, and that's nothing compared to what I think of him."

Lyndon Johnson played his cards cool and close in dealing with the personification of the Kennedy legend. He remained punctiliously considerate, even respectful, toward Robert Kennedy; he also became more and more the President of the United States dealing with a subordinate. On one occasion the Attorney General went to the Oval Office to discuss the handling of a particular matter, and he remarked that President Kennedy would have done differently. LBJ's voice was bland. "President Kennedy is no longer President."

Apart from Robert Kennedy, political proprieties dictated that the whole Cabinet remain until after the election of 1964. But the more realistic process, the shakedown of those who were to be genuine members of the Johnson Administration, was proceeding rapidly. Secretary of State Dean Rusk had a large psychological deposit in the bank. During the Kennedy Administration he had treated the Vice-President as a man of importance, regularly briefing him and seeking his counsel more than perfunctorily. The Secretary also had a rapidly accumulating interest on his deposit. Of all the Kennedy holdovers in the Cabinet, he was becoming the favorite target of the New Frontiersmen.

In addition, Lyndon Johnson thought Dean Rusk just about right as a Secretary of State. A President who assumes he is going to run his own foreign affairs wants a Secretary who is knowledgeable, prestigious and unassertive, and Rusk was all three. What President Johnson had heard of the Secretary's opinions on foreign affairs so far seemed "sound and sensible," and not at all in disagreement with his own.

Dean Rusk the man seemed about right too. The President was delighted with the fact that the Secretary had been a Rhodes Scholar and head of the Rockefeller Foundation—the kind of credentials he felt would help his Administration—and yet retained something of the Georgia farm boy's earthiness. He liked the maxim Rusk frequently quoted, "Pray as if it were up to God; work as if it were up to you," and he was sure that the Secretary also had that quality which LBJ praised so frequently, "the ability to understand what's on the other fellow's mind."

Vice-President Johnson and Secretary of Defense Robert S. McNamara had not been much in contact, but President Johnson and Secretary McNamara were hitting it off. The President admired the Secretary's swift, highly organized intelligence, his control over the peacocking generals and admirals, his practice of coming to the Oval Office with the feasible alternatives clearly defined. McNamara's stock soared during the early economy drive. He headed the department where savings could be made on the largest scale, he suggested practical cuts, and he presented them along with big multicolored charts which President Johnson could show to doubting congressmen and reporters. If there was anything Lyndon Johnson admired more than economy, it was economy displayed with garter.

In the immemorial way of politics, other Cabinet members were on their way out. Secretary of the Treasury C. Douglas Dillon, a Republican banker and an Eisenhower Undersecretary, had been brought into the Kennedy Administration because he was flexible and because of the advantages in making a Wall Street man the head of Treasury. Dillon was now talking of his need to get back to his private affairs after the election, and since LBJ looked forward to picking his own Republican businessman types, he was demurring only formally. The Secretary of Health, Education and Welfare, Anthony J. Celebrezze, and Postmaster General John A. Gronouski had been named to satisfy political obligations and because an Irish Catholic President has special pressures from the Italian and Eastern European Catholic communities of the United States. (Asked about his qualifications for Postmaster General, the Polish-American Gronouski had replied with a laugh, "I licked stamps during the Kennedy campaign.") Neither Gronouski nor Celebrezze had licked stamps for Lyndon Johnson, and as a Protestant he had his own ways of taking care of ethnic urges. The Secretary of Commerce, Luther H. Hodges, was a high-minded textile executive and former governor of North Carolina who had been appointed to represent the New South. He was sixty-five and anxious to go home, and his Texas friend in the White House felt no particular need for a representative of the South. Secretary of Agriculture Orville L. Freeman, Secretary of the Interior Stewart L. Udall and Secretary of Labor W. Willard Wirtz all wanted to stay in the Cabinet; they had assets, both in terms of politics and ability, and they were making the effort to become Johnson men.

On or around the White House staff, some key JFK aides were also fitting in—not only White House Special Assistant for National Security McGeorge Bundy, Director of the Budget Kermit Gordon and Peace Corps Director and Special Assistant Sargent Shriver, but also, to the surprise of Washington, Lawrence O'Brien. On the plane back from Dallas, O'Brien, as the chief JFK agent in dealing with Congress, and the new President had discussed the Soviet wheat-sale amendment which the Senate leadership had agreed to deal with by November 25, the day of the funeral. On November 25, O'Brien went home from Arlington

Cemetery, changed from his black coat and striped pants into a business suit, and returned immediately to his office for a head count on the amendment. Despite an intense attachment to John Kennedy ("My twelve years with him were a golden age. I never expect to know anything like them again"), O'Brien continued to labor wholeheartedly on political and congressional liaison tasks for the Johnson Administration. Cool-mannered, an instinctive politico but not without a controlled liberal's zeal, a craftsman in any task he undertook, O'Brien was held to the work by the vigor and skill of the LBJ drive for social legislation and not least by the feeling that "this is what Jack Kennedy would have wanted me to do."

Other important Kennedy aides were resigning or making their plans. The earliest and the prime symbolic exit came on February 29, 1964, when Theodore Sorensen left. He intended to write a book about President Kennedy, he said, "because doing the book is, I suppose, a subconscious way of doing the last thing I can for Jack Kennedy or his memory." I was struck by another of Sorensen's departing remarks. Three years before, when he entered the White House, I had spoken to him in preparation for writing an article on the beginnings of the JFK Administration. The first subject Sorensen brought up was that sentence at the close of James MacGregor Burns's Kennedy biography. Now, leaving Washington, Sorensen went back to the point, saying that he hoped his book would combat the "insidious myth" that John Kennedy "had no heart, that he didn't commit his heart, that he didn't feel passionately about issues." This was a sensitive subject to the closest of JFK's associates.

The Johnson men were more and more evident in the White House. They were gradually taking over and asserting themselves. President Johnson continued to make it plain that they were to go slow in seeking the better White House offices, and the Sorensen suite was vacant for weeks after he left. But in ways symbolic and practical the LBJ men were moving in.

Visiting the White House in the spring of 1964, Adlai Stevenson commented, "The atmosphere, the people—well, they are Johnsonian, or Johnsonized."

The Johnsonian staff had some peculiarly Johnsonian problems. The Bobby Baker affair was taking a much more troublesome turn. In January the Senate Rules Committee had turned up headline testimony. Don B. Reynolds, an insurance man in Silver Springs, Maryland, told the committee that he had taken Baker into his firm as a vice-president in order to exploit his political contacts. In 1957, Reynolds stated, Baker was instrumental in his placing a $100,000 life insurance policy on Senate Majority Leader Lyndon Johnson, just two years after the senator's heart attack. Then Reynolds unmistakably implied a kickback. Walter Jenkins, he declared, "suggested" that he buy $1,208 worth of advertising time from the Johnson family television station in Austin; he bought it, and having no use for it, sold it for $106 to a kitchen-ware manufacturer. In 1959 Baker had a "suggestion": Reynolds should send the Johnsons a stereo set, which ended up costing $584.75 for the purchase and installation. In 1961 Vice-President Johnson bought a second $100,000 policy through Reynolds.

Walter Jenkins, badgered by the press, was a worried man. Never happy to see reporters, he now fidgeted in his office, snappishly refusing to take any call which might be connected with Bobby Baker. President Johnson turned to Abe Fortas and that other lawyer-politico who was receiving more and more calls from the Oval Office, Clark M. Clifford. Both agreed that Jenkins should not appear before the Senate Rules Committee and thus give added publicity to the charges. Instead, Jenkins sent a memo to the committee stating that he had not known Baker was associated with the Reynolds firm, had never suggested to Baker or Reynolds the purchase of television time, and had thought the stereo was a gift from Baker, not Reynolds.

Fortas and Clifford also agreed that President Johnson should make a statement. At his next news conference, the President talked mainly about Panama and congressional activities and then himself brought up the newspaper stories about "an insurance policy that was written on my life some seven years ago, and I am still here." He did not mention a purchase of television time and he said of the phonograph, "The Baker family gave us a stereo set. We used it for a period, and we had exchanged gifts before. He was an employee of the public and had no business pending before me and was asking for nothing, and so far as I knew expected nothing in return any more than I did when I had presented him with gifts. . . . That is all that I have to say about it and all that I know about it."

Soon columnist Drew Pearson published a series of articles concerning the testimony. Citing FBI sources principally, Pearson impugned Reynolds's reliability as a witness, on the grounds that he had a record of making reckless charges and had been involved in overseas black-market as well as other unethical activities. The FBI publicly denied that it had given Pearson material; Pearson publicly denied that his source was the White House. The *New York Times* printed a front-page story by Cabell Phillips which stated flatly: "Persons within and close to the Johnson Administration have attempted to use secret government documents to impugn the testimony of a witness in the Robert G. Baker case." The article went on to detail alleged White House efforts to interfere with the news handling of the Reynolds testimony.

By March, Baker himself was before the Senate Rules Committee, waving to familiar faces among the senators with his immaculately manicured hands. The testimony wound through his sponsorship by Senate Majority Leader Johnson and by the Majority Leader's close associate, the late Senator Robert S. Kerr of Oklahoma; the miraculous way that Baker's $19,612-a-year salary became a fortune of some two million dollars; his friendship with "Miss Loudon County" of Tennessee (35-26-35) who served as hostess for him in an elaborate Washington town house; the Quorum Club, organized by Baker for congressmen and lobbyists, where Ellen Rometsch, a kind of political Lili Marlene, pleased gentlemen until the FBI deported her; the stock deals (Baker "knew a lot of people," explained Max Karl of the Mortgage Guaranty Insurance Corporation); the speculative land deals and the bank loans (he had borrowed $1,703,538, still owed $683,334 and was co-signed on another million); the motels and vending-machine concessions, including his investment in Serv-U, which promptly acquired the concession at three aerospace centers.

For the senators, Baker had a persistent cocky smile, the invocation of the First, Fourth, Fifth and Sixth amendments, and a suggestion: "Why don't you fellows call this whole thing off so we can all get a rest?"

In speaking of his aide Bobby Baker, Majority Leader Lyndon Johnson had been accustomed to using language that was not restrained. "I have two daughters," he commented. "If I had a son, this would be the boy." He is "my strong right arm, the last man I see at night, the first one I see in the morning."

Now President Johnson went on television and William H. Lawrence of ABC asked him about "your protégé and your friend."

In answering, the President called upon his minute knowledge of Senate affairs. Baker was already a pageboy in the Senate when LBJ was elected to the body. Technically, the secretary for the Senate Democrats, the influential position Baker came to hold, is recommended by the Democratic leader, approved by the Democratic caucus and ratified by the whole Senate; in practice, he is simply picked by the Democratic leader. President Johnson replied to Lawrence that Baker had been "no protégé of anyone; he was there before I came to the Senate for ten years. . . . He was elected by all the senators, appointed by no one, including the Republican senators—and I think that their investigation will be a fair one. . . ."

Lawrence pressed: "Quite apart from what the Senate committee may recommend, sir, have you formed a personal judgment, a judgment for yourself? You and Mr. Baker used to be friends. Do you continue to be friends?"

"I haven't seen him . . . or haven't talked to him since he resigned from the Senate." He wanted to see the evidence, "with which I am not familiar," before making a judgment.

Shaking off the Baker affair and Washington, the President and his family flew to Texas for the Easter weekend. One of Lyndon Johnson's joys in being home was the fast ride in his cream-colored Lincoln Continental, along eight-lane Texas highways or familiar ranch paths, zigzagging around piles of manure and shouting at the cattle. This time stories seeped into the press which described more than fast, noisy drives. They reported his careening up a hill and missing a head-on collision only because the other driver swerved to the dirt ridge. They also mentioned an afternoon drive when he was supposed to have taken four women reporters along and, a beer in one hand, driven up to ninety miles an hour in a seventy-mile zone.

The next week *Time* magazine was out with a lengthy, mocking article about the afternoon ride, entitled "Mr. President, You're Fun," and filled with details of presidential beer drinking behind the wheel, of his graphic description to the women reporters of the sex life of a bull, of bawling cow horns and tremendous speed. "Reporters in the cars behind could scarcely keep up, and all kept a wary eye on their speedometers. In the President's car, someone gasped at how fast Johnson was driving. Quickly, Lyndon took one hand from the wheel, removed his five-gallon hat and flopped it on the dashboard to cover the speedometer. . . ."

Press Secretary George Reedy dismissed the *Time* story as second-hand fantasy and it was correct that at least some of the details came from reporters' tales to one another. Whatever the exact truth, President Johnson had been hurt, and hurt with permeative effect, by stories emanating primarily from two powerhouses of the Northeastern press, the *New York Times* and *Time*. The combination of the articles on the alleged White House effort to control reporting of the Baker affair and on the Texas drive made him sound like what no national politician of the 1960's wants to sound like and what he in particular could not afford to appear: the wheeler-dealer with an elastic set of ethics and the overgrown country boy showing off in front of the girls. Johnson men in the

White House were thoroughly worried. Lyndon Johnson himself was volcanic.

Throughout his congressional career he had never really trusted the press. That is why he had fluctuated between courting it extravagantly and cutting it off. Now the distrust heightened to a great degree, causing him to swing the more violently between abnormal secretiveness and abnormal openness, all the while trying ever more to maneuver the reporters. During his later Senate career, when he was seeking to become a national figure, and during the vice-presidential years, he had felt that the Northeastern press was not giving him a break because he was a Southerner and, more specifically, a Texan. Now he was certain he had been right.

The Northeastern press, President Johnson stormed, would not have treated the Baker affair or the Texas vacation this way in the case of another President; they would not have done this to a Roosevelt, an Eisenhower, a Kennedy or even a Truman. They were out to get him because he was a Texan. The *New York Times* and *Time* went on his anathema list, to be given temporary exoneration only when it was politic. The whole Northeastern area which he associated with them, its whole "hoity-toity" approach to public affairs, became the more suspect in his eyes.

Early on April 8 the White House phone brought the surprise news. At 4:30 A.M. the railroad unions had suddenly struck the Illinois Central, so suddenly that four thousand passengers were left stranded in darkened cars. Clearly, the single walkout could quickly lead to a national railroad shutdown.

If the Illinois Central strike was a surprise, trouble on the railroads was not. The basic problem was technological change. Management wanted to eliminate featherbedding and to use new methods and arrangements for greater efficiency and profits; the unions sought to protect jobs, and as technology advanced, to see to it that their members got as much as possible of the resulting savings. Around this fundamental difficulty a thicket of secondary issues had gathered. For five years a Republican and a Democratic President, three Secretaries of Labor, Congress and a series of committees, commissions and boards had sought to bring stability to the industry. All had failed.

The chief negotiating representatives were men who had grown up to the clang and whistle of railroading and to the peculiarly respectable but dogged headbutting that marked railroad labor relations. Management's spokesman was James E. ("Doc") Wolfe from Shelbine, Missouri, sixty-one years old, who began as a coal-chute laborer on the Chicago, Burlington & Quincy, and had taken the management route. A short, brusque, plain-living man (he moved from a Washington hotel with French cuisine to get his beefsteak done right), Wolfe was difficult to budge at the negotiating table. His principal opponent was the portly Roy E. Davidson, sixty-three, Grand Chief Engineer of the International Brotherhood of Locomotive Engineers, from Fairmount, Illinois, who had begun at sixteen as a fireman on the Illinois division of the New York Central. Softer in manner and more bureaucratic in thinking, Davidson was no less obdurate.

The immediate genesis of the April 8 strike was a secret meeting of union heads, held six days before in the Hotel Hamilton a few blocks from the White House. In 1963 President Kennedy, faced with a national rail strike, had asked Congress to decree compulsory arbitration. The resulting legislation established a board which ordered the elimination of some forty-eight thousand jobs over a period of time. The union leaders were angry, and in early 1964 they twice planned national strikes, only to be stopped by court orders. At the Hotel Hamilton they decided to pick off the railroads one by one with walkouts staged so suddenly that the courts could not act; they chose the Illinois Central primarily because of the thoroughgoing dissatisfaction of its workers. Alert for management, Doc Wolfe had no intention of letting the dispute be maneuvered off the national level. As soon as he heard of the pinpointed Illinois Central stoppage he ordered new work rules posted, designed to force the unions to accept some of the economies management wanted or be responsible for a national strike. The union leaders immediately opted for the country-wide walkout and set the time: about two days after the beginning of the Illinois Central strike, 12:01 A.M. on April 10.

President Johnson asked Walter Heller for a quick estimate of what the results of a national rail strike would be, and he was particularly impressed by Heller's report that six million workers would be laid off almost immediately and that food shipments to New York City would be severely affected. Some advisers urged the President to stay out of the dispute. It had become so encrusted that he might suffer a humiliating failure; collective bargaining had broken down so completely in the rail industry that probably a confrontation was needed to restore it. Others were for his intervention. They stressed the adverse political effects if the country were tied up, and they predicted another congressional imposition of compulsory arbitration which could make a farce out of collective bargaining in a key part of the economy. From the beginning, Lyndon Johnson leaned toward intervention.

The very history and intractability of the problem lured him. What previous Presidents had failed to do, he would accomplish.

The White House phones went to work. At six o'clock in the evening of April 9, with the Illinois Central walkout holding firm and the national strike deadline six hours away, the bargaining committees entered the Cabinet Room. President Johnson opened with a prepared statement. The "extremely serious consequences" of a national strike were plain. Only forty-eight hours had been allowed for "last-ditch collective bargaining. This does not give the bargaining process a fair chance. It does not give the country a fair break." He asked the unions to call off the Illinois Central walkout, and management to withdraw the changes in work rules, for a twenty-day period while the dispute was negotiated.

With his audience obviously unreceptive, the President turned evangelical. His voice high, his arms out, he told the group that five years of battling had made both sides lose faith in each other. "On that tragic day in November," labor and management had pledged their support to the new President. He looked intently, first at Roy Davidson, then at Doc Wolfe, and asked each, "Have you lost faith in me?"

The two committees went off to their separate dinners. Management, which had nothing to gain and considerable to lose by a national strike, returned agreeing not to impose new work rules for twenty days. The union representatives, having little hope that more time would buy anything they considered important, had an unhappy dinner. They came back saying no, they were sorry, they felt they must continue the Illinois Central strike and hold to the national deadline.

President Johnson turned to the union leaders. "I am your President. All I want is for you to give me a chance. Just give me a chance. I want you to go into my office, talk it over, and tell me you'll do this for me." The labor chiefs filed into the Oval Office.

While the management men remained in the Cabinet Room, President Johnson entered the office of his personal secretaries and stood talking with two veterans of labor troubles he had called into the situation, Secretary of Labor Willard Wirtz and the Assistant Secretary for Labor-Management Relations, James J. Reynolds. After fifteen minutes, Wirtz went into the Oval Office. He came out shaking his head unhappily.

Lyndon Johnson, his negotiating antennae fully extended, thought he sensed that the labor leaders were not uniformly adamant. Something new in the way of seasoning should be thrown into the pot. He asked Wirtz and Reynolds for suggestions and chose two: Cut the postponement from twenty to fifteen days and bring in fresh faces, specifically the respected and skilled labor mediators George W. Taylor, of the Wharton School of Finance and Commerce at the University of Pennsylvania, and Theodore W. Kheel, the New York City labor relations expert. Wirtz cleared the two points with management and President Johnson took the proposals into the Oval Office.

The union men still did not accede. Now Lyndon Johnson paced the Oval Office, his face somber, his gestures pleading, pausing repeatedly to speak directly to an individual. He recognized, LBJ said, that there had been no real bargaining about the issues which concerned the unions most, and "I appreciate your patience. But give me time. Please give me time. I am your President. I'm new on his job. I'm coming to you for the first time. I urge you to give me the opportunity to give you good-faith bargaining. I will personally ride herd over the negotiations and see to it that there is good-faith bargaining."

The union leaders stirred uncomfortably but none spoke. "I want all of you to recognize," the President went on, "that we are in high focus throughout the world tonight. Please give me this opportunity to show that our system of free enterprise really works." In the United States itself, the future of collective bargaining was at stake. What's more, millions of men would be thrown out of work and the whole economy knocked askew. "As patriotic Americans, I tell you you must delay."

Union chiefs interrupted to say that they were good patriots, but they also had to protect their members. The railroad workers would get nothing without a strike, and they had already waited beyond all reason. The President turned on the sentimental pleas and that LBJ type of humor which had been throwing men off balance for years. To Charles Luna, president of the Brotherhood of Railway Trainmen, a Texan and a long-time acquaintance, he said, "Charlie, it's not one of those damyankees asking you."

Luna protested, "Mr. President, suppose you were in my place, suppose you had your responsibilities but I appealed to you on the ground that we are fellow Texans."

"Why, Charlie, I'd fasten the button over my purse, and put my hand over it too."

At about ten-thirty in the weary evening, the union leaders huddled in a corner of the Oval Office. They emerged agreeing to end the Illinois Central strike and to postpone the national walkout for fifteen days of negotiations. As Roy Davidson said, "What else do you do if the President looks you straight in the face and tells you that it is your duty as an American?"

When they heard what had happened, a number of the carrier

representatives exploded. "He was practically on his knees to them," a railroad president snapped. "The President demeaned himself with his begging and pleading." Not all of the union men disagreed. "He pleaded beyond reason, for a President of the United States."

Whatever people were saying, Lyndon Johnson had his postponement. He hurried to the television room of the White House —it was 11:05 now—to tell the country, and he took with him Davidson and Wayne Johnson, president of the Illinois Central. Both men made the proper polite remarks but the union chief had something to add. Staring doggedly into the cameras, he reminded everyone: Unless a settlement acceptable to the unions was reached within fifteen days, the national strike would begin precisely at the end of the period, at 12:01 A.M. on April 25.

President Johnson left to cover another front. He called the White House switchboard. "How many operators are on duty tonight?"

"Three, Mr. President."

"That's plenty. We're going to settle us a railroad strike. If any of these people want to phone me, put them right through."

He had calls of his own to make. Theodore Kheel and George Taylor may have been duly named as additional mediators but no one had asked them to serve. The President reached Kheel as he was dozing over a pro basketball game on television in his home in the Riverdale section of the Bronx. Taylor had just returned to his apartment in Rittenhouse Square in Philadelphia after taking his wife to the hospital for an operation. Lyndon Johnson made one more call, to the University of Pennsylvania Hospital. "I want you to know," he told Mrs. Taylor, "that your country appreciates what your husband is doing, coming down here to help us with you on your back." Mrs. Taylor was so moved the nurse had to steady the phone as she answered.

The next morning, April 10, with the fifteen days to go, the group assembled in the Cabinet Room. It included, in addition to the union and management representatives, Kheel, Taylor and Assistant Secretary Reynolds, with Secretary Wirtz serving as chairman. President Johnson opened the negotiations with some Johnsonian remarks that "it is a deep-seated principle with me, through more than thirty-two years of public service, that so long as men try conscientiously to resolve their differences by negotiation, so long as they will follow the philosophy of the prophet Isaiah to 'Come now let us reason together,' there is always a chance." He had a personal word about facing up to difficult decisions. "I know what it's like. The hardest decision I ever had to make was when I lost the presidential nomination and had to decide whether to take the vice-presidential nomination. I decided to because I felt it was necessary to a Democratic victory." The President left then but as the men proceeded with their work, periodically a head came through the door. "Hi ya fellows, how ya doing?" Lyndon Johnson would say. At times he paused for a pep talk or for a reading of the latest figures from Heller's office about the harm a rail strike would do to the country. Often during the negotiations Press Secretary George Reedy, who had been LBJ's labor man during the Senate days, was part of the scene, representing the President's sense of urgency and joining in the formulation of proposals.

April 12, thirteen days to go. There were no signs of real progress. The complexity of the issues, the heavy pressure from the people behind both sets of representatives, the sensitivities and suspicions of all the previous battles kept throwing up blocks. The negotiations were shifted to the Executive Office Building, not only to clear the Cabinet Room but to provide more space and make it easier to avoid reporters. Each side was given an ancient cavernous office, and a still larger room was available for joint meetings.

The afternoon of the shift, the negotiators had a caller again. LBJ was still one of the boys, understanding everyone's problems, but he stepped up the pressure by reading two more memos prepared in Heller's office. The first presented figures proving that rail profits had been rising in recent months. The second pointedly described the hard line of the unions in past efforts at a settlement.

The President was also turning on the heat in public statements. Neither side really wanted another compulsory arbitration decreed by Congress. The unions were afraid of a second unfavorable award and management feared losing what it had gained from the first board. Yet with the deadlock continuing, all hands could easily assume that the only way out was more compulsory arbitration. President Johnson found several public occasions to say how imperative it was to avoid a rail strike and just as many to avoid saying what he would do if the negotiations failed. There was only one answer—go to Congress—but he never expressed it. He was doing nothing to remove that threat and nothing to encourage a fatalistic assumption that there was no point in really trying to make the negotiations work.

Twelve, eleven, ten, nine days to go. Minor agreements were reached; the groups came a little closer on certain major issues. Yet there was no breakthrough. Charles Luna, good-humored as well as hard-driving, had caught the spirit of the Oval Office and was acting as something of a cheerleader. One gloomy night Luna decided that a coffee pot would help. He went foraging in EOB, where almost anything can be found, and produced a battered pot. Secretary Wirtz's limousine was dispatched to the all-night drug-store several blocks away for several cans of coffee, and magnificently inept hands took over the brewing. "The worst coffee I ever tasted," one management man, who emphatically does not want to be named, recalls, "even worse than what I've been drinking at my wife's hand for years. But it helped get us through those impossible nights and was about the only thing we could agree on."

April 17, eight days to go. Reynolds, Kheel and Taylor, who were doing most of the hour-by-hour mediation, decided to concentrate on one important issue and try to set a pattern for compromise. They chose the problem of the pay for road crews and yard employees. Reynolds, who was particularly skillful in handling Doc Wolfe, persuaded management to offer a considerable concession, and Kheel and Taylor went to the union men. "That Taylor," a labor leader recalled. "He'd push you so gently that you didn't know you were being pushed. But pretty soon, you'd be standing out in the hall wondering how you got there." Another union chief added, "Kheel made us a speech that cut us up pretty good, although he did it in such a nice way we didn't know we were bleeding until he left the room." But the issue involved the rivalry for members between the unions as well as money. They made only a tiny concession.

April 19, six days to go. At one o'clock in the morning the unions budged a little more and the mediators, convinced this was all they could get, told Wolfe where things stood. His reply was a blast. "I'm getting a little tired of these concessions which amount to asking for more than they know they will ever get and then giving a quarter of an inch. I'm in a foul mood."

That evening the whole group went to the White House to report to President Johnson. He had another pep talk and more patriotic pleas to offer. He also had tougher words for both sides than he had ever used before. To the union men he said they would have to have the courage to tell their members they could not get everything they wanted. To the management leaders he declared, "Don't let the almighty dollar stand in the way of a settlement." Not all of LBJ's tactics pleased the tired and disgruntled men. Asked what happened during the session, one union leader muttered, "Lyndon has a flag in the corner of his office. He picked it up and ran around the room with it." But one way or another the President was getting across the point that he insisted upon a settlement.

April 20, five days to go. The negotiations went into a marathon session which would last until six the next morning. The union men were showing signs of fear that the talks actually would collapse and the dispute go to compulsory arbitration. In the middle of the night Reynolds was smiling as he murmured to Wirtz, "It reminds me of something Tagore wrote: 'Faith is the bird that sings while dawn is still dark.' "

At about three o'clock in the morning Luna, George Harris, representing the Order of Railway Conductors and Brakemen, and Neil P. Speirs, president of the Switchmen's Union, took a slow stroll around EOB. The mediators had stated they would make no proposals for an overall settlement unless both sides requested them. Harris, Luna and Speirs decided that the time had come, and when they consulted their colleagues, all the union chiefs agreed. Speaking for the carriers, Wolfe assented too but with a condition. He recalled the unaccepted mediation proposals that had been introduced as evidence during last year's congressional and arbitration proceedings and insisted, "If this thing is not accepted, I want to be damn sure that it doesn't wind up as Exhibit One before some congressional committee."

The mediators promised that this time there would be one handwritten copy, to be destroyed and never described orally if the terms were not approved.

April 21, four days to go. Late in the morning the mediators appeared with eighteen sheets of long yellow paper filled with penciled handwriting. The proposals gave important concessions to each side, denied important points each group wanted. One issue had produced the greatest intransigence—the "interdivisional run," the trip that went beyond areas traditionally called "divisions." The carriers, pointing out that trains now ran much more swiftly, demanded the right to use the same crews beyond divisions and to effect other savings in labor costs. The unions stood rocklike against these changes. Now the mediators suggested that the interdivisional issue should be suspended and referred to a national committee for further discussion. It is impossible to put a dollars-and-cents valuation on their total proposal, particularly since the terms were tangled with the awards made under the previous compulsory arbitration. Most objective observers later declared that the mediators' program, if it leaned either way, was something of a victory for the unions.

That afternoon the union negotiators accepted the terms. Wolfe was far from agreeing. He did not have the final power of acceptance or rejection, he emphasized. That had to come from the nine rail presidents who at the moment were hurrying to

Washington. Moreover, he was not at all sure he would recommend approval because the program did not settle the interdivisional issue.

April 22, three days to go. Just after breakfast, Wolfe, an exhausted and none-too-happy man, arrived at the White House for a talk with President Johnson and Secretary Wirtz. He spoke forcibly of the importance to the rails of the interdivisional issue; he wanted assurance that the mediators' proposal did not mean that the matter was being swept under the rug. Wirtz promptly gave him an ironclad guarantee.

Wolfe then pressed two management grievances. A bill giving the railroads greater freedom in setting freight rates was stuck in the House Rules Committee because of the opposition of water carriers; the Treasury Department had ruled that the railroads could not depreciate for tax purposes a $4 billion investment in tunnel and bridge construction, a decision which cost them $25–$30 million a year.

Lyndon Johnson leaped at the possibility of a trade. The Administration would act to get the freight-rate bill out of committee, he told Wolfe, and he would personally arrange a meeting between an industry representative and Secretary of the Treasury Dillon to review the tax question. If there is "justice" in your position, "you are going to be treated right."

At midday, when the rail executives had reached Washington and Wolfe reported to them the conversation, the group was reluctant to accept the settlement. Hearing of the situation, President Johnson invited the industry men for late-afternoon coffee, adding to the cordiality by having Mrs. Johnson and Lynda Bird present for introductions. Once the family left, several of the executives spoke up to voice their disquietude about a program that did not definitely solve the interdivisional dispute. They meant no "disrespect" or "disloyalty" to the President, but they really did not feel they should go along.

Now the presidential persuasion started again, but in a different tone. The April 17 issue of *Time* had carried the rail executive's remark that President Johnson had demeaned himself by the way he pleaded with the union leaders for a strike postponement. Not mentioning the article but obviously referring to it, Lyndon Johnson replied with unwonted aloofness that he wanted to assure the executives again how interested he was in the prosperity of the industry and how determined he was that the negotiations over interdivisional runs be pushed. But that was that: it was as far as he would go. "I hope you realize that if you say no on this proposal, I accept your decision. That is the kind of country this is. There can't be any question of disrespect or disloyalty. You know how strongly I want a settlement. I don't know what I will do if there isn't one. However, there will be no demeaning of this office."

As the executives went on talking, their opposition dissolved. Wolfe took his group aside. Soon he turned back. "Mr. President, we are prepared to accept this proposal."

Never since he entered the White House had Lyndon Johnson been so jubilant. He sent word that he wanted all the participants at the White House in half an hour for the announcement of the settlement on television. When the men arrived, the President was talking with Walter Lippmann. Ebulliently he introduced Lippmann. "I want you to meet Walter Lippmann. He's smarter than all of us." He told Lippmann, "These men have just saved collective bargaining. They did a wonderful job for their country."

Then Lyndon Johnson learned that it would take more than an hour to make arrangements for a telecast from the White House. He bundled Davidson, Reynolds, Wirtz and Wolfe into a limousine and the car shot out of the driveway ahead of its escort of four motorcycle cops. When the police caught up, one befuddled officer was shouting to another, "Where are we going?" They were going up Wisconsin Avenue to WTOP-TV, where the President could go on the air immediately.

During the nine-minute ride LBJ asked Wolfe to hand him the phone. "Honey," he said to Mrs. Johnson, "I'm going on television at six forty-five. Now, I want you to watch me." Wolfe was still disentangling himself from the telephone cord as they reached the studio.

"This agreement," President Johnson told the nation, "is American business and American labor operating at its very best. . . ."

He introduced Roy Davidson, then Doc Wolfe. And he had a letter to read:

"Dear President Johnson:

"I am seven. My grandmother lives in New York. She is coming to see me make my first Holy Communion. Please keep the railroads running so that she can come to see me. Thank you.

> "Cathy May Baker
> "36 Hemlock
> "Park Forest, Ill.

"So," the President said, "Cathy's grandmother can now go to see her and all my fellow Americans can be proud that the railroad management and the railroad brotherhoods came, labored, worked and reasoned together and, in the American way, found the answer."

The letter happened to be ten days old. Cathy May's grandmother had already made the trip to Park Forest, stayed three days and returned home. But now, a few more exultant words from the President to the nation, and the cameras were off.

As Roy Davidson left the studio, a reporter asked how it happened that a dispute which dragged on through five years had been settled in thirteen days.

"There's your answer," Davidson replied, pointing at Lyndon Johnson.

"Roy," said Secretary Wirtz, "that's the shortest, most accurate speech I've ever heard."

Whereupon Roy Davidson and Doc Wolfe fared forth down Wisconsin Avenue for a drink.

The spring of 1964 went along, as spring in Washington has a way of doing, now lovely and lilting, now chill and soggy.

The whole nation was filled with contradictions and crosscurrents. Prosperity rolled across the country in great fat waves. Yet among the poor, especially the Negro poor, real incomes were lagging. International crises rarely crowded the headlines; the polls indicated that almost fifty percent believed the big war was only a matter of time. Never had the average American lived in such comfort, with so rapidly increasing a sense of status, with a more delicious feeling of constantly breaking across barriers of privilege. At the same time every index of personal anxiety swung upward, whether a resort to psychiatry, the kinds of books read, the themes of popular movies and television shows.

The results of whirligig change, of social dislocation, of attitudes uprooted without being replaced, were everywhere. These were the months when middle-class purchasers set a record buying houses in the suburbs and made a million-sales hit out of the song that sneered, "Little boxes on the hillside/Little boxes of tickytacky/All the same"; when Lloyd Goodrich, Director of the Whitney Museum of Art in New York City, turned away crowds with the observation, "In America today there seems to be a little margin for sensitivity," and across the city, in a respectable area of Queens, thirty-eight adults saw Catherine Genovese stabbed three times within a span of thirty-five minutes and not a one called the police; when religious ecumenicism produced Cardinal Francis Spellman's first attendance at a Protestant funeral, and research organizations reported a sharply increased sense of ingrouping in the ethnic populations; when the young voted the Peace Corps the "most admired institution in America" and made a cult out of Humphrey Bogart because, as Shirley Fayes, a coed at the University of Washington, explained, he was "tough, anarchistic, and believed in nothing."

Amid it all, incontestably, Lyndon Johnson had taken over as President of the United States. LBJ men or transformed Johnsonians now manned the key federal posts. His policies—and the modifications he had placed on the JFK policies—dominated the government. His tone echoed on every level. No one questioned who was running the United States, or that it was being vigorously run.

Irritation at cornpone and wheeler-dealer and a vague general leeriness marked the public attitude toward Lyndon Johnson. The Kennedy nostalgia was flourishing. In March a write-in movement, "Bobby for Vice-President," mushroomed in New Hampshire and its leader explained, "We don't want to embarrass President Johnson. It's just that the name Kennedy is magic up here." Yet the Administration stamped "LBJ" was functioning with remarkably wide acceptance if not enthusiasm.

The rail settlement was the final breakthrough for the new President. An agreement which two previous Presidents and five years of effort had failed to achieve—commentators were calling it a "miracle," a "tour de force," and most were adding that it was a capstone to a highly successful five months. Republicans and Democrats agreed that Lyndon Johnson had handled the transition after the assassination with skill—by far the best performance of this type, many said, in American history. Beyond transition, his leadership of Congress, dramatized by the passage of the tax-reduction bill and the progress of the civil rights legislation; his simultaneous push for social legislation and for economies; his role as what Walter Lippmann was calling a "healer," a "bridger of unbridgeable chasms" in public opinion; his air of action and decisiveness—all had built a genuinely national following. The LBJ general-performance polls were a sweep—a hearty seventy-three percent or better in every month from March through June of 1964. The Republicans were in disarray. The G O P leader Leonard W. Hall of New York, could only sigh, "He's the first President I ever heard of with both prosperity and poverty going for him." Even Norman Thomas, now seventy-nine and six times the Socialist candidate for the Presidency, mustered subdued approval. "I rub my eyes in amazement. The Johnson Administration is much better than I feared."

Basking in success, Lyndon Johnson did everything with re-

freshed confidence. Golf was not his game and he rarely played
it but now he was showing up at the Burning Tree Club and
whacking away. "He hits a pretty long ball," the report came back
to the White House, "but you never know where it's going." From
the day he became President he had shied away from risking
comparison with John Kennedy's effective live television news
conferences. In April LBJ took the plunge, fielding eighteen questions in a highly self-possessed way.

He was laughing in his public remarks, and kidding as well
as berating his critics. Republican Robert McNamara as the vice-
presidential candidate? "I've never been a man who believed in
guilt by association." To the ambassador from Argentina, who
was about to begin a cross-country tour, he remarked so that reporters could hear him, "Be careful on the roads. The country is
full of crazy drivers." He picked up his beagles, Him and Her, by
the ears, and editorials denounced him as cruel. This time he saw
no plot against Texans. He picked up Him by the ears all over
again and a newsman noted that the dog did not yelp with pain.
The President observed, "He doesn't yelp unless an A.P. photographer gets too close to him."

Before lunch one day, LBJ took off for a walk with Bill Moyers
around the White House grounds and noticed a crowd of tourists
outside the Southeast Gate. He ambled up. "Would you like to
take a walk with me?" The visitors tumbled in and President Johnson instructed, "All you ugly men get up front and all of you
pretty girls come back here with me."

He trooped everybody around the black-topped drive which
circles the South Lawn. C. L. Prashar from India, an architecture
student at Howard University, found himself strolling beside the
President. "Is Mr. Nehru getting any better?" Lyndon Johnson
asked. Mr. Prashar said he believed the Indian Prime Minister
was improving.

A woman from Rhode Island and a young man from Minnesota
fell in beside the President. "We sure think a lot of Senator John
Pastore down here," the President assured the woman from Rhode
Island. He turned to the young man. "You a student?"

"University of Minnesota."

"Well, that's a wonderful state."

A Danish tourist went up to a White House aide in amazement.
"Excuse me, sir, I just came in on the plane from Copenhagen
and happened to come by the gate. Er . . . [pause], er . . .
[pause], does this sort of thing happen very often?" It did, three
more times in twelve days during Lyndon Johnson's exuberant
spring.

The whole Johnson family was doing what comes naturally. Mrs. Johnson said she was feeling much more at home in the White House. Along the public corridors she was placing sculpture by the Western artist Frederic Remington, and in the private quarters and near the President's office, paintings by Porfirio Salinas, Jr., of San Antonio, who specializes in Texas scenes of bluebonnets, cactus, hills and creekbeds, and who had been the LBJ favorite since the 1940's "because his work reminds me of the country around the ranch."

Lynda Bird was exercising the prerogatives of being a female and twenty years old. She announced that she had broken her engagement to Lieutenant (j.g.) Bernard Rosenbach of Comfort, Texas. Lucy was becoming a very public sixteen. She let it be known that her name was now to be spelled Luci ("more elegant") and that her father would not let her go to the railroad station to meet the Beatles. Named Queen XXXVII of the Shenandoah Apple Blossom Festival, Luci had further comment. Would the President attend the coronation? "I don't know. I can't ever tell what he is going to do. He can't either."

Social life at the White House was becoming unabashedly Johnsonian. The first state dinner was for President Antonio Segni of Italy. Across-the-board ethnicity reigned; both Joe DiMaggio and Gian-Carlo Menotti were present. So was Perle Mesta, who had supported LBJ for President in 1960, and when JFK won, had come out for Nixon and been banned from the Kennedy White House. The entertainment represented its own definition of consensus. Robert Merrill, the Metropolitan Opera baritone, sang Rossini and Verdi, and the New Christy Minstrels, in their white blouses and green jumpers, flaked the paint from the East Room with a hootenanny of "Cotton Picker," "Brandywine," "Green, Green" and "Saint's Train."

Then came the first entertainment of royalty, the visit of the Arab leader King Hussein I of Jordan. The invitation list was drawn up to pay back old obligations, to promote present and future projects, congressional and otherwise, above all to represent all occupations, all interests, all points of view. And the affair was constructed to build to what Lyndon Johnson considered a real evening, dancing.

After the dinner for King Hussein, the President headed for the waxed parquet of the Blue Room. "Throw open the windows," he ordered, and with that the Air Force "Strolling Strings" struck up a waltz and he was off in a whirl. Connoisseurs noted that LBJ preferred the fast numbers and that whether the orchestra played a waltz, a samba, cha-cha-cha or Dixieland, he churned ahead with an assured two-step. The general terpsichorean verdict: "Not bad," to "Real good." A particular favorite sent the President's toes twinkling—"Alexander's Ragtime Band."

One of the guests on the carefully balanced list was Miss Trude Feldman, the correspondent for the Los Angeles *Reporter*. Since Hussein was a king, protocol required that the women ask him to dance. After holding back most of the evening, Miss Feldman went up to the king.

Hussein, making small talk during the dance, asked, "What does your father do?"

"He lives in California."

"Yes, but what does he *do*?"

"My father," Miss Feldman replied, "is a rabbi."

CHAPTER 6

The Johnson Men

As Lyndon Johnson took over the Presidency in the spring of 1964, the White House staff settled into a routine, or rather into as much of a routine as it would ever achieve.

The White House has a severely simple physical design. At its center are the presidential living quarters and the entertainment and display rooms. On the two sides are the working offices. The West Wing begins with the Oval Office of the President, the Cabinet Room and a conference area called the Fish Room because President Franklin Roosevelt decorated its walls with his deep-sea trophies. Then come the West Wing staff offices. The East Wing is of later origin, and was not constructed in its present form until World War II brought pressure for space. Upstairs in the East Wing are the offices for the First Lady's activities, social planning and the military aides. On the first floor are more rooms for the President's staff and for administrative purposes.

It is none too clear what went on in these various areas in the past, for surprisingly little of the workaday history of the White House has been recorded. (Near the end of the campaign of 1964, President Johnson tentatively approved a suggestion that he deliver a speech centering around famous events which had taken place in specific rooms of the White House. With all the willing help of Washington, I could discover little of just what happened where.) In the Johnson Administration, one fact was quite clear. The West Wing offices were the prestige staff quarters. The East Wing was considered too far away from what Jack Valenti called "the action" and too close to what the President called "the womenfolk."

East or West Wing, the work pace remained furious; the day beyond ten hours continued to be normal. To a considerable degree, duties were still not sharply defined. President Johnson liked to call his aides "valuable hunks of humanity who can do anything," "switch hitters" or "triple-threat men," and on a given day any one of them was likely to be passing, running and kicking, not to speak of kicking while running. They did what the President told them to do or what they thought he wanted done, or they worked away at a memo—and telephone calls—to get him to do something they thought he ought to do.

"We staff men," Bill Moyers said, "are like spokes in a wheel, all leading to the center, the President." Lyndon Johnson ran the White House as he had run his Senate office, under his hat. No one on the staff had the overall supervisory powers which Sherman Adams exercised in Eisenhower days. The President insisted that all his men were equal, paid them much the same salaries, saw to it that they received similar raises. He usually dealt with them one by one.

The personalization of the White House was increased by other habits of President Johnson. As he became more accustomed to his office, he intervened less. But he was still likely to pass on the assignment of a secretary, check word for word some inconsequential document or determine what newspapers were delivered to which office. Like Presidents before him, he often deliberately asked several men to prepare a memo or draft a speech on the same subject and then used the product he liked best. Unlike other Presidents, he stayed with the process, at times phoning an aide at seven o'clock in the morning or past midnight to see how the assignment was going, and dropping a remark which caused the man suddenly to shift the whole direction of his work.

Presidential appearances were a daily trauma. During this period it was rather easy to get President Johnson to commit himself to attend a particular function. The problem started once he had agreed; it merely meant that he might or might not appear. Almost always he did but only after hours of denying that he would, which led to frantic contingency planning.

The White House cannot be and should not be an operation dominated by the demands of efficiency. The genius of presidential leadership lies in the free play of a President's relationships not only with the nation but with the people around him. The most efficient administrators who have occupied the White House in modern times, Herbert Hoover and Dwight Eisenhower, were not among its most effective Chief Executives; FDR was constitutionally and joyously allergic to the man with an organization chart. Moreover, as the double layer of JFK and LBJ men in the Johnson White House gave way to a single file of Johnsonians, procedures became somewhat more regular. Yet the hyper-personalized ways of Lyndon Johnson were so pronounced and so overwhelming that at times they could confound helter-skelter into downright chaos.

President Johnson's attitude toward his staff was essentially feudal. He was the head of the duchy with all rights thereto appertaining. When he did not like the length of a Special Assistant's hair, he told him to go to a barbershop; he ordered a secretary to enroll in a charm school. He expected aides to be available at any time for any function. They were as likely to be asked to phone the tailor ("These damn pants hitch up too much") as to confer with an ambassador. One evening Jack Valenti, thinking that the next few hours looked calm, left for New York on a late plane to join his wife for the last act of a play. The night turned out to be the one on which LBJ came down with flu and was taken to the hospital. The next few days were not happy ones for Valenti.

The President could berate his aides in lashing language. Sometimes he did this collectively, as when he exploded at three of them in his office, "How can you be so goddamn stupid! Why can't I get men with the brains of the Kennedy bunch?" More often, he would turn on a single staff member. On a number of occasions I saw an aide emerge from a presidential session white-faced and shaking, swearing that he could not stand it another day.

All effective Presidents have used a carrot-and-stick technique with their staff in order to keep the men on their toes and in their place. President Johnson carried the tactic to his own extreme. He would heap praise on a particular aide for a period, much to the discomfiture of the others, then suddenly shift his attitude, giving the man no assignments, rejecting his suggestions *in toto*, scarcely speaking to him. Just as suddenly, the assistant would be lifted from hell and transformed into an angel once again.

But if LBJ exercised the full rights of the feudal lord, he did not forget the duties. He gave responsibility and genuine personal concern to the human beings around him. The reason that the chaos of the White House did not often have serious consequences is that basically Lyndon Johnson ran everything. To do this, he gave of himself profligately, not only the grinding hours of the two-shift day but a herculean readiness to take on any task at any time. He may have tongue-lashed his aides but he also lauded them, not only lavishly but with sincerity, particularly when an outsider criticized them.

Almost always President Johnson was sorry for his spells of anger and found his own ways to say so. One morning when I was to make a plane trip with him, the *New York Times* printed a front-page article containing information which the President emphatically did not want known. A friend on the staff telephoned me. "I've just seen him. Get ready—he's furious at you. _____ told him you leaked that story to the *Times*." When I entered the plane, the President ignored my "Good morning." Since it was a small jet, we all sat only a few feet from each other, and for twenty minutes or so he continued to ignore me, talking to others through or around me. I was thoroughly embarrassed and I seethed. Finally, trying to keep my anger down to a respectful tone, I said, "Mr. President, I am aware that you have been told I leaked that story in this morning's *Times*. I had nothing whatsoever to do with it, and I ask you to accept my word." He did not even turn to me as I spoke. Ten minutes later, when he called the steward for a soft drink, he added, "Get Eric one too. He's not always as bad as he seems." He drew me into the conversation, and that was the last I heard about the leak.

LBJ was full of acts of *noblesse oblige*, some eminently practical, others the gestures of sentiment that can mean a great deal. A staff member encountering financial trouble because of serious illness in the family found the medical bill quietly paid by "a friend." When another assistant was celebrating his wedding anniversary, two unexpected guests arrived: a beaming President of the United States and the First Lady, carrying a touching gift. Down through the ranks, Lyndon Johnson had a sense of camaraderie for his whole staff. People working with him often found themselves invited to stay on for lunch or dinner with the family, and the invitation might go to a Cabinet officer or to a secretary who had just been taking dictation in the Oval Office.

If President Johnson kept things swirling by his sudden moods, he also kept them moving ahead by his highly developed ability to give a firm answer. He tried to keep each evening free after ten-thirty, when he would climb into bed and start through the pile of memos which made up what he called his "night reading" (Valenti estimated that he consumed as many as two hundred thousand words a week this way). It was not true, as was often said in the press, that he would tolerate only one- or two-page memos. It was only necessary that the space be justified by the substance, and that the communication point to a clear set of recommendations. He particularly liked the memos that could end with a clean-cut "Approved _____," "Disapproved _____" or "Approved with the following changes _____." A message of this type might well be back the next morning with a handwritten *L* at the top to indicate that the President had read it, and with a check mark opposite one of the alternatives.

By the spring of 1964, the staff was shaking down to the point where some of the men had fairly specialized responsibilities. This was particularly true of the transformed Kennedy aides, most of whom continued to work in their specific areas. McGeorge Bundy still dealt primarily with foreign affairs; Kermit Gordon and Walter Heller with economic matters; Lawrence O'Brien with Congress and political problems. It was the LBJ men whom the President tended to draw into everything and to include in a way which made their influence pervasive. It was they who were most likely to be invited to a family meal or for a late-evening drink, when they had a better chance to learn what was really on President Johnson's mind and to say things which might influence him. It was they, "the people who have been with me to the well and back," to whom he spoke with his hair completely, or almost completely, down.

Significant as aides like Bundy, Gordon and O'Brien were, it was the Johnson men—now beginning to include, in a curious way, one ardent Kennedyite—who were the backbone of the new White House.

In the first hectic days the man with a conspicuously special relationship to President Johnson had been Walter W. Jenkins, and nothing was changing that now. Jenkins, forty-six years old, sat in his big office in the West Wing, suit baggy, his middle collecting fat, his dark hair graying and his face turning the more florid the wearier he became, endlessly doing a sweeping variety of tasks. The office continued to be a hubbub: the two secretaries and assistant Richard Nelson in the one room, the stream of people in and out, the whole somehow held together by Jenkins' low-voiced talking to President Johnson on the telephone, sometimes as much as two or three hours a day. Jenkins did not picture himself as a "policy" aide; in his shy, modest way he said he merely "helped the President get things done." But he helped LBJ get so many and so many different kinds of things done that only a man of far less ability and substance could have performed his role without influencing policy.

He was as close to a chief of staff as the Johnson White House could have. Publicly, no assistant questioned his primacy; privately, none acted without reckoning with it. In administrative matters, Jenkins was President Johnson's right hand—to the extent that the President wanted a right hand. He determined details that could make or break the influence of other aides; if a jurisdictional dispute arose and anyone but President Johnson was to settle it, the decision was made by Jenkins. He did the screening for many high-level appointments in the federal government, and sat in judgment on FBI and political reports on the candidates. Inside the White House, the surest way to get a memo into the "night reading" was to route it through his office. For the outsider, the fastest way to get to see the President was to interest Jenkins. He passed on a number of important presidential letters and documents, and had the authority—or rather simply assumed the authority in an entirely natural way—to instruct that President Johnson's name be signed.

All the while Walter Jenkins was doing all kinds of other jobs. Along with O'Brien he kept in touch with congressmen, usually handling the large and powerful Texas delegation himself. He sat in on Cabinet and National Security Council meetings, taking notes in his swift shorthand and preparing the advisories on Administration policies which went out to the departments. The shorthand added to his authority; the recipient knew that he was reading not someone's interpretation of Lyndon Johnson but the President verbatim. Jenkins rode herd on things President Johnson wanted done, finding out why the expected had not happened and why the unexpected did.

And of course the trivia descended in irritated flurries from the Oval Office. One day I walked in to encounter the crisis of the moment. When at the ranch, President Johnson delighted in handing out to especially honored visitors Western-style hats with a sketch of the ranch and the LBJ cattle brand inscribed inside. The President bought the hats by the dozens from a firm which sold them to him at a small profit. The Jenkins office saw to it that the company provided them at cost.

Above all, Walter Jenkins was the man who was close to the President. The relationship was never confused. One was the boss, the other the employee. But the men and their families were like Johnson City neighbors, the one having done better in the world but each understanding and moving easily with the other. A Jenkins son was named Lyndon; Luci Johnson's closest friend was Beth Jenkins. The night that Lyndon and Lady Bird Johnson moved into the White House, they had dinner at the Jenkins home, and Mrs. Johnson observed her first birthday as First Lady at a party the Jenkinses gave for her. There was nothing about the President that this assistant did not know. During the first spring of the LBJ Presidency, Jenkins disappeared for a few days, "on assignment" the press was told; he was in the old vice-presidential suite in EOB making up Lyndon Johnson's income tax. The President had absolute confidence in the judgments of his friend. He did not ask him what to do about the railroad strike or the Panamanian crisis. He did talk to him about everything, including railroad strikes and Panama, and what Jenkins said in his quiet, shrewd—and very respectful—way counted.

The affairs of Lyndon Johnson had dominated the adult years of Walter Jenkins. Born to a none-too-prosperous Texas farm family in Jolly, near Wichita Falls, Jenkins attended Wichita Falls Junior College, then managed two years at the University of Texas before his money ran out in 1939. Both he and a friend sought a job from the fount in that area, Representative Lyndon Johnson. The choice was Jenkins, who began as a politically appointed policeman in Washington, then was taken on in the Austin office of Representative Johnson, starting as an accountant-clerk and gradually taking over as general manager. During the next two decades Jenkins left the Johnson employ only twice—once to serve in the Quartermaster Corps in Africa and Italy during World War II, the second time in 1951, to run unsuccessfully for Congress, which was hardly outside the LBJ orbit.

For all his outward simplicity, Jenkins was a man of tightly coiled springs, with few ways of releasing them. He yearned for color and movement and excitement but had found no road to them. At the University of Texas his one extracurricular activity had been the theatrical group, the Curtain Club. The star roles went to others and the president was the future governor of Texas, the charmer John B. Connally. To Walter Jenkins, Lyndon Johnson—so smart, so flamboyant and so successful—was the epitome of what life could be. From the beginning he gave LBJ long hours, unbreakable loyalty and an indefinable emotional identification which was the strongest tie of all.

After returning from World War II, Jenkins found his bride, Marjorie Whitehill. To this plain-faced, plain-mannered, painfully introverted man, the interest of the attractive, bouncy Miss Whitehill was a tremendous boon. For her he gave up generations of Protestant background to convert to Catholicism. (In time there were to be interesting ramifications. Beth Jenkins went to the Catholic Marquette University in Milwaukee, her friend Luci Johnson followed her, fell in with Beth's circle of friends, converted and met a young Catholic from Waukegan, Illinois, Patrick J. Nugent.) But back in 1945, long before the White House days, a telephone call came in the middle of Walter Jenkins' honeymoon. Lyndon Johnson said he needed him, and grousing only mildly, Jenkins bundled up his bride and returned to Austin.

What was most significant about Jenkins' attachment to his boss was that it was no simple loyalty. Jenkins is an enormously decent human being, not because of any theories of man or ideology but because, from something inside himself, he seeks fair play and kindliness in the dealings between men. With no expression of liberal doctrine—a product of roughhouse Texas politics, he simply did not think in terms of liberalism or conservatism—he had a straightforward conviction that America is different, and that this special land, with all its talent and wealth, should create opportunities for ordinary people, like those from Jolly, Texas, to have better housing and food, a chance to finish college and higher odds on being able to enjoy the sunnier aspects of living. If Jenkins' loyalty to Lyndon Johnson was in part a fastening on to a rocketing career, it was also an attachment to a man who Jenkins believed would get done, through hard-headed politics, some of the things he himself very much believed should be done.

Jenkins' attitude toward President Johnson had its full component of protectiveness. Let anyone give a hint of taking a line that could hurt LBJ—the mild manner hardened and Walter Jenkins would be as tough as any Austin ward heeler. But again, the protectiveness was not a narrow attitude. Jenkins was indifferently educated and read little; his imagination was limited. Yet somewhere in his experience he had acquired the conviction that he would serve the President best by seeing to it that all the avenues to his mind were kept open. He was remarkably broad-gauged in his judgment of whom President Johnson should see and what he should read, and these included a number of people he personally did not like and points of view to which he was opposed.

Jenkins himself could take unexpected positions. In the school of politics where he developed, the first rule was to reward your friends. In 1964 a powerful friend sought his reward. Ellis Island had been closed but its disposition not settled, and the head of a major corporation, whose support in the coming election was important to President Johnson, approached Jenkins. The executive was avid about a pet charity—a school for underprivileged children—and he asked, in a way which assumed an affirmative reply, that Ellis Island be turned over for this purpose.

Jenkins gave no immediate answer. He consulted a number of people, including me, and asked me for a recommendation. As I'm sure others did too, I urged that the publisher's proposal be rejected and that Ellis Island be turned into a national park. Of course the school was a worthwhile project, I argued, but such causes should be taken care of in other ways. Ellis Island was of genuine emotional meaning to millions of our people. It would be quick and easy politics to give the publisher what he wanted; there was also a higher politics—the President as the guardian of the country's heritage. The man from roughhouse Texas politics saw to it that the publisher's request was turned down, and was largely responsible for initiating the moves which in 1965 made Ellis island a national preserve.

More and more, on a number of important matters, Walter Jenkins would say, "Better have Bill handle it." In this, as in most things, Jenkins was reflecting the President, for the fastest rising star in the White House was Bill D. Moyers.

Moyers' career is the classic story of the young man in a hurry. He was born at the height of the Depression in run-down little Hugo, Oklahoma, the son of an odd-jobs man. Then came the family move to Marshall, Texas, a stronghold of oil, gas and the Baptist Church, where the father did little better as a truck driver and candy salesman; the high marks at Marshall High School, North Texas State College and the University of Texas, combined with forays into local journalism to pay for his schooling; the jump to the big time—a letter to Senator Lyndon Johnson asking for a job, and subsequent work for the senator and at KTBC-TV in Austin; the early marriage to the winsome coed from North Texas State, Judith Davidson; a Rotary Fellowship to the University of Edinburgh and the tour of the newlyweds around Europe; the fumbling for a career—study at the Southwestern Baptist Theological Seminary, keeping a hand in journalism and in the LBJ operation, talking with Dr. Bill Pinson at the seminary about how he himself planned to run for office someday; the full-time commitment to Lyndon Johnson during the 1960 campaign; after the victory, the shift to the high post at the Peace Corps, one of the youngest men ever confirmed by the Senate, while maintaining close ties to the Vice-President; the rush to make it to *Air Force One* before it left Dallas; and now, at twenty-nine, Special Assistant to the President of the United States.

The relationship of Moyers to Lyndon Johnson was ready-made. To the President, the halcyon years in his own life were the period when, at twenty-seven, he ran the National Youth Administration in Texas. He responded to any young man who wanted to run things. He responded with particular warmth because like so many men, particularly those from a background where he-manness is the prime virtue, he felt that life without a son is incomplete. President Johnson had always felt a little cheated, almost embarrassed, at being surrounded by three women; in a vague way, he kept looking for a Lyndon Baines Johnson, Jr. He thought he had found him in Bobby Baker and was bitterly disappointed. He felt he had found him in Bill Moyers ("If I had a boy, I'd like him to be like this young fellow").

So many of Moyers' characteristics fitted him for the role. When a television interviewer, commenting on his slight twang, asked, "Do I detect a Texas accent?" Moyers replied, "Not only in my speech, sir, but in my heart." He was smart, and recognized as such, willing to labor without stint for Lyndon Johnson ("That boy has a bleeding ulcer. He works for me like a dog, and is just as faithful"), and he spoke in the right way about this leader, "whose full scope of thought, fervor and personality can never be known to one man alive." He had a natural Johnsonian zest for politics, as well as LBJ's tendency to talk about it in uplifted phrases. "That's what drew me into public service," he would say, pointing to a quotation from Jefferson which hung in his office. "The care of human life and happiness . . . is the first and only legitimate object of good government." Moyers also had the Johnsonian instinct for smoothing over differences. The President said, "He gets along with people. He can sit down with three people when they are miles apart in their thinking and get an agreement on what policy ought to be." Even his sense of humor was one that kept President Johnson guffawing; Moyers was an indefatigable practical joker.

If Lyndon Johnson responded to Moyers, Bill Moyers certainly responded to the President of the United States. Over the years Washington has known an unending series of fiercely ambitious men; Moyers certainly had a continuous and enveloping drive for power and status. The drive went side by side with his careful pleasantness and earnestness; it was evident in his sudden toughening if anyone or anything threatened his relationship with President Johnson. A detractor in the White House called Moyers "Elmer Gantry." The phrase was caricature and unfair, but it did suggest the air of completely satisfying rationalization with which he sometimes used stiletto tactics. As one staff man who found himself the victim of a Moyers thrust remarked, "Whatever he does, he does with every assurance that he is carrying out the will of John the Baptist."

In its angry way the Elmer Gantry slur also caught something of the special nature of Moyers' ambition. Marshall, Texas, represented the peculiar bifurcation marking many Southern communities. Amid the oil and gas establishments, the brick enterprises and the machine factories, four religious colleges were located in this town of sixteen thousand people. A careering young man took one of the two routes. The oil-and-gas group sought status through blatant money; never eschewing money, the Baptist college set sought status through occupations that could be defined, in a way satisfactory to themselves and to those they cared to impress, as service to man.

Moyers was also young, quite a bit younger than most other major members of the White House staff and young in a way which mattered a good deal more than mere chronology. He came along with a generation many of whose most articulate members thought of youth not as part of growing up, but as a movement; they were the most self-conscious young people in American history. Moyers delighted in being part of this wave. He talked to youth groups as if they were organized labor or the chamber of commerce: "God save us from that day when we must say to the young men and women of America, 'We cannot trust you.'"

In an earlier period, bright young men from Marshall, Texas, rarely went to Europe. In the fifties and sixties the fellowships were available and the lure of cosmopolitanism and intellectualism was strong. Moyers went to Europe and returned eager to be an intellectual, still stressing that he did "sensible reading" but including in that definition *The Economist* of London and snatches of Arnold Toynbee, James Baldwin and Norman Mailer. To his quotations from the Scriptures he added some from the Greek classics, and he talked about "the dangers of moral absolutism. No one has a monopoly on virtue or truth. Those that peddle this line, under whatever label, subvert the very thing that they want to obtain."

When LBJ won the Vice-Presidency in 1960 and Moyers had the pick of federal jobs before him, it was not surprising that he chose the Peace Corps. At the time it was a mecca for all kinds of young people, some of them as wide-eyed as any settlement-house Vassar girl of the 1900's, and many of its field workers performed prodigies of unadorned decency. But at the administrative level in Washington the Peace Corps in a number of cases attracted the youth-movement types, eager to commingle idealism with the prestige of cosmopolitanism and proud of their ability to conceive tactics not much different from those of traditional ward heelers. The headquarters were a natural habitat for the government careerists of a generation which believed in little except that it was important to believe in something ardently, which mixed the nineteenth-century American missionary instinct with twentieth-century managerial attitudes and cynicism. Moyers, having decided upon a high administrative post in the Peace Corps, no doubt assumed that the Vice-President would be reluctant to let him leave the immediate entourage, and enlisted the intervention of an old friend of Lyndon Johnson's. Urging that Moyers be permitted to make the shift, the friend described him as an "idealist-operator." At the Peace Corps headquarters, Moyers was idealistic and he operated.

In imitation of his mentor LBJ, he began building his empire. He started binding to himself—by camaraderie, by favors given and favors hinted, by a general air of pushing ahead together—a number of younger men throughout the federal government. After the assassination and his move to the White House, Moyers accelerated the process. Alone of the Special Assistants, he had a genuine organization, many of the members of which were eager to give the allegiance that permitted them to rise with the leader.

While building this following, Moyers cast himself in a particular role. He was the only old-line Johnson man to have served in a thoroughly New Frontier agency like the Peace Corps and who knew well many New Frontiersmen; he would be the bridge between the LBJ and JFK men. The synthesis was adroit. President Johnson was happy to have an aide who was so close to him and yet had a real line into the Kennedy fortress. The role made Moyers even more the model of the youthful, intellectualish hard-nosed idealist. It gave him a double power base—and if the Johnson one disintegrated, an escape hatch.

Moyers soon fixed his eye on Richard N. Goodwin, thirty-two years old, for whom John Kennedy, as Goodwin said, had been "a hero" and who continued to be an intimate friend of Robert Kennedy's. The son of a Boston engineer, Goodwin had come to Washington with an impressive academic record—first in his class at Tufts College and at Harvard Law School—and then he had served in the intellectually prestigious post of law clerk to Supreme Court Justice Felix Frankfurter. His tastes were exceedingly broad; he was developing a remarkably wide knowledge of literature and art and personal friendships with leading authors and artists. He was an occasional poet, could be intrigued by the project to save the Nile monuments from the waters of the Aswan Dam and at times remarked that what he really wanted to be was a writer. But Goodwin evidenced little sustained taste for the intellectual life as such. His delight was Washington and its intrigue. He roamed the corridors of power like a court manipulator out of the Middle Ages—dark, disheveled, brilliant and sardonic.

Goodwin had been an early recruit to the JFK drive for the Presidency, and after the victory he held a series of positions in and around the White House. Whatever the title, he was an "insider," with easy access to President Kennedy and his key aides and with a special interest in Latin American affairs, cultural activities and new projects like the Peace Corps. Whatever he was doing, he moved in an atmosphere of recognition of his brains and of uneasiness about the way he used them.

Part of this distrust came simply from his personality. Like a number of able men, Goodwin was blatantly arrogant. Another part came from a fact that was a decided credit to Goodwin. His basic attitudes were those of the American non-Communist left, and whatever the merit of these ideas, he had sincerely pushed to write them into policy, particularly in Latin American affairs. Inevitably, conservatives and routineers sharpened their knives. But a good deal of the distrust of Goodwin came from something quite different—his chameleonlike air, the feeling that he was a good bit of an adventurer with a highly developed ability to confuse advancing policies with advancing Richard Goodwin, and no great fastidiousness in the methods he used in either case. The general uneasiness was not diminished during the early LBJ period when Goodwin, a Kennedyite of the Kennedyites, hung on to a nondescript relationship to the new Administration, bemoaning Lyndon Johnson in private while maneuvering to become an important member of the LBJ group.

But Bill Moyers was decidedly interested in Goodwin. His extensive contacts with the Kennedy camp could be valuable. Important commentators were criticizing President Johnson for the literary barrenness of his speeches; Goodwin could write well— and the speeches could go to the President edited by Moyers. LBJ kept wanting "ideas." Goodwin and his friends were full of them and these too could go into the Oval Office, properly pruned and given the approval of successful idea-finder Bill Moyers.

Perhaps most important, Moyers was simply fascinated by Goodwin. Marshall, Texas, even the University of Edinburgh and the Peace Corps, were never like this. Here was a former aide to the illustrious Felix Frankfurter, a connoisseur of the latest in literature and art, who, at the age of thirty-two, last week's soup stain on his suit, puffing his cigar and twirling his gold chain enigmatically, talked of power and policy with a faintly weary smile. Richard Goodwin and Bill Moyers were becoming close allies. If Moyers gained from Goodwin and was bedazzled by him, Goodwin was so completely a Kennedyite that he could not hope for a real entrée without the intervention of an old Johnson hand. More and more Moyers saw to it that Goodwin was assigned to write speeches and was moved into the President's circle.

Moyers was also continuing to consolidate his own role. Every so often his ulcer flared up and he had to leave the office; then he was back, hard-driving as ever. With the confidence and affection of President Johnson, and with staff lines so amorphous, he was in a freewheeling position. He carried on some activities like those of Walter Jenkins—determining who was to meet with the President, conferring with congressmen, working on appointments to high positions. He also supervised the planning of presidential trips and had a good deal to do with determining not only where President Johnson went but how he projected himself. But the Moyers role was sweeping well beyond. He was being given a major part in shaping the Administration's legislative proposals, and he was writing a number of important speeches and heavily editing the drafts others prepared.

Increasingly Moyers sat in on presidential conferences and talked for long hours alone with President Johnson. He was acquiring the reputation of being the only man in the inner circle who said no to Lyndon Johnson. No one said no to Lyndon Johnson and stayed in the inner circle long. But Moyers was mastering the art of the occasional sidewise suggestion, which sometimes diverted the presidential course. He was exercising the prerogative of a son to commit an irreverence—especially in front of reporters —which LBJ would grinningly accept. Of larger importance, Moyers was getting a name for being the aide who could speak for President Johnson, and this reputation was certainly justified. The more Moyers spoke for the President, the more people asked him to speak for the President and the more his influence widened.

In a way, the greatest significance of the Moyers role in the LBJ White House came from the fact that President Johnson considered Bill Moyers his personal representative of the youthful, intellectual idealism of the 1960's. In general, the assistant's attitudes did fall within the broad liberal tradition, and to a degree he spoke for educated American youth of the 1960's. In this respect his role was highly salutary. Yet basically President Johnson was getting a thoroughly unrepresentative representation.

This resulted only in small measure from Moyers' intense ambition, which could make what he said so flexible. The root of the matter was simply that Bill Moyers thought and reacted within the conventions of decades of middle-class American youth. He shared little of the temper of mind which was so deeply influencing the lower-age groups of Metroamerica in the 1960's: their ambivalence toward the operating values of American society; their skepticism about big organizations and about power; their reaching for the offbeat in everyday living; their worried, irritated feeling that somehow, after World War II, American civilization had gone off the track. Bill Moyers, in his careful dark suit, so doggedly on the right side, so anxious for the approval of the successful, was not this youthful America.

Moyers was for civil rights, against poverty and concerned with better education. He spoke respect for books, artists and the man with a cause. He had all the gestures of liberal intellectualism while never having been immersed in its tradition, and he lacked both its essential style and content. His religious orientation was a clue; he was a product of the reformism of Billy Graham, not of Reinhold Niebuhr. American liberal intellectualism, whether that of Niebuhr or of Theodore and Franklin Roosevelt, has shown a persistent gift for expressing the American experience with all the rich nuances of the American language. It was Moyers who wrote the phrase "Cool it" into a presidential speech addressed to liberal intellectuals. Whatever its convolutions, the liberal tradition continued to produce a combination of passion and subtlety. It has thundered that America means endless possibilities; simultaneously it has never lacked leaders who emphasize that life is complex and human beings imperfect, and that the possibilities are achieved by using the tension between what is and what could be. Gesturing earnestly to a group of deeply troubled Negro leaders, Bill Moyers could say, "Now, there's just no reason why men of good will cannot move forward together."

In the spring of 1964 a visitor pressed President Johnson on the subject of why he did not pay more attention to the "new voices" in America. The President was less annoyed than puzzled. "New voices? I hear them all day from Bill Moyers. He's a fine young idealist, and he couldn't be closer to me."

One spring afternoon the big black limousines rolled along a road near Johnson City and the lead car suddenly stopped. A small olive-complexioned man wearing a golfer's cap and white buck shoes got out. He picked up a soft-drink bottle and threw it aside.

"That could have cut somebody's tire," Lyndon Johnson remarked with satisfaction.

Jack Valenti returned to the limousine. "I see you're still wearing those Harvard shoes," the President said.

"Couldn't do without 'em, Mr. President," Valenti replied, making the expected response to the familiar needling.

Jack J. Valenti, forty-two years old, was the bottle pickerupper, the chief butt of the presidential gibes and anger, the man who adjusted the Teleprompter, hurried to fetch Lyndon Johnson a pad of paper, counted the applause when the President didn't want to bother—and a decidedly important LBJ aide.

A Valenti in the White House would have seemed incredible to Grandfather Valenti, who had migrated from Sicily to Texas, or to the father, who earned $150 a month as a courthouse clerk in Houston. Jack Valenti, bantam in size and aggressiveness, was determined to do better. As a youngster he sacked groceries and ushered in the movies. Then he went to work as an office boy at the Humble Oil & Refining Company to pay his way through night classes at the University of Houston, scoring a high academic record, serving as president of the Student Association, director of Varsity Varieties, and news editor of *The Cougar*, and all the while dreaming of Harvard. When World War II came, Valenti chose the tough, glamorous road. A bomber pilot, he won the Distinguished Flying Cross and a sheaf of other medals flying fifty-one low-level missions over southern Germany and Italy.

After the war Valenti did not forget Harvard, making his way into the Harvard Business School. "I still remember," he remarked years later, "how I felt walking the Lars Anderson Bridge over the Charles that first day." He returned to Houston as supervisor of advertising and sales promotion for Humble Oil. In 1952 Valenti and a University of Houston classmate, Weldon T. Weekley, set up their own advertising and public relations agency, which was soon flourishing.

Weekley has recalled, "We worked well together. Jack was short and outgoing. I am tall and quiet. He was Mr. Outside and I was Mr. Inside." Mr. Outside was all over the place, drawing in the clients, dating the prettiest girls in town, writing a column for the Houston *Post*. He was emerging the model of the new-type public relations man, Texas style. He was imaginative, quick-thinking and fast-talking, with a vocabulary that ranged from the florid to the profane as the occasion demanded. His dress was natty, the silk suits set off by narrow lapels, a vest and often a two-toned white shirt with spread collars and French cuffs. A lively, friendly, sentimental human being, he liked parties, movies, opera, the theater, golf and poker. To his natural warmth was added all the conversational argot of his group. Secretaries immediately became "honey." Conversation was likely to begin with a hand around the shoulder and the greeting "My friend . . . ," and the first-naming came quickly.

In 1956 Valenti met Lyndon Johnson for the first time at a reception for businessmen. He devoted his Houston *Post* column to this tall man, "tall in the cord-lean frame," with "gentleness of manner" but "no mistaking either the feel of strength, unbending as a mountain crag, tough as a jungle fighter." After that column, the two men saw more and more of each other. The Weekley-Valenti agency received the account for the 1960 Kennedy-Johnson campaign in Texas, and Valenti functioned with the Johnson entourage in capacities that often went far beyond those of a public relations man. A strong personal tie between LBJ and Valenti also began developing. There was, moreover, Mary Margaret Wiley, a petite, lively blonde, her sheath skirts gay and her bouffant hair piled to a bow, a University of Texas graduate working as a secretary in the Johnson office. Miss Wiley became Mrs. Valenti in 1962, with Vice-President Johnson giving away the bride.

When the assassination occurred, Valenti was in the motorcade. "Jack, you stay with me," the new President said, and Valenti boarded *Air Force One* without a change of shirt. For nine weeks he lived with the Johnsons, first in their Washington home, The Elms, then at the White House, until he found time to arrange a Washington house for his family. Thereafter six mornings a week —and often on Sundays—Valenti drove up to the White House at six-thirty. The butler brought tea and melon and the two men began going over the day's work. Until the President went to sleep, Valenti was at his side much of the time.

By now Lyndon Johnson was Jack Valenti's hero, without qualifications and with considerable emotion. White House amateur psychiatrists had a field day with the Valenti attitude. They smiled and said that a wiry little man of five feet six inches, an Italian-American growing up in hyper-Texan Houston, naturally identified with the rugged LBJ, so unimpeachable a Texan. For Jack Valenti no involved explanations were necessary. Lyndon Johnson was his hero because he was sure that Lyndon Johnson was a genuinely heroic figure.

On his part, President Johnson enjoyed this aide's adulation, his bright, exuberant company, his absolute loyalty, all the things that made him the perfect crony and confidant. Sometimes the men, once the work was done, would sit up into the small hours, the President tired but relaxed, talking with Valenti about whatever came to his mind.

President Johnson also had a high regard for Valenti's abilities. It was true that he played the role of valet; it was also true that much of his time went to important tasks, which he executed with a shrewdly underplayed savvy. Basically, the Valenti job was to serve as custodian of the LBJ schedule, with all the significance that had. Beyond the schedule, the President frequently turned to him for getting done quickly and diplomatically whatever needed to be done. Valenti was a major liaison with Senate Minority Leader Dirksen; soothed the feelings of congressmen whose districts had lost an appropriation; moved projects through the bureaucratic web; served as President Johnson's ambassador in telling important people things they did not want to hear.

If Moyers wrote and edited speeches, Valenti edited far more of them, often adding significant passages. When LBJ was a boy, he heard a newspaper editor say that an effective sentence should never be longer than twenty-five words. He had not forgotten this, and he had other rules. Sentences should be not only brief but simple. Force is more important than ornateness. Use semicolons sparingly, if at all. "Keep things short, sharp and punchy." Valenti became an expert at the short, sharp and punchy.

President Johnson also liked the colorful in his speeches, especially the colorful that was sentimental. Valenti was good at this too. One of the things he admired about the President was that "he doesn't like cold intellectuals around him. He wants people who will cry when an old lady falls down in the street." Valenti urged staff members, "Get some tears in it." He himself wrote into the speeches considerable sentiment, sometimes moving, sometimes an unfortunate goo.

"Jack is really an intellectual," President Johnson commented. "People would admit it if he didn't come from the wrong side of the Mason-Dixon line." This characterization, whatever else might be said of it, did pinpoint a significant part of Valenti's role. During his life he had met up with a good deal besides middle-class attitudes, and he did not go through the experiences unaffected. His loyalty to Lyndon Johnson had a quality not unlike that of Walter Jenkins: he believed it important for the President to be brought into contact with a wide variety of people and ideas. In his own way, Valenti was a friend in the White House of the offbeat, or at least of the new.

From high school days, he had been a voracious consumer of books, and he installed in his Washington house a device which permitted him to read even while in the shower. Anthologies of quotations from famous authors were in his office and home. The Valenti taste in reading ran mostly to the non-fiction popularizers, or to curious throwbacks to the ringing and the exciting, such as the history written by the nineteenth-century Englishman Thomas Babington Macaulay. The thorough Lyndonologist could often tell what Valenti was reading by noting the quotations that appeared in LBJ speeches. Most of these quotations did not work too well; the authors Valenti chose, like Macaulay, hardly seemed natural to Lyndon Johnson. And in delivering the passage, the President had a way of pausing before it with the manner of a man who did not recognize what he was about to say, and then stumbling over it.

All the while Valenti was becoming the ringmaster of the White House staff. President Johnson thought it important to keep his photograph and words dominating the news media; public relations man Valenti heartily agreed. For a while Valenti conducted weekly meetings of the top staff—attended or not attended with tense concern about how an appearance affected position in the hierarchy—at which Valenti would bring out the next week's calendar and point to blank spots in the President's activities. Any suggestion that had Lyndon Johnson doing something which would make news won an enthusiastic hearing from Valenti and was often snapped up by President Johnson.

Some of these forays were assets to the Administration. But the experienced observers I knew thought that on the whole they were a detriment. They were transparently contrived; they overexposed the President, often in situations where he showed to little advantage; they encouraged an emphasis on sheer public relations, a kind of thinking toward which Lyndon Johnson was only too prone. In time they would lead to major blunders like the Hawaii conference on Vietnam in 1966, hastily and obviously staged to shift attention from Senator Fulbright's critical Senate Foreign Relations hearings and permitting the South Vietnamese Premier to put President Johnson in an awkward position before the world.

In the spring of 1964, when Pierre Salinger abruptly resigned as Press Secretary, the President did not think twice. He turned immediately to George E. Reedy.

The call reached Reedy in Doctors Hospital, near the White House. Oddly, the long hours of the post-assassination period had put weight on this assistant, and he was in the hospital on a rigid diet to lose some of his two hundred and eighty-five pounds. At Doctors Hospital, Reedy was taking the opportunity to catch up on reading, including Paul Tillich and—a coincidence he did not fail to savor—Cecil B. Woodham-Smith's history of the Irish famine, *The Great Hunger.*

Good books and George Reedy went together. He was easily the most deceptive of the Johnson staff. Six feet two inches tall, the loose body barely contained in sagging suits, ponderous in walk and speech, Reedy had a swift, powerful mind, a delight in books and talking about them, an instinct for philosophical conundrums, and a quiet, subtle religious faith.

Reedy was the only one of the old-line LBJ men not a Texan. He was pure Chicago, the son of a Chicago *Tribune* crime reporter, George E. Reedy, Sr., a well-known figure in the city during the Capone era. The boy had an IQ which put him in the child-prodigy class; he attended the University of Chicago as one of the intellectual elite groups President Robert M. Hutchins established.

George Reedy had a wonderful time in college. He ransacked the library, talked away the nights in hamburger bistros, harassed the dean, got a summer job on the Philadelphia *Inquirer*, announced that he was a socialist and became president of the university Socialist Club.

Emerging in 1938 with an A.B. in sociology, he went to work reporting for the Washington bureau of United Press International. After service in World War II as an Air Force intelligence officer in the Pacific, Reedy returned to UPI, now covering Capitol Hill. During this assignment he met Lillian Greenwald of New York City, a reporter for the International News Service and a young woman with her own probing mind. Appropriately enough, their son Michael is a gifted mathematician and a chess whiz.

Reporting from Congress, Reedy also came to know Senator Lyndon Johnson. He was acutely aware of the senator's faults. But he was drawn by the intensity of the LBJ operation ("he has almost unbelievable concentration on whatever problem is immediately before him"), an admiration for his ability to get solid legislation passed, and a conviction that the Senate would not be the peak of the Johnson career. In 1951 Reedy left newspaper work for a position on the Johnson staff. A friend chided him, "How can you leave reporting to work for some politician?"

"Because Lyndon Johnson is a first-rate man," Reedy replied. "He's the senator who's going to get useful things done, and he will be President someday. I'm hitching my wagon to a star."

By now the campus socialist was a pragmatist, interested in reform but preferring to call it "change," as much fascinated by the processes of politics as he was fervid about any particular measure. Whatever his title, he functioned as Senate Majority Leader Johnson's policy staff director, giving much of his time not only to relations with labor but to developing legislation, including the Space Act of 1958 in which LBJ took great pride. Reedy also served as press representative, and he had learned the Johnsonian concept of news. He gave out what Lyndon Johnson wanted given out in the way that Lyndon Johnson wanted it given out, and nothing else. George Reedy was a man who delighted in conversation. He started his day on Capitol Hill at the press table in the Senate restaurant and he was full of talk about everything— everything except his boss.

When Reedy received President Johnson's call at the Doctors Hospital, he hastily put on his clothes and headed for the White House. A few hours later Mrs. Reedy arrived at the hospital to pay his bill and the clerk said, Well, she guessed it was all right but they never before had a patient who just walked out. Reedy was in a hurry but he was not jumping for joy; he knew he was in for a rough time. He puffed on his pipe and observed, "It's like shoving a man into the front line of the trenches. If he survives, he gets the victory medal."

Reedy was only too aware that relations between President Johnson and the press were not good. Despite LBJ's new confidence in the spring of 1964, he still tended to view reporters as so many enemies to be told as little and manipulated as much as possible. He kept a tight rein on what his Press Secretary could say. As much as he thought feasible, he avoided the type of press conference which newsmen wanted: the set conference, announced ahead of time, for which they could prepare. He preferred briefings suddenly assembled, in his office, walking around the White House grounds, or by a haystack at the ranch. "I like to look my questioners in the eye," the President said; he also liked to keep them off balance, of which they were fully cognizant. He seemed to have a constitutional inability to do what was of importance to reporters—make a travel plan and let the Press Secretary inform them of the details so that they could tell their wives, pack a suitcase and not feel like so many menials being pushed around. The press was growing increasingly suspicious of what was told them. Too often President Johnson was making statements that did not check out and denying rumors which turned out to be facts.

Reedy set to work to try to heal the abrasions. At times he pressed LBJ on the point that a presidential Press Secretary is not a public relations man. But Reedy is essentially a gentle man; moreover, he knew what happened to assistants who pushed LBJ too hard about his mistakes. Most of the time he gave his emphasis to trying to keep himself informed about what was really on President Johnson's mind and transmitting as much of it as he felt he could in a way which would protect the President from charges of misleading statements.

In this effort, he labored under a serious handicap. President Johnson liked and respected Reedy enormously. "Next to Bird," the President once remarked, "the person who means most to me is George Reedy." President Johnson often turned to this aide for an opinion on the same type of problem for which he called Abe Fortas. But the President did not sit talking a great deal with Reedy; he was not enough of a one-two-three man. "You ask him what time it is," LBJ said in affectionate impatience, "and he discusses the significance of time before he tells you it's eleven-thirty." Reedy had trouble keeping the press informed about the President's thinking or plans because in many instances he simply did not know.

Under the circumstances, the loyal Press Secretary tried more and more to avoid giving out misinformation by the expedient of avoiding answers. At his two-a-day press briefings he frequently resorted to "I don't know" or "No comment." Often he deflected the question: "I'll have to refer you to Defense"—or the State or Commerce Department—"for that." Sometimes he resorted to circumlocution, and his natural heaviness of speech could turn these dodges into performances that sent the reporters away fuming.

Tormented by queries concerning the speed-and-beer drive, Reedy stated, "Your question is assuming some conclusions based upon some facts of which I am unaware. As a casual newspaper reader, I have some awareness of the stories to which you have alluded. As far as I can gather from these stories, I know of no particular occasion that could be identified from them on which I was present. Consequently, I cannot draw conclusions on a series of facts which are not known to me."

Reedy's problem was further aggravated by members of the staff. Ever since the 1930's, when the White House staff was organized in its present form, presidential aides had been told to be circumspect in dealing with the press. The Welsh politico Thomas Jones had invented the phrase often ascribed to FDR: White House aides need "high competence, great physical vigor and a passion for anonymity." President Johnson made it plain that the passion for anonymity was to be all-consuming. He, not others, was to determine the news, and if an assistant talked to reporters, it was to be at his instruction. But some of his men were not ready to accept this rule. They got together with reporters on their own, putting themselves forward in the light in which they wanted to be seen. The LBJ White House was one vast sieve. Because these leaks were surreptitious and often unrelated to the President's own purposes, they contributed to the confusion in news. George Reedy was a Press Secretary with a severely limited amount of information that was authoritative to announce, while other statements were constantly making their ways to the press.

When things were particularly troublesome, Reedy was likely to be on the phone to Horace Busby. "Buzz," people said of Horace Busby, "is one hell of a nice guy." He was a genial man, just turning forty, stocky, soft-mannered and rarely without a good-humored word for everyone. But beneath this outward serenity was another part of the man. Busby had a sharp, inquiring mind; he was restless, intellectually and in his thoughts about himself; his humor included a touch of quinine. A person of paper-thin sensitivity, he reacted quickly to a breach of his own dignity or any harshness in human relations.

The son of a well-known Church-of-Christ evangelist, Busby grew up in Fort Worth, Texas, red-haired and freckle-faced, seeming every inch the all-American boy. The nice minister's son enrolled in the University of Texas and proved quite a hellion. His writing skill quickly developing,—he was mastering the clean, pungent sentence—Busby became editor of the *Daily Texan*, a college newspaper with influence far beyond the campus and one that was carefully read by Texas politicians. At first he took on the usual college-boy's devils, like student housing and student food. Toward the end of World War II he headed into the storm center. The university was under the control of Texas' powerhouse, an oil-and-gas cabal, and its president, Homer P. Rainey, had turned out to be part of the group that was trying to move the state into twentieth-century liberalism. When the board of trustees fired Rainey, Horace Busby repaired to his typewriter and produced a series of stinging editorials. By now he was considered so much the campus heretic that the university's minuscule Communist cell tried to recruit him.

Busby left the university without formally graduating—he departed one course short because he wanted to be out and doing things—and took a job covering the Texas State House for the International News Service. But his *Daily Texan* editorials had been read by Lyndon Johnson, then about to run for the Senate as the candidate of the liberal forces and moderate conservatives against the thoroughly conservative Governor "Coke" Stevenson. In 1948, at the age of twenty-five, Busby began working for the future President.

It proved a long but not continuous relationship; Busby kept going on and off the LBJ payroll. He admired Lyndon Johnson in much the same way that George Reedy did, but unlike the unflappable Reedy, he found it impossible to take the lashings for any length of time. Indeed, he found it almost as difficult to accept the praise of Lyndon Johnson, who, despite all his vaunted skill in handling people, could show a strange obtuseness in his relations with a certain kind of man. There could be no question of how fond LBJ was of Busby and how highly he valued his work. Yet he could make a remark like "Buzz is a very sound, solid, able, good boy." The very sound and solid and able—and very adult and complex—Horace Busby would hear about the remark and flare.

There was also the matter of income. Busby had married Mary Virginia Alves, the pretty and spirited daughter of a division head in the U.S. Office of Education, who had been working as a secretary to Lyndon Johnson's successor as congressman from the Austin area, Homer Thornberry. Busby was a man with a sense of the dollar; he kept in mind doing better for his wife and three children. During his absences from LBJ, he did public relations work in Austin and founded a newsletter, the *Texas Businessman*. Later he moved his base to Washington, established the American International Business Research Corporation, and converted the *Texas Businessman* into the lucrative *American Businessman*.

Although nominally in and out of the Johnson operation, Busby always remained close to it and to politics. As he said, he was "hooked." Not only did he share Reedy's admiration for Lyndon Johnson and his conviction that the senator was a comer; even more than Reedy, he was fascinated by the processes of power. Busby, whether or not he was on the senator's roster, was at his side during the bid for the presidential nomination in 1960, went along as a speech writer and general aide on the Vice-President's overseas trips, spent long evenings at The Elms, and in 1963 drafted Vice-President Johnson's most notable address, the Memorial Day speech at Gettysburg during the centennial celebration of Lincoln's Gettysburg Address.

"To ask patience from the Negro," Busby wrote, "is to ask him to give more of what he has already given enough. But to fail to ask of him, and of all Americans, perseverance within the processes of a free and responsible society would be to fail to ask what the national interest requires of all its citizens." The speech was widely praised—so much so that Sorensen let it be known that it was the addresses of the President, not the Vice-President, which were to receive special attention.

Meanwhile Busby was acquiring the reputation of having become a standpatter. In the course of his Texas political activities, he had supported two prime targets of Texas liberals—Governor Allan Shivers and Senator Price Daniel, and for a year he served as administrative assistant to Senator Daniel. His newsletters had a businessman's ring and occasionally talked of liberals with asperity. Like a good many people who had worked with reformers, Busby was developing his degree of disillusionment. He was the more inclined to talk conservatively because by and large that was the way to get ahead in Texas political circles, and that was the way his leader, Lyndon Johnson, talked most of the time. If his public-relations and newsletter work were to make the money he sought, they had to speak to businessmen. Yet just what all this meant in terms of Busby's deeper attitudes is not clear. His mind remained open and freewheeling, his conversation roamed left and right, his humaneness was undiminished.

Liberal, conservative or agnostic, Busby was now officially back on the LBJ roster, installed as a Special Assistant in a rambling East Wing suite of offices that had formerly housed both Arthur M. Schlesinger, Jr., and Brooks Hays, an ex-Congressman from Arkansas. Like other LBJ aides, Busby functioned all over the lot. He handled his quota of congressmen, kept up contacts with businessmen for the President, carried on a number of quasi-foreign policy activities, including relations with the USIA and international organizations.

Basically President Johnson looked upon Busby as a speech writer, a special-projects man, and above all the fellow with the smart suggestion. Day after day and night after night—sometimes spending the few hours left of the night on a couch in the office—Busby turned out speeches, some major, some of the "Rose Garden" variety with which the President greeted visitors or presented awards. Attuned to the LBJ mind, his typewriter deft and indefatigable, he managed to write into even Rose Garden speeches a surprising amount of substance. Busby's special projects were significant; he had a sense of the potentialities of the Office of the Presidency not only for promoting the advantage of its occupant but for moving ahead worthwhile trends in American life. Of greatest importance were his carefully formulated memos to the Oval Office on domestic affairs. They were specific and they were unabashedly political, which were two of the reasons why LBJ read them so closely. They were also based on a sensitive understanding of the needs, material and otherwise, of the American people in the 1960's. And frequently—LBJ liked to have Horace Busby around him—this aide was up in the President's private quarters, pressing his points in his soft, subtle manner.

More than any other member of his staff, Lyndon Johnson believed, Horace Busby thought and felt like him. This did not leave Busby entirely comfortable, but at least with respect to a number of hour-by-hour situations, it was accurate and Busby was most often the man who served as LBJ's other self. On the night of the inaugural balls in 1964, Busby preceded the presidential party to each hotel, mingling with the crowd, and when Lyndon Johnson entered, handed him a few notes. President Johnson confidently followed the notes, in his remarks, in the people he singled out, and in his general conduct at the occasion.

Busby and Reedy often worked closely together in the LBJ White House. They were an important source of integrity in dealing with the press and with the country, of knowledgeability and sophistication, of a general attitude of, Let's get on with the American job. Essentially secure men within their own lives, they kept their personal ambitions subordinated to an effort to call from within Lyndon Johnson the qualities of greatness which they were sure—whatever their moments of anger and despair—were there.

"People sometimes ask me about that phrase, 'Johnson men,' " Horace Busby once mused. "Well, there is such a thing. A man is that way or he gets that way."

The Johnson men were quite different in many important respects, and one of them, Richard Goodwin, had so little in common with the rest that he cannot be included in generalizations. But Busby's remark was essentially accurate. Some Presidents, like FDR, deliberately grouped around themselves sharply contrasting types. Lyndon Johnson had Johnson men.

LBJ was a devotee of the young, or at least of the relatively young. He liked their quick reactions, their durability under relentless hours, their greater amenability to being ordered around. The oldest of the Johnson men was George Reedy, forty-six, and the average age—in this one case including Goodwin—was only thirty-nine.

They were men who not only worked furiously but who had, or had adopted, the President's attitude that life is earnest. The Johnson White House was not a merry place. Moyers might play his practical jokes, Busby get off his wry remarks, but the long hard days went by with a sobriety altered only by the general air of frenzy. The Johnson men saw relatively little of the ever-flowing Washington cocktail circuit. They were not particularly that kind of people, they had little time, and the President's wishes were plain. Even Jack Valenti now lived a different life.

At one of his staff get-togethers, Valenti conveyed to us a presidential order that aides were to stay away from "all" cocktail and dinner parties except family affairs or those of intimate friends. The redoubtable Mrs. Elizabeth Carpenter, chief aide to

Mrs. Johnson and the most independent and outspoken member of the whole Johnson group, exploded. "My husband is a newspaper reporter. He makes his living going to parties and finding out things. If I'm going to see him at all, it will be by going with him —and I intend to see him." Then she caught herself and laughed along with the rest of us. The order was obviously a product of an LBJ mood and was not to be taken literally. But it was an indication of his general attitude.

The careers of the Johnson men bore a striking similarity: almost all had spent the whole or a considerable part of their adult lives associated with LBJ. This was as true of Busby, Jenkins and Reedy, in their forties, as it was of Moyers at twenty-nine. Valenti, of Weekley & Valenti, was a nine-year LBJ man.

Feudalism has its long-running ties. At one stage in my White House work I made several trips to Texas, and was amazed at the number of President Johnson's old associates who had remained part of his activities—many of them a direct part—ever since his youthful NYA days. In the White House, not only the upper but the lower echelons were a maze of relationships extending over years. Jenkins' chief "secretary"—so trusted that she helped make up the Johnson income tax and evaluate FBI reports—was Mrs. Mildred F. Stegall, an LBJ employee for many years and the widow of a man whose first job, as a House doorkeeper, had been arranged by Representative Lyndon Johnson. At Busby's side was Mrs. Dorothy J. Nichols, who had met Lyndon Johnson when he was a schoolteacher in Cotulla, Texas, and whose husband, Philip Nichols, Jr., kept moving up with him until President Johnson named Nichols a judge on the United States Court of Claims in 1966. The chief assistant in Reedy's office was Mrs. Willie Day Taylor, University of Texas '47, a second mother to the Johnson daughters and such an old hand at family matters that the President designated her to decide which wedding presents for Luci should be accepted, which rejected.

One fact remained constant, both before and after Lyndon Johnson entered the White House. He almost never fired a high-level aide, and a high-level aide almost never completely left him. Usually they had no real independent base; their base was Lyndon Johnson. A man might leave out of weariness or anger or a desire for more money or because LBJ had decided it was best for the particular assistant not to be with him during the particular period. But whatever their personal feelings, they departed without a storm, and for the most part they remained within the Johnson orbit.

Men desirous of living in such a relationship are not apt to be strong individualists, the free spirits of the world. They are practical men with controlled habits and modulated emotions. Visitors to the White House frequently commented on the pleasantness of the LBJ aides; they were pleasant indeed, and flexible in all kinds of circumstances. But since they were all also intelligent and anything but spiritless, the situation had its consequences. The Johnson men had for Lyndon Johnson a rampant love-hate relationship.

They might have the adventurism of a Moyers, the hero worship of a Valenti, the moth-and-flame fascination of a Busby and Reedy. Whatever the feeling, it was complex. They had staked their careers and a good deal of their inner selves on Lyndon Johnson. They delighted in rising with him, in riding with his strength and cunning; they hated the dependency and the demeanings which came with the advancement. At Camp David, after midnight, berated for a statement he had to prepare in ten minutes, one aide announced that this time he was surely going back to his old occupation. Another morning another assistant, after working much of the night only to be awakened at seven-thirty for a presidential castigation, shook his head and said, "This is it." Neither resigned; neither had an allegiance to Lyndon Johnson marked by the affection which most White House aides had given to previous Presidents.

"The trouble with Lyndon," one of his oldest friends and strong admirers once remarked to me, "is that he is a sonofabitch. The next worst trouble is that he is a great sonofabitch. He will probably do more for the United States, destroying everybody around him, than any other President." His aides felt this too—in awe, irritation, wonderment and subservience.

Above all, the Johnson men were Johnsonian in that they were nonideological activists. Some had a background of emotional reformism; others, more than a flirtation with chamber of commerce crusading. By the time they reached the White House, there was not a passionate liberal or conservative among them. All had gone through a blunting of ideology; all, in their mental outlook, were pragmatists. With one exception they were Texans, and they were Texans not only in a geographical sense. They had the standoffishness toward the Northeast marking so many from that state, not least in their case because they thought of it as a region which bred ineffectual ideologues.

For the most part the LBJ men were on the liberal side of major issues. Their habit was to see a problem and ask how it could be solved. This meant, What is the sensible, effective solution? It also meant, What will the existing line-up of political forces in the country permit? In twentieth-century America, the workable solution to most problems has been the liberal or quasi-liberal one, and the political spectrum has favored the national leader who follows the New Deal-Fair Deal-New Frontier tradition. With seasoned practicality and enormous energy, and without fervor, the Johnson men generally took the liberal path.

At bottom what tied together the Johnson White House, leader and aides, was a zest in getting problems solved, and solved quickly. Late in the Spring of 1964, the President was asked whether it was not strange that he, urging sweeping liberal programs, had so close to him men associated in the past with a sharply different world. "I didn't pick them as conservatives or liberals or anything," Lyndon Johnson replied. "I picked them as men who know how to get things done."

The Johnson men knew how, and they were getting things done.

Ideas, Tomorrow

*F*or me, the spring of 1964 meant a considerable intensification of my own experience as a Johnson man, in whatever way and to whatever extent I was one. During my entire Washington period, for one university semester I commuted a day a week from Washington to Princeton to do some lecturing which the university department of history particularly felt it needed. I continued to moderate an NBC intellectual discussion television program, *The Open Mind,* which I had been doing for five years and to which I was devoted. My base was in Washington and beyond these things I was giving five to six days of the week to the White House, often working the LBJ elongated hours.

Of course I was engaged in putting the "quiet brain trust" into operation. I had planned the project in two stages. First, I would set up a group concerned with domestic problems; later I would organize another panel for foreign affairs. In conceiving the domestic group, I naturally thought in terms of areas of problems, labor, education, public finance, and so on, and I added places for a number of topics which seemed to me especially important for the 1960's, including the poor, science and technology, federal-state-local relations, the administration of justice, youth, and "the quality of American life." For each of these I chose one or more experts, but of course all members were to be free to make suggestions in any field.

Except for the meeting in the Cabinet Room when the State of the Union address was also discussed, I was left largely alone in making the selections, though Abe Fortas was always available for consultation. I sought telephone advice throughout the country and was careful to spread my choices around the nation. No consideration was given to a man's occupational base, whether a university, foundation or commercial corporation. What I was after, above all, was that rare man or woman, the expert who was also endowed with both exceptional imagination and a sense of the feasible.

I sent my final choices to Walter Jenkins for FBI clearance and managed to get all the names approved—not without difficulty in a few cases. I was learning that Jenkins, reflecting the President, had little tolerance in such matters. The list went to President Johnson in January 1964, and he okayed it without change.

Since I had the whole United States to call upon, the group inevitably was a distinguished one of great diversity. The categories and people were: the administration of justice, Paul A. Freund, professor of law, Harvard University; agriculture, John L. Fischer, professor of agricultural economics, Montana State College, and Earl O. Heady, professor of agricultural economics, Iowa State University; education, elementary and secondary, Richard H. Sullivan, president, Reed College; education, higher, David Riesman, professor of social relations, Harvard University; federal-state-local relations and the metropolitan areas, Homer C. Wadsworth, director, Kansas City Association of Trusts and Foundations, and Paul N. Ylvisaker, director, Public Affairs Program, Ford Foundation; government and business, Edward H. Levi, provost, University of Chicago, and Eugene V. Rostow, dean, Yale Law School; international trade and finance, Harry G. Johnson, professor of economics, University of Chicago; labor, Clark Kerr, president, University of California; medical care, Robert E. L. Faris, professor of sociology, University of Washington; migrant workers, Daniel H. Pollitt, professor of law, University of North Carolina; minorities, Leonard Broom, professor of sociology, University of Texas; minorities, the Negro, John A. Davis, professor of political science, The City College of New York; natural resources, conservation and regional development, the land and internal waters, Joseph L. Fisher, president, Resources for the Future, Inc., Washington, D.C.; natural resources, conservation and regional development, oceanography, Roger Revelle, director, Scripps Institute of Oceanography, University of California at La Jolla; the poor, rural, John Ehle, special assistant to the Governor of North Carolina, and Edward Higbee, professor of agriculture, University of Rhode Island; the poor, urban, Robert C. Wood, professor of political science, Massachusetts Institute of Technology; the Presidential Office, Clinton Rossiter, professor of American institutions, Cornell University; public finance, Richard A. Musgrave, professor of economics and public affairs, Princeton University; the quality of American life, John Kenneth Galbraith, professor of economics,

Harvard University, and Richard Hofstadter, professor of history, Columbia University; science and technology, Edwin H. Land, president, Polaroid Corporation; women, Margaret Mead, curator of ethnology, American Museum of Natural History, New York; and youth, Eli Ginzberg, director, Conservation of Human Resources Project, Columbia University.

While I was enthusiastic about the quality of this "domestic affairs group"—the name we usually used—I was not without considerable misgivings. Shortly after President Johnson approved the list, I had a trial run, inviting to the Fish Room a small number of people—Fortas, several from the projected domestic affairs group, and others—who were experts on federal-state-local relations, especially as they applied to the problems of the metropolitan areas. The gathering brought together men who had been doing some of the most interesting thinking about the cities, and Fortas was at his best. The talk was fertile and exciting; at least for me, it had the effect of confirming the conviction that some new governmental instrumentality was needed if anything substantial were to be done about the metropolitan areas. But as the day's session ended and the men hurried for their planes, one who was a personal friend took me aside and said, "It's grand to have this going on in the White House. But do you really think, all things considered, that it's going to work?" I offered the proper reply of a Johnson man, "Let's make it work," and returned to my misgivings.

When I got in touch with the men on the list for the domestic affairs group and asked them to serve, of course everyone accepted. But I could not fail to sense the same undertone which marked my phone conversations at the time of the preparation for the State of the Union message: Was President Johnson genuinely interested in what intellectuals thought?

Other problems were inherent in the very way the President expected the group to function, of which I had seen hints when he first gave me the assignment and which were now becoming increasingly obvious. Young Richard Nelson had a playful name for President Johnson, "The Maximum Leader." At the session on federal-state-local relations he had slipped me a note which read, "The Maximum Leader will be expecting ideas tomorrow." Nelson's kidding had its point. As I watched President Johnson in action and talked with long-time associates of his, I came to an uneasy conclusion concerning what he meant when he said he wanted "ideas." An idea was a suggestion, produced on the spot, of something for him to do tomorrow—a point to be made in a speech, an action, ceremonial or one of substance, for him to take promptly, a formula to serve as the basis for legislation to be hurried to Congress.

First-rate "experts" or "intellectuals"—the "best minds" the President sought—are rarely idea men in this sense. The people in the domestic affairs group had been so intensively concerned with the problems in their fields that inevitably they would have certain immediate suggestions. Over the long pull, instant ideas were not their specialty; indeed, men of this type have little use for them.

The circumstances under which the President wanted the group to operate complicated the situation further. Since the days of Theodore Roosevelt, and especially since the 1930's, intellectuals have performed brilliant services in devising and encouraging new programs. But they have done so mainly by writing seminal works and letting others do the implementing, or by functioning inside the government. Being inside gives them a firsthand understanding of the nature of the problem, makes them aware of what has already been proposed and why it was not adopted, and puts them in a position to advance their proposals through the thickets of bureaucracy. Inevitably, some of the men on my list were already deeply involved with government as consultants, and their membership in the new group was largely superfluous except as it might give them a more direct access to the President's ear. In the case of others who did not happen to be in this position, President Johnson expected them to be continuously useful while spread across the continent, busy with their regular tasks and cut off from the intimacy and immediacy of government.

The President's injunction to keep my White House connection and the domestic affairs group secret continued. I was beginning to understand the complexities of his attitude. He genuinely wanted a liaison with the intellectual world. He was curious about intellectuals, and in a way that was not without its poignancy, sought to understand them and have them understand him. They were "educators"; he had the belief of the superficially educated man in the magic of education and a feeling that if he could only find the right formula, he would loose an unending stream of "ideas." These personal attitudes joined with rudimentary political considerations. LBJ wanted to remain distant from no large group of voters—particularly one that talked and wrote so much, and most especially, one that JFK was supposed to have had in his hip pocket.

Yet President Johnson was leery. In the years immediately before the White House, he had arranged a few get-togethers with leading intellectuals. He had not enjoyed the sessions; besides, not one of the men supported him in his drive for the nomination in 1960. Now he was close to a presidential campaign and eager to win over Republican businessmen, to many of whom intellectuals were not educators but eggheads. If politically he felt he should pay attention to John Kennedy's celebrated rapport with intellectuals, nevertheless in this, as in everything else, he was edgy about appearing to imitate JFK. And reinforcing all these considerations was the President's general secretiveness in dealing with the press. So the order remained that nothing, nothing at all was to be given reporters.

For the most part I managed to keep myself out of the papers, if at the price of some extraordinary statements which I found myself making to the persistent inquiries of newsmen. The domestic affairs group remained under wraps, and with the natural consequences. Everything connected with it was marked by tension lest a reporter learn of its formation, and just because of the concealment, write a lurid story. The extreme secrecy confirmed the impression of a number of its members that President Johnson was merely going through the motions that he thought were expected of the successor to John Kennedy. To some of the men, my insistence on the tight lid seemed downright insulting. "What's the matter, Eric?" one said to me bluntly. "Is the President ashamed of us?"

Steadily, I kept pressuring for a low-key White House statement to the press, simply saying that President Johnson naturally wanted as much help as possible and had asked me to maintain an informal liaison with experts in various fields. The statement would include a list of the people forming the domestic affairs group but would emphasize—what was certainly accurate—that this was in no sense a super or exclusive panel and that the White House intended to be in touch, as it had been for years, with many other authorities in many other ways. Naturally, then or later, I would say nothing about specific proposals which members might be making. Any President would and should object to this because it was a sure way to get the suggestions mired down in ugly controversy before the Administration had adopted any part of them or even before they had been fully worked out.

At this stage it was easy for staff members to see President Johnson. A call to his top secretary, Juanita D. Roberts (another seasoned, pleasant LBJ aide, a product of Port Arthur, Texas, who had married Congressman Ray Roberts of Collin County, Texas), would lead to a quick get-together. But my feeling was that this matter, which touched so many sensitive spots, was best handled through one of the President's veteran Texans. I also knew myself.

I am quick-tempered too, and an LBJ outburst could cause me to say things that would impede any serious relationship between President Johnson and intellectuals.

I worked away through Walter Jenkins, who was unfailingly understanding. Jenkins was also unfailingly insistent that the President wanted no press notice of what I was doing, and that was that.

What changed the situation was another spate of news stories which indicated that I was replacing Arthur Schlesinger, Jr., on the White House staff, and the mounting irritation of the President and of Jenkins against Schlesinger. There was something about my fellow historian, to his glory or demerit, which peculiarly roused the Johnsonian. President Johnson would soon vent his feelings during the troubles in Santo Domingo, when he got off his remark that infuriated or titillated the several Washingtons: "What do you want me to do—send Arthur Schlesinger to take care of things?" The President and Jenkins were particularly stirred up by a syndicated column of a friend of Schlesinger's, Joseph Alsop, which stated that Schlesinger had "recommended" me as "his successor in case President Johnson still wanted a resident White House scholar. The fact that Goldman will eventually replace Schlesinger is now public knowledge."

Jenkins received an okay from the President to release an announcement, and on February 3, 1964, it was given to the press. The statement was a Johnsonian document. I was no replacement for Schlesinger; my activities represented a "unique approach." President Johnson wanted "ideas," "fresh, new and imaginative ideas for the benefit of the Government." He was establishing a "wide-open window" for them, and I would "co-ordinate" them while serving as "consultant and adviser to the President." No mention was made of the domestic affairs group. The work of the "nation's scholars and specialists" would come to the White House at no cost to the taxpayer. In a jumble of words which, if they meant much of anything, intimated inaccuracies, the statement had me co-ordinating away while continuing to teach at Princeton and without even a per diem payment from the government.

At that afternoon's White House press conference Pierre Salinger, who had not yet resigned as Press Secretary, manfully continued this line. Goldman "would serve without pay," function "most of the time" at Princeton, and his work was "the collection of ideas."

"Does he become the new Dr. Schlesinger?" a reporter asked.

"I anticipated that question," said Salinger, taking a protective puff on his cigar. He went into the stance of "for background only," meaning that what he said could be used in a general way but not directly quoted or attributed. Salinger stressed heavily that my role had been conceived by President Johnson and was quite different from Schlesinger's position under President Kennedy. Emerging from the "backgrounder," he stated, "I could not compare the two roles."

Another reporter cut in, "Are you sure you don't want to be quoted on it?"

This time Pierre Salinger's puff on his cigar was slow and definitive. "The more I think about it, the less I want to be quoted on it."

Near the end of the press conference the newsmen brought Salinger back to this subject. Was President Johnson creating a brain trust? If so, just who was picking its members?

On the few occasions when I had dealt with Salinger, I found it difficult to communicate with him. He seemed preoccupied with playing the buffoon; in the emotional Kennedyite way, he appeared to assume that if you were engaged in intellectual matters, you belonged with the RFK faction. Regardless of these characteristics, in the particular instance at hand he had little understanding of the kind of problems involved and was under instructions to dissociate my appointment from any similar activities of the Kennedy Administration.

No, Salinger answered the reporters, this was not a brain trust; "it is just a search for ideas." Then he uttered a gaffe: Goldman would have "a great deal to say" about the composition of the group and had been in contact with a number of the men, "but the situation is that any ideas are welcome." The Associated Press, understandably, immediately spread the word: The White House would "welcome the ideas from any person."

The form of the announcement impelled reporters to press me with two questions: Did President Johnson really expect me to do a job of this magnitude part time and unpaid? And did he really want "ideas" from the general public too? No matter how much the President wanted me to stay out of the papers, I could not avoid some answer to these questions without recreating an air of stealth. Obviously it was not my place to contradict official White House statements, and I could hardly declare that President Johnson was not interested in suggestions from ordinary citizens. I spoke the necessary weasels. Of course, of course, I replied, we would feel our way along about working arrangements. Of course the White House was interested in suggestions from citizens, although the main emphasis of my work would be on a liaison with experts.

Americans like nothing better than to tell the President how to run the country, and they now had what they thought was an invitation. The letters came through the "wide-open window for ideas" like an invasion of bats, piling into Washington and Princeton by the thousands. Someday someone trying to understand the America of the 1960's will take a look at this correspondence, now ensconced in the central files of the White House. It reflects how many of our people are, in plain English, irrational. A high percentage of the communications were, by any definition, the products of kooks, and no small number of such letters were written on the stationery of substantial citizens or of reputable firms. The outpouring also reflected the American unease in the 1960's. Through many of the letters ran the theme, We are doing okay, we are meeting the mortgage and the children will make it to college, but why doesn't the President do something to lessen the rat-race quality of American life?

As far as much of the press was concerned, I was now the "idea man," a silly title and one obviously damaging to what I was trying to do. On the other hand, the more responsible news agencies tried to understand and to be favorable. But what had been said—and not said—was such that they could hardly avoid some degree of skepticism. They questioned whether President Johnson was not simply making a clumsy attempt to please the intellectual group; they expressed doubt or at least puzzlement over what appeared to be the nature of my assignment and the conditions under which it was supposed to be done. As a matter of fact, the White House had managed to surround the appointment with such confusion that James Reston, just about as well-informed a man as Washington possessed, based his comment on a complete misconception of what my function was supposed to be, not to speak of his making the usual assumption that I was expected to perform it with the little finger of my left hand.

Reston had recently been on a plane trip with President Johnson and had been urging on him the importance of setting up some better way of recruiting high-level talent for regular government posts. The President had appeared interested, and Reston assumed that I was named to do the job. "Every President since Franklin Roosevelt has complained that he could not find and keep enough talent to work for the federal government," Reston wrote, "and President Johnson is now going through the same routine. His answer to the problem has been to appoint a distinguished historian, Dr. Eric F. Goldman of Princeton, to serve as a part-time consultant. . . . This whole project is too serious and important to be handled on a part-time basis. Dr. Goldman will go on teaching and writing and running a television program, and serve the President on the side. This is as good an illustration as any of what's wrong with the whole program of recruiting talent for the public service."

Under any circumstances, a person undertaking an assignment like mine is asking for trouble. The naming of a presidential assistant to provide proposals, however his role is defined, inevitably raises the hackles of some entrenched experts throughout higher levels of the government, who see the new man as a threat to their entrée to the White House. Inevitably, too, some White House aides of a long-standing relationship with the President, particularly those who are anxious to be known as intellectuals, view the new man as an undeserving interloper and one who could be dangerous to their own purposes. The announcement of my appointment, in the strange guise of unpaid, part-time "idea man" collecting ideas on the street corner, gave these naturally hostile forces a potent pool of ridicule.

It also projected me in an unfortunate way into the enmity between the Johnson and Kennedy forces. Even more than Salinger, many Kennedy men assumed that the intellectual life was peculiarly Kennedy territory and peculiarly not Johnson territory. On my appearance in Washington as an LBJ man, a number of JKF appointees in and outside the White House had been cordial and helpful. Others treated me as a wayward soul who had naïvely wandered into a ridiculous situation, or as a kind of traitor to the intellectual class. Some sought to save the wayward soul and I spent more than a few lunches or dinners during which Kennedy men more or less directly urged me, in the language of one of them, to "come over to your natural group," that is, to become what he was, a man working in the Johnson Administration but doing so on behalf of the "Kennedy movement." Whatever the attitude, the nature of the announcement of my appointment tended to confirm for many Kennedyites the opinion that Lyndon Johnson had little understanding of what working with intellectuals meant. To those who remained personally friendly to me, it was an invitation to clobber the President and, incidentally and regretfully, me; to those personally hostile, it ran up the flag of open season on me.

The tendency of some LBJ men to strike back did not help. During this period a respected reporter who was strongly pro-Johnson took me to lunch and devoted most of the meal to a denunciation of the "assumption of the Kennedy people that they own intellectual life." In the manner of offering me a weapon, he told me how President Kennedy had related to him with relish an anecdote which put one of the JFK associates, an intellectual, in a demeaning light. I had no way of knowing whether the account was true. I did know that I did not want to hear it and that I was uncomfortable at being in a position where people thought telling me such stories was appropriate.

Worried, unhappy at the White House handling of my appointment, depressed by the poison in the air, I debated with myself whether I ought to violate what I knew to be President Johnson's desire and speak more openly with the press. Why not see to it that the simple facts were emphasized—that I was living in Washington and working five or six days a week on White House tasks, that I received a government per diem, and that far from being an idea factory of the general public, the so-called ideas project was an informal liaison with experts that was hardly unusual in the modern White House? But I reminded myself that I was not the President of the United States and that I was in Washington to help carry out his policies and wishes. Continuing to avoid the press as far as seemed sensible and talking with reporters in a way that left the real definition of my role to what President Johnson chose to say, I pushed ahead with the domestic affairs group and with a variety of other unrelated White House functions.

One of the effects of working in the White House is a sharpened awareness of what the President of the United States has come to mean to the people of the United States. For more than a century the presidential office had seemed largely a distant political institution, but by the 1960's millions of Americans felt a highly personal relation to its occupant. He was no longer simply the governmental leader but the ultimate guardian of the national security, of the national welfare and—in a vague but potent way— of the national sense of the meaning of America. Moreover, unless he was a singularly unimpressive man, he had become the head of the national family, with all the emotional ties this implies. You sensed this in the bulk and nature of the mail that flooded into the White House, in the comments that were made to people who worked for the President, even in the way that tourists entering the building would lower their voices or straighten their ties. This gives the modern President tremendous power in setting public standards, and it had long seemed to me that the White House had been using the power too little.

Feeling this way, I was the more impressed by a particular correspondence. Early in 1964 I had asked a small number of thoughtful American authors to write me not about specific actions which they believed the Administration should take but about what its general thrust should be. The group included David Donald, Robert L. Heilbroner, Norman Podhoretz, Richard H. Rovere and Barbara W. Tuchman. Of course, the letters varied considerably in emphasis but they were remarkably alike in one way. They agreed that it was important, even urgent, for President Johnson to use his Office in a conscious effort to alter American values.

Barbara Tuchman wrote: "Since Jamestown and Plymouth Rock our progress has been governed by the pursuit and acquisition of material things. . . . In our time, the New Deal, in response to urgent and tragic necessity, dedicated itself to the abolition of want among the ill-fed, ill-clothed and ill-housed. Since then the battle against poverty, though not won, is now a process more or less self-propelling. . . . It is one of the tragedies of history that gain in one direction is never made without loss in another, and our loss has been in the realm of morality and quality. The public is suffering from it, I think, as from a deficiency disease.

"Has the time not come to shift the emphasis from the material to the moral? Have we perhaps learned from experience that the more concern we give to goods and services and entertainment, the less is left over for values for which the human being has an equal need: virtue, for instance, and standards, critical, aesthetic and moral?

"Standards, it seems, require spokesmen or they fade. As liberty needs eternal vigilance, standards need to be eternally reiterated by persons who carry authority by virtue of their office or character or both. . . .

"In less than six weeks in office President Johnson has . . . established his authority. . . . He could from now on become the spokesman of standards which we need. He could help us recoup the moral loss. It might be his place in the history of American development to begin to redress the balance between the material and moral."

Norman Podhoretz stated: "How can we learn to live in a society in which goods are abundant and work loses its force as the organizing principle of the individual's existence? This ought to be an enormous blessing, but it can only come as an ironic curse to a culture which is spiritually unprepared to cope with it. If we are looking for the 'New Frontier,' we will find it somewhere in this neighborhood—in the necessity for effecting a spiritual revolution in the American character in order to cope with affluence and automation. I would like to see President Johnson take public cognizance of this necessity; I would like to see him discuss the need for a revision of many of the basic values we have inherited from an age of scarcity and that are built into our educational system, our moral vocabulary, our very souls; I would like to see him help to get this strange predicament recognized for what it is and called by its right name."

Robert Heilbroner commented: "I must raise a . . . difficult problem, but one that I cannot in good conscience omit, for I believe that it goes to the very heart of things. This is the overpowering force of commercialism, spearheaded by the ubiquitous influence of advertising, and its effect on American life. Everyone, in private and public life, notices and laments the decline of serious purposes among so many of the younger generation. Yet few draw the connection between the 'fun morality' of youth and the climate of relentless and ceaseless exhortation to eat, smoke, ride, dress and live in the manner glorified by glossy photos and television advertising 'dramas.' . . .

"This is not an illness which can be quickly put to rights, but if it is to be cured, the cure must begin immediately. To begin with, I would like to see attention called to our state of affairs—forcefully and repeatedly—from the very summit of the nation. . . .

"I am very much aware of the difficulty of coping with this problem. At the same time, the conquest of commercialism strikes me as perhaps the acid test that America must undergo in this period of its national existence—the test that will determine whether it survives not merely as a nation but as a meaningful society. I am also sufficiently optimistic to think that the President, in his own earnest and very warmly human way, might be able to force a reconsideration of this gradual debasement of American life before it has gone irreversibly far."

David Donald wrote of the need for a "Crusade Against Ignorance"—not simply a drive for genuine schooling but in a far more sweeping sense of the phrase. "It is time for us to take a new look at our situation and to recognize a fundamental flaw in our previous approach. . . . To put it concisely, that problem is one of alienation. In our vast, diffuse society, Americans rarely have a sense of belonging, of meaningful membership in a national social order. The rapidity of our nation's physical expansion, the melting-pot character of our populace, and the speed of our economic transformation have inhibited the slow organic growth of ties of kinship, neighborhood, and culture that knit together the inhabitants of other lands. . . . Lacking a sense of identity, Americans are prone to delinquency, vandalism, hysteria, and—as recent events sadly show—senseless violence. Lacking a common purpose, Americans fall into warring, selfish groups, of parochial outlook, and these, exploited by interest politics, have prevented the elimination of blatant social injustice. . . .

"Of course it will take great courage to break from the political patterns of the past, and it will take great leadership to summon Americans to arms in the war against ignorance. But for President Johnson this is both a challenge and an opportunity. We look to him for leadership, because, as Woodrow Wilson said long ago, the President is the man to whom 'the voices of the nation . . . unite in a single meaning and reveal to him a single vision, so that he can speak what no man else knows, the common meaning of the common voice. Such is the man who leads a great, free, democratic nation.' Such, I conclude, President Lyndon Johnson can be."

None of the authors would have disagreed with Richard Rovere, who expressed his "hope that in the planning of a presidential campaign against poverty, thought would be given to the finding of means that would bring our dispossessed into an American community of which we could all be proud. There seems to me to be very little gain in economic growth when it is achieved by stimulating the production, distribution, and consumption of trashy things, the creation of trashy houses and landscapes, the dissemination of trashy education and ideas. We will face, always, the danger of becoming a well-fed, well-housed, well-clothed people in a land of moral and intellectual squalor and desolation. If we have the will to eliminate poverty, we should have the intelligence to plan a campaign against it that will do more than spread the blight of mediocrity and impoverished imaginations into the distressed areas of our country."

Certainly the impoverishment of the American imagination came partly from the prestige the general population gave to money, social position, athletic stardom and the aura of a celebrity—almost to the exclusion of status for intellectual and creative achievement. One pastime of a particular group of Johnsonians was to take apart President Kennedy's reputation for interest in the cultivated life. It was like his name for being a connoisseur of food, they said; when not putting on a display in the White House, his choice was clam chowder and hamburger. They told of the celebrated Casals evening that, as soon as politeness permitted, he made his way to a corner to talk politics with a Boston henchman. In all of this there is some general truth, inaccuracy in details and a crashing irrelevancy; the point is not what a President himself likes but what he encourages and holds up before the country as good. I had been happy with President Kennedy's emphasis on the intellectual and creative life and wanted President Johnson to further it. In fact, it seemed to me that a President who was known to be rough-and-ready could be particularly effective in saying to the country that the man with a flair for broken-field running and the one with a gift for mathematical equations are both part of a vital American community and that both deserve status and encouragement.

Obviously the place to start in attempting to influence the American order of prestige values was among the young, and in February 1964 a thought occurred to me which I shaped into a detailed memo for President Johnson. It proposed a system of "Presidential Scholars," which would recognize intellectual achievement among the students about to graduate from the nation's public and private secondary schools. Annually the Chief Executive would name two Presidential Scholars, a boy and a girl, from each state and territory; the designees would be honored at a White House ceremony and given a four-year all-expense college scholarship. After this system was working, a program would be added for young people outstanding in the arts. I was now too accustomed to the LBJ way not to emphasize that the whole project would cost the government little. The main expense, the scholarships, would be financed by foundations.

President Johnson liked the proposal, and as was usually the case when he reacted favorably to a suggestion, wanted it executed forthwith. The plan for a forthcoming honors system in the arts proved impractical. There seemed to be no reasonably objective way—at least none sufficiently objective for a President of the United States—to judge artistic achievement at the youthful stage. The speedy financing of the scholarships for intellectual achievement also ran into a wall. I received unenthusiastic replies from appropriate foundations (later learning that foundations generally felt they should spend their money on projects conceived by themselves rather than serve as a financial tail to the kite of the White House).

Necessity has a way of providing its own rationale. Was a monetary award really important—wouldn't students so able almost certainly receive scholarships from other sources? I had asked five men to advise me on planning the Presidential Scholars program; when I consulted them on the financial point, they concurred with my trend of thought although most did so reluctantly.*

* *The five men, who gave unstintingly of their time and expertise, were Henry Chauncey, president of the Educational Testing Service; Francis Keppel, U.S. Commissioner of Education; John Miles, manager of the education department of the United States Chamber of Commerce; John M. Stalnaker, president of the National Merit Scholarship Corporation; and W. Homer Turner, executive director of the U.S. Steel Foundation.*

They felt that it was a pity not to use this occasion to add to the scholarship resources of the nation, and that—American values being what they are—the award would mean more if it brought not only honor but money. Reluctantly too, I removed the scholarships from the program.

The Presidential Scholars would receive honor—a medallion presented to them by the President at a White House ceremony, with all the attendant recognition. Thus the total cost to be paid by the government would be only about $40,000 a year, for administrative expenses and for travel funds to bring the students to Washington. The tens of thousands of high-ranking students would be screened, without profit, by the National Merit Scholarship Corporation, using its own records and those of every other major scholarship agency. These nominees would go to a blue-ribbon White House Commission on Presidential Scholars, which would make final recommendations to the President.

I have no way of judging precisely President Johnson's motives in approving the Presidential Scholars program. Obviously it had political advantage; it not only put him generally on the side of the worthy but brought kudos in his name to specific families and communities throughout the nation. Yet my own impression is that he agreed to the proposal at least as much because of that marked enthusiasm of his for education—I really should say his extravagant enthusiasm, which came close to a belief that education can cure the world's ills—and his ardor to have his Administration associated with education in every possible way.

At any rate, the Presidential Scholars program involved some political risk as well as sure advantage. Several testing experts emphasized that because of the enormous differences in the cultural backgrounds of students, the final list might well be dominated by names from upper-income families; worse still from a political point of view, it might include no Negro. Partly to minimize such contingencies, partly to take care of the great disparity in the population of the states, I added fifteen Scholars to be chosen at large, and the machinery was geared to take into account striking promise as well as established achievement. But a degree of possible political embarrassment remained, President Johnson was aware of it and he ruled, Go ahead.

Soon the President decided on a formal television press conference and the scene which usually preceded such a session took shape. LBJ liked to open with specific news-making favorable items, large or small, and the White House was turned upside down to produce them. Two days before the press conference I was informed that the Presidential Scholars program and its awards commission were to be announced—which was fine, except that as yet there was no Commission on Presidential Scholars.

I scrambled together a draft of the announcement and a suggested commission. It was headed by Milton S. Eisenhower, president of the Johns Hopkins University, and along with appropriate school and university figures it included Leonard Bernstein and Katherine Anne Porter. President Johnson had no objection to this but he made an LBJ addition I should have thought of, a congressman. The inclusion of Senator J. William Fulbright came about in a way that caught the atmosphere of a pre-press conference period.

My first knowledge of it was when I noticed the senator's name on a release about to go out of the Press Secretary's office. The Press Secretary did not know how the name got on the list or whether it really belonged there. Hurriedly I checked. It was correct that Fulbright had been appointed to the commission; the President thought it was a good idea but neglected to tell anybody. I thought it was a fine idea. I felt it was an even better idea after the White House switchboard had chased down Senator Fulbright and I had asked him to serve, and after I had informed Chairman Eisenhower that the commission he headed happened to have another member.

President Johnson announced the Presidential Scholars program on April 16, 1964. Once it was under way, he grew increasingly enthusiastic about it and as always his enthusiasm was something to behold. The Commission on Presidential Scholars held its first meeting in the Fish Room of the White House on a Sunday afternoon in May. Shortly before it assembled, the relative Sabbath calm of 1600 Pennsylvania Avenue went to pieces. It had never occurred to me that the President would want to take time to open a meeting of one of his commissions, and a minor one at that. Now he had learned of the session and was stalking around the Oval Office. "What do you people do—stay up nights figuring out ways to keep things from me?" Jack Valenti and I threw together some remarks for him, and he headed for the Fish Room. LBJ was in high fettle. He started to read off the prepared sentences but they were much too restrained. "This program," he declared, "will revolutionize American education." A little nonplused, the commission set to work revolutionizing American education by honoring one hundred and twenty-one gifted youngsters.

The functioning of the panel left me impressed once more by the dedication which distinguished and extremely busy Americans are ready to give to the White House. All but one of the commission remained through two days of hard work in their regular meeting place, a dismal room in the Executive Office Building. They took enormous care, going through the dossiers again and again. I stayed away from the sessions, to preserve the symbolism as well as the fact of the total independence of the choices from any interference, White House or otherwise. But once I went into the room to ask about a detail and I was decidedly moved by the spectacle of the president of one of America's great universities, the chairman of the United States Senate Foreign Relations Committee, and the nation's best-known serious musician huddled over a file of papers arguing the intellectual merits of three teen-agers.

Meanwhile, there was the matter of the medallion to be presented to the Presidential Scholars. In its design—and of course it would include a profile of President Johnson—I wanted to avoid the banality of customary government aesthetics, and John H. Naisbitt, the art-minded aide to Commissioner of Education Francis Keppel, undertook to canvass critics throughout the country. Overwhelmingly they recommended Jacques Lipchitz, the seventy-two-year-old American sculptor of world renown. I hesitated; Lipchitz had begun his career a cubist and gone on to works which did not exactly express the taste of Johnson City. But they did represent precisely the distinction I sought. President Johnson approved the choice without comment.

When I phoned Lipchitz I added apologetically that on top of asking him to undertake the work, time was short and I must ask that it be rushed. His response was an enthusiastic yes. Lipchitz had fled the Nazi armies advancing in France and migrated to the United States in middle-age with virtually all possessions gone; he spoke with deep feeling of what the haven of America had meant to him. He was overloaded with commitments, he must leave for Europe shortly, but of course he would quickly design the medallion for the President of the United States.

Soon the artist got down to actual plans, and trouble was in the air. He could not work from photographs, Lipchitz said. He usually required twenty-five or thirty sittings, but in this special case he would make do with about eight hours. The thought of Lyndon Johnson sitting still for eight hours, particularly for an artist, was one which could come only to a man miles away from Lyndon Johnson. I backed-and-filled. I would hurry to him photographs for any possible preliminary work (they went off with the notation always made when anything involved President Johnson's face, "Please use left profile"), and I would do what I could about appointments.

President Johnson was informed of Lipchitz's need for time,

cut down to a diplomatic, "Well, about a total of three hours while you are doing other things." "Three hours?" said LBJ. "Tell him he can look at me for three minutes."

If the President could be tough about time in the case of a person in whom he had no special interest, when a man was actually on the scene he was just as likely to say, Have him in, and then drop everything and sit talking away to him. Lipchitz was asked to come to the White House with the explanation that he would be worked into the Oval Office for as many and as lengthy periods as possible. At the appointed hour, the White House guard telephoned. "There's a funny-looking guy out here with a crate. He says he has an appointment with the President and he won't let us look in the crate."

Richard Nelson rescued the sculptor, and Lipchitz came into the White House a gray little man in a disheveled suit, a beret atop an unshaved face, socks drooping over his ankles, carrying by a piece of thick string an orange crate which held his preliminary forms. Nelson and I looked at each other; Lyndon Johnson was not well disposed toward people who neglected trim appearances. We ordered coffee, went to work on the Oval Office and got nowhere. Lipchitz kept saying how wonderful it was that he, "a simple Jewish artist," had been invited to the White House, and we were embarrassed both by his remarks and by our inability to arrange some time. Finally we suggested that he leave his orange crate with us, return to his hotel and await a message.

Lipchitz left, and Nelson and I looked inside the crate. Of course at this stage the casts looked like nothing so much as some debris from Death Valley. Suddenly President Johnson called for "the sample," and Nelson and I again exchanged wan smiles. Fearing that he might break the casts if he removed them from the orange crate, Nelson carried the box into the Oval Office. He emerged a shaken young man. "He thinks it's the goddamnedest thing. He doesn't want it, he won't see Lipchitz, and the hell with it."

The next three days had their special quality. Lyndon Johnson was angry at Jacques Lipchitz, and Jacques Lipchitz was angry at Lyndon Johnson. Tuesday, Wednesday, Thursday went by, and still the President would grant no time. The White House staff took its stance; this one was "trouble" and members became became terribly busy when the subject came up. In the middle of it all, Lipchitz began intimating "anti-Semitism" at cocktail and dinner parties in Washington, which did not increase my ability to deal with the Oval Office. Finally Abe Fortas, a friend of Lipchitz's and an admirer of his work, effectively intervened; he was instrumental in arranging two brief sessions, which the President and the sculptor endured with pained politeness.

The next week Lipchitz finished his white plaster mock-up for President Johnson's approval and left it with Fortas. I had to be out of Washington that day and Richard Nelson loyally went the last mile. It was Sunday, May 24, his birthday, and in the late morning he showed up at the Fortas home full accoutered with date and with blithe, if wary, spirit. Fortas presented him with the mock-up, a bottle of Champagne Dom Ruinart, a declaration that the Lipchitz design was "great art" and an encouraging pat on the shoulder. Then the expedition was off to the White House.

Nelson counted up his assets. President Johnson would be returning from church, probably in a relaxed mood and with the soothing Mrs. Johnson. He had his date along and attractive young women brought out the most genial in Lyndon Johnson. He looked at the white plaster casts and was struck by the superb quality of the designs. The form for the front of the medallion showed an LBJ left profile of character and force; the reverse was a powerfully wrought Prometheus strangling the vulture of ignorance while holding aloft the light of learning. But there was also no doubt that the LBJ profile had a sharp nose, a conspicuous ear and a chin that could be called double, and that the Prometheus was not done in the style of Porfirio Salinas' bluebonnets. Nelson wondered just how much his assets were worth.

He and his date set the two forms up on the desk in the Diplomatic Reception Room of the White House, through which the President and Mrs. Johnson would enter. When LBJ arrived, he asked pleasantly, "What are you two doing over here at this hour on a Sunday?" Edging the President and First Lady toward the desk, Nelson said, "Oh, we just dropped by to show you something, the final Lipchitz models."

Lyndon Johnson looked down and his eye fell on the Prometheus. "Is that *me*?"

Nelson rushed in with an attempt at diversionary humor. "That's Barry Goldwater rising out of Phoenix. This one, sir, is you."

Lyndon Johnson stared at the profile, stepped aside and stared at it again. "Looks like I've been dead three weeks, and maybe ought to be." He turned to Mrs. Johnson. "What do you think of it, Bird?"

"Lipchitz is a great artist, Lyndon."

The President poked his head closer. "Still looks like I've been dead for three weeks. How many people gonna see this thing?" he asked Nelson.

"We're only giving out a hundred and twenty-one of them."

Lyndon Johnson paused, took one more look at the profile. "Well," he said, "as long as there are only a hundred and twenty-one."

Richard Nelson, no man to tarry when he was ahead, hurried his date off to the Champagne Dom Ruinart.

Like a Texas twister, the LBJ spleen came with sudden force, then as quickly swept away. Jacques Lipchitz accepted or at least tolerated, President Johnson soon recaptured his enthusiasm for the Presidential Scholars program and nothing happened to break the mood.

When the Scholars arrived in Washington for the ceremony in June, they testified to the extraordinary talent in all strata of American society. Without any heavy use by the commission of the at-large category or the criterion of promise without top achievement, the group included a sizable number from poor backgrounds and it did not lack Negroes; this pattern has been repeated each year as the program continued. For the first awards, the White House cars went to the planes and trains to pick up a Southern boy about whom the high school principal wrote, "He comes from a home so poor one would hardly believe it"; the son of a Rocky Mountain laborer; the daughter of an Eastern elevator operator; a Far Western orphan for whom home was a shunting back and forth between destitute relatives; and the child of a hospital orderly, one of the first Negroes integrated into the high school system of Little Rock, Arkansas.

The Presidential Scholars had quite a day. It began with briefings and question-and-answer sessions with Secretary of State Rusk, Chief Justice Warren, space scientists and the astronaut Alan B. Shepard, Jr., and was interrupted by lunch with their senators or representatives. Then they were swept on to the huge gilded East Room of the White House for a reception by President Johnson, Mrs. Johnson and Lynda. In his expansiveness about the project, the President had approved a large guest list for the reception which ignored any consideration except achievement and which included some people whose work he emphatically did not like. The celebrities of talent ranged through the authors Gwendolyn Brooks, John Hersey, Marya Mannes, Ogden Nash, Philip Roth and Robert Penn Warren; Nobel Prize scientists; the figures of the press Walter Lippmann and James Reston; leaders in the performing arts, whether George Balanchine or Helen Hayes; the cartoonists Herbert Block, Jules Feiffer and Bill Mauldin; the painters Willem de Kooning and Ben Shahn; and on through

Alfred A. Knopf, Thurgood Marshall, J. Robert Oppenheimer and Edward Durrell Stone.

For the evening's entertainment, Sidney Poitier emceed a program consisting of the Gerry Mulligan Quartet and the Kingston Trio, José Ferrer reading from Shakespeare, Leonard Bernstein in a rare appearance at the piano, and the Metropolitan Opera tenor Nicholas di Virgilio. This was my first view of the lovely South Lawn of the White House dressed for a summer evening's party, and I will not forget it.

The scene and the brilliance of the assemblage did not overshadow the conduct of the hosts. At the reception President Johnson radiated personal warmth and his pride in the Scholars; the famous handshake was rarely used to move the line forward. Mrs. Johnson and Lynda stayed from the beginning of the reception through the close of the evening at about ten-thirty, engaging in genuine conversation with scores of the Scholars. The President returned to work after the reception but as the evening neared its end the lights went out in the Oval Office and he reappeared on the South Lawn. Husband, wife and daughter sat quietly in back seats, ready to bid good night in the outgoing way that a family sends home guests it was especially pleased to have.

Throughout the Presidential Scholars occasion the Johnsons had been at their best and this episode, early in the Administration, brought an intimation of the situation that was developing, especially among younger and better-educated Americans. In my conversations with the Scholars, they naturally spoke the proper words of appreciation to President Johnson. But again I sensed an undertone. Curious as to whether I had been correct, after I resigned from the White House staff I wrote to the first group of Scholars and asked them to comment, in a quite general way, about the experience. By now they were seeing it at a remove of three years, when they had changed and a good deal had happened to the whole nation's relationship to Lyndon Johnson. Yet with all necessary discounting, the undertone clearly had been real. In fact, it had been less an undertone than a politely muffled roar.

For these intelligent young men and women, from all areas under the American flag, the memory of John Kennedy or the JFK legend had seriously undercut Lyndon Johnson. Letter after letter said in effect that it was great to receive the honor, but how much better if it had come from President Kennedy. As William G. Sinkford, of the Walnut Hills High School in Cincinnati, Harvard, '68, put it: "My feeling was probably best expressed . . . by a friend who said, 'It's too bad you couldn't have gotten the award from Kennedy. It would have meant more then.' "

My letter of course had associated the Presidential Scholars program with the Johnson Administration. In a number of the replies, the impulse to connect this kind of project with President Kennedy took the form of surprise at discovering that it was actually initiated by President Johnson. It was planned by JFK, the assumption had run, and put into effect by LBJ. All of the students with this impression also had assumed that President Johnson went ahead with the program for reasons of political expediency.

Political expediency—this was the theme which dominated the replies, whatever the shadings of reaction to it. Some of the students were irritated to the point of bitterness as they spoke of the "cheap politics" behind the program. Others, like Donald A. Mac-Gillis, William Hall High School, West Hartford, Connecticut, Yale, '68, took it as a caper: "Being a political pawn at the age of 17 or 18 is kinda fun." A number were simply resigned. Elaine A. Leachman, Los Alamos High School, Los Alamos, New Mexico, Stanford, '68, quoted the remark of another Presidential Scholar: " 'It was an election year, wasn't it?' "

What the Presidential Scholars were thinking, in their youthful way, was a premonition of what would prove so major a problem of the Johnson Administration. The Presidency of Lyndon Johnson was full of ironies. Not the least of them was the fact that one of his great strengths—his political skills, particularly as evidenced by his success with Congress—was already turning into a serious liability. The American people recognized him as a master politician. They applauded this; they were glad the bills were being hurried through the House and Senate. But they attached a price to the approval, and the price was nothing less than the severely damaging assumption that every move of LBJ was made for political and only for political reasons.

This is a reflection of the fact that the transcendently great politicians—Jefferson, Lincoln, FDR—managed to be highly political without appearing so in a blatant form, and while leaving the impression that politics were harnessed to a larger nonpolitical purpose. The attitude toward LBJ also was strongly influenced by Metroamericans, who were inclined to take it as a sign of culture and sophistication to look down on the "politician." Certainly the intensity of the reaction to the conspicuous politicality of President Johnson was connected with the assassination and the subsequent urge to halo John Kennedy, who had such difficulties with the House and Senate. In much of Metroamerica in the 1960's, the definition of a statesman was coming close to being a man who was too educated, too decent and too sensitive to get bills through Congress.

One morning, musing about this situation, I remarked to a
longtime LBJ man, "You know, sometimes I think that the best
thing that could happen to the boss would be for him to fall flat
on his face in some political move."

He straightened irritably, then grinned and went on to another
subject.

The flood of letters from the public to the "idea man," politely
discouraged, was subsiding. The work of the domestic affairs
group went ahead and was accompanied by correspondence, phone
calls and visits from a host of other people who had expert and
significant things to say. My office was also occupied with a variety
of possible presidential projects, to be considered, tested and perhaps developed. There were endless letters from important or at
least influential people to be answered in the name of the President—you leaned back in your chair and dictated authoritatively,
"The President feels . . ."—and there were discreet appearances
to be made as the "house intellectual," and occasional speeches to
draft for the President. Increasingly I became involved with Mrs.
Johnson's tasks. The "resident intellectual" is inevitably drawn
into the work of the First Lady, for she and he represent "culture";
besides, she has a woefully small staff to help with her speeches
and the manifold activities in which she must, or does, participate.
Needless to say, most important were the memos to be prepared
for the President with observations and suggestions about domestic
or foreign affairs.

One project, of no great significance in itself, offered insights
into the LBJ White House. It started with Horace Busby, who was
urging on President Johnson a strategy for the campaign of 1964,
presumably against Barry Goldwater, in which Lyndon Johnson
would be the commanding figure of experience and judgment
running against the trigger-happy tyro. Simultaneously, Busby had
his totally nonpolitical fascination with the Office of the Presidency and his drive to discover ways which would make it more
effective for the general welfare. These two interests combined
when Busby considered that 175th anniversary of the inauguration
of George Washington, and hence of the Office of the Presidency,
which would occur on April 30, 1964. He suggested to President
Johnson a White House observance; the President gave the go-
ahead the week before the anniversary, and Busby asked me to
work with him on the project.

Our basic thought was that whatever was done should fit into
a general call for an anniversary year of study of the Office of the
Presidency, in schools and at higher levels, with a view to increas-

ing the public understanding of the Office and encouraging research projects that might improve its functioning. President Johnson cleared the plan, Busby and I drafted a presidential proclamation, and all seemed to be moving smoothly. Then, as the short period for preparation raced ahead, the habits of the LBJ White House asserted themselves. Each detail had to be okayed in the Oval Office, with the inevitable delays. Three days before the occasion I was informed that the observance was to include a suggestion of mine for a presidential luncheon for writers who had distinguished themselves by their books about the Presidency or their biographies of individual Chief Executives. Telegrams of invitation were rushed out, but by this time LBJ's on-again, off-again way of keeping dates was operating. He said he doubted that he would attend the luncheon.

The arguments were pressed. The opinions of these guests counted with groups influential in determining the public picture of his Presidency at the present time, and they could have a lot to do with fixing its place in history; the President's absence from the luncheon, unless there was an emergency, would be particularly felt because he had just spent a highly publicized lengthy session with members of the United States Chamber of Commerce. No, Lyndon Johnson insisted, he really didn't think he would come. Finally, about half an hour before the guests arrived, it became clear that he actually would attend. I recall my emotions, and they were several.

The group was an interesting one, consisting of Catherine Drinker Bowen, George Dangerfield, Sidney Hyman, Margaret K. Leech, Arthur C. Walworth, Samuel Flagg Bemis of Yale University, James MacGregor Burns of Williams, Clinton Rossiter of Cornell, David Donald of Johns Hopkins, Louis W. Koenig of New York University, Richard E. Neustadt of Harvard, and Roy F. Nichols of the University of Pennsylvania. When they assembled with President Johnson in the Fish Room before the television cameras, I had my first full impression of just how uneasy Lyndon Johnson could be with a group of intellectuals. The situation was not helped by one celebrated academic who kept maneuvering, almost to the point of using his elbows, to stand beside the President in the photographs. I am afraid I knew only too well what was going on in LBJ's mind as he glared down that long nose of his.

But quite apart from this, the President was awkward and things kept going wrong. He tried to read from his prepared text the title of Dangerfield's book *The Era of Good Feelings;* it came out *The Era of Good Tidings.* He ad-libbed an intended pleasantry which, because it barged into an obvious sensitivity of one of the writers, fell with an embarrassing thud. Attempting to recoup, he went on to say that he was sure his guests understood that he had spent so much time with the Chamber of Commerce because "I was doing missionary work then, and I feel like this is my home congregation."

In the course of reading the formal proclamation, President Johnson's uneasiness was particularly plain. I had written into the document the sentence, "The Presidency has made every man who occupied it, no matter how small, bigger than he was; and no matter how big, not big enough for its demands." Busby wanted to delete the passage but I held out; I should have paid more attention to his understanding of Lyndon Johnson. Of course the President had okayed the proclamation before the ceremony, but when he was actually reading it aloud in front of this particular group, he pronounced the phrases "no matter how small" and "not big enough for its demands" with a look not so much of irritation as of hurt, as if he felt his listeners were applying the words to him. I was sorry I had been stubborn.

At the luncheon, held in one of the charming small rooms on the second floor of the White House, President Johnson was thoroughly cordial. He was also just about as uncomfortable a human being as I have ever seen. He talked and talked, in a compulsive monologue.

Some of his remarks concerned what it was like to be President of the United States and to try to represent the national interest. Along with everyone else in the room, I believe, I was seized by the directness, the vigor, almost the fury of his words. "Somebody," Lyndon Johnson declared with a jab at his food, "has got to assert the good of the country and I'm it, at least at the moment." He charged into a description of the railroad strike negotiations. "There really wasn't a bad man on either side—well, hardly any, except one or two. The point is they've got problems, you've got problems, I've got problems, and somehow we have to work them out without messing up each other too much." For more than fifteen minutes he spoke of how the settlement was reached, in a pyrotechnic display of knowledge of the American operating system and of the human beings called Americans.

Then, from time to time, one of the guests ventured a remark. The President replied warily, as if he were negotiating with an alien force. More and more, his insecurities came to the fore. He spoke of his fine staff and stressed that Jack Valenti "has more Harvard degrees than Bundy" (Valenti is an M.B.A. from the Harvard Business School; Bundy, a Yale A.B., was named to the high honor of being a junior fellow at Harvard, which brings no additional degree). President Johnson moved into a defensive, complaining description of his problem as a "Southern President."

Disturbed by these self-torturing themes and trying to break the luncheon into a general conversation, I attempted several times to bring up other subjects. The moves did not work. The President shook off my remarks and drove ahead with his near-monologue.

I was concerned. There was so much that educated Americans ought to understand about this President: his fervor for educational advances and certain other types of social legislation; his drive to be a President of the national interest, which came from idealistic as well as political motives; his congeries of difficulties, arising from a highly complex and most unusual set of circumstances; the general enormous potentialities in the Presidency of such a man if only he could achieve a genuine relationship with the part of America that was also able and also cared. Certainly little of the most hopeful LBJ was coming through.

It occurred to me that a small book should be written on the emerging Johnson Administration, an avowedly friendly volume, openly done in co-operation with the President and the White House, but one which rigidly preserved the right of independent judgment and critical statement. I did not want to do such a book alone, both because of lack of time and because the collaboration of a first -rate journalist would add much to its quality. I discussed the idea with a friend, Richard Rovere, an astute political and social observer and a thoroughly civilized human being. Rovere shared my view of the situation and expressed interest in doing the book with me. I asked him if he would, out of his sophistication in such matters, draw up a memo stating the sensible and proper basis for a "friendly" and "co-operative" but "independent" and "critical" work.

The statement Rovere wrote seems to me a model for an enterprise of this type. In view of the discussion that arose later about books written with the co-operation of powerful public figures, I think it is worth the space to print his memo virtually in full:

> I see no great problem involved in reconciling independence with co-operation. It should be clear that independence is important to everyone involved—to us, to readers, and to the White House people with whom we would be dealing. No work can be of any value to anyone if it comes from men who have surrendered or suspended their critical judgment.
>
> . . . Where co-operation, or privilege, is granted, simple courtesy requires that the writers advise those who have granted it as

to what use is being made of it. In other words, the manuscript should go to the President and to those of his staff who are concerned. We should hear with sympathy, and a readiness to reappraise, any objections that are made. In some matters—for example, breaches of confidence or invasions of privacy—we should feel bound to make the appropriate changes. In some matters—for example, opinions clearly attributable to the authors and to them alone—we should not feel bound.

It can, of course, be said that some tricky definitions are involved. There can be differences over what actually constitutes an invasion of privacy or a breach of confidence. And there can be differences as to what are matters of fact and what are matters of opinion. But in my experience, reasonable people do not find it difficult to settle these questions.

The procedure, as I see it, would be somewhat as follows: (1) the President and members of his staff would talk with us, responding to our questions, pointing out to us those things they regard as important; they would make clear when they were speaking on the record and off the record; (2) we would produce a manuscript; (3) we would submit it to them for purposes of criticism, correction and amplification; (4) they would criticize, correct and amplify; (5) we would feel morally bound to hear their criticisms with sympathy; to make corrections where we had erred as to fact, invaded privacy, or—through what could only be misunderstanding—broken confidence. Judgment on all these matters would have to rest with us, but then no undertaking of this sort makes much sense unless our judgment is respected.

So we had a fine potential basis. But the more I thought about the undertaking, the more dubious I became. Every book about Lyndon Johnson written with close ties to him had proved a disaster of sycophancy—whether *The Lyndon Johnson Story,* by his former Senate aide Booth Mooney, or *The Professional: Lyndon B. Johnson,* by his long-time friend, the Pulitzer Prize biographer William S. White. I began to wonder whether the project would not produce constant trouble and, ultimately, no book. I wondered further whether even proposing such an undertaking to President Johnson would not make him think me deserving of that most opprobrious of words in the LBJ lexicon: "disloyal."

I took the problem to a man I occasionally turned to for advice, a wise person, outside the White House, an intimate of the President for years who had the same critical loyalty to him that Rovere and I did. "A book like that would certainly do the President a world of good," he commented. Then, tactfully, he gave me his opinion. We both knew the President's "peculiarities"—he "perhaps a little better" than I. Lyndon Johnson did not have the same "habits of mind" as men like us; "perhaps"—with a smile—"that is why he is President and we are not." It must always be remembered that "the President has his own clear-cut picture of the world. It consists of two kinds of people, his friends and his enemies, and there are no in-betweens. The idea of a friendly but critical study makes little sense in that world." He would think the proposal over carefully, very carefully, *before*—he pronounced the word with special emphasis—I mentioned it to the President or anyone close to him.

I went back to my office and phoned Rovere. "Dick, I have wasted a lot of your time. I have become convinced that our project won't work. I've also become convinced that even proposing the book on our terms would ruin me with the President." Rovere understood, and that particular effort to help build a bridge between Lyndon Johnson and educated America ended.

It was high time that the occasion take place which was part of the original plan for the domestic affairs group—a White House gathering at which the members would meet President Johnson and begin co-ordinating their work. This was now scheduled for the Fish Room on March 19, 1964. The agenda I suggested included brief opening remarks by the President and a five o'clock reception. I prepared a draft of his welcoming words and a short, straightforward news release stating the names of the men and the hope of the President that from their work would come "fresh approaches and specific proposals, or reformulations of old ones, in the field of domestic affairs."

The day before the meeting President Johnson vetoed the press release and eliminated the reception without comment. He was scheduled to make his welcoming remarks at eleven o'clock. About an hour before, Bill Moyers called to say that the President had a cold and would not appear.

Did he really have a cold or was this some more of his back-and-forth about keeping an engagement, complicated by his skittishness toward intellectuals? Did Moyers want President Johnson to appear? "Bill," I replied, "I'm coming to see you."

When I arrived at Moyers' office, I was tense and no doubt showed it. "If the President is ill in his quarters, of course—"

"No, he's in his office."

"Or if he is in his office and feels poorly or something urgent has come up, okay. Then let's just tell the men the truth. But if there's anything else involved, he ought to know that staying away from this meeting is no casual matter. These people are not Boy

Scouts or garden-club ladies who've come to shake the hand of a President. They are influential, nationally and internationally. What's more, by serving in this group they are symbols—symbols of knowledge in the service of the nation. They have dropped their regular work and come here to help because they were asked to do so in the name of the President; they were also invited, among other things, to meet him. If he won't walk the few feet to the Fish Room and give them fifteen minutes, they can hardly think he gives much of a damn about them or what they might be able to contribute. I would feel irresponsible if I did not let the President know how I view this, and I'm going in to talk to him."

Moyers was listening with a look of agreement, but he reacted sharply at my last words. "Why don't you let me try?" he said.

I hesitated, not at all sure what attitude he would express to President Johnson. But I agreed, assuming I had made it clear that I did not intend to drop the matter if the answer was no, and that if Moyers really wanted the President to attend, he had a better chance than I of reversing the decision. Moyers telephoned shortly to say that President Johnson would be coming.

When he appeared the President did indeed have a cold and he did not look happy. As I took him around the room and introduced him, he was methodically pleasant. Moyers had edited out of the welcoming remarks anything reaching for substance or pith, and inserted sentences like "This Administration feels no discomfort in the presence of brains"; "no man, or no group of men, holds a monopoly on the truth"; and "I want to urge you always to speak frankly, to speak forthrightly, but above all to speak what you believe is right for America." President Johnson delivered the text and ad-libbed with an effort at warmth.

As the group got to work and the day went on, the worry that had now become habitual reasserted itself—the continued injunction that the domestic affairs group was not to be mentioned publicly. At lunch one of the men said to me with unconcealed irritation what a number were plainly thinking, "Well, Eric, are we still a band of outlaws meeting in a dark cellar?" Quite apart from the question of the members' morale, they had entered the White House through the customary route, the Press Lobby, and some of them might well have been recognized or at least aroused curiosity. Again I envisioned headlines about the clandestine egghead conspiracy.

In the LBJ White House there were times when you simply went ahead and did something, knowing that it was contrary to President Johnson's wishes but feeling that it had to be done and taking the chance that it would help, not hurt, his purposes. Early in the afternoon I asked Press Secretary Salinger to make a casual statement at his five o'clock press conference to the effect that a group of experts had been meeting in the White House for an informal discussion of domestic problems, and that their names were available. Salinger was in the mood to be casual; it was the afternoon of his resignation and his departure for the California senatorial race. He got off a quick sentence about the group, said the list of names was lengthy and was on the bulletin board if anybody wanted it, then hurried on to his resignation and the appointment of George Reedy, which of course was the splash news.

The next day's press carried little notice of the meeting, and there was no explosion from the Oval Office. The oppressive secrecy was gone. The President had greeted the group and given his blessing. The first get-together, largely organizational, led quickly to a two-day working session. Before and after these meetings, the members were producing both long-range memos and specific suggestions. As I had hoped, they were also sparking useful communications from experts outside their immediate membership.

No good purpose would be served by attempting to assess specifically the contributions being made by this project. The suggestions were of such different types—ranging from the extremely detailed to the broadest kind of consideration—and the results took such different forms that to single out particular instances would be confusing and invidious. Moreover, the ways of government being what they are, it is difficult to disentangle just what produced a given action.

To cite an instance from outside the domestic affairs group, the journal of the American Council on Education, the *Educational Record,* carried an editorial entitled "Memorandum for Eric Goldman" which urged the establishment of an "Urban Extension Service" attached to selected universities—a program comparable to the farm extension activities of state universities which over the years had done so much for the rural areas. Relayed by me in a slightly altered form, this editorial was directly responsible for the fact that President Johnson approved the urban extension concept in a June 20, 1964, speech and announced that he was asking Commissioner of Education Keppel to meet with educational leaders to work out the details; such a program was included in the Higher Education Act of 1965. Yet the realistic story was nowhere near that simple. Urban extension had been in the air for a long time; during its progress from concept to law, many men and many factors played key roles quite apart from an editorial in the *Educational Record* directed to an individual White House aide.

My own estimate would be that in the two months after the March 19 meeting of the domestic affairs group, proposals coming from members or produced by the existence of the project had a significant part in initiating two substantial Administration programs and a lesser role in one more. In time, long-range memos were to affect in discernible ways two major policies of the Administration. Some members, I am sure, would consider this estimate egregiously low; others might deem it high. I go along with the dictum of one of the domestic affairs group, Margaret Mead, who observed, "When dealing with what happens in government, you are talking about a labyrinth compounded by human beings."

In some ways, the spring of 1964 was a rather pleasant period for me. Obviously I was the target of my share of the LBJ irritations, but I avoided the beratings by making no particular effort to see the President and by dealing with him largely through memos—a procedure that had another advantage, since talking with him could result in an inconclusive monologue whereas his replies on paper were usually swift and categorical. This undoubtedly cut down on my "in-ness" at the White House, but you made your choices.

On April 21, 1964, President Johnson officially named me a "Special Consultant to the President." (There are a variety of titles for White House aides but the two most common are Special Assistant, which denotes "full time" and bans outside activities, and Special Consultant, which signifies that you are paid by the day and permits other income-producing activities like my television program.) Shortly thereafter Horace Busby, in his offhanded way, remarked that he was "getting tired of rattling around in all these offices," meaning his suite of four rooms in the East Wing of the White House previously occupied by Brooks Hays and Arthur Schlesinger. Would I like to move my office over from the Executive Office Building if the President approved? I would, and the President did. And President and Mrs. Johnson kept bestowing those gestures so acutely recognized in the White House—invitations to a particular type of social event, conspicuously warm words at public functions, thanks and praise conveyed directly or indirectly.

Of course the old rigmarole did not disappear. I was sworn in as Special Consultant behind closed doors and it was hinted that I not follow the usual practice of hanging my commission in my office. When the time came to move from EOB to the White

House, President Johnson made one emphatic stipulation: I was not to occupy the part of the suite previously used by Schlesinger.

All of this was not without its amusing aspects, but basic worries also remained. The group on domestic affairs might be producing—people of that quality inevitably do—yet how long could they continue to be useful functioning in the way that President Johnson had made necessary and within his definition of purpose? Already the difficulties inherent in the setup were showing, and a number of the men were restive or losing interest trying to operate within a framework which I was free neither to change nor to explain.

If the total secrecy had ended, the President's sensitivity about press notice of the proceeding had not diminished to any significant degree. In June the *U.S. News and World Report* informed me that the magazine had scheduled an article on the group and wanted to interview me and its members. Of course I avoided the reporter, but trying to prevent the other men from talking to him could only have given him the impression that there was something to hide. When the article appeared the experts had discussed their lines of thought in a way that was fresh and lively but so responsible it aroused little hostile comment. President Johnson read his copy of the magazine in high dudgeon. "Those people," he stormed, "will defeat me yet."

The President's drive to trim the cost of operating the White House continued, and such economizing—no doubt compounded by his skittishness about having the group visibly gathering—threw another block in its path. The members received no compensation but of course I assumed their travel expenses would be paid. Weeks after the first Washington meeting, I discovered that no checks had gone out. Lamely apologizing to the men for a "bureaucratic slip-up," I finally pried the money out of Walter Jenkins. I ran into still greater difficulty over the larger vouchers for the second, two-day session. With some embarrassment Jenkins told me that the President thought that inviting the group to Washington was "awfully expensive." Couldn't it all be done by mail? Jenkins did not have to add that there were to be no more meetings.

I was also experiencing increasing problems in working with Bill Moyers and Richard Goodwin. On the surface, they were cordial; as long as President Johnson continued to show signs of favor for a man, White House staff members were exceedingly careful. Moyers in particular would go out of his way to compliment my work. Yet both were exerting themselves to bring my activities under their control. At one point Goodwin phoned to say that he and Moyers thought it would be a good idea if my memos, instead of being sent directly to the President, were to be routed through him. When I overlooked the message—in the LBJ White House, often the tactful way to decline was to ignore— it became difficult for me to get answers from Moyers, who more and more had the surest knowledge of the trend of Administration policy.

With the desire of Goodwin and Moyers to solidify their positions as White House thinkers, anything having to do with the intellectual world was likely to be turned into a competition. It occurred to me that it might be useful to invite for lunch, in the privacy of the White House Mess, with whatever members of the staff cared to come, an occasional writer or academic of stature who represented some of the current further fringes of thinking about national problems. The first guest I chose was James Baldwin, an important spokesman of the emerging militant black feeling. When Moyers heard of the invitation, he let it be known that this was "political dynamite," and told me that he was to do the inviting of "such people." Goodwin acted as if I had invaded a private reserve. He knew "Jimmy" well; he would "take care of everything." By now most of the staff men shied away from getting involved, and in the end Baldwin, the imperturbable McGeorge Bundy and I were at the lunch table. Baldwin came, ate, talked and left. There was no explosion—in fact, I saw not a word in the papers—and I spent the next half-hour reporting to inquiring colleagues what Baldwin had said, which was plenty.

Quite beyond the expected tussles of palace politics, there was a far deeper concern. However my role at the White House might be defined, inevitably it included serving as a liaison between the Johnson Administration and the intellectual class in the United States. From the President's point of view this might mean that he wanted intellectuals to like him, to give him ideas and to vote for him. Intellectuals sought a symbol of their importance and an understanding ear in the White House. The general educated public thought it good to have their government influenced by the knowledge, attitudes and criticism of a class of men they admired. Whatever the reasons, serving as a White House liaison with intellectuals was a job which had come, rightly or wrongly, to be considered significant by people I respected and I wanted to do it right.

When I first arrived in Washington, a friend wired me: "Congratulations and condolences. As Johnson's envoy to the intellectuals nobody has had a better job since the NAACP sent a man to Mississippi." It was not long before I knew full well what he was talking about. In time the attitude of the intellectual toward President Johnson would be profoundly influenced by foreign policy developments. Here in 1964 and quite apart from international affairs, it was already clear that American intellectuals as a group did not respect, admire or like Lyndon Johnson.

The correspondence in which I was engaged, the phone calls and conversations, all pointed the same way. Intellectuals might be less bearish about President Johnson now than immediately after the assassination. When he put through Congress bills which they had wanted so long, they praised him. Some were even developing a theory that it was a good thing—for a while—to have the national leadership in the hands of a "gutter-fighter activist," to use the phrase of a leading academic. But the basic attitude remained. In July 1964 John P. Roche, professor of politics at Brandeis University, published an article in the *New York Times Sunday Magazine* on the relationship between the Presidency and intellectuals. Of LBJ, he wrote: "President Johnson has achieved little standing among intellectuals."

In 1964 it was common to assume that President Johnson's low rating with intellectuals came largely from a comparison with his predecessor. Needless to say, this was a factor, but I do not believe it should overshadow another consideration. From whatever evidence I had, Lyndon Johnson seemed to provoke in the intellectual community his own pristine, particular distaste. After a session of the domestic affairs group broke up, I walked one member to a cab, and our conversation drifted into the Kennedy-Johnson comparison. My colleague said directly what so many conversations and letters had politely implied: "I don't want to embarrass you about your boss, and of course I'm glad to do anything I can. But I must say I couldn't work up enthusiasm about Johnson if his predecessor had been Rutherford B. Hayes."

Most LBJ aides were not concerned about this disaffection. Before Roche published his article, he sent me a draft of it and later telephoned. In the conversation, he went beyond the essay and added a colorful description of what many of his friends "really" thought of Lyndon Johnson. I did not send the article to the President—he would be roused enough when it was printed—but I did show it or talked about it around the staff, using it as another argument that we should pay more attention to this worsening situation. Busby and Reedy went along with my point, but for the most part I roused little reaction.

Johnson men were inclined to be unconcerned because they thought of intellectuals as just one more, relatively small pressure group, perhaps temporarily out of joint but handleable. They overlooked the millions of Metroamericans, strategically located across the nation and so rapidly expanding in influence. Only one of the authentic LBJ aides had grown up in genuine Metroamerica. They had little feel for the junior executive, the lawyer, the accountant and his wife in the suburbs of New York, Chicago, or San Francisco, both deriving a sense of status from reading Saul Bellow's *Herzog,* John Kenneth Galbraith's *Affluent Society* and David Riesman's *Lonely Crowd,* tending sincerely to react to public figures and public issues in a way similar to these intellectuals, caring about political leaders who cared about men like Bellow, Galbraith and Riesman.

In a way, I was a strange person to be part of so cabalish an operation as the White House staff inevitably is. I might have tried to increase my effectiveness by heading into the intrigue and doing my own wheeler-dealing. But temperamentally, as a Princeton colleague once remarked, I am something of "a loner." I would rather sit in my office and worry a thought or a sentence, try to drive something through to completion, or just muse with a friend over a slow drink, than participate in any maneuver, single or collective. Having spent a good many of my adult years at *Time,* in television or on university campuses—those special habitats of *Homo operatusorum*—I had developed a pronounced, perhaps arrogant disdain for the whole process of manipulation, no matter how laudable its purpose. Besides, on the few occasions when I had tried to play the game, I abundantly proved to myself and everybody else that I was the least artful politician since Harold Stassen.

So I took a different road and plugged away. It was obviously quixotic to go ahead and establish a second group of authorities on international affairs. So far as domestic problems were concerned, I attempted small changes in the procedure of the existing panel which were possible within President Johnson's instructions, but fundamentally I was becoming convinced that he would be much better served by a series of task forces into which some members of the domestic affairs group could be integrated. Moyers wanted such task forces; setting them up would mitigate that difficulty. If established in connection with him, they were much more likely to be financed and to operate in close association with regular government officials. Since each task force would concentrate on a specific problem area of immediate concern to the President, all of them would be temporary, and the LBJ urge for secrecy could be satisfied without so much trauma. The pinpointed nature of the assignments would probably also increase the usefulness of the committees. Continuing to work with the existing group on domestic affairs but letting its activities taper off, I joined in the switchover to task forces.

The disaffection of Metroamerica was a more intricate matter. No doubt the heart of the problem was the general impression made by President Johnson, and much of this could not be altered. If LBJ had a record as a blatant political operator, that was history's dictum. If he reminded Metroamericans of their country cousins, his manner was, as he said, "mine—that's the way I am." The most practical place to bring about a quick and effective change in the Lyndon Johnson being projected to the public was in his speeches. For the most part they had been singularly lacking in the qualities which distinguish a presidential address for an educated audience: substance, a large and inspiriting theme, a sense of the American experience and character, and interesting use of language.

I had been thinking about this not only because of the President's problem with Metroamerica but because I myself was scheduled to make two speeches in April and May, one before an American University seminar in Washington and the other at Lindenwood College in Missouri. The theme I had been developing for these occasions was hardly one of particular originality. It represented, I suspect, just about what most well-informed Americans, or at least what most historians of the United States, would have emphasized in 1964.

The United States, it seemed to me, had gone through three phases. During the first period, running into the late nineteenth century, we peopled the continent and built a highly productive economic system. During a second era, extending through the first half of the twentieth century, we put controls on the flourishing economic system in order to increase the standard of living and the opportunities of the lower- and middle-income population. Now a third period was emerging. Material concerns were still pressing —particularly the disgraceful and dangerous economic position of the Negro—but the nation had reached a general affluence which permitted it to give attention not only to the quantity but to the quality of American living. My remarks before the American University seminar consisted almost exclusively of this exposition. At Lindenwood College I started from a different base but ended the same place—emphasizing the 1960's as a new era, the "post-affluent society," engaged in its own effort against the "dull society," the "overmaterial society," the "ugly society."

While I was writing these speeches, Richard Goodwin and I fell into conversation in the White House Mess. He was not a happy man. Engaged largely in drafting speeches for President Johnson, he was badgered by the President for a "big theme" that would characterize the Administration. With his own sense of the great tradition of presidential addresses, Goodwin was restless at the level of the speeches he and the rest of the staff were hurrying out. I commented that I and a lot of other people were troubled too, and mentioned the possibility of using themes like the three periods of American development and their implications for the Johnson Administration.

A few days later Goodwin gave me a ring and we had a long conversation in his office. I had been thinking further about the subject, and I now pushed more vigorously and more directly. President Johnson, I urged, should take the occasion of a full-dress speech to place his Administration in the perspective of the long-running American experience. The President should then go on to state that his Administration proposed to clean up the unfinished business of the second American era—the creation of a generally affluent society—while envisaging and working toward what lay beyond. I used some of the language I was writing into my remarks for Lindenwood College, including the drive against the "ugly society" and the "dull society," and I suggested that in terms of a popular slogan, the goal of "post-affluent" America was probably best caught by the title of Walter Lippmann's book of some years back, *The Good Society*.

Goodwin quite went along with me. But he obviously preferred "great society" to "good society." In speeches drafted since March, he had been using the phrase, without any particular thematic development behind it, and President Johnson seemed to like it.*

The President had an address scheduled at the University of Michigan commencement on May 22. Goodwin asked whether I could rush to him suggestive memos from members of the domestic affairs group who were experts on the metropolitan areas, obviously the central problem of post-affluent America. I did, and Goodwin drafted the speech.

The phrase "great society" has an interesting history. At least in its modern usage, it originated in The Great Society, an influential book published in 1914 by Graham Wallas, a Fabian socialist professor at the London School of Economics. When Walter Lippmann published The Good Society in 1937, he acknowledged the influence of Wallas' book and included a discussion of its doctrine. Since then "great society" had been called upon for a number of purposes. Speaking before the Economic Club of Detroit in 1939, Henry R. Luce urged businessmen to be social-minded and recognize that the "business of business is to take part in the creation of the Great Society." The 1958 edition of a widely used college textbook, International Politics by Professor Frederick L. Schuman of Williams College, used "great society" to refer to relationships between nations.

Setting his remarks within the framework of the three stages of American development, President Johnson told his Ann Arbor audience: "For a century we labored to settle and to subdue a continent. For half a century we called upon unbounded invention and untiring industry to create an order of plenty for all of our people. . . .

"The challenge of the next half-century is whether we have the wisdom to use that wealth to enrich and elevate our national life, and to advance the quality of our American civilization. . . . For in your time we have the opportunity to move not only toward the rich society and the powerful society, but upward to the Great Society.

"The Great Society rests on abundance and liberty for all. It demands an end to poverty and injustice. . . . But that is just the beginning.

"The Great Society . . . is a place where men are more concerned with the quality of their goals than the quantity of their goods." Then the President went on to offer specific applications, with heavy emphasis on the cities and not omitting attention to "ugly America."

Naturally I was happy that President Johnson had made such an address but "Great Society" bothered me, as it did some other members of the White House staff. Spoken by Lyndon Johnson, it smacked of a Texas tall tale (the President himself once used it interchangeably with the "glorious society"), and it invited snickers about instant Utopia. When the ridicule came, President Johnson backed away, saying that the words simply "express an aspiration—this is a great society now and we are going on improving it." For a while he even let it be known in the White House that he did not want the phrase used. But there it was, as Johnsonian as a roar down the highway, and the press soon made it the permanent slogan for the domestic program of the Administration.

Preparations for the University of Michigan occasion also brought the final decision to establish task forces, and they were mentioned in the speech. The reference was unmistakably Johnsonian. John Kennedy had set up "task forces"; these were to be "working groups." They were, if not secret, camouflaged; the statement sounded as if their main purpose was to arrange White House "conferences." And of course they would represent the greatest assemblage of wisdom since the Nicene Council. "We are going to assemble the best thought and the broadest knowledge from all over the world. . . . From these meetings and from this inspiration and from these studies we will begin to set our course toward the Great Society." Six days after the University of Michigan speech Moyers sent to the staff a memo making plain that the plan was for him to establish and supervise the groups. They would help develop the platform for the 1964 campaign, the 1965 legislative program and President Johnson's "blueprint for the next four years."

Of course I read the memo without surprise, and with a mixture of emotions. I was glad that all the efforts and headaches had helped produce some solid results. The broad sweep of the Ann Arbor address had given the Administration a genuine context. Producing additional expertise for the White House in the form of these task forces would work reasonably well. I was relieved of the major responsibility for bringing to President Johnson the products of the "best minds" via the "quiet brain trust," that surreal creation in view of the White House circumstances. Now I could work with the new groups to whatever extent seemed fruitful, and carry on any other contacts with specialists that appeared promising. Quite apart from the "best minds," however organized, I had mounting White House tasks that were worthy of any man's efforts.

Yet as the summer of 1964 came on I could hardly settle back in a mood of serenity. I was physically tired to the point that I had difficulty getting to sleep once I did go to bed. I was tired, too, of trying to interpret Lyndon Johnson to Metroamerica, and Metroamerica to Lyndon Johnson, which more and more appeared like attempting to interpret Mao Tse-tung and Senator Everett McKinley Dirksen to each other. And I was tired, I'm afraid very tired, of some of the attitudes and activities rampant in the West Wing.

On a sticky July morning in 1964 I ran into a friend on the staff as we made our way across Lafayette Park to the White House. After a few grunts of conversation, I broke into, "Damn it, it's time for me to resign. I've probably done whatever good or harm I can do, and anyhow. . . ."

My friend looked at me, at first taken back by my vehemence and then laughing. "I was about to call you and say the same thing."

We were both going through the emotional release of the LBJ White House. Aides regularly resolved to resign and then did not. There were always a dozen reasons, noble and not so noble, for any of us to stay.

Besides, who resigns when there is a campaign coming up, and against Barry Goldwater?

CHAPTER 8

Confidently, Warily

On July 15, 1964, the Republicans did it. Time after time since 1936 a sizable number, if not a majority, of the delegates to G.O.P. national conventions had yearned to nominate for President a thoroughgoing conservative and then had settled for a middle-roader who was supposed to be able to win. This year the delegates gathered at the Cow Palace in San Francisco hellbent toward the right. In a scene that resembled a lynching of liberalism, with a crushing vote of 883 on the first ballot, they chose Senator Barry M. Goldwater.

The senator promptly underscored the decision. Disdaining an overture to the liberal faction in his party, he delivered an acceptance speech which Governor Nelson A. Rockefeller of New York called "frightening." Ignoring the opportunity to balance the ticket by choosing a moderate as the vice-presidential nominee, he picked Congressman William E. Miller, a contemptuous enemy of federal aid to education, Medicare, the anti-poverty program, public power and agricultural subsidies, and a sniping exponent of the doctrine that the White House had been "appeasing" Communism. The delegates went on roaring, booing, stomping and jeering, with a passion against the twentieth century that startled veteran political reporters.

President Johnson stayed up late to watch the nomination of Senator Goldwater and switched off the television set with a broad smile. Barry Goldwater was every Democrat's favorite candidate; when the senator walked to the Cow Palace podium to accept the nomination, the President had in his pocket a poll which indicated a possible projected vote of 70 percent for Lyndon Johnson, 30 percent for Goldwater.

The nomination brought immediate evidence of the most serious split in the Republican party since Theodore Roosevelt stomped out of the 1912 convention to found the third-party Bull Moosers. As Goldwater finished his acceptance speech, Senators Jacob K. Javits and Kenneth B. Keating, accompanied by more than half the New York delegation, rose and left the Cow Palace. Michigan's record Republican vote-getter, George W. Romney, soon commented, "Well, we're going back to work just as hard as we can to assure Republican victories in Michigan." A reporter asked, "Don't you mean Republican victories all over the United States?" "I mean exactly what I said," Romney answered.

If the Republican ticket seemed pathetically weak, the Lyndon Johnson candidacy had powerful positive assets. The legend of JFK may have cast a shadow over LBJ, but it also inclined people to vote Democratic. For forty-one months the United States had enjoyed prosperity without a single serious storm signal of recession. The nation, if scarcely at peace, was not sending American troops into combat and the scarifying headlines were relatively few. President Johnson had his own strong appeal—his skillful takeover after the assassination, his can-do reputation, the legislation he was moving through Congress or proposing, accompanied by his emphasis on economy—the attractions which had developed by the Spring of 1964 and which now continued.

It was difficult to envisage just how LBJ could lose. Late one night another aide and I sat concocting a hypothetical situation. The economy would go into a recession; a foreign crisis brought the use of American combat troops; the President proved himself thoroughly maladroit in handling further ramifications of the Bobby Baker affair or a similar situation. But even if any or all of these circumstances occurred before the election, would the voters really prefer a Goldwater-Miller ticket? Like any experienced politician, President Johnson talked of running scared, and he called up hobgoblins galore which could defeat him. Shortly before the Democratic convention, he even walked the lawn of the White House musing out loud whether he should run at all. (Yes, the aide accompanying him replied, he thought he should run.) Plainly, the issue in Lyndon Johnson's mind was not whether he would run and win but whether he could win in a tremendous sweep, "the biggest of them all," as he put it. He knew well, and a bit ruefully, that one goal was unattainable even if he limited the comparison to modern times. In 1936 Franklin Roosevelt had garnered every electoral vote except the eight of Maine and Vermont; in 1964 the Democrats were certain to lose at least the seventeen electors of Alabama and Mississippi. Beyond that, the sky was the limit, and LBJ looked to the sky. He meant biggest in several senses—a leviathan electoral majority, a record popular victory, an unprecedented across-the-board backing from all the major elements of the population.

President Johnson had an entirely practical reason for his vaulting ambition. When entering the House of Representatives shortly after President Franklin Roosevelt's great victory of 1936, he had been lastingly impressed by how much trouble FDR experienced with Congress despite the size of his win. LBJ was determined to enact a sweeping Great Society legislative program after the election of 1964. He wanted to carry the nation by so large a majority, representing so dramatic a cross section of voters, that he would take his program before a House and Senate which was impressed, subdued and ready to follow him.

Beyond the practicalities of Congress, President Johnson looked to an alluring vista. Most politicians seeking national office extol unity; it is the obvious political ploy. LBJ had his own political reasons when he declared that he sought to be "the President who unified the nation." But he also kept repeating this because he meant it—in fact, because he hoped and planned that his most ringing accolade from history would be that he brought about a degree of national unity never before attained.

Lyndon Johnson may have grown up in purest Texas but it was an area without the usual regional characteristics. Johnson City is where Southern-style Texas ends and Western-style Texas begins, and it is really neither Southern nor Western. He was not a man of strong partisan feelings; he was a Democrat because, coming from his family and his state, it had never occurred to him to be anything else. Throughout his pre-presidential career he had worked as easily—and on a number of occasions more easily —with Republicans than with men of his own party. The strongest facet of his personality was not an ability to rouse passions of interest or of ideals, but to subdue both in some common denominator. President Johnson simply did not believe in disagreement, did not feel that there was anything creative in tension, was convinced by instinct and by his own thought processes that the quickest road to progress was the one with the smallest number of cross-roads. His view of America was that it had grown strong and prosperous because, except in moments of aberration like the Civil War, most Americans could brush aside differences and have at the common job. "Anybody can tear down a house," he liked to say. "It takes a real man to get together with others to build one."

To promote a national working together, the President had certain specifics in mind. He was sure that the United States in the post-World War II period had wasted enormous energy and talent in essentially unnecessary clashes between labor and management, urban interests and the rural regions, blacks and whites. He intended to find the formulas to smooth over these conflicts. He particularly sought to mediate the ancient quarrel between North and South. As the first Southern President of modern times—he complained about the role but cherished one aspect of it—he proposed to use his background to "bring the South back into the Union, not in a lot of words but for real."

Lyndon Johnson could speak with intense emotion of this unifying goal of his Presidency, particularly in referring to the North-South clash. One newsman, hardly a sentimentalist about politicians, has recalled an occasion when he was near tears as he listened to the President talk of his ideal of ending the Civil War once and for all. For President Johnson, 1964 was a political campaign not only to win but to win by the kind of mandate that would put him in a position to create an era of rapid national progress through national good feelings.

Above all, Lyndon Johnson wanted to win in a thunder roll because he was Lyndon Johnson. Shortly after the campaign began, I heard my first telling of a story originating with a Texan who had known the President for thirty years. "Lyndon reminds Texans of old Mrs. Lurana Fidelia Stribling, who put together one of the biggest ranch empires around Johnson City in the early 1900's. Once her overworked lawyer got maybe a little exasperated at the way she insisted on buying one ranch after another. He said to her, 'Mrs. Stribling, how much land do you want? Do you want all there is in the country?' And Mrs. Stribling answered, 'No, I don't want it all. All I want is all my own and all that joins it.' "

In dusty, dreary Johnson City, the boy had dreamed of running for President of the United States and winning it by himself, for himself. Wealth, family happiness and enormous political power had come to him, but the supreme prize seemed more elusive with every passing year. He had lunged for it in 1960 and been knocked flat. He moved into the White House in 1963, but was President only because of Dallas. Now was his chance. He would show patronizing Kennedyites, who had squeaked by with those 119,000 votes in 1960. He would show the political commentators, who for years had declared that no man from south of the Mason-Dixon line could win the Presidency; the liberal savants with their confident analyses that the big Northern cities would never roll up FDR majorities for an LBJ; the Southern politicians who were saying that Democrats in his own South were deserting him. Lyndon Johnson would win the Presidency of the United States with a sweep as big and wide as all Texas.

But there were problems. Confidently, warily, with rapt attention to every detail, he went after them.

The day the Republican convention ended—Thursday, July 16 —three Negro teen-agers got into a scuffle with the white janitor of an apartment building at 215 East Seventy-sixth Street in New York City. Police Lieutenant Thomas R. Gilligan happened along, and in the course of the trouble, shot and killed fifteen-year-old James Powell. On Thursday and Friday, Negroes gathered in angry clumps along the sticky streets of Harlem. Saturday night the crowds were much larger and the speeches much more bitter. At West 123rd Street, an impassioned speaker demanded the immediate suspension of Lieutenant Gilligan. He pointed to the precinct station a few blocks away. "Let them hear our demands. Let's go! Let's do it now!" The crowd, swollen into a mob, headed for the station house.

The precinct captain shouted through a bull horn, "Go home, go home. It's better for you."

From somewhere in the mob came a deep-voiced singsong: "We *are* home, baby. We *are* home. We *are* home."

For five nights and four days the violence ricocheted across Harlem, hopscotched into the Bedford-Stuyvesant slums of Brooklyn. Negro teen-agers ran wild. Negro adults tried to stop the rioting, sullenly did nothing, joined it in a bewilderment of feelings. A Harlem domestic worker, the mother of five without a husband, told a bystander, "I clean the white man's dirt all the time. I work for four families and some I don't care for and some I like. That night I worked for some I like. But when I got home and the trouble began, I felt like something was crawling in me, like the whole damn world was no good, and the little kids and the big ones and all of us was going to get killed because we don't know what to do. And I see the cops are white and I was crying. I said to me, Dear God, I am crying. And I took this pop bottle and it was empty and I threw it down on the cops, and I was crying and laughing."

As New York City quieted, Rochester erupted. Across the nation, and particularly in the North, moderate Negro leaders had the same message for the White House: serious trouble could occur at any time in their cities. The summer was bringing a fear, almost an assumption, of widespread racial rioting.

The comprehensive and tough Civil Rights Act of 1964 had been signed into law. But legislation and the crumbling of the walls of discrimination for some Negroes, instead of quieting the black ghettos in the North, were stirring them. Congressman Adam Clayton Powell, Jr., of Harlem, who could be penetrating as well as cockatoo, got off a private comment on the "two phases of the black revolution." The first, now ending, was the "Southern phase," which emphasized "middle-class matters," points of status, the right to sit up front in a bus or to sit down in a restaurant. The "Northern," "proletarian," "rough" phase was at hand. The New York or Chicago Negro had long been able to sit where he pleased; now he was heading into the "gut issue of who gets the money" and, Powell added, "watch out."

North or South, each advance of the Negro was leading to demands for more advances, more swiftly. The American Negro strikingly resembled the people of the underdeveloped nations who, in the scholar's phrase of the day, were going through "a revolution of rising expectations." The whole political context of the black revolution seemed to be changing. Much of the white South, with Negro rights jammed down its throat, was in a mood of sullen resignation. The white North, which had gone along with earlier developments in a burst of common sense, idealism and guilt, now showed signs of balking. Riots and fears of riots were hardening this resistance, particularly in the ethnic industrial-worker districts.

Before the Republican convention, George C. Wallace, the stridently segregationist governor of Alabama, had declared himself a candidate for President and entered Democratic primaries in Indiana, Maryland and Wisconsin. Most experts conceded him about 10 percent of the vote. His actual average in the three states: 35.4 percent. What was happening was plainest in the May 5 Indiana primary. Lake County, Indiana, with its day-and-night smoke and glare of steel furnaces and smell of oil refineries, had a population which was about 17 percent Negro and 24 percent recent immigrant stock, largely from Eastern Europe. In a spectacular upset, Wallace carried Lake County against the stand-in for President Johnson, the Indiana Governor Matthew E. Welsh. The steel nub of Lake County, Gary, was a prime example of urban ailments of the 1960's—congestion, air pollution and tension between its 22 percent recent immigration stock and its 39 percent Negroes. Wallace carried every all-white precinct in Gary.

For new times, new phrases. Eliot Janeway, the New York City economic consultant and editor of a newsletter, *The Janeway Service*, was an old hand at New Deal politics and a longtime friend of Lyndon Johnson. His instincts told him that the race issue might be ending, or at least significantly altering, the traditional Democratic coalition in which labor and Negroes voted the same ticket. Janeway was particularly convinced that the continuing effects of automation combined with an economic downturn that squeezed the job market would swing labor against the Negro. As he once laughingly remarked of himself, Janeway was something of an "economic philologist" (when working at *Time* he had coined "guesstimate"). In the summer of 1963, *The Janeway Service* was pointing to the possibility of "white backlash" among low-income whites against Negroes. After Indiana, and without any involved effects of automation or an economic recession, political commentators made "white backlash" a part of the American vocabulary.

Governor Wallace, out of his own tactical planning, soon withdrew from the presidential race of 1964, and Senator Goldwater was emerging as the candidate of white backlash as well as of the diehard Southern opposition. His speeches contained all the code words of white resistance; many of his agents went well beyond code. In the twentieth century, no presidential candidate of a major party had so angered and alarmed Negroes and white friends of the Negro cause.

Lyndon Johnson did not underestimate Goldwater's pull on the race issue. "I know those people out there," he said with a wave of his hand across the country. "We've been moving fast and they are troubled." He labored not so much to win pro-Negro votes, which he knew he had in abundance, but to prevent disturbances which could trigger white votes for Goldwater. Publicly President Johnson declared again and again that the progress of the black man could only be impeded by violence, and that he stood for the law and order which protected the rights and property of all. Privately he and White House aides urged influential Negroes to get the word into the ghettos that every bottle thrown was a help to Goldwater.

The leaders needed little persuading. They were worried by what had happened in New York and Rochester, both because of its backlash potential and its evidence that they themselves might be losing control of the civil rights movement. Shortly after the New York-Rochester disturbances Roy Wilkins, the soft-mannered but extremely effective head of the National Association for the Advancement of Colored People, called a conference which included the chief figures of the five other principal civil rights organizations: James Farmer (Congress of Racial Equality), Martin Luther King, Jr. (Southern Christian Leadership Conference), John Lewis (Student Nonviolent Coordinating Committee), A. Philip Randolph (Negro American Labor Council) and Whitney M. Young, Jr. (National Urban League). In a two-hour session the group hammered out two documents—both signed by all except James Farmer and John Lewis, heads of the increasingly militant CORE and SNCC—which represented an unprecedented statement.

Never before had major civil rights organizations tried to curb the zeal of their followers. Now these leaders stated that the Goldwater forces were injecting "racism" into the campaign and were a threat to the "whole climate of liberal democracy in the United States" and to "the implementation of the Civil Rights Act and to subsequent expansion of civil rights gains." The situation was so "serious . . . [that we] propose and call upon our members voluntarily to observe a broad curtailment, if not total moratorium, of all mass marches, mass picketing, and mass demonstrations until after Election Day, next Nov. 3." Negro energies, North and South, should go to "political action"—getting Negroes registered and seeing to it that they voted.

With a flicker of a smile Roy Wilkins told reporters, "This is a civil rights document, not a Johnson document."

Suddenly, the week after the Wilkins conference, a war 9,500 miles from Washington came crashing into the campaign.

The conflict in Vietnam had been grinding on, a dirty, ruthless, chaotic war with no end in sight but with few appearances that it was likely to draw America into deep involvement. In all his public discussions of Vietnam, President Johnson was holding firmly to the policy that "the United States, at the request of the Republic of South Vietnam and in accord with our obligations under the Southeast Asia Treaty Organization, is helping South Vietnam defend its freedom with military advisers, ammunition and matériel. It is not engaged in the war and does not intend to be."

On August 2 the Administration released the news that the United States destroyer *Maddox* had been attacked by North Vietnamese torpedo boats in the Gulf of Tonkin, a body of water bordered by the Communist Chinese island of Hainan, China itself and North Vietnam. A second announcement followed quickly: on August 4 North Vietnamese guns had fired on both the *Maddox* and the *C. Turner Joy*. That evening President Johnson ordered a single but heavy retaliatory bombing raid on North Vietnamese torpedo boats and their bases and went on television to tell the American people: "Aggression by terror against the peaceful villages of South Vietnam has now been joined by open aggression on the high seas against the United States of America. . . . Yet our response, for the present, will be limited and fitting. We Americans know, although others appear to forget, the risks of spreading conflict. We still seek no wider war."

In time the Tonkin incident would appear a turning point in American foreign policy, raise important questions of whether the North Vietnamese actions were provoked and whether the second attack actually took place, and serve as a focus for bitter discussions of the whole American role in Vietnam. But in August 1964 the dimensions of the Tonkin incident were much more limited.

Aides working with President Johnson at the time of the decision noted that he had the air of a man who believed only one course tenable and was ready to discuss merely the details of executing it. It was axiomatic in Lyndon Johnson's thinking—points that will be amplified in a later chapter—that "respect for the flag" must be rigorously maintained and that aggression must be stopped and stopped hard when it first shows itself. He knew the *Maddox* had been fired upon, and he was satisfied that in the second episode, torpedoes had been launched against the *Maddox* and the *C. Turner Joy;* these attacks represented "disrespect" for the American flag and "aggression." With the ineluctability of a syllogism, the necessary course of action emerged: stern retaliatory bombing.

Other considerations reinforced the decision. Vietnam presented patent political pitfalls. Of all the things which most Americans did not want, a shooting war was first on the list. On the other hand, since the late 1940's a considerable part of the population had been nagged by the feeling, however vague and confused, that the United States was not standing up to the Communists, and more and more the Goldwater campaign was striking this note. "Something has gone wrong," the senator was declaring. The "moral fiber" of America had been corrupted in a way which showed itself not only in the failure to take action against "crime in the streets" but in "timidity before Communism." No sentences brought louder roars from Goldwater audiences than the statements that "the Good Lord raised up this mighty Republic to be a home for the brave and to flourish as the land of the free . . . not to cringe before the bullying of Communism. . . . The tide has been running against freedom. Our people have followed false prophets. . . . Failures cement the wall of shame in Berlin. Failures blot the sands of shame at the Bay of Pigs. Failures mark the slow death of freedom in Laos. Failures infest the jungles of Vietnam."

Lyndon Johnson was running for President as a man of peace, but he had not the slightest intention of permitting Barry Goldwater to appear as the spokesman of the land of the free and the home for the brave. For the man of peace and the resolute defender of American principles, a bombing thrust against Communist attackers of United States ships—but only a single thrust—was ideal campaigning.

LBJ also remembered well that not many years before, another Democratic President had taken armed action in the Far East,

Harry Truman in Korea, without accompanying Republican approval and without formal congressional authorization. At first even that unreconstructable anti-Trumanite, Senator Robert A. Taft, hailed President Truman's move against "Communist aggression." Then the armed action escalated into large-scale war, the war became "Truman's war," and "Truman's war" turned into the prime emotional issue by which the Democrats were driven from the White House. President Johnson hoped and expected that the air strike he was ordering would not lead to American participation in the Vietnam shooting war. However it turned out, he intended to be protected during the campaign.

Apart from the Tonkin incident and the election, he was not at all sure what course of action he might in time want to pursue in Southeast Asia. Already the President was issuing a number of confidential deployment orders which made possible quick American strikes in the area. Consequently, in the hours immediately before his order to bomb North Vietnam, he took steps to use the Tonkin incident to throw a shield around himself not only for the campaign but for whatever later road he took and for however far he traveled it.

Thinking short range, he had phoned Senator Goldwater on a vacation yacht off California, and asked his public support for the coming air strike. The senator, who was hardly in a position to do anything else, promptly issued a statement that "we cannot allow the American flag to be shot at anywhere on earth if we are to retain our respect and prestige." Thinking short and long range, President Johnson summoned the leaders of both parties in the House and the Senate to the White House.

Speaking with the congressmen, he had the manner of the decisive leader in a time of national trouble. He was ordering the air strike as Commander in Chief, the President stated, and he did not believe that his action should be "embroiled in partisanship or in the political campaign." He further believed that Congress should speedily pass a joint resolution backing "your President." He was specific about what he had in mind: "a joint resolution of Congress like those passed at the request of Presidents Eisenhower and Kennedy to meet the threat to Formosa in 1955, to meet the threat to the Middle East in 1957, and to meet the threat in Cuba in 1962."

As part of its normal contingency operations, the State Department had stored away drafts for such a possible need. Following the outline of these documents but adding LBJ touches, President Johnson reeled off what he thought the resolution should say. Like the actual resolution presented to the House and Senate, his wording was cumbersome and it was not clear on one matter. But it conveyed three basic points. Congress approved the air strike against North Vietnam; for all practical purposes, it authorized the President to take whatever further steps he might deem necessary to combat aggression in Southeast Asia, "aggression" to be defined by the President; and this resolution remained in force until the President declared it was no longer needed or until it was repealed by a majority of the House and the Senate.

President Johnson left the clear impression that his conception of the sensible way to handle "aggression" in Southeast Asia— except for a sharply limited punitive thrust like the air strike against North Vietnam—was to do so without committing American combat forces. He gave no indication that he was at least considering a far different course in the future. Under the circumstances, the congressional leaders discussed the three points of the Tonkin resolution only briefly, and the document was hurried to the House and Senate the morning after the bombing of North Vietnam.

So sweeping a joint resolution of Congress supporting the foreign policy of a President is without any real counterpart in other modern democracies, and it is relatively new in the United States. The tactic developed after World War II from a laudable desire to express to the world an overwhelming, bipartisan support for the Chief Executive's moves in the face of foreign danger, and to strengthen his freedom of action in an age when the technology of war might make it necessary for him to make critical decisions within hours or minutes. In so far as such a document approves measures already taken by a President, as in this case the bombing of North Vietnam, it simply serves to present a united front. But when a resolution goes on to give blanket endorsement to any future decision a President deems wise, under circumstances which he alone defines—as the Tonkin resolution did—it enters an entirely different and far more troublesome area.

One opponent of the Tonkin resolution, Democratic Senator Wayne L. Morse of Oregon, insisted that it was unconstitutional. Morse is an able lawyer and his argument was not without point. The Constitution states that only Congress can declare war; in effect the Tonkin resolution said that Congress approved of the President's waging war, without asking for a congressional declaration of hostilities, if at some time in the future he considered war necessary to repel aggression.*

* *Senator Morse's challenge directs attention to the ambiguity in the Tonkin resolution. Of its three sections, Section 1 empowered the President to take armed action without any mention of the Constitution and therefore without recognition of Congress' exclusive right to declare war. But Section 2 stated*

But whatever the technical validity of the Morse contention, his point has an irrelevant ring. If the Constitution gives Congress the right to declare war, it also makes the President the Commander in Chief of the Armed Forces. With or without a congressional joint resolution, with or without a congressional declaration of war, the Commander in Chief is in a position to take the United States into a shooting war whenever he deems it wise, and no man who has the political agility to become President is likely to lack the techniques to win powerful public support for such an action.

The more practical problem lies in a different sphere; so broad a resolution entraps Congress. A Chief Executive may or may not be entirely candid in telling the House and Senate the future moves he is considering, and in this case President Johnson was not forthright. Regardless of the Chief Executive's presentation, the House and Senate are asked to write a blank check which can be filled in at a later time when the nature of the Administration's foreign policy, congressional attitudes, public opinion or any number of other factors may have significantly changed. Yet the House and Senate can hardly vote down such a resolution if it involves a nation considered to be an enemy or potential enemy; the refusal smacks of giving aid and comfort to that nation. Nor can they easily repeal the resolution in the future if the Chief Executive uses it as authorization for moves of which they disapprove. The repudiation undercuts the national leader at a time of war or other foreign crisis.

The entrapment is the more effective when a resolution is requested at a time near a national election. Congressmen of the President's own party are eager to demonstrate that they are upholding the hand of their chief. Congressmen of the opposite party are just as eager to show that they are patriots who understand that politics should stop at the water's edge.

It has been argued that if a President operating with the backing of a joint resolution desires to change his foreign policy in an important way, he should go to Congress and ask for a fresh authorization. But what Chief Executive is likely to encourage the

---

that he could move only in accord with the Constitution, which would assume Congress' prerogative. In the debate, Senator Morse made a distinction between the joint resolutions on Formosa, the Middle East and Vietnam, on the one hand, and the resolution at the time of the Cuban crisis. The first three gave blanket support to armed action by the President and were, in the senator's opinion, unconstitutional. The fourth supported action by "the United States," presumably meaning the three branches of the federal government operating in their appropriate roles. In Morse's view, this difference made the Formosa, Middle East and Vietnam resolutions unconstitutional and the Cuban resolution constitutional.

implication that his foreign policy is subject to the constant chec[k] of the House and Senate? And what significant purpose does th[e] original resolution serve if it does not approve wide freedom of ac[-] tion for the President?

Human beings, in or out of Congress, do not like entrapment The Formosa, Middle East and Cuban joint resolutions requeste[d] by Presidents Eisenhower and Kennedy brought no such congres- sional feeling because the crises which produced them were soo[n] solved, or at least disappeared from prime national attention. The Tonkin resolution concerned a situation that turned into a major war, and in the months to come an ensnared Senate flailed about in frustration and rage. By asking for the resolution, Lyndon John- son thought he was protecting the future as well as the present. Actually he was creating what he least desired—a future serious friction with Congress.

The trouble with the sweeping foreign policy resolution as a governmental technique is simply that it has no place in a democ- racy.

The problems it engenders showed themselves as soon as the House and Senate discussed the Tonkin resolution on August 6 and 7. The House confined itself largely to the clause supporting the air strike against North Vietnam, and on that subject Repre- sentative Henry S. Reuss from Milwaukee, the former general counsel of the Marshall Plan and now vice-chairman of the For- eign Policy Association, said all that needed to be said. The res- olution's *ex post facto* approval of the bombing, Reuss remarked, reminded him of a story. The bartender in a saloon calls the owner on the intercom to ask, "Is Casey good for a drink?"

"Has he had it?"

"He has."

"He is."

The Senate spent more time on the blank-check clauses of the document and produced a discussion that had the weird quality of being thoroughly troubled while its result was preordained. Sen- ator after senator, of many different types, took the floor to an- nounce a vote for the resolution and to add worried questions or statements.

Senator George S. McGovern, Democrat, South Dakota, a for- mer professor of history and director of the Food for Peace Pro- gram, a strong liberal: Was there any danger that the resolution could be taken to mean that the United States was going along with the call of the South Vietnam government to carry the war North? "I do not wish my vote for the resolution to be interpreted as an endorsement of our longstanding and apparently growing military involvement in Vietnam. . . . It could set the stage for World War III, involving this time the forces of Red China. . . . Let us seek a political settlement as soon as possible for a problem that is basically political."

Senator Daniel B. Brewster, Democrat, Maryland, Marine Corps veteran of the Pacific fighting in World War II, a middle-roader: He had experienced warfare in Asia and "would look with great dismay" on anything involving significant numbers of American troops in Asia. Did anything in this resolution "authorize or recommend or approve the landing of large American armies in Vietnam or in China?"

Senator Jacob K. Javits, Republican, New York, a leader of the liberal Republicans: "May a senator voting for the resolution assume that the United States with all its means, diplomatic and otherwise," will continue to press for maximum SEATO consultations and contributions and will use to the fullest the UN and other agencies to try to bring peace to Southeast Asia? Might he assume that congressional approval of the resolution will not "make everything else perfunctory"?

Senator John Sherman Cooper, Republican, Kentucky, a moderate, former diplomat, a pillar of the Senate and as such named to the Warren Commission: There were two essential points to the resolution—the first, protecting American armed forces from attack, and the second, the defense against aggression. About the first, there could be no question. About the second, "looking ahead, if the President decided that it was necessary to use such force as could lead into war," would the Congress be giving him the authority by this resolution?

He had confidence in President Johnson's "good judgment." But "I have not believed that Southeast Asia is the chief area of interest to the United States. We are committed in Europe and believe our chief interest is in the Western Hemisphere and Europe. In the Pacific we are committed to the defense of Formosa, Korea, Japan, and the Philippines. I do not know how widely we can spread our resources and our men. . . ."

Senator Frank Church, Democrat, Idaho, a member of the Foreign Relations Committee and a youthful liberal senator who was becoming increasingly articulate in foreign affairs: He had "serious misgivings" about American policy in Southeast Asia, which seemed to him "more the product of our own addiction to an ideological view of world affairs—an affliction which affects us as well as the Communists—rather than a policy based upon a detached and pragmatic view of our real national interests." These misgivings have been intensified by the "ominous events of the past few days. . . . Who can say that these events are not the natural consequence of the hazards we have assumed by the policy we have adopted in this part of the world?"

Senator Albert Gore, Democrat, Tennessee, a member of the Foreign Relations Committee and an ideologically freewheeling senator: Although he had not previously expressed his attitude publicly, he had stated his "deep concern" over American policy in Southeast Asia in executive sessions of the Foreign Relations Committee.

Senator Frank Carlson, Republican, Kansas, a member of the Foreign Relations Committee and a Midwestern conservative type: He too had been "greatly" concerned by our policy. "It seems that we take step after step that involves us in a situation from which it is most difficult to extricate ourselves."

Senator George D. Aiken, Republican, Vermont, a member of the Foreign Relations Committee and a widely respected elder statesman: "For some months it has appeared to me that an expansion of military operations in Southeast Asia was inevitable. I have been skeptical of the repeated assurances of high government officials that no such expansion was contemplated.

"I have repeatedly stated to those officials, including the President of the United States, that I was opposed to an expansion of the war. . . . I sincerely hope that the fears I have entertained over the past few months may prove to have been groundless."

Always the answers to these troubled questions and statements were the same, whether they were provided by Senator Fulbright, chairman of the Senate Foreign Relations Committee and floor leader for the resolution, by some other senator, or by the man himself who was stating the concern. The resolution contemplated no change in American policy in Southeast Asia; the President of the United States had asked for it without delay because he felt it important for the national security; a political campaign was going on and that made quick, sweeping bipartisan support even more desirable.

Near the close of the discussion, Senator Gaylord A. Nelson, a liberal Democrat from Wisconsin, took the floor to point out that some senators had construed the resolution to mean a toughening of American policy in Southeast Asia. He therefore proposed a "clarifying" amendment, in which the key sentence read: "Our continuing policy is to limit our role to the provision of aid, training assistance, and military advice. . . ."

Senator Fulbright replied that he had no objection to the amendment as "a statement of policy." It represented his own view and it was also "an accurate reflection of what I believe is the President's policy, judging from his own statements." However, as floor leader for the resolution he could not accept the addition. President Johnson had asked for swift support, and any amendment would require a time-consuming conference with the House.

The Senate approved the Tonkin resolution after just eight hours of discussion, by a vote of 88 to 2. The House took forty minutes and voted 414 to 0. President Johnson signed the document the same day, August 7, and Secretary of Defense McNamara reported that the American air strike was "very successful." Sixty-four planes went over North Vietnam, destroying twenty-five PT boats—a "substantial part" of North Vietnam's total number—and damaging all four of its PT-boat bases. There were no signs that the retaliatory raid was provoking North Vietnam or Red China to hostile actions against United States forces.

The Vietnam issue was, for the moment, quieted.

Meanwhile, there were other matters to be taken care of on the Hill. Before and after the Tonkin incident, Democratic House and Senate leaders were urging the President to let the congressmen go home and get ahead with their campaigning. But Lyndon Johnson was not done. He was putting through the House and Senate additional legislation, largely of JFK vintage, and leading a major congressional effort for the Economic Opportunity Act of 1964 (generally called the "poverty bill." Efforts were made by some of us in Washington to end the use of the phrase, which was scarcely a help to the pride of those the measure was intended to aid, but people went right on saying "poverty bill").

As early as March 16, President Johnson had sent EOA to Congress with a special message calling for a multipronged attack on hard-core poverty. The message stated his "total commitment" to the bill, and the phrase was no mere rhetoric. Here was a case where personal attitudes and feelings combined with a leader's political needs, his sense of timing, and his grasp of a national need to create a thoroughgoing sincerity.

"The President of the United States," LBJ told Congress, "is President of all the people in every section of the country. But this office also holds a special responsibility to the distressed and disinherited, the hungry and the hopeless of this abundant nation." Poverty must be fought "because it is right that we should"; EOA was an effort "to give people a chance." This was the voice of the heir to Jim Ferguson, the youth who had felt trapped cracking rocks between Johnson City and Hye, the man who never ceased to think of himself as a product of poverty. In discussing EOA,

Lyndon Johnson invariably spoke with an emotion that recalled New Deal days. Corporation executives were taken aback—and moved—by a President who told them, "You live on the side of the tracks where you have never seen this poverty. These people are human beings. They get hungry, like you and me, and they have feelings like you and me. They deserve something better of our country." And then, usually, the LBJ addition: "Doing something about poverty is economical in the long run. You don't have to be loose with a dollar to prove you are liberal—or callous to prove you are conservative."

Apart from President Johnson's intense personal involvement, he agreed with the social commentators who were maintaining that in the America of the 1960's, widespread hard-core poverty was a threat to the health and stability of the whole society. Politically, he considered EOA a must. Kennedyites might argue that an anti-poverty program had been conceived before Dallas and that the late President intended to recommend such a bill to Congress. But to Lyndon Johnson and to much of the country, EOA was the first major LBJ legislation sent to the Hill, and his prestige rode with it. He also considered it a major weapon in quieting Negro discontent, a lure for low-income and liberal votes, and a central component of the picture of himself which he wanted the nation to have: frugal and hard-headed but—to use the word he was making a White House staple—"compassionate."

The Senate acted on EOA first and amended the measure in two ways that the Administration did not like. It cut the appropriation and gave each governor the right to veto any poverty project undertaken in his state. But the bill passed by a large majority and without a serious struggle.

In the House, the Administration saw to it that the floor leadership for EOA went not to the chairman of the Committee on Education and Labor, Adam Clayton Powell, Jr., who was already acquiring something of the aura of Bimini, but rather to Phil M. Landrum, chairman of the subcommittee which considered the measure. Landrum was one of the more interesting characters in the extraordinary collection of human beings that compose the House of Representatives. A small-town Georgian, six feet tall, husky and hotheaded, delighting in his broadbrim colonel's hat and speaking his Southern vowels with a slight Scottish burr, he moved about the chamber like some relic of Georgia's ante-bellum past. Generally the representative was a strong conservative—he was best known for the Landrum-Griffin Act, an anathema of organized labor. But Landrum had a tough, independent mind and had learned from watching attempts to develop an industrial force from agrarian labor in his northeastern part of Georgia and from his Subcommittee on Labor Statistics.

His major speech for EOA was a curiously effective one that called up the attitude of another product of small-town America at the other end of Pennsylvania Avenue. "Poverty—what is poverty?" Representative Landrum asked. It could not really be defined at "a dollar level. . . . But there is a level at which you can establish whether a man or groups of men are able to enjoy the full benefits of American citizenship and, likewise, able to discharge the full responsibilities of citizenship." When "we were boys and when our forefathers were boys, poverty could be dealt with on an individual or small-group basis. The family could pick up and move to a new frontier." But now the poor were piling up in urban slums, where the "hopelessness" came, "then frustration, resentment and violence." Landrum paused and roared out, "Mr. Chairman, that is what we are faced with today. We are dealing with social dynamite."

The measure, he went on, was "the most conservative social program I have ever seen presented to any legislative body." It was a bulwark against "anarchy" and fiscally it was prudent. Last year, Georgia alone had spent $96,445,000 on public assistance. We are going to create "taxpayers instead of tax eaters," to end "the ever-increasing cycle of a child of poverty becoming a parent of poverty."

Look up there at the ceiling, said Congressman Phil Landrum of Jasper, Georgia, look at the carved words of Jefferson and Mason and Webster saying to us, "Do something to call forth the resources of this land; do something to develop its powers; do something to promote its general welfare; do something so that you and I may be remembered for what was accomplished in our day and time."

As Landrum finished, the House saw an unusual scene, a heartfelt standing ovation. But by midsummer the word going to the White House was grim. EOA was not only in trouble in the House of Representatives; it stood a good chance of going down in outright defeat.

Candidate Goldwater, appearing in Western shirt and boots at a Nevada rodeo, talked a breezy "conservative's objection to just this sort of thing—a dole for the poor, offered cynically for votes." Candidate Miller, clothed in homburg, chesterfield and vitriol, asked the New York State Association of Professional Men, "Who knows anything about poverty in this Administration—Bobby Baker?" Except for a small liberal phalanx, Republican members of the House gave indications of voting against the measure as a bloc.

EOA would obviously benefit many more Negroes than whites. Worried about the backlash reports from their districts, a number of Northern Democrats were hesitating. Southern Democrats hardened in opposition. Representative Howard W. Smith of Virginia, the powerful chairman of the House Rules Committee, took the floor to entangle racism and anti-poverty. "Any Southerners who plan to vote for this bill," he said in his aged rasp, "are implementing the civil rights bill that you opposed." He scored the proposed Job Corps installations as a devious way to establish "integrated camps," and hinted that under the legislation federal funds would go to the NAACP. In a magnificent irrelevancy of wrath, Smith added, "Is there anything in this bill that would stop them from establishing a nudist camp in your community?"

Southern or Northern, Republican and Democratic, wavering congressmen were finding reasons to vote no because of the hasty, jerry-built nature of the bill, the opportunities it opened for blatant politicking and corruption, and the danger that EOA would become a bureaucratic mishmash. (In 1967 the Administration itself would send to Congress recommendations for a major overhaul of the program.) Representative Peter H. B. Frelinghuysen of New Jersey, the Republican floor leader against the measure, probed these problem areas persistently and skillfully, and he did not neglect another tactic. He kept referring to EOA as "the Powell-Landrum bill."

LBJ's phone went into high digit, to bring Democrats back into the fold and to pick off detachable Republicans. Most of his arm twisting was the usual effort to add an affirmative vote, but in a case where the representative clearly would not support the bill, the forcible suggestion was made that he "take a walk"—find himself inextricably busy some place other than the House chamber at the time of the vote. President Johnson relentlessly pressured congressmen and relentlessly pressured other people to pressure congressmen. He went after not only the usual allies of such legislation but publishers, industrialists and bankers. A Republican congressman from Pennsylvania was startled to receive a lobbying call for EOA from Stuart T. Saunders, chairman of the board of the Pennsylvania Railroad, president of the Wabash Railroad, a director of the Buckeye Pipeline Co., the Chase National Bank, the Equitable Life Assurance Co., the Great Southwest Corporation and U. S. Steel. Lyndon Johnson threw everything he had into the fight, including the White House photography room. Doubtful congressmen suddenly found that they were cordially welcome at the White

House for a joint photograph with the President, along with a few words on how sensible it would be to vote for EOA.

The compromises, okayed from the Oval Office, came. The Administration forces gave up any effort to remove the distasteful Senate amendments. They accepted House changes eliminating two rural programs and requiring a loyalty oath from all enrollees in the Job Corps. But even with these concessions the report to the White House continued to be that EOA was in serious trouble in the House of Representatives.

By August, Administration pressure focused on an uncommitted group of Democratic representatives from North Carolina. At White House instigation, on August 6, the day before the crucial vote, Speaker McCormack arranged a meeting in his office. It included not only the North Carolina congressmen but Sargent Shriver, whom President Johnson had publicly designated to head the Office of Economic Opportunity established by EOA. The North Carolinians soon made plain their terms: most of them could be brought over to the bill, but Adam Yarmolinsky must go.

Yarmolinsky was one of those occasional Washington figures who are custom-tailored to rouse the dankest suspicions of Southern congressmen. He was from New York City, a Harvard graduate, short, dark, Jewish, militantly liberal, brilliant and quite aware that he was brilliant. As a high school junior, Yarmolinsky had attended several Young Communist League meetings with a friend; he did not like what he heard and stopped going. Later, under Robert M. Hutchins, he served as an officer of the rambunctious Fund for the Republic ("We are a wholly disowned branch of the Ford Foundation," Hutchins said with his serene heresy). A member of the Harvard group who came to Washington with President Kennedy, Yarmolinsky served as the special assistant to Defense Secretary McNamara, where he accumulated a superb record and highly articulate enemies.

When the Defense Department dismissed the dangerously crackpot Major General Edwin A. Walker, the ex-General went up and down the magnolia-and-oil circuit of the South shrilling how Yarmolinsky, "this Communist conspirator," had driven him out of the service of his country. Actually, Yarmolinsky played little or no role in the Walker case, but he did take actions equally offensive to segregationists. He had helped set up a commission to investigate racial discrimination in the Armed Forces and led the effort to implement the proposals of the group. Now on loan from Defense, he had been a major architect of EOA, that "blueprint for mongrelization of the races," as Congressman Smith described it, and it was common knowledge that at the strong recommendation of Shriver,

President Johnson planned to name Yarmolinsky deputy director of the Office of Economic Opportunity.

In Speaker McCormack's office a number of the North Carolina delegation pressed hard. They insisted they would vote against the bill unless Yarmolinsky was excluded from any role in administering the program. Shriver tried to dodge. All matters of executive personnel were uncertain, he said, and they were up to the President in any case.

Telephone the President, the congressmen demanded.

The next day Representative Landrum cut off a floor discussion of Yarmolinsky by announcing that he had it on the "highest authority" that Yarmolinsky would have no role in the Office of Economic Opportunity. When the critical vote came an hour later, Democratic congressional leaders were astonished. They had wrought better than they knew; EOA was supported by a secure, if not rousing, majority of 38. Only 8 votes were, beyond question, won by the decapitation of Yarmolinsky.

Whether or not the action was necessary to bring approval of the bill, Yarmolinsky was an able and dedicated man and a vaunted New Frontiersman. President Johnson's sacrifice of him provided critics, especially those of a Kennedyite bent, with another argument that LBJ politics were politics at any price.

At his press conference two days later, the President did not help the situation and he did not improve his reputation for talking realities to reporters. Edward T. Folliard of the Washington *Post* brought up the subject.

Q. Mr. President, I want to ask a question about Adam Yarmolinsky. . . . He had been with the Department of Defense—

A. He still is.

Q. I thought he had been working . . . on the poverty bill.

A. No, your thoughts are wrong. He is still with the Department of Defense.

Q. I was also asked to ask you, sir, if he was going back to the Pentagon, but you say he is still there.

A. He never left.

President Johnson signed the Economic Opportunity Act in the Rose Garden on the perfect summer morning of August 20, 1964. "On this occasion," he said with emotion, "the American people and our American system are making history. For so long as man has lived on this earth poverty has been his curse. . . . Today for the first time in all the history of the human race, a great nation is able to make and is willing to make a commitment to eradicate poverty among its people." Not veiling the fact that he was answering the Goldwater forces, Lyndon Johnson added, "This is not in any sense a cynical proposal to exploit the poor with the promise of a handout or a dole. We know—we learned long ago—that answer is no answer. The measure before me this morning for signature offers the answer that its title implies—the answer of opportunity."

When the seventy-two pens were given out, one of them went to Adam Yarmolinsky. He took it and stepped aside with a tight smile.

CHAPTER 9

The Matter of a Vice-President

*I*n midsummer 1964 the atmosphere of the White House was going through another change. The helterskelter of the immediate post-assassination days, the drive to establish Lyndon Johnson as President were giving way to a different kind of frenzy, the election of a candidate.

Old faces from the LBJ past showed up for specific chores. New people, obviously signed on temporarily, filled more rooms in the inexhaustible Executive Office Building. The LBJ economy rule for the White House staff was modified, and in an LBJ manner. People were added to the staff not by being put on the White House budget but by "assignment" from another part of the government or by being peremptorily inserted on the payroll of some hapless bureau. My own office burgeoned, including the addition of a gifted young historian and writer Daniel J. Kevles, now a professor of history at the California Institute of Technology. I trust it will not impair the professor's stature if I mention that he performed brilliantly as a White House staff man while being paid as assistant to the chief of personnel of the U. S. Weather Bureau, an estimable institution inside which Kevles never set foot before, during or after his work with me. As it does almost every quadrennium, the White House was turning into one big handsome frenetic campaign headquarters.

Just ahead, scheduled to open on August 24, was the Democratic convention. Before the assassination the Kennedy Administration had picked Atlantic City as the convention site. Beyond that all decisions were open, and LBJ was like the mother of the bride, considering, controlling, fussing over every detail. This was to be *his* convention, leading to *his* triumph. He personally chose where his aides would stay, the brand-new motel the Pageant Motor Inn across from Convention Hall, and he supervised bloc by bloc the allotment of spectator's seats in the auditorium. He specified that a forty-foot photograph of himself would flank the stage; that he would be nominated in a way nobody had ever been nominated, by "co-nominators," the Catholic California Governor Edmund G. Brown and the Protestant Texas Governor John B. Connally; that "Hello, Lyndon!" sung to "Hello, Dolly!" would be the theme song. Endlessly the President invited people to the Oval Office or upstairs to talk over some phase of the convention. Sipping at a low-calorie orange drink, offering heaping dishes of "oovies" but shunning the hors d'oeuvres himself (Juanita Roberts kept a rigid calorie count), he solicited opinions from an amazing variety of people.

Everyone in the White House was becoming involved in campaign matters, large and small. I had never thought of my role as political; in fact, it obviously called for the reverse and in any event that was my natural inclination. But campaigns have their siren call and to me as to virtually all the people I dealt with, opposition to Goldwaterism hardly seemed a matter of party. I was particularly repelled by the Republican vice-presidential candidate, William Miller. It was not only the policies the man represented; he had about him a slick sleaziness which made me wince at the thought that the election conceivably could put him in a position where he would be President of the United States.

One summer evening I made some remarks to this effect to Frank E. Smith, a director of the Tennessee Valley Authority, a decent, thoughtful Mississippian who was about to publish his autobiography, *Congressman from Mississippi*. The book told how Smith as a congressman had tried to stay in the House of Representatives and bring economic advances to Mississippi by paying lip service to racism, even voting regularly against civil rights bills, but was driven out in 1962 because of his general liberalism. Smith agreed with my reaction to Miller and added, "You know, what you're talking about is illustrated by a story in my book about an anonymous member of Congress. I didn't know that Bill Miller was going to become a famous man or I would have identified him." The passage stated that "another member"—Representative Miller—had offered to Congressman Smith a monthly pay check for work that was vaguely defined and which Smith became convinced was intended to influence his votes on legislation affecting enterprises in which Miller had a financial interest. Smith told me he was quite ready to identify Miller.

I put the facts in the hands of Walter Jenkins, and Jenkins passed them on to Drew Pearson. The Pearson column, this one written by his associate Jack Anderson, carried a detailed account of the incident and other news media picked up the story and played it hard. Of course Miller cried smear, but he was labeled in a way that he did not shake off throughout the campaign.

My first reaction was one of pleasure that the public was learning what kind of politician William Miller was. Then came second thoughts and an uneasiness. In the existing American political organization, the only quick, effective way to make public such a story is through a leak to the press. Had the material been turned over to the Democratic National Committee, it probably would have been bumbled around for a while and then issued in a way that made it sound like some more political gossip off the mimeograph machine. We simply have not developed a tradition and a system which would make it possible for an appropriate body, perhaps a different type of the party national committees, to take over a charge like this, issue it responsibly, let it be answered or ignored by a comparable organization of the opposing party or the individual himself, and then permit the public to decide. Using the technique of the newspaper leak means that the indirectness of the attack invites the inadequacy of the answer; of more significance, had Miller been a grossly abused innocent in this case, he could never really have removed the smudge. But the habit of the sidewise accusation had become rampant in America, and not only in political circles, long before I took a stab at it. Looking back, I regret my participation in it, however strongly I believed that putting William Miller in a position to be President would have been risking disaster.

From the Oval Office word came that President Johnson was looking for a phrase. He was not only out to combat white backlash by discouraging Negroes from militant activities which could create Goldwater votes; he was on the offensive and wanted a slogan expressing his confidence that he was winning over more business votes and more Republican votes in general than the number of Democrats who might be deserting him on the race issue. The White House staff offered its suggestions, but it was the pollster Oliver Quayle who came up with the expression that the President rightly seized upon: the simple opposite of "backlash"— "frontlash." Happily Lyndon Johnson wielded the phrase as he worked away to make it more and more of a reality.

With the passing summer months, frontlash campaigning turned the White House into that revolving door of guests which had brought me my sense of how LBJ had scored with his highly publicized call to turn out the lights. Once or twice a week, usually at lunch and occasionally at dinner as well, large groups were

invited to dine with the President. The men and women represented a variety of occupations, but most of them were influential
business or professional leaders who were habitually Republican.
The agenda was usually the same—a handshake with President
Johnson in the receiving line, the meal with LBJ seated at the
head table amid the most important or most recalcitrant nabobs,
the brief presidential speech, a warm, informal good-bye.

LBJ was a master at this gastronomical politicking. His
speeches, wandering far from the text, were persuasively nonpartisan and had an appealing undertone of "We responsible
people—you and I—understand that a pretty irresponsible fellow
is presuming to run this nation." At the table he usually controlled
his tendency to go into monologue and made interesting remarks
about the problems that were on his mind interspersed with family
tidbits. If the affair were stag he might be bawdy and bawdy in a
way which made the men feel they had been singled out for the
smoking-room talk of the great. With any table companions, the
President could be very presidential, and in a moving way. One
group of guests left the White House repeating President Johnson's
comment on how he felt after giving the order for the air strike
against North Vietnam: "It was a bad night for me. I suppose
Presidents get hardened to this sort of thing, but I'm not used to it.
I kept thinking, I sent those young men into that flak, and I am
personally responsible for getting them back."

At most of the luncheons, a White House staff member served
as host for each table of ten. If this duty sometimes proved a chore,
it could also be an education, particularly so far as the business
executives were concerned. At this high level of corporate leadership, a sizable percentage of the guests made the old stereotype
of the American businessman seem thoroughly outmoded. They
were anything but Babbitts; well-educated and having continued to
keep up with things, they had a variety of interests besides the
financial page and the golf links. Far from being narrow-gauged
chauvinists, they welcomed internationalism, talked coexistence
with Communism, and had a ready, if pragmatic, understanding
of the ferment of the have-nots around the world. In domestic
affairs, they went along with the assumption that the federal
government would continue to play a major role in the economic
and social affairs of the nation. They were sympathetic to legislation like the anti-poverty bill and civil rights, partly because of
their educated social sensitivities and partly because they saw that
such efforts would increase consumer power. "We're really post-
Keynesians," a Yale graduate, now heading an industrial empire,
remarked to me with a chuckle. "Keynes only wanted to spend dur-

ing depressions. We're ready for it any time, even if we also love politicians to talk about economy in government."

Barry Goldwater had little chance of holding the customary Republican votes of men like these. In fact, as you listened to them, they seemed so much more attuned to modern Democratic thinking than even to moderate Republicanism that you wondered whether Goldwater was not costing the G.O.P. a good deal more than defections in 1964. In instance after instance the businessmen at my table stated that they were casting their first Democratic vote in a presidential election for Lyndon Johnson. It seemed likely that having lost their political virginity, a number of them would continue their new and congenial liaison in the circumstances of ordinary national elections.

One summer campaign day brought a sharply different group to 1600 Pennsylvania Avenue. There is an old saying around the White House that if you want to get something done, go after it during a campaign. Presidents are more likely to give their time and are more ready to accept suggestions that will make news stories. In my historical work, I had been impressed by the role of the state universities in the early 1900's; the University of Wisconsin in particular had proved a staging point for an attack on the problems of its state and region, providing the zeal, organization and brain power to launch imaginative reform programs. President Johnson wanted to have influential people come to the White House and he wanted to appeal to Republicans, with their traditional interest in local rather than federal action. Why not invite the state university presidents and ask them to assume leadership in setting up machinery, statewide and regional, to analyze the long-range problems of their areas and to work out plans to meet them? President Johnson gave his okay and on August 13 the presidents of eighty-one state universities from all fifty states and the territories assembled at the White House. The day-long schedule included conferences with appropriate Cabinet officers and other officials, working sessions among the university heads, and luncheon with the President.

LBJ was in high form that day. He thought the occasion "excellent, *excellent*" for political purposes. Apart from the campaign, he was among educators, which pleased him, and among non-Ivy League educators, which pleased him even more. In his buoyant mood, he ad-libbed into the speech I had prepared for him a terse definition of federalism which was happily quoted by the dourest conservative press ("I never would want my county commissioner to recommend the plan for the Tonkin Gulf. . . . But I wouldn't necessarily want the Chairman of my Joint Chiefs of

Staff to grade the road that leads to my schoolhouse"); got off a hyperbolic compliment to me that caused some of my colleagues to eye me suspiciously for days; and took the occasion to launch a populistic recruiting drive for high-level government talent from the state universities which "grant more than half of the Ph.D. degrees—those of you here. You would never think so when you walk around the White House and see where these folks come from."

In the midst of all this, I'm afraid the President had forgotten the stated purpose of the gathering. But things have a way of happening in the White House in a confusion of effects. At the end of this day it was a Republican university president who offered a glowing resolution of appreciation to President Johnson and let it be known that he intended to vote for him. That evening the executive committee of the National Association of State Universities and Land-Grant Colleges met to plan a program by which the universities would address themselves to the long-range problems of their areas. In time the Association linked hands with the Governors Conference in this effort, obtained foundation support, made the project the theme of one of its national meetings and moved toward the actual studies.

Perhaps the spirit of the University of Wisconsin was stirring again in the sixties.

University presidents, corporation executives and a host of others—they came and they went but they interrupted little the avid attention Lyndon Johnson was giving to the most important detail of the convention, selection of the Democratic vice-presidential candidate.

For months political observers had speculated whether President Johnson would pick Attorney General Robert Kennedy, and some of the most seasoned of them had been saying that he would be virtually forced to choose the living symbol of the Kennedy legend. Actually, LBJ never seriously considered RFK. This was not simply a result of the President's intense personal dislike of the Attorney General and the fact that he had no intention of strengthening the Kennedy faction of the Democratic party. President Johnson believed that a possible Chief Executive should have "a little gray in his hair" and that Kennedy lacked other prime qualifications, especially a potential to lead Congress and the understanding that the United States is "a big place, with lots of different kinds of people with different thoughts and interests, who are not to be brought together by playing the game of royal family." Above all, Lyndon Johnson wanted to win the election on his own, and certainly not in a way which would permit the country to say that he had needed a Kennedy.

There were also the public opinion polls. For years LBJ had shared the traditional politician's belief that his own sense of the voters' mood was the best gauge of public opinion. He also remembered well the Joe Belden poll, which Texans had been paying attention to since the 1940's. In 1952 Belden announced that he was basing his results on the work of "seventy-seven researchers who conducted hundreds of carefully planned interviews." He predicted that Adlai Stevenson would defeat Dwight Eisenhower in Texas by 53 percent, and Eisenhower won the state by approximately that percentage. But during the campaign of 1960 John Kennedy, a devotee of polls, had begun changing Lyndon Johnson's mind, and the process was furthered by JFK's favorite pollster, Louis Harris, and particularly by the vice-president of the Harris organization, Oliver A. Quayle, 3d. In 1963 Quayle became head of his own polling firm, and he was just the person to complete the conversion.

A square-shouldered, pleasant man in his vigorous forties, the son of a former official of the Democratic National Committee, Quayle was absorbed in politics to the point of frequently running for local office as a Democrat in his hopelessly Republican home area of Bronxville, New York. His zest for politics was accompanied by considerable savvy; he not only invented the expression "front-lash" but was one of the first observers to sense the trend. His polling reports, abhorring pollsterese, used the professional politician's language, and spoke not of "upward mobile ethnic groups" but of "people on the make." And Quayle was accurate, so accurate in prediction after prediction that Lyndon Johnson would hmmm and say, "That boy seems to know what he's doin'." By the summer of 1964, Oliver Quayle & Company were an important part of the White House operation. Lyndon Johnson was not only converted but close to transfixed. He went around with his pockets stuffed with polls, always ready to pull them out for a stentorian reading.

On the subject of a vice-presidential candidate, Quayle had a striking report. President Johnson was running so strongly across so wide a cross section of voters that no vice-presidential candidate was likely to help the ticket to any significant degree. On the contrary, it could be hampered by any one of the men being prominently discussed. The practical question was close to being, Who would hurt Lyndon Johnson the least?

The polls indicated that Kennedy could weaken the ticket seriously and weaken it just where President Johnson was especially eager to be strong—among Southerners and businessmen. The

South remembered RFK as the Attorney General who had taken strong civil rights actions during his brother's Administration. Many businessmen recalled with resentment his role in the steel-price rollback of 1962, and they told bitter stories that he had used the FBI to obtain information for his purposes. They had, Quayle reported, a "cop image" of him.

If President Johnson had no thought of choosing Kennedy, he nevertheless kept talking about the possibility. After functioning some nine months as the successor to John Kennedy, he had developed a razor-edge sensitivity to anything connected with the family. To him, they were ever present and ever active, pestering everything he tried to do. He kept worrying the subject of RFK as the vice-presidential nominee until the White House staff and much of Washington were referring to the "Bobby Problem." Wouldn't Catholics be offended by rejecting him? Wouldn't his powerful friends in the Democratic party sit on their hands during the campaign? Wouldn't the general public take rejection as a slap at the memory of his brother?

One aspect of the Bobby Problem was anything but a product of Lyndon Johnson's state of mind. Kennedy wanted the nomination and he and his allies not only sought it for him but believed that he had a right to it. As time went by, President Johnson became convinced that the RFK faction intended to try to get it regardless of his wishes, and this was not beyond the realm of practicality. Ordinarily, if he cares to, the presidential candidate picks the vice-presidential nominee and that is that. But the 1964 convention was no ordinary one. The Kennedy political forces were belligerently active; many of the delegates were the same men and women who had nominated John Kennedy in 1960; powerful sentiments and political ties ran to the Kennedy organization. The situation held highly charged emotional possibilities resulting from the assassination, and the proper conjunction of events could explode them.

Such a conjunction seemed to be shaping up. The Arrangements Committee of the convention had scheduled a twenty-minute memorial documentary to President Kennedy—a deeply moving film—for the evening of the first session. Mrs. Jacqueline Kennedy had stated that she did not intend to go to Atlantic City, but in July the correspondent Nancy Dickerson, a friend of President Johnson's, made known that she had talked with Mrs. Kennedy and that she seemed to be changing her mind. Mrs. Kennedy now spoke of attending the convention and of "helping Bobby." A tribute to the murdered President, with Jacqueline Kennedy in her box, before a convention permeated with Kennedy emotions and interests, could ram Robert Kennedy down the throat of Lyndon Johnson.

On July 26 President Johnson called a meeting of the Arrangements Committee at the White House. He wanted to be brought up to date, he explained. His eye ran down the program for the opening session. Oh, that's too bad, he said, he wanted to be present for the memorial film. But with all the pressures on him, he didn't see how he could possibly get to Atlantic City for the first evening. The Arrangements Committee got the point. It scheduled the memorial documentary after the choice of the vice-presidential candidate.

With that, President Johnson could have dropped the Bobby Problem and simply gone ahead and named his man. But he felt, probably correctly, that a good chance still existed that Kennedy would be nominated from the floor of the convention. He did not want to be put in the position of crushing an RFK nomination, and he was becoming convinced that Kennedy devotees throughout the country would be less offended in the long run if he settled the matter promptly, publicly and once and for all.

Lyndon Johnson went into another intense brain-picking effort, especially with his lawyer-politico friend James H. Rowe, Jr. Montana-born and Harvard-educated, an alumnus of the New Deal, able, urbane, rocking back and forth in his chair in his comfortable middle years, somewhat idealistic and also fascinated by power traffickings, Rowe had been a Humphrey man in the 1960 battle for the Democratic nomination, then when Humphrey was eliminated, the chief LBJ lieutenant. Now in 1964 he was a major figure in Oval Office campaign planning, and his opinion was emphatic. The faster Robert Kennedy was publicly eliminated, the better.

A strategy was worked out. President Johnson would tell Kennedy that he did not intend to choose him as the vice-presidential nominee. He would attempt to get Kennedy himself to make a public statement of withdrawal. If that failed, the President would convey his decision to the press, making every effort not to appear hostile to the Attorney General.

LBJ telephoned RFK and asked him to come to the White House for a talk. The appointment was set for 1 P.M. on July 29, and this time Lyndon Johnson did not move to the informal rocker and sofa at the far end of the Oval Office. He sat at the desk of the President of the United States, with Kennedy in the chair to his right. He made plain that he did not intend to name the Attorney General. Then he added many warm words about Kennedy's political future and offered him his choice of almost any post he might want in the 1964 campaign or in the next Administration.

What happened beyond that is the subject of thoroughly confused reports. The record is completely contradictory on one crucial point—what was said or not said about how the decision was to be made public. President Johnson has stated that he brought up the matter and that Kennedy asked for time to think it over. Accounts of the meeting from RFK sources included no mention of this subject. After the meeting Lyndon Johnson tried some oblique prodding, including asking the JFK appointee McGeorge Bundy, a Republican who had never played any political role, to speak to Kennedy and ask that he announce his withdrawal. Bundy and Kennedy talked; RFK said that any public statement would have to come from LBJ. Kennedyite Washington promptly filled with more talk about Bundy "the traitor."

At 6 P.M. the day after the Oval Office confrontation, the President hastily summoned a press conference and executed the alternative strategy. He told the country that he had "reached the conclusion that it would be inadvisable for me to recommend to the convention [as my running mate] any member of the Cabinet or any of those who meet regularly with the Cabinet." He had "personally informed" all the men affected by the decision whose names had been mentioned in the press as vice-presidential possibilities.

In later conversations with reporters, President Johnson insisted that this move was not directed at Kennedy. He simply wanted to keep all his Cabinet men from being pestered by politics; they were too valuable and too busy for that. For instance, home-state campaigns were beginning to boom Secretary of State Rusk and Secretary of Agriculture Freeman for the Vice-Presidency. The newsmen could only conclude that the President's vaunted political antennae must be even more wondrous than they had imagined. No one else in Washington, let alone in Georgia or Minnesota, had heard of a single such effort.

The whole affair was fantastically circuitous and a little silly. A group of Democratic congressional candidates roared with laughter when Kennedy remarked to them, "I must say I stand in awe of you. You're not members of the Cabinet, and you don't meet regularly with the Cabinet, and therefore you are eligible for the Vice-Presidency." The room rocked again when Kennedy added that he was going to send "a little note to Cabinet members saying, 'I'm sorry I took so many nice fellows over the side with me.'"

But it was done, and Lyndon Johnson was like a man who had exorcised his devil. "Now that damn albatross is off my neck," he chortled to an aide. The whole White House sighed with relief.

Right after the Oval Office conversation I ran into a staff member who had been talking with the President. He broke into a Texas-style buck and wing and headed for the door. "Me, I'm going to have a drink, a long, slow couple of them!"

Lyndon Johnson was so exuberant that he did something which experienced politicians simply do not do. He sneered at a vanquished but still powerful foe, and one without weapons comparable to his own during the contest. The day after his announcement, President Johnson invited three White House correspondents to lunch, and the talk rambled on until late afternoon. As time went by, he grew more relaxed and spoke in detail of the elimination of RFK, telling the story as he wanted it told. Leaning back from the table, his skilled mimicry cutting, he imitated Kennedy's "funny voice" when he first telephoned him for the appointment, the "gulp" as he heard that he was eliminated, the looks on his face while they talked of the aftermath of the *fait accompli*.

Within hours the lunch was the talk of Washington. Heretofore Robert Kennedy had emphasized, at least in the statements he intended for circulation, how much President Johnson had gone out of his way to avoid a rupture with him during their meeting. Now RFK boarded a plane for a Hyannisport weekend with a look of cold fury. For Kennedy, who had always viewed Lyndon Johnson with distaste and who had been having difficulty controlling his bitterness during Cabinet meetings, this was the total, final break.

As the U. S. Ambassador to the UN, Adlai Stevenson "met regularly with the Cabinet." When informed of the President's elimination of all Cabinet-rank men from consideration for the Vice-Presidency, he immediately phoned an old friend. "Hubert," Stevenson said, "it's you."

For weeks much of knowledgeable Washington had been betting that the final nod would go to Senator Hubert H. Humphrey of Minnesota. LBJ and Humphrey had both entered the Senate in 1949, the Texan hellbent for the Senate Establishment, the Minnesotan hellbent to raise hell. Yet from this unlikely start they had developed a personally warm and politically close relationship. They shared a small-town, non-Eastern background, great admiration for FDR, a bent toward policies of his coloration despite LBJ's conservatism in the Senate years, a delight in politicking and in making the legislative process work.

"Lyndon," Humphrey recalled, "was about the first of the Southerners I found I could talk to." Lyndon Johnson said, "Hubert wasn't like the other liberals. He wanted to get the job done."

Rapidly heading toward the Senate Majority Leadership, Senator Johnson had been exceedingly outgoing to Senator Humphrey, lecturing him on playing the game, teaching him the fine points, edging him into the favor of the inner circle. On his part, HHH functioned as the LBJ liaison man with the growing band of liberal senators. When Lyndon Johnson became Vice-President and the talk started that he would be dumped from the 1964 ticket, Senator Humphrey promised to do all in his power to stop such a move. After the assassination the President and the Senator had grown still closer. The two men talked long and intimately almost every day, by phone or at the White House, and HHH served as an LBJ lieutenant in the Senate.

In addition to President Johnson's respect and affection, Senator Humphrey had all kinds of other assets as a vice-presidential nominee in 1964. At that time he presented the picture of a man of widely recognized presidential stature, a political leader of seasoned skills, a tireless and colorful campaigner and an engaging human being with few mortal enemies. He was from the Midwest, an area that was one of the better bets for Goldwater, and had long since established a reputation for liberalism which balanced the lingering impression that LBJ was essentially conservative. This liberal appeal was the other side of Humphrey's one important liability. Though he did not raise the hackles of the South and of business to the extent that Robert Kennedy did, he certainly was no favorite of either. But in recent years, he had managed to soften even much of this antagonism and was now blunting it still further by persistent cultivation of these groups.

There is considerable circumstantial evidence that from the first, President Johnson had intended to name Humphrey as the vice-presidential candidate. Yet the senator had no real assurance that he was the choice until the day before he was nominated, and the convention and the country learned it still later. Lyndon Johnson was the most zealous practitioner of the cat-and-mouse game the White House has ever known. He liked to avoid revealing a decision until the last possible moment because he believed it would be better received if he slowly prepared the way by "building" opinion around it. He was also anxious, in his phrase, "to keep the options open"; he wanted to remain free to change his mind if circumstances suddenly altered. He was eager to have the maximum publicity for his decisions, and the longer he delayed announcing them, the more reporters filled the media with speculation about them. These hard-headed reasons were thoroughly entangled with LBJ personal traits. He reveled in the mastery over a situation which he achieved by creating an air of mystery and confusion; in suspense for the sake of suspense; in making sure that if something good came to a man, it came the hard way.

Before and after the elimination of Kennedy, President Johnson kept making it publicly plain that Humphrey was high on his list. All the while, at various times he spread the impression that he might well name Adlai Stevenson; Secretary of Defense Robert McNamara; Sargent Shriver; Mayor Robert F. Wagner of New York; Senators Thomas J. Dodd or Abraham A. Ribicoff of Connecticut, Eugene J. McCarthy of Minnesota, Edmund S. Muskie of Maine or John O. Pastore of Rhode Island; Governor Edmund G. Brown of California; Representative Cornelius E. Gallagher of New Jersey; even a mysterious university head whom the President would extol without naming and who was actually Clark Kerr, president of the University of California at Berkeley.

LBJ started these rumors through a variety of techniques, including an invention of which he was quite proud—the peripatetic press conference. He would let it be known that he felt like taking a walk and head briskly out of the Oval Office, usually for the driveway circling the South Lawn. The reporters scrambled after him, puffing along and clutching their notebooks, getting down his conversational hints about the vice-presidential choice with a maximum of confusion and a minimum of benevolence toward Lyndon Johnson.

The stocks of individual contenders went up and down. The news media kept talking the Vice-Presidency. Senator Humphrey's advocates grew more numerous, more concerted and more edgy.

Publicly the senator took it all with his accustomed good cheer. "Nobody has to woo me," he said with a laugh. "I'm old reliable, available Hubert. . . . The President sent Bobby Kennedy to the Far East. He sent Sargent Shriver to deliver a message to the Pope. Adlai Stevenson got to escort Mrs. Johnson to a theater in New York. So I asked the President, 'Who's going to enroll Lynda Bird in George Washington University? I'll volunteer.' "

But the quipping could not conceal the toll which the cat was taking on the mouse. Hubert Humphrey is an intelligent, proud and sensitive human being. Two weeks before the convention I watched him eating lunch in the White House Mess. Despite his ebullience, his face was that of a man who was being drained. These days he was telling friends the sad little story of the girl whose hero was the handsome captain of the football team. He would keep phoning her—always to ask her opinion of some other girl and never for a date.

. . .

As it became clear that President Johnson was going down to the wire with the announcement and the interest in the vice-presidential nomination mounted, it seemed to me that the situation might offer a special opportunity to the President. Perhaps he could simultaneously put his delay in a more favorable light, educate the public concerning the Office of the Vice-Presidency, and do something to make more sense out of it in terms of twentieth-century conditions. Like a good many Americans, I believed the Office could use a little sense-making. Perhaps someday the United States will adopt a constitutional amendment which provides for a merely caretaker government until a new President can be elected and—because he has been chosen in his own right —can therefore function without the stigma of having come to the White House through the accident of the Vice-Presidency. Meanwhile nothing can be done about the fact that the basic function of the Vice-President is simply to be there in case the Chief Executive dies or is incapacitated. But even under the existing system, a good deal can be changed to help prevent the vice-presidential Office from being a debilitating experience for any able and spirited man who occupies it, and to give more dignity and genuine usefulness to a high-ranking instrument of the United States government.

This involves both the manner and tone of the choice of the vice-presidential candidate and the definition of the functions of the Office. Nothing in the Constitution or in the laws of nature requires that the Vice-President must be, as Vice-President Harry Truman defined his role, "about as useful as a cow's fifth teat." Nothing decrees that he must feel as Vice-President Lyndon Johnson did. LBJ would wryly tell a no doubt apocryphal but symbolic story about his chauffeur, who had driven him as Senate Majority Leader and continued with him as Vice-President. Vice-President Johnson noticed that the driver, customarily a cheerful fellow, was becoming more and more grumpy. One morning he asked what was wrong and the chauffeur replied, "Well, I don't mean to be personal or anything like that, but my wife thinks I ought to get a job driving somebody important."

In midsummer, President Johnson had requested that I prepare a series of "background pieces"—historical and analytical memos—on various phases of past Democratic conventions. I usually sent these to him with the suggestions for his own actions implied rather than stated. (As always, the LBJ eye was fixed on FDR. Typically, the memo on acceptance speeches came back with a notation instructing, "Give me more on R in '32.") On August 16

I gave the President a ten-page memo concerning the vice-presidential nomination which was not only historical and analytical but contained a series of explicit recommendations.

The gist of it was that the public took the vice-presidential Office a good deal more seriously now than even a decade before, partly because of the assassination of John Kennedy and partly because of its slowly expanding activities. Consequently, the way that the President handled the nomination in the final stages was of considerable importance and could pay significant political dividends. To take advantage of the changing public attitude, I suggested, the process of nominating the vice-presidential candidate should not follow the usual pattern. In a few twentieth-century instances the presidential candidate had not been instrumental in naming his running mate. But customarily he chose the man and then the convention in a kind of demeaning afterthought went through the dreary rigmarole of pretending to pick him. "The basic premise of the following plan is that the choice should be accompanied by a maximum of dignity, candor and emphasis on the sense of responsibility you have felt in making it."

Trying to de-emphasize the appearance of cat-and-mouse, I proposed that President Johnson should avoid further public discussion of the vice-presidential candidate until after he himself was nominated. Attempting to dispose of any coy nonsense that the convention was making the decision, I went on to argue that near the beginning of his acceptance speech, the President should make the blunt statement that "you deem it to be your first important responsibility as a presidential candidate to recommend the vice-presidential nominee and that you will do so the next morning.

"The next morning—in an atmosphere of dignity in the White House—at a nationally telecast breakfast meeting attended by Congressional and Party leaders and a selection of prominent Democrats in business, labor, the professions and the arts, you would speak on the subject" of the Vice-Presidency, making the following main points:

"It has been traditional in America to treat the nomination of a Vice-President in a cavalier way. . . . But the country knows that it can no longer afford this attitude.

"Under our system, it is best for the presidential nominee to recommend the vice-presidential candidate and to do it forthrightly. Looking back over the political history of the twentieth century, a pattern is clear: in both parties, most of the highly qualified vice-presidential nominees have been named by the presidential candidate. Conversely, in most of the cases where an unqualified man was picked, the choice came about in a situation where the presidential candidate was not exercising a firm hand.*

"Naturally and understandably, the convention and party leaders—when left alone—are likely to pick a least-common-denominator vice-presidential candidate, out of some combination of the desires to placate a losing faction, achieve regional balance and recognize policy differences within the party.

"Because of the foregoing, you have been giving long and careful consideration to the matter. . . . In your thinking, you have not dismissed regional balance and the recognition of different elements within the party. These are entirely legitimate considerations under our system. But you have kept paramount the question: What man—by natural ability, character, temperament, governmental experience and political philosophy—is the best qualified to perform the expanding duties of the Vice-Presidency and, above all, to succeed to the Presidency?

"Having named the man and briefly stated his qualifications, you would then go on to say that with such a man in the Vice-Presidency, it is possible for you to move ahead with a program that is long overdue—real steps to increase the dignity, responsibilities and activities of the Vice-Presidency. . . .

"Consequently, after the election of the Democratic ticket, you intend to (a) set up an office of the Vice-Presidency *in the White House;* (b) have the V.P. continue to sit with the Cabinet and the Security Council; (c) assign to the V.P. overall supervision of two programs essential to the health of the American society—the amelioration of poverty and the elimination of discrimination; (d) assign to the V.P. the duty of making systematic trips to chosen parts of the world, with a view to reporting to the President and—if the President approves—to the Congress suggested steps that might be taken to advance peace; (e) assign to the V.P. particular types of ceremonial duties now performed by the President, thus starting the tradition that under certain circumstances citizens or foreign dignitaries can be honored in full measure by the V.P."

In other sections of the memo, seeking a further way to cut down the artificiality surrounding the choice of the vice-presidential candidate, I suggested that the President arrange with the

---

* *The breakdown I gave the President was as follows: Since 1900, six men have been nominated for the Vice-Presidency whose qualifications were highly dubious. Only one of these six was chosen by the presidential candidate. On the other hand, there were also six instances in which the qualifications of the men were outstanding. Five of these six were designated by the head of the ticket.*

convention leaders "to eliminate the wearisome and phony-appearing nominating speeches, roll call, etc."

Certainly Lyndon Johnson, who had sat brooding in the Vice-Presidency for three miserable years, could have found nothing revolutionary in this memo. He had not the slightest intention of following any suggestion that he stop talking publicly about the Vice-Presidency until after his own nomination; if anything, he stepped up his mentions of the subject. He also rejected the idea that he should discuss his attitude toward the Office in a full-dress speech. But the week after he received the memo he invited a group of newspapermen to the White House for a "background" session on the Vice-Presidency. President Johnson told the reporters that he had arranged to have "research done on the background and potentialities of the office" and that, having mulled it over carefully, he had reached certain conclusions. Then, as he often did when he found a memo congenial—this time frequently referring to white cards in his hand—he followed most of its points and much of its language down the line. This included his comments on the changed attitude of the public toward the Vice-President, the historical reasons why he was going to make a forthright choice of the candidate, the balance between traditional considerations and bedrock qualifications he was keeping in mind, the fact that he would name the man from the dignity of the White House, and the specifics of the changed circumstances and greatly broadened assignments he planned for the next Vice-President.

Reporters came away from the meeting writing that LBJ, in the words of one newsman, intended to "make his Vice-President the busiest and most influential in American history." But just who was this busy and influential man to be? During the weekend of August 22, right before the opening of the convention, President Johnson filled the media with another spate of stories on the theme that he was wondering whether the nominee had better not be a Catholic. With Kennedy eliminated, wouldn't Catholic voters feel they had a right to a Catholic substitution, and wasn't the Republican vice-presidential nominee, William Miller, a Catholic? Perhaps the choice should be a man not previously mentioned—the Catholic Senate Majority Leader, Mike Mansfield of Montana—or Senator Eugene McCarthy. Rumors from the White House particularly boomed McCarthy. Reporters spread the word that LBJ was listening attentively to his old buddy, Governor John Connally of Texas, who was pushing McCarthy not only as a Catholic but on the ground that he would annoy the South less than Humphrey.

The lowering of the odds on McCarthy, at the urging of Connally, added another strange note to the bizarre lottery. This second senator from Minnesota emanated little natural appeal for a Lyndon Johnson or a John Connally. He had a detached, faintly smiling, elliptical manner which his friends called intellectual and his enemies called cynical. His humor was not hail-fellow camaraderie; it was a cutting, at times mordant wit. He had not taken a major part in the day-by-day operations of the Senate, and no legislation of prime importance was associated with him. Though a Northern liberal, his name produced little response among labor or minority groups. McCarthy was a red flag to the Kennedyites, whom President Johnson was anxious not to rouse. At the 1960 convention, when the JFK bandwagon was in full evidence, he had stood up and made an eloquent speech for Adlai Stevenson which stole the show. "He's a goddamned pixie, that's what he is," a worried LBJ aide said to me when I arrived in Atlantic City.

But the pixie was not without characteristics which gave credence to the reports that he would be the vice-presidential choice. Having backed Stevenson in 1960, McCarthy made it plain that he next preferred Lyndon Johnson. He was a Catholic, just as authentic a Midwesterner as Humphrey, and handsome in a way to stir female Metroamerica ("a Stevenson with sex appeal," the same LBJ man remarked to me). McCarthy had another quality which was now assumed to be important to President Johnson; selecting him would be much more of a surprise than choosing Humphrey.

Over everything, vice-presidential or otherwise, a final air of mystery gathered. Of course the President was going to Atlantic City to accept his own nomination—or was he? At a press conference a reporter inquired about his travel plans.

A. With regard to the convention, I expect to go up later Thursday evening—I don't know what time—if I go at all. . . .

Q. Mr. President, did I understand that you might not go to Atlantic City at all?

A. No.

Q. I misunderstood.

A. Evidently. I didn't say I would, or I wouldn't.

Press Secretary George Reedy's press briefings now reached the ultimate travesty of communication.

Q. Can you give us any indication of timing?

A. No.

Q. Can you tell us anything about the President's travel plans?

A. I have nothing on the schedule yet.

Q. Do you know when you will have the schedule?

A. No.

Q. If Mr. Johnson is nominated by the convention, when will we get his speech?

A. I really couldn't tell you that yet. You have too many ifs in there. If you take the ifs out, that won't help either.

Finally, mercilessly badgered by the press, mercilessly reined in by his boss, Reedy had enough.

Q. Do you expect any additions to the President's published schedule?

George Reedy gazed out the window. "I am a man," he said, "who always looks forward to each fresh and inspiring experience of the day. I find I am always surprised by the delightfully unexpected."

The convention opened on a muggy Monday, August 24. Senator Humphrey arrived in Atlantic City with a flourish of high spirits that merely emphasized his nervousness. His men had set up headquarters on a whole floor of the Shelburne Hotel. Word came from an LBJ aide, "Take it easy," and Humphrey decided to share a modest, single-switchboard headquarters with McCarthy.

That first evening trouble broke. Mississippi had sent its usual delegation of lily-white party functionaries, and a second group, sixty-four Negroes and four whites, declared that they represented the Mississippi Freedom Democratic Party and should be recognized as the legitimate delegation. Angrily, the MFDP moved toward a floor fight.

Such a spectacle, televised across the country, could have its consequences. Depending on which way the decision went, it might alienate Southerners and increase white backlash, or anger Negro voters and white liberals. Inevitably Humphrey, as a leading civil rights figure, was involved. President Johnson left the senator on his own and his phone calls to Atlantic City went to others. Uneasiness spread through Humphrey headquarters that the President was indeed keeping his options open and that if the senator emerged from the fracas too controversial a figure, LBJ would discard him. By noon of Tuesday—in part through Humphrey's efforts—enough of a compromise was reached on the Mississippi quarrel to avoid a floor fight.

By now an overpowering pro-Humphrey opinion had built up within the Democratic party organization. Only hours remained to drain any further publicity from the vice-presidential choice. President Johnson arrived at final details. Proceeding along the lines indicated by his "backgrounder" with the press, he would announce his vice-presidential "recommendation" from the White House the next day, Wednesday, have the convention name him-

self and Humphrey on Wednesday evening without the folderol of
roll calls, and then fly to Atlantic City on Thursday to deliver his
acceptance speech. Hubert Humphrey, still not sure he was the
choice, sat in his hotel suite beaten into a limpness compounded
of soaring expectations and grinding anxiety.

On Tuesday afternoon LBJ acted. He phoned Walter Jenkins
in Atlantic City and told him to arrange a talk between James
Rowe and Humphrey. Jenkins took down the rest of the President's
lengthy, precise directions in his shorthand. Rowe hurried to find
Humphrey, led the senator and Mrs. Humphrey to his suite at the
Pageant Motor Inn, motioned Humphrey into the bedroom and
closed the door. Rowe told Humphrey: You are the Democratic
nominee for Vice-President. Then he gave the rest of the LBJ message, a detailed list of do's and don'ts, including an emphatic instruction that the senator read carefully the Washington *Star* story
resulting from the "background" session on the Vice-Presidency.
That article would make clear why the President had picked him
and what he planned for him as Vice-President.

In a state of exhausted elation, Humphrey turned to the door
to tell his waiting wife. Rowe stopped him; President Johnson had
ordered total secrecy.

Not even my wife? the senator exploded. Muriel has got to
know.

Rowe was embarrassed. All right, he said. But no one else,
absolutely no one.

So Senator and Mrs. Humphrey knew but the country did not,
and the game was not quite over. On Wednesday morning President Johnson rose at five o'clock, whirled through some White
House business and put in call after call to the Pageant Motor Inn.
He was bothered; the convention was proving a terrible television
show. As Jack Gould of the *New York Times* wrote: "You can almost hear people clicking off their sets all over the country." Worse
still, with little else to discuss, television newsmen kept interview-
ing delegates about the civil rights troubles of the Democratic
party.

In the course of the morning President Johnson happened to
talk on the phone with Pierre Salinger, who was in California campaigning for senator. When the President mentioned the convention doldrums, Salinger had a suggestion. Why not abandon the
plan of naming the vice-presidential candidate from the White
House, fly to Atlantic City ahead of time and announce him from
the podium of the convention on Wednesday night?

Lyndon Johnson jumped at the idea. No President had ever
designated his running mate in a speech made to the delegates.

This would be the final splash; this would get the television sets clicking on again. A new schedule was arranged so that President Johnson would arrive at Convention Hall about nine-thirty Wednesday evening—the start of the evening's television watching on the West Coast and not too late for the East.

In Atlantic City, Hubert Humphrey was following instructions. Late Wednesday morning he headed for the airport to board a plane for Washington, assuming that he would travel alone. That was not the LBJ plan; Senator Eugene McCarthy was also to be aboard so that reporters would not know which man was the vice-presidential nominee. But McCarthy had become convinced that he was not the choice, and he was irritated by being made part of what he considered a demeaning charade. Perhaps, too, he was influenced by a kind of fatalistic languor that seemed to mark many of his political activities—a languor that particularly applied to the Vice-Presidency.*

McCarthy sent a telegram to President Johnson removing himself as a contender for the vice-presidential nomination. Quickly Lyndon Johnson found a substitute. When Humphrey reached the plane at the Atlantic City airport he was taken aback to see Senator Thomas Dodd of Connecticut.

In Washington it was near lunchtime, and the President turned to a group of reporters in his office. "Y'all want to take a walk today?" The most peripatetic of all the peripatetic press conferences —the one that Rowland Sweeney of the Chicago *Sun-Times* called the "Death March"—was at hand.

Off the President went, trailed by some sixty reporters around the quarter-mile oval driveway in the 89-degree heat. Lyndon Johnson heard Him and Her yapping. "Let's get the dogs," he said. "They heard you talkin' and they want to go too." On the fourth lap the President turned the panting beagles over to a Secret Service man. The panting reporters kept walking.

Lyndon Johnson talked on and on—about how good Senator John Pastore's keynote speech had been ("My barber told me it made him proud to be an American"), about the decisiveness of Speaker McCormack as the convention chairman ("I must say I admired him when he seated that Mississippi delegation and said

* *In 1968, campaigning for the presidential nomination in Rushville, Indiana, McCarthy was asked whom he would name as his vice-presidential candidate if he won the nomination. He replied, "Actually, that's the last choice I would make. You fill all the important offices first. . . . The more important choices are Secretary of State and Attorney General. If you pick those right and you're succeeded by your Vice-President, he can't do much wrong anyway. At least we hope not. He's pretty much down the chute at that point anyway."*

in one breath, 'All those in favor say aye, all those opposed no, motion carried' "). He fished in his pocket for the results of a medical examination he had taken after a nine-lap walk earlier in the week. "Whoops," said the President, "that's a poll." He read off the poll. Sixty-eight percent of the women, 70 percent of voters aged twenty-one to thirty-four, 73 percent of the Catholics, 86 percent of the Negroes, 97 percent of the Jews favored Lyndon Johnson.

But what about the vice-presidential nomination? reporters pressed.

"How can I tell you something I haven't made up my mind about?" The President offered the information that Senators Dodd and Humphrey were coming to see him that afternoon to give him "their advice, recommendations, etc." about the Vice-Presidency.

By the tenth lap, reporters were dropping out to sit under the shade trees. Others peeled off their soaked jackets and fought on. The President had lots more to talk about, including the medical report, which he had now found. He read the words of the four physicians: " 'His exercise tolerance continues to be superb. There is no health reason why he could not continue an active, vigorous life.' "

After ninety-five minutes and fifteen laps—about four miles— it was over. Lyndon Johnson turned to the women reporters who had stuck with him. "I'm going to give you a medal," he said and handed them newly minted likenesses of LBJ.

Humphrey *and* Dodd on their way to the White House? Dodd was a Communist-chasing nonentity from the small state of Connecticut, Hardingesque of face and Hardingesque in tendencies, but a loyal trooper of Lyndon Johnson in the old Senate days, a Catholic and, above all, a spectacular surprise. Reporters filed stories that Dodd might well be the choice.

Dodd and Humphrey arrived at the White House and talked with President Johnson in separate sessions. Hubert Humphrey did not forget his instructions. When he emerged and newsmen asked the inevitable question, he said that he knew nothing about the vice-presidential choice and that he had "not talked with the President about the subject in more than a month."

At seven o'clock Lyndon Johnson called another press conference, this time in the Oval Office. He wanted the reporters to have a drink with him in celebration of his birthday which was coming the next day, but they would have to cut the occasion short. He was going to Atlantic City not tomorrow but tonight, in a plane with Senators Dodd and Humphrey, to recommend the vice-presidential candidate to the convention.

A newsman asked, "Are you going to tell the man privately before you announce the decision?"

"I have not gone into that. I have not thought of it. I will think of it and you will be on the plane, so you can ask me, and I will let you know what I decide—if you are available. I don't know whether I can reach him."

The reporters piled up the stairs to the private living quarters for the drinks and canapés. A woman correspondent peered around a half-open door, beat a hasty retreat. "My God, the President is in his underwear!" He emerged dressed for the convention and spent most of the party watching the convention proceedings on television. "I feel wonderful, very relaxed," he told a newsman.

At Andrews Air Force Base, Senators Dodd and Humphrey and the reporters gathered with the President for the flight to Atlantic City. Was it an LBJ impulse? Was it calculation that the suspense had been carried far enough? Was it sheer exuberance? On the landing strip Lyndon Johnson suddenly took Hubert Humphrey by the arm and led him over to a group of reporters. "I want you to meet the next Vice-President of the United States."

Beaming, the President boarded *Air Force One*, switched on the television set and turned to Senator Humphrey. "All right," he said, "we've got the show on the road."

The Prize

B y the time *Air Force One* set down on Wednesday evening, Atlantic City was in the full throes of being Atlantic City. The time-worn resort had not built a major hotel since the crash of 1929, and the delegates were scattered along five miles of ocean-front, most of them far from the friendly bourbon with old George and the gratifying handshake from the party chieftains. Many found themselves in hotels or boardinghouses that featured limping elevators, falling plaster, detachable doorknobs and dubious linen. Adlai Stevenson was established in yesteryear's splendor at the Hotel Traymore. He came grimacing out of an elevator carrying six bottles, sans bellboys, to a luncheon he was giving, sans waiters, and delivered himself of the observation, "I never thought one city could manage to get things so bitched up."

Along the boardwalk the food delicacies ranged from frankfurters cooked in champagne to bananas coated with chocolate. The souvenirs included a cocktail shaker shaped like a bedpan, rubber-and-nylon "Golden Goddess Shrunken Heads," and Kennedy mementos for every pocketbook and every variety of mawkishness —pistachio-covered Kennedy coins to be eaten (10 cents), sky-blue "JFK Drinking Glasses" for your highball ($1.95), a prayer, inscribed in gilt letters and entitled "Special Delivery from Heaven" ($2.95). Delegates passed around the gibes, "Welcome to Appalachia-by-the-Sea" and "This is the original Bay of Pigs."

But Atlantic City, like an aging harridan, had a way of adjusting to the customer, and she did not entirely fail her multimillion-dollar visitor. When the Democratic convention began, the most conspicuous object in town, atop the Million Dollar Pier, was a 160-by-36-foot billboard picturing a firm, friendly Barry Goldwater and declaring: "In Your Heart You Know He's Right." Good Democrats fretted, but soon all was well. For $365, at six A.M. the day President Johnson was to arrive, the billboard company added a forty-by-four-foot P.S. reading: "Yes—Extreme Right." Everywhere, everything was LBJ. The President's favorite entertainer, Carol Channing, the bubbly, fog-voiced star of *Hello, Dolly!*, was in town to belt out again and again, "Hello, Lyndon!" The barbecue was prescribed for entertaining, heaped seafood replacing heaped beef. The convention pet was seventeen-year-old Luci Baines Johnson, now impishly drawing press photographers into the surf to get a shot of her, now listening big-eyed in the buffet line while Senator Edmund Muskie of Maine explained how to tell a boy lobster from a girl lobster. The reigning hostess was that tried-and-true Johnsonian, Mrs. Perle Mesta. This week she swept into Atlantic City, once again the hostess with the mostest, each night partying seven to eight hundred VIP's and untold and none-too-unwanted gate crashers. Her base was a villa, Atlantic City style, with multicolored rock gardens, rampant foliage, a waterfall in the living room and a patio with a platform surrounded by cherubs, from which the hostess or a dignitary, when so moved, could address the assemblage.

The Pageant Motor Inn put on its best airs for the White House staff. The chrome bric-a-brac of the rooms was shining; the swimming pool was maintained at an immaculate chlorine green. The telephone operator would start to snarl, catch herself and say, "I'm sorry, sir, we're so busy, sir." The clerks remembered too, until the pressures came and they reverted to Runyonesque grunts. New Jersey's state police, straight-faced and portentous in their pale blue and orange-chevroned uniforms, kept scanning their lists to make sure, for the fifth time that day, that a staff member was okay to go upstairs. Only occasionally did they lounge around the balcony and ogle the secretaries and wives. Only once, at two o'clock in the morning, off duty and filled with beer, did they foam into a swimming party, tossing each other into the chlorine with happy oaths and bellows.

When President Johnson arrived on Wednesday evening, he was taken to Room 114 of the motel, where he watched on television as the convention finished its job of nominating him by acclamation. The President knew all the details about the towering gray Convention Hall across the street and they did not displease him. The hall itself, covering seven acres, is the world's largest auditorium. The 5,260 delegates were the greatest number at any American nominating convention up to that time. Now LBJ serenely watched the demonstration for him mount into a proper bedlam. Californians banged garbage-can lids together, Iowans yelled and waved cornstalks, balloons six feet in diameter floated toward the ceiling, Missouri-mule standards lurched along the aisles. The tremendous organ boomed out "Hello, Lyndon!" "Yellow Rose of Texas" and "The Eyes of Texas Are Upon You," took a huge breath and played them all over again. A large, sunkist and abundantly relaxed female delegate from Florida kept crowding the television screen with a poster which declared definitively, "We absolutely adore Lyndon."

As the demonstration neared the end of its planned twenty minutes, President Johnson left the motel and entered Convention Hall to name Senator Humphrey. He may have abandoned his vice-presidential plan to the extent of naming the selection at Atlantic City rather than the White House. But he made the announcement in a speech which briefly included the main points of his "background" session with the press, and when he designated "my close, my long-time, my trusted colleague, Senator Hubert Humphrey of Minnesota," the convention followed his original instruction and nominated the senator in a quick roar of acclamation. For the first time both men on the national ticket of a major party, their selection preordained, had been named without the farce of a long string of speeches and a roll call.

The next morning President Johnson flew to Winchester, Virginia, to attend the funeral of Mrs. Harry Byrd, the wife of his old ally and foe in so many Senate actions. Lyndon Johnson was an emotional man at funerals and weddings. As Senator Byrd was about to drive away, the President reached into the car, grasped his hand and kissed it. In the country where LBJ grew up, the kissing of men by men was a custom of close sentiment, and there are earlier photographs of this type. I cannot imagine anyone attributing effeminacy to Lyndon Johnson, but so intense was his concern with every facet of his public image that these previous pictures were always kept secret. The publication of the photograph at the Byrd funeral, a genuinely moving picture, produced one of the few moments of strong presidential irritation during the triumphal convention week.

On Thursday afternoon he flew back to Atlantic City, staying at the large white stucco house that had been loaned to the Johnsons by Hess H. Rosenbloom, brother of the owner of the Baltimore Colts. That evening the memorial film of President Kennedy was to be shown, introduced by Robert Kennedy, and President Johnson did not attend. Some delegates muttered that he was discourteous and afraid to face the Kennedy emotion. Actually, once the occasion was at hand, Lyndon Johnson simply felt that he did not want to intrude on a Kennedy occasion.

It was an hour unique in the history of American politics. As Robert Kennedy stepped forward to the podium, the delegates, first in the back rows, then up and down the hall, rose in a storm of applause. There was no music, no parading, no yelling, just the din coming from the heartfelt clapping of thousands of hands. The brother stood stock-still, looking small and thin in his black suit and black tie, most of the time his head bowed and his eyes closed, frequently biting his lip. Occasionally the applause receded and he would start, "Mr. Chairman, Mr. Chairman—" Again the ovation cut him off. Once he smiled, a wisp of a smile, and tears came to his eyes. After sixteen minutes the great hall, reluctantly, let him proceed.

"Mr. Chairman, I want—" Robert Kennedy began, and his voice broke. He started again and delivered his brief speech in a quiet voice, with few gestures and in sentences at times garbled by emotion. Near the end he spoke directly of his feeling for his murdered brother. "When I think of President Kennedy, I think of what Shakespeare said in *Romeo and Juliet:*

> When he shall die,
> Take him and cut him out in little
> stars,
> And he will make the face of Heaven
> so fine
> That all the world will be in love
> with night
> And pay no worship to the garish
> sun.

The memorial film took over on the giant screen. In the presidential box, sweeping low over the hall, Mrs. Johnson, the two Johnson girls and Mrs. Robert Kennedy sat in tightly controlled composure. The audience watched in a hush, the quiet broken only by starts of laughter as the familiar voice spoke a well-remembered witticism. When the lights went on again, thousands were wiping their eyes.

Lyndon Johnson was making last-minute changes in his acceptance speech. He was eager that this address, more than any he had ever delivered, should be memorable in the manner of FDR's ringing 1932 acceptance speech, which brought the phrase "New Deal" into the language. He had studied intensely the detailed analysis of that address he asked me to make, and he had kept after the whole White House staff to submit ideas and drafts and conferred with scores of other people. Picking here and there from various versions of the speech, he had the drafts rewritten and re-rewritten. At dinnertime on the evening of delivery, Horace Busby and Richard Goodwin were holed up in a second-floor room of the motel, tearing the manuscript apart once again and frantically reconstructing it. This time Lyndon Johnson was trying too hard.

Moments after the memorial film ended, the President entered his box at Convention Hall. He sat restlessly, hunching back and forth as Senator Humphrey delivered his vice-presidential acceptance speech. Hubert Humphrey had gone through years of political frustration, often boomed but never chosen for President or Vice-President. As I walked to Convention Hall I ran into one of his old friends who remarked, "What I'm remembering—and maybe what he's remembering—is the day Kennedy crushed him in the West Virginia primary and he sat in the hotel room choked up and saying, 'It was like the corner grocer running against a chain store.' " This night the corner grocer was in the big time; he seized the moment. Burnished, confident and impish, he waded into the convention crowd.

"Most Democrats and Republicans in the Senate voted for an eleven-and-a-half-billion-dollar tax cut for American citizens and American business—but not Senator Goldwater." Most had voted for the civil rights bill—but not Senator Goldwater. "Most . . . but not"—the crowd was taking up the beat and HHH broke into one of his enormous smiles. Jubilantly he and his audience chanted along in the cadence of assault.

It would have been difficult to follow this Hubert Humphrey with any speech; President Johnson did not have much of a speech. It contained not a single memorable phrase, no tang or vault, little to pull the delegates or the television audience out of their evening lethargy. But the roars came automatically, and except for the fact that the President kept asking people the next day, "It went over big, don't you think?" all was proceeding apace.

That Thursday, August 27, 1964, was Lyndon Johnson's birthday, and as soon as the proceedings ended, four thousand carefully chosen guests headed for the Grand Ballroom of Convention Hall. Caterer Roy Waldron, from Dallas, talked Dallasatian statistics: 18,000 hors d'oeuvre, 6,000 pounds of ice, 9,000 serving dishes, 36 coffee urns, 20,000 napkins and 12 giant birthday cakes. Toastmaster Danny Thomas intoned, "Fifty-six years ago a boy was born to the soil of Texas," and out from the wrappings came one of the cakes, a ten-by-six-foot production, baked in the shape of the United States with Arizona smaller than Arizona and Texas bigger than Texas. LBJ sheared off Arizona with one pass and cut up Texas for his family and the Humphreys. The roar of applause was like the Rio Grande in flood.

Outside, the celebration had begun well before the presidential acceptance speech, and it kept on mounting. Just beyond the breakers, a flotilla of two hundred small boats blinked and tootled. Along the boardwalk thirty-one school bands, Irish-American jiggers, Italian-American choruses, Russian-American folk dancers and eleven other ethnic groups blared, strutted, pirouetted. Everything was kept in careful balance. When "The Sons of the Auld Sod" and "The Sons of the Land of Milk and Honey" quarreled over position in the parade, the units were placed side by side. When the crowd yelled for an encore of an Irish jig, the marshal discovered that "popular demand" required another rendition from the Jewish chorus. Past one o'clock in the morning came the finale, three tons of gunpowder lighting the skies with a six-hundred-square-foot portrait of Lyndon Baines Johnson in red, white and blue.

Lyndon Baines Johnson, fifty-six years old, just nominated for the Presidency of the United States on a ticket that could not lose and nominated in exactly the way he wanted it done, looked tired, so tired that his massive shoulders seemed less support than burden. Still, he had a grin and an observation.

"I've been going to conventions since 1928 and this one is the best of all."

The next day President Johnson bundled his family and the Humphreys into planes for the ranch. It was time, he said, for some rest and a bit of strategy planning "in the shade of the live oaks on the banks of the Pedernales."

The oaks had never been more serene, the Pedernales more sparkling, but somehow it was not a restful weekend. President and Candidate Johnson kept tramping Hubert Humphrey, the press and anybody else in sight around the ranch, rushing them all off for an electioneering speech at a local birthday celebration, nudging them for reactions to his thoughts about the campaign. Back at the ranch, hour after hour LBJ sat in his big colorful living room, surrounded by a stream of summoned visitors, planning, worrying, talking and talking the right tactics against "this funny fellow."

A strange campaign was coming up, no doubt, with the Republicans led by the most improbable major party candidate of the twentieth century. In all the fury of pro- and anti-Goldwater feeling at the time, it was easy to forget just who Barry Goldwater was. He was the handsome, friendly son of Arizona department-store money. Life had been easy and he was easygoing. He ambled through a year and a half at the University of Arizona, ambled out into a front-office job in the department store. His executive manner, employees remembered, was "informal"; once, catching a mouse in the store, he put it in a pneumatic change tube and rushed upstairs to watch the cashier's reaction. He had occasional ideas, some of which were big sellers—most notably, men's shorts decorated with red ants which he called "Antsy Pants." After World War II service as a ferry pilot, largely in the India-Burma theater, Goldwater began dabbling in politics. In the Eisenhower year of 1952 he tried for the United States Senate and was elected, he remarked amiably, as "the greatest coattail rider in the business."

The senator liked to think of himself as a kind of twentieth-century frontiersman, the more so because in Arizona, Westernism was status and the Goldwater family, of Jewish merchant background, did not call up the Daniel Boone tradition. He delighted in he-man things—the rugged outdoors of Arizona, jet planes, man-to-man talks with generals and admirals, the Navajo tattoos on his left hand, electronic gadgets like the one at his home which at sunrise ran up the Stars and Stripes and at sunset brought it down. He admired the he-man approach to national problems. "The trouble with the so-called liberal today," Goldwater liked to say, "is that he doesn't understand straightforward simplicity. The answers to America's problems are simple."

The senator was not especially bright and he knew it. Casually he remarked, "I'm not even sure I've got the brains to be President." He had no compelling drive for power. In the Senate he was a well-liked backbencher, at first not taken very seriously by his colleagues. But with the death of Senator Robert Taft, conservative Americans were hungry for a leader and they began fixing their attention on the pleasant, good-looking Arizonan with the square jaw and the appealing way of speaking their opinions and interests. In turn he began to think of himself, with considerable pride, as "a salesman of conservatism."

When the movement to nominate Barry Goldwater for President developed, one of its less zealous devotees was Barry Goldwater. "It certainly wasn't something that was burning a hole in me," he recalled later. He had large doubts whether a "real conservative" like himself could possibly win; he did not know how much he wanted to try. Yet the enthusiasm of his backers was contagious and he came to look forward to running against President Kennedy in 1964—"not that I thought I would have beaten him but it would have given me a chance to put my ideas up against his on television." Then John Kennedy was murdered and that night Goldwater turned to his wife Peggy and said, "The hell with this Presidency thing." When his supporters kept pushing and the senator entered the New Hampshire primary in the Spring of 1964, only to be beaten by Richard Nixon, he shrugged. "Well, that's that." But as he was to learn, "I'd underestimated the 'Draft Goldwater' movement."

Now this most curious candidate was setting out on a most curious campaign. At times he was propelled by the fervor—in thousands of cases, the fanaticism—of his supporters and by the ambition, however flickering, that any man has. Then he sought election with driving vigor and hell-and-damnation themes. At other times he was dogged by a feeling of futility and his lack of pleasure in the hullabaloo of campaigning. He could come to the platform during a tremendous ovation, stand with the spotlights and the cheers beating down on him, waving and smiling without zest and looking as if he wished he were back with his planes and his gadgets and his desert.

From the day of Goldwater's nomination, commentators kept reminding him that in recent American elections the broad middle road had been the path of political victory and that he would benefit richly from shifting or at least softening some of his positions. Except in trivial ways, he did not alter the stance he had taken at the convention. He continued to speak extreme conservatism—opposition to almost every major piece of social legislation passed since 1929, hostility to the doctrine of coexistence with the Communist powers, distaste for most of the fundamental trends of American life since World War II. Many of his speeches sounded like those of a man who would much rather be right than President or at least of a man, pretty sure he was not going to be President, who saw no reason why he should not take the opportunity to be right.

On the banks of the Pedernales and in the strategy conversations that followed his return to Washington, President Johnson saw no reason to alter the campaign plan he was moving toward well before Goldwater became the definite choice of the Republicans. To him, the naming of an extreme conservative merely made the strategy seem that much more desirable. He would not run as a fighting liberal, as Franklin Roosevelt had done in 1936 or Harry Truman in 1948, nor would he campaign with the strong undertone of conservatism that marked the Eisenhower drives of 1952 and 1956. By the fall of 1964 Lyndon Johnson was more convinced than ever that a genuine consensus existed in the United States. He believed that it amounted, in domestic affairs, to an acceptance of the New Deal and of a continuing extension of New Deal-type legislation; in foreign affairs, to a willingness to move along, in however troubled a way, with efforts to find a workable state of coexistence with the Communist powers. He himself had become more and more emotionally committed to the attitudes associated with this consensus. He thought they were good politics; good for the national security and the prosperity of the country; above all, good for furthering that national unity which he valued so highly. He would campaign as a relatively nonpartisan candidate with an overriding appeal for harmony built around this consensus—as "President of all the people," to use the phrase that was becoming basic to his conception of the campaign. His major emphasis would be on domestic affairs, the area in which he was most interested and in which he believed the American people were most interested.

In discussions about more specific campaign procedures LBJ advisers kept bringing up party organization, but they were talking into the wind. President Johnson remained a devotee of the Texas tradition of personalized politics. The campaign was the candidate; you got together your friends and allies, raised the money and went at it. Tradition aside, he was as little ready to delegate political authority as he was to abdicate any other part of his realm, and he was the more standoffish about the Democratic National Committee because it contained a number of men who had made promises of support to him before 1960 and then, he was convinced, never really delivered.

Well before Dallas, the JFK forces had been planning for 1964. Since then many JFK aides may have resigned but some of the "Irish Mafia"—those whose role was primarily political—had stayed on and they gave every indication of being ready to work hard for the new ticket. With the advent of the campaign, LBJ bestowed upon them glowing words and important responsibilities, especially their leader Lawrence O'Brien. President Johnson was also drawing into the campaign his own people, not only James Rowe but two men who had long worked with him in Texas politics, Clifton C. Carter and W. Marvin Watson. Carter was now officially connected with the Democratic National Committee, partly to function for the committee and partly to keep an LBJ eye on the committeemen. Watson, executive assistant to the president of the Lone Star Steel Company in Daingerfield, Texas, was spending a good deal of his time performing political chores for the President, such as handling sensitive administrative tasks at the Atlantic City convention. O'Brien and Rowe tried to co-ordinate things, and at times they tried to co-ordinate each other. And that was about it at the top level. Throughout the campaign nothing approaching an organization of authority and duties existed, and the lines of communication from Washington down to the precinct levels were loose and confused. Lyndon Johnson never named a campaign manager; everybody knew who that was.

The President had a theory about campaigns which he had

tested over the years and in which he had considerable, if inter-mittent, confidence. He did not acquiesce in "Farley's law"—the dictum of FDR's legendary campaign manager that few votes are changed between Labor Day and the election. On the contrary, LBJ was sure that huge numbers of votes could be shifted by a campaign that moved through three phases which he summarized as "Inform, Convert, Agitate." In the first period, the voters were informed, that is, the candidate brought the issues to the fore in the way that he wanted them presented. The second period, con-version, put the emphasis on winning over the hostile or the doubt-ful. In the final stage, agitation, the candidate went into a furious effort to create an atmosphere of intense interest, and to make sure that the faithful and the converted actually went to the polls. Throughout—and this was of prime importance—the candidate gave every appearance of being so concerned with the issues that he had little interest in attacking the feckless fellow who pre-sumed to oppose him.

Some advisers urged that from the beginning President John-son should make extensive, openly political tours, and wherever he was, should campaign directly. Others strongly favored his follow-ing the precedent of a number of previous incumbent Presidents. Governor John Connally, so long an LBJ intimate, put the argument succinctly: Lyndon Johnson was way ahead now; he could lose votes only by making mistakes, and the less he campaigned openly, the less likely he was to make them. The President should campaign primarily by *being* President, remaining mostly in Washington and presenting a picture of a Chief Executive so concerned with the welfare of the nation that he had little time to chase votes.

LBJ responded to this argument. It fitted in with his desire to run as "President of all the people," and he was especially impressed by the fact that Franklin Roosevelt had adopted the stance for much of the campaigns of 1940 and 1944. By Labor Day he had definitely accepted the strategy for the period through "informing," perhaps in a modified form through "conversion," and even part of "agitation." "We have a job to do here," he was telling the country in September, "and we are going to try to do this first. When, as, and if we can, we will make as many appearances as we think we can without neglecting the interests of the nation."

President Johnson managed, when, as, and if he could, to make a remarkable number of appearances without neglecting the na-tion. There were dams and airports to dedicate and when Hurri-cane Dora struck, he was in Florida before people could start pick-ing up the pieces. He made sustained speaking trips, one all the way to the West Coast, and somehow his remarks got across forcefully the benefits to Americans from Democratic social legislation and the dangers of a reckless foreign policy.

But each trip had a conspicuous presidential aura, and whatever Lyndon Johnson said, in whatever tone, was always incidental to a higher theme. In Detroit he pounded the lectern, shouted until his voice broke, leaned so far forward that he was practically nose to nose with the front row of the audience. Nevertheless, the speech was set within the context of his statement that "I have come here in Cadillac Square to call for national unity." In Sacramento he was greeted by a shrieking partisan crowd of one hundred thousand. "Now how is *that* for a turnout?" he winked to an aide and launched into the declaration: "I come as no partisan. I come as President of all the people of the United States, to speak to all the nation, and for the nation, to all the world." In Harrisburg the occasion was a dinner sponsored by the Pennsylvania State Democratic Committee. President Johnson praised his Republican predecessor Dwight Eisenhower and Republican Governor William W. Scranton lavishly, and his text was from that eminent nonpartisan George Washington, who had warned against " 'factionalism' " or agitating " 'the community with ill-founded jealousies and false alarms' " and who, as the speech went on, sounded more and more like the kind of prudent, progressive leader who would readily have understood the need for Medicare and federal aid to education and for a foreign policy remarkably like that of Lyndon Johnson.

When President Johnson went to El Paso for the signing of a treaty with Mexico over the long-disputed Chamizal tract of land, I learned just how much above-the-battle and nonpartisan everything was being kept. I wanted the President to talk more about foreign policy in the campaign to soften the feeling that he was essentially only a domestic affairs man, and without regard to the election, I was concerned with getting his attention directed more toward international affairs. This could be, I believed then, decidedly good for the country; he had displayed flashes of a salutary pragmatic flexibility in thinking about world problems, as when he privately remarked shortly after the election of 1960 that he thought JFK should recognize Red China promptly and be done with it.

On September 17 I sent President Johnson a memo emphasizing that there was a widespread feeling that "you just aren't as interested or as experienced in foreign affairs as in domestic matters" and suggesting that he counter this by a campaign commitment to undertake "a systematic exploration for peace." Specifically, he would state that "in the years of your new Administration, you will meet with every major world leader, seeing some in Washington and others on trips undertaken for this purpose. At these meetings you will naturally talk about specific troubles but the main emphasis will be on broad new approaches which, in the context of the 1960's, could lead to a more genuine peace."

This memo was returned with the LBJ scrawl, "I like it," and an instruction to have the proposal gone over by Secretary of State Rusk. I expected the State Department, with its habitual distaste for procedures that went over or around its own channels, to shoot down the nub of the suggestion—the systematic exploration initiated by the President—and my expectation was fulfilled. When State was done, what went into the El Paso speech was the vague: "I pledge you here today I will go to any remote corner of the world to meet anyone, any time, to promote freedom and to promote peace."

This was the first appearance of the I-will-go-anywhere-for-peace formula which, when repeatedly used by President Johnson in connection with the Vietnam War, was to bring him so much woe from critics who believed he was ready to go any place except to the negotiating table. In September 1964 it had little or nothing to do with Vietnam or, in the purely rhetorical form in which it was stated, little or nothing to do with anything except making Lyndon Johnson sound a devotee of brotherhood, in and outside the United States. What struck me at the time was not the State Department sentence but the passage preceding it, which had the unmistakable ring of the Oval Office. Nonpartisan, very presidential President Johnson wanted everyone to know that all "the Presidents of the last twenty years" had the same willingness "to go anywhere, to talk to anyone, to discuss any subject" for peace and freedom.

El Paso, Detroit, Sacramento—but most of the time the President of all the people was busy being President at the White House. "This job," as LBJ used to say, "includes a lot of things," and so it did. He was finding it good for the country to step up the number of his press conferences and television appearances; to flood the press with statistics from the Council of Economic Advisers underlining the unprecedented prosperity the United States was enjoying; to meet in the Cabinet Room with the forty-five members of a newly formed "National Independent Committee for Johnson and Humphrey" and to tell them, "I did not, I do not, I shall never seek to be a labor President or a business President, a President for liberals or a President for conservatives, a President for the North or a President for the South. . . ."

The committee was the ultimate in frontlash; it was crammed with Republican leaders of finance and business who were refugees from Goldwaterism. What G.O.P. businessman could not pull the Democratic lever the more serenely when he read the pro-Johnson declarations of a group including members of the Eisenhower Cabinet, two Cabots from blue-chip Boston investment firms, Sidney J. Weinberg of Goldman, Sachs in New York City, Henry Ford II and Thomas S. Lamont—not to speak of the presidents or board chairmen of American Can, American Machine and Foundry, Bulova Watch, Curtiss-Wright, Inland Steel, Merck and Texaco? Johnson men used this committee with telling effect across the country. Specifically, Idaho probably went into the LBJ column by a one percent squeak because the prestige of the committee influenced Robert V. Hansberger, president of the Boise Cascade Corporation and the state's tycoon, to break with his lifetime Republicanism and throw his weight behind the Democratic ticket.

Then there was Congress—weary, fretting Congress, which for so long had wanted to go home and campaign. Lyndon Johnson, if he believed the campaign was the candidate, also believed that the candidate was the man plus the record he could display. He wanted the House and Senate to stay in Washington and pass more bills, particularly Medicare and an additional $1-billion anti-poverty appropriation for Appalachia. The White House pressure for this legislation did not work. Miracles, for the moment, were running out, especially with the miracle man so preoccupied.

Holding Congress in session did produce some dizzying political broken-field running. In June the Supreme Court had handed down its one-man, one-vote decision, requiring the reapportionment of state legislatures on a population basis, and thus undercutting the power of rural and small-town areas. Conservatives in both parties were up in arms, and never insensitive to them, Senate Minority Leader Everett Dirksen pushed an amendment to a foreign aid bill which stated it to be "the sense of Congress" that federal court orders forcing the reapportionment should be postponed. The farms and the small towns were fertile Goldwater territory; Lyndon Johnson had no intention of permitting any Republican, not even his intermittent ally Everett Dirksen, to emerge as their savior. Without revealing his hand, he persuaded Senate Majority Leader Mike Mansfield to serve as co-sponsor of the Dirksen amendment. Then the indignation came from the other side. Big-city mayors and congressmen besieged the White House with demands that it back the Supreme Court. Just as discreetly, LBJ reversed his field. Urban-minded senators launched a semi-filibuster against the amendment, and the White House saw to it that the talking was not discouraged. The Senate proceeded to pass the amendment and now Lyndon Johnson, the ball completely tucked away, went straight down the middle. The amendment was sent to a House-Senate conference committee, whose Democratic majority learned the White House wishes. They simply quashed the amendment, taking no position on its merits. And finally, on October 3, Congress was permitted to go home.

The next day the Seattle *Post-Intelligencer* mused: "It may be that Barry Goldwater will be elected. It may also be that Chase National will go broke, that Governor Wallace will get an honorary degree from Tuskegee, and that Mickey Spillane will win the Nobel Prize for literature."

By this time the polls said it, independent commentators agreed, Democratic politicians felt it in their bones, Republican spokesmen, apart from the fanatics, did not deny it. The election, for all practical purposes, was over. Everything pointed to a sweep for LBJ.

Lyndon Johnson took to what some of the less reverent members of his staff called "the pollarama." The opinion surveys— the Quayle polls and many others—were handled through Walter Jenkins' office; Richard Nelson did the work of arranging for special studies, collating the results, seeing to it that President Johnson was daily supplied with summaries. Every so often the President asked to have the figures put on large colored graphs, state by state. The charts were placed around one of the spacious rooms on the second floor of the White House and selected newsmen were invited for a drink. Then LBJ, spectacles down his nose, pointer in hand, staged the pollarama, moving around and expatiating on the finer points of the situation. Occasionally he paused and instructed Nelson, "Get me the latest"; the assistant came back with a poll which, sure enough, was almost always more favorable. There was elation and pride in these performances, and there was also the seasoned knowledge that the more hopeless the Goldwater cause seemed, the more tightly the purse strings would be drawn on the potentially vast Republican financial resources.

So it was all over for practical purposes—or was it? At least a generation will have to pass before American politicians get over the 1948 psychosis. The polls had made Thomas Dewey an easy winner; Harry Truman stayed in the White House. The 1948 election underlined another characteristic of American voting which had not been lost on Lyndon Johnson. When the polls indicate that a man is far ahead, his supporters may well not bother to vote. More important, an underdog tow can develop. In a society like the United States, where so many consider themselves ill rewarded compared to what really should have been bestowed on their talents and labors, the man disastrously low in the ratings has sympathizers regardless of what he advocates. Evidence exists which suggests that Harry Truman may have carried the winning states because enough men and women went to the polls intending to vote for the all-conquering Thomas Dewey but at the last minute felt, Poor Harry, kicked around like me, might as well give him a vote.

There was a further consideration. People like myself—and men closer to President Johnson—were pressing a possible sleeper issue, one that could eventually swing a fair number of votes if LBJ continued to appear to be winning in a romp. Republican candidates had been lamenting the loss of "freedom" and "individualism" in America ever since the 1930's but had made little headway with their gloomings. Goldwater was also bearing down on the point and in the atmosphere of the 1960's, he might be touching a nerve.

I tried to summarize the possibility for the President: "If there is any one thing that lies deepest in the American tradition, which affects both the mind and the emotions of people of all classes, it is the feeling that the American is—more than any other man—an individual, a sturdy fellow standing on his own two feet, making his own decisions, working out his own compact with his God and his fellow-man. Yet the history of the United States during the last fifty years, and particularly in very recent years, can easily seem like an almost unending series of assaults on this conception of the American.

"This is true whether you listen to the corporation executive growling against unions which impede his 'freedom of action'; the factory worker complaining about distant union leadership; the executive or the worker irritated at taxes which 'spend his money for him'; the backlasher protesting against the loss of his individual 'right' to pick his neighbor; the novelist railing against 'conformity'; or the nice club lady, uneasily wondering whether the 'breakdown of individual responsibility resulting from the welfare state' has not led to crime in the streets.

"In my opinion, it is this whole collection of things—coalescing into a vague, often unspoken feeling that the American as an individual is being destroyed—which creates Goldwater's deeper appeal."

Considerations of this nature, pressed on President Johnson from many quarters, were making him restless with the restrained, "informing" stage of his campaign. Far more powerful urges to swing out were coming from within the man. Every sign that he was winning big had only one meaning to Lyndon Johnson; he could win bigger. Another inner incitement was a downright goad. As the evidence of a landslide mounted, it also contained more and more indications that many LBJ votes were just as much anti-Goldwater as pro-Johnson.

Publication after publication was summarizing opinion in remarks like that of the St. Louis optometrist who commented, "Goldwater is beyond belief. Johnson leaves me cold, but I am going to ring doorbells for him." From New York City came the same point in its own West Side form. Ben Kaplan, operating in a slit of a store on West Forty-fourth Street, was hitting the jackpot with "loser's buttons." Especially good sellers were "Alfred M. Landon" (cost 7 cents, price 75 cents), "I'm for Willkie" (cost 5 cents, price 50 cents) and "Hurray for Harold Stassen" (cost 2 cents, price 35 cents); his hottest item was "Chiang Kai-shek" (cost 1 cent, price 40 cents). "I can't understand it," said Ben Kaplan, "but when I ask customers why, they say they're going to vote for Johnson but are down on both him and Goldwater and want something far out to protest." The public opinion analyst Samuel Lubell, intently studied in the White House, reported that the coolness toward President Johnson by LBJ voters was shot through with the impression that he was just another manipulating politician. Lubell gave the specific illustration of a Dayton, Ohio, precinct where nearly a quarter of those who intended to vote for the President questioned his fundamental honesty.

If there was anything Lyndon Johnson yearned for next to winning big, it was winning on a wave of respect and affection. He was choleric at all the talk of his being a "lesser evil" victor, and amid this mood he and the whole White House were rocked by a late-September statement of the Reverend Mr. Francis B. Sayre, Jr., Woodrow Wilson's grandson and the prestigious Dean of the Episcopal Washington Cathedral. We behold, the minister declared, both parties "completely dominated by a single man— the one, a man of dangerous ignorance and devastating uncertainty; the other, a man whose public house is splendid in its every appearance, but whose private lack of ethic must inevitably introduce termites at the very foundation. . . . Our people are in a great dilemma, and there is no corner of the country which you may visit today where you do not feel this profoundly. We stare fascinated at the forces that have produced such a sterile choice for us; frustration and a federation of hostilities in one party; and in the other, behind a goodly façade, only a cynical manipulation of power."

In the ensuing furor, commentators pointed out that Dean Sayre was an ardent Kennedyite, and some wondered aloud about what had happened in the Washington Cathedral to the Christian doctrines of humility and forbearance. But the White House atmosphere was not improved by the number of these commentators who went on to say that whatever the clergyman's bias or self-righteousness, his "harsh pronouncement"—to use the words of the Washington *Star*—"we suspect, sums up the real mood of a great part of the electorate."

All of these factors pushed Lyndon Johnson to move quickly into the "conversion" and "agitation" periods, perhaps telescoping them, and the pressure did not have to be too hard. Continuing an aloof run for the Presidency at least a little longer had its advantages, but it simply was not the way of the man, whatever his theories about the way to run for office. Franklin Roosevelt and Harry Truman may have responded to an election like McGinnis to the fire bell; neither they nor any other modern American presidential candidate had Lyndon Johnson's unadorned, unrestrained, unabashed joy in all-out campaigning. He savored every aspect of it: the conspiratorial conferences far into the night; the friends from old political wars gathering to meet you; the enemies attempting to catch you off guard and the counterpunch to foil them; the stage acting; the thunderings to the crowds and the roars back; the planes and the babies and the laying on of hands. "Some men are born to campaign," said Mrs. Johnson. "Lyndon was."

As September ended, the President of all the people, the constrained nonpartisan figure of the Oval Office, returned to Convention Hall in Atlantic City to speak to the thirty-five hundred delegates of the United Steelworkers of America. In sonorous presidential prose, he went along talking about extending prosperity to all Americans and harnessing technology, "the challenge of the future," to human needs. Then he came flailing down off the pedestal and made after Barry Goldwater. "We will do all these things because we love people instead of hating them; because we have faith in America, not fear of the future; because you are strong men of vision instead of frightened cry babies; because you know it takes a man who loves his country to build a house instead of a raving, ranting demagogue who wants to tear down one."

When the White House party returned to Washington, Press Secretary Reedy, still thinking in terms of a President magisterially above assailing his opponent, told reporters the passage should read "raving, ranting demagogues." Soon Reedy had another anouncement: The correct form was *a* "raving, ranting demagogue."

The Lyndon Johnson campaign, the real campaign, was on.

There had been nothing like it since the Yellowstone geyser. Up and down the country LBJ beat his way, a latter-day William Jennings Bryan borne by jets and wired for television, storming, pleading, cajoling, evangelizing. In the forty-two days between his Steelworkers speech and the election, he traveled well over sixty thousand miles, made at least two hundred speeches, chucked babies' toes and fingers from Miami to San Diego, shook so many hands that at times his right arm was limp and his right hand raw and bleeding.

Everything and everyone was thrown into the drive. It had become custom that the Secretaries of State and Defense do not campaign; Dean Rusk and Robert McNamara discreetly campaigned. No occasion was lost to move a White House staff man into action, and for the first time the entire family of a President undertook intensive electioneering. Mrs. Johnson made forays into stubborn Goldwater country west of the Appalachians, and led the "Lady Bird Special" that barnstormed through hostile Southern areas. The Johnson girls operated sometimes together, usually separately. Their joint speciality was the Young Citizens for Johnson, which staged barbecues from Long Island to Beverly Hills.

Walter Jetton would fly in from Fort Worth, portly, amiable, a God-fearing man who did not smoke, drink or curse, and who had long since been recognized as the nation's virtuoso of outdoor beef. Always frontlash glamour girls, like Henry Ford II's strikingly attractive daughter Charlotte, were present, and big-name entertainers provided the beat. The greensward rocked, the beef disappeared, and there were a few words. Lynda, serious-minded and studious, worked over her speeches and frequently sought help from the staff. Luci was not particularly interested in suggestions from anyone, including the man in her house who most people thought was rather good at politicking. Some of us in the White House wondered when disaster would break over her head, but I suppose Providence looks out for pert teen-agers who are daughters of the President of the United States.

Once in a while even the ebullient Hubert Humphrey was tired. But if it occurred to the vice-presidential candidate to let up, he received no encouragement from the Oval Office. His campaign wound on and on, and Hubert Humphrey spoke on and on. Mrs. Humphrey, accustomed to her husband's long-winded oratory, had sighed years ago, "A speech to be immortal does not have to be eternal." Yet HHH at his best was not only eternal but effective, and exhilarated by the vice-presidential nomination, he reached his heights in 1964. Many times his caravan thundered, crackled or twinkled in some of the most telling campaigning of the post-World War II period.

The Humphrey speeches were basically serious, hard-driving, colorfully worded, delivered with pounding on the podium and right index finger in the air. It was his assigned job to attack the Goldwater opinions point for point; he raked them over the coals until they lay in charred ruins. Always the puck was restless in the bottle, ready to break out with something unprepared and delightful. Goldwater and especially Miller took to referring to Humphrey by his full name, Hubert Horatio Humphrey, with a sarcastic emphasis on "Horatio." One spanking October day, Hubert Horatio Humphrey addressed himself to the matter. "Senator Goldwater thinks he has found a real issue in my middle name. In the spirit of charity, however, I must warn him. The hidden middle-name vote—all those youngsters blessed by loving parents with a middle name they choose to convert to an initial—may rise against him. He should beware of the midlash." Even the jaded reporters chuckled appreciatively.

HHH kept on his efficacious way, the Johnson circle did their duty, and more and more Lyndon Johnson benefited from his greatest asset—the Republican candidate for President. Barry Goldwater continued to talk in October as he had in September, and he became even more helpful. Two issues were turning into focal points of the campaign; on both, he made sure that he offended or worried the maximum number of voters.

For years the bedrock and symbol of New Deal-type legislation had been the social security system, established during the era of Franklin Roosevelt and expanded under every succeeding President. Before Goldwater's nomination, he had called for making social security "voluntary," which obviously meant dismantling the system. Now he dropped the word "voluntary" but insisted upon "drastic revision," to the fears of the nineteen million Americans who were receiving benefits and to the indignation of millions more who considered it the minimal criterion of modern and humane government.

Ever since Hiroshima, the fact of nuclear power had hung over American discussions of public issues like the possibility, in the realm of personal affairs, of a dread disease. Most people did not like to hear talk about nuclear bombs; when the subject was discussed, they assumed that the tone would be grave. Goldwater kept talking about nuclear weapons, and he spoke of them with an eerie mixture of casualness and a kind of cowboy bravado, more than implying that he would be a Chief Executive not so awe-struck he would be afraid to use them. Every time the senator touched upon the subject he managed to send shivers down the national spine, and the occasions included even his efforts to reassure. In Harwood, Indiana, trying to combat the anxiety that President Goldwater might be the man to push the nuclear button, he remarked that in all likelihood the Communists would strike so quickly "the President would not be around to push the button."

The Republican candidate was not only saying just the wrong things; he was caricaturing himself by picking just the wrong places to say them. He chose Charleston, West Virginia, bordered by some of the country's most dismal poverty, to assail the Employment Opportunity Act; in a sentence that must have brought great comfort to the hill dwellers of Appalachia, he added that the Johnson Administration defined poverty at a level which represents "well-being beyond the dreams of a vast majority of the people of the world." He picked Memphis, the cotton capital of the world, to declare that cotton subsidies had been "forced on the farmers by Washington." For Knoxville, center of a region transformed by the Tennessee Valley Authority, he reiterated his conviction that TVA should be sold to private utilities.

As Barry Goldwater kept stumbling, the campaign style of LBJ burst into full flower. On the jet he often slumped in his seat, weary and snappish. When the plane landed, he was a man transformed, down the ramp with the big shoulders back, the Stetson jaunty, smilingly heading for the hands. The Y. A. Tittle of handshaking was establishing new standards. In Riverside, California, he was seen taking care of eight voters almost simultaneously, quickly squeezing with one of his hands some part of an available arm. After St. Louis, when his fingers were usually too sore or too bandaged for shaking, he developed the technique of The Touch, which seemed to leave the recipient almost as pleased. One way or another, no opportunity was missed. Richard Rovere, covering the Louisville appearance on a dark, raw night, found himself standing among local Democratic chieftains who had come to the airport to greet the candidate. "My eyes and ears were absorbed by the rite I was witnessing, and my hands were enjoying the relative warmth of my topcoat pockets, when, all of a sudden, a long presidential arm shot toward me, removed my right hand from my right pocket, clasped it and returned it to me."

The motorcades were likely to be maelstroms. Lyndon Johnson would order the long black limousine stopped and out the window came a bull horn. "Come on, folks, come on down to the speakin'.

You don't have to dress. Just bring your children and dogs, anything you have with you. It won't take long. You'll be back in time to put the kids in bed." A few more blocks, the limousine stopped again and out came Lyndon Johnson, pushing into the crowd, both arms working, until the worried Secret Service got him back in the car for another stretch of the journey.

Something folksy kept happening. In Brooklyn Lyndon Johnson came to a boy with a scratch on his arm, reached in his pocket for a Band-Aid, applied it with an added pat on the rear. At Scott Air Force Base in Missouri, he saw a group across the way, leaped a four-foot construction ditch to get to them. In Memphis he climbed on top of his limousine for a talk, paused to hitch up his trousers, almost lost his balance as the crowd gasped. In Seattle he joined a marching high school band, autographed the drum, led the cheers: "All the way with LBJ!"

The "speakin's" brought back memories of an America long, long ago. Harry Truman whistle-stopped in short, punchy talks; Dwight Eisenhower was a thirty-minute man; John Kennedy rarely talked over twenty minutes. Often Lyndon Johnson went on for forty-five minutes, paused for more roars and then started up again. Everything was "you folks." "I want you folks to know," he would start, and what followed might be policy, political recollections or a bit about his family affairs.

Once in a while, the President told the crowds, he came upon "sourpusses carrying a picture of that other feller." They were not his kind of folks, not his kind of Americans, not the "smiling, friendly faces I want to walk the road of life with." He talked about "smiling, friendly faces" until one aide, asked at the White House Mess how a campaign trip had gone, stared into his soup and moaned, "Fifty thousand f---ing friendly faces." A few days later the assistant was back on the trail and he heard: "Yes, all day I have seen your smiling faces. All day I have looked into your happy countenances. All day I have seen the family life, the mothers and the children of America here in the heartland of the great state of Illinois. And those voices sound powerful to me. They sound clear. They sound free. And when I return to the White House, and the policemen turn the keys on those locks on those big black gates, and I get to those few acres that are back of our house, it is going to be folks like you that sustain me in my labors and in my thoughts."

The public-policy points were the same as in the first days of the campaigning, but now they were delivered in direct campaign style and old-shoe language. Lyndon Johnson would continue to be the President of all the people: "I came here to talk with all of you, Republicans, Democrats, and whatnots." As Senate Minority Leader under a Republican President he had been told, " 'It is the duty of an opposition to oppose.' I said no. It is my duty to support the President every time I can in good conscience, and to resolve any doubts in behalf of the cheer leader of this country." The stance was never neglected. At the news that Herbert Hoover was dying, nonpartisan President Johnson was so eager to bring a conspicuous halt to his campaigning for a day that an aide had to caution him, "But Mr. President, he isn't dead yet."

The more specific points followed what he considered the consensus that had been reached in the 1960's. On social legislation: "We are not going to kill social security and we are not going to sell TVA. We are not going to sell another river in America." The "decent laws" passed over recent years—"that's what Americans want and what they are going to get. . . . And if you don't believe in them, you can go you-know-where!"

On civil rights: "Some people say we passed an act up there that is going to take a lot of jobs away from white folks. . . . I want to meet that head-on." He wanted his audience to know what an Alabama friend of Mrs. Johnson had said to her the other day. " 'Lady Bird, I have been thinking about this problem a lot and they have got out a lot of stories about what has happened. But I would rather have a Negro beside me on a job than beside me in a soup line.' "

On foreign policy and nuclear power. "Let your President get one thing straight in everybody's noggin. . . . I admire a brave man, but some people have more guts than brains."

Often President Johnson would describe to crowds what it was like being in the White House at the time of the Kennedy-Khrushchev confrontation over Cuba. "As President Kennedy and the leader of the Soviet Union came eyeball to eyeball and the thumbs started inching up"—and LBJ's big thumb would start inching up—"as the thumbs started getting closer to that nuclear button, the knife was in each other's ribs, and neither of them was flinching or quivering."

Invariably the crowd hushed, mesmerized by the imagery. Then he would ask, "Which man's thumb do you want to be close to that button now, which man do you want to reach over and pick up that hot line when they say, 'Moscow's calling'?"

Candidate Johnson did not talk much about the Vietnam War. In his first post-convention speech, delivered at a birthday barbecue for him in Stonewall, Texas, he had described his general attitude in terms of his actions at the time of the Tonkin incident.

He had let the North Vietnam government "know that we meant what we said," and the retaliatory bombing he ordered was "a very serious act." But "we didn't bomb any cities. . . . We didn't kill any women and children. We didn't invade any metropolitan areas. We didn't provoke any great nations. . . . I get a lot of advice, and I need a lot. . . . I have had advice to load our planes with bombs and to drop them on certain areas that I think would enlarge the war and escalate the war, and result in our committing a good many American boys to fighting a war that I think ought to be fought by the boys of Asia to help protect their own land. And for that reason, I haven't chosen to enlarge the war."

Now, in the later stage of the campaign, Lyndon Johnson preserved this tone. But he became a bit more explicit, largely in terms of contrasting his attitude with that of Goldwater, whom he more or less directly presented as a man ready to involve the United States in the shooting war. Some of these later statements were ambiguous, at least in their insistence both that President Johnson did not intend to let South Vietnam "be swallowed up by Communist conquest" and was against American combat intervention. One of the speeches contained three escape-hatch clauses: he was opposed to "going north" and dropping bombs "at this stage of the game"; thought "just for the moment" that the United States was not ready for American boys to do the fighting for Asian boys; believed "dropping bombs around" should be used "only as a last resort." At the same time, the overwhelming impact of the LBJ campaign remarks on Vietnam was that he fully intended to stay out of the shooting war. In view of the fact that the President's campaign statements later became the subject of widespread bitter feeling—at times based on severely abbreviated forms of his remarks which he and some of his friends considered misleading and unfair—his chief campaign comments on the Vietnam War after Stonewall are given here in a way that attempts to convey the substance and nuances of what he said.

Eufaula, Oklahoma, September 25. There are those that say you ought to go north and drop bombs, to try to wipe out the supply lines, and they think that would escalate the war. We don't want our American boys to do the fighting for Asian boys. We don't want to get involved in a nation with 700 million people and get tied down in a land war in Asia.

There are some that say we ought to go south and get out and come home, but we don't like to break our treaties and we don't like to walk off and leave people who are searching for freedom, and suffering to obtain it, and walk out on them. We remember when we wanted our freedom from Great Britain, and we remember the people that helped us with it, and we'll never forget them. So we don't want to run out on them.

So what are we doing? We're staying there and supplying them with some of the things that we have, some of the things that the richest, most powerful nation in the world has developed. . . . and we're hoping that some way, somehow, these people that are invading them and trying to envelop them and trying to take their freedom away from them will some day decide that it's not worth the price and they will leave their neighbors alone and we can have peace in the world.

But we are not about to start another war and we're not about to run away from where we are.

Manchester, New Hampshire, September 28. Some of our people— Mr. Nixon, Mr. Rockefeller, Mr. Scranton, and Mr. Goldwater— have all, at some time or other, suggested the possible wisdom of going north in Vietnam. Well, now, before you start attacking someone and you launch a big offensive, you better give some consideration to how you are going to protect what you have. And when a brigadier general can walk down the streets of Saigon, as they did the other day, and take over the police station, the radio station, and the government without firing a shot, I don't know how much offensive we are prepared to launch.

As far as I am concerned, I want to be very cautious and careful, and use it only as a last resort, when I start dropping bombs around that are likely to involve American boys in a war in Asia with 700 million Chinese.

So just for the moment I have not thought we were ready for American boys to do the fighting for Asian boys. What I have been trying to do, with the situation that I found, was to get the boys in Vietnam to do their own fighting with our advice and with our equipment. . . . We are not going north and drop bombs at this stage of the game, and we are not going south and run out and leave it for the Communists to take over.

Now we have lost 190 American lives, and to each one of those 190 families this is a major war. . . . I often wake up in the night and think about how many I could lose if I made a misstep.

When we retaliated in the Tonkin Gulf, we dropped bombs on their nests where they had their PT boats housed, and we dropped them within thirty-five miles of the Chinese border. I don't know what you would think if they started dropping them thirty-five miles from your border, but I think that is something you have to take into consideration.

So . . . we are going to continue to try to get them to save their own freedom. . . . We think that losing 190 lives in the period that we have been out there is bad. But it is not like 190,000 that we might lose the first month if we escalated that war.

. . . We are trying somehow to evolve a way, as we have in some other places, where the North Vietnamese and the Chinese Communists will finally, after getting worn down, conclude that they will leave their neighbors alone. And if they do, we will come home tomorrow.

It is not any problem to start a war. . . . I know some folks that I think could start one mighty easy. But it is a pretty difficult problem for us to prevent one, and that is what we are trying to do.

Akron, Ohio, October 21. In Asia we face an ambitious and aggressive China, but we have the will and we have the strength to help our Asian friends resist that ambition. Sometimes our folks get a little impatient. Sometimes they rattle their rockets some, and they bluff about their bombs. But we are not about to send American boys nine or ten thousand miles away from home to do what Asian boys ought to be doing for themselves.

President Eisenhower said in 1954 to the Government of Vietnam, "President Diem, we want to help you help yourselves. We will give you advice, we will provide leadership, we will help you with material things, with your weapons and the things that you do not have, to protect your independence . . . and not be swallowed up by the Communists."

We have been doing that for ten long years under three Presidents. . . . The reports that come in are gloomy from day to day.

But we have a choice. We can seek a wider war. China is there on the border with 700 million men, with over 200 million in their army. And we could get tied down in a land war in Asia very quickly if we sought to throw our weight around. Or we could retreat and pull out and say "Goodby" to the rest of the world, that we are going to live on our own shores, and we would let Asia go to other people. But we don't seem to think that either of those alternatives is the wise decision.

We are going to continue to try to make these people more effective and more efficient, and do our best to resolve that situation where the aggressors will leave their neighbors alone. . . .

We are going to assist them against attack. . . . We will not permit the independent nations of the East to be swallowed up by Communist conquest.

And what was the campaign, LBJ style, accomplishing? There were those, like the editors of the pro-Johnson St. Louis *Post-Dispatch,* who were sure that "it was helping mightily to reduce everything to cornpone." Horace Busby, who traveled with President Johnson much of the time and carefully questioned local reporters and policitians, had a sharply different interpretation, one which he thoroughly believed and which was not stated to please his boss. Busby was convinced that President Johnson was conducting his own version of the Fireside Chat. The campaign was a "phenomenon," he thought, an astoundingly successful educational enterprise. With his whoop-de-dos and just-us-folks manner LBJ was personalizing the Presidency and the national and international problems that came to it as no post-World War II Chief Executive had done, and his audiences were hungrily responding.

Phenomenon or monumental exhibition of cornball, Lyndon Johnson was incontestably drawing larger and more responsive crowds than any previous presidential candidate. Place after place was like Louisville, where a record eighty-five thousand people packed the plaza of the War Memorial Building and spilled down the side streets as far as the eye could see, breaking into tumult every three or four sentences of the speech. Governor Edward T. Breathitt bestowed the ultimate compliment: "It's outdone the Kentucky Derby. That's the first time a human being has been able to draw a crowd like that in Louisville."

LBJ was going through October a happier man each day. As any politician knows, big roaring crowds are the harbinger of a big roaring majority, but for him there was more to it than that. At the end of the Louisville day, he was secluded in a private area of the airport when he spotted a familiar reporter and walked over to him. "Come with me. I read what you wrote about my not having rapport, about people not really liking me, and now I'm just going to show you something."

The President led the newsman out into the crowd and the din went up. Lyndon Johnson pulled away, cupped his hands to the ear of the reporter. "Now, why don't you write about that!"

No matter how hard President Johnson campaigned, he also kept the White House churning with election-oriented activities, one of which resulted in the establishment of a minor institution. From academics and others I was receiving increasing reports about the attitude of educated youthful voters—youthful in the sense that they were in college or still not out of their twenties or early thirties. A small percentage of them, observers told me, were pro-Goldwater and these were extremely enthusiastic. An overwhelming number were pro-Johnson but with little zest for their candidate. The reports were easy to believe. Lyndon Johnson may have been able to stir all kinds of groups but his occasional appearances before youthful audiences were woeful. There was something about the young that brought out the most evangelistic in him, and there was something about the young of the 1960's which made them recoil from evangelism.

William C. Friday, president of the University of North Carolina, just forty-four himself and sharply alert to national trends, had noted the enthusiasm of Goldwater campus forces. He believed that strengthening the commitment of the pro-LBJ group was important not only for the election but in order to provide President Johnson with greater support during the rest of his Administration from a vigorous and articulate section of the public. Friday thought that the best way to do this was through college student leaders, many of whom could vote and all of whom had natural ties to their contemporaries, and he suggested to me that some kind of a White House occasion should be staged which was directed toward this purpose.

Friday's comment sent my mind to a memo which I had received about six weeks before from John W. Gardner, president of the Carnegie Foundation of New York. He had urged a "national service plan," either privately executed or established by the government under the title of the "Presidential Corps." Each year one hundred particularly able and highly motivated young men and women would be selected for fifteen months of training and service in various parts of the federal government. Conceivably, Gardner wrote, this period could be substituted for military service. Some of the corps would stay in the government, but even those who did not would constitute "a natural resource," a group with a sense of "personal involvement in the leadership of the society."

Of course I strongly shared Gardner's purpose; it fitted the kind of thinking behind the Presidential Scholars by seeking to encourage a Jeffersonian elite of talent who, because they were more appreciated and were drawn further into leadership focus, would make themselves responsible for American society to a greater extent. Yet I was not much taken with details of the Gardner proposal. It was likely to produce more "government internees," and I believed an adequate number of programs of that type already existed. Also, I had become convinced that any plan under which government service could be substituted for military duty would be considered draft dodging by the general public and would result in actual draft dodging in more than a few cases. During a chance conversation with Mrs. Johnson, she had spoken warmly of her desire to draw more gifted young people into the federal service. Out of my respect for Gardner and the feeling that the First Lady might want to take up his proposal, I sent the memo to her, but she showed no interest.

Now, with the campaign in full swing, I decided to put together the possibilities prompted by the Friday and Gardner communications: a plan quite different from a national service Presidential Corps but having some of its overtones, to be announced at a White House college-student meeting. The combination might further the long-range purposes shared by Gardner and me—and I was sure by Friday too—and it might possibly build greater understanding between President Johnson and the younger age group during the election and for future years of his Administration.

My memo to the President cited Friday and Gardner, explained both the political and nonpolitical purposes I had in mind, and recommended a White House invitation to a cross section of college student leaders. During the day the students would have a chance to meet with men they were likely to respond to and who were responsible for affairs that were very much on their minds—Secretary of Defense McNamara talking about the draft, Secretary of Labor Wirtz on the emerging economic and social patterns of the nation, and UN Ambassador Stevenson on world trends. The evening's entertainment would express the taste of the upcoming educated generation—performers such as Bill Cosby and Barbra Streisand. President Johnson's speech—and here perhaps I skirted the edges of tact—"could be a quite unusual talk, in which the President comments, in an understanding way, on the special attitudes and the mood of the new generation." The speech would announce the establishment of the "White House Fellows" or the "National Fellows."

This would not be a national service, a government internee, or a government recruiting program. Men and women would apply, and on recommendation of a blue-ribbon commission the President annually would name just fifteen Fellows, thirty-five or younger, who had already established themselves in their various occupations by their abilities and personal qualities. They would not be assigned merely to parts of the government but at the highest level—one directly to the Vice-President, one to each of the ten Cabinet officers, and four to members of the White House staff. My mind was not on how to keep them in the government; having served for fifteen months, they would return to their regular professions, hopefully forming a growing body of talented and influential Americans who combined absorption in their own work with an active, knowledgeable concern for public affairs. Of course I closed the memo with the LBJ essential. However much I had changed Gardner's suggestion, what I was proposing moved along somewhat similar lines and I stated my strong impression that his foundation would finance a three-year trial operation.

The memo came back with an enthusiastic go-ahead from President Johnson and with notations by both him and Mrs. Johnson. (Mrs. Johnson's markings, as usual, were signed "CTJ." It was necessary for her to employ the initials of her actual name, Claudia Taylor Johnson, which she rarely used, rather than of Lady Bird Johnson, which everybody called her, to avoid the confusion of LBJ's.) CTJ seemed to like either "White House Fellows" or "National Fellows," LBJ made no comment on that point, I picked White House Fellows, and White House Fellows they were. The occasion was scheduled, at the President's wish, for just fourteen days away, October 3, 1964.

By now the pell-mell haste and the sigh and the apology ("I'm awfully sorry but I'm sure you understand the unusual circumstances") were standard. I requested that the Carnegie Foundation finance the trial stages of the program; Gardner called a special meeting of his board of directors and quickly a sum up to $225,000 was guaranteed. When I hurried together a President's Commission on White House Fellows, the presidential approvals of the names came back from the campaign jet over a radiotelephone which was acting up in a storm. The words were so garbled that it took me several minutes to make sure whether David Rockefeller, as chairman, was being okayed or berated. He was okay, bounteously so. One college president, to whom I had sent the presidential wire asking him to name a student leader, telephoned to say plaintively, "Campus opinion has been torn hopelessly for months. What do you want me to do?" It is one of the wondrous powers of the White House that under such circumstances you say sweetly, "That *is* a problem, but of course you want a representative here," and the person replies, "Of course. I will wire you the name later today."

At the occasion for the announcement of the White House Fellows program, President Johnson surprised me by delivering the speech I had prepared largely intact. It was not a Johnsonian exhortation to youth. In it he kidded himself; spoke sympathetically of a generation raised in the backwash of depression and war ("If you think your elders did not do so well, you certainly have reasons for it"); recognized the instincts of the "volunteer generation" and their restlessness with a "spectator society." I have no idea whether he made many votes or friends for himself, but I was pleased that the Fellows were launched in an atmosphere that was relatively free, so far as I could tell, of the customary youthful irritation and snickering at him.

In practice, the program did turn into something of a recruiting device for government and politics. During its first three years of operation, about twelve percent of the Fellows did not return to their former occupations. They stayed in Washington in higher-level positions ranging through the Departments of Agriculture, Labor and the Post Office, the Office of Science and Technology, and the Senate Labor and Welfare Committee. One went into politics, as an aide first to Senator Frank Church of Idaho and then to Mayor Joseph L. Alioto of San Francisco. Two became long-time members of the White House staff—Charles M. Maguire, from a mixed advertising and scholarly background in New York City, and Wyatt T. Johnson, Jr., from the business side of the Macon (Georgia) *Telegraph and News*. Tom Johnson, as he was called (he was not a relative of the President), began as an assistant to Moyers, then moved into the White House inner circle, and when President Johnson announced he would not run again he soon let it be known that Tom Johnson would be going with him to Texas to assist in post-presidential administrative and writing activities.

I watched the recruiting a little wistfully; this was not the original purpose of the program and it could impede application by the kind of people originally sought. But—sticking to my strongly held opinion that a project established by the White House under an independent commission should remain independent—I never really interfered. In any event most of the Fellows were returning to their communities, perhaps with some of the hoped for effects, and certainly the country benefited from many of the young people being drawn into government and politics through this procedure.

After the election, President Johnson showed increasing interest in the White House Fellows. He saw to it that the program received government financing and watched over the Fellows protectively, clobbering any bureaucrat who tried to shunt a Fellow away from important centers of action. His teacher's instinct was roused; he proposed to teach the Fellows government. Once in a while he gave a long evening to the group, and these occasions could display Lyndon Johnson, one of America's better authorities on the ways of government, at his most candid, most thoughtful and at times most heretical.

In 1968, shortly after he announced his retirement, President Johnson issued a statement which was lost in the spectacular political developments of the period. LBJ had a way of launching projects, major or minor, with fanfare and then forgetting them. He was a busy man; he was also LBJ. But one subject—the Office of the Presidency and ways to improve its functioning—kept intriguing him. The 1968 announcement picked up his interest expressed at the time of the 175th anniversary of the Office of the Presidency and joined with his paternal feeling for the White House Fellows. He stated that he intended to ask a small group, consisting of Cabinet members from the Roosevelt through the Johnson Administrations, to undertake a long-range study and to recommend changes in the Office of the Presidency "to improve it, strengthen it, do whatever we can to make it stronger," and that he proposed to have some of the '68 White House Fellows, "whom I will take great care in selecting," work with him toward the same end.

The results could be interesting.

The White House Fellows duly established, in early October campaigner Johnson swung West, then South. The Southern drive was particularly intense. Only eight states showed any real possibility of going Republican and five were below the Mason-Dixon line. But electoral votes were not the whole story; of equal if not greater emotional importance to Lyndon Johnson was the fact that the South involved both personal pride and his sense of historic mission. The South was his home territory, and he did not want to be repudiated by the neighbors. As the likely proportions of his victory grew larger, more than ever he sought an across-the-board sweep which would make him the truly national President and one who could genuinely reunite North and South.

The South was not easy pickings. President Johnson had not only put through Congress the toughest civil rights law of the twentieth century; the fact that he, a Texan, had emerged a strong advocate of the Negro enraged many Southerners, who now thought him a traitor to his own people. This feeling was not confined to the red-gallus back country. I was amazed by the number of letters I received from educated, generally desegregationist Southerners who nevertheless stated, as one Georgia author wrote, "I cannot stomach a man who leaves us and goes up there to Washington to lecture us."

Lyndon Johnson could be highly interesting on the subject of the Southern mind. Although not a Southerner in basic ways, an important part of him belonged to Dixie. When that strain came to the fore he sounded like most members of a group who feel themselves misunderstood and abused. He became intensely introspective; he talked about the Southern mentality a great deal, poked into it, defended and attacked it, kept trying to explain it to others and perhaps to himself.

There were only three ways, LBJ believed, to win the Southerner over to accepting civil rights or a civil rights candidate. One was to support the policy, clearly and firmly, and to support it to the Southerner's face. More than once he commented that Democratic presidential candidates had a habit of being very pro-Negro but of talking in watery generalities south of the Mason-Dixon line. "There are men down there," he said. "They may not like it, but at least they would like it straight."

The President's second tenet was to recognize that the South also had its habits of thinking, its own context for civil rights or any other issue. After the campaign, advising one of his Northern Cabinet officers on the way to handle the Negro question in the South, he leaned back and observed: "A Southerner is against civil rights, but he loves the Constitution. He's brought up on Constitution, Constitution, Constitution. Well, during the campaign I talked the Constitution, which happens to include equality for the Negro."

Most basic was the third tenet. While campaigning in 1964, President Johnson remained the heir of Jim Ferguson and the exponent of that special variety of liberalism. He did not appeal to the magnolia South of old families, not even particularly to the blast-furnace South of burgeoning industrial success. His attention went to the millions, products of the rural small-town areas, who had always felt themselves beleaguered by the moneyed and the prestigious, at home as well as in the North. Sometimes this South had turned to racism, sometimes not, but always it fought to rise another rung on the ladder, for more schooling, a bigger house, a new automobile, a chance for a greater sense of self-respect. These were the things, Lyndon Johnson was sure, which most Southerners really wanted and which had been denied them by politicians— creatures of Northern and upper-class Southern interests—who used fear of the Negro to divert voting power from such goals. An essential in talking to the South about the Negro, he stressed, was to point out that there were other things in the world, ones far more important to the average Southern family, than holding the Negro down.

In the early stages of the campaign, President Johnson had made forays into the South and emphasized all three of these points. He had especially practiced what one of his political aides called the "agricultural strategy"—reminding his audiences how many of them made their living directly or indirectly from the soil, how much their incomes had been increased by Democratic farm programs, and what would happen to these programs if Southern voters were lured by the civil rights issue to support a Republican candidate who favored the "prompt and final termination" of all farm subsidies. But his mentions of Negro rights, constitutionalism and the primacy of economic and social progress had usually been so blurred that they hardly met his own criterion of talking straight to the Southerner. Much of the point of what he said was lost in his exhortations to come along, folks, and march with the President of all the people.

President Johnson gave considerable thought to his October trip into the South. Shortly before his departure he sat talking about New Orleans, the last, climactic stop on the itinerary, with Senator Richard Russell of Georgia, a man whose political sagacity he continued to respect highly. During the conversation the President called for the latest Louisiana poll; it showed New Orleans and southern Louisiana about evenly divided but the state as a whole heavily pro-Goldwater.

"Maybe New Orleans is the place to make a real civil rights speech," LBJ remarked.

Senator Russell stirred uncomfortably. "In New Orleans? That's pretty strong stuff for New Orleans."

Was Lyndon Johnson thinking that since Louisiana appeared hopeless, he might as well use New Orleans as a dramatic platform to speak out in a way that could do him good in the North and in the South generally? Was he refusing to concede even Louisiana, taking the poll as a challenge? In either case, a "real civil rights" speech in New Orleans was a clear risk. It would have to be extremely effective to go down with the audience at all; effective or not, it could result in a hostile demonstration that would harm him throughout the South. LBJ seemed undecided, and turned the conversation with Russell to other topics.

In the late afternoon of October 9, *Air Force One* landed at Moisant International Airport outside New Orleans. Goldwater's strength was immediately evident, in the heckling from the crowd, the sneering placards, the well-advertised fact that some members of the Louisiana State University Band had even balked at playing "Hail to the Chief." President Johnson remained the LBJ of the weeks of campaigning, the regular fellow from next door, grinning and shouting his doctrine that Americans are really one big happy family. During the eleven miles of the motorcade he stopped eight times to wade into the crowd, shake hands and get off more of the same.

Nearing the heart of the city, he emerged with bull horn and boomed out, "Is this Goldwater territory?"

"No," the thousands responded. From far back in the crowd a deep Negro voice broke through the cheering. "Come on, baby, knock yourself out! Come on, LBJ, knock yourself out!"

Lyndon Johnson smiled but made it clear that he was a friendly man talking to friendly faces. "Don't y'all say anything ugly. Let's keep our shirts on and be nice."

At supper time President Johnson appeared at the train station to meet his wife, who was concluding her "Lady Bird Special" in New Orleans. Again the Goldwater sentiment was plain. The enthusiastic gathering inside the station was almost all Negro; outside in the plaza, the predominantly white crowd was subdued or openly hostile. Of course the Democratic Governor John J. McKeithen was present to welcome the President and First Lady, but when he was introduced, a glaring period of time passed before he appeared from behind the red, white and blue bunting. Then McKeithen came forward, waved, said nothing, quickly retreated. Lyndon Johnson smilingly applauded the non-speech and stepped to the microphone for a few pleasant remarks about helping "our people to forget their old animosities. We are all Americans."

That night he entered the Grand Ballroom of the Jung Hotel to address an audience of some nineteen hundred, at least two thirds of whom were enemies of his civil rights policies. Few news media reported his remarks in any detail or commented upon them; by now most reporters had enough of LBJ's folksiness and repetitions and were more inclined to write about the crowds and the hoopla than what he said. But the New Orleans speech deserves a place in history. It was Lyndon Johnson's finest hour of the campaign— finest in the nature of its central point, its political adroitness and its sheer boldness.

The prepared remarks lasted for about thirty-five minutes and were super-tactful. Again little that he said came close to filling his prescription for talking straight to Southerners. With a flourish to New Orleans the "Queen City" and to the South which Lady Bird, Lynda, Luci and I "love," he was done with his written text.

The applause had been frequent for such hostile territory, and the crowd seemed to be responding to Lyndon Johnson. He made a decision. He continued with an ad-lib almost as long as his prepared speech.

Looking down the head table to Senator Russell Long, the son of Huey Long, he said, "I don't want to conclude this talk . . . without telling you that some of my political philosophy was born in this state." Then, for the first time in public, President Johnson told of "the dark days of the depression" when "a young country kid from the poor hills of Texas" first went to Washington and made the standing arrangement so that he could hear every speech of Senator Huey Long. "The things that I am talking about from coast to coast . . . tonight and tomorrow and next week are the things that he talked about thirty years ago"—the right of every man to education, a job, the protection of social security, medical care when he was old and ill. Huey Long was "way ahead of them all because he was against poverty, *really* against it, and for the ordinary man, *really* for him." Long's voice was "still tonight," but "as long as the good Lord permits me, I am going to carry on."

The attention of the audience was heightening. Lyndon Johnson asked, And why had the South made such slow progress toward this better living for its people? Those who "would use us and destroy us first divide us. There is not any combination in the country that can take on Russell Long, Allen Ellender, Lyndon Johnson and a few others if we are together. But if they divide us, they can make some hay. And all these years they have kept their foot on our necks by appealing to our animosities and dividing us."

Many in the audience were sitting bolt upright; a hush was coming over the ballroom. LBJ plunged ahead to identify the source of that divisive animosity. He did not mention the words "Civil Rights Act of 1964" but this time there was not the slightest blurring. "Whatever your views are, we have a Constitution and we have got a Bill of Rights and we've got the law of the land. And two thirds of the Democrats in the Senate voted for it, and three fourths of the Republicans."

Lyndon Johnson paused. His shoulders went back, his right arm came up. "And I signed it, and I am going to enforce it, and I am going to observe it. . . . I'm not going to let them build up the hate and try to buy my people by appealing to their prejudice."

Now the whole room was tense. Scattered applause started, quickly stopped.

The President leaned over the lectern. He wanted to tell "you folks" a story about "a great son of Texas who came from an adjoining state—I won't call his name." (He was referring to Joseph W. Bailey, born in Mississippi, who served as United States Senator from Texas in the early twentieth century.)

When young Sam Rayburn first entered the House of Representatives, President Johnson went on, Rayburn visited the old senator and the two men sat talking late into the night. The senator got to discussing the South's economic problems and "how we had been at the mercy of certain economic interests, and how they had exploited us. They had worked our women for five cents an hour, they had worked our men for a dollar a day, they had exploited our soil, they had let our resources go to waste, they had taken everything out of the ground they could, and they had shipped it to other sections.

"He was talking about the economy and what a great future we could have in the South if we just meet our economic problems, if we could just take a look at the resources of the South and develop them. And he said, 'Sammy, I wish I felt a little better. I would like to go back to old'—and I won't call the name of the state. It wasn't Louisiana and it wasn't Texas—"

Lyndon Johnson's two arms stretched high and he slashed the air with both of them as he hammered the rest of the words of the old senator: " 'I would like to go back down there and make them one more Democratic speech. I just feel like I've got one in me. Poor old state, they haven't heard a real Democratic speech in thirty years. All they ever hear at election time is nigra, nigra, nigra.' "

The audience gasped. President Johnson quickly finished his ad lib, and for a long few seconds the room was quiet. Then, starting here and there, applause came and people stood up. Tentatively, slowly, the handclapping built into a standing, shouting ovation from almost every man and woman in the hall. It went on, a tremendous roar, for fully five minutes. The nineteen hundred Louisiana Democrats knew they had heard truth, political skill and audacity combined in one electric moment.

During the last weeks of the campaign, both sides shifted strategy somewhat. No one was more aware than Barry Goldwater that his campaign was not going well. None of his attacks had really caught on and anti-civil rights, on which his advisers had depended so heavily, clearly was not delivering enough votes to make the election even close. Now the senator began emphasizing more and more the point which from the beginning had instinctively been his central theme. The "individualism," the "values"—usually the phrase was the "morality"—of America were going to pieces; this was the "simple heart of the matter." Sometimes he spoke of "morality" in a broad sense, sweeping under it "softness" toward the Communist powers and in Vietnam, "crime in the streets," and the "destructive effects" of social legislation on the individual. More often he bore in with a narrower definition, the "corruption of politics LBJ-style," innuendos about the way the Johnson family fortune was built and the "curious crew" with whom President Johnson had been associated, especially Bobby Baker. "The people have looked at the man who occupies the White House," Goldwater was declaring, "and have found him shadowed by suspicions which no amount of handshaking and hurrah can wash away."

The handshaking and the hurrah were battering even Lyndon Johnson's tough physique. Deep fatigue lines showed in his face, his voice was giving way to hoarseness; increasingly he had to resort to The Touch. Security scares were piling up—in Phoenix,

Los Angeles and then in Buffalo, where police seized a man with a rifle at a place the President was expected to pass. Some associates pressed the advice that the all-out bull-horn campaigning was costing him dignity. Mulling over these considerations, President Johnson decided that he would slow down and give the preference to set, dignified occasions. He would keep on agitating but, as he remarked, "less like a windmill."

Immediately after the Republican convention, LBJ had expressed the judgment that the sentences in Goldwater's acceptance speech embracing "extremism" were a blunder from which the senator could never recover. Almost everything he did during the campaign was intended to portray the G.O.P. candidate as a dangerous radical, alien to the tradition of the Republican and Democratic parties alike. This had worked well, but as the weeks went on, he became convinced that it was particularly effective in the realm of international problems. Peace and a wise attitude toward nuclear power, he suspected, were the major considerations influencing voters who were still doubtful. Consequently, he was reversing his decision made at the beginning of the campaign. From now on he would talk more about foreign affairs than about domestic matters, or at least as much.

On October 14 President Johnson arrived in New York City for a major effort reflecting the new strategy, a dignified foreign affairs presentation at the Alfred E. Smith Memorial Foundation dinner in the Waldorf-Astoria Hotel. At about six o'clock, while he rested in his suite, Press Secretary George Reedy took a phone call and the President received his first report of the sensational fact: the week before, Walter Jenkins had been arrested as a homosexual, under circumstances that were as grimy as possible. The news media were about to reveal that the Special Assistant to the President of the United States had been seized in a pay toilet in the YMCA two blocks from the White House with a sixty-year-old veteran who lived in an old soldiers' home. Moreover, the press had discovered that Jenkins was arrested in the same washroom on the same charge in 1959.

The whole development was stunning, almost incredible to Lyndon Johnson. This was the first and only crisis of the campaign, but it was a crisis both personal and political. Walter Jenkins, his friend and confidant over the decades, the whole Jenkins family tied to the Johnsons by the most intimate bonds—the personal blow could not have been harsher. Walter Jenkins, his closest White House aide—the situation seemed custom-tailored for the Republicans. Would it not give real power to the Goldwater charges about morality? Since homosexuals are prey to blackmail, and since Jenkins was privy to all White House secrets, did not the disclosure invite the attack that the Johnson Administration had endangered the military security of the nation? Two years later Lyndon Johnson still insisted vehemently in private that the Jenkins arrest resulted from a G.O.P. frame-up, and "some day we will prove it." Whether he really believed this or not, the statement reflected the impact which the downfall of Walter Jenkins had made upon him.

Press Secretary Reedy, visibly shaken, assembled a makeshift news conference to announce the resignation of Jenkins. President Johnson sat forlorn on the dais in the Grand Ballroom of the Waldorf-Astoria, smiling wanly and replying mechanically to the guests around him who were trying to make conversation. When the time came to speak, he cut the address almost by half and delivered the remainder in a distracted monotone.

Lyndon Johnson was caught in a cross fire of emotions. There was his sense of responsibility, as President, for the men he had named to high posts and for national security; his feudal, sentimental loyalty to Walter Jenkins; his relentless determination that nothing was to be permitted to take votes away from him. He resolved the conflicts the LBJ way.

He did not make a prompt, forthright comment expressing his sympathy for an old friend and able public servant who was in trouble, and stating that as President and a candidate for the Presidency, he would say nothing further until he had checked whether the trouble hurt the national interest. He made no immediate public comment. Obliquely, he went along with Mrs. Johnson's strong desire to issue a statement and she gave reporters the words: "My heart is aching today for someone who has reached the end point of exhaustion in dedicated service to his country." Meanwhile Lyndon Johnson ordered a crash poll on the effects of the Jenkins arrest on voters and an emergency FBI check into whether security had been violated. As reassuring reports came back, he released a statement of sympathy for Jenkins, who "has worked with me faithfully for twenty-five years," with "dedication, devotion, and tireless labor," but with no appreciation for Jenkins the public servant.

The Jenkins case produced a strange atmosphere in the White House. Of course staff people talked of the possible consequences in the election, and since Walter Jenkins was well liked, there was strong sympathy for him, his wife and six children. Yet these were not the most striking reactions. Whatever the nature of Jenkins' difficulty, he was obviously no simple or habitual homosexual. He was a man who for years had been destroying himself in the service of Lyndon Johnson, ten to sixteen hours a day, six or seven days a

week, and finally something had snapped. All of us recalled the
way he had been looking, his face red and blotched, his gestures
coming in jerks of nervousness. Men moved about the White House
in troubled preoccupation, some of them speaking in bursts of
bitterness against Lyndon Johnson and with comments like "There
but for the grace of God go I." One of the LBJ circle remarked ruefully, "I suppose Walter really went to that washroom but whatever
he did, it's really not the point. He was finding his own way to try
to commit suicide—he was a desperate man seeking a way out of
the kind of life he had been living."

The Republican campaign took on a new vigor. Barry Goldwater made little direct use of the Jenkins issue, but he spoke in
refreshed tones about the importance of "clear and constant evidence of the highest morality" in the White House. Other Republican leaders were not so restrained. Vice-presidential candidate
Miller attacked Jenkins by name, deriding any contention that
"this type of man" did not "compromise the national security," and
frequently speakers linked together Bobby Baker and Walter Jenkins and demanded to know what kind of a President it was who
had chosen two such close associates. Across the country some
G.O.P. politicians spread blue jokes.

They were all wasting their time. An FBI report, made public
eight days after news of the arrest, stated that no evidence had
been found to indicate that Jenkins had infringed security "in
any manner." A rapid fire of sensational world developments
moved the story off the front pages. Within three days the headlines reported that Nikita Khrushchev had been ousted from control of the Soviet Union, that the Labour party had won the
national election in Britain for the first time in thirteen years,
and that China had exploded its first nuclear bomb. President
Johnson took full advantage of these developments. Speaking
gravely from the White House, reiterating the point on the road,
he talked of the need for "stability" and "responsibility" in "these
times of rapid change," in contrast to those who were "trigger-
happy."

Still another fact—one that is a commentary on changing
American attitudes—diminished the political repercussions of the
Jenkins disclosure. Fifty or perhaps even thirty years earlier, the
charge of a homosexual on the White House staff would have
loosed a flood of sustained and severely damaging moral indignation. But by 1964, a considerable portion of the American population was educated enough to view homosexuality not as a sin
but as a physical deviation or a form of sickness. An influential
section of church leadership was ready to speak out in these terms.

Forty-five nationally respected religious figures soon joined in declaring that the Jenkins case should not be permitted to obscure
genuine "moral issues such as the full civil rights of all citizens,
the shameful squalor and poverty in our cities and the danger of
nuclear war." So marked was the change in educated circles that
G.O.P. efforts to exploit the Jenkins disclosure actually may have
cost Goldwater votes. As one Republican businessman remarked to
me, "I've been swinging back and forth but this cheap vendetta
makes me really wonder whether my bunch is ready to run the
country. Don't they know the man is sick?" In any event, the polls
indicated little or no damage to the LBJ cause.

Lyndon Johnson himself had been hit so hard by the episode
that he found it difficult to leave well enough alone. Soon he gathered selected newsmen for a late-afternoon session in a private
room of the White House and embarrassed them by making dark
insinuations of what he knew about leading Republicans or members of their families and hinting that he would use the material
"if they keep after my people." Another time, while he was on the
road campaigning, a reporter brought up the Jenkins case, and the
President exploded into an inaccurate and unfair analogy with a
Republican instance of homosexuality some years back which
involved an individual who was not even in public office.

But by now nothing, not even LBJ mistakes, could stay the
Lyndon Johnson avalanche. Soon he was back in fine fettle, carrying around in his breast pocket the latest summary of the polls:
Johnson, 481 electoral votes; Goldwater, 57. He was mopping up,
making suddenly scheduled trips into doubtful areas, burrowing
after that last possible vote. He held to his new strategy, sometimes. He avoided mass scenes, except when people were there and
the bull horn was at hand, and suddenly he was out of the limousine cavorting and exhorting. He emphasized foreign affairs. He
had picked up a remark from a Southern politician that he was frequently using: "It just won't do for my opponent and Red China
to have atomic bombs at the same time." But Barry Goldwater, in
the name of freedom of the individual, kept criticizing LBJ proposals for social legislation. Now and again—and then again and
again—the President permitted himself a departure from the problems of the world. "Some people," he observed with a snap in his
voice, "keep talking about freedom. And just what are you going
to take home to Molly and the babies comes Friday night—freedom?"

The real change was in a kind of euphoria that was settling
over Lyndon Johnson amid all the bursts of strident campaigning.

Partly it was calculation; he wanted any doubtful voter to know that he might as well vote for so serene and confident a leader. Partly it was simply the way Lyndon Johnson felt.

He discussed his future plans with story-book expansiveness. "So here is the Great Society," he told a Pittsburgh crowd seven days before the election. "It's the time—and it's going to be soon—when nobody in this country is poor. . . . It's the time—and there is no point in waiting—when every boy or girl . . . has the right to all the education that he can absorb. It's the time when every slum is gone from every city in America, and America is beautiful. It's the time when man gains full dominion under God over his destiny. It's the time of peace on earth and good will among men."

More than anything else, Lyndon Johnson now strove to sound like, what he wanted so much to be, the wise, benevolent father to the nation. He talked and talked—in a period of a day and a half he was making speeches for a total of six hours—interspersing everything with homilies and surges of sentimentality. He said: "Let's always be nice. When your neighbor comes over to your house, and he has been living alone for a long time and he gets lonesome, even if he does kind of do all the talking you be nice to him and courteous, because everybody is entitled to associate with good company every once in a while. . . ."

"Love thy neighbor as thyself; do unto others as you would have them do unto you. No matter how long it may take, no matter how difficult it is, this above all else is the great horizon toward which we march united. . . ."

And always: "Let's keep a smile on our face, let's keep faith in our heart, let's keep hope in our vision, let's move on to conquer unknown frontiers."

Election eve, near dusk, Lyndon and Lady Bird Johnson flew into Austin to an old-home welcome. Surrounded by men and women with whom he had gone through the years, Lyndon Johnson spoke his inner feeling. "It seems to me tonight," he said to one friend, "that I have spent my whole life getting ready for this moment."

Next morning the Johnsons were up at six-thirty and reached the polling place in Johnson City seven minutes after it opened. The President lingered at the poll; it was in the squat little building of the Pedernales Electric Cooperative down the street from his boyhood home, to him a proud symbol of what he had done for the district when he was its congressman. The rest of the day LBJ was restless and moody. He took forty reporters on a tour of the house where he grew up; drove from Johnson City to the ranch, from the ranch to Austin; in midafternoon impulsively telephoned Carol Channing to thank her for popularizing "Hello, Lyndon!" "I've heard it in every precinct in the country. I almost feel as if I composed it myself." At dinnertime the Johnsons joined old friends in a suite of the Hotel Driskill in Austin, since the 1880's a beef-steak-and-bourbon center of Texas political activities. The President sat hunched in a horsehair Victorian chair, intently watching the returns from the three television networks that were coming in on sets placed side by side. He said little and shushed people around him.

Obviously his mind was fixed on one point. A call came to me in Washington inquiring about the exact details of Franklin Roosevelt's triumph in 1936. Vaguely recalling a bizarre statistic and checking and finding it to be a fact, as tactfully as I could—who likes to bring up the subject of the mother-in-law at the wedding feast?—I cautioned against any early statement about comparative popular pluralities. In 1936 FDR had no doubt won by the all-time record, 60.8 percent of the total vote. But it was entirely possible that LBJ might roll up a tremendous plurality and nevertheless still be excelled by, of all people, Warren Gamaliel Harding, who had carried the country by 60.3 percent in 1920.

At about ten o'clock the President and Mrs. Johnson left the Driskill for a reception given by John Connally at the governor's mansion. No one in the United States doubted that Lyndon Johnson was overwhelmingly elected, but he was edgy. To a reporter who asked for a comment on the results, he snapped, "I'll have a statement if you'll just hold your potatoes."

At the Municipal Auditorium in Austin, thousands had gathered to watch the returns projected on a huge screen, and to await the arrival of President Johnson and his victory statement. The auditorium was a carnival of bunting, banners and the blaring of Texas songs. On the front of the blue-draped podium was the presidential seal, prepared for John Kennedy's visit on November 22, 1963, and now used for the first time.

In future days analysts would note many aspects of the LBJ victory. Millions had voted at least in part against Barry Goldwater rather than for Lyndon Johnson. A significant number declined to choose either; one and two-tenths percent fewer eligibles voted in 1964 than in 1960. The gigantic plurality resulted in part from the increase in population; 1964 was the election year when most of the World War II baby boom came of voting age. The nature of President Johnson's campaign had irrevocably stamped him in the mind of Metroamerica as a figure of the old school, given to platitudes and bathos, and had not diminished the impression of him as a thoroughgoing politician in the country as a whole. Ardently presenting himself as the candidate of peace, he had made statements about his policy toward the Vietnam War that would recoil on him within months.

All of these things, and more, were to be said in time, but on the night of November 3, 1964, what was on Lyndon Johnson's mind and the mind of the nation was that he had won a thunderous, unprecedented victory. Except for FDR in 1936, he had scored the greatest electoral triumph, 486 to 52. Excepting no one including Warren Gamaliel Harding, he gathered in the largest plurality, both in actual numbers and in percentages, 15,951,296 and 61.1 percent respectively. He was sweeping in on his coattails the most Democratic and the most liberal Congress since the heyday of the New Deal. It was almost unbelievable but it was true: Goldwater had not carried a single congressional district in thirty-two of the states outside the South.

Lyndon Johnson had achieved his cherished goal of being the most broadly based, most national victor in modern times. In state after state he won a majority of whites and Negroes, organized labor and big-businessmen, city dwellers, suburbanites and farmers. He carried every state in the North, Midwest and Far West. In the inner Western area, counted upon by the G.O.P. forces as their preserve, he won every state except Goldwater's Arizona and even there the margin was so thin the result was uncertain for hours. The region most likely to break up his bid for across-the-board backing did not fail him. Goldwater took five states of the old Confederacy, but the other six voted LBJ.

Backlash proved only a flick. In the telltale areas, where George Wallace had run so well in the 1964 primaries, Goldwater scored little better than the usual Republican vote. Samuel Lubell offered the plausible explanation: many anti-Negro, lower-income voters, had decided—at least for the moment—that social legislation and peace were more important than the race issue. But frontlash was devastating. Louis H. Bean, the respected political analyst, estimated that it ran as high as seven million, almost half the President's plurality.

The frontlash produced a wild scramble of ticket splitting, which elected or brought to heightened attention Republican figures in states swept by President Johnson—John H. Chafee in Rhode Island, George Murphy in California, Charles H. Percy in Illinois, George Romney in Michigan, Hugh Scott in Pennsylvania, and Robert Taft, Jr., in Ohio. All election evening Lyndon Johnson closely watched one particular instance of ticket splitting. A

Kennedy was running in 1964, Robert Kennedy, candidate for United States senator from New York. LBJ carried the state by a plurality of approximately 2,600,000 votes, RFK by 720,000. The President was particularly interested in the senator-elect's victory statement on television. Robert Kennedy said that his win represented an "overwhelming mandate for the policies of John F. Kennedy and of course Lyndon Johnson."

A little after one o'clock in the morning Lyndon Johnson entered the Municipal Auditorium. All moodiness, all edginess were gone. He was gentle, playful, endlessly polite and gracious. He delayed making his victory statement; he was savoring every moment. At 1:40 A.M. he delivered his remarks, making only a soft reference to the extent of the sweep and tying it to the harmony theme which had dominated his campaign. The victory "reaffirms the achievements and policies which have emerged over generations from common American principles. It is a mandate for unity. . . ."

Lyndon Johnson called on his wife, Lynda and Luci to speak, then took the microphone back to talk about Hubert and Muriel Humphrey and the barbecue the Johnsons and the Humphreys were going to have on the Pedernales tomorrow. The cheers kept rolling up and he stood basking in them. All the yearning years, the tortuous climb through Congress, the try for the Presidency in 1960 that was quashed, the excruciating period as Vice-President, the gnawing, mounting feeling that his chance would never come—all of this was over. The prize was his, and in glittering form. He had won it, by himself, in his own way, the biggest of them all.

When Lyndon Johnson finished his remarks about the Humphreys, he introduced to the crowd his youngest sister and then her husband and then their daughter. He stood there, the towering body rocking back and forth, gazing around trying to think of some way to extend the golden moment.

Finally Mrs. Johnson whispered, "Come on, let's go." Reluctantly, he went.

CHAPTER 11

Muted Mandate

*P*resident and President-elect Lyndon Johnson headed for the ranch and remained there for most of the period until the new year. He led one hundred and fifty aides and reporters around the land, discoursing on soil and rain, the good sense of the American voter, the way Communist peoples also seemed to want television sets; invited the Georgia governor and senators, whose state had gone Republican, for a fence-mending deer hunt; presided over Thanksgiving, Christmas and the Johnsons' thirtieth wedding anniversary in cascades of sentiment; hammed it up for photographers with a scene of himself, his pants slung low in ranch-hand style, and Agriculture Secretary Orville Freeman in a sports coat, corralling a mournful-looking steer; announced he would wear no cutaway and top hat at the Inauguration but an Oxford-gray suit, black shoes and a fedora; took Lady Bird Johnson for a ride in an electric golf cart and careened with such sharp turns that once her hand went to her mouth in fright; welcomed President-elect Gustavo Diaz Ordaz of Mexico with a bear hug and entertainment which ranged from classical Spanish dancer Mary Moore to a demonstration of shepherding by hill-country collies; and talked and talked and talked with a stream of visitors he summoned in careful succession or invited on a moment's notice.

And President Johnson worked, with fascination in his job and a flagellating compulsion to do it superbly. The campaign pallor had not disappeared from his face when, despite all the antics and the vacationing, he was getting in a six- to eight- to ten-hour day. For a year he had run an Administration that was in part inherited, in part makeshift. Now he was free, in fact and in spirit, to shape everything as he wished, and he went at everything.

LBJ was preparing for history too. At the confrontation about the vice-presidential nomination in the Oval Office, Robert Kennedy had observed that the "On" button of a tape recorder was down. At the ranch and in Washington, the buttons on many tape recorders were often down. Visitors to the ranch were also noting that whatever they were doing—conferring with the President in high seriousness at the big mahogany desk in the living room or chitchatting with him during a walk along the Pedernales—they were likely to be accompanied by a slight, pleasant-mannered Japanese-American, his camera constantly clicking. Yoichi R. Okamoto ("Oki" to everyone), a photographer of marked gifts, was an employee of the United States Information Agency who, at the President's instruction, was recording the Johnson Administration so assiduously on film that he was creating an almost hour-by-hour pictorial history.

President Johnson gave much of his time to mulling over the legislative program he would send to the new Congress. Commentators kept talking about the ringing mandate he had received; he talked differently. He was skeptical how much any presidential election was a mandate for a legislative program. However great his pride in the returns of November and his eagerness to believe that the masses had risen up with hosannas for LBJ, he was restrained when he spoke of the public backing he could expect for his proposals. The huge majority, he would say, represented general approval for the way he had handled the transition and for his conduct of the Presidency during 1964, and beyond that, it confirmed his impression that the country was ready to "move ahead." To this extent, he had achieved the leverage with the House and the Senate which he had sought. But the landslide did not mean that the public had expressed backing for specific bills or for an attitude of legislative adventuring.

Lyndon Johnson kept measuring his situation against that of Franklin Roosevelt in 1936. In both instances an incumbent President had won a sweeping victory and carried in with him large congressional majorities. But FDR, his admirer LBJ was sure, had then proceeded to make one of his few important political mistakes. President Roosevelt, President Johnson believed, interpreted the size of his win as a mandate to try to ram down the throat of Congress too much, too little planned, too casually timed. He let loose his zealous New Dealers, and they climaxed their errors with the abrasive legislation to enlarge the Supreme Court. Lyndon Johnson had compelling personal memories of those days. When he first took his seat in the House of Representatives in 1937, he was startled to find the body in a mood of near-revolt against a landslide President. He was convinced that FDR's misjudgment had provoked this attitude, and he further believed that it created circumstances highly favorable to the formation of the Southern Democratic-Republican coalition in the House and Senate which was to harass every Democratic President from that point on.

Lyndon Johnson was also being Prime Minister Johnson. In dealing with a Congress, he stressed, a newly elected President starts out with a certain political capital. It may be large or small—and no one needed to tell LBJ how big his was—but whatever its size, it has limits. Sooner or later, more and more members vote against the Administration, out of the sheer cussedness of man, the desire not to appear rubber-stamps, and the inevitable pressures from interest groups as a Chief Executive's program unfolds. "I've watched the Congress from either the inside or the outside, man and boy, for more than forty years," Lyndon Johnson remarked shortly after the 1964 election, "and I've never seen a Congress that didn't eventually take the measure of the President it was dealing with." He was determined that his measure would be taken as late as possible. "I worked like hell to become President, and I'm not going to throw it away."

And Lyndon Johnson proposed to be circumspect because of his ultimate goal—to serve as, and be remembered as, the President of national unity. He might admire enormously Chief Executives like Theodore and Franklin Roosevelt, but it was not for the ruckuses they had stirred up in Congress. His eye was more on the possible opposition coalition than on the powerful phalanx of pro-LBJ representatives and senators. He was particularly conscious of the congressmen from the five states below the Mason-Dixon line which had gone for Goldwater—in Mississippi, by no less than 85 percent.

Hence he wanted no highly dramatic "Hundred Days." At least in the early stage, he would send to the Hill those bills which had been backing up public support over so long a period that most congressmen of either party would vote against them only with a full sense of an electoral ax over their heads. The measures would go to the House and Senate one by one, not in a clump which could set up an "automatic opposition." "It's like a bottle of bourbon," said Lyndon Johnson. "If you take it a glass at a time, it's fine. But if you drink the whole bottle in one evening, you have troubles. I plan to take a sip at a time and enjoy myself."

Other fine points in the art of congressional relations were to be practiced sedulously. A measure would be sent to the Hill when Congress was in a "receiving mood," when the agendas of the relevant committees made it possible to clear the legislation swiftly so that opposition would not build up, and when the interests of the most intensely concerned congressmen were most likely to coincide with support for the bill. Premature disclosure of the details of legislation was to be guarded against; that too brought a coalescence of opposition. A proposal of this period that had enormous potentialities—the plan of Walter Heller, chairman of the Council of Economic Advisers, to return to the states a portion of federal income tax money—would soon be rejected by President Johnson in large measure because it leaked to the press and, the President felt, proceeded to rouse too many hostilities.

All this caution certainly did not mean that Lyndon Johnson intended to dawdle or to avoid measures he deemed important because they had strong enemies. "I do not accept the definition of government as being just the art of the practical," he liked to say. "It's the business of deciding what is right and then doing it." He had a kind of mental clock ticking off the inevitable attrition of his control of the House and Senate. As the new Congress was about to convene he mused, "I was just elected President by the biggest popular margin in the history of the country—sixteen million votes. Just by the way people naturally think and because Barry Goldwater had simply scared hell out of them, I've already lost about three of those sixteen. After a fight with Congress or something else, I'll lose another couple of million. I could be down to eight million in a couple of months." Before the serious attrition set in, he proposed to use his victory.

Just as consciously, LBJ was laboring not only to hold but to increase public support for his coming moves. He knew the liberals were with him. As a matter of fact, he feared they might be too much with him; "their columnists will be on my neck each day I don't deliver Utopia." Publicly and privately, he was giving his chief attention to conservatives, the business community and skeptics at large.

His tone was usually like the one on an occasion when reporters were at the ranch and he strolled out of the house holding three fat black binders. These were "a display," LBJ said with a chuckle. They contained "impressive legislative recommendations," but he was "poring over them" and making no hasty decisions. To the press and others, he cut back the expansive connotations of the phrase Great Society. "I don't want to leave the impression that we expect to build a Great Society overnight, or in any one day or in any one week or in any one month, or in any one session of Congress." Constantly he talked budget and budget economies. Although "meeting the aspirations of the American people," his 1965 budget, like his 1964 one, would be "frugal."

In every presidential move establishing the new Administration, one theme dominated. Lyndon Johnson expressed it in a remark to an aide who was working on a legislative proposal: "Now, don't make people mad."

An approach and then of course the men to carry it out—now President Johnson had a Vice-President, an able and energetic one, and he had to decide what to do with him.

After the election, LBJ made a number of remarks which suggested that he would carry out his convention-time pledge to give more dignity and importance to the vice-presidential office. In specific fact, President Johnson approved a plan for an official residence for the Vice-President and would have pushed it through Congress except for the Vietnam War and his own strictures about nonessential expenses; established Humphrey in a suite of offices in the Executive Office Building more appropriate for a Vice-President than those which he himself had occupied; continued the practice of including the Vice-President in Cabinet and National Security Council meetings, and named HHH to his own old posts as chairman of the National Aeronautics and Space Council and of the National Advisory Council of the Peace Corps, neither of which positions was mere window dressing; added a thoroughly sensible post, the chairmanship of a new Council on Equal Opportunity, with limited but genuine powers to coordinate federal efforts in the civil rights field; kept bestowing ceremonial titles, out of which the bearer could make what he wished; drew the Vice-President into legislative planning and foreign policy discussions; at times used him for liaison with Congress and for other political tasks; and continued to have long, confidential talks with him though the intimacy, interestingly enough, tended to diminish after the election.

That was just about it, and the total did not notably increase the dignity and importance of the Vice-Presidency. Humphrey was eager to have fulfilled two key points in the convention-time LBJ prescription for the Office—overall supervision of certain important domestic programs of the Administration and significant foreign policy assignments—but he was asked to undertake neither. Lyndon Johnson was experiencing the same impulse that most Presidents feel on the subject of Vice-Presidents. He intended to make sure that the Number Two man remained securely Number Two. He was also showing the attitude that he in particular had toward any subordinate; he was going to break the Vice-President into line and keep him there.

The process had begun in the weeks before Atlantic City when he forced vice-presidential aspirant Hubert Humphrey into the role of suppliant, his cup conspicuous before the nation. That might have been forgotten, but the duly elected Vice-President of the United States never really recovered in public esteem from the accounts of his visit to the ranch immediately after the election. When Humphrey arrived he was handed one of LBJ's ranch outfits and set to clumping along at Lyndon Johnson's side, size 11 cowboy boots on size 9½ feet and a five-gallon hat on a head that was at least one gallon larger. The President called for horses, a frisky quarter horse for the Vice-President-elect; the photographers snapped pathetically ridiculous pictures of horseman Hubert Humphrey. Newsmen were noting that LBJ more than occasionally referred to Humphrey, in a particular tone of which he was a master, as "Umphrey."

The general impression of the attitude of the President was so strong that when Winston Churchill died in the winter of 1965 observers jumped to interpret—and misinterpret—the choice of the American representative to the funeral. President Johnson, suffering from a bronchial infection, could not go to London himself, and in his stead he named not the expected protocol choice, the Vice-President, but Chief Justice Earl Warren. The President had a sound reason for the decision. He thought he might be a good deal sicker than the public announcement indicated; Humphrey himself had a cold and under the circumstances he did not think it wise to send the Vice-President out of the country on a tiring trip. But with his usual secretiveness, LBJ offered no public explanation, and the widespread assumption was that he was engaging in some more cutting down of his Vice-President. About the only pleasure Humphrey could derive from the incident was Art Buchwald's exposé of the real reason he was not sent to the funeral: Hubert Humphrey simply could not look sad.

The situation was exacerbated by qualities of the Vice-President himself. Never forgetting his small-town, depression-ridden background and his political frustrations, Hubert Humphrey was profoundly grateful to Lyndon Johnson for the vice-presidential nomination ("Hell, I was just little Hubert from South Dakota. Now just think, I occupy the second highest office in the land"). Having developed a sophisticated understanding of the American government, he did not doubt that the second highest office in the land required a dogged second-fiddle attitude. As ambitious as ever, he sought to stay in the good graces of his boss as the way to greater power in the Administration and perhaps a real chance at the Presidency. No novice about human beings, he knew what staying in favor with LBJ meant and on the few occasions when he forgot, his knuckles were sharply rapped. A perceptive, sensitive man living close to the Presidency, he was keenly aware of the brutal demands of the first Office and the special needs of its present occupant for a sense of loyalty and support.

Throughout the Johnson years, Vice-President Humphrey agreed with the broad outlines of the Administration's domestic and foreign policies, and he felt that it was his plain duty to support them publicly. He turned away from the suggestion of friends that if he dissented on an important issue, he should resign. The voters, he insisted, had named a Vice-President basically for the purpose of having a Chief Executive ready if something happened to the President. Besides, if he removed himself, only the proverbial heartbeat stood between the leadership of the free world and its assumption by the septuagenarian Speaker of the House John McCormack, a worn routineer and a man marked by some of the worst attitudes of the Joseph McCarthy era.

"The best way to survive this job," FDR's first Vice-President, John Nance Garner, once observed, "is to keep your mouth shut." Hubert Humphrey not only could not keep his mouth shut; he could not, in what he said and did, mask his effulgent feelings. Warm, outgoing and with an addiction to overstatement and over-personalization, during his Vice-Presidency he increasingly re-solved all his impulses by a language and a stance of super loyalty to the President, expressed over and over again in word and deed. Some friends continued to object, at times in a billingsgate against Lyndon Johnson which they called criticism. The Humphrey re-sponse was to talk more, and not only to defend but to over-defend.

The HHH posture as Vice-President would become plainest as the Vietnam War issue mounted. If he agreed with the general Administration policy, in sessions with the President he also spoke for less emphasis on Asia at the expense of Europe, and in Vietnam itself, more effort at a political solution and skepticism concerning search-and-destroy military tactics; he expressed doubts about the wisdom of trying to bomb the North Vietnamese to the negotiating table. These points he made in strict confidence. He did not even speak up much at Cabinet meetings for fear of a leak and a display of disagreement at the top of the Administration. Publicly—badg-ered alike by friends, the unmistakable insistence of President Johnson on utter loyalty and his own feeling that he owed it—he kept overtalking. The stormy disrupter of the 1948 Democratic convention in the name of decency for Negroes, the generous-spirited pioneer of Medicare, the Peace Corps, the Job Corps and Food for Peace, the man with a sympathetic and flexible view of the world's social dislocations and a never quiescent drive for arms control, sounded more and more like a hawkish, maudlin, passé Throttlebottom.

Quite apart from Vietnam, the melancholy story of Hubert Humphrey as Vice-President was foreordained. It was implicit in the nature of the Office and was simply magnified by the conjunction of the personalities of LBJ and HHH. When the Founding Fathers wrote the Constitution of the United States they never intended the Vice-Presidency in anything like its present form, and today it has become less an office than a dilemma. If the political processes put a second-rater in it, statistically the nation is running more than a 20 percent risk of having a second-rater in the Presidency of the United States. If a man of ability and spirit is chosen, he is being placed in a role that is certain to be miserable, likely to be demeaning, and may well—depending on the personalities and circumstances—seriously corrode his potential for effective leadership in the future.

The Cabinet presented no such intricacies. During the period between Dallas and the election, President Johnson had kept the group carefully intact except for the special case of Attorney General Robert Kennedy. Now he had something of a rule of thumb in considering the retention of members. There were the JFK men, whom he considered for the most part able, dedicated to public service and quite capable of serving another President loyally. Then there were the RFK men; whether able or not, they were "sonsofbitches, plotting inside my own house."

Lyndon Johnson had every intention of keeping in his Cabinet five Kennedy appointees whom he thought of as "JFK men": Dean Rusk in State, Robert McNamara in Defense, Secretary of the Interior Stewart Udall, Secretary of Agriculture Orville Freeman, and Secretary of Labor Willard Wirtz. He not only wanted to retain Rusk, McNamara and Wirtz; he had come to value them so highly that he would have resisted strongly had they shown any desire to leave, which they did not.

As for the rest of the Cabinet, LBJ went about filling it out at a leisurely pace and in ways that expressed his debts, needs and enthusiasms. First he moved into the post of Secretary of Commerce John T. Connor, president of the drug firm of Merck and Company, who had contributed energetic service on the frontlash National Independent Committee for Johnson and Humphrey. Then over the months of 1965 he named as Secretary of the Treasury Henry H. Fowler, a ruddy-faced, profane veteran of the upper echelon of Washington bureaucracy, adept in handling congressmen or bankers; as Secretary of Health, Education, and Welfare John Gardner, nationally associated with the President's passion, advances in education, and—as LBJ emphasized in announcing the appointment—also an ex-Marine and a Republican; and as Postmaster General, the hallowed seat for politicians, Lawrence O'Brien, the JFK politico who had come through for LBJ.

One 1965 appointment to the Cabinet had its special overtones. During the conversation between President Johnson and Attorney General Kennedy concerning the 1964 vice-presidential nomination, RFK had urged that his deputy Nicholas deB. Katzenbach should succeed him in the Cabinet. The deputy was a first-rate lawyer, with proven skill in the difficult civil rights area and an exceptional composure under stress ("I am an under-reactor," Katzenbach used to say), but he was only too clearly an RFK man. LBJ sought a different Attorney General, was turned down, kept coming back to Katzenbach. There was, to be sure, an advantage in an RFK man if he would continue to do a superior job and remember who had appointed him. For months the President kept Deputy Attorney General Katzenbach dangling, tested him in ways subtle and unsubtle, and then—when convinced that the Katzenbach ties could be made to run to the Oval Office— named him Attorney General.

Whether a JFK man like O'Brien or an RFK man like Katzenbach, each no less than Vice-President Humphrey felt the pressure to prove their loyalty to Lyndon Johnson. Again the Vietnam War would be the ultimate testing ground. In October 1967, five months before he resigned from the Cabinet to manage the anti-war candidacy of Robert Kennedy, O'Brien summoned the dead in support of the Vietnam War. Speaking in Lexington, Virginia, he declared that if General George C. Marshall were alive, "no doubt" he would thoroughly approve the Administration policy. Katzenbach had already appeared before the Senate Foreign Relations Committee with testimony so loyal it played a role in political history. Defending President Johnson's escalations of the war with no authorization from Congress except the Tonkin resolution, the Attorney General stated that declarations of war had become "outmoded" and strongly implied that in foreign affairs a President can do what he pleases without regard to Congress. Senator Eugene McCarthy, a member of the Foreign Relations Committee, got up and walked out of the hearing muttering, "There is only one thing to do—take it to the country." The Katzenbach testimony was a factor in moving McCarthy to take the Vietnam War to the country by entering the 1968 presidential race.

Back in the happier days of 1965, Cabinet choices could move along in an atmosphere of LBJ omnipotence, but all-triumphant or not, the President had to do something about the White House staff. The abrupt departure of Walter Jenkins had removed the single cohesive figure. In the exigencies of the moment, President Johnson had announced that Moyers would "replace" Jenkins. Since the fallen aide had taken care of so many different things and was in some ways irreplaceable, the statement did little to clarify the structure inside the White House. In addition, most of the staff ended the campaign exhausted and jumpy. The year since Dallas had been quite a period in terms of excitement known and power exercised, yet almost all of them felt put upon trying to function under the LBJ system. The offices filled with talk of resignations, this time not only the usual White House self-therapy but also a ploy to get an improvement in one's situation for the long pull.

Shortly after the election President Johnson put his mind to the most obvious problem—simply providing more help. In May 1964 he had named S. Douglass Cater, Jr., a Special Assistant, setting him to work largely on campaign tasks, and now at the beginning of the new term Cater was taking over regular White House functions. The aide represented an increasingly familiar American type, the journalist who moves back and forth between the press and universities. After his education at Harvard, he had become a member of the original staff of *The Reporter* magazine, and went on to serve as its Washington correspondent. Periodically interrupting this work for fellowships or visiting professorships, he produced two books of a semi-scholarly, semi-reportorial nature, *The Fourth Branch of Government* and *Power in Washington*. Forty-one years old, ambling in manner and speech, with a well-stocked mind readily adaptable to the main chance, Cater had hard-driving ambitions which were obscured by his pleasant ways and his moments of ambivalence between the urge to lay hold of the levers of manipulation and a desire to be recognized as a man of humanistic values.

He also had characteristics which made him highly eligible for the LBJ staff. He was a Southerner born and bred, a product of Montgomery, Alabama; the son of a state senator, he grew up to the assumption that politics is the natural way of life. His wife, the statuesque Libby Anderson of Birmingham, had been the first woman elected president of the University of Alabama student body and the executive secretary to Congressman Laurie C. Battle of Alabama, and she did not lose her political instincts. In the early 1950's Cater had various connections with the Secretary of the Army and the Director of Mutual Security, and when

Senator John J. Sparkman of Alabama campaigned as Adlai Stevenson's vice-presidential candidate in 1952, Cater was along in the decrepit DC-3, writing speeches and serving as a general aide.

By the mid-1950's Cater was generally categorized as a liberal in his attitudes, and he was one of the few liberal journalists of any prominence who was finding warm words for Senate Majority Leader Lyndon Johnson. In 1955 he visited the ranch and came back emphasizing precisely the point that LBJ wanted emphasized. The *New York Times* had run a story, Cater wrote, that the Senate Majority Leader was becoming a powerful regional figure and a rallying point for the nation's conservative forces. This was not so; Lyndon Johnson was a "national" leader, one "who brings a perfectionist's craftsmanship to everything he does," and his "brilliant career" "has earned universal respect and admiration for his success at finding for the national Democratic party in the Senate the center at which it can operate with safe and enduring equilibrium." Against the background of this kind of writing, relations between Cater and the Senate Majority Leader grew increasingly cordial.

Bill Moyers pushed Cater's appointment to the White House staff, and while the President was considering it he leafed through the Cater book *Power in Washington,* which was published in early 1964. "He's pretty rough on Kennedy," LBJ said. Then he riffled a few more pages. "And he's pretty rough on me too." To Lyndon Johnson the passage was rough indeed; Cater had ventured to suggest that "many senators, both liberal and conservative, rankled under the intensely driving technique of leadership Johnson displayed." But the overall treatment was as understanding as ever. On the day he was named to the White House staff, Cater could quite accurately tell the press that his relationship with the President had been "very good for a number of years"; he had been "greatly impressed with the Senate Majority Leader," and "developed an admiration for the man." This appointment brought into the White House one of the few figures of the American intellectual or quasi-intellectual world who seemed ready to be a thoroughgoing LBJ man.

Several months after the election, President Johnson made official what had long been a reality by designating W. Marvin Watson a White House aide with the usual title of Special Assistant. Like Cater, Watson was just beginning his forties in age, but he was a man of markedly different background. He had grown up in Huntsville, Texas, near Houston, a lumber and oil town stretching over red sandhills, known for the house of Sam

Houston which was modelled after a Mississippi steamboat, the gray towers of the Texas State Penitentiary, and the production of hard-shell Baptists like the Watson family. The father, operator of a small auto dealership, could give the son little financial backing but he was all for his get-up-and-go. Marvin Watson helped pay his expenses through Baptist-oriented Baylor University by selling coveralls and after combat service in World War II as a Marine on Guam, Iwo Jima and Okinawa, he returned to Baylor on the GI Bill and took a master's degree in the business school. For a while he could find nothing better than selling hearing aids in San Antonio, but then he heard of an opening as manager of the Chamber of Commerce in Daingerfield, east of Dallas.

The big man in the Daingerfield area was Eugene B. Germany, the author of six pamphlets with titles like *And Passing Through the Valley of Baca He Made It a Well*, and as good a Methodist as Marvin Watson was a Baptist. Texans also knew Germany as an instance of their state's indigenous product, the man who combines fundamentalist religion, business success, antediluvian corporation practices and right-wing politics. Starting as a high school science teacher, he had tried oil prospecting on the side, struck it rich, used his resources to take over the presidency of the Lone Star Steel Company and then run the firm with labor attitudes straight out of the McKinley era. Meanwhile he was becoming a central figure on the Democratic State Executive Committee, usually throwing his influence behind candidates well to the right of Robert Taft. Germany promptly took a liking to the new young manager of the Daingerfield Chamber of Commerce and made him something of a protégé. By the late 1950's Watson, not yet out of his thirties, was executive assistant to the president of Lone Star Steel and a rising power on the State Democratic Committee.

The human being emerging from this life was a sturdily built man, with bright gray eyes beneath heavy dark brows, usually affable, almost gentle in manner, hard worker, nonsmoker, nondrinker, known for his clear, decisive thinking and his personal integrity. Watson permitted himself only one frippery. He was a natty dresser, given to hand-tailored seersucker suits, color-checked shirts, flashing gold cuff links and a jewel-flecked triangular watch.

Of course he was strongly conservative in business and political attitudes, though not an ultra-rightist like Germany. Basically, Watson's conservatism derived from his parochialism. With scarcely any imagination or intellectual curiosity, he knew no world except the moral credo of small-town Texas, the business

credo of Lone Star and the political credo of Austin. As businessman or politician, he was essentially an administrator—"the
greatest nit-picker around," one associate put it, "the master of the
paper clip." The affability would disappear and the gray eyes
flash when a subordinate took a dawdling lunch, made a slip
in some bureaucratic procedure, or in a moment of emotion or
opinion forgot that the function of business was to make money
and the function of politics was to win votes.

When Watson's political work brought him contact with Lyndon Johnson in the late 1940's, an alliance was natural. Watson
saw in the senator what he admired, a man who knew his job; the
senator saw in the Democratic State Committeeman what he
needed, another rising conservative to bolster the liberal-conserva-
tive coalition that he was trying to build in Texas politics. Watson
was a pioneer and indefatigable Johnson-for-President worker in
1960, and when that effort failed he continued to remain in close
touch. His assignment at the Atlantic City convention of 1964
was to "co-ordinate" it. Co-ordinate it he did, everything from
supervising the distribution of tickets to LBJ's birthday party, to
intricate decisions affecting the power and aplomb of political
leaders, to lecturing staff workers about too much partying and
making passes at the secretaries. Watson took over with his
customary obliviousness to the ways of the world beyond Texas.
After the delicate compromise was reached in the Mississippi
delegation battle, some angry Negro representatives decided to take
seats anyhow. Walter Jenkins was appalled to hear Watson's
drawl over the intercom telling the convention police to "clear
out those people." The forcible ejection of pro-civil rights forces
would have made quite a television scene, and Jenkins quietly
saw to it that the sit-in was handled by being ignored.

At the same time that President Johnson formally named
Watson to the White House staff he was also reaching out for
Joseph A. Califano, Jr., thirty-three, the special assistant to
Secretary of Defense McNamara and the only important LBJ
aide genuinely drawn from another part of the Executive branch
of the government. Califano was an unusual Johnson man in
other respects too. Brooklyn-born, the son of an Irish-American
mother and an Italian-American father who held an administrative
post at International Business Machines, educated at Holy Cross
and Harvard Law School, he had been rewarded for his excellent
law school record by a job at the New York firm headed by none
other than Thomas E. Dewey.

Except for his swarthy appearance, Califano looked like any
other well put-together junior executive, but he had his own variety

of demons of restlessness. He had never shown any interest in government or politics; he wanted to get ahead in the legal corporate world and to make money and wield influence. One day in the early period of 1960 when he was sick and stayed home from the office, his wife, the former Gertrude Zawacki, a devotee of tangy spaghetti dishes and New York reform politics, had some friends in for dinner and political talk. Califano was intrigued; this seemed much more interesting than "splitting stocks" at Dewey, Ballantine, Bushby, Palmer & Wood, and it was not at all removed from the world of influence and money.

That fall Califano did a little local work for the national Democratic ticket. After JFK's win he found a place for himself in the Defense Department, which in many ways is a branch office—some say the headquarters—of corporate America. His abilities quickly propelled him up. In time Califano, no ideologue, no fighter of lost or losable causes, eagerly taking to the systems-analysis approach of McNamara and adding to it a flair for politicking that the Secretary did not have, became McNamara's right-hand man.

Much of Califano's work involved liaison with the White House. Both President Johnson and Bill Moyers noted that his sharp intelligence included an ability to analyze a problem quickly and come up with clear alternative proposals; his political instincts permitted him to get apparently intransigent opponents to some measure of agreement; and his prodigious work habits and unstoppable manner (one of those subjected to it called it "the old hatchet man wired for computers") bespoke a drive to build a reputation as a man who knew how to get things done. The day after the 1964 election President Johnson phoned Califano and invited him to come to work at the White House. Secretary McNamara tactfully stalled the transfer, and for a while Califano virtually worked under both roofs. In July 1965, he was formally named to the White House staff.

As the President added aides, usually youngish men, a long-time associate observed, "Johnson may be the vainest man and the roughest boss who ever came down the pike, but he has always been keenly aware that what he achieves depends on the help around him. He especially leans toward young men. He himself was always the bright young man—at twenty-seven the administrator of the National Youth Administration for all Texas, a young representative and then a young senator, the youngest Majority Whip of the Senate and then its youngest Majority Leader. As he likes to say, 'Old men for advice, young men for action.' He stockpiles bright young men in his mind, and then somehow, sometimes by the damndest ways, he gets them working for him where he wants them to be."

During the Senate days Lyndon Johnson had stockpiled a young Texan, Harry C. McPherson, Jr., and now at thirty-five McPherson was beginning to function quietly as a White House aide with his formal appointment to come a month after Califano's. When the announcement was made a reporter remarked, "McPherson is the only Special Assistant to the President who once aspired to be a professional poet." Home for McPherson had been Tyler in eastern Texas, near Moyers' Marshall and Watson's Daingerfield, a community existing basically on oil and livestock. But Tyler was also different. With a population mounting over 65,000, the rose-growing center of the world as well as a service area for the ranches and derricks, it was proud of its lovely Municipal Park, its remarkably free-wheeling junior college, its civic theater and its more than competent East Texas Symphony Orchestra. The son of an advertising man and a mother who once aspired to be a novelist, McPherson grew up in a home touched by books and music and for his higher education, his sights went beyond Texas. He chose the University of the South in Sewanee, Tennessee, which was still stirred by memories of the "agrarian poets" who had given it a moment of literary prominence in the 1930's. For graduate work he went still further away, to Columbia, telling his friends he intended to be a poet and all the while being caught up in the liberalism that dominated the Northeastern campuses.

McPherson's military service as an air-target intelligence officer in Europe coincided with Senator Joseph McCarthy's rampage, which embarrassed and frightened any intelligent American who listened to the reactions of Europeans. "I saw us going into an era where everyone's rights would be in danger. I decided to be a lawyer." McPherson returned to attend the University of Texas Law School. He graduated a quick-minded, agreeable young man with soft good looks, strong ties to the Episcopal Church, and a questing way of talking about "social consciousness," David Riesman's observations on the changing American character and the "necessity of new views." Soon he wrote two plays, *Ground Zero* and *Missing Person,* staged in an Episcopal church and filled with social significance.

But Texas seems to have its puissance even over dramatists of social significance and poets and enemies of power-happy senators. For years a great favorite of University of Texas students—including the University of Texas student who became Lady Bird

Johnson—had been a breezy, sharp-spoken professor of economics, Robert H. Montgomery. The professor once sat in the Austin airport, his ranch shirt open at the collar, and explained his students to me. "In other parts of America," Montgomery said, "social reform or making it in the corporations or something else may be it. In Texas, even more so than in the rest of the South, politics is it. Politics is not just something an ambitious young man does. It is *it*—a way of life, as natural as riding a horse, or when you've made it, going to Neiman-Marcus for a mink for the wife." In 1956 the Senate Democratic Policy Committee needed an assistant counsel and the chairman of the committee, Lyndon Johnson, approved the addition "provided he's a Texan." Poet and worrier over the state of man, Harry McPherson, who was also a Texan, got the job.

From then on, whatever his nominal post—it ranged from counsel to a committee headed by Senator Mansfield to Deputy Undersecretary of the Army—McPherson was at least a part-time Johnson aide. He helped draft speeches and legislation for the Senate Majority Leader, did political chores and proved particularly useful in handling what LBJ called the "knee-jerk liberals." In the vice-presidential days, Moyers saw that McPherson's star was rising and took care to draw him into his own group of young comers. McPherson's first title in the Johnson Administration was Assistant Secretary of State for Educational and Cultural Affairs, a holding operation until he was formally transferred to the White House staff.

While he added new aides, President Johnson also moved to mollify grievances of the old hands. He brought Richard Goodwin out of the shadows of the Executive Office Building, named him a Special Assistant and gave him a White House office, let him talk to the press—without too frequent lashings from the Oval Office—about the fact that he was writing speeches. The President also moved Horace Busby from the East Wing to Jenkins' old office in the West Wing, with the implication that he would be more a part of hour-to-hour operations. He made an effort, sincere if short-lived, to decrease the drain on the energies and tempers of his staff. He even found the money to permit sprucing up a number of the White House offices, especially those in the West Wing, where the large-scale turnover in personnel had created the appearance of a well-slept rooming house. The choices of the men for the redecoration of the rooms where they spent so many of their waking hours were often strikingly characteristic. In particular. Marvin Watson's office became Watsonian.

He liked blue and in his dogged way, everything was blue—draperies with light blue urns against dark blue lines, a navy blue sofa beneath a painting of bluebonnets, a dark blue chair near his desk and two light blue chairs nearby, a color photograph of Lyndon Johnson in muted blue.

Busby and Mrs. Johnson took over redoing the Press Lounge and the Fish Room (the latter now renamed by the President—to the regret of all devotees of the whimsical—the West Wing Conference Room). Paintings were hung on the walls of the West Wing Conference Room, and the book shelves were filled with volumes about the Presidency, to replace the *World Almanac* of 1962, a biography of Boss Tweed and a vagrant copy of *Mr. Blandings Builds His Dream House*. Wherever Mrs. Johnson was involved, her quiet, firm interest in modern as well as Western painting was likely to show itself. Up on the most prominent wall of the Press Lounge went "Woman by Window," a large, decidedly contemporary painting by Richard Diebenkorn. Traditionalists muttered about this canvas so conspicuously displayed, and Lyndon Johnson went to see it. He looked at it, looked again, and remembered who had put it there. "Let it stay," said Lyndon Johnson.

The President was giving a little more specific shape to the duties of the staff. Continuing to insist that his men were absolutely equal, he permitted Bill Moyers to assume increasingly the role of chief of staff. In terms as clear as the matter can be stated, this meant that Moyers delegated many of the tasks within the White House; often spoke in the name of the President to officials from the Vice-President on down and to powerful people outside the government; sometimes okayed or vetoed proposals of varying importance without consulting the Oval Office; had a hand— on occasion, a decisive hand—in making many top-level appointments; and was likely to be called by the President for long talks about developments. In addition, he was becoming even more the key staff figure in doing the preliminary shaping of the legislative program in domestic affairs.

Earlier LBJ men were shifting in importance or function. Goodwin was now clearly the chief speech writer, particularly for addresses concerning race or urban problems. Busby and Reedy, continuing their other functions, gave time to a type of task they had become accustomed to in the Senate days, Busby carrying on relations with business and Reedy with labor, as he had done in the case of the threatened rail strike. More than ever Valenti was the jack-of-all-trades and whatever his assignment, exceedingly close to the President but with that intimacy threatened by Watson.

Among the new men, Cater specialized in education and public welfare, McPherson, in civil liberties and civil rights. Both did speech writing; McPherson especially showed skill at producing the LBJ cadence, and in addition was being groomed for the post of the President's legal counsel. For the moment Califano functioned as something of an aide to Moyers, particularly in working on the legislative program.

Of the recent appointees, the one quickly developing the most important role was Watson. He was taking over from the departed Walter Jenkins administrative supervision of the White House, and from Jack Valenti, most of the functions of the appointments secretary, confidently exercising the considerable power coming from these activities. Watson was also becoming an important political voice of the White House, to some extent in dealing with Congress and to a greater degree in dealing with Democratic chieftains around the country. His further role was intangible, but perhaps most significant. More and more it was Watson rather than Valenti who was likely to be at the President's side for long periods of the night and day, with all the confidant's potentiality for affecting decisions.

Like the earlier group of Johnson men, the four new appointees were youthful; their average age was thirty-seven. Three of the four had grown up in the South, two in small towns and none in Metroamerica; two had been closely associated with LBJ during most of their working lives; most were heavily dependent on the good will if not the patronage of Lyndon Johnson for their future careers. Ideologically, Watson may have come to the White House a conservative, Califano with many of the attitudes of Dewey, Ballantine, Bushby, et al., Cater and McPherson generally liberal in outlook, but the classifications meant little. The basic instincts of Cater, McPherson and Watson were political and of Califano, activist. Cater and Watson in particular took pains to shake off their past ideological identifications. Watson made it known that he was for right-to-work laws at Lone Star Steel and against them at the White House because his guiding principle was "loyalty to the man you are working for." LBJ had a way of referring to Cater as "one of my professors" and the aide, only too aware of what this meant, made quiet moves to indicate that he was just as "practical" as Watson or anyone else not tainted by a Harvard degree and the authorship of books. Fundamentally, the Johnsonian core of the LBJ staff remained what it had been since the first days of the Administration: able, hard-working, not inclined to go out on limbs of any kind, intensely political, a group who knew how to do well what the boss wanted done.

The most important difference continued to be that Walter Jenkins was gone. Since no one in the White House had questioned Jenkins' primacy on the staff, his understanding of President Johnson's thinking and moods, or his disinterested loyalty, he had been able to keep the group functioning as something of a unit and to delegate tasks with a minimum of irritated maneuvering by others. With his practice of seeing to it that the President had the benefit of all responsible points of view, power drives and personal opinions had less chance of cutting off staff members from maximum effectiveness and consequently of creating deep-seated dissatisfactions. Under the changed circumstances, the group of assistants fragmented even more than White House staffs usually do.

Bundy's foreign affairs operation went largely its own way. Cater, Califano, Goodwin and McPherson moved principally in Moyers' orbit. Valenti and Watson worked in uneasy relationship to each other, and both to Moyers. Busby and Reedy were off by themselves, sometimes functioning together, mostly singly. To a considerable extent, the staff was turning into a shifting band of individuals and groups moving in mutual suspicion around the commanding, demanding figure of Lyndon Johnson.

With this kind of a staff make-up serving a President who interpreted his landslide as a muted mandate and with the continuing obeisance of the Administration to almost all shades of opinion, it was hardly surprising that a heavy blandness marked Administration activities and that the tortuous realities of foreign policy were receiving short shrift. To be sure, President Johnson was already taking foreign policy actions, some of them with momentous implications. Yet he appeared to be making the moves with his left hand, and his bulging black binders contained relatively few significant proposals in the international field. In his background sessions for the press, he sounded as if he were saying that the world was in good shape and that if the United States only applied good will and common sense, things would go along fine.

This stance in foreign affairs was not reassuring, and in the field of domestic problems my old concerns about the consensus approach, when in the hands of a President of overweening political instincts and pragmatism, were flooding back. Again it was impossible to ignore that consensus can be a fancy name for third-ward politics—getting as many voters as possible behind you and doing what most people are ready to do—or it can mean bringing to enactment programs on which the general public has come to agree, in a spirit of opening the way to future-oriented legislation. But if no one was to be made mad, as President Johnson had expressed his attitude, how could consensus in the second sense be advanced? Occasionally he was ready to speak the more extended doctrine, as when he accepted sentences I had drafted for a speech the month after the election stating that "consensus can become a comfortable cushion on which a nation simply goes to sleep. Consensus can also be an active, dynamic, rolling credo. Consensus can be a springboard. . . ." But the fundamental tone did not change.

There were other concerns too. Could nothing be done about the general debilitating air of just-us-folks-doing-sensible-things? And what of the constant injection of transparent political craftiness, the absence of fire and lilt, the paucity of association of the new Administration with people of varied achievement, the rarity of things, little and big, which give dash, color and richer powers of leadership to a Presidency? Would Metroamerica, so put off by the LBJ campaign, respond to the emerging Administration? And without some degree of enthusiasm from Metroamerica, could the Administration have much real command of the late 1960's?

Not only the general picture but small episodes spurred my doubts. The incidents began with the inauguration itself. I had suggested that the ceremony include a three-to-five minute reading of a selection prepared for the purpose by a celebrated American author, specifically, a prose poem on the theme of the meaning of the American experience written by John Steinbeck. Not only was Steinbeck a Nobel Laureate in literature; he was a family friend of the Johnsons' and both the President and the First Lady admired his writings (*The Grapes of Wrath* was one of the few novels LBJ had ever read). Steinbeck also seemed thoroughly appropriate to a Lyndon Johnson ceremony because he was a Westerner and an author most famous for his stories about the troubles of ordinary people. The week before the inauguration, the President gave tentative approval to the proposal.

The White House switchboard reached Steinbeck in Dublin, and I explained that President Johnson had not given a final okay and that since the ceremony was imminent, the material would have to be written and cabled within thirty-six hours. Good-humoredly, Steinbeck went along. The text he sent was moving indeed, and I hurried it by the jet courier to the President who was at the ranch. Word came back that he had read it to Mrs. Johnson, remarked, "It's too good—it will upstage my speech," and vetoed it. What lingered of Steinbeck were a few themes and phrases that made their way into the inaugural address and an almost-verbatim section, one of the more routine of Steinbeck's passages, which proved to be the most quoted part of the President's speech: "I do not believe that the Great Society is the ordered, changeless, and sterile battalion of the ants. It is the excitement of becoming—always becoming, trying, probing, failing, resting, and trying again—but always trying and always gaining."

What did the veto mean? Vain or not, Lyndon Johnson could hardly have been serious when he spoke of being upstaged by a four-minute ceremonial reading. Conceivably he balked because the public might say that he was imitating Robert Frost's appearance at the inauguration of John Kennedy. But he had considered this point when the suggestion was first made and dismissed it. More than likely, once he came to the actual decision President Johnson shied away from anything suggesting what he called "artsy," and was further dissuaded by the fact that Steinbeck had spoken of the impatience, tensions and fears of the American people and LBJ wanted no such words spoken at his inauguration.

Soon Lincoln's Birthday was at hand—an observance that had added point because 1965 was the one hundredth anniversary of the end of the Civil War—and I decided to make another stab at associating the Administration with cultivated groups in the country and at emphasizing foreign policy and stating consensus in a more active way. I suggested a White House Lincoln luncheon. The guests would be about a hundred Lincoln writers and scholars and some of the nation's more interesting Lincoln buffs, and the President would make a major speech based on the famous quotation from Lincoln's 1862 Annual Message to Congress, "As our case is new, so we must think anew and act anew."

The nation might well be in a mood, I argued, to respond favorably to an address pointing out that one hundred years ago, the ending of the Civil War meant that certain problems were settled and that the country was entering a genuinely new era. But American leaders immediately after Lincoln did not think through the nature of this new age, and the results were the blunders of Reconstruction. "Now once again," my précis of the projected address went on, "we are entering a new era. A broad consensus in foreign and domestic affairs exists. . . . At this point, the speech would analyze where we are and where we are going, particularly discussing these points: (1) the vital difference between a passive and an active consensus; (2) the larger pattern into which the Administration domestic measures fall; and (3) the relative roles of foreign and domestic policy in this period."

President Johnson instructed me to arrange the luncheon and write the speech. In preparing the draft, I kept very much in mind his strategy of the muted mandate and the reasons for it. But I also made the address express explicitly the insistent demands of foreign policy and of a consensus which would not serve as a rationalization of severely limited objectives.

That Lincoln's Birthday gave me a warm feeling as I watched the belligerently activist, anti-"artsy" LBJ engage in genuine conversation with writers, scholars and other Americans who had an appreciation of the subtleties of the Lincoln story. As for the speech, the President scrapped my version almost completely and delivered a standard talk about the ideals of "unity" and "freedom" exemplified in Lincoln's leadership. Perhaps I had written a poor draft. Poor draft or not, I was learning just how determined Lyndon Johnson was to launch his program without stirring up anybody.

One aspect of this episode struck me with particular force. In reporting the event, the more Metroamerican the newsman, the more he was inclined to treat it as a political ploy. A typical account, by the syndicated columnist Mary McGrory, was entitled "Johnson 'Kidnaps' Lincoln" and described how the Democratic President had "stolen Lincoln for his own party and claimed him for his own." The luncheon was an "unprecedented" observance, not only for any President but particularly for a Democratic President, and its most remarkable feature was the number of Republicans invited. "The political abduction was disguised as a treat for scholars . . . and was a blend of homage and craft that no Republican could decently protest. . . . Lincoln's Birthday presented an irresistible opportunity to Mr. Johnson. He seized it in a bold and brilliant stroke that will be much noted and long remembered."

Well, maybe it was a bold and brilliant political stroke, but if so, it certainly was a remarkably concealed one. Not only was the event suggested and the guest list drawn up by a person who had totally different purposes in mind; the President who approved the affair gave no indication that he had any particular political motive. Abraham Lincoln is just about as national an institution as the United States possesses, and for a man elected to the Presidency twice on the Republican ticket, just about as nonpartisan a figure. To LBJ the occasion seemed simply "the kind of thing a President should do," as he remarked to me after the luncheon, and if he had some wile in the back of his head, it totally escaped me.

But what was striking about the press coverage was not whether observers like Mary McGrory were right or wrong; it was their assumption. As Lyndon Johnson entered his new Administration, his past and his posture in the present appeared to be provoking from Metroamericans in still more more magnified form that now so familiar reaction: whatever LBJ did was undertaken simply for political purposes.

Several months later there was talk in the White House about the coming Medal of Freedom presentations. In 1963 President Kennedy had established the award to honor citizens of the United States, together with a few foreigners, who had made particularly distinguished contributions to some aspect of American life. The recipients were to be named on July 4, and the program associated both the national holiday and the Presidency with highly interesting people of a great variety of creativity. President Johnson presented the first two groups of Freedom Medals to lists of men and women drawn up largely in the JFK days. But now trouble came.

For 1965 the awards committee included among its nominees Herbert L. Block ("Herblock"), the American Daumier who, having lacerated politicians for years, had not neglected to take a few cuts at President Lyndon Johnson. LBJ grumbled about "giving out medals to all these characters whose names will cause an uproar in the papers." Besides, "why should I go around honoring people who attack me?" He did not seem to understand, or did not choose to understand, that by presenting a medal to Herblock he was no more endorsing the cartoonist's opinions than he had, from previous lists, approved the theology of Pope John XXIII, the segregationist views of Representative Carl Vinson or the aesthetic judgments of Edmund Wilson. Nor did he appear to comprehend that by honoring a sometime satirist of himself who happened to be an American of extraordinary talent, he would be adding flavor to his Administration.

More trouble came from the limitations of men on whom President Johnson relied. One of his aides, out of sincere but narrow-gauged interest, involved himself intensely in the Freedom Medal recommendations and he had a candidate of his own, a well-known writer of skillful popularized history. Then friends of the assistant urged a different name on him. If a historian were to be honored, they felt it should be a particular academic who had produced major scholarly works that bore direct relevance to a serious American problem of the 1960's. One of the more frustrating conversations of my life resulted when the aide asked me which man was "the bettter historian." I tried to explain that they had been engaged in essentially different work; both had made important contributions to the national understanding of the past; either—or both—was worthy of the recognition; and if I were asked to make a choice it would be the scholar, not because he was a scholar but because I believed his writings were of deeper significance and influence. Clearly I was not getting across. In an entirely friendly way, the aide was obviously passing off my distinction between the two historians as academic condescension, and my statement that neither was "better" as an instance of the intellectual's indecisiveness. Between this sticky situation and Herblock, the Freedom Medal awards were ended for the rest of the Johnson Administration, depriving July 4 of something besides windy speeches, sunburns and accident statistics.

The recurring small incidents all fitted into a larger picture—at times I sat glumly in my office. I was still anxious to do things to help bring this enormously capable leader into greater rapport with Metroamerica, but the atmosphere of the White House was only too plain and only too surely being projected to the nation. Yet anybody with a wisp of sense does not sit glumly in a White House office for long. You continue to remember that a man who has won the Presidency of the United States no doubt knows a great deal more about running a country than you do, and that the phone is ringing with thoroughly worthwhile things to do or try to do. It was especially silly to moon over the Johnson Administration in early 1965, when the President was already scoring a resounding series of legislative successes.

I announced to my office the wisdom that I wanted embroidered on a sampler and placed in our foyer. It was a quotation from James R. Hoffa: "I may make a mistake sometimes but I am never wrong." And with that, I joined full-heartedly and proudly in President Johnson's drive to get through Congress, by the approach he considered best, legislation which the American people had needed so much for so long.

CHAPTER 12

The Great Drive

O n the evening of January 4, 1965, President Johnson entered the House of Representatives to deliver his second State of the Union message. All across the packed chamber, thoughts turned back to the year before, when a Vice-President suddenly become President had appeared for the same purpose. In many ways the scene was the same. Lyndon Johnson walked down the aisle with a smile and a greeting on all sides, the presidential box contained a carefully balanced group of guests, the speech had been honed to its final comma for maximum impact. Yet the occasion was also strikingly different. This was no accidental President putting on a demonstration of confidence and command, but a Chief Executive speaking with the aplomb of resounding election in his own right. Lyndon Johnson read in a relaxed slow drawl, his gestures natural and free, pausing so much to drive home his points and to accept the applause that he ran his planned thirty minutes to forty-nine. The speech was some four thousand words long, and not a one of them mentioned John Kennedy.

The address followed the approach he had been working out since the election. It was set within the context of the "quest for union." Less than a fifth of it concerned foreign affairs, and except for mention of efforts to increase contacts with the Communist countries of Europe, the section was a series of generalities; Vietnam received just one hundred and thirty-one words. In domestic affairs, Lyndon Johnson made it eminently plain that he expected action, and he went beyond bread-and-butter legislation to speak of establishing a National Foundation on the Arts and getting under way "a massive effort" to improve the appearance and increase the human rewards of the cities and countryside. But everything was countervailed, subdued, de-fanged.

The parts of the speech on beautification and the arts foundation came between paragraphs concerning budget economies and a section to please Goldwaterites who were exercised about crime in the streets. Though the sound of a battery of coming legislative proposals could be clearly heard, many were left in broad, accommodating outline. One of the most specific moves the President indicated—answering labor's demand for repeal of Section 14(b) of the Taft-Hartley Act—was promptly undercut by informal assurances from the White House that this point would not be pushed too hard. The frugality theme was hit again and again. A Great Society would cost money but it was to be accompanied by a cut in excise taxes, movement toward a balanced budget and a continuing pursuit of governmental economies. "Last year we saved almost thirty-five hundred million dollars by eliminating waste in the national government," Lyndon Johnson declared, his voice rising. Applause. "And I intend to do better this year." Louder applause.

The whole address had the tone of a leader who planned no roughriding of Congress. It was in this speech that Prime Minister Johnson spoke his most glowing public words about "This Hill, which was my home" for so long, described congressmen as "men whose first love is their country, men who try each day to do as best they can what they believe is right," and emphasized his "total respect" for Congress. It was fascinating to watch the representatives and senators as Lyndon Johnson poured it on, at first a little embarrassed as he described them as selfless patriots and then settling back with an air of "But of course, of course."

President Johnson was addressing a House and Senate hand-tailored for his purposes. This Eighty-ninth Congress contained the largest Democratic majorities since 1937 (a lopsided 295 to 140 in the House and 68 to 32 in the Senate), and most of the new members were friendly to the New Deal-type legislation the White House would propose. The shift was especially striking in the House of Representatives, where it particularly counted; except in the case of civil rights legislation, the lower body had been more frequently under the control of the Southern Democratic-Republican conservative coalition of which LBJ was so leery. The new House had a whopping ninety-one new members, about one-fifth the total membership. Cast up by the weird Goldwater candidacy, they were even more of a mixed lot than usual: a mortician from New York and a Michigan spice merchant, a one-time female singer on Don McNeill's *Breakfast Club*, the retired Navy captain who skippered the *Nautilus* under the North Pole, a Democrat from Maine who won by forty thousand votes and a Mississippi poultry farmer who ousted a Democratic veteran of twenty-two years. But seventy-one of the ninety-one freshmen representatives were Democrats. Most had in common relative youth—the average age was forty-four—a liberal attitude, and an eagerness to be associated with new and newsmaking legislation to help retain their precarious seats.

The House Republicans were in the disarray of a badly beaten army. Thrashing about in gloom and confusion, they unceremoniously deposed Minority Leader Charles Halleck, he of the weary jowls and dreary obstructionism, and replaced him with Gerald R. Ford of Michigan, a handsome University of Michigan star lineman and Yale Law School graduate who talked the need of an "attractive new image" for the Republican party. ("I've been through adversity before," Halleck growled, "but I've never had to run in a beauty contest.") Most of the time it was difficult to see vast policy differences between the Halleck doctrines and the "constructive conservatism" of Ford. But the new Minority Leader did represent an effort to get leadership with an accent of modernity; he paid much more attention to the younger Republican members; and he had a strategy that was discussed in G.O.P. circles with wistful excitement. Republican members would not simply be against a Democratic White House bill. They would turn to other techniques—voting to recommit it to committee for "revision and improvements," which would give them a chance to smother it, or introducing a substitute of their own, with G.O.P. representatives under party discipline to vote for the substitute measure. If such moves failed, they would be free to vote as they pleased. Thus they would have a chance to kill or bypass the Democratic bill, but if neither worked, they could support it and not be known as eternal naysayers.

The strategy was shrewd and in a way, genuinely constructive. There was no reason why Republicans or anybody else could not, if they really tried, present a potentially better measure. But the plan did not surmount a hard fact: like the whole G.O.P., Republican House members now had to pay for the party's fling with Barry Goldwater. Their candidate had created a House in which liberal or quasi-liberal Democrats had the votes, and even the power of a Southern Democratic-Republican coalition was critically weakened if not shattered.

Under gentle White House prodding, the new House promptly expressed its mood. The three key bodies were the committees on Appropriations, Rules, and Ways and Means, all of which had been strongholds of the conservative coalition. The Eighty-ninth Congress altered the formula by which members were chosen for

Appropriations and Ways and Means in a way that put not only more Democrats but more LBJ Democrats on the two committees. As Lawrence O'Brien remarked, "This change means that half the battle of enacting the Johnson program is over."

Another move concerned the Rules Committee, which had the power to prevent any bill from going to a floor vote and which was still chaired by the rancorously conservative Howard Smith of Virginia. Even in the atmosphere of 1965 the aged shamrock politician, Speaker John McCormack, was scarcely a grenadier of the Great Society, but he could usually be depended upon to go along with the White House. The House Democratic leadership now proposed to give the speaker the power to call out for a vote any bill on which the Rules Committee had not acted within twenty-one days. Democrats joined Republicans in wrathful opposition, recalling the state of affairs at the turn of the century—which this change would not recreate—when Speaker Thomas B. Reed, "Czar Reed," announced arbitrary decisions about legislation with the sardonic declaration, "Gentlemen, we have decided to perpetuate the following outrage. . . ." The proposal produced a real scuffle in the House. But Speaker McCormack received the power and Chairman Smith got the message.

A few days later, Lyndon Johnson commented to a friend on the situation in Congress. "It could be better," he said, "but not this side of Heaven."

The White House schedule was set. First the President would send to the Hill his medical and education bills—two monumental measures with long accumulated support behind them and an excellent chance of going through without serious trouble. Their passage would give momentum to the whole program. If difficulties came, it was better to face and settle them rather than permit them to entangle the rest of the White House legislation. Then, while these bills were making their way through the House and the Senate, LBJ would ask for a series of carefully timed lesser measures. Still later, he would press for additional laws—important but not indispensable to the success of the larger program—which might well be blocked in either house.

Two and a half months after the opening of the Eighty-ninth Congress, President Johnson, reacting to a new climax in the black revolution, would suddenly propose legislation that had not been part of his agenda for 1965—a sweeping voting rights bill. This measure and the medical and education legislation proved the milestones of his 1965 legislative drive. To each,

Prime Minister Johnson gave thorough and careful application of the Johnson treatment, and each represented a different form of the LBJ techniques in pushing major legislation through the House and Senate.

Three days after the State of the Union message, the President made his first move by sending to the Hill a special message entitled "Advancing the Nation's Health." The heart of the accompanying legislation was essentially the same as the bill sponsored by the Kennedy Administration and introduced in Congress by the Democrats, Representative Cecil R. King of California and Senator Clinton P. Anderson of New Mexico. It established what had come to be called Medicare, a national compulsory system of health insurance under social security for those sixty-five or older.

Lyndon Johnson had a favorite phrase for his Administration. He was, he liked to say, "the education President and the health President." These were the down-to-earth needs that came naturally from the Jim Ferguson and Huey Long traditions, and beyond that, sentiment for the aged was a marked personal attitude of LBJ. It had been drilled into him by his mother, and Johnson City still remembers how young Lyndon, out on a date, would excuse himself from the girl to assist some elderly person across the street. As a senator, he had opposed federal medical systems, but here again is the old story of the changes that came in him as he shifted from being a congressman to Chief Executive and experienced the particular circumstances of his new post.

As President, Lyndon Johnson's personal sentiment for a program like Medicare coincided with the fact that it was the kind of JFK bill which simply could not be left stranded and with his knowledge of the national support for it which had been steadily building over recent years. As long ago as 1945, President Truman had taken the unusual step of personally going before a joint session of Congress to urge a national medical insurance program. Harry Truman took hard the defeat of the measure; he had a number of bitter disappointments as President, he commented after his White House days, but this one troubled him the most. In the two decades that followed, the facts of American life kept piling up support for Medicare. The number of Americans sixty-five or over more than doubled, hospital costs soared, fewer and fewer families had an extra room where the grandparent lived and would be taken care of during minor ailments or in place of a nursing home.

Medicare had its expected enemies—conservatives and private insurance companies—but its serious problem was that peculiarly potent antagonist, the American Medical Association, which excoriated it as "socialized medicine." The AMA not only possessed large sums to spend on lobbying against Medicare; it had a self-righteousness which permitted it to condone all-out tactics and a special prestige in the eyes of Americans which it used to the hilt. Individual doctors could match the attitude of their organization leadership. Congressmen appreciated full well the story Representative Walter H. Moeller, a former Lutheran minister representing an Ohio district, told about the campaign of 1962. When Moeller informed local medical leaders that he had not made up his mind about Medicare and would not come out against it, some doctors spread the word that he was a socialist, gave anti-Moeller lectures to their patients before treating them, even threatened to stop taking care of them if they voted for him.

No one noted the potency of the AMA more closely than Wilbur D. Mills, chairman of the House Ways and Means Committee, which has jurisdiction over social security programs. A product of dusty little Kensett, Arkansas, Mills had run up brilliant records in the local schools and then at the Harvard Law School. At twenty-nine he was in the House of Representatives, at thirty-three, a member of the Ways and Means Committee, at forty-nine the youngest man ever to attain its chairmanship. Many Washington observers considered the stocky, plain-looking congressman from Kensett, with his quietly self-contained manner and his simple habits of living, the ablest mind in the House of Representatives. He had an awesome ability to comprehend complex legislation, a swift instinct for catching the essence of men and situations, and a well-demonstrated adroitness at shaping a bill in a way that would bring disparate elements to its support. Mills was also just about the most cautious man who ever held a major congressional post. He was innately conservative, kept a careful eye on opinion in the second congressional district of Arkansas, had an enormous political pride which made him shy away from backing legislation that could be defeated in his committee or in the House, and was marked by a certain congenital over-objectivity or indecisiveness of mind which sometimes had him stating both sides of an issue more cogently than the ardent advocates did. "Shakespeare wrote a play about him," a Kennedy aide once grumbled.

Mills had been cautious and more than cautious about Medicare. He had made it plain to President Kennedy that he would not sponsor the program in the Ways and Means Committee. Its plan to put medical care for the aged under social security, Mills stated, was not fiscally prudent and would endanger the monthly checks of the millions depending on other forms of social security. Moreover, the bill lacked a majority in his committee, and even if he found a way to push it through, the House was likely to defeat it. Some friends thought Mills had a third reason which he did not express—his conservative tendencies which made him susceptible to the AMA point of view.

But the Mills caution also included another element: he was cautious against being left standing by the roadside. By the time the Eighty-ninth Congress assembled, Medicare was booming. Candidate Johnson had made it a shouting issue on the road and had come home spreading the word that of all domestic issues, it was the surest producer of real applause. The AMA's tactics were backfiring, and strong pro-Medicare lobbies, most notably the AFL-CIO, were stepping up their activities. The changes in the House rules had created a Ways and Means Committee which probably contained a majority for the legislation no matter what its chairman did. Wilbur Mills himself was talking differently. He was, he said, "acutely aware of the fact that there is a problem here which must be met."

President Johnson had been watching all this with his craftsman's eye. Mills was no personal favorite of his—the man's self-possession and skeptical objectivity made LBJ uncomfortable —but he thoroughly understood the tugs and pulls inside the congressman; he had experienced most of them himself. He also understood that congressmen can change their minds and that the Ways and Means chairman, so powerful and respected in the House, was the key to passage of Medicare and to passage without the rancor that would impede other legislation.

The LBJ strategy for Medicare was to send the King-Anderson bill to Congress with the understanding that two changes were to be made to satisfy points of Mills. The basis for estimating the cost of the program would be revised, and Medicare income would be separated from other social security money and placed in its own trust fund. The President planned to keep in the most minute touch with everything concerning the progress of the legislation, primarily through Lawrence O'Brien and Wilbur J. Cohen, the legislative assistant secreary for the Health, Education and Welfare Department, who was a remarkable combination of masterful knowledge of public welfare programs and of adeptness on the Hill. Cohen and White House aides would always be ready to apply pressure to individual congressmen, and they would work in close alliance with Andrew J. Biemiller and Nelson H. Cruikshank, the two seasoned lobbyists of the AFL-CIO. Beyond these things, Lyndon Johnson would leave Medicare in the hands of the distinguished gentleman from Arkansas.

That gentleman assembled Ways and Means amid the potted

palms and long lugubrious curtains of its committee room. Mills's attitude had now clearly changed. He had decided that some form of federal medical insurance for the elderly was inevitable, that he was for it, that he would in fact lead the parade—all the while changing the bill in ways that made it better suit his ideas, shaping the tactics that would get it through the House, and associating the final triumph as much as possible with his name.

Soon Ways and Means had before it three quite different forms of the insurance. The first was the King-Anderson bill, amended in accord with the White House-Mills agreement, which continued to be called Medicare. The second version had been hurriedly introduced in the new House at the behest of the AMA and provided for "Eldercare." In desperation the AMA was shifting strategy. It continued to call King-Anderson "socialized medicine" but now added another charge: Medicare not only went too far but accomplished too little. Eldercare built on existing legislation, the Kerr-Mills Act of 1960 for the "medically indigent," those not on welfare but too poor to sustain many medical costs. Under Kerr-Mills, on the initiative of a state the federal government would subsidize an insurance plan for the medically needy of that state, worked out with a private insurance company, and the eligibles would voluntarily buy the insurance. Eldercare adopted this approach, broadening somewhat the categories of those eligible and the number of services included.

Proponents of Medicare responded with unveiled disgust. Eldercare, they pointed out, offered little that Kerr-Mills did not already provide and besides, in the five years since Kerr-Mills was enacted less than half the states had set up a plan under it. There were those who simply could not take Eldercare seriously. The New Jersey Democrat, Congressman Frank Thompson, Jr., rose in the House of Representatives to announce that Eldercare had inspired him to devise a still better system, "Doctorcare." It was to be financed by a two-percent tax on applesauce. The funds would be used to provide therapy for any doctor who felt himself suffering from an urge to make house calls. If he did not respond properly to the treatment, he was to be rushed to the nearest Cadillac showroom.

Dr. Milford O. Rouse, the Dallas gastroenterologist who was Speaker of the House of Delegates of the AMA, did not think the situation funny. The physician, a former director of the Life Line Foundation of the ultra-rightist oil billionaire H. L. Hunt, believed that capitalism itself was endangered by "the concept of health care as a right rather than a privilege." The campaign against Medicare, he told cheering AMA meetings, had reached the stage where it was a battle for "the American way of life" and "the protection of the sick. It must be won. . . . We are not a wealthy organization. But we have a modest reserve for a day like this." The reserve was $14,735,000 and the appropriation for this stage in the battle was $550,000.

The third bill before the Ways and Means Committee was a result of Minority Leader Gerald Ford's strategy of presenting alternatives to Democratic legislation. Congressman John W. Byrnes of Wisconsin, the ranking Republican on Ways and Means, worked with consultants from the private insurance industry to produce "Bettercare," which was something of a cross between Medicare and Eldercare. Like Eldercare, it was voluntary and functioned through private insurance companies; like Medicare, it put the overall supervision of the program in the hands of the federal government. Unlike Medicare or Eldercare, it offered a system of the "voluntary supplement," by which a person could pay more insurance and receive more services, including some doctors' fees.

Chairman Mills asked Wilbur Cohen to be present at a session of the Ways and Means Committee on March 2, 1965 and to go over the three bills, detail by detail, from the Administration's point of view. By about three o'clock that afternoon, Cohen was finishing with the last of the measures, the Byrnes bill. Naturally he emphasized its main characteristics—that it was a voluntary program and one which included the "voluntary supplement."

As Cohen stopped, Chairman Mills turned to Congressman Byrnes. "You know, John, I like that idea of yours."

The members of the committee stirred. Was Wilbur Mills really contemplating going over to a Republican plan? With a quiet smile, Mills went on with what he actually had in mind. The arrangement, he said, might form a "three-layer cake": the AMA expansion of Kerr-Mills making up the bottom layer, to take care of the poor; King-Anderson, the middle layer, providing basic hospital needs for the general population; and for the top income group, the "voluntary supplement" drawn from the Byrnes plan, by which those with greater resources could insure themselves for more.

Representative Byrnes sat with his mouth open. The whole room was stunned. "It was the most brilliant legislative move I'd seen in thirty years," Wilbur Cohen commented later. "The doctors couldn't complain because they had been carping about Medicare's shortcomings and about its being compulsory. The

Republicans couldn't complain because part of it was their idea. In effect, Mills had taken the AMA's ammunition, put it in the Republican's gun, and blown both of them off the map."

When the news came to President Johnson, he was surprised, amused and delighted. With a laugh he instructed, "Just tell them to snip off that name 'Republican' and slip those little old changes into the bill."

Wilbur Cohen had one worry. The little old changes would mean a $500 million increase in the cost of the bill at a time when the President was talking frugality as sternly as ever. He raised the point, and President Johnson replied, "I'm going to run and get my brother."

Cohen's face crinkled in puzzlement. He said he didn't understand.

"Well," LBJ continued, "I remember one time they were giving a test to a fellow who was going to be a switchman on the railroad, giving him an intelligence test, and they said, 'What would you do if a train was coming from the east going sixty miles per hour, and you looked over your shoulder and another one was coming from the west at sixty miles an hour, and they were heading for each other with just a mile to go? What would you do?' And the fellow said, 'I'd go get my brother.' And they said, 'Why would you go get your brother?' And he said, 'Because he hasn't ever seen a train wreck.'"

You have the $500 million, said Lyndon Johnson. And always watch out for trains.

The White House expected few problems for Medicare in the Senate, which had actually passed the King-Anderson bill during the Kennedy Administration. Yet the legislation had to go through the Senate Finance Committee, headed by a deeply convinced opponent, Senator Harry Byrd, and if Byrd delayed hearings, troubles could accumulate. The senator was as good a friend of Lyndon Johnson's as ever but that was not the point. Shortly before the House accepted the Mills version of Medicare, President Johnson arranged a bit of arm twisting, the first on nationwide television.

He asked nine leading Democratic representatives and senators, including Senator Byrd, to appear with him and "explain and discuss" the measure. Eight of the men found good things to say about Medicare. Harry Byrd said nothing.

The President turned to the senator. "I want to commend you for the fine job your committee in the Senate did [on another piece of legislation]. I know that you will take an interest in the orderly scheduling of this matter and giving it a thorough hearing."

Harry Byrd continued to remain silent and Lyndon Johnson asked, "Would you care to make an observation?"

Senator Byrd obviously did not care to make an observation, especially with millions of people watching. "The bill," he said gruffly, "hasn't come before the Senate. Naturally, I'm not familiar with it."

President Johnson went on. "And you have nothing that you know of that would prevent . . . [hearings] coming about it in reasonable time—there is not anything ahead of it in the committee?"

The senator shifted uneasily in his seat. "Nothing in the committee now."

The President leaned forward intently. "So when the House acts and it is referred to the Senate Finance Committee you will arrange for prompt hearings. . . ?"

Harry Byrd sighed. "Yes," he said.

Lyndon Johnson smiled broadly into the television cameras. "Good! Thank you very much, gentlemen."

Always a man of his word, Senator Byrd saw to it that the Finance Committee moved through some twelve hundred pages of hearings in fifteen days, frequently turning the chair over to the New Mexico Senator, Clinton P. Anderson of the King-Anderson bill. By this time the AMA drive was reaching its apogee, with twenty-three full-time lobbyists costing an estimated $5,000 a day and employing tactics as uninhibited as ever. But AMA men were now being viewed by many congressmen in a manner that would have seemed lese majesty only a few years before. The chief AMA spokesman before the Senate Finance Committee was its president, Dr. Donovan F. Ward of Dubuque, Iowa, who fully shared Dr. Rouse's sense of Armageddon. The AMA's fight, he declared, recalled Winston Churchill's stand against the Nazis in Britain's darkest days. To the amusement of much of the hearing room, Senator Anderson walked into Dr. Ward with sharp, sarcastic questioning which forced the AMA president to admit that he had been obscuring the number of prominent physicians backing Medicare and that while he accepted a national social security system in other respects, he wanted medical insurance associated with help for the poor. A lacerated President Ward went back to Dubuque, and Medicare seemed to be rolling through the Senate.

Then, on the day the Senate Finance Committee ended its public hearings, trouble struck. Out of the blue, Senator Russell

Long of Louisiana, now the successor to Hubert Humphrey as Senate Majority Whip and the Number Two Democrat on the Finance Committee, held a press conference to announce that he would offer two amendments to Medicare. The first removed any restriction on the length an elderly person could stay in a hospital or receive post-hospital care. To pay for this, the second amendment increased social security payments but graduated them according to income. The amendments were serious. Unlimited stays meant unlimited costs; a graduated scale of payment violated the basic principle of social security, which is to provide essentials not as charity determined by a means test but as an insurance paid for, and paid for alike, by the savings of all individuals. The AMA immediately supported the Long amendments, assuming that if adopted, they would never be accepted by the Administration and would kill Medicare in the inevitable House-Senate conference.

Senator Long had a variety of motives for his move, ranging from a simple desire to please anti-LBJ elements in Louisiana to his complex relations with the AMA, but they were not the whole story. To a degree President Johnson's Medicare was being endangered by a version—a quite different one but a version nevertheless—of the Fergusonism and Longism which were part of LBJ's own feeling for needy old people. Washington had known Senator Huey Long as "The Kingfish"; it called Senator Russell Long "The Princefish." Russell Long was very much the son of his father, with the same rumpled manner and shaggy friendliness, the impish grin and bulbous nose, the callithumpian rhetoric and the aisle-walking politicking, the genuine warmth for the problems of lower-income groups—and the same instinct for that boondocks liberalism which contained elements of a red gallus doctrine of the corporate state. Huey Long had threatened the New Deal by his flamboyant "Share-the-Wealth Plan," in which a benevolent government, run not so benevolently by Huey Long, would hand out enough so that "every man would be a king." The son also liked pyrotechnic proposals which made the poor recognize that they were poor and permitted him to take care of them.

For a few weeks Senator Russell Long did nothing formal about his amendments while the Finance Committee, now in executive session, went ahead with its clause-by-clause consideration of Medicare. The White House relaxed, thinking that the senator had simply been engaged in a bit of grandstanding. On June 17, Long appeared at the committee meeting, liked the line-up of senators present, and just as the group was about to adjourn for lunch suddenly offered his amendments. He presented them not in the customary printed form, which could be studied, but orally. In urging them, he at first addressed himself primarily to the liberal members of the committee and made a moving plea for giving the elderly "real protection, as long as they need it." Appealing to the whole committee—and here he was never more the son of Huey Long—he asked whether his colleagues, so engrossed in the technical features of the bill, had considered the political disaster the legislation could bring. It limited the hospital coverage to sixty days and would any senator who voted for it survive the outcry when the first old lady in his state was carried out of the hospital to die at the end of her sixty days? After about thirty minutes of hurried discussion, Long pressed for a vote. The hungry senators adopted the amendments, 8 to 6, and headed for lunch.

President Johnson heard the news during a break in a Cabinet meeting. He got out of his chair and stalked the room angrily. How could such a thing be permitted to happen? he demanded to know.

The situation was not easy to reverse. The President was on the best terms with Senator Long. By benign lack of objection, he had helped make Long Senate Majority Whip and the senator hoped that the same neutrality, or perhaps something better, might in time elevate him to Majority Leader. But at the moment Long had other fish to fry. When President Johnson asked him to withdraw his amendments he declined, with great protestations of loyalty to the White House. So far as other senators on the committee were concerned, the Long amendments, like his whole approach to public affairs, had an insidious, self-propelling nature. The amendments might be irresponsible, but they combined an arrant vote-getting quality with humanitarian appeal. Once such proposals were let loose, and especially once they had been voted upon favorably, what politician indeed wanted to put himself on record as being in favor of evicting an old lady from the hospital?

Soon further complexities emerged. Anxious to protect the elderly as much as possible but against irresponsibility, some senators were trying to take both positions, and they included as good a friend of sound social security as Senator Abraham A. Ribicoff of Connecticut, who had served as President Kennedy's HEW Secretary. When the AFL-CIO lobbyist Nelson Cruikshank spoke to Ribicoff, he found the senator favoring unlimited care but opposing payments on a graduated scale. His problem, the senator said, was political but only partly so; there were his personal feelings of compassion. "You won't have to walk along the street in New Britain, say, and have someone stop you and tell you about his dying mother and her need for more hospital care." The union man's efforts to argue that it made little sense to be for something and against the way to pay for it—a point he hardly needed to make to a man like Ribicoff—got nowhere. Cruikshank was talking into a tangle of emotion and politics, a realm not notable for its rationality.

Lyndon Johnson went to work. The telephone calls and invitations to the Oval Office were largely directed to the obvious targets, the liberal senators on the Senate Finance Committee. The nature of the appeal was equally inevitable: a hint at a compromise that would extend the number of days offered and increase the social security payments but keep the period of care limited and preserve the ungraduated system of deductions. The varieties of LBJ arm-twisting were called upon in indefatigible variety. To one senator, troubled about the effect on his shaky seat of a vote against the Long amendments, President Johnson promised a campaign appearance in 1966 and "probably there are other things we can do. You're too fine a senator to lose." When a second senator arrived at the Oval Office, he found the President riffling through a pile of documents. "You know," LBJ mused out loud, "it seems that your state may not be getting its fair share of conservation projects here of late."

HEW Secretary Anthony Celebrezze, about to leave the Cabinet, was doing his last job helping to get Medicare through. A man of rotundity and good cheer, Celebrezze observed with a chuckle, "When the President wants something badly enough, dogs' ears aren't the only things that get pulled." One wavering senator described his lobular experience: "Well, the President told me how he understood all my problems. Then, in the nicest way—he was pouring me a soft drink—he suggested what worse problems, and damn practical ones I must say, I would face if I didn't see the light."

With the crowning achievement of his career at stake, Senator Anderson labored relentlessly in the Finance Committee against the amendments. He was greatly aided by another member of the committee, the Democratic liberal veteran from Illinois Paul J. Douglas, who proceeded to do something highly unsenatorial. Douglas told his colleagues bluntly, "I made a mistake and so did you. We simply didn't think through these proposals."

Gradually the complex of pressures took hold. The Senate Finance Committee reversed its vote on the Long amendments, and reported the bill out essentially in the Wilbur Mills version plus the new compromise amendment approved by the White

House. On the Senate floor the power of the Democratic majority and of the bipartisan support for a workable Medicare was so great that the debate lasted only three days; a few changes of substance but none touching the core of the program were voted through. Senator Ribicoff delivered an impassioned plea for an amendment providing unlimited care and during a few hours it seemed so likely to pass that Senator Anderson went home sick with concern. The White House pressure and that of the AFL-CIO, in the words of one senator, came "like a hailstorm"; the Ribicoff amendment was killed, if only by four votes. A few more weeks of wrangling in the House-Senate conference committee and the signing of Medicare was set for July 30, 1965, just two hundred and four days after Lyndon Johnson's message to Congress calling for the legislation.

"This ceremony," LBJ said, "really ought to be something." The President had decided that major laws should not be signed routinely in the White House but at places around the country picked for their special appropriateness in each instance. This appealed to him sentimentally, and he was sure it would make more news. He had no hesitancy in choosing where to sign Medicare. The longer Lyndon Johnson served as Chief Executive, the more he admired Harry Truman's Presidency. "That little fellow was pretty much always on the right track, and he was able to spot a bastard two hundred yards off." President Johnson also remembered the lonely day twenty long years before, when President Truman had gone before Congress and pleaded for federal medical insurance. The White House planes roared off to the starch white Harry S. Truman Library in Independence, Missouri, carrying the President, the Vice-President, one Cabinet officer, two governors, twelve senators, nineteen representatives and an assortment of aides and others who had proved themselves special friends of Medicare.

The eighty-one-year-old former President had to be helped to the microphones, but the blue eyes were bright behind the steel-rimmed glasses and the voice took on all the well-remembered crackle as he read his little speech and, happily, did not read it just as it had been written for him. "Not one of these, our citizens, should ever be abandoned to the indignity of charity. Charity is indignity when you have to have it. We don't want these people to have anything to do with charity and we don't want them to have any idea of hopeless despair. Mr. President, I am glad to have lived this long and to witness today the signing of the Medicare bill which puts the nation right, where it needs to be right."

Then, in a way Americans did not associate with Harry Truman, the old man groped for words. After a few moments he added, "I thank you all most highly for coming here. It's an honor that I haven't had done to me—well, for quite a while, I'll say that to you."

President Johnson's words spoke his own emotion and his bursting sense of achievement. "No longer will older Americans be denied the healing miracle of modern medicine. No longer will illness crush and destroy the savings that have been so carefully put away. . . . No longer will young families see their own incomes, and their own hopes, eaten away simply because they are carrying out their deep moral obligations to their parents, and to their uncles, and to their aunts."

Then Lyndon Johnson sat down at the old-style mahogany desk at which the legislation embodying the Truman Doctrine had been signed. Of course there were pens, scores of them, and President Johnson handed one to Senator Russell Long, for his "effective and able work" in passing the bill.

January 7, 1965, the special message to Congress calling for Medicare; January 12, the second LBJ volley—another special message entitled "Toward Full Educational Opportunity," accompanied by a bill prescribing an expenditure of $1.5 billion on the elementary and secondary schools of the nation.

Even more than Medicare, this legislation had Lyndon Johnson's emotional commitment. It was also like the medical measure in that it emerged from a long history; had been proposed, at least in terms of its broad purposes, by the Kennedy Administration; was backed by demands which were rapidly mounting as the classroom population rocketed; and was strongly opposed by conservatives, who saw it as another thrust of federal interference into the life of the local community and of the individual. But the education bill was different from Medicare in a critical respect —it involved the issue of the separation of church and state.

For decades most American Protestants and Jews had taken their stand on the Bill of Rights of the Constitution and its stricture that "Congress shall make no law respecting an establishment of religion, or prohibiting the free exercise thereof." This, they were sure, meant that tax money should go only to public elementary and secondary schools. If anyone chose to send his children to a private institution, that was his business; let him and his church pay for the schooling. Over the years public money for parochial schools had been opposed by the National Education Association, the massive teachers' organization, the National

Council of the Churches of Christ, representing the major Protestant denominations, and the largest Jewish organizations.

Of the Americans counted by the churches as having religious affiliations in 1965, some forty million, or about 36 percent, were Catholics. There is no accurate information on the attitudes of Catholics toward the school issue, and there is evidence that they were considerably less monolithic on the point than was commonly assumed. But the National Catholic Welfare Conference, which spoke officially for them, had been clear-cut in its position. The NCWC maintained that the "free exercise" of religion guaranteed in the Bill of Rights included the right to educate your children in a religious-oriented school, and that asking Catholics to pay taxes for education funds of which they received none was a misinterpretation of the Constitution and a gross injustice. The NCWC also had a highly practical argument and a no less practical concern. In 1965 about six of the forty million American children attending elementary and secondary schools were in Catholic institutions. Did the American public refuse to recognize, the NCWC demanded, that it was avoiding responsibility for the cost of educating these students, about 14 percent of the whole group? The Catholic population was increasing at a rate greater than the general percentage and the parochial schools were jammed. Catholic leaders again and again expressed the fear that the influx, with no public funds to help pay the spiraling costs, would lead to rapid deterioration of their educational institutions.

The thorniness of the church-state issue had been made dramatically plain when President Kennedy sent his elementary and secondary school bill to Congress in 1961. For personal as well as political reasons, JFK was extremely sensitive to any implication that the fact that he was a Catholic would influence his public policies, and his Administration's measure aided public institutions exclusively. It died in the House Rules Committee by the decisive vote of Representative James J. Delaney, an ardent Catholic from an overwhelmingly Catholic district in New York, who ignored the choicest blandishments of the JFK forces ("he didn't want a thing," Lawrence O'Brien recalled ruefully) to stand immovable by the position that "aid to education should apply to the entire school system."

But the atmosphere was changing. Both the Catholic and non-Catholic groups were worried over the condition of their schools and more and more convinced that federal aid was the only salvation. Yet the Catholics, by demanding equal help for the parochial schools, were getting no help. The non-Catholics, by insisting upon nothing for religious institutions, were getting nothing for themselves.

The majority non-Catholic group also had reason to look to its political bastions. The growth in the numbers and influence of the Catholic population was increasing its power in both parties, particularly in the Democratic party which was the home of the movement for any variety of federal aid to education. Among the many notable characteristics of the new Eighty-ninth Congress was its religious composition. From the days of George Washington through those of John Kennedy, one of the Protestant denominations had always been able to claim the largest number of members of the House of Representatives, in modern America usually the Methodists. In the Eighty-ninth Congress, for the first time the Catholics led (Catholics 107, Methodists 88). Growing Catholic power suggested non-Catholic accommodation.

The political realities encouraged changes in attitude that were occurring independently. The opinion-formers among Protestants, Catholics and Jews were living side by side in Metroamerica, anxious to appear educated and emancipated beyond the religious group clashes that were now being called bigotry. Only a decade before the poet-historian Peter Viereck could write, "Catholic-baiting is the anti-Semitism of the intellectuals." Now, in the circles which read men like Viereck, an anti-Catholic gibe was as likely to produce flinching as an anti-Semitic dig. Among Catholics the oncoming generation contained tens of thousands whose thinking was permeated by the vague, nonsectarian humanism dominating much of educated America. The influence of Metroamerica on the general population joined with the spreading national popularity of ecumenicism to lessen the rancor over whose children received public funds for their schooling.

Under the circumstances, obviously some reformulation of federal aid to education—giving each group something while not requiring any one to back down too conspicuously—would win wide support, and just such a reshaping was under way. In 1947, in *Everson* v. *Ewing Township,* the United States Supreme Court had declared constitutional a New Jersey law authorizing the use of state funds to provide bus transportation for parochial school children; the benefit, a majority of the Court ruled, was going to the individual child, not to the school. This formula was taken up by a number of Catholic and non-Catholic leaders as a way of justifying a variety of indirect aids to parochial educational institutions. The approach figured in White House discussions in the early 1960's, but President Kennedy stuck to his refusal to propose any federal financial help to parochial schools, indirect or direct. As the JFK Administration gave way to the LBJ days, an additional element entered the discussions. With anti-poverty in the air, the suggestion was being made that the child-benefit theory should be used to justify indirect aid to parochial schools in the form of federal funds to lift the level of education for poor children, whatever the type of their school. John Kenneth Galbraith in particular took the lead in urging this approach, and it attracted the interest of three other men especially influential in Washington in matters of educational policy—Wilbur Cohen, as concerned with schools as he was with medical problems, John Gardner, at this time chairman of the LBJ task force on education, and Francis Keppel, the JFK Commissioner of Education who was continuing in that post under President Johnson. When the Gardner task force made its recommendation for education legislation to the President, its central feature was federal aid justified by benefit to the individual poor child.

President Johnson leaped at the formula. It fitted the anti-poverty emphasis of his Administration; an impeccable Protestant, he had far less concern than John Kennedy that he would be accused of favoring Catholics; above all, this approach offered a way around what seemed to him a boring religious imbroglio. In thinking about education or any other public problem, Lyndon Johnson was strikingly removed from religious or religious-group feelings. As a boy, when his ardent Baptist mother would read him stories from the Bible, he would ask skeptically, "Is it true? Did it really happen?" At the age of fourteen he went through what is so common among teen-agers, a burst of religion, and was duly re-baptized in the Pedernales River as a member of the sect numerous in the Johnson City area, the Disciples of Christ. And that was about it so far as LBJ and religion were concerned until, during his most anguished period of the Vietnam War, he did what other nonreligious Presidents have done in times of crisis, turned to the solace of prayer. In 1965 President Johnson was thinking in utterly different terms. Catholics, Jews, Disciples of Christ—he viewed them all as so many groups like union men, manufacturers and beet farmers, whom he was eager to understand—and did, as a matter of fact, understand remarkably well—in order to fit them into his governmental and political plans.

Even more than was his usual practice, LBJ gave minute personal attention to the drafting of the special message on education and to the education bill itself. However much public opinion was shifting, he knew he was walking on eggs in his reliance on the child-benefit theory and he was determined that there should be no heavy-footedness. He was convinced that the formula was a winner nevertheless and he was anxious that this monumental legislation, on a subject of such intense personal meaning to him, should be associated with him in every possible way.

President Johnson had assigned Horace Busby and me to a literary "sprucing up" of certain documents for Congress, and I wrote into the education special message a conclusion which seemed to me appropriate and led into it by a quotation from Lincoln. Back came the draft with an instruction to replace the Lincoln words with "that great quote from Lamar." I was not only ignorant of the great quote; I did not know who Lamar was. Judicious inquiry produced the information that Mirabeau B. Lamar, the second president of the Republic of Texas, was notable for his militancy against Indians and Mexico and as the "Father of Education in Texas." It was he who had been instrumental in having land set aside for schools and colleges, and for more than a century his words to the Texas Congress in 1838 had been the rallying cry of Texas friends of education: "The cultivated mind is the guardian genius of democracy. It is the only dictator that free man acknowledges. It is the only security that free man desires." The quotation, which turned out to be the favorite of President Johnson's second only to Isaiah, prefaced the conclusion to the message, giving the document an unmistakable LBJ flavor.

Like most such measures, the education bill itself was an omnibus. Some of the provisions were pioneering—appropriations to build up library and textbook resources for children in public and private schools, to establish experimental educational centers and to promote research into innovative teaching techniques. But the heart of the legislation was the billion dollars to improve the general primary and secondary school system. The federal government would provide each state funds in the amount of the number of children in the state from low-income families (less than $2,000 a year income), multiplied by 50 percent of the state's average expenditure per pupil. Although the largest impoverished populations were concentrated in the South and in Appalachia, poverty was so spread through the country that this provision meant some aid, and often a substantial amount, for at least 90 percent of the school districts in the United States. The money would be granted only to public school boards, but the boards were instructed to take into account the needs of students in private as well as public schools. They were specifically empowered to use the funds for "shared-time" programs, under which public and parochial school students took instruction in the same classroom, and for special services, like educational television, which would be available to all pupils. Estimates of the dollar value of this help to the Catholic schools varied widely; none was below the multimillions.

Throughout the preparation of the measure, President Johnson saw to it that Administration officials kept in touch with every important pressure group and with a number of organizations that were anything but important. Little changes were made to take care of the convictions, prejudices or private preserves of various education idealists, satraps and operators. The final form had the prior approval of all the most powerful organizations directly concerned.

President Johnson sent the education bill to the Hill with one overriding concern: he was determined to keep the lid on the church-state issue. His strategy was the reverse of his plan for Medicare. In this instance there was to be no dependence on a Wilbur Mills, no relaxable leash, no sympathetic receptivity to amendments. LBJ made his wish—he avoided the word "demand" —unmistakably clear. The education bill was to be put through with force-draft speed just short of provoking a congressional revolt, and it was to be passed, in the White House phrase, "without a comma changed." To congressmen who complained about such pell-mell procedure in the case of a complex and sweeping measure, the answer was to be blunt. No doubt the bill had its imperfections, but the important thing was to get a national system of aid to primary and secondary education established. The deficiencies could be taken care of another year.

The danger spot for the education bill was the volatile House of Representatives, and the possibilities showed themselves as soon as the House Subcommittee on Education opened hearings. The Republican and conservative concern over federal control in local school matters was ever present, and the church-state issue flared up in vigorous opposition testimony from representatives of Protestant and Jewish organizations. But the adroit nature of the legislation, the national atmosphere, the careful groundwork laid by the Administration and the Democratic muscle in the House showed their effects.

This was particularly not the hour for those who talked religious clash; most of the testimony sounded like an ecumenical chorale. For the first time the National Education Association, the National Council of Churches and the National Catholic Welfare Conference joined in support of the same legislation for the lower schools. Catholic and non-Catholic leaders, clerical and lay, praised the measure not only as a boon to the nation's schools but as a product of a hopeful "new mood" in all religious circles and as an "instrument of reconciliation" across denominational lines.

The chairman of the House Subcommittee, Carl D. Perkins, from the coal-mining area of eastern Kentucky, was an open-faced, open-mannered Administration stalwart who liked to see education and pro-union legislation pushed ahead and who disliked fusses; he hearkened to the word from the other end of Pennsylvania Avenue. Perkins hurried the hearings along and three days after their close, he called for a vote in the subcommittee. All the Republican members, protesting "the hasty and superficial consideration" given the measure, refused to vote. The Democrats pushed the bill through.

In the full House Committee on Education and Labor, the legislation ran into a thicket which even Lyndon Johnson had not anticipated. The year before its chairman, Representative Adam Clayton Powell, Jr., had been provided $225,000 in expense money for the committee. This year he wanted $440,000, and the House, edgy about his conspicuous junketeering, had not voted it. Chairman Powell, it seems, just could not get his mind on legislation until his committee, "the most important committee on domestic legislation on Congress," received its expense money. In these days the Democratic leadership was hesitant about pressuring the House in matters involving Adam Clayton Powell, but after two weeks Lyndon Johnson refused to risk further delay. He persuaded the leadership to make the push and the House gave in, providing the $440,000 by a concealing voice vote. Chairman Powell was a changed man. The committee would meet, he announced, every day, all day, including Saturday, until work on the education bill was completed. It did.

The form of the measure which reached the House floor included only inconsequential amendments. The White House and the Democratic leadership were relieved, but still wary. Using its overwhelming Democratic majority, the leadership rammed through a vote limiting the whole floor consideration of the bill to three days, and the caution proved well-advised. Soon the House was into a debate over the church issue so violent that members shouted at each other across the aisle. An unusual demand was heard and diverted with difficulty—the formal censure of a representative for the language he had used to another member.

At one point the House tangled itself in the question, Did the education bill authorize a person on the public payroll to teach in a parochial school? Representative Delaney's colleague from the Queens-Brooklyn area of New York, the Catholic Representative Hugh L. Carey, was a member of the House Subcommittee on Education. He replied with a buoyant yes. The Protestant floor leader, Carl Perkins, answered hesitantly, no, not really. A number of Democrats pledged to the bill were showing puzzled and worried faces. Congressman B. F. Sisk of California, a graduate of the Church-of-Christ Abilene Christian College and the representative of a largely Protestant area around Fresno, had spoken in favor of the bill. Now he said: "This example gets to the very guts of the problem. If the answer is yes, I shall have to vote against the bill."

Representative John Brademas of Indiana, a Rhodes Scholar on whom the leadership had been depending for the high road if the debate took this kind of turn, rephrased the question. Didn't the bill mean that local public administrators could send to a parochial school a teacher of "special subjects" but not an instructor in "general subjects"?

"Special like a guidance counselor, yes," Perkins replied with relief. "General, no."

"Amen," said Congressman Carey in a tone of loud satisfaction. The satisfaction was not shared by representatives who wondered just what "general subjects" meant and just what lay between vocational counseling and general teaching.

The activities of the White House and of the House leadership intensified. With his personal feelings so thoroughly involved, President Johnson's arm twisting particularly took the form of the emotional patriotic appeal, "as your President, to give these American kids what they deserve." He talked to congressmen a great deal about his own school teaching days, like the year when he was the principal in Cotulla, Texas, and it was "pathetic what those kids got. They were almost all Mexican-Americans. They went and smoked during recess. I said, 'Let's have volleyball,' and I bought a ball for them, and we got together some old musical instruments. We taught them to sing and we organized a band, and I had a debating team, although I couldn't talk Spanish and they couldn't speak English, and we debated whether the jury system was good. They were so grateful at this little bit of nothing that the Mexican people have been voting for me ever since." Lyndon Johnson's face hardened. People who kept finding things wrong with the education bill were like the "old fogies" around Fredericksburg, near Johnson City. When the railroad company announced a new train to San Antonio, they put on long faces and said, " 'Well, they'll never get her started, and if they do, they'll never get her stopped.' Well, we *are* going to get her started, and we are *never* going to get her stopped."

Amid the outbursts of the church-state issue in the House, further trouble developed on a surprise point from an unlikely source. Representative Edith S. Green from Oregon, the fourth-ranking Democratic member of the House Committee on Education and Labor, was generally a supporter of liberal measures and particularly of aid to education. But the congresswoman, a staunch Protestant and friend of the public schools, was none too happy about this bill, which she believed "opened the way" to increasing support for parochial schools. She also had a hard eye for her constituents' interests, and she had personal ambitions, specifically to become chairman of the House Education Subcommittee and generally to be recognized as an education power in the House. Now she waded into a key part of the education bill, the provision that federal funds were to be given on the basis of the cost of educating a child in the particular state —to use the two extremes, $241 per year in Mississippi and $705 in New York. Under this procedure, Mississippi would be granted an annual total of about $38 million and New York $92 million. Such an allocation, Representative Green declared, would make the rich states richer educationally and the poor states poorer. She did not emphasize so strongly that the formula would be no boon to states like Oregon, which spent a relatively large amount on the schooling of each pupil but did not have a heavy percentage of the impoverished. Representative Green proposed an amendment granting a flat $200 across the nation for each poor child.

Following the White House line of argument, the Administration forces answered that a fixed sum had been considered and rejected, because the cost of good schooling varied sharply in different sections of the country. Percentagewise, if not absolutely, poor states would be helped more than the prosperous ones, and the formula would stimulate additional spending on education by all states. In any event, the defenders added, the present solution seemed the best. Here was a prime instance where the plan should be tried and if a change seemed called for, it could be made another year.

But the Green amendment had considerable appeal. It brought a democratic aura of the same for everybody. Many congressmen from the South, where the expenditure per pupil was comparatively low, saw in it a way of getting a much more substantial slice of the appropriation for their states. A number of Republicans came from areas in a similar situation; furthermore, they

viewed the amendment as the one serious hope of leaving any
G.O.P imprint on this legislation which touched most homes in
the United States. For practical purposes, Minority Leader Ford
accepted the Green proposal as the "Republican alternative" under
his general strategy. President Johnson's reaction was immediate: crack the party whip. The amendment of Representative
Green, good Democrat that she was, went down under the power
of the Democratic majority.

From opponents, Democratic and Republican, came flailing
speeches. The iron resistance to amendments, the insistence on
speed, were "a relentless steamroller," "a travesty of the democratic process." As for dependence on the fact that the legislation
could be improved later, Representative Charles E. Goodell from
upstate New York, the ranking Republican on the House Education Subcommittee, called this "the weirdest doctrine I have heard
in all my years in public life. It justifies rushing through anything." Representative Green, her usually pleasant voice icy, assailed "this determined effort to cut off legitimate concerns about
the bill. . . . One reason I have been proud of being a Democrat
is because we have tried to protect the minority. I have never
interpreted this as just protecting an ethnic minority." Republicans rose in ovation and most Democrats, puzzled as to what
to do, stood up too.

Congressman Howard Smith moved in, irreconcilable and
grim, calling on all that he could from his worn decades of power.
Smith hated everything about the education bill—the extension
of federal activity, the inevitable use of tax funds to promote
desegregation, the aid from public resources to Catholic students,
the emphasis on changed circumstances which suggested that
something might be lacking in the thinking of an eighty-six-year-
old. In a 1923 decision, *Frothingham* v. *Mellon,* the United States
Supreme Court had ruled that an individual citizen could not
challenge in the courts the manner in which a federal law provided for the expenditure of funds. "This bill has been treated
like it has been sent down from Heaven," Congressman Smith
stormed, and he proposed to desanctify it by an amendment providing that a citizen could test its constitutionality. The move
had all the old man's seasoned shrewdness. What congressman
is not in favor of a citizen's right to challenge Washington? The
Smith thrust also had the potential of ungluing the coalition
Lyndon Johnson had so carefully put together behind the legislation; from the beginning, the National Catholic Welfare Conference had made plain it would withdraw its support if a provision
for constitutional review were added. The White House word was

the same: party loyalty. The Smith amendment was defeated the way that was easier for House members, an unrecorded voice vote.

The third, last day of House action stretched into twilight, then past the supper hour. The opposition tried everything, making points for the record and delaying for the sake of delaying —amendment after amendment, repeated quorum calls, more roaring speeches against "force tactics," a demand that the full House journal of the previous day be read, motions for teller votes requiring that members walk up the aisle one by one to be counted. After eight unbroken hours, the vote came. It was 263 to 153, with the acceptance of just one minuscule amendment beyond the minor ones already inserted by the House committees. Republicans, now released from party discipline and moving with the national tide, contributed substantial support.

The Senate action was fundamentally the same story. The venerable joke was that if the House passed the Ten Commandments, the Senate would amend them to nine or eleven. This time President Johnson let the Senate know that he wanted it to adopt the precise House version of the education bill, thus eliminating a House-Senate conference and any further chance of difficulties. The opposition in the Senate knew a stone wall when it saw one. The subcommittee and committee completed hearings and all action on the House measure with dispatch, and reported it to the Senate without a single change. On the floor, a few serious efforts were made at amendment, but the White House reaction was so formidable and the outcome so ordained that opponents exercised themselves less against the bill than against the situation. Senator Winston L. Prouty of Vermont became so agitated at "this relentless machine" that he found himself saying, "The principal issue facing the nation today is not education. It is the future of the Senate as a co-equal partner in the legislative process." The senator sat down and the upper house completed its legislative process in three days, not a day longer than the House of Representatives.

As the final vote began, the Colorado Senator Peter H. Dominick stood pounding his desk and shouting, "I for one resent the whole procedure." The count was 73 to 18.

Within a few years the possibility arose that the Education Act of 1965 might be the only major legislation of the Johnson Administration to be overthrown by the Supreme Court. In 1968 the Court, by an 8 to 1 vote, reversed its 1923 ruling to the extent of declaring that a citizen could challenge the constitution-

ality of a law involving the "establishment of religion" clause in
the Bill of Rights. A sharp test of the Education Act was ready
to make its way to the high court, and the suit was based not only
on legal considerations but on the contention that the legislation
as it was actually being administered was leading to "any number of constitutional violations."

1968—but this was April 9, 1965. The news that Congress
had completed action on the education bill reached President
Johnson as he entered the Astrodome in Houston to watch the
Astros play the Dodgers. His face dissolved into a huge smile.

The presidential statements came in a flood. "As a son of a
poor farmer, I know that education is the only valid passport
from poverty. . . . Health is important. So is beautification, civil
rights, agriculture, defense posture, but all of these are nothing
if we do not have education. . . . Since 1870, almost a hundred years ago, we have been trying to do what we have just
done—pass an elementary school bill for all the children of America. . . . We did it, by all that's good we did it, and it's a wonderful, proud thing." Then, in the full burst of his feelings: "I
will never do anything in my entire life, now or in the future,
that excites me more, or benefits the nation I serve more, or
makes the land and all its people better and wiser and stronger,
or anything that I think means more to freedom and justice in
the world than what we have done with this education bill. . . .
This is the most important bill I will ever sign."

Again the President directed all praise toward Congress—
"most of the members of both parties voted for it . . . it's not
partisan." These representatives and senators would be "remembered as pioneers of a new day of greatness in America. And as
long as your name is called, your descendants are going to be
proud of it. You mark that prediction."

Lyndon Johnson did not mention a spectacular fact. With
something more than co-operation from the White House, the
Congress had passed a billion-dollar law, deeply affecting a fundamental institution of the nation, in a breath-taking eighty-seven
days. The House had approved it with no amendment that mattered; the Senate had voted it through literally without a comma
changed.

The President's jubilation was such that he permitted himself
moments which a more sober Lyndon Johnson would never have
allowed. Reminiscing publicly about his school teaching days, he
talked about Cotulla "and then I became a lobbyist for the
Houston Teachers Association. I went to Austin and had to deal
with that Texas legislature—and that will try a man's soul, won't

it?" And alongside those congressmen whose descendants were going to be so proud because they voted for the education bill were the representatives and senators who opposed it—their "folks are going to be proud" because their ancestor was fortunate enough to serve in the Congress which enacted it. Lyndon Johnson grimaced, extricated himself with a boyish laugh. "You ought to strike that. That was not in the text."

The President would brook no other suggestion; the bill would be signed a mile and a half east of the LBJ ranch in the little building, now an unoccupied shambles of sagging walls and rusty galvanized siding, where Lyndon Johnson first went to school. He had the people he wanted hurried there—congressmen and government officials, seven Mexican-Americans from his classes in Cotulla and four members of a debating team he coached in Houston High School, the barber Hugo Kline from Fredericksburg who took his first lessons with Lyndon Johnson, and of course his first teacher, Miss Katie, now Mrs. Kate Deadrich Loney, seventy-two years old and living in Rough and Ready, California, who had taught grades one to eight all in one square, bare room.

Battered school furniture was scattered on the scraggly lawn. President Johnson pointed to a scarred bench and called out, "Come over here, Miss Katie, and sit beside me, will you? Let them see you. They tell me that I recited my first lessons while sitting on your lap." And so it had been; the President's mother was busy with five children and chores, and besides, she thought her eldest son, who seemed so bright, should begin learning as soon as possible. When Lyndon was four, she started taking him down the road to Miss Katie, asking her to "keep him busy and teach him something, anything worthwhile."

Now Lyndon Johnson sat down on the bench, signed his full name to the Education Act of 1965 with a single pen, handed the one pen to Miss Katie. The old lady did not understand; a pen was a pen, and this one was not hers. She left it on the bench as she walked away.

The President frowned and started toward her. Then once again the tremendous sense of accomplishment came across his face in a glowing smile. He took the wheel of his white Lincoln Continental and led a cavalcade of forty automobiles on a roar down the dirt road, the plumes of dust swirling off into the clear blue Texas sky.

A few days before the special messages on the education bill and on Medicare had gone to Congress in January 1965, Martin

Luther King, Jr., summoned the press for his own news. In the South of 1965, about two million Negroes were registered to vote; almost three million were not. The Negro leader announced that he was about to sweep together the half-starts and local campaigns of the past decade in an all-out drive to register the Negroes of the South.

From one point of view, it was surprising that the civil rights movement had waited so long to concentrate on the vote and focused most of its attention on desegregation, particularly of the schools. The ballot was the surest road to all changes, including desegregation; the right to vote was the clearest constitutional right of the Negro, stated in incontestable English. Yet as Justice Thurgood Marshall once observed, Negroes had reasons both practical and emotional for emphasizing the classroom first. Education was the prerequisite for jobs, for the creation of an effective leadership group, and above all, for a sense of self-respect. Moreover, as Marshall said, "there is something especially humiliating and infuriating about being told that your child cannot sit beside another one in an American schoolroom, of all places."

In turning to their massive voting rights effort, Martin Luther King and his strategists picked the starting point with adroitness. Alabama lay under the governorship of George Wallace, by now a national symbol of racism. Stretching off to the west from the state capital at Montgomery was Dallas County and its county seat, Selma, which looked down on the languorous Alabama River from a high bluff. Selma was straight out of a thousand novels about the unreconstructed South, lovely to look at and ugly just beneath the surface.

The city had a population of about 29,000, some 14,000 whites dominating 15,000 Negroes. It methodically used ancient legal tricks for preventing the registration of Negroes, including a test of the governmental process in which a white clerk asked applicants questions which few Americans could answer (Sample: What two rights does a citizen have after indictment by a grand jury?), and then told the Negroes their replies were wrong. Selma's voting rolls stood at 97 percent white, 3 percent Negro. The old families, living well from the surrounding cotton, livestock and dairy areas and a sprinkling of industries, occupied graceful homes on the rise of the city, some of the houses dating back to the congenial 1830's and '40's. The Negro men did the menial jobs around town; most of their women worked as domestics up the shaded avenues.

The old families left to custom and to the white workers and middle classes the task of keeping the Negroes in line. Custom had not been working too well. Even before King arrived in Selma, the city was feeling the winds of the black revolution; for two years SNCC had operated from a house on First Avenue and Tremont Street, supported by Negroes from most segments of the black community. But the workers and the middle classes had not neglected their function. They provided the bulk of the membership for the first White Citizens' Council in Alabama and went along with James G. Clark, Jr., Sheriff of Dallas County, a bully-boy figure who was also perfectly cast.

Six feet tall, two hundred pounds, few of which were excess, Clark walked with the appropriate swagger and talked with the appropriate bluster. He had started out as a farmer on the Pea River, taken a fling at politics, ended up the happy sheriff of his county. He delighted in his gold-braided sheriff's cap, his night stick and burnished pistol, the cattle prod hanging from his tooled-leather belt, his volunteer mounted posse of two hundred which followed him worshipfully. Only one thing about his work annoyed the sheriff, "all this nigger fuss here of late. We always git along. You just have to know how to handle them." When Negroes in Selma started demonstrating in the early 1960's Sheriff Clark handled them. The Negroes took to singing a local ballad about a Jim Clark of long ago—no relative of the sheriff and, ironically, a Reconstruction scalawag who was pro-Negro for purposes of plunder. "Ain't gonna let no Jim Clark turn me round," the Selma Negroes of the 1960's chanted in a song that was to become a hallmark of the black revolution. This Jim Clark was quite ready to turn them round with night sticks and cattle prods.

The day Martin Luther King entered his target city, January 8, Selma started making sure that he would be successful. Recently given the world-wide prestige of a Nobel Prize, he went to register in the Hotel Albert, and a woman in the lobby screamed, "Get him! Get him!" James Robinson, a twenty-six-year-old gas-station employee, punched King twice in the head and aimed kicks at his groin. As police pulled Robinson away, the Negro leader became the first of his race to register at the Hotel Albert and for his $5.75 room bill, received $500,000 worth of national indignation.

From that point on, Selma and Sheriff Clark kept the anger mounting across the United States. King organized the Negroes for marches to the courthouse to register and Clark and his posse responded with mass arrests and, on occasion, with billy clubs and wet bullwhips. Soon he arrested one hundred and sixty Negro boys and girls who were milling outside the courthouse. With the

Selma jail filled, Sheriff Clark forced them to go by fast trot to a lockup six miles away, the sheriff following part of the way on foot, then turning the job over to possemen in cars. Children began vomiting and dropping on the roadside; after three miles, they were permitted to "escape." The next day Clark entered the Jefferson Davis Hospital in Selma declaring, "The niggers are giving me a heart attack." Outside the building two Negro children, James Maith, seven, and Olanda Reeves, fourteen, stood with signs which expressed, among other things, what was happening in the mass media of the country. The placards read, from one to the other, "Get well fast sheriff—we miss you."

Governor George Wallace now began making his contributions to the cause of Martin Luther King. When the Negro leader proclaimed a "March of Freedom" down the fifty-two miles from Selma to the state capital at Montgomery on Sunday, March 7, Wallace forbade the demonstration and ordered the Alabama state police to enforce his decree. Sunday at three o'clock, six hundred and fifty Negroes assembled at the old red brick Browns Chapel Methodist Church in the heart of black Selma. Two abreast, bedrolls and knapsacks on their backs, they filed through the quiet back streets and headed for the Edmund Pettus Bridge, which spans the Alabama River on the route to Montgomery. Just the other side of the bridge, the marchers confronted the state troopers and Sheriff Clark's mounted posse. The troop commander ordered the Negroes to return to Selma; they did not turn around. Troops and possemen, bullwhips and billy clubs flailing, waded into the demonstrators. White and yellow clouds of tear gas swirled across the road; choking, bleeding Negroes fled in all directions. Troopers and possemen chased them, lashing away, the possemen trampling the fallen with their horses.

Martin Luther King immediately announced a second march for Tuesday, March 9, this time appealing to the "conscience of the nation." More than four hundred clergymen of all three faiths and prominent white laymen converged on Selma. Governor Wallace went to federal court to enjoin the demonstration and Judge Frank M. Johnson, Jr., a mild segregationist, issued an injunction banning the march until he had studied the situation. King, in a difficult position, started the march but when it crossed the Pettus Bridge and he was met by a federal marshal bearing the court order, he waved his followers back to Selma. One of the demonstrators was a slight, thirty-five-year-old Unitarian minister, a father of four, the Reverend James J. Reeb, known in Boston for his welfare work in the black slums. That night Reeb and two other white ministers had dinner in a Negro restaurant in Selma and then went for a walk. Four whites came running toward them yelling, "Hey, nigger-lovers!" and swung at them with heavy boards, smashing Reeb on the temple. Customers in a white eating place sat watching the assault through the large front window. None went out; none called the police. Reeb died two days later.

By now indignation was sweeping the United States. When the hundreds of Negroes marched in Selma, tens of thousands, white and black, marched in other cities. In St. Louis, nuns stood an all-night vigil; in Mobile, the concert pianist Byron Janis cancelled his performance to express "my sense of horror"; in sixteen cities well-known entertainers raised a half-million dollars in forty-eight hours to aid "Martin Luther King's fight for humanity." Individuals and organizations inundated the White House and Congress with demands for federal action.

In the Oval Office, President Johnson was moving cautiously. He was no great admirer of Martin Luther King, among other reasons because he questioned how well his judgment would hold up over the long pull. LBJ also was no enthusiast of mass demonstrations. To a man of his turn of mind, the Negroes would do themselves more good by using their energies and their resources working on their politicians to get beneficial legislation. His opinion of demonstrators was not improved when, two days after the second Selma march, twelve white and Negro teen-agers entered the White House under the guise of tourists and staged a sit-down in the East Wing. They were not one of the glories of the civil rights movement. They sprawled across the floor, shouted songs interspersed with crude insults directed at the President, demanded that he speak to them and that he "speak right." By afternoon they had taken a position not far from my office. As I walked by, one of the girls yelled, "Where you going, fink bastard—going to get him his bullwhip?"

The prime element in President Johnson's caution was his reluctance, like that of any modern Chief Executive, to use federal military power in a state when the governor had not asked for it. Such a move could easily make a hero out of the governor, result in serious violence, and impede solution of the immediate crisis while embittering feelings for years to come. With his goal of bringing the South emotionally back into the Union, he was particularly anxious not to appear the iron fist of federal power. Early in the Selma developments, Lyndon Johnson commented: "People talk about my reluctance to use troops in Selma. Well, as President I *am* reluctant to use the strength of the defense establishment for such a thing. When you sit in this chair, you think three times before you say 'go.' "

At the same time, he had no intention of appearing a weak President, afraid to tame gasconading governors. Whatever he thought of Martin Luther King or of demonstrators, he did not question the legitimacy of their goal to establish the right of Southern Negroes to vote. He was keenly aware that if King should be discredited by failure, far less responsible Negroes were likely to take over the leadership of the civil rights movement. He was just as cognizant—he was being told it in every possible way—that if he expected to hold the Northern cities behind him and his general program he could not let George Wallace best Martin Luther King.

For the moment, President Johnson tried to calm both sides while seeking ways to permit the demonstratons to go on without violence. He called upon Vice-President Humphrey, who still carried the aura of Mr. Civil Rights, and the Vice-President talked day and night with Negro leaders, maintaining that the real point was not whether the federal government would use troops at any given time but how it could—with or without troops—help achieve substantial long-range gains for the Negroes. The President dispatched to Alabama conciliators under the leadership of the former governor of Florida, LeRoy Collins, the type of man he liked to use in dealing with the South on race matters. Unchallengeably Southern, a recent convert to desegregation and then on the grounds that it was the "sensible thing," allied both with the past and the new commercial class who wanted to avoid trouble, astute but easy-mannered, Collins, LBJ said, "is the kind of fellow who glides you across, not shoves you and makes you balk."

Judge Johnson in Alabama finished his deliberations and removed his injunction against a Selma-Montgomery march. King set the date, March 21, and declared that this time he and his people were going through, come what might. President Johnson could no longer leave the question of the use of federal troops in the vague realm of presidential efforts at conciliation.

George Wallace now prepared to bestow his supreme gift on Martin Luther King. The governor remembered his splash in the 1964 primaries and decided that he was a big leaguer, destined to be President or to make a President beholden to him. Such a national figure deals only with national figures and in the full spotlight. Wallace wired President Johnson requesting a conference between national leader Lyndon Johnson and national leader George Wallace. The President was most receptive and the meeting was promptly arranged.

At the conference President Johnson made it plain that he would not tolerate continued violence against peaceful demonstrators, but he also went well beyond that. He was not satisfied—at least without a try—to accept the prevailing national picture of Wallace as simply a reactionary racist demagogue. He sensed the possibility of an immemorial Southern type, the politician with some genuine sympathy for the needs of the mass of human beings but driven by a personal contempt for Negroes, an instinct to use racism to whip up votes and a redneck's rancor toward upper-income educated Northerners who looked down on rednecks while backing the Southern Negro. LBJ knew well the Wallace story—son of a dirt farmer, berry picker, magazine peddler, kitchen helper, dump-truck driver, professional fighter, marrying a sixteen-year-old girl who was clerking in a five-and-dime store, and then, as a state legislator and as governor, amid his incessant shrilling about "segregation forever," showing a real interest in providing more trade school and college scholarships, anti-racketeering efforts, the expansion of hospitals and similar legislation. The key to such a politician, Lyndon Johnson believed, was not necessarily to assume that he did not care; it was to recognize that he might have a complex of reactions dominated by the black man and all that surrounded the issue of the black man.

The conference lasted more than three hours and much of the time was used by Lyndon Johnson in trying to get beneath or around the obsession. His approach was that of the New Orleans speech during the campaign of 1964—Let's move Alabama beyond "nigra, nigra," on to important things. The Governor said that he too wanted to stop violence in his state. Very well, the President replied, the way to end demonstrations was to take action to meet the Negro discontent which produced them. "You can't stop a fever by putting an ice pack on your head. You've got to get to the cause of the fever."

With his usual appeal to a man's vanity and ambition, LBJ spoke of Wallace's abilities and urged that instead of using them to combat the Negro, he ought to put them to work lifting the poor of both races. He should "stop looking back to 1865 and start planning for 2065." Sooner rather than later, the President went on, Negroes were going to vote in Alabama and they would not support an enemy; moreover, there was a special place on the national scene for a Deep South governor who became a symbol of race harmony and general social reform. Immediately and specifically, Wallace should begin by issuing a public declaration of his support for "universal suffrage in the State of Alabama and the United States of America," his readiness to back the right of peaceful assembly and his intention of calling a biracial conference in Alabama to start working out the state's social problems.

George Wallace, the sly, nervy little infighter from roughhouse Southern politics, was not accustomed to talk like this. He went home saying privately that President Johnson "was as nice to me as could be." As for the points made, "I have much more respect for him than I thought I'd ever have. I can understand now why he gets his legislation through Congress." LBJ in comparison to JFK? "Johnson's got much more on the ball." And with an enigmatic little smile: "If I hadn't left when I did, he'd have had me coming out for civil rights."

But once settled back in Montgomery, Governor Wallace returned to "nigra, nigra." He arranged a televised joint session of the Alabama legislature to denounce the coming Selma march as being like the Communist "street warfare" that "ripped Cuba apart, that destroyed Diem in Vietnam, that raped China—that has torn civilization and established institutions of this world into bloody shreds." He concocted a strategy; he would shift the whole problem to Lyndon Johnson. Declaring that the protection of the "so-called demonstrators" would cost $350,000–$400,000 and that Alabama did not intend to spend funds "which otherwise would be used for the care of our sick and infirm, both white and Negro," he wired the President with fanfare, calling upon the federal government to provide "sufficient civil authorities" to enforce the ruling of its federal judge, Frank Johnson.

Now President Johnson had just what he needed—an official request from the governor of Alabama to ensure the safety of the marchers. In an immediate public reply, he brushed aside talk of using civilian personnel as so much nonsense. "It is not a welcome duty for the federal government to ever assume a state government's own responsibility for assuring the protection of citizens in the exercise of their constitutional rights." But since such was Governor Wallace's decision, he was federalizing units of the Alabama National Guard and adding federal marshals, military police and FBI agents "to assure the rights of American citizens pursuant to a federal court order to walk peaceably and safely without injury or loss of life from Selma to Montgomery, Ala."

One of the fascinations of history is to observe what a certain type of politician is capable of believing, or of trying to convince others that he believes. A year later Governor Wallace's press secretary, Bill Jones, in a book obviously speaking for the governor, *The Wallace Story*, described this episode with great pride as one in which George Wallace had "set" and "sprung his trap" on Lyndon Johnson by getting him to send in federal troops.

So much for the immediate problem; the Selma marchers would go through to Montgomery without carnage. But there was also, as the President had told the governor, the basic matter of removing the cause of the demonstrations. Six Southern states— Alabama, Georgia, Louisiana, Mississippi, South Carolina and Virginia—and some counties in other Southern and border states continued to use various legalistic devices, particularly unfairly administered "literacy tests," to prevent Negroes from voting in large numbers. The situation could be changed only by the cumbersome and uncertain process of amending the Constitution, or by congressional action giving the federal government the power to intervene effectively in state election procedures.

In carrying out the JFK program in 1964, Lyndon Johnson may have pushed through Congress the sweeping Civil Rights Act of that year. But a voting rights bill was a long step beyond, and he had an even longer record of opposition to civil rights measures. As a new member of the House of Representatives in 1937, he cast his first vote against an anti-lynching bill; as a representative and as a senator between 1937 and 1956, he opposed all civil rights legislation. Along the way he kept making standard Dixie declarations, and on the specific issue of federal intervention in the South to guarantee Negro voting, his most explicit statement came straight from decades of defense of the Jim Crow ballot: "The framers of the Constitution of the United States were plain, specific and unambiguous in providing that each state should have the right to prescribe the qualifications of its electorate." This was an intriguing figure to be emerging as the sponsor of a voting rights bill. Was President Johnson, in that persistent word, "sincere"?

The answer again lies in the ambiguities of the adjective when applied to leaders in a democracy. Lyndon Johnson grew up in an area where race feeling did not run high. The Johnson City region contained few Negroes; with no particular venom and a degree of kindliness, it assumed the separation of the races and the inferiority of the Negro. As a youthful Fergusonite, LBJ drew considerable feeling from his political associations for all people low on the economic ladder, and that early experience of teaching in Cotulla gave him a steadfast sympathy for Mexican-Americans, affecting his attitude toward any minority.

For most of his congressional career he simply "went along" on the subject of civil rights. They were not a prime issue of the pre-Eisenhower years; he represented a district and then a state which were against civil rights legislation; and he accepted the doctrine that a congressman owes his primary allegiance to his constituents' wishes. He had no burning personal desire to do otherwise, and he was perfervid to rise swiftly in the congressional hierarchy which —especially when he reached the Senate—meant working with the Southern powers who largely controlled the body.

But by the late 1950's civil rights were no longer a side issue in the United States or in Congress. LBJ had now taken specific aim on the White House, and constantly before him was the example of Senator Richard Russell of Georgia, one of his own mentors, a man of distinction in many ways who had been blocked from serious consideration for the Presidency because he was stamped as another Southern Democrat on the subject of race.

Ambition coalesced with changing attitudes. As Senate Democratic leader, Lyndon Johnson may have remained a senator from Texas but he was also given on occasion to thinking of his constituency as the whole Democratic party, including its pro-civil rights wing. Increasingly his Fergusonism was taking the shape of seeking to bring the South back into the Union on the basis of de-emphasizing race and pressing for economic and social change. He was annoyed and impatient at the way civil rights issues, like some ugly reef of cant and cynicism, kept wrecking sensible consideration of major congressional legislation in the Senate.

In 1956 the headlines reported a "Southern Manifesto" denouncing the Supreme Court school desegregation decision. It was signed by eighty-one representatives and nineteen senators, including Senators J. William Fulbright of Arkansas and John J. Sparkman, of Alabama, Adlai Stevenson's running mate in 1952— by every senator from the old Confederate South with the exception of Lyndon Johnson and the two senators from Tennessee, Albert Gore and Estes Kefauver. Though Senate Majority Leader Johnson presided over the serious compromising of a civil rights bill submitted by the Eisenhower Administration in 1957, he also saw to it that the measure became the first such legislation to pass the Senate since 1875. The three years in the Vice-Presidency deepened his sense both of the urgency of the Negro problem in terms of the national welfare and of the importance of his own political future of shaking off his anti-civil rights record.

The Presidency brought a whole concatenation of forces pushing LBJ toward complete and emotional advocacy of civil rights. The change in his constituency was sharp and compelling; it now included 22 million restless Negroes and 169 million whites, many of whom seemed ready to respond to the black man's agitation. As President, and especially as one seeking to be known as the architect of national unity, he obviously could achieve his goal only by moving white-Negro relations toward a new plateau marked by legal and political equality and by increasing economic opportunities for the black man. As a politician, especially one hurt by the lingering impression that he was an old-style Southern Democrat, vigorous pro-civil rights leadership had great lure. And as a human being, sitting in the Oval Office which has roused the better angels of every man who occupied it, he was moved by the influences of a long past, whether the distant voice of Jim Ferguson, the pinched faces of Mexican-American children, or his slowly mounting contempt for the racial clichés that diverted attention from pressing human needs.

Well before Selma, it was clear that the issue of Negro voting rights in the South would soon take its place on the civil rights agenda. As early as mid-1964, President Johnson had asked Nicholas Katzenbach, still Acting Attorney General, to prepare recommendations about the form such a move should take, particularly whether the device should be a congressional bill or a constitutional amendment. The assignment was long-range and was to be kept out of the press. Lyndon Johnson had no intention of handing Barry Goldwater more Southern votes in the election of 1964. He also did not want the matter brought up in the post-election Eighty-ninth Congress. He sought time for the South to digest the Civil Rights Act of 1964, and feared that a second pro-Negro move so soon would provoke a Senate uproar snarling all other legislation.

The voting rights campaign of Martin Luther King, Alabama's handling of it, and the national reaction produced a hasty revision of the schedule. As soon as Selma exploded, President Johnson gave new instructions to Katzenbach, now duly named Attorney General: drop consideration of the slow procedure of constitutional amendment; prepare a voting rights bill quickly.

It was the nature of Lyndon Johnson that once he had made a decision, it became an all-encompassing one. People spoke of his sense of political timing, and he certainly had this to a high degree. But there was also a kind of inner timing, the process by which something happened inside the man to pull together all sorts of convictions, political considerations and personal likes and dislikes into a consuming composite of thought and action. Such a moment occurred as the Selma crisis developed. Suddenly his strategic hesitancies and his reservations about demonstrations receded. Suddenly his bent toward civil rights, his conception of the role of the President, his impatience with the politics of "nigra, nigra," and the political needs and opportunities presented by Selma rushed to the fore, and all complexities merged into a simple, sharp issue to which a son of Johnson City easily responded: the right of an

American citizen to vote. Suddenly everything took fire from the fact that the millionaire President, the wheeler-dealer who delighted in manipulating power groups, also remained responsive to the little fellow yearning for a break, the uneducated, the elderly sick, the minorities who needed a hoist. Suddenly Lyndon Johnson resolved that he would not only send a voting rights bill to Congress; he would envelop the black revolution and stand forth as what he had always wanted so much to be, the President of all the people.

Early in the LBJ Administration I happened to have called to President Johnson's attention two phrases of Theodore Roosevelt. The President of the United States, TR had said, is "the steward" of the nation, and when some basic issue is at stake, his office can be a "bully pulpit." It was noticeable how much President Johnson used the phrases during this period. It was high time, something within Lyndon Johnson told him, to mount that pulpit and exercise that stewardship.

Not for nineteen years—since 1946 when Harry Truman went to the Hill to ask legislation to break a railroad strike—had a President personally gone before Congress to appeal for a domestic law. President Johnson proposed to deliver his message calling for voting rights legislation standing before a joint session, at the prime television time of nine P.M., on March 15, midway between the second Selma march and the day when federalized troops would protect those American citizens who chose to walk peaceably, pursuant to a federal court order, from Selma to Montgomery, Alabama.

The day the decision for the address was made, he assembled his key staff men about seven o'clock in the evening. Until midnight he poured out what he wanted to say, going over and over alternative approaches, philosophizing, nailing down specific sentences, restlessly seeking to "get it said, really said." Other sessions were frequent and lengthy. Aides did their usual drafting of versions, but to an extraordinary extent the final manuscript was Lyndon Johnson in Lyndon Johnson's own language.

Word had gone out in Washington that this speech was not to be missed. The Cabinet, Supreme Court Justices, and ambassadors accepted their invitations; every possible seating place, even the usually forbidden aisles, was filled. The jam accentuated the fact that the entire congressional delegations of Mississippi and Virginia, as well as many individual Southern congressmen from other states, had chosen to absent themselves.

When President Johnson entered the chamber of the House of

Representatives he offered few hail-fellow handshakes and smiles, and carried himself in a way that made his six feet, three inches more towering than ever.

He began in his usual style for formal addresses, the low, slow voice. "I speak tonight for the dignity of man and the destiny of democracy. . . .

"At times history and fate meet at a single time in a single place to shape a turning point in man's unending search for freedom. So it was at Lexington and Concord. So it was a century ago at Appomattox. So it was last week in Selma, Alabama."

Veteran congressmen could not recall when the room had been so hushed. Even the clicks of photographers' cameras were clearly audible.

The President's voice rose and quickened. In Selma, "long-suffering men and women peacefully protested the denial of their rights as Americans. Many were brutally assaulted. One good man, a man of God, was killed. . . . The cries of pain and the hymns and protests of oppressed people have summoned into convocation all the majesty of this great government—the government of the greatest Nation on earth.

"Our mission is at once the oldest and the most basic of this country: to right wrong, to do justice, to serve man. . . .

"The issue of equal rights for American Negroes is such an issue. And should we defeat every enemy, should we double our wealth and conquer the stars, and still be unequal to this issue, then we will have failed as a people and as a nation.

"For with a country as with a person, 'What is a man profited, if he shall gain the whole world, and lose his own soul?' "

The first applause, strong and sharp, crackled across the chamber. No one in the room, friend or foe of the Negro, could fail to feel the sense of inexorable history. The first Southern President of modern times, the one-time congressional opponent of civil rights bills who had assailed precisely the kind of legislation he was now advocating, was throwing the whole moral power of the presidential office behind the most basic of civil rights. Further, he stood at the podium the first President in American history to identify himself, publicly and in words of unqualified intensity, with the cause of the Negro. (Just how unqualified was indicated by the fact that he omitted from the prepared text a line stating that "the right of free speech does not carry with it the right to endanger the safety of others on a public highway," an obvious criticism of the tactics of some demonstrators.)

Lyndon Johnson swept on, his voice taking on unwonted qualities, now ringing, now slashing. His thumb would go up in emphasis, his lips purse in tension, his fists clench. Vigorous applause followed every few sentences.

Television cameras sweeping the room caught striking vignettes: in the presidential box, Mrs. Johnson and Lynda on the edge of their seats, their guest, J. Edgar Hoover, staring into some world of his own; Vice-President Hubert Humphrey, presiding over his first joint session of Congress, roseate and solemn; some Supreme Court Justices applauding strong lines, others sitting in judicial restraint; the usually contained Senate Majority Leader Mike Mansfield close to tears at one emotional moment; Senator Allen J. Ellender of Louisiana slumped gloomily in his seat.

The issue was clear-cut, the President declared. "There is no Negro problem. There is no Southern problem. There is no Northern problem. There is only an American problem. And we are met here tonight as Americans—not as Democrats or Republicans—we are met here as Americans to solve that problem."

The United States "was the first nation in the history of the world to be founded with a purpose." The purpose was to assure "to every citizen that he shall share in the dignity of man," and the dignity was impossible without the right to choose his leaders. Parts of America had set up barriers against voting, of such a nature that the only way to pass them "is to show a white skin." He was sending a bill to Congress to end this, and he called upon the House and Senate to brush aside their usual wrangling over civil rights. "The Constitution says that no person shall be kept from voting because of his race or his color. We have all sworn an oath before God to support and to defend that Constitution. We must now act in obedience to that oath. . . .

"This time, on this issue, there must be no delay, no hesitation and no compromise with our purpose."

The applause started again. Little Emanuel Celler from Brooklyn, seventy-seven years old and dean of the House of Representatives in years of service, chairman of its powerful Judiciary Committee, proud Jew and well-tested friend of all minorities, had waited for decades to hear a President of the United States talk like this. Representative Celler stood up, his hands pounding above his head. The House and Senate, the Supreme Court, the Cabinet and the ambassadors followed him in roaring ovation.

The demonstrations in Selma, President Johnson continued, focused on voting rights for the Negro, but they bespoke considerations beyond that and beyond the black man himself. The Negroes were declaring that they wanted both the vote and "the full blessings of American life"; they were also pointing to an urgent national need. "Their cause must be our cause too," for they were summoning the United States not only to end discrimination against the black man but to "overcome the crippling legacy of bigotry and injustice" in all parts of American life.

Then Lyndon Johnson paused. His long arms went up and he spoke the words that had made their way into the national tradition by slogging feet on scores of dusty roads, by children singing above the swish of whips and by men, women and children chanting into the snarl of dogs. With slow, bulldozer force the President of the United States said, "And . . . we . . . shall . . . overcome."

This time Emanuel Celler did not have to lead. The whole chamber was on its feet again. In the galleries Negroes and whites, some in the rumpled sports shirts of bus rides from the demonstrations, others in trim professional suits, wept unabashedly.

President Lyndon Johnson had one more thing to say. He wanted to state why he spoke with such feeling about this particular legislation, and it concerned Cotulla. "My students were poor and they often came to class without breakfast, hungry. They knew even in their youth the pain of injustice. They never seemed to know why people disliked them, but they knew it was so, because I saw it in their eyes. I often walked home late in the afternoon, after the classes were finished, wishing there was more that I could do. . . .

"Somehow you never forget what poverty and hatred can do when you see its scars on the hopeful face of a young child.

"I never thought then, in 1928, that I would be standing here in 1965. It never occurred to me in my fondest dreams that I might have the chance to help the sons and daughters of those students and to help people like them all over this country.

"But now I do have that chance—and I'll let you in on a secret —I mean to use it. And I hope you will use it with me."

Lyndon Johnson left the emotional chamber head high with a quiet smile. He threw a kiss to his wife and his daughter Lynda in the presidential box. In the same manner as his entry, he paused for few gestures of political camaraderie.

Lynda came down to the swarm of reporters with her face flushed. How did she feel about the speech? She replied in a way that her father liked very much. "It was just like that old hymn, 'Once to every man and nation comes a moment to decide.' "

The President's instructions to Attorney General Nicholas Katzenbach for the voting rights bill had stressed three points. The legislation must be prepared in close concert with the bipartisan leadership of the Senate, particularly Minority Leader Everett Dirksen, so that the Senate votes would be available to invoke cloture and end a filibuster. It should be constitutional beyond a doubt; a measure approved by Congress and then voided by the Supreme Court would be worse than no law. Lastly, it had to be effective— the national mood would not be satisfied by innocuous legalese.

The legislation that was emerging met the prescription. It was being worked out in conferences between Katzenbach and his men, particularly Deputy Attorney General Ramsey Clark, and Majority Leader Mike Mansfield and Minority Leader Everett Dirksen; Dirksen was a full partner and the meetings were sometimes held in his cluttered lair in the Senate Office Building. The bill was based squarely on the declaration in the Fifteenth Amendment to the Constitution that the vote shall not be "denied or abridged by the United States or by any State on account of race, color, or previous condition of servitude. The Congress shall have power to enforce this article by appropriate legislation."

The central operative provision was practical. Disenfranchisement was declared to have taken place in all counties where on the date of November 1, 1964, literacy tests or similar restrictions on voting were in effect, and where less than 50 percent of the voting-age citizens had been registered and actually voted in the 1964 presidential election. This covered Alabama, Georgia, Louisiana, Mississippi, South Carolina and Virginia, and thirty-four counties in North Carolina. It also included the entire state of Alaska; Apache County, Arizona; Elmore County, Idaho; and Aroostook County, Maine. But as Katzenbach remarked, "It may have snowed in Maine on election day," and a discretionary clause absolved areas where racial discrimination was clearly not intended. The provisions of the bill went into effect by an automatic triggering device. In the case of any county declared discriminatory by the definition of the legislation, all literacy tests and similar regulations were declared void, and the Attorney General was given the power to supervise federal elections by sending in examiners to register anyone who met the basic tests of citizenship, age, sound mind and absence of criminal record.

The voting rights bill went to the House and Senate two days after the President's appearance before Congress, on March 17, and its chances appeared excellent. LBJ's bipartisan preparations continued indefatigably; national opinion remained forcefully behind the legislation. As Senator Dirksen intoned in one of his magnificently mixed metaphors, "The fever will not subside; it is in the air." All but the magnolia congressmen seemed eager to assert themselves as pro-civil rights. Democratic members were not missing a bandwagon, especially when the calliope was so loud, and Republicans were not forgetting that in the presidential election just held, Negroes voted more than 90 percent for the Democratic candidate. The Senate, with its proffer of the filibuster technique to the Southerners, had been the graveyard of most civil rights bills, but the voting rights law started through the upper house co-sponsored by the two party chiefs, Mansfield and Dirksen, and sixty-four other Democratic and Republican senators—a total already only one vote short of the two-thirds necessary to invoke cloture.

Alabama, continuing as Martin Luther King's best friend, saw to it that national sentiment stayed roused. When King led the third march out of Selma, rifle-bearing troops under the orders of the President protected the demonstration, but murder came anyhow. A white sympathizer, Mrs. Viola G. Liuzzo, wife of a Detroit union official and the mother of five, was killed by a bullet fired at her temple by slayers tentatively identified as Ku Kluxers. Alabamians lined the route of the march to yell four-letter words at a nun from Kansas City as she trudged along, and slapped their thighs in glee when they thought of just the right cadence to shout at a one-legged marcher from Michigan: "Left, left, left. . . ." The one hundred and forty-one members of the Alabama legislature solemnly —and unanimously—got to the heart of the problem by passing a resolution thundering against "the evidence of much fornication at the marchers' camps." And Governor George C. Wallace continued, imperturbable and compleat, George C. Wallace.

Having agreed to receive a petition from the demonstrators when they reached Montgomery, he reneged on the promise, with the humpty-dumpty observation that a peaceful demonstration sanctioned by a federal court, protected by federalized troops, for the purpose of acquiring a plainly stated constitutional right, was "a prostitution of lawful process." Next day, Wallace was up bright and eager to discuss the murder of Mrs. Liuzzo on the network television program, *Today*. "Of course, I regret the incident," the governor told the nation. "But I would like to point out that people are assaulted in every state in the Union." Unwilling to leave bad enough alone, he added: "With twenty-five thousand marching in the streets and chanting and maligning and slandering and libeling the people of this state as they did for several hours on this network and the other networks, I think the people of our state were greatly restrained."

Nevertheless, smooth passage of the voting rights bill was not assured. The legislation had inherent difficulties, and forces were not lacking to pounce upon them. With its transparent relationship to votes in future elections, it was also an invitation to Northern Republicans to try to amend it significantly and thus give themselves a degree of credit for it. Over the whole venture hung the worry that the simmering national racial tension might flare up in a way that would sharply diminish public and congressional support for pro-Negro action. If there was little chance that the voting rights bill would be defeated, there was a distinct possibility that a combination of circumstances and interests could lead to months of debate, derailing other LBJ legislation, or to amendments that would render the measure ineffective or vulnerable to court action.

Under the circumstances, President Johnson's strategy for getting the measure through Congress was somewhere between the approaches he used for Medicare and for the education bill. As in the case of aid to education, he pushed for quick action. As in the case of Medicare, he depended heavily on one key figure, Senate Minority Leader Dirksen, and he was ready to slacken his lines of control to the extent of permitting Southerners to play to their publics and of allowing Northerners or Southerners to put through amendments that did not go to the core of the bill.

In the Senate, the voting rights legislation went to the Judiciary Committee, chaired by James O. Eastland of Mississippi, who took great pride in the fact that since he became head of the committee, it had effectively buried one hundred and twenty civil rights bills. Eastland was particularly adamant about a voting rights bill; it roused both his deepest prejudices and his most practical political fears. Now he expressed his "shock" at the new Administration measure, and declared that he would fight it "as long as God gives me breath." Majority Leader Mansfield and Minority Leader Dirksen did not intend to wait that long. Using the power of their bipartisan bloc, they put through a Senate vote instructing the Judiciary Committee to report out the measure in fifteen days, by April 9.

Much that happened at the hearings before the committee had a familiar enough ring, whether the cultivated Senator Sam J. Ervin, Jr., of North Carolina, using involved constitutional arguments to oppose votes for Negroes, or stubby Leander Perez, the Democratic boss of Plaquemines Parish in Louisiana, chomping on his long black cigar and muttering about the "Communist plan" behind the voting rights bill and the "immoral character" of Negroes, whose "only interest is to get welfare checks. . . . They are a low type of citizenship."

But all the while Perez and Ervin talked, the real problems of the legislation were emerging. The Twenty-fourth Amendment to the Constitution, ratified the previous year, abolished poll taxes in federal elections but said nothing about state and local voting, and the voting rights measure remained silent on state and local voting taxes. The civil rights leaders, especially Martin Luther

King, wanted this legislation to complete the abolition of poll taxes; they pressured vigorously the liberal members of the Judiciary Committee, most of whom themselves leaned in the direction of such a ban.

Senator Dirksen, the ranking Republican on the Judiciary Committee as well as Minority Leader, was also on the move. He might back the voting rights bill but he liked to leave the Republican stamp, not to mention the Dirksen stamp, on major legislation. The senator had a group of legal assistants, known without affection in Democratic circles as "Dirksen's Bombers," who devoted themselves to ferreting out problems in Administration legislation, and now they found two real ones. The formula for detecting discrimination left out Arkansas, Florida, Tennessee and, of all places, Texas—states that imposed no rigged tests but nevertheless contained about one-fourth of the unregistered Negroes in the country. Civil rights leaders argued that areas in these states used nonlegislative measures, particularly threats of job reprisals, to effect disenfranchisement. The formula also included counties which had literacy and similar tests and where it was not clear, as it was in Alaska or Maine, whether the regulations were administered for racist purposes. Senator Dirksen proposed an amendment which he called "truly national." It would exempt counties with literacy tests and similar devices which could prove in court that at least 60 percent of their voting-age citizens were registered, or less than 20 percent of the population was "non-white."

The Administration strongly opposed a poll-tax ban in state and local elections as a part of the voting rights bill. It believed the prohibition would probably be ruled unconstitutional, and it was further concerned about the difficulty of proving in any particular case that the tax was established for the purpose of disenfranchising Negroes. It was against the Dirksen amendment on the ground that it could prove a way by which some hard-core discrimination areas escaped the effect of the legislation by increasing the registration of white voters. It had adopted its formula because it was convinced that any other one would end up creating still more problems, that is, include even more counties which practiced no disenfranchisement of Negroes or omit still larger discriminatory areas in the South and border states.

Senator Dirksen and the anti-poll-tax forces persisted, other senators pushed amendments of substance, and the fifteen days went by. On April 9, with the clock moving toward the midnight deadline, the Judiciary Committee reported the bill favorably, in a tone that left the real settlement of the issues to the Senate floor. This was just the sort of situation the Southern forces had hoped for. If they could feed it by delaying tactics and more divisive amendments, perhaps they could split the bipartisan coalition behind the measure and talk it into oblivion or at least load it with crippling amendments. With an air of refreshed confidence, Senator Eastland announced that a long period would be needed "to explain this bill to the American public."

If the senator was actually heartened, he completely misunderstood. The White House kept the phones active but not demanding, depending on Mansfield and Dirksen, and the reliance was justified. Everett Dirksen might be as partisan, as McKinleyesque and as eel-like as ever, but again he would emerge—strewn hair, bloviated words, zigzagging strategies and all—a man who did not want the Republican party trailing too far behind the 1960's and who did not forget the national interest.

Majority Leader Mansfield was almost as deceptive a political figure as Minority Leader Dirksen. Mild-mannered and somewhat retiring, he hardly appeared the type for a Senate Majority Leader. In fact, some of his colleagues insisted that Mansfield had been hand-picked by Vice-President Johnson after the election of 1960 so that LBJ could continue to run the Senate. But if Mansfield was no strong-armed leader of wile, he was a capable, proud man of genuine convictions. He believed in the voting rights bill and he had been stung by criticisms of his leadership. He intended to lead this measure firmly and surely to adoption in a clear and effective form.

During the debate on the Senate floor, Mansfield and Dirksen worked together with a closeness rarely, if ever, seen in the upper house before, and both were given constant if judicious support by the White House. A few changes of consequence were adopted. The Administration did not dare to risk Dirksen's withdrawal from the coalition, and his amendment had some merit; in modified form, it was voted through. The poll-tax dispute was circumvented. Local and state poll taxes were not voided; instead, the Attorney General was instructed "forthwith" to file suit against their constitutionality in Alabama, Mississippi, Texas and Virginia, the only states where they remained law. A third amendment was accepted both because of its source and because it was not objectionable to any powerful faction. Senator Robert Kennedy had almost a million Puerto Ricans in his new political home of New York State. He proposed and got an amendment waiving English literacy requirements for citizens who had completed the sixth grade in any school under the American flag.

The amendments kept coming, the speeches went on, and the Southern senators were clearly heading into what amounted to a filibuster. Anxious as he was to get the bill through before more problems arose, President Johnson cautioned against swift invocation of cloture. David West, of the Dallas *Morning News*, remembered the attitude of Senate Majority Leader Johnson when Southern senators were filibustering against the civil rights bill of 1957. "Let 'em talk for a while," LBJ said. "This is their job. This is what they were sent here to do, just as you fellows have to report it. You wouldn't like it if I interfered with your job and caused your publishers to jump down your throats."

After twenty-four days President Johnson and Mansfield and Dirksen agreed that the Southerners had amply demonstrated to the home folks that they were against votes for Negroes. On May 21 came the petition for cloture. Everett Dirksen offered his "regrets that I must cut off the voices of my distinguished colleagues, but with some measure of assurance that in the long veil of history, over the transient concerns of this fleeting day, they will find me not too far wrong," threw full G.O.P. support behind the move. Four days later, on a rare occasion for the Senate, every one of the hundred members was present for the cloture vote, which in effect was the decision on the bill. Cloture was invoked 70 to 30—the second time in American history on a civil rights issue but also the second time in two years, the other occasion being the Civil Rights Act of 1964.

Action in the House of Representatives came more slowly because Representative Howard Smith was successful in bottling up the voting rights bill for five weeks in his Rules Committee. But the Southern strategy was more of the same: delay, seek amendments, hope to split the coalition. The Republicans also were in an identical position, trying to make the bill in some measure their own. Once again the chief sticking points were the poll tax and the Administration formula for establishing discrimination.

The civil rights leaders were exerting particularly strong influence over members of the House. The Administration stood aside while the representatives passed an amendment abolishing taxes on local and state voting, assuming that the provision could be removed in the House-Senate conference which lay ahead. The main contest came over the discrimination formula, and the House tossed up the problems of the plan in balloons of oratory. Howard H. ("Bo") Callaway, a socialite enjoying his one term in the House of Representatives as a Republican member from Georgia, had an especially good time with the specifics of the Administration triggering device. Much better, Callaway said, would be to "select all states which have an average altitude of 100 to 900 feet, an average yearly temperature of 68 to 77 degrees at seven A.M., average humidity of 80 to 87 percent, and a coastline of 400 miles. With this formula we encompass all the southern states attacked by . . . [the Administration bill], but have the added advantage of including all of North Carolina and excluding Alaska."

The G.O.P. Representative John V. Lindsay, soon to run for mayor of New York City, wanted to be serious about votes for Negroes. There must be a better formula, he insisted. Take Newton County, Arkansas, where there were no impeding tests but 78 percent of the whites were registered and not a single Negro. The next day Senator Fulbright took Newton County, Arkansas. Lindsay, the senator replied, was entirely correct in his statement, but had failed to note that exactly two non-whites lived in Newton County and "there is some question in the collective mind of the Census Bureau as to whether either of them is Negro."

The test came shortly. House Minority Leader Ford continued his strategy of the alternative Republican bill and it was offered by William M. McCulloch of Ohio, a thoughtful legislator who, as the ranking Republican on the Judiciary Committee, had proved his commitment to civil rights during the debate over the 1964 measure. Not questioning the need for voting rights legislation, McCulloch argued that the Administration plan had a "punitive tone" toward the South, would ultimately raise constitutional questions and did not cover all areas in which the Negro was disenfranchised. His bill eliminated automatic triggering by any percentage and substituted a system under which, on the receipt of twenty-five meritorious complaints from a voting district, federal registrars would be dispatched with the power to waive impeding tests.

The White House was alarmed by the McCulloch bill. To the Southerners, it offered a way of harassing the Administration measure; to the Republicans, a method of not voting for another LBJ bill without appearing anti-Negro. It was also a genuine measure, not a mere political ploy, and an argument could be made that it was superior to the Administration legislation both in being less arbitrary and more comprehensive. But President Johnson and the civil rights leaders were sure that it would do little to give the vote to the Southern Negro because it lacked the one essential—the power of the federal government, without depending on local action, to go in and register voters. The President and the House Democratic leadership began the process of stiffening Democratic backs and of seeing how many Republicans could be detached from the G.O.P. bill. The prospects were dubious. Southern Democrats flocked to the McCulloch version, and G.O.P. lines were holding so firm behind it that the Administration could count just ten Republican votes for its own measure, considerably less than it needed for passage.

At this juncture, an overarticulate Southern congressman— not an Alabamian, for a change—did the work for the civil rights leaders. The obvious strategy for the Southerners was to go on attacking voting rights legislation in general, to show no enthusiasm for the McCulloch bill but to back it in the hope that it would create an impasse in the House-Senate conference. Instead the floor was taken by Representative William M. Tuck of Virginia, "Genial Big Bill Tuck," tobacco grower and banker, former governor of Virginia, member of the Board of Governors of the Jefferson Memorial Foundation, and a man the Southerners took pride in having speak for them. Tuck declared: "The plain, unvarnished truth" was that a vote against the McCulloch substitute meant a vote "to foist upon your constituents this unconstitutional monstrosity" of federal intervention to guarantee Negro voting. The McCulloch bill was "milder" and therefore "far more preferable."

Minority Leader Ford sat listening with the look of a man betrayed. He tried to repair the damage by declaring that the McCulloch bill should be passed because it was a "better bill," not because it undercut Negro voting. But Ford was wasting his time. "It's not for me to advise my Republican friends," Speaker McCormack commented, "but I think Governor Tuck put them in a very untenable position." By evening Ford learned that fifteen Republicans had already deserted the McCulloch bill. The House vote on it and then on the LBJ measure were repeats of the Senate story. The House balloting was less notable for the size of the majority than for one element in it. Times were changing; an awareness of those oncoming Negro votes filled the chamber. Twenty-three congressmen from Florida, Georgia, Louisiana and Texas—most of whom had never cast a pro-civil rights vote—backed the Administration voting rights bill.

The House-Senate conference wrangled on for more than three weeks, with the Administration seeking to hold together the bipartisan coalition behind what it considered essential. President Johnson's arm twisting now was more open, but probably his most telling move was not pressure at all. During the conference sessions, congressmen who wanted important changes kept pointing to Lyndon Johnson's long anti-civil rights record and his opposition to the voting legislation he was now advocating. The references hurt; they threw an air of crass expediency over the whole Administration effort. The situation was exacerbated by the fact that in a thoroughly uncharacteristic move, LBJ had hailed the House passage of the voting rights bill with remarks that included a slap at the Republican effort for the McCulloch bill. Ford and McCulloch replied in a stinging statement that "the President is obviously sensitive to his own 'Lyndon come lately' congressional record on civil rights." With a mocking thrust that stirred up again all the difficulties of the Administration formula, they asked, Why was Texas not covered by the original LBJ bill?

As the tangles of the House-Senate conference continued, on July 13 Lyndon Johnson made the most effective press conference statement of his Presidency. He said what was certainly not easy for him to say—that he had been wrong. "I think that all of us realize that at this stage of the twentieth century there is much that should have been done that has not been done. . . . I am particularly sensitive to the problems of the Negro. . . . Perhaps it is because I realize, after traveling through forty-four states and after reading some twenty thousand or thirty thousand letters a week, digests from them, that it is a very acute problem and one that I want to do my best to solve in the limited time that I am allowed. I did not have that responsibility in the years past, and I did not feel it to the extent that I do today. . . . I am going to try to provide all the leadership that I can, notwithstanding the fact that someone may point to a mistake or a hundred mistakes that I made in my past."

The Kennedy amendment went through the House-Senate conference without much difficulty, but removing the poll-tax ban imposed by the House was not so easy. Attorney General Katzenbach had to produce assurance from Martin Luther King that the "forthwith" provision was acceptable in order to win the acquiescence of the most recalcitrant House conferees, two congressmen from polyglot districts in Massachusetts and New Jersey. The Dirksen amendment, enveloping all the strands of discontent with the Administration formula for identifying discrimination, continued to be a problem, and at the showdown, Senator Dirksen continued to be a sincere friend of the legislation. The upshot was a settlement that preserved the original formula as the basis of the law but added a provision so complex that it is impossible to determine its effect, if any, except in terms of the senator's personal and political needs.

The voting rights bill was ready for signing on August 6. This time the scene was on the Hill, in the ornate President's Room where, precisely one hundred and four years before, President Lincoln had signed the law freeing slaves who had been forced into the Confederate armed forces. But the occasion was more notable for the men and women around President Johnson—not only Martin Luther King and other embattled leaders of the civil rights drive but two figures from the poignant past. One was Mrs. Rosa Parks, the seamstress who had decided she would not give up her seat to go to the back of a bus in Montgomery in 1955, gray hair braided back, frail-looking and serene as ever, now working as a reception- ist in the office of the Detroit Negro congressman, John Conyers, Jr. The other was Miss Vivian Malone, daughter of a Mobile handy- man, who had decided in 1963 that she wanted to enroll in the University of Alabama and had proceeded to enroll after Governor Wallace was removed from her path by federal troops, now hand- some and smiling radiantly, with her A.B. from the University of Alabama and her job as a researcher for the Department of Justice of the United States.

Promptly the symbolism of the signing ceremony was dwarfed by action. The results of Medicare and of the education bill could come only over the months and years. President Johnson signed the Voting Rights Act on a Thursday. On Friday the Department of Justice designated the affected areas under the definition of the legislation and filed suits against the poll-tax law of Mississippi. That weekend, lights burned all night in the Justice Department. On Tuesday additional poll-tax suits were filed in Alabama, Texas and Virginia, and forty-five federal registrars, all Southern-bred and all rushed through a three-day training course, fanned into Alabama, Louisiana and Mississippi.

They arrived in Selma, Alabama, to a mixed reception. Sheriff Clark was ready to tell everyone from the sidewalks, "The whole thing's so ridiculous I haven't gotten over laughing at it yet." A by- stander asked, "Would the Negroes who were registered actually be able to vote?" The Sheriff laughed uproariously. "If they can find their way into town."

An elderly Negro woman, her brightly colored cotton print dress crisply ironed, found her way into town and into the county courthouse. She struggled with a ballpoint pen, conquered it and as she left, remarked, "I'm going to vote now. I'm going to vote be- cause I haven't been able to vote in my sixty-seven years."

A no-nonsense voting rights bill signed into law after being before Congress just one hundred and forty-two days; the sweeping education bill, eighty-seven days; far-reaching Medicare, two hundred and four days—and all the while, other important meas- ures were being marched, squeezed, wheedled, glided, exhorted and shoved through the Eighty-ninth Congress.

The signing ceremonies came in a rapid fire: March 9, 1965, an additional large anti-poverty program, $900 million for Appalachia; April 26, significant manpower-training extensions; June 21, a $4.7 billion excise-tax reduction; July 14, the Older Americans Act, establishing an Administration on Aging in HEW; July 15, greatly expanded drug controls; August 10, omnibus housing legislation, including a provision for rent supplement payments to low-income families; August 26, the Public Works and Economic Development Act, consolidating and encouraging regional development; September 9, establishment of a new Cabinet Department of Housing and Urban Development; September 29, creation of the National Foundation for the Arts and the Humanities; September 30, the High-Speed Ground Transportation Act, opening the way to a serious attack on mass-transit problems; October 2, the quaintly labeled Water Quality Act, an effort to diminish water pollution; October 3, abolition of the decades-old discriminatory quota system for immigration; October 6, establishment of a system of regional medical centers to give substance to the announced campaign against heart disease, cancer and stroke; October 9, more large-scale anti-poverty legislation; October 20, air pollution controls; November 4, omnibus farm legislation; November 8, $2.4 billion more aid to higher education.

The first, 1965 session of the Eighty-ninth Congress sat from January 4 to October 23. In those nine months it approved eighty-nine Administration-sponsored or Administration-backed measures of importance. President Johnson lost only three bills which he had declared to be of any particular significance: the appropriation for rent supplements, home rule for Washington, D.C., and the repeal of Section 14(b) of the Taft-Hartley Labor Act—and it was not at all clear that he really wanted the last.

In the twentieth century, two previous Congresses had been especially notable for the amount and scope of legislation passed, the opening periods of the Wilson and the FDR Administrations. It was the more productive of the two, the Hundred Days of FDR, which had particularly challenged Lyndon Johnson. He may have wanted to avoid the drama of the Hundred Days but certainly not its fruitfulness, and as the first hundred days of his new term ended in April, he could not resist a little comparative public preening. Whether the FDR or LBJ Congress actually was the more productive depends on how you define "major legislation"; nevertheless, objective observers were ready not only to forgive President Johnson's pride but to add two points that he himself could not publicly make. Unlike FDR, he was functioning without the co-operating pressure of a national economic crisis, and he was sending most of his bills through in a carefully planned and timed pattern. During the period between the close of the LBJ hundred days and the adjournment of the first session of the Eighty-ninth Congress, the pace of legislation, far from slackening, accelerated. At the end, President Johnson, with another pardonable flurry of adjectives, could call his Congress "the greatest in American history. . . . This has been the fabulous Eighty-ninth Congress."

Republicans could only console themselves with epithets. Barry Goldwater called the first session of the Eighty-ninth "the Xerox Congress"; the National Republican Congressional Committee labeled it "the Three-B Congress—bullied, badgered and brainwashed." James Reston spoke with more serenity. "He's getting everything through the Congress but the abolition of the Republican party, and he hasn't tried that yet."

Again certain qualifiers must be added in assessing this 1965 legislative score. President Johnson was still being aided by the climate of opinion created by John Kennedy's assassination, which made both the country and the Congress more ready to accept JFK-type legislation. A number of bills similar to the LBJ 1965 legislative program, as in the case of his 1964 successes, had been presented to the House and Senate during the Kennedy Administration. The Eighty-ninth Congress had a make-up and a mood to go along because of the landslide in the election of 1964, which was a creation of Barry Goldwater as well as of Lyndon Johnson. Yet with all these things said, they only qualify and do not undermine the achievement. And whatever the qualifiers, they must be accompanied by the statement that after all it was Lyndon Johnson who got the bills passed.

If he had a favorable climate of opinion, he knew how to use it. If he could call upon commanding majorities in the House and Senate—as other Presidents before him could—he saw to it that the majorities were put to work to an extent as great or greater than any previous Chief Executive. Much of the legislation may have come from the Kennedy agenda; some of it did not and that which did was often given a different twist. The rent supplements bill was the most striking of several that pointed in a pioneering direction. Of the big three of 1965 legislation—Medicare, aid to education and voting rights—the first two had been sent to Congress in the JFK years but not the third. Moreover, the health insurance plan was significantly altered as a result of the arrangement with Wilbur Mills and the school law rested on the newly adopted theory of aid to the individual poor child.

Working in the White House during this period produced on occasion an almost eerie feeling. The legislation rolled through the House and Senate in such profusion and so methodically that you seemed to be part of some vast, overpowering machinery, oiled to a purr. You were reminded of the most striking physical characteristic of the President, those eyes beneath the half-lowered lids, clear, steady, all-seeing and unrelenting. Once in a while I would amuse myself by kidding colleagues about what the boss could *not* get Congress to approve, and the reaction to such banter made clear how many areas were off limits even in the heady atmosphere of 1965—whether I mentioned a genuine tax-reform law or the kind of legislation which recognized that American cities were headed for real trouble. But whatever the limitations and moments of oppressiveness, working in the White House of 1965 also brought intense excitement. There was an exhilarating feeling of being part of the command post of a nation—the lead nation of the democratic world—while it was bringing itself up to date under one of its most authentic citizens, as authentic in some of his worst defects as he was in strong virtues, but withal a man who kept on that phone expressing to congressmen some dogged version of the credo that America means a better shake for the ordinary man.

As the first session of the Eighty-ninth Congress moved ahead, Lyndon Johnson stood at a peak of success certainly unexcelled, and perhaps unequalled, in American political history. By the spring of 1964 he had established himself as a man who had taken over the Presidency at a moment of national shock and restored confidence and movement. Now he had gone on to score a record win in 1964, and was using the victory to enact a rich legislative program directed toward meeting human needs. He seemed to be moving toward his personal objective of being the President of national unity, and especially of reuniting North and South. In the fall of 1965, the polls indicated that during the three decades of opinion surveys, no President had so consistently enjoyed strong support across all major segments of the population. As for the South, Lyndon Johnson had imposed on it the two toughest civil rights laws in American history. Yet the region was not in revolt against him; on the contrary, it showed many signs of accepting his doctrine of less "nigra, nigra" and more economic advancement. Rising just ahead, glimmering and intoxicating, was the ultimate goal—to be considered a great President, even the greatest of them all.

The pinnacle of political success and the goal visible—but something was wrong, drastically wrong. Amid the push for domestic legislation, President Johnson was embarking on foreign policies in the Dominican Republic and in Vietnam which were producing a troubled atmosphere for him. Yet quite apart from international affairs, his difficulties were plain, and Lyndon Johnson himself was only too aware of them. His support, he remarked with a brooding look on his long face, was "like a Western river, broad but not deep." At the height of the movement of bills through Congress, he was showing the testiness which came when he knew things were not really going well. He would belligerently refer to the White House as "Lonely Acres." He flew off to his ranch, usually balm for any discontent, then abruptly cut the visit short. He staged the swearing-in ceremony in the Cabinet Room for General William F. McKee as Administrator of the Federal Aviation Agency, customarily the kind of occasion that brought LBJ effusions, and he bolted from the room with scarcely a handshake.

The press was not hailing Lyndon Johnson. It was generally circumspect, and often it was riding him in a way that no Chief Executive had been subjected to since the most hapless days of Harry Truman. In July 1965 President Johnson instituted what seemed to him the proper cure for troubles with the media, a shift in Press Secretaries. He announced that George Reedy, who had long been suffering from a painful foot ailment, was going off for an operation at the Mayo Clinic, and named Bill Moyers to replace him. Moyers was given more latitude to answer questions, and being closer to the President, he knew more answers. But the general press treatment of Lyndon Johnson did not notably change.

The public was raising no hosannas. All Presidents of marked personalities have cruel stories told about them. Yet the Copperhead snipings at Lincoln, the parlor-car smearings of Theodore and Franklin Roosevelt, the smirking tales about John Kennedy were rarely as cutting as the anecdotes directed at Lyndon Johnson. They left him little except being a smallbore cheat. Moreover, most previous Presidents had enjoyed a compensating adulation from at least parts of the population. Few signs of popular affection for Lyndon Johnson were appearing. There were no "Teddy Bears" that had marked the heyday of Theodore Roosevelt, no rash of "Franklin Roosevelt Avenues," no rush to the younger generation, as in the Kennedy days, to imitate the President's gestures and haircut.

For two decades liberal professionals in a dozen fields had called for a Chief Executive who could get liberal legislation enacted. Now they had one, and they were not happy. I spoke or corresponded with hundreds of them during this period and their tone rarely varied from a snappish disdain for LBJ. In September 1965, some three thousand academics gathered at a meeting of the American Political Science Association in the Sheraton-Park Hotel in Washington. Their attitude toward the sweep of legislation through Congress was typified by Nelson W. Polsby, professor of government at Wesleyan University, who dismissed it as just the result of "a swollen Congressional majority that Barry Goldwater handed the Democrats, passing programs that have been kicking around since New Deal and Fair Deal days."

The White House filled with talk of an "image crisis," and all kinds of things were tried. President Johnson appeared more and he appeared less on TV. He made statesmanlike private remarks intended to reach and to impress the public, and he stringently banned leaks from his living quarters. Everything that was done seemed to worsen matters.

In June 1965, Jack Valenti was scheduled to speak before the Advertising Federation of America in Boston and he decided—incidentally, entirely on his own—to go down the line for his boss. What may well be some of the most remembered phrases of the Johnson years resulted: "The President, thank the Good Lord, has extra glands," an "extra prescience," a "fuller measure of important things that is beyond the dimensions of ordinary men"; he is a "sensitive man, a cultivated man, a warm-hearted man. I sleep each night a little better, a little more confidently because Lyndon Johnson is my President." The giggles and snickers were heard across the country. Herblock promptly produced a cartoon to stand beside his other classics: Lyndon Johnson with a cat-o'-nine-tails walking away from brutalized aides, and at the bottom the words, "a sensitive man, a cultivated man, a warm-hearted man, I sleep each night. . . ."

Loyal Lyndon Johnson refused to criticize loyal Jack Valenti, even in private. "What's wrong with Jack's admiring me?" he growled. "They just attack people close to me to get at me." But the sense of "image crisis" in the White House was not alleviated.

The close of the triumphant first session of the Eighty-ninth Congress coincided with President Johnson's gallstone operation. After the surgery, he had time in the hospital for some mulling, and he thought and talked a great deal about the press and about "those people out there."

"What do they want—what *really* do they want? I'm giving them boom times and more good legislation than anybody else did, and what do they do—attack and sneer! Could FDR do better? Could anybody do better? What *do* they want?"

In time he would find out.

Lady Bird

*I*n the final days of the 1965 session of Congress, attention was fixed on a measure officially designated the Highway Beautification Act but which everyone called the Lady Bird bill. Mrs. Lyndon Johnson liked flowers, trees and unspoiled scenery, and she had a husband who shared her feeling about the outdoors. As the end of the Congress approached, she persuaded the President to put the "must" tag on legislation that dealt with the regulation of billboards and junkyards along highways. The Senate passed the bill. Now the House was finding out what pressure could really be, and the voices on the White House telephones included one with a soft feminine twang expressing its own version of the Johnson treatment.

The legislation was fought by strong lobbies and it had other enemies among House members who thought it unworkable and still others who were simply tired of being pressured and wanted to go home. To get the measure through reluctant committees, President Johnson and his wife had accepted weakening amendments, and during the floor fight they were working on congressmen until the opposition leader, Representative William C. Cramer of Florida, protested, "Never, never has this body known such arm twisting." But on October 7, the day Congress was originally expected to adjourn, the Lady Bird bill still was not law.

The White House had planned a gala evening to salute the Eighty-ninth Congress, with entertainment including Mahalia Jackson, Frederic March doing a reading and a combo called "Your Father's Moustache." At seven-thirty the senators and their wives arrived, "Your Father's Moustache" took up the beat, but no representatives appeared. They were still in the House chamber, shouting at one another in a fourteen-hour hassle over beautification and their wives were in the galleries, their White House finery drooping. President Johnson sent a message to the House floor: he certainly hoped the members would make it to the party, *after* they had passed the bill. His aides conveyed more detailed and harsher words. At 1:15 A.M., when the President had gone to the Bethesda Naval Hospital for the gallstone operation scheduled the next day and the gala had gone to sleep, the House passed the Lady Bird bill.

After recuperating, appearing in the East Room to sign the Highway Beautification Act, President Johnson remarked, "There is a great deal of real joy within me, and within my family, as we meet here." As in the case of the Education Act, he used only one pen, and he handed it to his wife with a kiss on the cheek. Mrs. Lyndon Johnson stood behind her husband at the ceremony, fifty-two years old, five feet, four inches tall, dark-haired, brown-eyed, her complexion fresh and her figure trim as a teen-ager's, dressed in an unassailable coral wool suit, calmly doing and saying just the right things. The composure had been a long road in the making.

The First Lady was born in Karnack, a speck of a town that was the center for a scattering of about a hundred white and five hundred Negro families. Karnack was in Texas but barely so—from the top windows of the houses you could see Louisiana—and the terrain had none of the invigorating hills, challenging caliche soil or the sweep of cattle land that characterized other parts of the state. This was bayou country: dark pine forests, quiet Caddo Lake shrouded by cypresses, alligators slithering into muddy banks, tired land yielding a scrabble of cotton and somewhat more rewarding vegetables and timber. In this kind of world, as Mrs. Johnson's brother Anthony remembered, "Families lived far apart, and the cock crowed only once, for there was no answering call."

The forthright brother said about their parents, "They had nothing in common except that they were in love." At the turn of the century Thomas Jefferson Taylor, a strapping young dirt farmer in Autauga County, Alabama, had picked up his few belongings and headed west, across Mississippi and Louisiana into Karnack, where he decided to settle and try his luck. He opened a general store and liked the possibilities. Soon he returned to Alabama for Minnie Lee Patillo, the tall, graceful granddaughter of a Confederate officer who had accumulated large holdings of land in Autauga County, eleven heirs by two marriages, and considerable patrician status. Minnie Lee Patillo's parents announced that a marriage between their daughter and a dirt farmer was unthinkable; she thought about it and married him. (Later the battle in the

Patillo family over the inheritance led to a Faulknerian scene in which shares of land of varying value were put in sealed envelopes and scattered on the floor. Uncle John Patillo, blindfolded, crawled around, calling out the names of heirs in alphabetical rotation and picking up an envelope for each person.)

Taylor now had some capital from income his wife received. Shrewd, hard-working, hard-fisted, in a few years he owned the two local cotton gins, and his general store had become a long box-like wooden building that was the busiest enterprise for miles around. "T. J. TAYLOR—DEALER IN EVERYTHING," the sign on the store read, and it scarcely exaggerated. Most nights, sometimes until four o'clock in the morning, he was busy supervising the cotton gins or working on his ledgers. Farmers who borrowed money from him paid as much as 10 percent interest; he foreclosed more and more mortgages and bought up land, all the while extending his farming activities to the citrus-growing which the region favored. T. J. Taylor was becoming the big man in the area. He purchased the one imposing home in Karnack, "Brick House," a rambling mansion built by slaves in the 1840's, with a fireplace in every room and the first indoor plumbing in Karnack.

Mrs. Minnie Lee Taylor was turning into something of an American original. She was mercurial as a Deep South summer day, moving suddenly from moods of energetic exhilaration to ones of languid introspection. She was quite capable of the eccentric. For a while she would brook no violation of a succession of food fads in her home; she favored sweeping ghostly dresses and heavy veils, and an occasional inexplicable turban. Other habits were ones that Karnack simply happened to consider eccentric. She filled her home with good books, which she read, and with quality Red Seal records, especially of Caruso, which she never tired of playing. Almost every year she would entrain, alone and majestic, for the opera season in Chicago. Back home, she toured the muddy roads in her black Hudson Super Six, its top down, stopping here and there to visit a sick child. What seemed downright incredible to Karnack was that Mrs. T. J. Taylor declared herself a suffragette and an integrationist of whites and blacks. Votes for women she could only talk about, but integration she practiced by inviting Negroes into Brick House for long conversations, leaving T. J. Taylor shaking his head. But somehow none of this really affected the deep bonds between this magnificently incongruous couple.

The first two children, both boys, Mrs. Taylor dispatched to out-of-state boarding schools. The third, the girl Claudia Alta, she kept home. One day Claudia's Negro mammy, Alice Tittle, looked at her charge, thought of the brightly colored, gentle little ladybird beetles of the region, and remarked, "Lawd, she's purty as a ladybird." A gentle little ladybird Claudia was; chirping she was not. Alice Tittle was a wonderful mammy, as far as a mammy could go. Mrs. Taylor fussed over her daughter and sometimes read to her for hours, particularly from the Greek and Roman myths, but often the mother was wilting in her room or rushing off to do something that attracted her attention. The brothers were away at school for most of the year, and there were few playmates in Karnack who felt at home with the daughter of T. J. Taylor. While still quite young, Claudia developed the habit of taking long walks by herself. She would go to "special places" and sit for hours, a wistful little girl.

Just before Claudia's sixth birthday, Mrs. Taylor died, and the loneliness deepened. T. J. Taylor was a doting father, but business was business. Sometimes he took the child with him to the store at night, putting her to sleep while he worked on his account books. The only cot available was on the second floor of the store, between two rows of wooden coffins which were part of the stock that offered everything. "Daddy," she asked, "what are those things?" "Dry goods," T. J. Taylor said quickly, but Claudia did not remain unaware for long.

Soon the father summoned help from Alabama, Mrs. Taylor's spinster sister Effie Patillo, who came to live in Brick House. The kindly, sensitive, almost ethereal aunt conveyed to her niece her own delight in raising flowers, identifying trees and hunting for the first violet of the season or the earliest bursts of redbud and dogwood. She kept the girl reading from Minnie Taylor's well-stocked library, everything from Dickens, Shakespeare and Mark Twain to Zane Grey, then on to the new titles that she ordered by mail from Austin. But the other-worldly Aunt Effie knew little about the needs of a growing girl and particularly a growing girl in the 1920's. She was sickly, or thought she was, and sometimes in Brick House it was not clear who was taking care of whom. During her childhood Claudia had three women who were devoted to her—her mother, Aunt Effie and Alice Tittle—but never a mother in the simple, confidence-building sense that a clerk in her father's store might have a mother.

When the girl was sixteen, her father and Aunt Effie conferred and the decision was to send her to a private school in Dallas, St. Mary's Episcopal School for Girls. The new enrollee had a peaches-and-cream appearance and she was studious and sweet; she was also the shyest girl in St. Mary's. When another student had a party at her home, Claudia would edge toward a corner or make her way upstairs to talk to the mother. She hated the nickname "Lady

Bird," and was continually teased trying to escape it. The clothes she picked were tacky, and she bought little of them or of anything else; what she had learned from her father's grinding away at his ledgers was to be economical to the point of parsimony. She lacked small talk, did not know how to dance and had little skill at making a young Texan feel, what was of no small moment to a young Texan, that he was a comer.

She found a few close friends, especially the bouncy Eugenia Boehringer (later Mrs. E. H. Lasseter, the wife of an attorney in Henderson, Texas), who had a way of taking over people she liked and whom she thought were doing themselves injustice. Gene prodded Claudia about everything from clothes to attitudes, and persuaded her to join a group of St. Mary's girls who were enrolling in the University of Texas in Austin. At first Claudia trudged the campus, filled with the sons and daughters of Texas boomsters, head tucked down in an old coat of Aunt Effie's. But her father as well as Gene was at work. He gave her a swank new Buick coupe, a Neiman-Marcus charge account, and a stern lecture to use both of them. Claudia was changing. She abandoned the struggle to get rid of her nickname ("I learned to live with it"). Her clothes perked up; she started to date as well as to make high marks; and she learned to dance, specializing in the hard-pounding Louisiana stomp. By the time she took her A.B. in 1933, she thought Austin "a most wonderful town" and stayed on for an additional year while taking a second degree in journalism.

Lady Bird Taylor left the University of Texas an attractive, pleasant, strikingly intelligent young woman, still somewhat shy but with a rapidly emerging vivacity. Though no longer stingy, she was frugal, and had a careful eye for the practical. She might be the daughter of an ever more prosperous man intending to get married "to a nice nine-to-five fellow, with a white house and a dog," but, as she said to her friends, "you never can tell what is going to happen." She had made sure she included in her college work typing and shorthand, and enough credits in education to qualify as a schoolteacher. No one could fail to recognize the daughter of T. J. Taylor in Lady Bird Taylor, A.B., B.J.

But she also remained the child of Minnie Lee and Effie Patillo. She spoke of both in a glow of admiration because "the very way they lived kept reminding you, each in her own way, that it could be such an interesting world if you would only reach out for it." She knew she wanted to go back to Karnack for a while, to redecorate Brick House for her father and give him the companionship he needed, but she was equally certain Karnack would not hold her long. At the university, in addition to keeping up with the meat-and-potatoes courses she had read Hemingway, Dreiser and Edna St. Vincent Millay, sipped bootleg cherry wine, asked dates to take her to see Anton Chekov and Eugene O'Neill at the university theater and quoted Dorothy Parker with the right air of nonchalance. If the University of Texas had what could be called an *avant garde* in the late twenties and early thirties, Lady Bird Taylor was not far *après*. She might be a teacher, if things turned out that way, but it would be in "some faraway place, maybe Hawaii or Alaska." She had chosen to spend her extra year in journalism school because journalists "lead less humdrum lives."

To such a young woman anything might happen, and it promptly did. Shortly after graduation, Lady Bird planned a sightseeing tour to Washington, and Gene Lasseter told her she knew someone she simply had to meet, a young man named Lyndon Johnson who worked as the secretary to Congressman Richard Kleberg from the Austin area. She gave Kleberg's Washington phone number to Lady Bird, who put it in her pocketbook and left it there. She might read Hemingway and sip bootleg wine, but the girl from Karnack was not going to call up a strange man.

Several weeks later Lady Bird was visiting Gene in Austin and in walked Lyndon Johnson with a date. Mrs. Johnson never forgot her first impression. He seemed "excessively thin but very, very good-looking, with lots of black wavy hair, and the most outspoken, straightforward, determined manner I'd ever met. I knew I had met something remarkable, but I didn't know quite what."

The remarkable young man kept looking intently at her and directing his conversation to her; he found a moment away from his date to ask her to have breakfast with him the next morning at the Hotel Driskill, where he was staying. She gave a vague answer ("I had a sort of queer moth-and-flame feeling"). The next day she had an unusually early appointment in the building next to the Driskill, and as she left it she saw Lyndon Johnson sitting at a table by the hotel window. Impulsively she entered. The pair had breakfast and went for a drive in the country.

Mrs. Johnson never forgot this occasion either. "He told me all sorts of things that I thought were extraordinarily direct for a first date—about how many years he had been teaching, his salary as a secretary to a congressman, his ambitions, even about all the members of his family, and how much insurance he carried. It was as if he wanted to give me a complete picture of his life and of his capabilities." Then, after this Dun & Bradstreet review, Lyndon Johnson asked Lady Bird Taylor to marry him. She was so staggered she could scarcely get out a no.

He had a week before he must return to Washington, and he wasted no hour of it. He swept Lady Bird off to Johnson City to meet his mother, who pleasantly, carefully surveyed her; his boss Representative Kleberg at the fantastic King Ranch owned by the Kleberg family, a holding larger than the state of Connecticut presided over by the *grande dame* who maneuvered Lady Bird aside and told her to marry Lyndon; and his friends in various places, droves of them, helter-skelter, including the cocky redhead Daniel Quill, a clerical worker and politico in the office of the San Antonio deputy county clerk whom LBJ later made postmaster of the city. The young men were close for many reasons, among them the mountainous appetite of Lyndon Johnson and the specialty of the Quill home, mother Quill's roast beef, brown gravy and cornbread.

For the introduction of Lady Bird to Dan Quill in San Antonio, Lyndon insisted on a splendid dinner, but he and his friend had a problem: neither had the money to pay for it. Quill, who knew everything about San Antonio, thought of a gambling house where the dinner was elaborate and free to start customers upstairs to the roulette wheels in the right mood. Miss Taylor and Messrs. Johnson and Quill dined royally on steak and walked out into the sparkling fall evening. What was the couple like in courtship? Quill was later asked. "Well, Lyndon was always the aggressive one, you know. Yes, she was shy—but also you had to be shy if you were around Lyndon."

As the week neared its end, Lyndon Johnson set up all kinds of involved arrangements to make it possible for him to get to Karnack and meet Lady Bird's father before his departure. After the get-together, in the sidewise manner that daughters have with fathers, Lady Bird sought a comment on her whirlwind suitor. T. J. Taylor was direct: "You've been bringing home a lot of boys. This time you've brought a man." That night Lyndon Johnson again urged Lady Bird Taylor to marry him. Again she said no; they had known each other only a week and she was a "prudent person." But she sent him away with a warmth she made sure he understood.

From Washington, Lyndon Johnson bombarded Brick House with telephone calls and letters. He mailed his photograph too. Below the serious face with bright eyes was the carefully written inscription: "For Bird, a lovely girl with ideals, principles, intelligence and refinement, from her sincere admirer Lyndon." In Lyndon Johnson's Texas, young men who intended to amount to anything married up in the social scale. His father, a scrabbling farmer-politician, had picked the granddaughter of the president of Baylor University, just as Lady Bird's dirt-farmer father had entered a family of patricians. Yet marrying up did not mean the girl with money in many cases. If the marriage of T. J. Taylor helped considerably toward his financial success, the granddaughter of the president of Baylor University brought virtually no dowry. The desirable attributes reflected in the sentiment on the photograph seem to have been much more important. In the rough-hewn world of this type of Texas man—a world they delighted in thinking of as rough-hewn—the wife was to have "ideals" and "refinement," the better pedigree and education, the interest in "culture" which, as Lyndon Johnson used to say, was "the business of womenfolk." Lady Bird Taylor could not have fitted the prescription better; besides, she was "the prettiest girl I ever saw."

Lady Bird Taylor was not so much a type in her attitude toward the man to marry. In her private sphere one sought a "real man," a phrase with its connotations. Of course one took a close look at the respectability of the family, and gave thought to what the future provider would be like. But then too, Lady Bird was the daughter of a poor nobody who had become the leading citizen of his area. To her, the nuances of the phrase "real man" had less to do with present standing than with impressions like her feelings when her father and suitor met and she watched the two men. "My father was six foot two," she later recalled her thoughts. "Lyndon was six foot three"; T. J. Taylor may have lived in "a tiny world," but he was "the head man there and people called him 'Cap'n Taylor.'" There was an air about Lyndon Johnson too of take-charge, of outer and inner strength, and also an air hinting at a far and mysterious future which intrigued the daughter of Minnie Lee and Effie Patillo.

After six weeks of daily telephone calls or letters, Lyndon Johnson came cannonading back to Brick House. "Let's get married. Not next year, after you've done over the house, but about two weeks from now, or right away."

Lady Bird gave a vague answer. She was not at all sure she wanted to marry anyone yet. She was enormously attracted by this fireball of a young man, but he also overwhelmed, almost frightened her. She went with him to look at rings in Carl Myer's jewelry store in Austin, then would not let him buy one. She talked to Aunt Effie, who was thoroughly against her marrying a suitor she had known less than two months and who added plaintively that she was sick and wanted Lady Bird to spend the winter with her in Florida. The girl talked to her father who said, "If you wait until Aunt Effie is ready, you will never marry anyone. Do what you think best." Several times Lady Bird told her father she thought she ought to go with Aunt Effie to Florida and not marry until the next summer, if then.

On a Saturday morning, November 17, 1934, Lyndon Johnson, twenty-six years old, took Lady Bird Taylor, twenty-one, for another drive. A technique that congressmen were to know in years to come went to work. "If you say no, it just proves that you don't love me enough to dare to marry me. We either do it now, or we never will." At the St. Mary's School for Girls Lady Bird, raised a Methodist, had been drawn by Episcopalianism and joined that denomination. Two days before the drive she had taken out her Episcopal prayer book and read the solemn, beautiful marriage ceremony. Now she turned to Lyndon Johnson: Had he really stopped to think how serious a step marriage is? Shouldn't they keep seeing each other and wait? Lyndon Johnson had one reply to all questions. "Do you or don't you love me?" "Simply because I didn't want to lose him," she finally said yes.

The driver let out a yip. He knew just the right place—San Antonio, where there was a fine old Episcopal church on the square, St. Mark's, and where Dan Quill would take care of everything. He whirled the car to the nearest phone booth. Quill had become accustomed to working with his friend during the Kleberg campaign for Congress. "When we had to ask someone to do something difficult, we'd say, this is what's got to be done, then we'd say, ever so much obliged, and just hang up the phone and stay away from it until the thing was done." Lyndon Johnson told Quill that he and Lady Bird would be arriving in San Antonio about six o'clock, they were going to get married that night in St. Mark's, they would meet him in the lobby of the Hotel Plaza, and he would be ever so much obliged if Quill would arrange things. Then Lyndon Johnson hung up.

There were things to be arranged. To get married in St. Mark's Church, you needed the minister of St. Mark's. The San Antonio license bureau closed at three o'clock, and Texas law required that both applicants appear in person with approved physical certificates. Quill, a member of St. Mark's, hurried to its minister, the Reverend Arthur R. McKinstry, who said he was sorry but he never, absolutely never, performed a marriage ceremony without knowing the couple's background and having a serious talk with them. Quill pleaded that these were fine young people and they just weren't available for a talk; they were on U.S. Highway 81. He kept on urging and besides, the Reverend McKinstry was "kind of indebted to me." On a trip to Washington, Quill had worked out a less expensive mailing permit for the church's bulletin. At last, reluctantly, the minister consented. As for the physical exam and personal appearance requirements, after all Quill worked in the office of the deputy county clerk. When the couple drove up to the Hotel Plaza dusty and excited, he was standing outside grinning, in his hand Marriage License No. 104,133 duly issued by the county of Bexar, Texas.

In the flurry of greetings Lady Bird asked, "You have the ring, Dan?"

"Ring? Gosh, you've been passing jewelry stores all day. You mean you didn't get a ring?"

The Sears, Roebuck store nearby was keeping late Saturday hours. Quill asked for a wedding band and the clerk said, "What size?" No man to be stopped, Quill persuaded the clerk to let him put bands of assorted sizes on a jeweler's measuring stick and take them to the hotel; he and Lyndon Johnson supervised the trying on. Quill hustled the other rings back, and paid the $2.50 for the one they chose. It was his wedding present to his friends.

There was one more detail. The couple had been able to reach only a single friend apiece who could make it to the ceremony, and Dan Quill believed a proper wedding required people. He phoned ten friends, none of whom had ever laid eyes on the bride and groom, and they assembled, threw the rice, joined in a gay dinner of steak and champagne at the San Antonio landmark, the St. Anthony Hotel.

In 1954 Senator Lyndon Johnson was scheduled to speak in San Antonio. Quill telephoned Mrs. Johnson and said she must come too, no questions asked, and when she arrived he presented her with her marriage license. In the hubbub of the wedding, the certificate had never been given to the Johnsons; it found its way to the courthouse because its information was so incomplete it lacked an address for either party. For twenty years, until Quill's accidental discovery of it, it lay in the courthouse office, and for twenty years the husband had been saying to the wife, too bad you lost our wedding license, and the wife had been saying to the husband, too bad you lost our wedding license.

In 1934, Lyndon Johnson could not have cared less about a piece of paper. He bundled Lady Bird in the car, waved his long arms wildly out the window and shouted, "Mr. and Mrs. Lyndon B. Johnson are off to Mexico—wherever we land." They landed in Monterey.

The first home of the Johnsons was a two-room furnished apartment, with a rollaway bed in the living room, at 1910 Kalorama Road, N.W., in Washington, D.C. The bride soon learned a number of things about her sudden husband, including that LBJ respect for a dollar which was as thorough as her own. From her mother and her mother's family she would receive an inheritance of some $60,000 and considerable acreage in Autauga County, Alabama, which did not begin to pay any real income until it was later shifted from cotton to timber. By entire agreement between Mr. and Mrs. Johnson, the management of the land and the money and the returns from them were left in the hands of T. J. Taylor. Lyndon Johnson's salary as secretary to Representative Kleberg—the $267 a month President Johnson liked to talk about —was the sum the couple spent. In her first twenty-one years Lady Bird Johnson had never swept a floor or cooked a meal; on Kalorama Road, she swept the floors, bought a recipe book and cooked the meals.

Most of the things Mrs. Johnson was learning about Mr. Johnson were not what they wanted but what he wanted. He declared a good wife should be a "good manager." It was a matter of "Lyndon's personality," Lady Bird once remarked in her diplomatic way. "He wants me to handle anything I am capable of. He's a little incensed if I want help on trivial things." Eager to be a good wife, she decided that the "secret is organization." She revived her University of Texas shorthand and developed a habit that never left her, carrying a pad and pencil at almost all times to make notes on items to be done. She managed virtually everything in the Johnson household, from paying the bills to getting her talkative husband out the door.

A wife also "ought to look like something." This meant "style," high heels, sharp lines to the suits and dresses, bright not "mule" colors, especially red. Mrs. Johnson gave up low heels, which she enjoyed for daytime, and turned to bright colors, which she had long wished she had the nerve to wear. "Style" was not too easy to achieve on $267 a month, but her husband kept after her, often going along for the shopping and passing judgment. Lyndon Johnson made it equally clear that he wanted people around, for a drink at the end of the day, for supper, or to spend the night on the rollaway bed. He wanted them around because he liked them around and because he aimed to get ahead, and he expected his wife to help him by being with him, talking to the folks and not off in the kitchen. The bride took a grip on her shyness and her recipe book, specializing in dishes that required less attention, and forged ahead.

Above all, Mrs. Johnson was learning that Mr. Johnson was the sun and everything had to orbit around him. His temper was quick and sharp, and he made little effort to control it. He was given to jubilant enthusiasm and deep gloom, and he could go from one to the other in minutes. He made little effort to control these moods either. He was relentlessly demanding, whether about the look of the living room, the press in his suits, or the comments she made to visitors. He enjoyed exhibitions of what he felt like doing, when he felt like doing it. At a social gathering he might tell stories full of four-letter words until his wife's face flushed, then amble across the room and roundly kiss her while loudly declaring, "I love you."

On the honeymoon, Lady Bird Johnson had received a letter from her mother-in-law. In part, it was a welcome into the family; in part it was also a scarcely veiled statement of how fortunate Lady Bird was to have captured Lyndon. Of the five Johnson children, the eldest boy was the apple of his mother's eye. When the father had laid down rules of discipline, she often saw to it that they were not enforced. When at fifteen Lyndon refused further schooling and ran off in a jalopy to the West Coast, she explained it all away. On his return she patiently waited for him to want to go to college and then took care of getting him in. As he made the first steps in his career, she praised him in extreme language. She was particularly rapt at his political bent; her father had run for Congress and been defeated and she saw in her son, "the first born of his first born," as she would say, the coming vindication. The son had responded in kind. He kept telling people, "There is no one like my mother"; at college, in his twenties, he sent her sentimental and often lengthy letters almost every day and when a reply was delayed in reaching him, he was depressed. He had an intense dependency on her and the thoroughgoing spoiling that comes from such a relationship. Unusual as it may seem to apply the term to a gangling hellion furiously pushing ahead in the grapple-and-grab of Texas politics, Lady Bird Johnson had married something of a mama's boy.

After nine months in Washington, the couple moved back to Texas, to Austin where Lyndon Johnson took over as Texas administrator of the New Deal agency for the youthful unemployed, the National Youth Administration. Mrs. Johnson set up a home in half of a small rented duplex, kept managing a tight budget and a schedule organized around a husband who worked ten to twelve hours a day and came trooping in for dinner with assistants, a politician he was sure would be useful or somebody from the old days in Johnson City he had run into down the street. Now the wife was learning a basic fact about her husband: he needed politics as much as food and water.

Eighteen months after the Johnsons arrived in Austin, in 1936, the congressman from the district suddenly died. Nine aspirants announced for the seat, some of them men of long-accumulated political power in the area. Lyndon Johnson, twenty-eight years old, from the district's smallest county, who had never met the mayor of Austin or most of the other local Democratic leaders, left no doubt that he wanted to be the tenth candidate. The Sunday after the congressman's death, Mrs. Johnson listened while Mr. Johnson talked over the situation with a pro he had come to know in the course of his Kleberg activities, State Senator Alvin W. Wirtz. The senator gave his diagnosis: Lyndon Johnson had a bare chance, but it would take at least $10,000 to get anywhere in the race. The rest of the day Lady Bird Johnson watched her husband's face as he talked about being a congressman.

That evening she went to the phone and called Karnack. "Daddy, do you suppose you could put ten thousand dollars from my inheritance in the bank for me? Lyndon wants to run for Congress."

"Well, today's Sunday," the doting father said. "I don't think I could do it before the morning, about nine o'clock."

Mrs. Johnson always remembered this first campaign with mixed feelings. "Lyndon was never so young, and never so vigorous, and never so wonderful. I only regret that I did not have the gumption to go with him." Claude Arnold, Sr., the campaign manager, added, "I can see him now, up and down the streets, a long, skinny thing, his hand stretched out and saying, 'I'm Lyndon Johnson. Now, I think . . .'" Neophyte or not, Lady Bird Johnson pitched in, calling up voters, licking envelopes, cheering on her man, and she received a permanent impression of all campaigns: "They represent early sunups, cold pancakes and total confusion." Hit by appendicitis and utter exhaustion, Lyndon Johnson was taken to the hospital on election eve. The next day his wife chauffered voters to the polls from dawn to dusk, then hurried to the hospital to celebrate the victory with him. She wondered why she felt so queer until she realized she had not stopped for breakfast, lunch or dinner.

The twelve years in the House of Representatives—the girl from the nature walks in Karnack and University of Texas literary circles was reading books, when she read at all, in snatches before sleep, almost never attending the theater and finding nature mostly in the grass of Capitol Hill. She was busy taking an unending stream of constituents to watch the House in session and playing hostess. Going to the Johnsons' was becoming quite the thing in congressional circles, particularly among the Southern and Western delegations. There was the shrewd, ebullient talk of Lyndon Johnson; there was also the charm of Lady Bird Johnson. The shyness had disappeared and given way to a vivacious warmth and constant thoughtful little gestures that made every guest feel especially wanted. More and more the wife's political knowledgeability and astuteness developed and made itself evident. And the Johnson home now included that ornament whom Mrs. Johnson had achieved from the home economics courses of tiny Wiley College in Marshall, Texas, Mrs. Zephyr Wright, "the best Southern cook," as Speaker Sam Rayburn pronounced her, "this side of heaven and if I felt qualified, I would go further in my statement." Mrs. Wright was especially a master of the Johnson favorites, roast with a helping of "Pedernales River chili" or fried chicken and spoon bread, and a dessert of chocolate soufflé or what she firmly described as "old-fashioned" fruit ice cream.

During the earlier years of Lyndon Johnson's period in the House of Representatives, the couple kept moving back and forth from a rented place in Washington, occupied while Congress was in session, to another rented home in Austin, used to keep the political fences in repair. Lady Bird Johnson packed and unpacked and arranged and rearranged until, as she sighed to a friend, "I feel like a weary octopus." One day Representative Johnson was sitting in his Washington living room talking politics with John Connally when his wife came bursting in. She had just found the most wonderful house to buy, she enthused, and went on with the details. Lyndon Johnson grunted and resumed his political talk.

By now Lady Bird Johnson had a reputation as a wife who never showed irritation to her husband, but at this moment the reputation went into stormy suspension. "I want that house! Every woman wants a home of her own, and all I have to look forward to is the next election!" With that, she stomped out of the room.

Lyndon Johnson scratched his head in puzzlement. This wasn't like Bird at all, he said to Connally. What did Connally think he ought to do?

"I'd buy the house," Connally said.

From the new home Representative Johnson went off to military service in World War II. Mrs. Johnson took over running his congressional office, and not in a nominal sense. Eight months later, President Franklin Roosevelt ordered all congressmen mustered out, and Lyndon Johnson returned moody and restless. The household was running up debts; he had been beaten in a try for the Senate in 1941; he was not skyrocketing in the House's tough seniority system. Maybe, he said to his wife, they ought to get out of politics and return to Texas and make some money.

Things were also happening in Mrs. Johnson's mind. Her father was pressing her to take the rest of her inheritance; he had remarried, he was aging and he wanted to get his property responsibilities straightened out. Skeptical as she was about her husband's talk of leaving politics, she was eager that he should have all possible choices in the future. The experience of running the congressional office had stirred her latent feelings that a woman ought to be doing something on her own in the workaday world. Never far below the surface were the business instincts of T. J. Taylor's daughter and the lingering insecurities of her college days that "you never can tell." Her interest in journalism had not disappeared, and she thought of radio and the emerging television industry as a part of journalism.

In 1942 the Johnsons heard that station KTBC in Austin was up for sale. It was ramshackle but could be purchased for a total of about $30,000; KTBC had a monopoly position in Austin, a rapidly growing mass-media market. Mrs. Johnson bought KTBC with part of her inheritance and a bank loan, and the Johnson family fortune was in the making. When Lyndon and Lady Bird Johnson entered the White House twenty-one years later, they were probably the wealthiest family ever to occupy it except for the Kennedys, and certainly the richest who had built rather than inherited their fortune. However the total value was estimated, it included the Texas Broadcasting Corporation with an annual income in the hundreds of thousands, large investments, the ranch which is generally considered a three-quarter-million-dollar property, and extensive holdings in land and livestock.

Secretive as Lyndon Johnson was, he became most rigid when the family property was discussed. Yet there was no great mystery, at least about most of it. The basis of the Johnson fortune was the wife's inheritance, her hard work and acumen in using it, and the good fortune of owning a strategically located franchise at the opening of the television era. When Lady Bird Johnson bought the rundown KTBC, with a midget 250 watts, no right to broadcast at night, no network affiliation and nine employees, she temporarily moved to Austin by herself. In the best manner of T. J. Taylor, she sat in a little office, taking up one by one the unpaid bills, planning expansion of the station's facilities and offerings, sorting out employees, prodding old and new salesmen to sell commercials. After eight months, when KTBC showed its first profit, she returned to Washington, but for years she received weekly reports on the business and returned them with detailed instructions. She also supervised the transformation of part of her land in Alabama from cotton to timber, and added to her acreage. There is no doubt who the businessman in the Johnson family was, and that Lady Bird Johnson started the sharp upswing of the Johnson holdings without need of political influence.

Beyond that came the preservation of KTBC's monopoly in Austin and the expansion of the company holdings into other parts of Texas and into Oklahoma (all requiring the approval of the Federal Communications Commission), as well as the real estate deals in Texas. Husband and wife were now operating as partners, with Lyndon Johnson proving to have a sharp eye for Texas land. Whether at this stage the fortune would have mounted so swiftly if the head of the household had not been an increasingly powerful politician in Texas and Washington is a matter of anyone's conjecture.

In the period when Lady Bird Johnson was straightening out KTBC, all the while remaining very much the busy Mrs. Lyndon Johnson, friends in talking about her more and more used two adjectives, "self-disciplined" and "compartmentalized." As one intimate commented, "She's the Neiman-Marcus of women, everything in the right department. She takes care of one type of problem with full attention, then shuts off that part of her mind and moves to another." Lady Bird Johnson had a different word for it. "I hope," she remarked, "I have developed some degree of elasticity."

The year of the purchase of KTBC was the eighth year of the Johnson marriage. During that time Mrs. Johnson went through four miscarriages. In the tenth year, Lynda was born, and three years later, Luci came. Now the woman who remembered so keenly what her own girlhood was like had two daughters of her own, and everything within her yearned to envelop them in affection and attention.

Lyndon Johnson treated his daughters to great bursts of pride and spoiling. When Lynda was born, he called up everybody on his staff in the middle of the night to announce the news. When Luci wanted a dog and her mother, with new rugs on the floor, showed no haste to respond, the door flew open one evening and in walked Lyndon Johnson, snow dropping off his coat, with a big smile and a big box; he had driven in a blizzard to Winchester, Virginia, to get just the right dog. (It was the family's first beagle, "Little Beagle Johnson," sire of the celebrated "Him" and "Her.") But then too Father was always very busy and always doing something for which he needed Mother.

In 1948, when Lynda was four and Luci one, LBJ undertook his most difficult campaign, a second try for the Senate in a primary against nine other candidates, including Governor Coke R. Stevenson who had not lost an election in thirty years. Campaigning day and night in the first systematic electioneering by air travel

Texas had ever known, he managed to force a runoff but came in second, a formidable 100,000 votes behind Stevenson. Again the Senate seemed beyond his reach. He was an unhappy man.

However deep her involvement in her husband's politics, Lady Bird Johnson had never gone on the campaign trail. She wondered whether public opinion of the day would approve it. She hated to fly; planes frightened her and sometimes made her nauseous. She dreaded making a speech—her hands literally shook—and she was embarrassed to stand up in front of strange women and praise her husband. Above all, she did not like the thought of leaving her young daughters. Lady Bird Johnson took to the campaign trail. For the care of the girls, she now began her dependence on the sensible and gentle Willie Day Taylor. Bracing herself, Lady Bird Johnson climbed into the planes, flying with and without her husband. She made speeches, at first ones that were barely more than a "Hi y'all," then full-blown efforts itemizing and praising her husband's record.

The day before the primary she was in an automobile that turned over twice. She crawled out into the mud, her arm and back bruised, stood in a reception line in a dress borrowed from her hostess, then hurried on to San Antonio to join her husband on the platform and make another speech. She did not mention the accident to him. That night she went on by herself to Austin. She had a plan; she phoned her mother-in-law and her two sisters-in-law, took the Austin telephone directory and tore it into four parts. The women sat at phones, calling all the names they could manage from A to Z. LBJ won the primary—by the famous eighty-seven votes.

The Senate years, the heart attack, the 1960 drive for the presidential nomination, the Kennedy-Johnson campaign, the fretful vice-presidential period—more and more, and especially after the coronary, Lyndon Johnson wanted his wife to be doing something with him or for him. Increasingly Willie Day Taylor spent the many hours with Lynda and Luci.

In a way there was a glowing relationship between Mrs. Johnson and her daughters. She adored them, and they responded with a feeling not always accorded mothers. Some of Lynda's happiest girlhood moments came when she could sit talking about "the thoughts inside me to my wonderful mother." Lucy never forgot that when the question of a curfew on dates came up, her mother said, "It's up to your good sense. I trust you." When Luci told the story, she added fervidly, "You don't let a person like that down." But a mother like that is a mother you want to be with.

Once, when Mrs. Johnson was again tied up by something of the father, Lynda snapped, "We are the deprivileged children." Luci remembered "screaming and stomping my feet because my mother was pulled away from me by something father wanted her to do. My resentment was aimed at him because he seemed to be always taking my mother away, and I knew I loved her.

"Even when my father was around, I'm afraid I didn't do much to help our relationship. So eventually he stopped trying too. This bothered mother a great deal. She tried her best to smooth things over, and to keep us a closely knit family. She loved us both and tried to bring us together. She felt a sense of loyalty to father; but she also felt a tremendous sense of conscience toward my sister and me. Quite often she was torn between the two obligations.

"Finally, I decided: why buck it? So I stopped thinking of him as a father and started thinking of him as a friend. Eventually, I learned to love him as a person, not as a father who seldom had time to be a father."

Often, when Mrs. Johnson was about to go off with her husband, she would linger for a few minutes with the girls. She would give each a long hug and say, "Remember how much you are loved."

When the Johnsons entered the White House Lady Bird Johnson, who had been through so many roles, was assuming one that was in many ways the most ambiguous. Shortly after coming to Washington, I received my first request for assistance from Mrs. Johnson, beginning the years when I worked a good deal with her and her staff, along with my duties for the President. Such an experience sets one to thinking about the Office of the First Lady. Obviously over the centuries the First Lady has played two roles: the private one, in which she influenced her husband to a greater or lesser degree, and her public position with its potential power in forming opinion or taste. But the one role seems to have had little to do with the other. Mrs. Ulysses Grant may have had women all over the country filling their homes with tazzas and lambrequins in imitation of the way she redecorated the White House, and their great granddaughters marched to art museums and took to pillbox hats to be like Mrs. John Kennedy; neither woman influenced her husband's conduct of public affairs beyond a minuscule degree. Perhaps somewhere somebody imitated the horsehair sofa and embattled hair of Bess Truman—perhaps. Yet President Truman listened to his wife closely on public as well as family matters.

The Office of the First Lady also lacks any steady line of development. Inevitably the private influence of the wife has varied from Administration to Administration, and her significance in forming opinion or taste has shown the same irregularity. With an occasional exception, the wives in the earlier history of the United States seem quaint footnotes rather than part of the substance of their eras. Mrs. John Adams is best remembered for hanging laundry in the East Room while insisting on receiving visitors from a chair modeled after an imperial throne; Mrs. William Howard Taft, for going to Cabinet meetings with her husband and, when accused of attempting to influence policy, explaining that she went to keep the President awake; Mrs. Calvin Coolidge, for her unlikely beauty and her still more improbable insistence that her husband was a talkative man. With the passage of another decade, observers said that from now on the First Lady inevitably would wield considerable public influence. Was there not the precedent of the redoubtable Mrs. Franklin Roosevelt, and the growing power of the mass media to spread the activities and attitudes of the President's wife? Yet Mrs. Roosevelt's successor, Mrs. Truman, moved through seven years of the White House leaving only the vague impression of a displaced housewife. Mrs. Eisenhower followed with two terms that suggested an army officer's wife on another pleasant tour of duty. Then, in the unpredictable ways of the First Ladyship, they were succeeded by the crashing impact of Mrs. Kennedy.

After more than two years of watching a First Lady in action, I wrote what seemed to me the simple fact into the draft of a speech for Mrs. Johnson commemorating Eleanor Roosevelt: "The Constitution of the United States nowhere mentions the First Lady. No other official document defines or limits her functions. She is what she—and her husband—wants her to be." After more than two years of functioning as First Lady, Mrs. Johnson saw no reason to alter the description, as it applied to both private and public aspects of her role.

So far as the private part was concerned, many knowledgeable people commented that Mrs. Johnson might well turn out to be the most influential First Lady in American history. She was not simply a wife; unique among the First Ladies, she came to the Office an established business success and a woman with decades of direct political experience. She and LBJ had traveled the long road to the White House very much together. Yet they had been together much more in the process of getting there than of deciding what to do once they arrived. Informed and sharp-minded though she was, Mrs. Johnson had no strong interest in the particulars of public policy. She was even less ideological than her husband, and had an uninflatable modesty about the value of her policy opinions, especially in foreign affairs. In the White House she tended to use her breakfast-table power directly only in a few areas of strong personal concern, like the Highway Beautification Act.

Still, the observers were right in predicting for her a significant policy role. By the time he became President, Lyndon Johnson, whatever his peacocking, had developed a thoroughgoing respect for the judgment of his wife in all matters. He talked with her about everything, and he paid close attention to her reactions. She rarely took a rigid position or argued; as she once said in a phrase that was only half joking, "I infiltrate." The infiltration was the deeper because to a man of the President's serpentine mind, nurtured in the webs of Texas politics, the crowning virtue was loyalty. He spoke magniloquently of the great loyalty of particular associates and he believed it, more or less. There was only one human being whose loyalty he questioned not at all.

This influence of Mrs. Johnson operated more in a negative than a positive way. The one real naysayer in the White House was the lady with tenure. The instances ranged in importance from a note she passed to him while he was evangelizing away in a speech—"that's enough"—to bothered looks and sympathetically questioning words that affected a number of minor and at least four major decisions of the LBJ Presidency. The negative operated most effectively in a general sense. Mrs. Johnson had always thought it important to create in the home an "oasis of calm" for her husband. In the White House, when the President displayed his propensity for the excessive, her balanced, quieting presence, apart from any words she spoke, tended to remove the far edges from what he was thinking of doing. "Lyndon," as Mrs. Johnson commented, "believes that anything can be solved, and quickly." Around her, he was less likely to try to solve the world yesterday.

The First Lady was less diffident in assessing human beings than she was in discussing proposals. She had one unspoken but unbreakable rule: if a man seemed to fill a personal need for her husband, she was for him, no matter what she thought of him. Once her associates tried hard to bring about the removal of an aide close to LBJ because they thought him harmful to the President's actual purposes. There was every evidence that Mrs. Johnson shared the opinion, but her answer was a firm "No, Lyndon needs him." Beyond that, a good many important figures, in and outside the White House, were advanced, eased out, or went up or down in influence depending on the impression they left on Lady Bird Johnson. Her judgments were not always beyond question. More than her husband, she tended to think well of the "nice person" who could turn out to be someone, particularly a Southerner, with a softly accented, self-seeking line. But in general she was remarkably sound in assessing who had brains, a usable combination of stability and verve, and a degree of disinterest. And she was not so much put off, as LBJ could be, by urbanity or past associations.

In a quite different way, Mrs. Johnson importantly affected personnel in the case of those who functioned in close relationship to President Johnson. Without her, probably it would have been impossible for the President to hold an adequate number of able aides—or rather, probably it would have been impossible for him to keep enough men of ability who were not ready to sacrifice self-respect for the glitter of the White House. The cat-o'-nine-tails featured in Herblock's cartoon was used too often and too humiliatingly. Lady Bird Johnson heard about the worst incidents; she was likely to learn of them from her husband, who told them to her in a mixture of sheepishness and the hope that something would happen which almost always did. She would be on the phone to the man, or perhaps to his wife. She might or might not refer directly to the incident but she did convey, with words that were politic but had every mark of sincerity, how much she and the President appreciated the work that the individual was doing, despite, as she remarked on one such occasion, "the strains we all find ourselves under." And the phone call was likely to be followed by another healing gesture, usually an invitation to an especially intimate and enjoyable White House social occasion.

In matters of pure politics, the First Lady functioned with the least diffidence of all. She was a pro; she knew it and her husband dissented not at all. He believed, perhaps rightly, that people either are born with "political sense" or they are not, and he believed, certainly rightly, that his wife had such political sense. Unique in the history of the White House, the President and the First Lady talked politics, all aspects of it, on a basis of equality or something very close to it.

As political colleague, Mrs. Johnson brought to a high stage of development a venerable function of the First Lady. Wives, including the wives of Presidents, have a habit of telling their husbands how they are doing in the opinion of other people. Most previous First Ladies moved about so little, and were so inexperienced in assessments of public reaction, that their comments were little more than chit-chat. But Eleanor Roosevelt, a pioneer in many things, was different; as reporters said, she was "the eyes and ears of the President." Lady Bird Johnson liked the phrase,

and she liked the concept. Being Lady Bird Johnson, she system-
atized it. She kept on the move, taking along her shorthand
pad and returning with a clear written report summarizing and
evaluating comments on the Administration's conduct and policies.
Washington is a city in which every first person is writing a
memo to every second one, and every third person is employed to
to shield his boss against memos. Lady Bird Johnson's memos
were read by the boss.

Her pencil was also active, day by day, in the basic political
tasks of keeping allies happy and of placating enemies. As First
Lady, she intensified a long-standing practice of Mrs. Lyndon
Johnson, picking up behind the cyclone of her husband and
bringing organization. The man who was sure he had been done
wrong, the woman who was infuriated by a feeling of slight was
caught up in Mrs. Johnson's soft net and somehow assuaged.
She was especially adept in her use of the White House guest
list. It might be gone over by both husband and wife but the
two processes were not the same. Lyndon Johnson tossed names
on or off with swoops reflecting his likes and dislikes of the
moment. The editing of Lady Bird Johnson was as trim as her
newlywed's grocery list on Kalorama Road—rarely a politically right name omitted, scarcely a politically dubious name
wasted.

And the ultimate testing ground of politics, the big campaign
—in 1964, the once-shy girl from Karnack added an unprecedented
performance to the folklore of American elections. If the South
was her husband's special concern, she had something special
to offer; she was as Southern as pralines and white colonnades.
Lady Bird Johnson suggested what no wife of a major presidential
candidate had attempted, a solo whistle-stop tour, the chief
terrain to be the heart of the disaffection, the small towns and
backcountry of the South. LBJ hesitated. He wondered how
Southerners would react to a First Lady's campaigning alone, and
he envisioned the headlines if anti-civil rights incidents occurred.
But he also saw the potential effectiveness.

On October 6, 1964, the sixteen-car "Lady Bird Special"
left Alexandria, Virginia. Three experienced Southern politicians
were aboard to help with the soothing of wounds and to take
care of possible explosions. Lynda was along for the first part
of the trip and when she returned for college classes, Luci arrived
to add the extra fillip. There were sixteen attractive hostesses,
drawn largely from the wives of the strongly Southern Johnson
White House staff. Nothing was overlooked, certainly not bright
yellow "Lady Bird Special" matchboxes, LBJ hats and Lady Bird

streamers, and for the small fry, whistles, balloons and candy kisses.

Five days, eight states, 1,682 miles, forty-five stops and forty-five Lady Bird speeches the Special wound on. Much of the time it traveled over rails that had been used only for freight for years—to Suffolk, Virginia; Ridgeland, South Carolina; Jesup, Georgia; Chipley, Florida; even Ashokie, North Carolina, where a passenger car had not stopped since 1952 and the last celebrity to get off the train was Buffalo Bill in 1916.

The male politicians would whip up things with some stem-winding. Then Lady Bird Johnson came on, usually in a demurely colored suit, her voice never more Southern, her words soft-sell. This is a "journey of the heart," she would say. "To the President and to his wife, the South is a respected and a valued and beloved part of the country. I am deeply attached to the South. I am fond of the old customs, of a special brand of gentility and courtesy." Gently she glided into the main point of the LBJ formula for appealing to the South. She might love the old ways, but she was "even more proud of the New South, the glistening skylines, the prosperity both in the factory and on the farm, and"—now came a smile—"I would be remiss if I didn't point out that these years of growth were Democratic years."

Before Mrs. Johnson left on the trip, Harry S. Ashmore, the former editor of the Arkansas *Gazette*, had prepared a draft of a speech for her which contained strong civil rights sentences, including mention of "the dark stains on our history." The First Lady had pondered the passage, then commented, "This ought to be said—am I brave enough?" She consulted her husband. At the beginning of the trip, just outside Washington, she took a clear-cut civil rights stand, omitting mention of the past, and on the rest of the swing she occasionally brought up the issue briefly but firmly.

Frequently she spoke before signs saying: "Lady Bird, Lady Bird Fly Away," "Welcome to Goldwater Territory," "U.S.A. Needs LBJ Like It Needs Graft, Hypocrisy and a Hole in the Head." At four stops she was loudly booed. The noisiest heckling came in South Carolina, where chants of "We want Barry" interrupted her speech. The male politicians in her party rose to try to quiet the disturbance, and that night Lady Bird Johnson called them into her car. "Look," she told them, "I know you're chivalrous and they make you mad, but I didn't expect this would be an easy assignment. I'll handle it." The next time the heckling started, she stopped her speech, squared herself and said with a vigor that obliterated her drawl, "My friends, this is a country of many viewpoints. I respect your right to express your viewpoints. Now it's my turn to express mine." The shouts died away.

The heckling, widely publicized in the South, proved a bonanza for LBJ. For many conservative Southerners opposition to civil rights legislation may have been a near-obsession, but so was courtesy to Southern womanhood, especially a Southern woman who was well-born and well-arrived. The strikingly large crowds drawn by the Lady Bird Special ("My God," said the mayor of Suffolk, "she's got out more than the football team") also had their effect. Dan J. Moore, the segregationist Democratic candidate for governor of North Carolina who had refused to mention Lyndon Johnson's name in his campaign, sent his wife to scout the reception of the Special as it crossed into his state. Before Mrs. Moore could get home to report, she herself was reaching for microphones to urge, "Vote the Democratic ticket from top to bottom," and phoning her husband to make sure that he appeared with Lady Bird Johnson.

More subtle results came too. Governors in every state on the itinerary except Wallace of Alabama felt it wise to visit Mrs. Johnson's car and pay personal respect, and Governor Wallace sent a huge bouquet of red roses. In the tradition of Southern politics, a warrior is no less a warrior if he lays down his arms before a lady. For politicians who wanted to go along with Lyndon Johnson but were worried by opinion in their states, the Lady Bird Special was a convenient bridge by which they could cross over from neutrality to a degree of support. For most of those who did not want to back the President, the First Lady's visit put them in a position where they thought it best to soften their attacks for the remaining weeks of the campaign.

Mrs. Johnson carried on the routine of her White House work on the second floor of the mansion with her personal secretary, the attractive and efficient redhead Mrs. Ashton G. Gonella, a Louisianan who had been a secretary to Senator Johnson. The rest of the more important members of the staff were on the second floor of the East Wing, with the spit and polish of the office of the military aides in between. Tension may have run through the Lady Bird staff; the possibility was always present that stormy intervention would come from the Oval Office. The group continued to be overworked; Lyndon Johnson held tight the string on funds for the womenfolk. There was all the jostling for favor implicit in the situation. But the Lady Bird operation was sharply different from the LBJ staff concentrated in the West Wing. Taking its structure and tone from its head, it was much more organized and efficient and more friendly and humane in dealing with people and situations, and it had a general attitude based on a respect and affection for the First Lady without jabbings of love-hate feelings.

The types were more varied, reflecting the many facets of Lady Bird Johnson. The Social Secretary was the strongly political Mrs. Elizabeth C. Abell, "Bess" Abell, daughter of the longtime LBJ ally Senator Earle C. Clements of Kentucky, a tall blonde who put together social affairs with the same calculation and aplomb that had taken her father into the Senate establishment and then to his post as chief lobbyist for the American tobacco industry. Mrs. Johnson never ceased to respond to journalism. In addition to the Press Secretary, two skillful assistants, Mrs. Marcia M. Maddox, of Washington, D.C., and Miss Simone Poulain, Canadian-born, had close ties to the field. For most of the LBJ Presidency, the chief aide for the White House activities of Lynda and Luci was a product of the long feudal ties of LBJ, the pretty young Texan, Mrs. Marta M. Ross, granddaughter of Roy Miller, the "boy mayor" of Corpus Christi who had helped arrange the hiring of "a long-legged schoolteacher" as secretary to Representative Kleberg. The head of the correspondence section was the cultivated, gracious wife of a foreign service officer, Christine Stugard of San Juan, Texas. In the largest suite of offices, forty-five years old, short, stout and bustling, her mass of gray hair askew, the voice coming through on the phone heavy-breathing and hearty, reigned Mrs. Elizabeth S. Carpenter, whom no one knew for more than five minutes without calling Liz.

Liz Carpenter was as Texan as the Alamo, a fifth-generation Texan born in Salado in an antebellum mansion of twenty-five rooms, a slave quarters and no indoor toilet. The father, Thomas Sutherland, a building contractor, was better at lusty psalm singing and joking than at making money. In time he took his wife, four sons and the daughter off to Austin. His income went up, but the Sutherlands, who delighted in long bantering dinner hours, remained more successful at laughing aside the Depression of the 1930's than at licking it.

Liz was merry too. She was smart, imaginative, so energetic she walked in a churn, and immensely likable, the girl of the big smile and the gay quip. At Austin High School, the University of Texas and the University of Texas School of Journalism, she was into everything and her classmates wanted her into everything. In high school she had dated Leslie E. Carpenter. He never let her get away, and two decades after they were married he spoke of her as if he were the luckiest man in America. Before the marriage, graduating from journalism school in 1942, she made off, like a good Texan, to her congressman's office in Washington for help in getting her bearings. Representative Johnson was away at war, and Lady Bird Johnson and the constituent fell to talking. After that the Johnsons never let her go either.

Mr. and Mrs. Carpenter, both practicing journalists, set up the Carpenter News Bureau in Washington, and became intimate friends of the Johnsons. When LBJ was nominated for the Vice-Presidency, Mrs. Johnson asked the newspaperwoman to serve as her press aide. Liz Carpenter had about the same opinion of airplanes as Lady Bird Johnson (one of her contributions to the 1964 campaign was, "In my heart I know the Wright brothers were wrong"), but the lure was too much. She accepted, and stayed on as the press secretary of the Vice-President's wife. No man to overlook a Liz Carpenter, LBJ named her his "executive assistant" too. It was, she said, "the two-way stretch."

When Mrs. Johnson became First Lady, the two-way stretch did not entirely end. Liz Carpenter continued to send well-read memos to the Oval Office, and to supervise a number of activities that involved both husband and wife. She was also the one regular member of the White House staff, male or female, who showed any degree of genuine independence. In the vice-presidential days, Lyndon Johnson had once yelled at her on the phone, "Why don't you use your head?" and she yelled back, "Because I'm too busy using yours." That sort of thing had ended now, but she was still capable of resisting some of the nonsense that could come out of the Oval Office and of getting away with it.

Of course Mrs. Carpenter functioned primarily for Mrs. Johnson, a day-and-night job in itself. Her official title was "Press Secretary and Staff Director for the First Lady," but that was about as descriptive as saying that Walter Jenkins had been a Special Assistant to the President. A remarkable relationship existed between the First Lady and this aide. There was no false camaraderie; Liz Carpenter, who had known Lady Bird Johnson for years as "Bird," now called her Mrs. Johnson with complete naturalness. Between the two women were bonds of affection, similar views and confidence in each other that did not require inappropriate familiarity. Their empathy was so great, and Mrs. Carpenter had so much to do with everything the First Lady did, that Washington snipers liked to say, "Lady Bird is nothing without Liz." The statement was malicious extravagance, but it was true that Liz Carpenter performed an extraordinarily effective job of projecting Mrs. Johnson in the way that she wanted to appear.

In the course of this intricate process she was Press Secretary, idea woman, personnel chief, schedule maker, advance woman, stage manager, instant speech writer, speech editor, co-ordinator of batteries of volunteers, court jester and intimate and deeply understanding friend.

Like the boss, the aide was a pro, and this showed itself most plainly in one of her key functions, Press Secretary. The term had not been used in connection with a First Lady until the regime of Mrs. Eisenhower, who designated the Social Secretary, Mrs. Mary Jane McCaffree, to serve also as Press Secretary. Mrs. Eisenhower was pleasant when available, which was hardly ever, and with the female reporters Mrs. McCaffree had the manner of a press secretary for the CIA. Mrs. Kennedy saw the news people only when she felt it necessary. She named as Press Secretary a winsome socialite, Miss Pamela Turnure, who had never been near a typewriter, and for the reporters the JFK period seemed three years of the blind leading the uncooperative. Mrs. Johnson and Mrs. Carpenter put the whole relationship on a different basis.

The First Lady made herself available for periodic news conferences and for individual interviews. Frequent briefings were held by Press Secretary Carpenter, and she was always ready for a reporter's phone call to her office or home. Constantly there were the Liz touches. On one hectic campaign trip, by the third day the press car of the train was a rolling slum of mashed cigarettes, soggy coffee containers and sandwich crusts, and one hundred and fifty females had found no opportunity to debark long enough to go to a hotel and have a bath. Liz Carpenter had posted one notice on the bulletin board pointing out that the reporters had to abide by the schedule. "The train does not wait. If you get left, just take out residence in the nearest town, register, and vote." Now she put up another one: "On the theory that the press that bathes together stays together, we have reserved three rooms, baths, and showers and one hundred and fifty towels at the Duval Hotel in Tallahassee tonight."

Whatever the warming conviviality, Press Secretary Carpenter remained the pro, and she was political and she was tough. She stated her function bluntly as one of helping the First Lady "to project a good image in order to help the President." She was even more concerned with public impressions than Mrs. Johnson, and she watched intensely what she called the "reviews" of East Wing activities. When the coverage did not suit her, she sat down with the First Lady to learn what they could from the criticism, all the while making plans in her head to take care of the worst culprits. She wielded news tips, unusual story opportunities and prestige invitations for reporters and writers as carrot, and the stick could come down hard.

But once when asked about her chief aide, Mrs. Johnson replied with a string of laudatory adjectives, then paused and added, "She is kind, very kind—and I like that." Liz Carpenter might guard the First Lady like an embattled fury; in an instinctive way, in both personal relations and public matters, she usually threw her influence on the side of the proposition which represented the more humane thing to do. Poverty particularly touched her, and one of my fond White House memories is of Liz Carpenter, in a flurry of tough talk, shunting aside for activities that would help or encourage the poor a number of proposals that would have taken the First Lady into more impressive and perhaps more politically profitable functions.

In the laughter-starved Washington of the Johnson era, the wisecracking Liz Carpenter was soon eagerly sought out for speeches. She became something of a stand-up comedian, at times getting off gags which were none too edifying for a First Lady's lady. But the more genuine Carpenter humor came snapping out, privately and at times publicly, in remarks that caught up the foibles of the whole lot of us, including herself and the mighty man in the Oval Office. Her remarks would get back, and then too she remembered to laugh.

At one press conference, Mrs. Mary C. Pakenham of the Chicago *Tribune*, an implacable pursuer of dog stories, kept questioning Press Secretary Carpenter about the new White House collie, Blanco. "How did the First Family acquire Blanco?"

"He was a gift from a little girl in Illinois."

"He is an Illinois dog, then?"

"That's right."

"Is he a Chicago dog?"

"No, he's a northeastern Illinois dog."

"Where does he live?"

"In the White House doghouse."

"Is he happy?"

"Yes."

"How do you know?"

"Because I'm there most of the time."

In working out the specific programs of the First Lady, Mrs. Johnson and Mrs. Carpenter had a constant collaborator. Lyndon Johnson had no intention of being casual about activities with such potential for shaping the general view of his Administration. On her part, Lady Bird Johnson was no more interested in a contest of assertiveness with her husband as First Lady than she was as wife. With naturalness, she consulted him on all moves of any consequence. As things worked out, the two were in such agreement on the broad definition of her public role, and the President had so much confidence in the way she would implement it that—considering his usual habits—the details were handled with little interference or furor.

On one basic point the President and the First Lady could not have been in more complete agreement: Lady Bird Johnson would do nothing that gave the appearance of imitating Jacqueline Kennedy. In part, this reaction was as simple as anything human can be. Obviously, Mrs. Johnson and Mrs. Kennedy were very different women. Out of self-respect and pride, the Johnsons wanted Lady Bird to be her own First Lady; out of basic political considerations, they knew that any semblance of imitation would be an invitation to ridicule.

But the situation went beyond that. Mrs. Johnson had stood beside her husband while he went down to defeat before the Kennedys in 1960, and she had lived through the three years of the Vice-Presidency in a Kennedyite Washington which she knew considered her a bourgeois bore. She had heard quoted and requoted Mrs. Kennedy's remark that "Lady Bird would crawl down Pennsylvania Avenue on cracked glass for Lyndon Johnson" —and she had her opinion of any woman who would not do the same for her husband.

Yet there was also Dallas. As a woman, a mother and the wife of a President, Mrs. Johnson was deeply sympathetic to another woman, the mother of two small children, who had watched her husband murdered because he was President. A year and a half after the assassination, sitting on a platform in San Marcos, Texas, she sobbed when her husband made an emotional reference to John Kennedy. In the days immediately after the assassination, she had tried everything she could think of to· make things easier for the young widow. "I cannot serve her happiness," she would say. "I will try to serve her convenience."

Mrs. Kennedy had her feelings about the Johnsons too— especially about Lyndon Johnson as President of the United States. Mrs. Johnson was not to know the full bitterness of Mrs. Kennedy until midway in the Johnson Administration, when the White House became aware of the contents of the book commissioned by the widow, William Manchester's *The Death of a President*. But from the beginning, the new First Lady could hardly fail to sense that her predecessor did not reciprocate her extended hand, and sharply pointed incidents kept happening in the relations between the two women to deepen that impression. The personal as well as political Kennedy-Johnson split was strongly felt in the East as well as the West Wing of the LBJ White House, and its effects were far from trivial.

Mrs. Johnson believed that her role as First Lady in public affairs consisted basically of two parts, unequal in importance. The minor one was the encouragement of certain values that she considered good to the women and families of the nation. The function she deemed more significant was expressed in the straightforward sentence: "As a public figure, my job is to help my husband do his job." She meant this literally, and she generally accepted or rejected an activity according to the criterion of how much it helped the President's broad purposes, specific programs or political position.

The general rule had a qualifying corollary. Once I took to her a proposal given me by a well-known writer that would have enlisted her prestige in attempting to make libraries more a part of the life of American communities. The program fitted the library legislation the Administration had already won from Congress, would have made favorable news, and could easily have had impressive political backing. Mrs. Johnson listened carefully and responded warmly to the proposal as such. But then the corollary went to work. Probably as much as any First Lady, Lady Bird Johnson cherished books, but she was not a woman of the libraries. She doodled a bit on her pad and then said decisively, "I haven't been in a library since I left college. This is not *me*." The support to the President was to be given in ways which she felt were *her*.

Everything was to be carried out with a careful eye to the nature of the impact. Mrs. Johnson was not only political; she was cautiously so, as a matter of conviction as well as temperament. If FDR was the hero of her husband, Eleanor Roosevelt was the President's wife she most admired, but she did not approve the storms the great lady had stirred up. Both Mrs. Roosevelt and Mrs. Johnson visited impoverished areas in Appalachia. Mrs. Roosevelt emerged trailing hosannas and denunciations and a famous cartoon, and Mrs. Johnson returned with politely approving or scoffing news stories and no cartoon at all. She wanted it that way. The support for her husband, she was sure, should be given in a supplementary, low-key manner and without "creating controversy."

After a little more than six months of settling in the White House, Mrs. Johnson was ready for a broad statement of the kind of values she wanted to represent to American women. The speech was to be made as the Baccalaureate Address at Radcliffe College on June 9, 1964, and it produced a request to me for assistance. Mrs. Johnson, Liz Carpenter said, was becoming concerned about the speech. "She wants this one to say something. But she has never spoken before an Ivy League audience, and she isn't at all sure how to approach them or how they will receive her."

At this early stage of the Administration, I had never been in Texas except for a quick trip on a university matter, or talked much with those purebred Texans, Mrs. Johnson and Mrs. Carpenter. I had little conception of what the First Lady thought the role of a woman should be, and I found it puzzling if interesting to try to figure out the ideal of a woman of her experience. My conclusion, written into a draft of the speech, was that she did not want to be "the long-striding feminist in low heels, engaged in a war with men" but "pre-eminently a woman, a wife and mother." Yet she claimed in addition the full rights of involvement in a career and public affairs. In some ways her goal seemed to me like that of many educated girls reaching maturity in the 1960's who sought to be "natural women"—free to go where their natures took them both as females and as human beings. I was also struck by the fact that Lady Bird Johnson's formative environment had included overtones of the Western United States, where the "natural" women emerged in the sense that they pioneered in running for office and asserting themselves beyond the household.

Apparently my draft hit enough of the right note, and then followed the interesting experience of watching Mrs. Johnson and Mrs. Carpenter work together. The First Lady would not like a phrase, reach for a replacement, and the aide, in perfect attunement, would have it. Mrs. Johnson would feel that an idea was a bit off; Mrs. Carpenter understood just how it was off. Other changes were a lesson in politics, Lady Bird style. Pointed sentences were fuzzed; a passage about the involvement of women in politics was converted into a direct sell for the President's major programs; a quotation from the Bible was placed at the end of the speech. And when the editing was done, there was a last-minute caution. The phrase, "natural woman"—wouldn't that call up a picture of nature girl or even a naked woman? I said I didn't think it would. Protection was added, "the natural woman, the complete woman."

The day of the speech proved that Mrs. Johnson had not been without justification in her nervousness about Radcliffe, so deep in Kennedy territory. When she rose in the white-and-orange velvet of the University of Texas, more than a few of the Radcliffe seniors chose to listen to the First Lady of the United States by reading newspapers and noisily rustling them. That had its effects in the White House. There was also a revealing flash of the relationship between the Oval Office and the East Wing. The address received a good press, including an editorial in *Life* which declared that of the season's "crop of commencement speeches, we judge the graduates at Radcliffe had the best of it. . . . Lady Bird did quite a lot for zest and sanity that day." Another occupant of the White House, who had contributed heavily to the season's crop of commencement addresses, read the *Life* editorial without notable enthusiasm.

The natural woman, the First Lady had no doubt, was a cultivated woman. "Of all the talents I wish I had," she said in another speech, "the one I admire most is the ability to make words march and sing and cannonade." She remained fascinated by the serious theater and when the reviews of a play attracted her, she would try to arrange a trip to New York. A longtime latent interest in art intensified during the White House period, and she zestfully involved herself in her own program of embellishing the rooms. Some Sunday afternoons she would slip off with Lynda to a Washington museum and wander happily, talking about the paintings and sculpture with her daughter.

But the word "culture" was not used favorably in the East Wing. Here was a prime case where Mrs. Johnson could appear to be imitating Mrs. Kennedy. Moreover, Lady Bird Johnson's own inclinations made her shy away from the connotations frequently attached to the word. She did not consider herself a devotee of "culture," and did not like people who thought they were. "My experience," she remarked in discussing the values she wanted to represent to American women, "has been as a wife, mother, businesswoman and politician. I have no apology for that. I also enjoy what people create, if the book or painting says something to me. I believe every woman should explore the world of the arts to find out what talks to her. I don't believe she should make a fool out of herself running after art for art's sake."

The First Lady was well aware that *To Kill a Mockingbird*, by Harper Lee, was considered middlebrow. The book was about Mrs. Johnson's kind of South and it had absorbed her more than any other modern fiction; Harper Lee's name often led the list of White House invitations to literary people. Tennessee Williams was a writer who sounded as if he would have understood Karnack, Texas; he was Mrs. Johnson's favorite playwright. Her preference in art was primarily for paintings, Western or the old masters, along with a variety of contemporary American works that also "touched something" in her. Mrs. Johnson was happy if the press was interested in these choices of hers. She was just as happy if it let her alone on the general subject of culture, and on certain occasions—like her museum visits with Lynda—she took every possible precaution to keep her cultural interests unreported. As Liz Carpenter said, "Mrs. Johnson believes it right that she should help open to other women the rewards she has derived from good books or fine paintings. She does not believe that it is her role to represent culture with a capital 'C,' any more than she should speak for plumbing with a capital 'P.' "

The general values she wanted to represent occupied Mrs. Johnson intermittently, but her main effort went to the support of Administration policies which seemed congenial to her. Especially in the early LBJ years, President Johnson put emphasis on bringing women into high government positions and on offering general encouragement for their equality in the business and professional worlds. Obviously this was partly political, but it also reflected his conviction, derived in large measure from his admiration for his mother and wife, that the country was not using sufficiently the talent represented by its women. Whatever the motivation, no program could be more authentically Lady Bird. She gave to it sustained effort, her activities taking political shape in the unfortunately titled "women-doers" White House luncheons, and more important form in the use of her Office to move ahead able women in the federal service and outside of government.

Though no social crusader, the First Lady felt still more strongly about poverty, especially its stunting effects on children. Want offended her both as a decent human being and as an organized mind which was repelled by the unnecessary cruelties people inflict on each other. "I could make a lifetime work," she once declared with unusual fire, "doing something, anything about poverty children."

The First Lady's anti-poverty work was made more effective by her easy relations with the director of the Office of Economic Opportunity, Sargent Shriver, who had a way of understanding people like Lady Bird Johnson. Some of the Lady Bird activities were public relations gimmickry; a "seminar and tea" to launch the enlistment of volunteer teachers for the Headstart Program included guests like Gina Lollobrigida, who hardly impressed the nation as the anti-poverty type. Another function made eminent sense. Mrs. Johnson used the atmosphere of the White House and her personal charm to bring together in ice-breaking sessions government officials and nongovernment experts who were flooding into Washington to assist OEO. And she did the chores, like the trip to St. Petersburg in February 1965 to dramatize VISTA (Volunteers in Service to America) by serving as the commencement speaker to its first graduating class.

At seven o'clock in the frigid morning the First Lady was at the Washington airport. She settled in her seat, took out her light-colored glasses, and went over the white cards on which her speech was typed, making a few changes and re-absorbing the contents. Then a conference or two with Liz Carpenter and others, a trip down the aisle of the plane for pleasantries with the press, and she returned to her seat. She rested her head on her arm; she looked a tired woman. As the plane was about to land, Mrs. Johnson redid her make-up and came down the ramp with the needed smile and cheerful wave.

By eleven o'clock she was walking into the sticky St. Petersburg auditorium appearing, as she usually did, more fragile than she was and as always, completely poised. She made her speech with almost no appearance of reading and gave moving effectiveness to the key lines: "America is many things. But above all— more than any country in the history of man—we have been a nation of volunteers. . . . Democracy means human spirit that sweeps beyond mere laws, the vision which calls upon us to use our resources so that every American can walk with head high in the tonic air of self-respect. . . . To be at the forefront of a great national effort is an opportunity which comes to few in a generation, and the personal satisfaction it brings is deep and lasting. You will know, as nothing else could help you know, that we are all of us brothers, every one of us to every one of us." As the First Lady neared the end, and was expressing not only her congratulations but, "let me add, more than a bit of envy," she ceased to depend on the cards at all and was turned fullface to the nineteen volunteers, ready to hand each his diploma with a constantly varied few sentences.

Then the real grind began: a visit to a remedial reading class, squeezed in one of the school desks for twenty minutes and leaving with an emphatic "Y'all sure read that fast"; lunch in the steaming, clattering cafeteria of the VISTA school for cooking, seated between two of the VISTA graduates, a garrulous fledgling minister and an overwhelmed middle-aged spinster; the consumption, down to the last strangely colored glop, of student-cooked avocado stuffed with Gulf shrimp, banana nut bread, and "Lady Bird Delight," a cream puff in the shape of a bird filled with peanut-butter ice cream, sprinkled with confectioners' sugar and floated in papaya sauce; a trip to the VISTA project in the nearby Negro slum where she went tramping over rocks and brambles to admire the work of the volunteers, ducked into trailers to tell the occupants how fine their improvements were, sat through another twenty-five minutes of a class, her lap full of azaleas and periwinkles pressed upon her; standing patiently for five minutes, waving back a Secret Service man, while a Negro tyke managed to make his battered camera work; a ten-minute change of clothing and the drive to the reception for the local powers at the new St. Petersburg Museum of Fine Arts, the walks down still another long corridor to look at "this one more collection you simply must see"; and at eight-thirty in the evening, after more than thirteen hours, back to the plane. Lady Bird Johnson settled in her seat, and now she looked a very tired woman indeed.

Constantly rising in importance in her mind and gradually taking over the bulk of her time, was "beautification," the counterpart to President Johnson's interest in conservation. The coiner of the word, happily, is lost to history. "Beautification" is an uglification of the language, as Mrs. Johnson knew, but until something else came along, and nothing else did, she accepted it and worked with it. The White House has never had a First Lady who took such delight in a sweep of uncluttered hills and swirling clean rivers, a well-planted urban development or her own plantings. One of the first things she had done when the Johnsons bought their Washington home was to get out a shovel and place three saplings on the back lawn. She kept turning acres of the ranch into wild flowers until her husband growled in mock annoyance, "She's going to beautify us right out of grazing land." In the sober LBJ White House, there was something joyous about the spring mornings when she and her entourage, equipped for horticultural foray, came clattering down the corridor, husky Secret Service men carrying potted seedlings to be placed in some drab area of Washington.

The Lady Bird drive for beautification headed into a tangle of attitudes. Some represented the traditional garden club urge for prettification. Others were a continuing manifestation of the kind of *noblesse oblige* which seeks an overlay of flowers on the slums. Always there were the women who lay in wait for an entrée to the White House and are ready to take the necessary measures, including giving large sums to beautification programs, to achieve it. But a significant number of the Lady Bird allies, like Laurance S. Rockefeller, the spindly, forceful Rockefeller brother who was the chairman of her national committee, represented a new breed of beautifiers.

Over the years, appearance had slowly become a workaday issue in the United States. The rampage of junkyards and billboards along the highways, the air and water pollution resulting from the same attitudes, the physical deterioration of the cities were too obvious to ignore. Efforts at urban reform constantly ran into aesthetic concerns. Planners throwing up vast new complexes were forced to decide whether they were really satisfied with a steel and concrete civilization, and slum problems could touch matters of appearance in startling ways. City after city reported that when you painted a school building and put trees around it, the teen-agers were less likely to throw bricks through the windows. A more educated corporate leadership, and one with a more enlightened self-interest, was taking over many executive offices. These men noted studies like the 1964 survey commissioned by the Shell Oil Company, which left no doubt that landscaping was a lure for motorists who figured, not unreasonably, that a gas station which bothered to landscape would also bother to keep its rest rooms clean.

Lady Bird Johnson worked with all the attitudes. She put on white gloves with the right thumb painted green and went with garden clubs to the slums. She picked up litter on Pickup Day and planted trees with chrome-plated shovels from Washington to San Francisco. She made her committees a magnet for contributions to beautification projects, and saw to it that the philanthropists were rewarded with White House attention. She had Liz Carpenter, and then a special team within her staff, working out arrangements with corporations that would combine profits with pleasantness. And she carried the word, in her own way. During a three-week period in 1965 she made seven trips for beautification, including a visit to Milwaukee. There she took on the subject of litter but did not forget that beer had made Milwaukee prosperous as well as famous. She called litter "one of the greatest detractors of beauty" and mentioned not a beer can.

The results? Many of them were long term or, alternatively, quite transient, superficially undertaken to win favor with the White House, and in the hangdog later days of the Johnson Administration the First Lady's efforts slackened. But in 1965–66, when her campaign was in full swing, progress was incontestable. The pioneering highway beautification bill, however weakened, was the law of the land. Across the nation, she was giving heightened status and popularity to gifts or appropriations for beautification, and the results had a cash register ring in the multimillions. Leaders in twenty-three cities, working with her office, were setting up influential cross-section committees, some with the eager backing of the mayors. Corporation officers were hiring additional junior executives, to keep in touch, as one chairman of the board put it, with "this Lady Bird thing, very interesting, might be important." Mail was flooding into the East Wing, "quality mail" and "dollar mail," like the proposal from a major corporation to discuss a national program for burying transmission lines. And at least for a time, the beautifiers of all stripes, inclinations and aberrations knew that they had an able and dedicated friend in the White House.

At the height of the beautification campaign the staff of Mrs. Johnson filled with indignation. The Gallup poll was out with its annual survey on the subject of what women Americans admire. At the top of the list was Mrs. John Kennedy; second was the First Lady of the United States. Apart from this comparison, Lady Bird Johnson was obviously gaining no great place in public esteem and affection. The general reaction was less enthusiasm or dislike than a shrug.

As First Lady, Mrs Johnson functioned with a major liability. She was her husband's wife, and the national attitude toward LBJ cast a strong light on whatever she was and whatever she did. She had another serious problem, television; she may have made a fortune from it but, like Lyndon Johnson, she was finding it no friend. Many students of democracy have long argued that television injures the democratic process by putting a premium on irrelevant or trivial characteristics. The whole Johnson family on the screen raises another question—whether the box in the living room gives anything close to an accurate portrayal of public personalities. Lady Bird Johnson was transformed most of all, and totally to her loss. Her charm, which was as great as it was reserved, appeared mechanical. Though an unusually attractive mature woman, on the screen she seemed all mouth and nose, with little grace of figure, and the drawl that was simply a regional accent in personal contact emerged an abrasive twang. Her intelligence and humanity disappeared into some mystery of the medium. Very soon I had become accustomed to the experience of talking to someone who had formed his impression of Mrs. Johnson from television and then come away from a meeting with her exclaiming, "I never had the slightest idea she was like *that*."

Yet it was also true that basic characteristics which produced the general national reaction were the purest Lady Bird. Unusual as she was, she had a constant air of the woman next door, and ordinary people have seldom excited ordinary people. She put exceptional talents to the service of a rigorous circumspection; she rarely made a mistake. But First Ladies who rarely make a mistake never score a coup.

The real Lady Bird Johnson was the middle-class woman who had developed that role to near-perfection. As such, she particularly had little appeal to Metroamerican women and in many instances was downright offensive to them. Struggling with overextended budgets, occupationally yearning husbands and uncertain status in their communities, they were in no mood for middleclass verities. They wanted identification not with traditional attitudes and sentiments—especially those that called up the breadand-butter existence and the prestigeless South and Texas—but with the breakaway to a life characterized in many ways precisely by the connotations of the word "Culture." They would not have enthused over a First Lady named Lady Bird had she been Lady Bird Joan of Arc; they were not responding to "y'all," efficiency, the good wife, the model of the controlled life. They might approve of what a beautification campaign would bring; at any given moment, they preferred a place of exquisite scenery and exquisitely chilled daiquiris which managed to omit guests who pursued beautification as "women-doers." Lady Bird Johnson was beige, and beige ladies did not command the cocktail parties of the 1960's.

There is irony in all this. Mrs. Johnson brought to the Office of the First Lady basic qualities superbly suited to its needs. No doubt, after her the Office will continue its erratic way. Yet she gave it such organization and so firm a sense of purpose and usefulness that it is doubtful whether it will ever completely return to its traditional aimlessness.

There is special irony in Mrs. Johnson's relationship to Metroamerican women. Of all First Ladies, none knew more about, or had greater sympathy for, the problems of a wife with the careering husband, of money that was so important but had to be talked about as if it were not, of the whole tortuous path of the American woman who had been emancipated into a doubly demanding position. None had a more sincere interest in the essence of culture with or without a capital "C."

Lady Bird Johnson, no saint, had her moments of discouragement and irritation that so little of this was understood. Occasionally too she showed her exasperation with the LBJ way of life. And once in a while a look would come over her face, an expression which in a more grandiloquent age, for a more pretentious person, might have been called inscrutable. Perhaps it was not really inscrutable at all. Perhaps it called up things that might have been: the free-wheeling ways of Minnie Lee Patillo and the gentle ways of Aunt Effie; the footloose hour when reading did not have to be snatched at and gardening was not organized into a campaign; the thoughts of a life, which some other people seemed to have, in which there was time to smother little girls with attention and the wife was not all self-discipline and the husband all-commanding; the memory of First Ladies who, by feeling much more free, had known the tang of being widely worshiped and roundly disliked.

The look came, once in a while, and quickly disappeared. Lady Bird Johnson had a rich sense of living the good life. On U.S. Highway 81, fighting it every mile, she had stumbled into years of excitement far beyond her girlhood fancies. If she realized that as First Lady she was no national heroine, she had a solid confidence that "I've done a job, a good and useful one." She had her daughters and the older they became, the more she saw in them parts of herself that delighted her—Lynda, "my Miss Purpose," Luci, "just a little bit of way out yonder." Above all, she was with the man she wanted to be with.

Lady Bird Johnson was well aware of her husband's gargantuan faults, and occasionally, when it could not possibly hurt him, she mentioned them. She was also well aware that she had married him because she did not want to face losing him, she had stayed married to him for the same reason, and in her view of life, such a man you sought not to remake but to fulfill. For Lyndon Johnson, she had the eyes of a woman who cared deeply, and who saw what she wanted to see. His domineering? "He has the strength that wears well." His fussing into everything? "He stretches you. I might get annoyed at his telling me how to dress but I do look better." His lashing ego? "Men who achieve things drive things."

She cared deeply, and she had the sustaining assurance that he did too. No President and First Lady have been more simply, more straightforwardly, more securely husband and wife. There were not only the demands by the husband on the wife; over the years a dependence came, not simply one of convenience but of entangled emotional needs, and one that ran both ways. Lady Bird Johnson knew she held the ultimate emotions of her husband, however sporadically or crassly they might be displayed. She knew that he genuinely appreciated her attitude toward him. "Bird," Lyndon Johnson was ready to tell anybody, "has never failed me. Your friends, your relatives—they let you down sometimes. Bird has never failed me." She knew what so few wives have the glory of knowing, that her husband thoroughly respected her as a human being, a mind and a partner in everything he did.

And over the decades, she had never lost the feeling that came to her when her father and her suitor stood in front of Brick

House. The man she had married, she remained sure, was a real man. Along with all the painful recollections of her years with Lyndon Johnson, other memories accumulated: his long-legged, shouting bound into the house when, as NYA administrator for Texas, he had managed to get one hundred and seventy-one more kids out of boxcars and into jobs; the time of the first try for the senatorship, which they thought he had won only to have the prize slip away, and the jaunty way he walked to the plane and waved goodbye to make her feel better; the courage at the time he knew the full heart attack was coming, lying in Bethesda Naval Hospital and carefully husbanding the twenty minutes the doctors had given him to take care of his responsibilities to her, their daughters and the Senate; the anger and burst of activity when, as Vice-President, he learned that one of his Mexican-American students from Cotulla had scored second in a test and been discriminated against for a job in the Federal Home Loan Administration; the few sentences he spoke quietly to her on the day in Dallas when they waited to learn if President Kennedy would die, a few sentences about his country and its people.

CHAPTER 14

"No More Munichs"

I just hope," Mrs. Johnson remarked in mid-1965, "that foreign problems do not keep mounting. They do not represent Lyndon's kind of Presidency."

Some modern American leaders, most notably Franklin Roosevelt, Adlai Stevenson and John Kennedy, have felt at home in international affairs and despite the worries brought by crises, went at foreign policy with zest. These men came from or had been imbued with the attitudes of the eastern United States, where concern with the rest of the world traditionally has been strongest. Inward-looking Texas was inclined to assume that the business of America is America; Lyndon Johnson tended the more toward this attitude because he was so much a creature of the New Deal 1930's, which had rolled up its sleeves not to confront the world but to reshape America. Until his role as Vice-President took him abroad, he had never gone outside the United States except for trips to Mexico and his World War II service. It was a striking fact that of the authentic LBJ men who came into influence after the assassination—whether aides in the White House or associates of the President who remained outside—only a few had any particular international bent.

Lyndon Johnson entered the White House not only little concerned with the outer world but leery of it. "Foreigners are not like the folks I am used to," he remarked, and he was only half joking. At first he was so uncomfortable with the stream of ambassadors arriving to present their credentials and to get in a word with him that he avoided the occasions ("They're your clients, not mine," he told Secretary of State Rusk) or because he was so uneasy, turned the meetings into a carnival of rudeness. Then, realizing that this would not do, he swung to the other extreme and had

Jack Valenti arrange ambassadorial luncheons at which he appeared near the end of the occasion and engaged in excessive camaraderie. President Johnson had a further wariness. In his opinion, politicians, whether comfortable with foreign policy or not, ventured into the field at their own peril. He did not forget that the Korean War had been the emotional issue which gave the Republicans their only occupancy of the White House since 1932.

Early in the LBJ Presidency an aide remarked sympathetically, "He wishes the rest of the world would go away and we could get ahead with the real needs of Americans." At hostile cocktail parties, people passed around the japery: "In this Administration, you know, we are not going to bother with foreign policy." Sarcastically or sympathetically, it may accurately be said that Lyndon Johnson became President without a foreign policy. But it is important to clarify what is really meant by such a statement.

It means that President Johnson preferred to think about and deal with domestic rather than international affairs; that he lacked extensive acquaintance with foreign leaders or significant knowledge of foreign civilizations; and that he had no carefully thought out conception of the workings of the international system, few broad-gauged premises concerning diplomacy or war, even less feel or sense of things international. The statement does not mean that in most of these respects he was markedly different from two of the three men who presided over America's twentieth-century wars—Woodrow Wilson and Harry Truman—and it can be argued how much genuine foreign policy Franklin Roosevelt brought to the White House, even if he had long been interested in it and shown an instinct for it. Nor does the statement eliminate the crucial fact that Lyndon Johnson entered the Presidency with a set of assumptions, attitudes and prejudices which, together with his personality, amounted in practice to a foreign policy.

He had little respect for American relations with other nations after the Truman Administration, and this judgment very specifically included the Kennedy years despite his admiration for a few specific JFK actions in the international sphere. The basic trouble, President Johnson believed, was that the United States is a nation easily misunderstood by foreign leaders, and that it had failed to make itself clear. The most serious international problems of America came from the fact that the United States permitted a "miscalculation" of its intentions and will. Foreigners thought of America, to use a frequent LBJ phrase, as "fat and fifty, like the country-club set." They did not believe that it had a hard-headed understanding of its self-interest or a willingness to act upon it.

Consequently, he was sure that the United States should move promptly and vigorously to counter anything which was significantly harmful to American interests. It was like a Senate maneuver; you had to show that you were ready to play your cards. What he considered significantly harmful to the United States encompassed many things, including a concern—more often associated with nineteenth-century leaders—over the importance of "respect for the flag," with all the connotations attached to that phrase. But the prime worry clustered about the word "aggression."

President Johnson had little patience with those who went into involved definitions of the term. "Aggression is when one country won't let another one alone. Everybody knows when that is happening." To him, aggression was the nub of the world problem in the twentieth century. A series of aggressions turned into tragedies because the United States did not sufficiently make plain, and make plain quickly enough, that its interest—peace—was threatened by aggression and that it proposed to do something about it. Some men who knew LBJ well have said that he was "obsessed" by this feeling about aggression and the importance of an American stand against it. The term rings wrong for Lyndon Johnson. He was not obsessed by anything unless it was his personal need to stay ahead of the game, all games. Yet his concern over aggression was certainly the core of his foreign policy attitudes.

Looking back over the past, he saw the United States as having been endangered by two major waves of aggression, first the fascist and then the Communist. The fascists of the 1930's, he remarked again and again, did not believe the United States understood and would fight for its interests in Europe. They listened to FDR's critics, not to FDR. The Communists of the 1950's did not believe that the United States understood and would fight for its interests in Asia. They listened to Harry Truman's critics, not Harry Truman. That was the heart of the trouble.

In all of this President Johnson, like so many people who do not read history, was peculiarly a creature of it, and perhaps a prisoner of one particular interpretation of it. When Communist North Korea invaded South Korea in 1950, President Truman was visiting his home in Missouri. On the three-hour flight back to Washington he wrestled with the crisis, and what went through his mind was the memory of Hitler, Mussolini and the Japanese fascists in the 1930's and the failure of the democracies at Munich to stand up to their aggressions. This, he believed, had brought on World War II. Now the Communists were repeating aggression in Asia. He "felt certain" that if South Korea were allowed to fall, Communist leaders would be emboldened to attack nations closer to the United States, and small nations would lack the will to stand up to threats or actual aggression by stronger Communist neighbors. Permitting the aggression in South Korea to go unchallenged "would mean a third world war, just as similar incidents had brought on the second world war." What President Truman considered the Munich parallel was the prime reason for his decision to use American combat power in Korea.

In the early period of the Johnson Presidency, on several occasions Harry Truman and Lyndon Johnson talked about the Korean intervention, and the new Chief Executive thoroughly agreed with the retired President's analysis. The point had long been on his mind when he thought about foreign policy. During the nomination fight of 1960, he had attacked John Kennedy through his father, Joseph P. Kennedy, who supported the Munich settlement while American ambassador to Britain. Candidate Johnson heatedly told delegates, "I wasn't any Chamberlain umbrella man." Harry Truman looking back to Munich, Lyndon Johnson looking back to Munich and to Harry Truman's decision in Korea—with the double force of what he was sure represented historical parallels, President Johnson was determined, as he once snapped, "No more Munichs."

LBJ had also talked, as Vice-President, with President Kennedy after the Cuban missile confrontation. The two men may have had sharply different attitudes in Latin American policy, but they were in total agreement that JFK's forceful moves had been correct. As President, LBJ drew from the Castro experience the conviction that "any man who permitted a second Communist state to spring up in this hemisphere would be impeached and ought to be." The memory of Cuba underlined his sustained edginess about Communist "aggression" anywhere. To him, no more Cubas went along with no more Munichs.

Whatever was to be done in foreign policy was to be done the LBJ way. Ever conscious of public relations, he was ready for endless speeches on international affairs, the announcement of concordats, the flow of ceremonial gestures, the long-range building of amity. But he did not put much stock in them; he relied on the efficacy of action. As one associate of many years remarked, "President Johnson doesn't believe that relations between nations turn on minor understandings, on cultural differences, on what you say in speeches or formal diplomatic exchanges. He thinks relations turn on fundamentals, on what you do and the motives you show by doing it, on whether other nations think you have a tough-minded view of your own self-interest. He believes that the persistent misunderstandings of America make it necessary for the United States, more than any other country, to communicate its purposes and its awareness of its self-interest loud and clear and over and over again, by deeds rather than words."

The LBJ deeds, it has been said, were impulsive. Certainly he could explode and berate the ambassadors of Britain, Chile and Denmark: "I just don't know what's wrong. Here are innocent American civilians killed by Vietcong bombs and you complain that we bomb bridges in the North. Bridges don't bleed. Americans do." His first reaction to the news of rioting in Panama had also been no model of deliberation. But impulsiveness in important matters was not the customary LBJ way, in foreign policy any more than in other fields. Except when certain emotional nerves were touched, he would keep walking around an international problem, poking at it, looking at it from this and that angle, checking with all kinds of people. The impression of impulsiveness came from what happened once he made up his mind. Then grimly, no holds barred, and at times utterly pell-mell, he went for the jugular. I ran into an LBJ associate who had spent a good deal of time with the President on a particular foreign crisis and his greeting to me was, "Whew—he's decided that one, finally. Now God help them, or God help somebody."

The jugular approach in foreign affairs fitted in easily with the LBJ tendency to go it alone. President Johnson was never hostile and rarely indifferent to international organizations for peace; he genuinely recognized the usefulness of the United Nations and of the battery of regional bodies created since World War II. But his cardinal doctrine—the necessity for America to move decisively to protect American interests—did not encourage him to worry long over the opinion of other nations. His spread-eagle patriotism, his disdain for the irresoluteness of group diplomacy, and his delight in barnyard language combined to build few bridges between him and diplomats assembled in international organizations. Of the Latin American regional group, the Organization of American States, LBJ said on an occasion when he knew his words would be repeated, "It couldn't pour piss out of a boot if the instructions were written on the heel." As a matter of fact, the description was not too inaccurate; the OAS had been notoriously indecisive and ineffective. But it did, as one OAS diplomat solemnly remarked to me, "have a tendency to make us think that your President does not consider us too important."

Foreign organizations were one thing; the voters and the Congress of the United States were another. Of course Lyndon Johnson was political in thinking about foreign policy. He was political when he got up in the morning and considered which tie would look best on color television, and he was political when he went to bed at night, making those last phone calls to Schenectady, Butte and Dripping Springs, Texas. Just because he knew he was no veteran in foreign policy and assumed that international affairs were a snare for any President, he was the more determined to touch all bases. He had a basic principle in the political handling of foreign policy, and it came from his revered master, Franklin Roosevelt: "It's fine to be a leader, but you better make sure that when you turn around, somebody is following you."

In international affairs, Lyndon Johnson remained not only the politician but the man of the Hill. No modern President has shown so intense a concern with maintaining broad approval for his foreign policies in the House and Senate, though the pursuit of this harmony was not without its special LBJ characteristic. One perceptive United States senator caught the nuances of President Johnson's attitude: "I am sure that if he really believed Congress was against any major part of his foreign policy, he would abandon it. He feels in his bones that a President will become a cropper if he fights Congress on foreign policy. But then, of course, comes the question of what Congress really thinks. Lyndon has some interesting views about that. He believes that he can help Congress considerably in figuring out what it thinks. He also believes that the nub of what Congress thinks is not contained in the noise of clashing factions. It is contained in the balance between the factions or in a least common denominator, which a President must figure out and help to shape."

The President must figure out and help to shape—LBJ was determined to keep foreign policy firmly in his hands. He had a degree of populistic skepticism about the State Department ("Lots of words, lots of reports, little"—tapping his head—"up here"). He had come to know the military well during his period as chairman of the Senate Aeronautical and Space Sciences Committee and of the Preparedness Subcommittee of the Armed Services Committee, and he respected a number of military leaders as men of ability and decisiveness. But he was also often put off by their tendency to seek the military decision ("The State Department wants to solve everything with words, and the generals, with guns") and by the military's free-spending ways. Shortly after he became President he called in the Joint Chiefs of Staff and told them, "You've done a good job of protecting my two girls for years, but you're the biggest wasters and spenders in the country." President Johnson, like some of his predecessors, delighted in devising ways to get around the regular procedures of State and Defense. In foreign affairs, during the formative stage of the major policies of the Administration he relied heavily on those two close advisers in so many things, Clark Clifford and Abe Fortas, and on three officials quite apart from their titular roles—Secretary of State Dean Rusk, Secretary of Defense Robert McNamara and Special Assistant for National Security Affairs McGeorge Bundy. Unlike most other Johnson aides, Rusk, McNamara and Bundy went up and down little in his estimation; from the beginning of his Presidency he thought them dedicated and extremely able. Nevertheless, Lyndon Johnson made the decisions, little and big.

Intertwined with all aspects of his foreign policy was the President's ambition. Much as he wished that international affairs could be de-emphasized, he was too seasoned a political leader not to know that they were certain to play an important part in the overall judgment of his Administration. He was determined that when he did have to deal with them, he would do so with effectiveness and splash. Lyndon Johnson was going to be a great President, a very great President, in all ways.

And then there was JFK. The more Kennedyites praised the dead President for knowledgeability and deftness in international matters, the more irritated LBJ became. It was not simply that he failed to see anything especially good in President Kennedy's general foreign policy performance; the annoyance reached back over the years. He did not forget that it was he who, as Senate Majority Leader and a man consulted by Presidents in international as well as domestic matters, had seen to it that freshman Senator John Kennedy was granted his wish to be named to the Senate Committee on Foreign Relations. As the contest for the 1960 Democratic nomination sharpened, and JFK workers made comparisons between their man and LBJ in the field of international problems, Lyndon Johnson had exploded to one group of delegates, "This young fellow I appointed to a foreign relations committee claims he knows more about foreign affairs than I do. You know, there are some people who will throw crutches at their doctors and get smarter than their daddy." For a while Daddy had no opportunity to show them; now he did.

A drive to distinguish himself in international matters joined with a wish that the world would not bother him; a foreign policy partially attuned to a mercurial Congress; a readiness to saber-rattle at the ripple of a flag, along with an insistence on pinpointing hard American interests; a conviction that big wars were prevented by fighting smaller wars—was there anything beneath this congeries of attitudes that provided a larger context for the Johnson foreign policy?

There was, and it emerged from a powerful American tradition. Over the generations, Democrats and Republicans, liberals and conservatives, had tended to assume a general international trend, a trend so certain in their minds that it took on the cast of a law of history. Human beings everywhere, the law ran, sought peace and democracy, wanted to get ahead to a farm of their own or a house on the right side of the tracks, preferred to do it all gradually and with a decent regard for the amenities. Consequently, the real history of man was a long, slow swing toward a world consisting entirely of middle-class democracies. Once in a while trouble came when some country fell under an evil leader or leaders who forced it along a road proscribed by the law of history. Then it was only necessary to remove the pernicious element and let the aspirations flow back along their proper path. (Characteristically, the United States conducted its wars not in the name of fighting a whole people but against wicked leaders— the tyrannical King George III, the militaristic Kaiser, the brutal fascist dictators, the Communist conspirators.) Since the natural movement of the world was toward peaceful, democratic, middle-class ways, foreign policy was essentially a problem of encouraging this trend, and when necessary, of removing an unnatural growth by diplomacy or war.

President Johnson brought to the White House this traditional American assumption that Americans and the peoples of the rest of the world had in common a bedrock interest in ruling themselves and in advancing economically and socially. As a result, sensible foreign policy was to be based on the working out of the shared attitude in concrete ways. As far as foreign leaders were concerned, LBJ carried over from his experience in domestic affairs a conviction that techniques must exist to reach them and to arrive at accommodations with them. If they were men of good will, this could be done by concentrating on their genuine concern for the advancement of their nations toward democracy and a higher standard of living. If the leaders were types unmoved by such considerations, the need was for some of the many forms of arm twisting available in the international sphere, not excluding the form of dropping bombs. Then the leaders would give way to the popular desires which Lyndon Johnson was sure existed, or their replacement would be forced.

Those who thought along the lines of the law of history often gave it a particular emphasis. For many decades a feeling had been growing in America that the Asians were the special mission of the United States under the law of history. It was the American duty to help feed them, educate them, convert them, nudge them along toward the middle-class life. The sentiment was plain in President William McKinley's declaration that "there was nothing for us to do but to . . . educate the Filipinos, and uplift and civilize and Christianize them." Over the years the attitude was spoken from a thousand pulpits by missionaries returning from China with fervid reports of how many more Chinese had chopped off their pigtails, learned to wear pants or marched to the baptismal font. The emotion made its way into hundreds of speeches by politicians of the modern era—not to speak of the dictum of United States Senator Kenneth S. Wherry, who told a wildly cheering crowd in 1943, "With God's help, we will lift Shanghai up and up, ever up, until it is just like Kansas City."

Senator Wherry was from Nebraska, and in the vast span of middle states swinging from the Canadian to the Mexican borders, millions of Americans had been isolationist or little interested in international affairs. But their attitude was isolationism or indifferentism with a twist. They responded little to Europe; they disliked economic and diplomatic arrangements with it and shied away from fighting in its wars. Yet in many cases they were not only willing but eager to be involved with Asia. The habit of thinking reached a temporary climax at the time of Pearl Harbor. Significantly, the influential Chicago *Tribune,* savage opponent of FDR's "finaglings in Europe," swung happily behind war in Asia, "our natural area."

Perhaps someone will eventually write a study of this bifocalism. It would be an important book, and it would have to be a lengthy one. Many long-time developments are entangled in the attitude: the fact that most Americans came from families who left Europe by a deliberate act of rejection; the participation in transatlantic wars which left millions sure that they had been "suckered"; an anxiety about the "hordes" of Asia and an assumption of superiority to yellow peoples—feelings which in combination inclined Americans to believe that they need not fear dealing with Asia and that they had better do it; the difference between the commercial and financial ties that ran East and West; and the long-pervasive influence of American missionaries and traders who crossed the Pacific. Just because of the many strands that went into it, the attitude had particular emotional potency.

Lyndon Johnson was of this bent of mind. He found it hard to get really interested in European affairs, but Asia lit all kinds of candles in his mind. This was especially true because rural, impoverished Asia, in contrast to industrialized, prospering Europe, evoked memories of his native central Texas. When the

President was growing up in Johnson City, as he never tired of saying, the surrounding country was a land of grudging caliche soil, scrub cedar and periodic devastating floods; by the time he entered the White House, it had been transformed into a region of pleasant living, largely through irrigation and rural electrification. Of all his prepresidential achievements, LBJ took greatest pride in his congressional leadership in harnessing the lower Colorado River for the benefit of a sweeping area including his home district. In his late Senate days he was happily working away with engineers on a plan for a canal that would connect all the rivers in Texas from the Sabine to the Rio Grande and multiply by seven the water available for irrigation. It is no accident that in time the man who did so much to put Lyndon Johnson into politics, Texas State Senator Alvin Wirtz, and the man who did so much to keep him there, Abe Fortas, were both closely associated with the Interior Department and its land-blossoming projects. When President Johnson looked at Asia he saw central Texas—its needs and what had been done about them.

Two years before the LBJ Presidency, an accident of history brought into sharper focus Lyndon Johnson's thinking about international affairs. In 1961 President Kennedy had, among his myriad problems, two that kept pressing for attention. One was a very able and energetic Vice-President with very little to do. The other was the growing skepticism in Southeast Asia, especially in the government of President Ngo Dinh Diem of South Vietnam, whether the United States meant anything substantial by its declared opposition to Communist advances in the region. As Presidents have a way of doing, JFK found one solution for the two problems. In May 1961 he sent Vice-President Johnson on a trip to reassure Southeast Asia.

The thought of Lyndon Johnson on a diplomatic mission had a depressing effect in the State Department ("Like some wines," an assistant secretary murmured, "Lyndon does not travel well"), and part of the press had a field day with LBJ's Asian tour. Seeking to convince President Diem that the United States would stand behind him in important ways, the Vice-President proclaimed Diem—corruption, ineffectuality and all—the "Winston Churchill of Asia." He got going again and found Diem to have "the qualities of George Washington," along with "the courage" of Andrew Jackson and "the astuteness" of Franklin Roosevelt. In Thailand, embassy officials briefed the Vice-President on the Thai tradition of not shaking hands. LBJ went riding through the streets of Bangkok, gathered a crowd and burst from the car, hand extended. In India, he was impressed by the Taj Mahal; he let out a whoop to test its echo.

Yet for Lyndon Johnson the ten-day trip was the most satisfying episode in his whole three years as Vice-President. He had something significant to do and, press gibes or not, it was generally conceded that he did it well. Most American and foreign observers agreed that he had handled the task in a way which, as the Manila *Times* declared, "gives a shot in the arm to Southeast Asia. . . . He has erased a few of the grave doubts and [his] trip, more than anything else, will serve to rekindle faith in America and in its intentions."

Away from his top-hat role in Washington and the arched eyebrows, Lyndon Johnson felt he could be himself, and it seemed to him to work beautifully. In Saigon he attracted unheard-of throngs by repeatedly stopping his car to step into the crowds. He was sure that faith in America increased when, coatless, tieless, hand outstretched, always ready for an impromptu little speech, the Vice-President walked the dark alleys of the settlers' village at Bien Hoa and the filth-strewn gullets of the refugee camp at Honai. On the way to the airport for departure, LBJ was suddenly out of the limousine again, taking with him Nguyen Ngoc Tho. Vice-President Johnson handed Vice-President Tho an American flag, took a South Vietnamese one himself and beaming marched through a cheering crowd the last half mile to the plane.

Manila brought a prickly situation. Lyndon Johnson thought it important that he address a joint session of the Philippine Congress, but the House leaders opposed it, partly because no Number Two man had been so honored and partly because they were irritated at what they deemed America's weak attitude toward the Communist threat. The U.S. embassy prevailed on the congressional leaders to relent, and the Vice-President took over. He cut his long address to twenty minutes, ad-libbed into it vigorous promises that "America will honor her commitments to the cause of freedom throughout the community of free nations." Before and after the speech he had a personal word for everybody, including the pageboys. They dropped their stiffness as he walked over to them and told them, with a wink, about the days when his father was in the Texas Legislature and "my greatest ambition *then* was to be a pageboy." Down the streets LBJ went, shouting "*Mabuhay,*" delighted at the *Mabuhay*'s which roared back and the subsequent local press report: "The greatest reception since General MacArthur."

On to 24 hours in Formosa, the formalities with President

Chiang Kai-shek, and a street speech in purest Johnsonese: "I assure you on behalf of President Kennedy that we love our friends, and expect to stand behind them every day, today, tomorrow and every day to come." The Vice-President liked the newspaper coverage of this occasion too: "Violent enthusiasm. . . . It was carnival when the New Frontier came to Taipei."

In Bangkok LBJ left his conference with Prime Minister Sarit Thanarat to board *Rua chang* and visit floating shops, offering the greetings of *"wai*'s." The Thai reserve was in evidence; *wai*-ing was not working well. The Vice-President tried something else. He pulled out an old Senate card and gave it to a little girl. Now more *wai*'s were returned, followed by loud cries of *Kobchai,* the thankyou. Then he ventured on the proscribed handshaking, got a pleased if startled response.

Bangkok was the headquarters of the eight-nation SEATO defense organization, and Lyndon Johnson decided on a prod. "Meeting here today, we are confronted with a moment of decision. It is time to be tested. As we say in the language of my hill country, it is time to separate the men from the boys." He left, grinning to an aide, "I'm not sure they understood the words, but I think they got the message."

In New Delhi, there were added features: distribution of old LBJ campaign ballpoint pens, and a story about Lynda, who had an Indian college classmate she liked so much "we are going to invite her over for Sunday dinner as soon as we get back to the ranch." One crowd was listless, but the Vice-President pumped away: "America stands for peace for every man, woman and child." The response was satisfactory.

Pakistan was the last stop and it was more than satifying. In the capital Karachi, at Elphinstone and Preedy streets, a wild demonstration was triggered by the gifts, handshaking and a speech which the buffeted, perspiring interpreter translated as "I need more education and health and housing. You need more education and health and housing."

In a quieter interval, near the Drigh Station, the Vice-President saw a camel cart loaded with straw. He stopped his car, went over to the cart and pulled out a few tufts. "What do you do with the straw?" he asked the driver.

"It's for cattle fodder," Bashir Ahmed replied. But, he added sadly, his horseshoe mustache drooping, "My camel is getting old."

Lyndon Johnson brooked no sagging spirits. "We have come to see you and your camel. Our President wants to see your camel. He has plans to make things better for you."

Bashir Ahmed looked at the Vice-President, murmured a few words of Urdu which are difficult to translate except as "Is this for real?"

LBJ put his hand on the camel driver's shoulder. "Would you like to come to my country?"

"Why not? Why not?" Bashir Ahmed sighed.

The Vice-President forgot about the incident until, back in Washington, he noted a mention of it in a clipping from the Karachi *Dawn*. Why not, he thought, and reached for the phone to set up the invitation. Now skeptics did not even bother to be skeptical; this, they groaned, was cornballism on the global scale. On the day of Bashir Ahmed's arrival at the New York International Airport, Lyndon Johnson himself looked apprehensive. Bashir Ahmed emerged, his *Shalwar* trousers, his *Sherwani* long coat, and his *Jinnah* fur cap impeccable. The trip was his first experience with wearing shoes; he walked serenely.

He was sorry, Vice-President Johnson ventured, that the weather was so cold.

"It is not cold weather," said Bashir Ahmed, "but the warmth of people's hearts that matters."

The Vice-President blinked; the reporters blinked. The camel driver, in the wondrous way of an LBJ story, was turning out to be a man of sharp wits and inherent dignity, with a touch of the folk poet about him. At the ranch he went to bed imperturbably in the room occupied a short while before by the President of Pakistan. He was more interested in looking over things from the saddle of a prime quarter horse, which he thought might be a fair trade for a camel; in meeting Lynda ("A daughter in the family is like spring among the seasons"); and in a visit to the State Fair of Texas, where he was presented with a blue truck by the Ford Motor Company and gently indicated that he preferred green. When he was flown to visit Harry Truman, his manner was so courtly that the flustered ex-President addressed him as "Your Excellency," and on recovering, gave him a steak breakfast and a good-luck token.

Ensconced in a suite at the Waldorf-Astoria in New York City, Bashir Ahmed learned that his wife, Chidoo, amid great fuss from his four children, brother-in-law and neighbor women, had moved from their slum hut to an uptown apartment. Strong tea had sustained him throughout his visit. Now he asked for a cup, and observed with a thoughtful pull at his mustache, "A woman is like a camel. You never know what she will do next."

In Pakistan, Bashir Ahmed, who was carrying it all off with such aplomb, was a hero; the American press laid off snide stories.

From the office of the Vice-President came trumpets of triumph for person-to-person diplomacy.

Buoyed by everything connected with his trip, Lyndon Johnson found in his firsthand contact with Asia confirmation of what he had so long instinctively believed. The region was enormously important, "greatly appealing." The law of history seemed written all across it. "You can sense how these people feel," he had remarked after a trip to a Vietnam village. "They want the same things we do." In the cruel refugee huts outside Saigon, his concern over Communists and his anger at them had magnified. "It's the same old story—aggression against decent people, leading to danger of war for all decent people. Aggression is the evil of the twentieth century."

The trip particularly drove more deeply into Lyndon Johnson's thinking the conviction that Asian Communist "aggression" must be stopped, and what he saw made him the surer it must be stopped the LBJ way. In a memo to President Kennedy prepared after his return, the Vice-President spelled out his conclusions. The need was not talk but "a clear-cut and strong program of action." The basic problem was "hunger, ignorance, poverty and disease." In attacking it or in establishing more immediate economic and military programs, the United States would have to take the lead. "The key to what is done by Asians in defense of Southeast Asian freedom is confidence in the United States. There is no alternative to United States leadership in Southeast Asia. Leadership in individual countries—or the regional leadership and co-operation so appealing to Asians—rests on knowledge and faith in United States power, will and understanding." The Pacific international defense organization SEATO "is not now and probably never will be the answer because of French and English unwillingness to support decisive action."

The alternative was the same dangerous one that had come from previous American failures to act with sufficient vigor against aggression. "The battle against Communism must be joined in Southeast Asia with strength and determination to achieve success there—or the United States, inevitably, must surrender the Pacific and take up our defenses on our own shores. Asian Communism is compromised and contained by the maintenance of free nations on the subcontinent. Without this inhibitory influence, the island outposts—Philippines, Japan, Taiwan—have no security and the vast Pacific becomes a Red Sea. . . . The basic decision in Southeast Asia is here. We must decide whether to help these countries to the best of our ability or throw in the towel in the area and pull back our defenses to San Francisco and a 'Fortress America' concept." Moreover, without effective aid the United States would be saying to the world that it does not "stand by" its friends. Such a policy, Lyndon Johnson added crisply, "is not my concept."

On the subject of just what to do, the memo was less crisp. Of course more attention should be given to the area; there should be greater economic aid and military advisory help, and the efforts to create regional programs in Southeast Asia should be intensified. But what if the Communists kept succeeding? In sentences that carry an eerie premonition of the onrushing future, the Vice-President stated that the decision "must be made in a full realization of the very heavy and continuing costs involved in terms of money, of effort and of United States prestige. It must be made with the knowledge that at some point we may be faced with the further decision of whether we commit major United States forces to the area or cut our losses and withdraw should our efforts fail."

And then there was a river, the Mekong, long, majestic, unruly and mocking. Gathering its waters sixteen thousand four hundred feet up in the Tibetan plateau, the Mekong extends some twenty-six hundred miles, swirling through China (the Chinese call it Lan-Tsan-Kiang, "the wild river"), then flowing with intermittent turbulence through its lower basin, including parts of Cambodia, Laos, South Vietnam, and Thailand, and just below Saigon, emptying annually four hundred million acre-feet of water into the South China Sea. Twenty million people live in the watershed of this lower basin; for them, the chief product of the Mekong has been devastation, its spring rise reaching as high as twenty-five feet. As early as 1952 the UN started planning a project which would bring Cambodia, Laos, South Vietnam and Thailand together to control the lower Mekong for the purposes of flood prevention, electric power, irrigation, fisheries development and more practical navigation. But the program was discouraged by the instability of the area and the fear of an insufficient market for large-scale electric power.

Shortly before Vice-President Johnson left for Asia, two of the ubiquitous friends he had acquired over the years got in touch with him. One was Arthur E. ("Tex") Goldschmidt of San Antonio, who had worked in the New Deal as a public-power expert, gone on to United Nations technical activities, and was at this time the highly respected Senior Director for Special Fund Operations of the UN Department of Economic and Social Affairs. (In 1967 President Johnson—to considerable applause among the knowledgeable—was to make Goldschmidt an ambassador, as U.S. Representative to the UN Economic and Social Council.) The other friend was Cesar Ortiz-Tinoco, an alumnus of LBJ's schoolteaching days, who had left Texas for the cosmopolitan life, acquired a British wife with a Sunday-supplement reputation for Mexican cooking, and was now serving in Bangkok as chief of the information services of the UN Economic Commission for Asia and the Far East. Goldschmidt and Ortiz shared zeal for the UN Mekong project, and both urged the Vice-President to look into it on his trip. If the river were harnessed to the use of human beings, Goldschmidt emphasized, rice production could be jumped 500 to 600 percent, and the overall results "would make TVA look like a minor operation."

They were talking to the right man. The Mekong project seized Lyndon Johnson's mind and emotions. Here was a chance to build something, to get Asia going the way of central Texas, to transform the law of history into the reality of bigger crops, schools, hospitals and, in the LBJ phrase, "an extra little helping in life." While in Southeast Asia, the Vice-President saw to it that he learned everything he could about the Mekong development program. Meeting with its planning committee in Bangkok, he let them know, "I am a river man. All my life I have been interested in rivers and their development." He listened to their talk of plans, endless plans, and he grew restless in a way he remembered long afterward. "There's been talk for years, planning for years. When do we get some action?" The Mekong project, so exciting in promise and affecting a critical part of Asia, was just the sort of program to fill out and underline the emerging lines of Lyndon Johnson's thinking about the world.

Later his intimate, William S. White, commented on that thinking as it had taken shape when the Vice-President returned from his mission for President Kennedy. White mentioned a number of points, but he stressed particularly that LBJ came back with a full-blown "Asia Doctrine," one that was "a big bite."

CHAPTER 15

Jackrabbit
Hunkered Up

*I*n the flush of his election triumph, in December 1964, President Johnson sat musing at the ranch about the world situation. It was a sparkling day, and for the most part his thoughts were sunny too. He skipped around the globe, finding cause for optimism in many areas, and he was particularly pleased that relations between Russia and the United States seemed to him less strained than at any time since World War II. Then an edge of exasperation entered his voice. There was Vietnam, of course, and that was "a mess." For twenty years the problems created by the collapse of the old French empire in Southeast Asia had been "a headache to the whole West," and inevitably the United States was involved. There was "no easy solution, none at all," for the dirty little war thousands of miles away. Abruptly the President stopped, went back to more pleasant matters.

Lyndon Johnson was not only reasonably satisfied with the state of the world; he was more than satisfied with the way he had been handling it. In the spring of 1964, when he had been asserting his mastery of the Presidency, Panama acted up and he liked the way he had managed to quiet down that trouble. When the long-running Cyprus problem brought a threat of war between two NATO countries, Greece and Turkey, he left the situation largely to the British and to his subordinates, and they kept Greece and Turkey from each other's throats. Other flare-ups, other handlings of them—LBJ was pleased that they had not really distracted him from the election and then the launching of the 1965 legislative drive in Congress.

On April 24, 1965, shortly after the voting rights bill went to the Hill and at the height of the maneuvering over Medicare, the ruling military junta in the Dominican Republic was attacked by rebel forces, with danger to the lives and property of United States citizens. The news reached the White House without warning, and it hit straight at the LBJ emotionalism concerning standing behind "the flag." He told the National Security Council: "It's just like the Alamo. Hell, it's like if you were down at that gate, and you were surrounded, and you damn well needed somebody. Well, by God, I'm going to go—and I·thank the Lord that I've got men who want to go with me, from McNamara right on down to the littlest private who's carrying a gun." Quickly he ordered Marines into the island, and built the number of armed forces to twenty-one thousand.

President Johnson publicly justified his intervention in the same tone he had used before the National Security Council. "I knew this: This was no time for indecision, or procrastination, or vacillation. The American people hadn't elected their President to dodge and duck and refuse to face up to the unpleasant. . . . We covet no territory. We seek no dominion over anyone. All we want to do is live in peace and be left alone if they will do it. But if they are going to put American lives in danger—where American citizens go that flag goes with them to protect them. . . . As a little boy I learned a declamation that I had to say in grade school. I don't remember all of it but a little of it is appropriate here this afternoon. It went something like this: 'I have seen the glory of art and architecture. I have seen the sun rise on Mont Blanc. But the most beautiful vision that these eyes ever beheld was the flag of my country in a foreign land.' " *

However beautiful the vision, the flag of his country was not the only consideration President Johnson had in his mind. The rebel forces included some Communists or Communist sympathizers. Observers disagreed concerning how many and how influential they were; to LBJ, that was not the point. There were *some;* they *might* take over the revolution. No more Cubas—the Communist issue made the President the readier to move all out against the rebellion, and to make clear to everyone that he would brook no further Castroism. In fact, shortly after the intervention his public statements began to sound as if the prevention of a Communist takeover was the primary reason for his action and the protection of life and property only secondary. He talked darkly of an "international conspiracy . . . [the people] who came in there to have a Communist seizure of the island," and declared, "We don't propose to sit here in our rocking chair with our hands folded and let the Communists set up any government in the Western Hemisphere."

---

* *The quotation, a bit garbled, is from a favorite schoolroom declamation of LBJ's boyhood days, the 1878 apostrophe to the flag by Senator George F. Hoar of Massachusetts.*

Whatever the point being made, Administration declarations about the Dominican episode were beginning to take a remarkable freedom with facts. At the time of the rebellion, the American ambassador in Santo Domingo, W. Tapley Bennett, had cabled: "American lives are in danger. . . . If Washington wishes, they [American troops] can be landed for the purpose of protecting evacuation of American citizens. I recommend immediate landings." In a speech of May 3 President Johnson transformed this cable, still in quotation marks, into " 'you must land troops immediately or . . . American blood will run in the streets.' " At a news conference of June 17 the President took the occasion to state "Some fifteen hundred innocent people were murdered and shot, and their heads cut off, and six Latin American embassies were violated and fired upon over a period of four days before we went in. As we talked to our ambassador to confirm the horror and tragedy and the unbelievable fact that they were firing on Americans and the American embassy, he was talking to us from under a desk while bullets were going through his windows and he had a thousand American men, women, and children assembled in the hotel who were pleading with their President for help to preserve their lives." The reports of most American newsmen were that no embassy had been fired upon, no one had been beheaded, no considerable loss of life was visible and no American civilian was hurt.

From the U.S. embassy in Santo Domingo came a list of "Communist and Castroist" leaders in the rebel movement. Three correspondents who had just returned from the Dominican Republic discussed the list in a television colloquy.

Dan Kurzman, Washington *Post:* "When American reporters pushed the American embassy for evidence that the Communists were taking over, they finally agreed to give us a whole list."

Tad Szulc, *New York Times:* "No, they didn't agree, they forced it on us."

Kurzman: "Okay. Well, first they gave us a list of fifty-three hard-core Communists. Later they gave us a thirteen-page treatise."

John Barnes, *Newsweek:* "Which they had distributed in the U.S. before."

Kurzman: "Apparently, so we couldn't check it on the spot. And then we started checking it. I found that of the three who were supposed to have been given jobs by the Caamaño government [a previous Dominican regime, from which a number of the rebel leaders came], one turned out to be a die-hard conservative, another was a naval officer known to be a conservative, and another—"

Szulc: "One of them was ten years old."

Kurzman: "No, let's not exaggerate. He was fifteen years old, and he'd never had an official job."

There was a further consideration. In subscribing to the Charter of the Organization of American States in 1948, the United States had agreed not to intervene in the affairs of another American country except in the case of "aggression" or a situation which endangered the peace, and then it would act only after consultation. The Dominican crisis had developed with such speed that it permitted little time to consult the leisurely Organization of American States. The first decision whether to send troops had to be made at about six P.M.—cocktail time along the Latin American embassy row. But President Johnson had not only failed to consult; he did not even inform the OAS. Its executive secretary heard of the action when he happened to switch on the television set.

If the Administration's handling of the Panamanian incident had created a ripple of criticism, the Dominican intervention brought stormy waves. In the Senate days, the Johnsons and Senator and Mrs. J. William Fulbright had been on good terms, though not intimates. Vice-President Johnson had urged President Kennedy to name Fulbright Secretary of State, and after the assassination Mrs. Fulbright helped Lady Bird Johnson with the sudden tasks of her new position. Now the chairman of the Senate Foreign Relations Committee publicly expressed strong and worried criticism of the President's policy in the Dominican Republic. He and other critics pointed to comments like that of Alberto L. Camargo, the former President of Colombia, who had always been a friend of the United States. Camargo, in Europe at the time, described the "general feeling" abroad "that a new and openly imperialistic policy in the style of Theodore Roosevelt had been adopted by the White House and that, if there was intervention with Marines in the Hemisphere, against unequivocal standards of law, one could only expect—in Asia, in Africa and wherever—new acts of force and, perhaps, the escalation of the cold war to the hot in a very short time. . . ."

President Johnson was annoyed but not upset. He turned to the polls; at the height of the intervention, the public was approving his Presidency overwhelmingly. He kept talking to congressional leaders of both parties, and most were behind his Dominican policy. He looked at results. The Dominican situation was heading to a point where a relatively free election would be held, and an anti-Communist, apparently stable government installed. Lyndon Johnson allowed that he rather thought Senator Fulbright owed him an apology. He saw in what was happening confirmation that the LBJ way in foreign policy was the effective way—for the Dominican Republic or for more serious problems like Vietnam which, by the time of the Dominican intervention, was becoming serious indeed.

Presidents Truman, Eisenhower and Kennedy had taken action in Southeast Asia, but largely with their left hands and in ways irrevocably committing them to very little. It was Dwight Eisenhower who established something of a policy. He believed it a matter of "importance" to the security of the United States that Communists be prevented from taking over South Vietnam lest a "crumbling process" in Asia be set in motion. Expressing his concern at a press conference in 1954, he added a phrase to the American vocabulary: "You have a row of dominoes set up, you knock over the first one, and what will happen to the last one is a certainty that it will go over very quickly."

Agreeing with this "domino theory," some advisers, military and civilian, urged President Eisenhower to use combat power. He rejected such a program, going along with the Army Chief of Staff, General Matthew B. Ridgway, and the Army Chief of Plans, General James M. Gavin, who opposed any policy that could involve American ground troops in Asia. While in the White House, Dwight Eisenhower aimed for what was coming to be called in Washington a "political" rather than a "military" solution. He sought to fend off a Communist takeover of South Vietnam by providing its government with economic aid and noncombat military help. The hope was that this would permit and encourage the government to build up its armed forces, fight off the Communists by itself, and undertake the economic and social reforms that would make it more popular and stable. President Eisenhower made a commitment, but a highly qualified one. In a public letter to President Diem of South Vietnam, he stated that the United States would continue to give noncombat aid, provided that the help was met by assurances of "performance" on the part of the South Vietnam government, both in building the military capability to resist "attempted subversion or aggression" and in "undertaking needed reforms."

President Kennedy agreed, in some measure, with President Eisenhower's domino theory about South Vietnam, and hence with his estimate of the area's importance to the United States. In 1963 JFK described the goal of American policy in Vietnam as the creation of "a stable government there, carrying on a struggle to maintain its national independence. We believe strongly in that. . . . In my opinion, for us to withdraw from that effort would mean a collapse not only of South Vietnam but Southeast Asia." He was even more cautious than President Eisenhower about a combat commitment. With a mind shaped by the policy attitudes of the new generation, JFK was skeptical of applying military force to a problem that was so largely political and social, or of easy dependence on the doctrine of fighting Communism, and he was heavily conscious of anti-colonial and race feelings in Asia. Fundamental to his approach was the French experience in Vietnam. If the war were again converted into what appeared to be a white man's colonial war, President Kennedy was certain, the United States would surely be on the losing side as the French had been. "In the final analysis, it is their war. They are the ones who have to win it or lose it. We can help them, we can give them equipment, we can send our men out there as advisers, but they have to win it—the people of Vietnam—against the Communists. . . . But I don't agree with those who say we should withdraw. That would be a great mistake."

As a result, in basic outline President Kennedy continued the Eisenhower measures. Avoiding the smallest commitment of U.S. combat power (a little such help was like "taking a drink. The effect wears off, and you have to take another"), he provided economic and military aid, particularly the latter, so that during his Administration the number of American military advisers in South Vietnam rose from about eight hundred to seventeen thousand. He also continued to try to exact, in return, performance on the part of the South Vietnamese government. But as the JFK years ended, South Vietnam was not safe from the Communists; its government was a caricature of stability and was doing little reforming. As Arthur Schlesinger, Jr., has commented, President Kennedy realized that he never really gave Vietnam "his full attention."

Lyndon Johnson, suddenly President and suddenly finding Vietnam along with a number of other matters on his desk, was just as ready not to give Vietnam full attention. Certainly he agreed with his predecessors' estimate of the importance of the area, and he shared their apprehension over the commitment of land forces in Asia. Stressing this second worry, he told an almost incredible story about his last visit to see General Douglas A. MacArthur in Walter Reed Hospital. The aged warrior might be a world-wide symbol of American belligerence in the Far East but as LBJ repeated the conversation, the general had counseled him, "Son, don't get into a land war in Asia." So President Johnson went along with the Eisenhower-Kennedy program, providing economic and military aid but restricting it to aid only.

There was only one thing wrong with the Eisenhower-Kennedy-Johnson policy for Vietnam: it was not working. It sought, fundamentally for reasons of American national security, to keep South Vietnam from falling to the Communists by bolstering its anti-Communist government and its armed forces and by encouraging social reforms. At times during the years 1954–63, at least parts of the program had seemed to be functioning well. That is why President Kennedy, shortly before his death, stated that he expected to be able to withdraw all American military advisers by 1965, and why President Johnson repeated the hope during the assassination weekend. But during the LBJ years, as 1964 gave way to 1965, the periods of optimism in the White House were increasingly few. It was becoming clear that either the United States would do something different or South Vietnam would fall. The problem could no longer be handled with hopeful in-between policies.

By early 1965 President Johnson had three realistic alternatives. One was for the United States to find the most graceful way to pull out. Another was some version of the enclave theory—the use of limited American combat power simply to occupy ports, airfields and military bases, and to help repulse attacks on areas held by the Saigon government, thus hoping to bolster the South Vietnam regime and to disintegrate Vietcong strength by demonstrating that they could not win a decisive victory. The third was to employ U.S. combat forces in the way that seemed best calculated to end the fighting on terms that would leave South Vietnam safe from Communist domination.

A great deal has been said about the influence of particular groups and individuals on President Johnson's Vietnam decisions, especially the military, the "military-industrial complex" and close advisers. It is certainly correct that LBJ continued to listen attentively to the military; he had no aversion to the "military-industrial complex" because he did not think of it as such. Clark Clifford and Abe Fortas were as important in discussions of Vietnam as of other international matters, and the President's official aides in foreign policy, Rusk, McNamara and Bundy, were consulted more than ever. All five of these men now favored American combat action in Vietnam, even if Secretary McNamara ("He's a perfesser type," the President would say in affectionate joshing) evinced considerable reluctance on occasion.

At the time some surprise was expressed in White House cir-

cles that Rusk and Bundy were proving tough talkers in international affairs. The surprise came from the assumption—which
certainly does not hold up in many cases—that "perfessers" are
fairly uniform types in foreign policy, and from overlooking facts
concerning the Secretary of State and the Special Assistant for
National Security Affairs. Secretary Rusk, although a man of
academic and foundation background, had spent much of his
formative foreign policy experience under Secretary of State John
Foster Dulles, who wanted to fight in Vietnam even before the
French were driven out. Special Assistant Bundy, in addition to
having been a professor and dean, was closely connected by birth
and upbringing to a Republican group which had long favored a
stiff stand against disturbers of the peace on the international
scene. His chief scholarly book is a collaborative work with Henry
L. Stimson, President Hoover's Secretary of State, who had sounded
the first call for American action against aggression in the Far
East as long ago as 1931 when Japan invaded Manchuria.

President Johnson listened closely to them all. He was also
listening to a lot of other people, some of whom were for withdrawal or enclave action. He was stalking the subject in his customary way. But to picture Lyndon Johnson's decisions as emerging from the capture of his thinking by particular individuals or
some group is to misunderstand the man. Faced with the alternative possibilities in Vietnam policy, his own general attitudes
toward international affairs were taking over. They might be
amended, speeded or slowed in execution by his consultations, but
above all they were confirmed by what he chose to hear from
everyone to whom he was listening.

To President Johnson the nub of the matter was that the South
Vietnam which was falling to Communists was in Asia, and Asia
was of prime importance. The immediate issue was "aggression."
A large and complex literature has grown up about whether what
was going on in Vietnam was in fact aggression in the customary
sense of the word. The Johnson Administration scarcely added to
the clarity of the debate; soon the State Department would issue
a white paper, *Aggression from the North*, which was a ringing
exercise in oversimplifications and questionable inferences. LBJ's
attitude toward such documents was a smile and the assumption
that these things were part of the complicated business of running
a complicated country. He had his own clear picture in mind.

Of course the Vietcong represented, in part, indigenous social
discontent in South Vietnam, and the Vietnamese Communists, in
North or South Vietnam, were not simply puppets of Red China

if they were puppets at all in any significant sense of the word. But for Lyndon Johnson, these facts also were not the point. He was sure Red China sought a Communist Asia; however complex the relationship between China and North Vietnam, China stood behind Ho Chi Minh's North Vietnam regime; Ho was helping the Vietcong with supplies and the infiltration of trained manpower. Just when he started to help them with a substantial quantity of regular troops remains a matter of dispute, and in his book *The Abuse of Power*, Theodore Draper has effectively challenged a number of Administration statements on that subject. Once again, to LBJ this was all a matter of detail and of the handling of public opinion. The essentials were plain to him: whether by supplies, infiltration or regular troops, North Vietnam—with Red China behind it—was an aggressor, and the aggression was succeeding. American policy faced another 1930's, when Hitler went on the march, or another 1950, when North Korea backed by Red China invaded southward. The United States could either stop the new aggression with armed force or step aside and allow a Munich. And Lyndon Johnson was no President to preside over what he considered a Munich.

All the while a subordinate factor, but one not insignificant in the President's thinking, was asserting itself. Two days before the 1964 presidential election, the Vietcong had leveled a mortar barrage against the Bien Hoa airfield in South Vietnam, killing five American military men, wounding fifty-six and destroying six B-57 bombers. On Christmas Eve they undertook a bolder stroke. In broad daylight they bombed an American officers' billet in downtown Saigon, killing two and wounding sixty-three, and television sets across the United States showed pictures of young American officers being pulled out of the smoking shambles. To Lyndon Johnson, these attacks were an outrage against the American flag. They were just the sort of thing he had in mind when he said he thought it important for the United States to indicate, loud and clear, that it was ready to stand up for its honor and its interests. Moreover, the Vietcong assaults, particularly the Saigon attack and its televised results, directed his attention to that subject for which he always had the keenest eye, the state of American public opinion.

The words "hawk" and "dove" were now coming into wide usage. They did as much to confuse as to classify, particularly in describing the attitudes of Administration officials. (To call McGeorge Bundy a hawk, for example, overlooked a number of parts of his thinking.) Yet in a rough way, the phrases did identify one strand of public opinion which was ready for powerful military moves in Vietnam, and another which was for withdrawal, or against the use of any combat power, or for its use only as part of some enclave program. The President disliked the words "hawk" and "dove," and even more the word "dawk." Nevertheless, his thinking about Vietnam was dawkish in the sense that he was ready to use combat force but in the form of limited war, and he was convinced that his chief problem in doing this would come not from the dove but from the hawk sentiment in the country. He had not failed to note that during the campaign of 1964 Barry Goldwater's greatest asset in the eyes of many voters seemed to have been his hawkish stance. He had also been impressed by the angry roar that went up when the television pictures of the Saigon attack were shown. I and a lot of other people doubted the President's estimate of relative hawk and dove sentiment, and believed that he was getting his impression primarily from Congress, which did have strong hawk tendencies at the time. But whatever the facts were, LBJ's judgment of public opinion played its role in shaping his policy toward Vietnam.

Under all the circumstances, President Johnson saw in the three alternative proposals for Vietnam little choice at all. To him, withdrawal was out of the question; it would be a disgraceful Munich, and one that would enormously increase the number of hawks. An enclave approach appealed to him because of its restricted use of American combat power; yet in his eyes it had overwhelming defects. It too would not satisfy basic points of the hawks, and he accepted the preponderant advice of the military that it would lead only to a protracted, ugly stalemate.

The third procedure—the direct use of military power in certain ways—seemed to the President to get to the heart of the matter. Bomb North Vietnam. This would keep the hawks off his back and declare, so loud and clear that it would be heard around the world, that the United States would not tolerate offenses to the American flag or aggression in Asia. The bombing, LBJ agreed with its proponents, would lead to the desired goals. It would strengthen the South Vietnamese government and stiffen the morale of the population; reduce the flow of men and supplies from North Vietnam to the Vietcong; and make so harshly plain to Hanoi the price of its actions that Ho would eventually be ready to negotiate on a basis acceptable to the President. Only the most extreme air-power devotees in the Pentagon believed that the war could be ended by bombing alone, and President Johnson accepted the corollary. United States ground troops would have to be used in the fighting.

Just what did this policy ultimately entail? The President

agreed with the calculation that Red China, though it might help indirectly more and more, would not turn the conflict into a Chinese-American struggle, and hence the most dreaded Asian land war—against China's millions—would be avoided. How long would it be before Ho was ready for LBJ-type negotiations? Here President Johnson was given estimates of the widest variation. He made his own guess, and arrived at the most monumental miscalculation of his career. He figured that the war would be over within twelve to eighteen months, before it could cut too deeply into American life. It would, he said, be like a "filibuster—enormous resistance at first, then a steady whittling away, then Ho hurrying to get it over with."

Early in 1965 the President made the final decision. For years he had been saying, "Never move up your artillery until you move up your ammunition." Now he saw to it that meticulous care went into planning the military action in Vietnam. "I want no Bay of Pigs," he ordered. Meanwhile he readied public opinion, kept up a stream of congressional conferences and waited for the right moment.

By February 1965 Vietnam had become a major item in the catalogue of American worries, and an influential part of the press and of congressional comment had the tone Lyndon Johnson wanted: it was pushing the President. Then the Vietcong made their contribution. On February 6, guerrillas struck Pleiku, 240 miles northeast of Saigon, the headquarters of South Vietnam's II Army Corps and the site of the American-operated airstrip at Camp Holloway. Four miles across the rolling Viet plateau, other Vietcong tossed into American billets homemade grenades wrapped in bamboo or placed in beer cans. The toll of the attacks: eight American dead, one hundred and eight wounded. The television coverage was extensive and infuriating.

President Johnson came into the hastily assembled National Security Council meeting clutching the latest Pleiku casualty list. "I've had enough of this," he said, and he spoke in the manner of a man who was sure that a lot of other Americans had more than enough. He went on, talking with his habitual emphasis on the loud and the clear in foreign policy. "The worst thing we could possibly do would be to let this go by. It would be a big mistake. It would open the door to a major misunderstanding."

Twelve hours after the Pleiku raids, forty-nine U.S. A-4 Skyhawks and F-8 Crusaders streaked off air carriers in the South China Sea, heading with their bombs for Donghoi, a major staging point for Communist guerrillas one hundred and sixty miles above the 17th parallel dividing North and South Vietnam. Twenty-one days later the President ordered continuous bombing of North Vietnam, no longer in retaliation against raids but "to force the North Vietnamese into negotiation." Within four months American troops were engaged in the full fighting, offensive and defensive.

No sooner had the bombing taken the United States into the Vietnam War than a good many influential people wanted it to get out. The pressure came to the White House from UN Secretary-General U Thant, the Soviet Union, General de Gaulle, discreet emissaries of the Western powers, neutral nations, congressmen and a flood of letters. My own mail increased fivefold, much of it suggesting, more or less directly, that by continuing to work for Lyndon Johnson I was party to a kind of frontier massacre.

The mail disturbed me. Ever since the Vietnam issue became important in the Johnson Administration, I had been troubled. I was satisfied that the United States could not simply withdraw. I was partially persuaded, but only partially, that holding South Vietnam was important to American national security. Beyond these two considerations, the basic trend of President Johnson's thinking about world problems now seemed to me full of disastrous possibilities.

Like much of the general criticism, the burden of the mail coming to me was, Why doesn't the President make more of an effort to negotiate? I shared the concern, but at least I knew the actual reason. Lyndon Johnson did not make more of an effort to negotiate because throughout the earlier stages of the war, he did not want to negotiate. Now that the United States was in the conflict, he was more eager than ever to rid himself of the Vietnam "mess." But the mess was there, and according to his foreign policy ideas, there was nothing to do except fight until the North Vietnamese "let their neighbors alone." He did not believe, certainly at this stage, that negotiations would help at all toward that end.

On many private occasions, the President spelled out his attitude. The Communist military position in South Vietnam was strong, the South Vietnam-American position weak. As a veteran poker-playing politician, he saw no reason why Hanoi would want to negotiate at this time except to insist on terms that would give them control of South Vietnam. The more he studied the peace feelers, the more he was convinced that he was right. All of them came through third parties. If Hanoi "seriously" wanted to talk peace, LBJ declared, it could reach him or an appropriate American official in "five minutes." He was not getting a single such indication; "no one in authority over there has said to me, 'I want to sit down and talk.' It takes two to negotiate." At a Cabinet session in the Spring of 1965, after Senator Jacob Javits of New York had made a speech urging more effort to negotiate, President Johnson twisted in his chair irritably. "Who the hell am I going to negotiate with—Senator Javits?" His attitude was strengthened by a man whose judgment he greatly respected and whom he did not fail to consult on a number of occasions. Dwight Eisenhower said to him, "When I hear the talk about negotiations, I wonder why people don't recognize that there must be someone to negotiate with, and there must be someone willing to negotiate."

Of course, the opinion that the other side did not want genuine negotiations was based on the President's estimate, and that of advisers like Secretary Rusk, concerning the nature of the peace feelers coming in (Rusk publicly spoke of having judged them by his "antennae"). Influential sources urged President Johnson to try negotiations anyhow and see if he could not get someplace. What did he have to lose, they argued, and the alternative was more of this grisly war.

But Lyndon Johnson thought he had plenty to lose. He was convinced that a seeming eagerness for negotiations on his part would worsen the situation at home and abroad. In Asia, the North Vietnamese would believe that the United States lacked the will to stick it out. The confidence of the Saigon government would be undermined, and other Southeast Asian nations would wonder too. At home, his hurrying to the conference table would produce a tide of hawk feeling that would be difficult to control. Still worse in all these respects would be the kind of negotiations which seemed to him highly probable under the circumstances, negotiations that failed. At Camp David the President leaned back, stared out into the dark forest and observed solemnly, "The need now is not for negotiations but to get the message across to them—leave your neighbor alone and we can all have peace and get ahead with our business."

Still the criticism kept mounting, especially on the point of negotiations. Much of it came from people who linked President Johnson's lack of enthusiasm for the conference table to a general attitude of bulldozing militarism—"an outmoded imperialism," in the words of Senator Wayne Morse of Oregon, "which ignores the fact that Asia's real problem is food and clothing and schools." Lyndon Johnson was infuriated by this kind of talk. Was there anyone who was more of an apostle of food and clothing and schools for people everywhere? he demanded to know.

McGeorge Bundy was scheduled to speak on American foreign policy at the Johns Hopkins University in Baltimore on April 5, 1965. Minutes before he took the podium, he learned that the President had accepted an open-end Hopkins invitation for April 7. LBJ had decided "to get a few things said," and to say them himself. Frantically the Special Assistant reorganized his remarks to confine them largely to comments on Vietnam critics, leaving the path clear for the boss.

Two hours before President Johnson delivered his address, he inserted a passage stating his readiness for "unconditional discussions" of peace. The offer was for unconditional talks with the "governments concerned" thus excluding the Vietcong, the chief military force that the United States was fighting; the negotiation situation was left substantially where it had been. But to appease his critics, LBJ had altered his tone.

The major portion of the address was no mere gesture of placation. It articulated the full-blown Asia Doctrine—the repulse of aggression, then the remaking of the nations. His arms out in messianic appeal, the President called for a concert of Asian countries which, with the leadership and help of the United States, would undertake sweeping programs of economic and social improvement.

The law of history marched with his phrases. What do "the ordinary men and women of North Vietnam and South Vietnam—of China and India—of Russia and America" want? "They want what their neighbors also desire: food for their hunger; health for their bodies; a chance to learn; progress for their country; and an end to the bondage of material misery." And they would find these things through the path of "peaceful association."

Lyndon Johnson was with them, he wanted them to know. He intended to expand and speed up the sending of American farm surpluses to "the needy in Asia." He proposed a "greatly expanded" co-operative program for social upbuilding in Southeast Asia, with the aid of the United States, the United Nations and, "I would hope," all industrialized nations, including the Soviet Union. He would "shortly name a special team of outstanding, patriotic, distinguished Americans" to plan the U.S. participation. "The vast Mekong River can provide food and water and power on a scale to dwarf even our own TVA." Of course the end of the Vietnam fighting would be "necessary for final success. But we cannot and must not wait for peace to begin this job."

At the close, the President referred directly to his 1961 experience in Southeast Asia and, quite emotionally, to roots that reached much further back. "We often say how impressive power is," Lyndon Johnson told his audience, his voice taking on a low, highly personal quality. But guns and bombs, rockets and warships, however necessary "to protect what we cherish," are actually "witness to human folly.

"A dam built across a great river is impressive.

"In the countryside where I was born, and where I live, I have seen the night illuminated, and the kitchens warmed, and the homes heated, where once the cheerless night and the ceaseless cold held sway. And all this happened because electricity came to our area along the humming wires of the REA. Electrification of the countryside—yes, that, too, is impressive.

"A rich harvest in a hungry land is impressive. The sight of healthy children in a classroom is impressive. These—not mighty arms—are the achievements which the American Nation believes to be impressive."

If the doctrine was authentic LBJ, the presentation did not lack the Johnsonian touches of reassuring the right people, of concern for Congress, of helter-skelter, of plans vaulting into the grandiose. Remaking the world cost money, a lot of which Congress had to appropriate and more of which, hopefully, the world would contribute. The naming of a man with the proper appeal to head the program was important. In the last hasty decisions about the Johns Hopkins speech, the President decided that it was essential to identify the director of the plan then and there. He considered one man desirable above all: Eugene R. Black, the urbane New York banker, former president of the World Bank, a figure of esteem in international finance and diplomatic circles, approved by liberals in Congress because of his broadly internationalist views and admired by conservatives as a planner of stern fiscal standards.

Several hours before the Baltimore speech McGeorge Bundy placed a telephone call to Black and reached him in the executive dining room of the Chase National Bank, where he was lunching with Henry Ford II. Black's reply was firm. He was sorry, but he could not take on the job; he was already hopelessly overloaded. Bundy persisted, Black persisted. Finally Bundy said, "Here's someone who wants to talk to you."

The President came on the phone, but still the banker backed away. Lyndon Johnson declared he wanted Black to realize just how important this was, and while the lunch in the Chase dining room went cold, he read his entire speech over the phone. Catching the drift of the conversation, Henry Ford II whispered to Black that he just could not turn down President Johnson. The banker agreed.

Hurtled to Washington the next day in *Air Force One,* Black walked into a hastily assembled meeting of Cabinet officers and White House aides. The President introduced him, announced that Mr. Black would now explain the Asian development plan, settled back in his chair.

Black got by, mostly by asking questions himself for about two hours, and then LBJ called in the press. A reporter wanted to know if the President had named the "special team of outstanding, patriotic, distinguished Americans" mentioned in the Hopkins speech.

A long finger went out to Eugene Black. "There's my team, right there."

No group was ever named. The plan to expand the sending of U.S. farm surpluses to Asia faded away as well; it had been suggested before and always dropped, largely because the farm blocs in the United States and other Western countries feared it would depress world food prices. Yet the LBJ emotion and method, however chaotic their path, did get things going. Within sixty days Eugene Black, in concert with the UN, had a program ready, and the President soon obtained from Congress $89 million as an initial American appropriation. That fall the first meeting of the Asian Development Bank was held in Bangkok. Within eighteen months Takeshi Watanabe, the bank's Japanese president, could announce a total capitalization of $1.1 billion, a membership of nineteen Asian states and eleven non-Asian nations in addition to the United States, and a scattering of projects actually under way.

A seed had been sown, whatever the climate it would face. As for Lyndon Johnson, he was as sure as ever: "That Asia—things can be done there."

Shortly after the Johns Hopkins speech, on May 23, 1965, David Wise, the White House correspondent of the New York *Herald Tribune,* published an article over which the copy desk put the words " 'Credibility Gap.' " Probably this was the first use of the phrase in print. But the headline writer put it in quotation marks; it had certainly been expressed before, and the thought was in the air.*

A sharply pointed joke was being told in Washington, includ-

---

* For connoisseurs of famous phrases, it should be noted that a number of Washington reporters believe that "credibility gap" received its principal popularization from a later article (December 5, 1965) by Murrey Marder of the Washington Post. Marder devoted almost two columns to a detailed analysis of the "growing doubt and cynicism concerning Administration pronouncements" and wrote: "The problem could be called a credibility gap."

ing some Johnsonian enclaves and not excluding an occasional closed-door recitation in the White House. "Do you know when Lyndon Johnson is telling the truth?" the person would ask. "Well, when he goes like this"—finger beside nose—"he's telling the truth. When he goes like this"—pulling an ear lobe—"he's telling the truth. When he goes like this"—stroking the chin—"he's telling the truth." Then: "But when he starts moving his lips, that's when he's not telling the truth."

At work again were all the troubles of President Johnson in creating public trust. They may have started during the days of his emphasis on domestic problems, but they intensified greatly after he undertook important moves in foreign policy—to some extent as a result of his anything-goes statements during the Dominican crisis, to a much greater degree when the United States entered the fighting war in Vietnam. In foreign or domestic affairs, the widespread sense of a credibility gap came in part from the same facts: Lyndon Johnson's reputation as the incessant politician; his conspicuous delight in the secretive and the devious; his sky-high barnstorming when he got going before a sympathetic audience; his undeniable habit of simply playing fast and loose with facts. Yet there were additional specific reasons why foreign affairs, and most especially Vietnam, magnified vastly the national feeling of credibility gap.

There were, perhaps most basically, that Tonkin resolution rushed through as the election battle of 1964 got under way and those Lyndon Johnson statements concerning Vietnam made during the campaign. Some of the President's friends might be outraged by charges that these were evidence of deceit, or at least of a deliberate blurring of the truth. They asked, Was it not true—and it was true—that during the campaign the Vietnam War was not to the fore of the President's thinking; that the likelihood of a Communist victory was not as great in 1964 as later, the President in 1964 had as yet made no decision to enter the war, and if he took steps to ready the possible deployment of American forces, this was a procedure any responsible Chief Executive would have ordered; that the Tonkin resolution, with its broad grant of future authorization to make war, had precedent in the Presidencies of Dwight Eisenhower and John Kennedy, men not generally assailed as tricksters; and that during the campaign, when LBJ spoke of his opposition to "going north" in Vietnam and attacked Goldwater as trigger-happy, at least on one occasion he qualified his statements by phrases which indicated he was describing his thinking "just for the moment" and "at this stage of the game." Defenders went beyond these indubitable facts to challenge: Even without qualifiers in speeches, was it not common sense to assume that a President cannot bind himself for the future, when circumstances may change? And apart from all other considerations, was it not traditional—and traditionally understood—that candidates speak in the heat of a campaign with a good deal of oratorical license, especially on such subjects as being friends of peace? Explanations and defenses there might be; Lyndon Johnson was not exonerated in a good deal of American public opinion, and a glance backward helps to explain why.

In the final stage of the presidential campaign of 1916, Woodrow Wilson also swung to peace as his keynote, assailed the Republicans as "the war party," brought crowds to their feet with declarations like "I am not expecting this country to get into war." The most successful slogan of the Wilson forces, probably invented by the publicity man for the Democratic National Committee, Robert W. Woolley, was: "He kept us out of the war."* Four months later President Wilson went before Congress and asked for a declaration of war against Germany. In the campaign of 1940 Franklin Roosevelt told a Boston audience with grave emphasis, "And while I am talking to you mothers and fathers, I give you one more assurance. I have said this before, but I shall say it again and again and again: Your boys are not going to be sent into any foreign wars." Fourteen months later American boys were fighting in Europe and Asia.

These statements were seized upon by detractors of Presidents Wilson and Roosevelt, yet overall they did little damage to the men during or after their Administrations. The two Presidents were generally liked, admired and trusted, and the statements were taken more as an expression of hope and a bit of campaign flummery than of innate or serious dishonesty. Whatever the tone of some of his speeches and the activities of his backers, Woodrow Wilson never personally and clearly committed himself against intervention in the European conflict. Franklin Roosevelt did not "send" American boys into a foreign war; he responded to the Pearl Harbor attack. There was also the important matter of context. Candidate Wilson, who had just led a preparedness movement from the White House, and Candidate Roosevelt, who had been rallying the nation against the threat of fascism, were hardly men you would vote for if you wanted a strongly anti-war candidate.

The campaign of 1964 was another matter. Americans might be preparing to vote for Lyndon Johnson in record numbers, but

---

* *In one of the unending quirks of history, Woolley turns out to be the grandfather of Lynda Johnson's husband, Charles S. Robb.*

he was not generally liked, admired and trusted. A clear-cut foreign policy issue had emerged. Goldwater urged the use of American military forces in Vietnam, including the bombing of North Vietnam and the bolstering of the South Vietnamese forces with American combat troops. LBJ denounced these proposals as dangerous warmongering. If he used qualifying clauses on occasion, it remained a fact that the unmistakable inference from his speeches was a pledge against intervention in the shooting war. He also did not hesitate to declare categorically, as he did in Pittsburgh on October 27, 1964, "There can be and will be, as long as I am President, peace for all Americans. . . ." The whole context of the election of 1964 was radically different from 1916 and 1940. A sensible person wanting to stay out of World War I and World War II conceivably could have voted for Woodrow Wilson and Franklin Roosevelt or for their opponents. A sensible person wanting to avoid combat commitment in Vietnam had to vote for Lyndon Johnson—or, as many did, against Barry Goldwater.

With the development of President Johnson's Vietnam policy after the election, its sheer nature brought out his worst instincts. In a very real sense he had adopted a compromise program, leaving large numbers of both hawks and doves unhappy. More forthright political leaders than Lyndon Johnson, attacked from both sides, have been known to try to be all things to all men. In a way, Lyndon Johnson's decision to fight in Vietnam was the logical consequence of the policies of past Presidents. In a way he was upholding American commitments. In a way . . . and LBJ, being LBJ, transformed those facts to all the way. It was certainly true that Presidents Eisenhower and Kennedy had publicly stated the serious American concern with South Vietnam's "struggle to maintain its national independence," to use again the JFK phrase. It was not true that either had been ready to commit combat forces to achieve that end. It was certainly true that the United States was a member of the Pacific defense organization, SEATO, which pledged all signators to consult about military aid when requested to do so by a member faced with a threat to its independence. It was not true, as President Johnson repeatedly stated or implied, that SEATO membership required the United States, on penalty of bad faith, to send bombs and troops to defend a signatory.

The problem of negotiations was the sorest temptation. With the utmost sincerity the President believed that for the good of the United States, he should make no moves toward negotiations in circumstances he believed unpropitious. He could have explained his thinking to the public, at least in part, or avoided saying much of anything on the subject by diplomatic doubletalk. But both of these procedures entailed political risks, and they did not ringingly present Lyndon Johnson as the man of peace who, in order to fulfill his responsibilities as Chief Executive, was forced to fight a war. He succumbed fully to the temptations of the situation. He sought to exorcise the whole tortuous problem of peace feelers by trying to obliterate them. Out from the Oval Office, or from subordinates, would go the statements that no "meaningful" peace feelers had been received, when in cold fact feelers had come which might have been of considerable meaning.

Beneath everything else, and fundamental to the creation of the sense of credibility gap, was Lyndon Johnson's conception of the role of the Chief Executive in important matters of international affairs. If he believed that a President had a certain right to "protect his options" in all decisions foreign or domestic, where war and peace were concerned he extended the right even to the point of wanting to cut off press speculation about his coming moves. Bill Moyers once stated the LBJ attitude: "It is very important for a President to maintain up until the moment of decision his options, and for someone to speculate days or weeks in advance that he's going to do thus and thus is to deny to the President the latitude he needs in order to make, in the light of existing circumstances, the best possible decision in grave matters affecting the national security."

Newspapermen might answer, as James Reston did: "If all presidential options are to be protected from speculation until the very last minute, what redress will there be the day after the President has opted to dispatch the Marines, or bomb Hanoi, or publish a decision to wage war all over Southeast Asia as he deems necessary? These are hard questions, and the answers are not that the Commander in Chief must telegraph all his punches in advance. But at the same time, the doctrine of no-speculation-before-official-publication . . . is something new in the catalogue of presidential privilege." New or not, President Johnson claimed and sought to exercise that privilege.

He went further. Well before Lyndon Johnson entered the White House, in his own mind he had erected the Presidency into a near-omniscient, almost unassailable institution so far as the ultimate questions of foreign policy are concerned. The President was "the only President you have." The safety of the nation was at stake. The President studied the situation, sought advice, arrived at a decision. He should be supported by the people of the United States. To withhold this backing was to split the unity of the country and to weaken the national effort at a time of confrontation with potential or actual enemies. Worse still, it gave aid to hostile forces.

To most congressmen, bipartisanship in foreign policy has meant the effort to reach a broad agreement on essentials and the avoidance of narrowly political attacks. To Lyndon Johnson as Senate Democratic Leader, bipartisanship had come close to meaning that the President's decisions were not to be questioned or criticized. He had not only believed this; to a considerable extent he practiced it during the years he led the Democrats in the Senate while Republican Dwight Eisenhower occupied the White House. As President, LBJ took great pride in the attitude he had maintained. He reminisced, "People said to me, 'Why don't you get up and criticize?' I replied, 'We ought not to do anything that might be misunderstood by foreign countries. He is the only President we have, and I am going to support that President, because if I make him weaker I make America weaker.'" Lyndon Johnson's type of patriotism could take wing on this subject. "When they lead your boy down to that railroad station to send him into boot camp and put a khaki uniform on him to send him some place where he may never return, he doesn't debate foreign policy. They send you to defend the flag, and you go."

Once LBJ entered the White House, his conception of the Presidency in relation to international affairs received the most powerful kind of reinforcement. Now *he* was the only President the country had. *He* had a right to expect support. As American participation in the Vietnam War heightened, it was becoming clear how reluctant President Johnson was to approve the right of dissent against presidential decisions in foreign policy. He did not want to approve the right for the simple reason that he did not really believe in it. Or to put the matter more precisely, he believed in the right but did not believe that it should be exercised.

Thinking and feeling this way, he was all the more ready to suppress or distort facts. The critics were engaged in an impropriety that hurt the country, and a little impropriety in handling them was his privilege and even more, his duty. He felt this especially in dealing with reporters, whom for so long he had considered an enemy force. And, whether dealing with the press or other molders of public opinion, he felt this with added force as a result of his conviction that he would never be given a fair break because he was Lyndon Johnson of Johnson City, Texas. More than once during 1965 LBJ said in varying forms, with an acridness touched by wistfulness, "I don't think I will ever get credit for anything I do in foreign policy because I didn't go to Harvard."

Critics so unfair were critics who deserved to be—in fact, had to be—maneuvered.

Another American war, the third in twenty-five years, in far-off rice paddies amid baffling Asians, under an unloved and none-too-trusted President, bringing fears of a nuclear World War III— as 1965 went on, the American people were marching into the Vietnam War with few banners flying. That summer I ran into a senator from the Far West and asked how people in his state were taking the war. "I guess the same way they're taking it in your part of the country," he replied. "They're taking it."

Lyndon Johnson was taking it too, in a gamut of moods. At times he was glum and irritable at this foreign mess, the worst of a whole bunch of them which kept shoving their way into the proper business of an American President. "I don't know what will be written about my Administration. Nothing really seems to go right from early in the morning until late at night. When I was a boy growing up, we never had these issues of our relations with other nations so much. We didn't wake up with Vietnam and have Santo Domingo for lunch and the Congo for dinner."

At other moments the Vietnam decision, now finally made and being executed, brought a shoulders-back sense of command, a feeling of the Churchillian role. More and more President Johnson wanted phrases like "the defender at the gates of freedom" in his speeches. He told an aide, "I know some of you think I get a little irritated at times, but it's always about minor things. When the bullets start whizzing around my head, that's when I'm calmest." And it was true that, on the subject of the Vietnam War, Lyndon Johnson dropped a good deal of the Lazy-L manner and old-shoe language and spoke and acted with a low-voiced gravity and firmness.

Most of the time he was neither the indomitable Churchill at the gate nor the misused leader. The critics—hawks and doves and semihawks and semidoves—hammered away more and more. All of this he took, amid the spurts of anger, as a test of his political skill. He had adopted the "dawk" policy; it was good for the country, he was sure, and it was sound politically. He would build around it the same kind of consensus he had constructed for his domestic program. Expecting more troubles in public opinion, and also expecting to conquer them, he grinned and said, "I'm like a jackrabbit hunkered up in a storm."

The scene was not all discouraging. In the earlier stage of American participation in the Vietnam War, the LBJ general approval rating in the polls remained high. On the Vietnam issue itself, polls and the other usual indicators all told a similar story: the public might not be waving flags, but at least 60 percent of it was saying that it favored the Johnson policy. Some indicators suggested that President Johnson's dawk war program might actually be increasing his overall support. At this stage it could have been losing only pockets of those who had voted for him in 1964, while winning over a large number of Goldwater hawks who were happy to find the United States at last in the fighting.

So LBJ went to work to convert or at least mollify the dissidents, hawk and dove. He called critical reporters into the Oval Office for long talks about Vietnam, spiced with an occasional hint that a newsman might suddenly find himself endowed with an important exclusive. He dispatched aides for "some good talk" behind closed doors with influential groups. Above all, he saw congressmen at breakfast, lunch and dinner, and at a long series of White House receptions.

Virtually all the senators and representatives and their spouses were entertained with an attention to the human ego unprecedented in the long history of White House cajoling. The heart of the effort came when the President introduced Secretaries Rusk and McNamara for background talks on Vietnam. "Ask anything you want, classified information or not," Lyndon Johnson would say. "You can also ask *me* anything you want, and I'll answer it."

For each question to the President, a tailored answer. The Republican senator from Pennsylvania, Hugh Scott, prided himself on his Phi Beta Kappa key, his seventeen honorary degrees, his service in UNESCO and the NATO parliamentary conference. Would the South Vietnamese prove a "viable" fighting force? Senator Scott asked the President.

Statesman to statesman, Lyndon Johnson ran down the statistics of South Vietnamese casualties ("Compared to our population, these casualties are three hundred and fifty thousand. The Vietnamese are a valiant force for freedom"), and discussed the partially classified Saigon plans for further mobilization.

Senator Ross Bass, the Democrat from Tennessee, was proud of his log-cabin birth in Giles County, his past presidency of the Association of United Postmasters of Tennessee, his membership in the American Legion "40 and 8," his reputation as "just folks." He asked the President, "Why do we permit all these coups in South Vietnam? Why don't we move in, pick a man and say to the South Vietnamese, 'Look, this is the guy we want, and he's staying in charge'?"

Now Lyndon Johnson was just folks too. "Let me tell you about the time we needed a good sheriff down in Blanco County in my state. We got a guy to run and he was great for the first two years. Then he got himself a fancy car and the next thing you know he was keeping a woman, and we couldn't get rid of him. If I can't get rid of a sheriff, how can I get rid of a government in South Vietnam?"

Senator Bass chuckled appreciatively. Senator Scott came out of his session announcing, "I have had the benefit of the most candid kind of briefing. For the first time in my experience, the President of the United States not only gave us a briefing but invited questions which he answered himself. I think this is better than the equivalent British system, with its question period on the floor of Parliament. We were not only complimented by the procedure, but immensely helped because we posed to the President rather pointed questions, and received answers with which I found myself in agreement."

Meanwhile, the ladies had been with Mrs. Johnson. She offered her special treat, the tour of the family quarters, and her own occasional conversational remarks about her husband's Vietnam policy. Host and hostess overlooked no gesture. Guests were invited in flatteringly small groups. People who might not have been on a strictly protocol list were included. The Honorable Kenneth B. Keating, the New York Republican rendered an ex-senator by Robert Kennedy in 1964, was invited and toasted by the President. He went away musing: "When the Republicans were in the White House, I didn't even get a square meal." A representative or senator seeking the bathroom might find himself being escorted by Lyndon Johnson, and not to a guest facility but to the private quarters. One congressman reported nonchalantly to his wife, "In case you're interested, the President uses Ipana toothpaste."

And amid all the pleasantries, there was the occasional intimation of the whip. During another presidential escort, LBJ fell into conversation with a Republican senator who was known for his delight in spreading word of the White House mood in the Senate chamber. "You're getting solid support from our side," the senator remarked. "What about the people in your party—the cut-and-run boys?"

The host's face turned grim. "The world shouldn't be misled by differences of opinion. I'm going to talk to those boys—personally —every one of them."

CHAPTER 16

The President and the Intellectuals

*I*n February 1965 the White House Social Secretary, Mrs. Bess Abell, stopped by my office. She had been looking ahead on the White House calendar, Mrs. Abell said. Spring would soon be here and how about doing something "cultural" that would go well with the season? After all, the Kennedys had made a great hit with the dinner for the Nobel Prize winners and the Casals concert. Of course we didn't want to imitate the Kennedys, but could I think of something different along that line?

Bess Abell had a way of talking about "culture" that made me wince, and at the moment my mind was far away, concentrated on a quite different type of project for the President. But her inquiry brought to the fore several thoughts that had been in the back of my head. I was more interested than ever in having the White House throw its prestige behind the recognition and encouragement of an elite of talent in the United States. A Great Society of Medicare, air pollution controls and similar reforms was fine, but the beginning of President Johnson's legislative successes in these fields simply made more glaring how little the nation was doing to bring intellectual and artistic creativity closer to the daily lives of its people. I also had not lost my urge to help in trying to establish some degree of rapport between the President and Metroamerica, and obviously that purpose would be furthered by a demonstration of White House interest in the arts. Then too, my office contained its own pressure group—my chief assistant at this time, Dr. Barbaralee D. Diamonstein, a gifted and dedicated young woman with a special flair for the arts. (Later she served as special assistant for cultural affairs in New York City and there pioneered the trend for municipal outdoor exhibitions of large-scale sculpture by arranging the Tony Smith show in Bryant

Park.) For weeks Miss Diamonstein had been urging me to give greater attention to ways by which the White House could encourage the cultural renaissance occurring in many American communities. And withal, there was the matter of the newly established National Council on the Arts, which could use a little projecting into public awareness.

All of these considerations coalesced in my mind as Bess Abell talked in my office, and I suggested a specific project: a "White House Festival of the Arts," an outgoing, warm, colorful White House salute to the Americans who were building up the museums and symphonies in the local communities, organizing reading and discussion groups, staging their own arts festivals. Let's ignore all the elements of phoniness and status-seeking in these activities, I added. There are better and worse ways to strive for status and to be phony, and there is also something genuine and healthy in all this.

The festival could be appropriately Johnsonian as an across-the-board representation of many of the arts. It would give the new council a prominent and appropriate role, and associate the White House with the interest that was exciting the suburban communities. In the way of such conversations, the more I talked the more enthusiastic I became. I saw the halls of the White House covered with contemporary American paintings, the South Lawn alive with sculpture, composers' works being performed in the beautiful old rooms, and writers reading from their works beneath portraits of John Adams and Abraham Lincoln. The President of the United States would greet his guests with the appropriate and convincing attitude: A lot of this is not my kettle of fish but it is live and interesting and part of the America of the 1960's and the White House is happy to join in celebrating and encouraging it, as it is glad to salute the vitality of our people in all fields.

Bess Abell liked the "splash" such a festival would make. But the more specific I became, the more she pulled back. "Writers and artists," she said. "These people can be troublesome." I shifted from the subject and went on to a routine matter that mutually concerned us.

In the LBJ White House of this period, autonomy reigned—or rather, autonomy was the polite word for it. The spokes ran to the center of the wheel, as was said, and if you wanted something done you moved along your own spoke, avoiding other ones which you knew might well foul the machinery. As soon as I got a pressing matter out of the way, I had a talk with Roger L. Stevens, the Special Assistant for the Arts and chairman of the National Council on the Arts. He liked the suggestion, and I sent a memorandum to the President recommending a White House Festival of the Arts.

   In view of the purpose later widely attributed to the festival, and the insistence that it was hastily put together to blunt the criticism of President Johnson's foreign policy among intellectuals and artists, it should be noted that the memorandum was sent to the President on February 25, 1965, before he ordered systematic bombing of North Vietnam and before the Dominican intervention, and hence before there was any great outcry against his foreign policy. The original date suggested for the festival was April 12, the day before Jefferson's birthday (LBJ was already scheduled to be out of town on the birth date), which gave a little more than six weeks for preparations, an ample period with the special resources of the White House. The festival was not directed primarily to intellectuals and artists. The basic guest list, the memo stated, would consist of "the people who have been encouraging the arts in their local communities. These would be the chairmen of existing state commissions on the arts (about twenty-two are functioning) and the heads of representative local symphony associations, art societies, museum boards, etc." In further consonance with this approach, the presentations at the festival would be confined to the major interest being shown in communities around the country, contemporary works by Americans.

   The purposes of the festival presented to the President had nothing to do with foreign policy. "There has never been a White House Festival of the Arts," the memo ran. "Consequently, this would be an especially striking way of stating the interest of the White House in all the arts" at a time when that interest was becoming important in the lives of large numbers of Americans. It went on to argue that the festival "would underline the new National Council on the Arts because the members would be prominent throughout the day."

   Nothing in the memo suggested that Lyndon Johnson was supposed to emerge faunlike as a devotee of the arts. In the manner of the LBJ White House, the memo included a "suggested scenario" (the word "scenario" was *de rigueur* in the days of Jack Valenti), outlining just what would happen when and what the role of the President and the First Lady would be. The festival would run from 10 A.M. to 10 P.M. Mrs. Johnson's participation was left to her own inclinations; the President's was pinpointed. He would appear at 6 P.M. for the reception and for his brief remarks, which I planned to draft as ones in which he would express a flexible Presidency, with the Chief Executive encouraging new and worthwhile trends in the country whether or not he had a particular personal interest in them. He would eat buffet dinner with the guests and then, if the world stayed quiet long enough, remain for the evening's presentations.

The memo came back with notes by both the President and Mrs. Johnson. The First Lady was enthusiastic, especially about the considerable attention given to drama in the plan. She was no less Lady Bird in another notation: the effort required for executing such a festival properly would be the kind that "works & shoves, & *works* & *shoves*." LBJ scrawled: "I like this Ask Bill M & Jack [Valenti] to see me about it before I take final action—"

Just what happened thereafter I do not know except that Valenti was strongly supporting the project. Such an unusually long time passed without a definite answer from President Johnson that I asked him whether the delay meant he wanted the project abandoned. His reply was no, but final clearance did not come until May 22. Valenti and I got together to fix a new date. In view of the President's schedule, the latest feasible day before full summer was June 14. We did not want to carry the festival over into July or August because many of the key guests were likely to be out of the country, and since it was obviously desirable to use the summer beauty of the White House grounds as a backdrop, we could not delay until the fall.

What was President Johnson's motive in approving the festival? Of course I have no way of being sure. No doubt he thought it would help ingratiate him with people interested in the arts. But my distinct impression is that he originally reacted favorably to the suggestion largely because, to use once more his phrase for such matters, he considered it a "nice thing" to do. Between the time of his first interest in the festival and the final approval, he had ordered systematic bombing of North Vietnam, and the criticism had flared in intellectual and artistic circles. Perhaps then he started thinking of the festival in terms of a tool to quiet opposition to the war. But I doubt whether this was ever a major consideration; he simply did not take the festival that seriously. Overall LBJ appeared to think of it as a pleasant day, the sort of thing a President ought to do in view of all the interest in art around the country, one that would particularly please the ladies, and that was that.

May 22, the okay; June 14, the festival—only twenty-two days. Never had the leisurely world of the arts had it so furiously. At that time my staff consisted of Miss Diamonstein and two secretaries, Mrs. Lenora G. Haag and Mrs. Patricia C. Siemien, who once again proved how much more than secretaries they were.

"Well," said Mrs. Siemien in her wry way, "artists were never my favorite playmates. But anything for my country." She and Mrs. Haag did anything and everything, day and night, with finely honed professionalism, often solving problems before I knew they existed.

Miss Diamonstein was Miss Festival. A petite blonde behind two phones in a huge barnlike office in the Executive Office Building, endlessly imaginative, quick and sparkling in manner, she persuaded, pushed, enthused, scolded and charmed the festival ahead. Her ambition for the festival was sweeping; it was she who suggested including the cinema, "that art of the upcoming generation," and thus for the first time the White House gave serious recognition to this art form. People kept telling us that after all, the White House was the White House, and that Presidents had been known to express their opinion of some modern art in highly unpresidential language. Miss Diamonstein would brook no timidity; her criterion was quality and quality only. Of course we had no money, not a penny, for the festival, and museum directors, for example, were asked to assume the expense of packing, insuring and often, because of the time shortage, air-freighting their paintings or sculpture to and from Washington. More than a few directors boggled at the request. No matter; Miss Diamonstein was on the phone and the *objet d'art* went on the plane. (Her prize was probably the 3,500 pounds of Peter Voulkos' "5,000 Feet," air-freighted from California courtesy of the Los Angeles County Museum of Art.) Ideas kept spilling out of her. During the twenty-four years that the National Gallery of Art occupied its present building, its lovely garden court had never been used for a luncheon or dinner. The festival guests would have a respite from the formality of the White House and lunch and listen to George F. Kennan speak on "The Arts and American Society" in the court because she had thought of it.

We divided the festival into seven major categories: painting, sculpture, literature, music (serious and jazz), the dance, the cinema and photography. (Photography also was being given its first serious recognition as an art form by the White House.) Of course the painting, sculpture and photography would be exhibited; the films would be shown; the music, drama and dance performed; and the literature presented by having authors read from their works.

No effort was made to pick the "best" in any field; in addition to being silly, this would have been inappropriate for the White House. The whole selection process was informal. In each field certain people and certain works obviously should be included.

Beyond that, Miss Diamonstein and I consulted, in a bedlam of phone calls and conferences, various experts and critics around the country, taking care to see to it that they represented a variety of taste. We sought to choose the artists in each form who, in the opinion of knowledgeable people, were doing work of the highest distinction; to make sure that each significant genre was represented; and to designate that particular creation which authentically represented the artist. Occasionally, puzzled over which specific work of an artist should be chosen, we asked the man which of his creations he felt best represented his work in general; interestingly enough, the answer invariably was that he did not know. When two or more works of an individual seemed equally appropriate, we picked the painting, sculpture, or photograph that came from a collection which would increase the geographical distribution of the White House exhibition.

In the field of writing, where I felt most at home, I simply went ahead and made some choices, inviting authors who were generally esteemed as fine craftsmen in their various fields. Here it seemed to me interesting to have the person make his own choice of what he cared to read from his writings. I asked John Steinbeck to chair the session, and when he proved to have an unbreakable commitment in Europe, I turned to another distinguished literary figure, Mark Van Doren. For a poetry reading I chose Robert Lowell; for light verse, Phyllis McGinley; as novelists of contrasting types, Saul Bellow and John Hersey; and to represent a few of the many nonfiction strands, Catherine Drinker Bowen, E. B. White and Edmund Wilson. Despite the superb writing being done in American history, I invited no historian because, with so many possible nonfiction fields, I did not want to emphasize my own.

All the writers accepted, and graciously indeed, except Wilson and White. Wilson declined with a brusqueness that I never experienced before or after in the case of an invitation in the name of the President and First Lady. White said no with the charm of a "Talk of the Town" column. "Of course I'd do anything for the White House but, believe me, you don't want me. I've tried reading from my essays and for some reason, probably my good taste in literature, I just can't do it. When I try it's awful. It's torture for me and worse torture for the audience." I did not go to a second choice in the nonfiction field. In a procedure like this, there are no first and second choices, and even more I did not want a fine writer possibly publicized as a substitute.

Whatever the creative field, no attention was given to the politics, ideology, opinions or personal habits of the people chosen.

To my certain knowledge, one had been a member of the Communist party well after the Nazi-Soviet nonaggression pact; the photograph of Edward Steichen's selected was a portrait of Paul Robeson; one sculptor had so firmly established a reputation as a devotee of the bottle that on the afternoon of the festival I asked a White House policeman to keep a gentle eye on him after his initial visits to the bar. Nothing was eliminated, as long as it seemed significant, on the ground that it was inappropriate for the White House. The paintings included "The Calumet," a pop work of Robert Indiana, and the op painting of Richard Anuszkiewicz, "Squaring the Circle." Of the eleven works of large-scale sculpture for the magisterial South Lawn, one was Jason Seley's seven-by-four feet of welded chrome automobile bumpers and grille, "The Masculine Presence."

In all the hurly-burly of the choices, one set of circumstances particularly struck me. I had expected trouble in arriving at any considerable agreement among the experts we consulted, especially in the fields of painting and sculpture, and the trouble came. Well-known cognoscenti cajoled, shoved, maneuvered, offered more or less subtle bribes and—in one case—made a highly unsubtle threat to try to get certain artists included, sometimes for commercial gain, in more cases to promote a particular collection, in still more instances out of sheer arrogant dogmatism. Yet this was not the dominant note. Nationwide, we found expert after expert who immediately and sympathetically comprehended the purpose of the festival, made no effort to push his own interests or taste and unstintingly gave of his time to the project.

Furthermore, with the art adventurers fended off, there was a remarkable agreement among experts as to what was significant in the whole spectrum of contemporary art. Speedily there was little doubt about more than two-thirds of the painters and half of the sculptors who should be included. If this experience is a sound indication, it is simply not accurate to say that art standards—or, for that matter, standards in a number of other forms covered by the festival—are chaotic in modern America.

Yet the process of arranging a White House Festival of the Arts still retained its ample quality of the rococo. Cultivation, so the wise men tell us, makes men civilized. No doubt, but culture in the America of the 1960's can make intelligent men act like idiots—including high government officials who schemed to have some favorite work presented; thousands of otherwise sober citizens, duly organized into associations, who really believed that their group should be permitted to name a representative to read a poem or sing a song at the White House; and the masters of great corporations—the presidents, not the public relations men—who were on the phone seriously attempting to have a "corporate cultural presentation" at the festival.

The invitation list was another carnival of pressures. The White House does not have capacious resources for entertaining; it can seat comfortably only about four hundred and fifty, and the sole place for numbers beyond that is the South Lawn. We had to adopt stringent rules for the festival. There were two basic categories to be taken care of: the men and women who were the outstanding leaders in encouraging the arts around the country, and artists and writers. Since the festival was being staged primarily for the first group, they were invited for the full event. Artists and writers were invited for the climactic function, the presidential reception, speech, dinner and the evening performances, most of which would occur on the South Lawn. In order to avoid naming one artist or writer over another and in order to have a group of manageable size, we invited only those artists and writers who were participating in the festival either through a reading or through their works. Even with these restrictions, the projected number was impossible, and a further rule—possibly unique in White House entertaining—had to be added: the appropriate person, but not his or her spouse, went on the list.

Invitations to White House functions are and should be cherished. But during my period in Washington, I never experienced anything like the assault for an invitation to this event. One prominent Eastern socialite had both his senators and his congressman intervene. When that failed, he added a member of the Democratic National Committee and a broad hint that he was close to people who could help my career enormously. A much esteemed corporation executive wired and then phoned me twice to make it ever clearer that he had given thousands to the 1964 Democratic campaign fund and that he was thinking of not giving another penny. I doubted if he had given thousands and I suspected that he would continue to give more than a penny, but anyhow, I got his point, and I also ignored it. Not to be invited to the White House Festival of the Arts, it seems, was to be uncultured, and in 1965 that was bad, very bad.

Inside my little staff, the baroque of life in the Johnson White House kept emerging. We *were* a tiny group, budgetless, putting together an octopus project in twenty-two days. The high Republican chairman of a museum board called to say that he was all for the festival, but it happened that the constitution of his institution, inviolate since the nineteenth century, categorically forbade loaning works when the expenses were not paid by the recipient. I could only suggest, "Where Presidents of the United States are concerned, has a Constitution ever really been a stumbling block?" There was a noise on the phone, which I like to recall as a chuckle; in any event, the painting arrived. For the presentation of Arthur Miller's play, *Death of a Salesman*, we wanted Mildred Dunnock who had created the role of the wife, Linda. The White House operator tracked down Miss Dunnock in a beauty parlor and, with her head pulled out from under the dryer she said, "Yes, of course, but, oh dear, this *is* sudden. I was just about to . . ." Three days before the festival opened, Mrs. Stewart Udall gently pointed out to me that an American festival of the arts might be considered somewhat lacking if there was no representation of Indian art. René d'Harnoncourt, director of the Museum of Modern Art in New York City and a long-time student of Indian art, and Donald G. Humphrey, director of the Philbrook Art Center at Tulsa, Oklahoma, were forthwith pulled from what they were supposed to be doing to help pick and get transported to the White House an appropriate painting, which turned out to be Blackbear Bosin's plain but strangely enigmatic "Prairie Fire."

And in the long run, in a Johnsonian or any other enterprise of this type, some degree of the totally arbitrary inevitably entered. We might have experts galore, we might listen to them closely, they might arrive at a high degree of agreement. At some point somebody simply had to say yes or no.

Down to the final wire, there was total disagreement about the relative gifts and significance of two painters. I asked Mrs. Haag for the photographs of the works in question and examined them for a few minutes. "Let's put that one in," I said.

"But why?" Mrs. Haag said.

"Because it's better."

Lenora Haag looked at me in a way that only a secretary who has been working with a man for a long time looks at him. "You're going to put it in just on the basis of your own personal opinion?"

Grinning sheepishly, I retreated into the absurd. "Well, we're in the White House. It's like Teddy Roosevelt, asked to explain one of his actions. He said, I did it because it was the right thing to do. And when the questioner asked, How do you know it was right? Teddy replied, Because I did it."

Lenora Haag smiled weakly and sent the order through.

Amid the final whirl of preparation I received a letter from

Robert Lowell requesting that I give an accompanying letter to the President. The enclosure read:

DEAR PRESIDENT JOHNSON:

When I was telephoned last week and asked to read at the White House Festival of the Arts on June fourteenth, I am afraid I accepted somewhat rapidly and greedily. I thought of such an occasion as a purely artistic flourish, even though every serious artist knows that he cannot enjoy public celebration without making subtle public commitments. After a week's wondering, I have decided that I am conscience-bound to refuse your courteous invitation. I do so now in a public letter because my acceptance has been announced in the newspapers, and because of the strangeness of the Administration's recent actions.

Although I am very enthusiastic about most of your domestic legislation and intentions, I nevertheless can only follow our present foreign policy with the greatest dismay and distrust. What we will do and what we ought to do as a sovereign nation facing other sovereign nations seem now to hang in the balance between the better and the worse possibilities. We are in danger of imperceptibly becoming an explosive and suddenly chauvinistic nation, and may even be drifting on our way to the last nuclear ruin. I know it is hard for the responsible man to act; it is also painful for the private and irresolute man to dare criticism. At this anguished, delicate and perhaps determining moment, I feel I am serving you and our country best by not taking part in the White House Festival of the Arts.

Respectfully yours,
ROBERT LOWELL

My first reaction to the letter was fury. This, I told myself, was arrant troublemaking and publicity seeking—the acceptance of a White House invitation, then turning it down, the injection of irrelevant grand issues in high-sounding language, the play to the newspapers. Then, studying the actual contents of the letter and reflecting on what I knew of Lowell (I had never met him), I decided that my initial reaction was off base and that the letter had been written by a sincere and troubled man. He was wrong, it seemed to me, but for reasons I had to respect.

Secluding myself in my office and putting my thoughts together for five minutes or so, I telephoned Lowell. I did not urge him to attend and read from his poems; if he felt uncomfortable doing that, I said to him, he certainly should stay away. I did urge him to withdraw his letter and to let it simply be said that he had discovered he could not attend for personal reasons. The participants in the festival had not yet been widely publicized and his abstention in this way would cause no hubbub.

I believed the letter should be withdrawn, I stated, because its basic assumption seemed to me wrong. As we all know, the President plays two roles. In the one he is the Chief Executive, Commander in Chief, the leader of his political party, and the proponent of certain policies, foreign and domestic. In the other role, he is the nonpolitical, nonpolicy, ceremonial head of the nation, filling an office in which it is his duty to encourage all good values and activities of the nation. Obviously it was in the second role that President Johnson was sponsoring the arts festival and had invited Lowell. No ideological or policy tests had been applied to the people invited; in turn, they should apply none to their host. Acceptance of an invitation implied no approval or disapproval of his policies, subtle or otherwise.

Moreover, I went on, I believed that the letter would have an important effect which was contrary to Lowell's own wishes. He wanted, I was sure, to broaden appreciation of the arts in the United States and to make them a more integral part of American living. He also sought as much interchange of ideas as possible between Presidents and men like himself. Toward these ends it was helpful to have Presidents and intellectuals and artists get together. It was more than helpful to have the President of the United States—particularly one who was known to have no great personal taste for the arts—celebrate them from the nation's first house, declaring, directly or in effect, that whatever one's personal tastes, the arts were a vital part of the national life.

I did not know, I added, Lowell's picture of President Johnson's personality and of the workings of his mind. But it was my opinion that the letter would infuriate him and that he would deem it an insult to him personally and to the Office of the President. The effect would be particularly disastrous just because of Lowell's distinction. The episode would give President Johnson the feeling that intellectuals and artists were his hopeless enemies and would seriously diminish any desire on his part to spread appreciation of the arts, to have further contacts with the groups, or to listen to what they had to say on policy matters.

Lowell replied that he had thought the matter over carefully before sending the letter, and that he had talked with a number of friends, some of whom had argued as I was doing, and others who had urged him to withdraw from the festival. He did not particularly discuss the points at issue. Rather, Lowell emphasized that he could not escape the feeling that his presence would express, in some sense, support of President Johnson's Dominican and Vietnam policies, and he found these so morally reprehensible he could not appear.

He apologized, Lowell said, for having accepted thoughtlessly and for the position in which he had placed the President and me. But his mind was made up and in good conscience he could take no other path.

In the course of the conversation I mentioned the release of the letter to the press. It was already in the hands of the *New York Times,* Lowell stated. I did not bring up the propriety that a letter is not given to the newspapers before it is received by the addressee, particularly when the addressee is the President of the United States. It did not seem appropriate to argue protocol when a man was acting on such strong inner feelings. I did offer, if Lowell agreed to withdraw the letter, to call the *Times* myself, and I assured him that the withdrawal would be handled in such a manner that there would be virtually no possibility that the episode would become public.

No, Lowell replied, he wanted to go ahead.

Throughout the conversation the poet was gracious, free of self-righteousness about the position he was taking, and thoroughly understanding of the complications he was causing. I hung up the telephone with the impression of a fine human being. I also hung up with the feeling that all hell was about to break loose.

I sent the letter to President Johnson, together with a description of the situation and with a suggested reply to go out over the President's signature:

DEAR MR. LOWELL:

I have your letter in which you state that you are withdrawing from the program of the White House Festival of the Arts.

I regret your decision both because the occasion will be deprived of your great distinction and talents and because of the reason you give. Mrs. Johnson and I have planned the Festival as a way of honoring and encouraging all the arts in America without regard to political affiliation, public questions, or temporary disagreements over foreign or domestic issues which may arise among our people. I fully and deeply respect your disagreement with certain phases of the Administration's foreign policy but I regret that you have seen fit to inject that disagreement into an occasion where it is quite irrelevant.

Sincerely,
LYNDON B. JOHNSON

The roar in the Oval Office could be heard all the way into the East Wing. The instruction came back, Answer the letter under my own name and make it "just an acknowledgment." I decided that "just an acknowledgment" could include this much:

DEAR MR. LOWELL:

As you requested, I have sent your letter on to President Johnson.

Needless to say, I regret very much that the White House Festival of the Arts will be deprived of your great distinction and talents.

Sincerely yours,
ERIC F. GOLDMAN

The next morning the *New York Times* carried the Lowell story on the front page. In view of its inherent news interest, I was scarcely surprised that the *Times* played it prominently, but I was interested to learn that President Johnson took the placement as another example of the hostility of the *Times* toward him.

By a conjunction of circumstances and personalities, some actions acquire an immediate and continuing symbolic significance. Such was the refusal of one of America's leading cultural figures to appear at a cultural occasion sponsored by the President of the United States. For many academics, writers and artists, the Lowell rejection bespoke their own feelings toward a President who had conducted the Dominican intervention and ordered entrance into the Vietnam War.

In the period immediately before the White House Festival of the Arts, on March 24, 1965, at 8 P.M., some three thousand faculty and students showed up in four auditoriums of the University of Michigan in Ann Arbor for faculty lectures and seminars directed against the Vietnam War. Hour after hour of passionate speeches and discussions; the 2 A.M. breakfast break that was eggs, coffee and anti-LBJ; more hours of angry talk; the final massed outdoor meeting with everyone turning to watch the clock approach 8 A.M., and the air of triumph as the prescribed twelve hours were reached; the six hundred proud survivors going off to bed, classes, or the coffee shoppes—the first "teach-in" against the Vietnam War had been staged.

As the teach-ins spread to campuses from Bowdoin in Maine to Pomona in California, major intellectual figures stoked the dissent. From Paris, Jean-Paul Sartre announced that he was canceling a lecture tour in the United States; he could have "no dialogue" in a nation which practiced "the politics of violence" in Vietnam. Archibald MacLeish, long recognized as something of an unofficial minister of culture for the United States, declared that he did not presume to pass judgment on the Administration's foreign policy.

But he did want to say that Vietnam, coming on top of the Dominican action, "had raised the question whether the nation has become indifferent to the opinions of mankind and outgrown its old idealism." Lewis Mumford, the urban philosopher who for a whole generation had expressed the quest for the civilized life amid the chrome and roar of American cities, was more than ready to pass judgment.

In 1965 Mumford was president of the American Academy of Arts and Letters, and on May 19 he took the occasion of the customary presidential address to express his "shame" and "anger" at American foreign policy. Men "devoted to the pursuit of the arts and humane letters have . . . a special duty to speak out openly in protest on every occasion when human beings are threatened by arbitrary power: not only as with the oppressed Negroes in Alabama and Mississippi and our neighbors in Santo Domingo, but the peoples of both North and South Vietnam who must now confront our government's cold-blooded blackmail and calculated violence." The American government's "unctuous professions of reasonableness, peacefulness and restraint have been undermined by the incontinent actions it has taken, and by its repeated threats to widen the scope of its destruction unless its conditions are met." The United States had no more right to exercise "military coercion" in Vietnam than Soviet Russia did to establish rocket bases in Cuba. By asserting "high-handed power," the Johnson Administration was doing "more to rehabilitate totalitarianism and to corrupt responsible democratic government" than the whole Communist movement could hope to achieve. Some of the celebrated writers and artists present at the meeting objected to Mumford's speech; many applauded vigorously.

The "intellectuals," people said, were rising up in wrath against the Vietnam War. The dissent was plain enough; the meaning of the word "intellectual" was not. French in origin, it identified a European class with a usable degree of accuracy. But it had never really applied in the American scene, and by 1965 it was often being employed in a way that led to misleading and at times ludicrous generalizations. Academics and professional writers, for example, were customarily put together under the rubric. Yet many in each group had little in common either in way of life or in fundamental attitudes toward public and private questions. Within the academic community, varying types of institutions and different regions of the country produced sharply contrasting types of men and of ideas. Within the same university, a professor of anthropology or of history was as likely to be as different from a professor of chemistry, or for that matter from a professor of

English, as he was from the public relations vice-president of a steel company.

Some commentators on the 1960's, attempting to escape the confusion of the word, defined an intellectual not in terms of occupation or of attitudes but of mental characteristics. Like Tom Wicker, now head of the Washington Bureau of the *New York Times*, they said that "what an intellectual is all about . . . is a particular turn of mind—questing, challenging, skeptical, analytical, toughly fibered. He thinks for himself. His impulse is to reason, his gift is to perceive." This was fine as an expression of the intellectual ideal. The trouble was that it applied a good deal more to people like Wicker, who did not call himself and was not usually called an intellectual, than to thousands who did, very noisily, adopt the name and who were, in strident approval or denigration, generally accepted as such.

Perhaps in the long run an American intellectual should be defined in the way that Louis Armstrong responded when he was asked what jazz is. The great Satchmo, so legend has it, replied, "Man, if you got to ask, you ain't ever gonna know." At any rate, for the most part what seems to have been meant in 1965 when Americans referred to intellectuals was—without much regard to abilities, achievement, habits of mind or way of life—a large, amorphous group of academics, writers, editors, staff people at foundations, certain types of lawyers, and a scattering of others who made their living primarily from talking, writing, research or some combination of these. Painters, sculptors and other artists were sometimes put under the classification, often not. It is in this very general sense, keeping the artists separate, that I will use the word.

Judging from my contacts with intellectuals and artists and from the other available evidence, in 1965 they had no composite attitude toward the Vietnam War. On the contrary, they seemed much like the general population—most of them going along without any great enthusiasm, some hawkish or dovish. Certainly they were not overwhelmingly anti-war. From one week's mail sent by intellectuals and artists in the summer of 1965, I made a tabulation of attitudes on Vietnam. The correspondence was split, 35 percent anti-war, 30 percent pro, with the rest somewhere in between. As late as 1967, when the protest had become thunderous, two University of Michigan sociologists, Howard Schuman and Edward O. Laumann, undertook an intensive poll in that institution, which was not only the birthplace of the teach-in but was generally assumed to be strongly dovish. Their conclusion: the idea of a "faculty consensus" against the war was "campus folklore." The teaching body divided almost evenly on the crucial question of an unconditional end to the bombing. Furthermore, if a significant dove-hawk breakdown existed, those who wanted the Administration to escalate outnumbered those who wanted it to slow down. One revealing statistic indicated that pro-LBJ men were especially numerous among faculty who had not previously expressed their opinion in any public form.

That same year, 1967, the Citizen's Committee for Peace with Freedom in Vietnam was established, led by Dean Acheson, Omar Bradley, Dwight Eisenhower and Harry Truman, all strongly pro-war. It was still able to command the names of such leading academics as J. Douglas Brown of Princeton, an architect of the American social security system; James MacGregor Burns of Williams, the FDR and JFK biographer; the outstanding historians, Oscar Handlin of Harvard, Allan Nevins of Columbia, and T. Harry Williams of Louisiana State University; well-known writers or editors like Marc Connelly, Ralph Ellison, James T. Farrell, Howard Lindsay and Ralph E. McGill; E. L. Tatum, Harold C. Urey and Eugene P. Wigner, all Nobel laureates in science or medicine; and other figures long esteemed in intellectual circles from a variety of fields, such as Thurman W. Arnold, James B. Conant and Paul H. Douglas.

Yet these very signs of support for the Vietnam War pointed to the essence of the situation. The organizer of the Citizen's Committee for Peace, Paul Douglas, was seventy-five years old; of the luminaries listed above, more than two thirds were over sixty, and about one third past seventy. The University of Michigan survey, for all its lack of consensus, did find noticeable trends. The younger faculty were more likely to be anti-war (and this did not correlate particularly with whether they were draft eligibles). The faculty man's field of work mattered even more. Three out of four professors in the social sciences wanted the bombing stopped unconditionally, and professors in the humanities tended in the same direction, though by a closer margin. The professional schools were sharply divided. Among the natural scientists, the pro-Administration group dominated.

What was happening in 1965 was that a particular group among the intellectuals and artists, probably a minority, was becoming strongly critical of the Vietnam War. Among the intellectuals, this opposition was made up primarily of academics and writers; among the academics, the ranks were filled chiefly by professors in certain fields; the academics and the writers were doing most of the expressing of the dissent. And at the center of the agitation, the source of its large-scale support, were the professors in those certain fields, the social sciences and the humanities.

In some ways, and in the case of some members of this opposition group, the attack on Lyndon Johnson's entrance into the Vietnam War was hardly edifying. More than a few of the letters that came to me and of the comments I heard and a number of the published statements revealed an unmistakable characteristic. In these instances, the LBJ policy was not really being considered on its merits; it was being attacked in considerable measure out of snobbery, social and intellectual.

The aspect of the snobbery that was social came from the simplest of facts. Intellectuals and artists, after all, are human beings, and the desire to associate yourself and what you think with what you deem to be the upper rung of society is a reasonably well established part of the condition of man. These social aspirations blended with an intellectual snobbery to form a more intricate and more important element in determining the reaction to the war.

Different generations of American intellectuals and artists have varied a great deal in their view of their place and of their role in society. Some periods, like the 1930's, produced a widespread yearning in the groups to be part of a people's movement. Joseph Mitchell expressed the attitude with classic brevity in his stories about "McSorley's Wonderful Saloon." The phrase "little people," Mitchell declared, was "repulsive. . . . There are no little people in this book. They are as big as you are, whoever you are." Many intellectuals and artists re-created this spirit in the 1960's; many others, however, found little attraction in declaring themselves at one with the masses.

They sought a sense of camaraderie not with truck drivers or struggling writers, in or out of a saloon, but with what they felt were the elite of their generation—an elite not necessarily defined by talent. They looked at the new middle classes in Levittown watching *Bonanza* on television, beer can in hand and a paperback of *Peyton Place* on the end table, and they felt amply confirmed in their attitude. They thought of themselves as special people, the last custodians of values in a mass-corrupted society, ready to attack and to reconstruct it without in any way being ready to risk being contaminated by it. In this kind of atmosphere it was noticeable how much British publications were the standard. On books, one quoted the *London Times Literary Supplement* and one kept *Encounter* on the coffee table—or one did until it was revealed that the CIA had been subsidizing it. The mood was essentially that of Tory radicalism, every man his own Disraeli.

Within these circles, some carried elitism even further. The word "alienation" had long been current, and it had often been taken to mean a stance not inappropriate for an intellectual or artist—enough distance from and skepticism of American society to be able to criticize it fruitfully. But for one group, "alienation" was now amounting to an attitude of removal from the society, a feeling of such superiority to it and contempt for it that they were more interested in sneering at it than in changing it. Some of these alienates also proudly called themselves "anarchists." The word was inaccurate only in that the old bomb-throwers had plans to build a new structure once they had destroyed the existing one.

Similar developments had their significance among the intellectuals who were proving the bulldozer of the opposition to the Vietnam War, the professors in the social sciences and the humanities. For decades, a certain type of faculty man, for example the professor of medicine or of engineering, had been something of a figure in the community. He made the better salary, carried on private professional activities that brought not only more income but an aura of moving with the established groups, was likely to be invited to dinner parties on the social side of town. Most faculty men had not been enjoying this life. They were preserved in genteel poverty, and were respected in the way that nice ladies engaged in good works were respected. But things had been changing.

In the new America, governments and corporations more and more were seeking the expertise of economists, sociologists, psychologists and men in related disciplines. The general cultural explosion tossed off an added prestige for all academics. The baby boom of the World War II era and the spreading affluence brought hundreds of thousands pressing against the college admissions offices. Somebody had to teach them, even if at the ratio of 3,000 to 1, and professors in every field were savoring the delights of a seller's market.

Faculty men in the humanities and social sciences, in short, were undergoing their own revolution of rising expectations. Like the Nigerians and Indonesians, they were headed toward the better life, and the more they got, the more they wanted. They sought a higher income, but that was only part of the story. Now that it was possible to become somebody, they were the more eager to be somebody in all senses of the word.

A change in personnel added impetus to the drive. The shift

had been occurring throughout the American intellectual and artistic worlds but, proportionately, it was more extensive among the academics. In previous generations, most professors had come from middle- or upper-class backgrounds, and from families whose sense of social position was secure in all senses. Charles A. Beard, the prominent historian of the twenties and thirties whose father was the leading citizen in his part of Indiana, once remarked, "We were working from inside the top of the system, and assumed with ease that America belonged to us, whether we were attacking its leaders or not." From the thirties on, the democratization of American life had been rapidly opening professorships to men from the less confident backgrounds, economically and otherwise. For the most obvious and understandable reasons, they had a special sensitivity to all matters of status and a sharp concern with the great American game of getting ahead.

And what were the measurements of success in this intensely upward-mobile group? Establishing a name as an excellent teacher did not count high; for many, such a reputation was actually a minus point. They were having none of that old situation where professors were ranked along with ministers as "teachers and preachers." A common phrase of the faculty lounge was "my work" ("Now that the students are away for the holidays, I can do my work"). My work was the pursuit of foundation money to acquire a leave from teaching, the research for an article which might produce an offer from a more prestigious institution, consultancies for government or business in that bright, lucrative outer world, a speech or community activities which would win invitations to the socially more prestigious homes. And the stance to be adopted in all this? An air of having to put up with America, a special sniffishness toward the mere middle classes, a liberal intellectualism that was more waspish than obstreperous, a general identification with the attitudes, manners and dress of the top layer of Eastern America or of Britain. This type of the new professor may not yet have decided that he was one of the beautiful people, but he was certain that he wanted the beautiful people to find him congenial at a cocktail party.

In 1965 the American intellectual and artistic groups, both in and out of universities, were much larger in numbers and, in terms of positions held in government and business and attention given by the press, more influential than at any time in the history of the United States. Tens of thousands of them were able, dedicated, professionally and personally admirable and engaging, and remarkably free of snobberies social or intellectual. Yet these other attitudes did characterize many individuals in the groups—and these attitudes did matter, among other reasons, because of their confrontation with the fact that Lyndon Johnson had taken the United States into the Vietnam War.

The President had a habit of dividing politicians into the "lucky" and "unlucky." John Kennedy, he thought, had been lucky. How else could such a "lightweight" have made the big time so quickly and easily? He was inclined to think of himself as unlucky. Take the Vietnam War itself, LBJ would remark. Presidents Eisenhower and Kennedy had skidded by it and it was dumped on him at a stage where drastic action had to be taken. Then there were the endless little matters. One of the more Johnsonian moments of the LBJ years came when, minutes before the President was to appear on television, he dropped his contact lens in the bathroom adjoining the Oval Office. A military aide, a civilian staff member and the President of the United States were on all fours looking for the lens as LBJ mournfully muttered, "Oh me, I try so hard. Why do these things have to happen to me?" President Johnson was unquestionably unlucky in one respect. If his circumstances and characteristics had been chosen for the purpose, they could not have been better contrived to call out the worst in the intellectual and artistic communities, especially where foreign policy was concerned.

The personal snobbery and social aspirations? To intellectuals and artists of this bent, Lyndon Johnson was no alluring figure as a domestic leader but at least he was effective in the right direction, and after all, domestic policies were only domestic policies. Foreign policy was different; in the sixties it was the status area in public affairs. These intellectuals and artists liked to think of it as being carried on by patricians or near-patricians—an Acheson, Harriman, Stevenson or Kennedy—or at least by establishment figures, and they wanted their ideas about it identified with men of this kind. Yet here was Lyndon Johnson of Johnson City presuming to lead in international affairs and to take them into war. "I look at that Texas cowhand and listen to him mangle the language," one Midwestern professor remarked to me, "and I say, 'No, dammit, go fight your own war.'" And that, so far as the professor was concerned, was definitive comment on the Johnson foreign policy.

The intellectual elitism? LBJ himself had a comment on that. "Until I got in this job, I didn't realize you had to look down your nose to understand foreign policy. I apologize." The yearning for a sense of greater recognition and importance? The doctrine, regardless of accuracy, was fixed: Lyndon Johnson does not love intellectuals and artists (which was mostly true), and President

Kennedy did (which was true to a certain extent and in some ways). A man who does not appreciate me, especially on the subject of foreign policy, cannot be right and what's more, I'm going to let him have it.

A section of the intellectual and artistic communities— naturally the intellectuals made most of the public statements— proceeded to let Lyndon Johnson have it on the subject of the Vietnam War in a way that was not their finest hour. The argument whether men engaged in the arts or in academic specialties removed from the specific public issue at hand have any special claim to be listened to is a stale and tedious one. Of course they do—to some degree. They are generally more intelligent, better educated and more concerned than the cashier at the supermarket, and at least they have read their *New York Times*. Yet there are salutary restraints in asserting the claim. Secretary of State Rusk, beleaguered on the subject of the Vietnam War by eminent postexpressionist painters, enzymological biologists and authorities on Scandinavian literature, reminded the country of the comment made about Albert Einstein—that he was a genius in mathematical physics, an amateur in music and a baby in public affairs. The poet W. H. Auden, asked for his opinion about the LBJ policy in Vietnam, gave it, a strongly negative one. Then he went on to express his continuing puzzlement that "writers should be canvassed for their opinions on controversial political issues. . . . Their views have no more authority than those of any reasonably well-educated citizen. Indeed, when read in bulk, the statements made by writers, including the greatest, would seem to indicate that literary talent and political common sense are rarely found together." Salutary restraints there may have been, but not when things inside you egged you on to lambast Lyndon Johnson.

In the pell-mell assault, intellectuals long noted for their advocacy of modernity and flexibility could resort to the mustiest of dogmas. Some of the arguments being advanced against the Vietnam War had a ring clearly reminiscent of Senator Robert M. La Follette orating against World War I, or Senator Burton K. Wheeler calling down imprecations on Franklin Roosevelt because of his pro-war moves at the end of the 1930's. The Columbia University historian, Henry F. Graff, in an article for the *New York Times Sunday Magazine*, struggled to be fair to this kind of thinking whatever its source, but he could only conclude: "The unadorned truth is that isolationism is reviving in our midst." Determined to beat LBJ over the head with JFK, some academic intellectuals talked the kind of iffy history that would flunk a freshman. President Kennedy may have increased the number of "military advisers" in South Vietnam from eight hundred to seventeen thousand and may not have made his final decision for or against combat intervention; John Kennedy, they nevertheless stated categorically, would never have entered the Vietnam War.

A group among the anti-Johnson intellectuals not only declared the unknowable; they distorted the known. Particularly during the teach-ins, they delighted in declaring that "Eisenhower himself had admitted" that Ho Chi Minh would have won 80 percent of the vote in an election including both North and South Vietnam. What the former President actually said, in his memoirs *Mandate for Change*, was that if a Vietnam-wide election had been held during the French fighting to hold the area, with Ho running against the playboy Chief of State Bao Dai, Ho "possibly" would have won as much as an 80 percent victory, and he stressed "the lack of leadership and drive on the part of Bao Dai." An election held subsequent to the armistice, with Ho running against another candidate and after he had instituted his collectivization program, was a totally different proposition. Obviously the misrepresentation of the Eisenhower statement tended to make Ho something of the grand old man, the hero of the Vietnamese people North and South, and the Johnson Administration, even more than it might be, the backer of reactionary, antipopular forces. Its widespread use, a travesty of any intellectual or scholarly method, did not—as some White House people insisted—indicate considerable pro-Communism among the intellectual dissidents. It did reflect a spirit of anything-goes in attacking Lyndon Johnson's policy in Vietnam.

Anything goes—the tone could be one of vicious irrelevancy. The British journalist Henry Fairlie visited the United States in 1965 and went home shaking his head sadly. "I have found nothing more strange or unattractive than the way in which American intellectuals take pleasure in reviling President Johnson," he wrote. The attack was "personal," a "fastidious disdain for the man. . . . He is a slob, one of them said to me. . . . Others say much of the same, if less briefly."

Fairlie was spared reading my mail and answering my telephone. One day an acquaintance, a nationally known academic, called to read me a letter of protest against the Vietnam War and to have my assurance that it would go straight to the President. I listened. Some of the letter criticized the policy, but most of it was a denigration of Lyndon Johnson, especially in comparison to John Kennedy "who understood the importance of brains," and an assault on the President's personal background, intelligence and motives. "Stupid," "blundering," the phrases ran, "Bismarck out of Southwest Texas State Teachers College," "cheap politics to please the yahoos." When I suggested to the professor that he keep the criticism of foreign policy in his letter and omit the personal aspersions, he declared, "I never thought that you, just to hold a White House job, would turn into a lackey for a Texas nothing." He announced that he would get the letter to the President by another route, and I agreed that was best. Perhaps now, if he reads this book, he will understand how much I sympathized with his policy points and how little tolerance I had for the rest of the letter.

Generally, this was proving no happy period for me. I had decided on the "intellectual life" only after considerable wavering. After college, I had been tempted by a variety of occupations, especially journalism, and during two separate periods I worked as a writer for *Time* magazine. But for a young man like myself, emerging from an impoverished and broken home, the university world and the kind of teaching and writing one can do there had a strong lure. A tremendously exciting ideal had been held up before me by some superb human beings I was lucky enough to meet among professors and writers, the ideal of a band of men devoted to the freewheeling pursuit of intelligence, decency and kindliness in human affairs and to passing on this tradition. I had elected the intellectual life, enjoyed it, and by a quirk was in the White House, so people said, representing it. Now with the chips down, with a grave public issue at stake, I was appalled by a good many of the group I represented.

I was appalled—and at times thoroughly impressed. A deeply informed, trenchant criticism was being mounted against President Johnson's policy in Vietnam, some of it coming from intellectuals and artists who were in no way petty, some of it from those who were also petty indeed. Again, and for natural reasons, writers and academics were the most frequent and effective spokesmen of this dissent.

An eerie pattern has marked modern American life. "It would be an irony of fate," Woodrow Wilson remarked shortly before he began his Presidency, "if my administration had to deal chiefly with foreign affairs." The irony not only happened; it kept repeating itself. President Wilson, the vigorous reformer in domestic affairs, turned into Wilson the war leader, and World War I was followed by the anti-reformism of the twenties. President Roosevelt's crusading New Deal merged into World War II; then came the conservative Congresses of the late forties. President Harry Truman the Fair Dealer fought the Korean War and gave way to

Eisenhowerism. Now Lyndon Johnson, architect of the Great Society, had gone to battle in Vietnam, and a school of intellectual critics saw the cycle of reform, war and then the cessation or slowing of efforts for social improvement about to occur once again.

And this time, they were sure, it was all so unnecessary. They viewed the Johnson policy for Vietnam as one based on a set of outmoded ideas. They had broken with the American law of history which envisaged a world seeking—if only evil leaders were removed—tidy middle-class democracy. They were reconciled to a situation in which history, with a mocking toss of her head, seemed off on a tear with shaggy and troublesome suitors. The democratic-Communist clash, as these intellectuals conceived it, came fundamentally from a long-running, worldwide social revolution. They doubted whether the resulting problems could ever be solved in a way that satisfied all the national interests of the United States; they were positive they could not be solved quickly. They emphasized that America would make little gains with any policy based on simplistic anti-Communism because the Red surge represented, in a viciously distorted way, the legitimate and irresistible aspirations of millions for independence, social reform and self-respect.

Consequently, their great desideratum in foreign policy was flexibility, a constant wariness of ideas or analogies from the past, a ready experimentalism in programs for the present and future, and a supple understanding of, and a large degree of sympathy with, what was happening in the underdeveloped world. They particularly sought flexibility in analyzing the nature of world Communism at any given time. In the early years of the Cold War, American policy had been heavily influenced by a concept of a monolithic global Red movement. The approach, such intellectual critics contended, was questionable in the days of Harry Truman or John Foster Dulles; in the sixties, any policy which carried even overtones of it was dangerously inadequate.

This way of thinking led to a challenge of every fundamental of President Johnson's policy in Vietnam. It denied that the issue was: Munich or fight. Vietnam was no simple question of aggression; basically the long-running conflict was a civil war inside South Vietnam and inside all of Vietnam, arising essentially from nationalist urges and social conditions. The alleged lurking figure of Red China, controlling and egging on the Vietcong and North Vietnam, was just too pat. For centuries Vietnam, North or South, had shared a powerful emotion—fear of China and a desire to stay away from its tentacles.

The intellectual critics questioned whether the holding of South Vietnam was important to the security of the United States. As John Kenneth Galbraith would soon posit, Suppose North Vietnam had quickly taken over South Vietnam in 1954. Would any vast cry of calamity have gone up? Would not the real issue have been, then as later, the long-range orientation of Asia in world affairs? The domino theory split the ranks of the intellectual dissidents. Some agreed with President Kennedy that there was a degree of validity in it. But none accepted it in the LBJ form of a virtually automatic 1-2-3, largely removed from other factors which could change the rules of the game. Vast China had gone Communist in 1949, these men emphasized, and nevertheless most Asian countries were still not so much Communist—or anti-Communist—as they were nations seeking their own ways to satisfy the explosive expectations of their masses.

Those expectations, so explosive and so justified—here was the heart of the intellectual attack. Faced with such yearnings, the critics balked at allying the United States with a series of corrupt and mainly reactionary Saigon governments. The Johnsonian insistence on asserting American interests in Asia loud and clear seemed to them to be handing hostages to the Communists. For more than a century Asians had been hearing the voice of American interests. Rightly or wrongly, they had their own version of what it was saying: imperialism, landlordism and racism. Above all, the intellectual critics repudiated the application of American combat power to a problem which they considered basically political and social. For such a situation, resorting to war was what you did when you did not understand what to do and, in a nuclear age, when you proceeded to compound miscomprehension with bravado.

If there was one figure from whom intellectual America in the 1960's took its special guidance in foreign policy, that man was George Kennan. A striking combination of the hard-headed thinker and unabashed idealist, Kennan bore the credentials of a distinguished scholar in international affairs, a diplomat of long experience, and the governmental activist who was the principal architect of the highly successful Marshall Plan. In addition, Kennan wrote and spoke with force and verve. In 1950 he published the lectures he had given at the University of Chicago, under the title *American Diplomacy, 1900–1950*, and this volume proved the first in a series of books, articles and speeches that had an extraordinary impact, directly and indirectly, on campuses and throughout educated America.

Kennan's central theme was that ever since the United States became involved in world affairs at the turn of the twentieth century, it had tended to pursue a spuriously moralistic foreign policy. It fought self-righteous battles in the name of "freedom" and ignored both essential realities and essential moralities. The intelligent as well as the ethical approach was to determine just what was needed to protect the national interests of the United States and to further its conception of a better world; to calculate how much of this was practical without neglecting the high-priority claims of the American people themselves; and then to seek these limited goals by skillful diplomacy and economic and technological aid, and without the brandishing of arms. The permeative influence of the Kennan approach had prepared the way for the whole intellectual criticism of American intervention in the Vietnam War, and it did more. It threw into question even the one element in President Johnson's Asian policy which he thought would appeal strongly to intellectuals, his call for the rapid economic and social development of Southeast Asia.

As the designer of the Marshall Plan, Kennan had emphasized that the essential in any such program was to apply it to a region which had a viable economic and social system, one which simply needed pump-priming to make it work. Western Europe had such a system, he emphasized; Asia did not. When the Marshall Plan went before Congress, China was not yet controlled by the Communists, and powerful senators demanded to know why there was no Chinese appropriation. Kennan stoutly maintained that money for China was just dollars down the drain, a sop to domestic political prejudices, and that an aid program for Asia should come later, in a much different form. Only over his continuing protest did President Truman recommend an appropriation for China, and even then it was kept outside the regular Marshall Plan funds. Now, with the Vietnam War on, President Johnson had proposed what amounted to a crash Marshall Plan for Southeast Asia, and Kennanite skepticism was endemic among intellectuals.

One center of the intellectual attack on the President's foreign policy was the *New York Review of Books*, a journal which in a way was an accident of American trade unionism. At the end of 1962 the New York City newspapers were closed down during a long strike, and two New Yorkers who were going along without their daily *Times* were Jason Epstein, an editor at the publishing firm of Random House, and his wife Barbara, a staff member of the *Partisan Review*. The Epsteins were people who, in the words of the husband, felt the urge to "withdraw" from American culture in its usual forms; in the mornings, walking to work, he often detoured through Central Park to avoid passing the Lincoln Center for the Performing Arts. One evening during the strike, the Epsteins were entertaining friends at their West Sixty-seventh Street apartment and the talk turned to how "pleasant it was to live in New York without newspapers; how, now that there were no newspapers, there didn't seem to be any news either; that things didn't really happen in fact but happened only in the *New York Times*. A hundred or so pages of events had to be invented every day to accompany the ads, and on Sundays a thousand pages—most of them trivial—had to be concocted." Epstein remarked how especially glad he was not to be reading the *New York Times Book Review*, that "monstrous" collection of the "work of tired hacks, lame professors, breezy illiterates." For several years Epstein had been urging the founding of a new book review, and at the gathering in his apartment the thought came up: Now, with the *Times Book Review* blacked out, was the chance to start a book journal on the British model, like the *London Times Literary Supplement* or the *New Statesman*.

It was primarily the Epsteins, along with Robert B. Silvers, who launched the *New York Review of Books*, with Silvers serving as the operating head. Just thirty-two years old, Silvers had already established himself as a successful editor, with an astute blue pencil, a quick sense of trends and a rapidly widening circle of friendships among writers and academics on both sides of the Atlantic. He was also an Anglophile, a master of name dropping in a way that did not clatter too loudly, a devotee of the more lofty in all things. His attitude toward American civilization was indignation leavened with pity.

Under Silvers' editorship, the *New York Review of Books* emerged a coterie journal on the British model. The reviews were of exceptionally high quality in terms of both the seriousness of the points discussed and the pith of the style. They were concerned less with the book than with whatever else the reviewer deemed more important, or at least more interesting to himself, and the whatever else was increasingly political. Authors and reviewers were entangled in a tight literary incestuousness ("The *New York Review of Each Other's Books*" was the current quip). And though the journal attracted writers of a wide variety of attitudes, it maintained the general stance of the personal and intellectual elitism of the sixties. In time it would run a series of advertisements which declared: "The *New York Review of Books* has been called cliquish, intellectual, opinionated and snobbish. For $7.50 a year you can be, too. For $7.50 a year you too can be feared and envied. What will your middle-brow friend say when you point out to him. . . ."

Most of the inner circle of the *New York Review* had gone along with President Johnson in the early phase of his Administration, approving his domestic policies but with a marked distaste for his Administration in general and for him personally. The emergence of Lyndon Johnson as a foreign policy leader outraged many in this group. It offended their serious ideas about international affairs, which were generally those of the intellectual opposition; it offended things deeper and more personal. They became emotional and contemptuous opponents of the Dominican intervention and of American participation in the Vietnam War.

The wife of Robert Lowell, the novelist and critic Elizabeth Hardwick, was a friend of Robert Silvers', and on the Sunday just as Lowell was about to withdraw from the White House Festival of the Arts, Silvers telephoned Elizabeth Hardwick about another matter. She told him of her husband's decision and added that he was preparing his letter to President Johnson. That afternoon Silvers stopped over at the Lowell apartment and was shown the letter. He thought it "superb." As Silvers later described his attitude at the time, Lyndon Johnson had "contrived the festival to present a false front to the world that writers and artists are backing the Vietnam War," and was "trying to use" Lowell for this purpose. There was a "moral duty to attack the festival"; there was also "the plain politics of the situation," making sure that the Lowell withdrawal "hurt Johnson as much as possible with intellectuals and artists who voted for him in 1964."

The next day, not at the suggestion of the Lowells, Silvers mounted a campaign. He got together with the poet Stanley J. Kunitz, and the two men drafted a telegram to President Johnson stating support for "Lowell in his decision not to participate in the White House Festival of the Arts. . . . We would like you to know that others of us share his dismay at recent American foreign policy decisions. We hope that people in this and other countries will not conclude that a White House arts program testifies to approval of Administration policy by the members of the artistic community. . . ." Silvers and Kunitz drew up a list of writers and artists, and divided the task of telephoning them for signatures. They wanted the story to appear in the papers the day after the publication of Lowell's letter and hence had little time to gather names. They dispatched the wire to the White House with twenty signatures; Kunitz said that he had received 90 percent acceptance from those he approached. A number of the names were drawn from the immediate *New York Review* circle, but they also reached well beyond that, and in general represented an impressive array of talent.*

In the White House, communications to the President about a specific project are sent to the appropriate aide, who then decides whether to take them up with the President. When the telegram reached my desk, my eye was drawn quickly to three signatures, those of Dwight Macdonald, Larry Rivers and Mark Rothko. These men were on the invitation list to the festival.

Rivers and Rothko were there as artists whose paintings had been chosen for exhibition, Rivers' "The Final Veteran" and Rothko's "Ochre and Red on Red." Macdonald came under a different category. For each field of the arts, we had included on the invitation list a group of able critics of varying taste. In addition to his work as a staff writer for *The New Yorker* and his occasional pieces for the *New York Review*, Macdonald was the film critic of *Esquire* magazine. There were those who said his basic critical tenet was that all American films are bad. In general, he had emerged as something of a prophet of elitism, helping to popularize "anarchist" as a description of his type of attitude toward American civilization, coining the word "Midcult" in derision of his special target, American culture, calling for "alienation from every statistically significant group or trend in American political life today," especially any group or trend which could produce that "tasteless, crude" Lyndon Johnson and "his Vietnam War." A pungent writer and a man knowledgeable about the cinema, Macdonald was on the festival guest list representing film criticism of the elitist point of view.

White House invitations are hand-lettered, and because of the jam-up in the calligraphy office, the festival group were being mailed in small lots. When the Silvers-Kunitz telegram reached me, Macdonald's invitation had just gone out. Those of Rivers and Rothko had not been mailed, but telegrams had been sent to two galleries requesting the loan of their paintings. The Macdonald case, at least as far as I was concerned, was simple. He had been invited to the festival and he could accept or decline, as he chose. That aspect of the Rivers-Rothko situation seemed to me equally clear-cut. Any host, even a President of the United States, has a right not to invite to his home a guest who had publicly announced

---

* *The full list of signers was: Hannah Arendt, John Berryman, Alan Dugan, Jules Feiffer, Philip Guston, Lillian Hellman, Alfred Kazin, Stanley Kunitz, Dwight Macdonald, Bernard Malamud, Mary McCarthy, Larry Rivers, Philip Roth, Mark Rothko, Louis Simpson, W. D. Snodgrass, William Styron, Peter Taylor, Edgard Varese and Robert Penn Warren. Silvers, as an editor rather than a writer or artist, did not sign.*

that he does not want to come. But the question of the exhibition of the Rivers and Rothko paintings at the festival was a quite different matter, the more so because it involved that special kind of human being, Lyndon Johnson.

If the President had been infuriated by the Lowell letter of withdrawal, the publication of the Silvers-Kunitz telegram stoked his anger. As his rage mounted, it found a broader target. Of course intellectuals and artists as individuals had never been favorites of his, but now he was lumping them all together in one repulsive conglomerate. He was making few distinctions between the various types of critics of his Vietnam policy, even between those pro- and anti-Vietnam. He was furious at "these people," all of them, who had insulted him and the Office of the Presidency. The mood went deeper. The Johnsonian conception of the role of the President in foreign policy was at work, and he saw "these people" as ones who were quite ready, by demeaning the President and by making a public spectacle of their attitude, to hurt their country at a time of crisis. They were not only "sonsofbitches" but they were "fools," and they were close to traitors. A minor event, a mere ceremonial festival of the arts, was blowing up into a situation which could have anything but minor significance.

At various moments LBJ declared that he "had enough of these people" and was going to call off the festival, which of course he would not do, or that he "simply won't show up at the thing," which he might very well do. Listening to these and similar statements from the Oval Office, I did not doubt that what happened in the next few days might seriously affect the President's receptivity to anything proposed or argued in the future by "these people," who included some of the most fertile and dedicated minds in the country; could cause him to do and say things that would cut him off further from Metroamerica; and in the peculiarly inflated possibilities of the situation might make him react in ways which would diminish him and the United States in a world that was only too ready to believe that at bottom all Americans were Texans, and that all Texans were boors.

Obviously my general role was to try to keep to a minimum the inherent abrasiveness of the circumstances while preserving the quality and integrity of the festival. But there were also specific and pressing matters, not the least of them the paintings by Rivers and Rothko which were scheduled to be hung in Lyndon Johnson's home. I hastened to get in a word with him before he acted and instructed me to cancel the requests to the galleries. A wrathful Lyndon Johnson reading was much more persuadable than a wrathful Lyndon Johnson being talked at, and I hurried off a memo.

It pushed the practical point: cancellation would almost certainly leak to the press and the White House would be "embarrassed." But with the probable developments of the coming days in mind, I emphasized most strongly the question of the general point of view to be maintained for the festival, the "right position—that the festival has nothing to do with foreign or domestic policy and the paintings were picked, after consultation with appropriate art authorities, as being worthy of inclusion on the grounds of sheer painting quality." Chosen on that basis, they should be hung on that basis, no matter what Rivers and Rothko thought of the Vietnam War and whether or not they wanted to attend the festival. For the White House to act otherwise would be to duplicate what Lowell and the signers of the telegram had done, interject an irrelevant issue into a ceremonial arts occasion.

To my relief Jack Valenti called within half an hour. He said that President Johnson had asked him to tell me to go ahead with the paintings.

"I'm glad, Jack," I responded. "I'm sure that's the correct decision. But what did the President say generally? It would help me to know."

Valenti gave a tense little laugh. "I don't think you want to hear what he said."

A large number of intellectuals and artists, publicly or privately, were taking positions on the issue that had been raised: What is a proper and healthy relationship between government and the arts? More specifically, did an intellectual or artist, by accepting celebration at a White House ceremony, implicitly commit himself to support of a controversial Administration policy? The mail was heavy and there were many statements to the press, but no real trend of opinion showed. The points made ranged all over the place, and without much correlation to the distinction of the man in his field. Of the one hundred and two writers, artists and critics invited to the festival, only four besides Lowell declined on his grounds.* But these statistics also mean little. Fourteen more declined—an unusually large group for a White House function—without giving any reason except a purely social one, and most of them may have been politely avoiding stating the Lowell posi-

* They were the drama critic of the New Republic, Robert S. Brustein, soon to be named dean of the Yale Drama School; the sculptor Alexander Calder; the painter Jack Levine; and the photographer Paul Strand.

tion. Among those who replied affirmatively, to my knowledge at least fifteen attended with serious doubts in their minds.

The two novelists who had agreed to read from their writings made public statements which also reflected the variations in opinion. Saul Bellow told the reporters that he considered the Dominican intervention "wicked and harmful" and that he was against the Vietnam War. But the festival was not a "political occasion," the President was "an institution" as well as the country's chief policy maker, and President Johnson was seeking "in his own way, to encourage American artists. . . . I accept in order to show my respect for his intentions and to honor his high office. I am sure that he does not expect me to accept every policy and action of his Administration together with the invitation."

In a quite different tone, John Hersey stated to the press that his decision to go to the White House was firm only "up to the present." Furthermore, under the circumstances he did not plan to read from one of his novels. "Like many others, I have been deeply troubled by the drift toward reliance on military solutions in our foreign policy. . . . It has been my intention to attend the festival because I felt that rather than by declining or withdrawing, I could make a stronger point by standing in the White House, I would hope in the presence of the President, and reading from a work of mine entitled *Hiroshima*."

Amid all the controversy, one development gave me a particular personal twinge. For years I had delighted in the painting of Jack Levine, with its sharp social satire that combined gusto with gentleness, and now Levine's declination on the grounds of principle had arrived. But at least I was pleased that unlike some of the comment I was hearing from the intellectual and artistic communities, Levine stated his position, however firmly and candidly, with respect for the President of the United States and with a sense of what the festival was trying to say to the nation. His wire to President Johnson read: "I am grateful for the honor shown me by your invitation. To me the invitation is especially moving because in my work I have always criticized our customs and institutions. But I must decline. With Robert Lowell and others I believe it is impossible to divorce U. S. culture from our policies in Vietnam, and I think our policies in Vietnam are appalling. Respectfully, Jack Levine."

Meanwhile Dwight Macdonald was busy. Without an invitation to the festival, he had signed the telegram stating that he approved of not attending. Now that he had an invitation, he wondered whether he did not want to appear after all. He kept discussing the matters with friends. It was a chance to "get Johnson," he said, to "strike out at his war." In a conversation with Robert Silvers the idea came up that Macdonald should attend the festival and write an article about it for the *New York Review*.

These facts I learned later. At the moment the fact was a telegram on my desk from Macdonald, addressed to me. It accepted the invitation to the festival, mentioned that he was one of the signers of the Silvers-Kunitz wire, and went on to say, "I assume you would have no objection to my writing something later about my impressions of the festival if the spirit moves me since you were kind enough to invite such an inveterate writer and critic as myself but it seems something I should mention. . . ."

I telephoned in reply. My distinct impression from the conversation was that Macdonald hoped I would disinvite him because of his signing of the Silvers-Kunitz telegram and the indication that he planned to write an unfavorable article, or that if I let the invitation stand, I would make the point that it was not proper for him to come as a guest to the festival and then write an attack on it. Whatever mistakes I might be making, I was not going to put an obviously hostile writer in the position of being able to claim that the White House Festival of the Arts was a collection, insofar as possible, of those artists who approved of President Johnson's foreign policy and were ready to say nice things about the festival. Apart from my desire to protect the President and the festival, personally I had no stomach for any such rules. When Macdonald asked me, in effect, if he was still welcome, I replied that he had been invited without any test of his attitude toward the President's foreign policy—in fact, with full knowledge of his hostility to the Vietnam War—and that he continued to be welcome, again without policy criteria. As for what he might publish, he was certainly entirely free to write an article and to write it as he pleased.

In the Oval Office, the festival kept grinding on sensitive nerves. John Hersey may have thought that what he was expressing in his statement to the press was his ambivalence on the question of whether a man as opposed as he was to the Vietnam War should participate in a White House occasion. But his words were carefully noted by President Johnson, and to him they indicated no ambivalence at all except how best to hurt Lyndon Johnson and the war effort. The Hersey statement was another insult from "these people." Within earshot of the press LBJ declared, "Some of them insult me by staying away and some of them insult me by coming." Privately he added, "Don't they know I'm the only President they've got and a war is on?" The festival day was a Monday. The President was scheduled to spend the preceding weekend in Texas, and he let it be known inside the White House that he saw no reason to leave the ranch while "this bunch" was in Washington. His attitude, swirling out of the Oval Office in dark, sullen clouds, permeated the staff.

In the LBJ White House, projects either "had it" or they did not —meaning that they were or were not pleasing the boss. At the beginning the festival had it, to the extent that at times getting things done was difficult because of the offers—and the interference—of co-operation. Now, suddenly, the festival no longer had it, and most West Wing aides were scurrying to dissociate themselves from it. At the staff meetings Jack Valenti arranged, he made no direct criticism of me, but he was decidedly nervous over "the upset" of the President and talked of the need "to get this over with, the best way we can."

At one Valenti session Richard Goodwin leaned back, flicked his cigar and remarked wearily, "Yes, it's all a mess. Of course Lowell should never have been invited in the first place."

I tried, and failed, to contain my anger. When I invited Lowell, I exploded, it was by virtue of his high quality as a poet, which was generally recognized. Furthermore, while I didn't happen to agree with the action Lowell took, his was certainly a defensible position. Around the White House, it was too easy to forget that President Johnson's foreign policy—any President's foreign policy —was not beyond criticism, and that the Vietnam War in particular raised among sensitive men moral issues that made them want to declare themselves.

That said, my anger subsided. I had noticed that Valenti was listening to me intently, and I was sure that as always he was loyally trying to figure out what was best for President Johnson. It occurred to me that I ought to say more, in the hope that it would be passed on to LBJ through Valenti, which would make my remarks far more palatable than any direct approach by me.

All this hand wringing over the festival, I continued, was not what we ought to be doing. The festival was a minor event, a very minor one. It was the White House attitude that was magnifying it. The papers were beginning to fill with talk about the way the President was reacting—as if a poet, by expressing his convictions and emotions, would somehow endanger the national security. The President greatly admired Franklin Roosevelt and thought Woodrow Wilson was a self-righteous prig. Well, how had FDR reacted to criticism, particularly of his foreign policy? He parried it and laughed. And what had Wilson the self-righteous done? He acted wounded and bitter and won himself more enemies.

Goodwin yawned, said he had to leave, and departed. I kept going. What we ought to be doing, I said, was to help the President relax and turn this situation to his purpose of being a truly national leader. One of the reasons the intellectual and artistic communities reacted against him was their feeling that he really didn't give a damn about them. Why not give a damn and take some occasion to bring up the point raised by Lowell's withdrawal, with the attitude that it was an interesting, important point and one worth discussing. For years the intellectuals and artists had been saying that government should encourage and support their work without imposing restrictions on what they did or said. Well, a President had now pushed legislation through Congress to encourage and support them without restrictions, and was about to stage a festival to honor them without policy tests—in fact, honoring a host of his critics. Then *they* tied politics to the arts; *they* said, We don't like LBJ's foreign policy, and therefore we don't want to come to his house for a ceremonial occasion.

Shortly before this staff meeting, John Steinbeck had made a comment about the festival controversy. "It used to be," he remarked, "that we worried about protecting the intellectuals and artists from the government. Now it looks like we have to protect the government from the intellectuals and the artists." I had just heard the comment and now I repeated it. Why shouldn't the President use this quote—from a man certainly respected in intellectual and artistic circles—and mull it over a bit publicly? Intellectuals and artists might get the impression that he really cared, and was ready to think about their problems and attitudes.

There was a crisscross of comment in the room, all of it impatient. Realizing that I was conducting a futile monologue, I stopped, and the subject was quickly changed. Perhaps Valenti did convey something of what I had said to President Johnson; I never knew. At any rate, that was the last of the Valenti staff gatherings at which I was present. When the usual hour arrived, a secretary phoned to say that the time had been changed. Twice my secretary inquired about the new hour and when she was given vague answers, I told her to stop asking.

The Social Secretary, Bess Abell, was stirring, and so was her chief assistant, Mrs. Barbara Keehn. A carry-over from the JFK days, Mrs. Keehn was, if the conception makes much sense, a kind of career person in the Social Secretary's office. Sturdily efficient, she drove ahead with the clear goals of pleasing whoever happened to be the President and the First Lady and more immediately, their representative the Social Secretary. These ladies had two concerns. They guarded over the prerogatives of the Social Office, or what they deemed to be its prerogatives, with jealous intensity, and the planning of the festival had been rushing ahead with only a polite relationship to them. Their second concern had formidable buttressing. Bess Abell inherited from her father Senator Clements a closeness to President Johnson, and independent of that, LBJ valued her highly for what he considered her political shrewdness. As the troubles over the festival developed, she made plain to me that the President had instructed her to keep a careful eye on it.

The actual planning of much of the festival was being done so quickly that there could be little interference from anyone. My staff was further protected by the ignorance of the Social Office about the world of the arts. Neither Mrs. Abell nor Mrs. Keehn, it turned out, had ever heard of Edmund Wilson. Mrs. Keehn at first thought that Willem de Kooning was a musician, and Mrs. Abell was puzzled that I had chosen George Kennan, that year's president of the National Institute of Arts and Letters, as the luncheon speaker. "What does he have to do with culture?" she asked, then added, "Oh, well, never mind—he's a good Democrat."

Other matters were not so simple. When Bess Abell learned that scenes from Arthur Miller's *Death of a Salesman* had been chosen as part of the drama section of the festival, she called me, her voice steely. "Miller," she said, "was a Communist. We can't have him and his play in the White House."

I had no way of knowing whether she was speaking for herself or President Johnson, and at that moment I saw no point in trying to find out. At that moment I also saw no point in arguing the larger question of whether Miller or any other writer should be banned from the festival on ideological grounds. I replied only by saying that I was sure Miller had not been a Communist, and that I would double check the details and let her know.

The story is well known. In 1956 Miller appeared before the House Committee on Un-American Activities, testified that he had never been a member of the Communist party and spoke of his associations with some Communists. He refused to name the Communists, was cited by the committee for contempt because of this refusal, and was subsequently exonerated. When I stated these facts to Bess Abell, I felt it necessary to say that apart from the legalities I thought that Miller ought to be honored, not criticized— "don't you?"—for his refusal to name the Communists. Then, trying to get rid of the whole tawdry business with a little joke, I added, "Besides, Miller married Marilyn Monroe. That ought to kill any suspicion that he's not a red-blooded American."

Mrs. Abell was in no mood for joking. "I have to be out of town this weekend. But I am very worried about this; I don't like it at all. You'd better think it over."

I'm afraid I did not think it over. Monday morning when she came to my office and brought up Arthur Miller, I told her that I simply could not agree with her. I didn't believe the President should be pestered with such details, but if she thought the question should be referred to him for decision, then let's go to him and have it out.

Bess Abell did not reply, went on to other matters, finally came back to Miller. "I don't understand why you are being so stubborn. These people of yours—and this festival—have done nothing but cause trouble for the President. But if you insist, I'm tired of trying to make the festival sensible. Remember, Miller is your responsibility." So it was Bess Abell and not President Johnson who had wanted to use McCarthyism against Arthur Miller. Relieved to learn this, I turned to last-minute festival details and to other tasks, including drafting a speech for Mrs. Johnson.

The First Lady was scheduled to give the commencement address to the first graduating class of the College of the Virgin Islands and I wrote into the speech: "I remember, not many years after I graduated from college, listening on the radio to a great American President, Franklin D. Roosevelt. He came to the part of his address which concerned the young, and President Roosevelt said: 'There is a mysterious cycle in human events. To some generations much is given. Of other generations much is expected. This generation of Americans has a rendezvous with destiny.'

"Many of us were deeply moved by these words. We rolled up our sleeves and tried to translate the words into a better America. We did a lot of good, I believe, and we also committed errors both of omission and commission.

"Now we know that your generation, in a far deeper sense, has its rendezvous with destiny. It is not for those of us who too often fell short to lecture you, but perhaps one word is permissible.

"Perhaps there was in yesterday's generation a greater emphasis on saving the world in general. I believe I see in this generation the happy tendency to apply ourselves to our own areas. . . . Today, around the world, a strong new trend is showing itself"—youth driving to bring their ideals into reality "in their own backyards, and therefore the more surely and the more quickly."

Looking back now on the speech, this passage must have

sounded somewhat on the melodramatic side, especially being spoken at a languid tropical scene in Mrs. Johnson's drawl. As can happen with speech writers, I was injecting into her remarks my own mood and I was feeling a bit dramatic, or grim, or, as LBJ would say, hunkered up. The festival of the arts had once seemed so minor and so pleasant a task. Instead it kept raising the nastiest kind of problems and ones which only too plainly could escalate. Friends from the intellectual and artistic community, who had no way of knowing what was actually going on in the White House, called me to say sadly or bitterly, Why have you made yourself a tool of this sham propaganda festival? From the other side, criticism within the White House constantly grew sharper. That was the situation; that was that. The festival, as the Lady Bird speech said, was my backyard; I proposed to take care of it. The President had asked me to come to Washington to help him and I intended to help him in a way I considered important. Come hell or high water, come my friends, enemies, the West Wing, Bess Abell or Lyndon Johnson himself, I was determined to do everything humanly possible to see to it that the First House of the United States, when it chose to put on a festival of the arts, put it on with an inflexible commitment to quality and to intellectual and artistic freedom.

Clearly, the chief remaining potential for trouble was the opening session, the readings by literary figures. Of the five authors originally scheduled to read, by now one had withdrawn and three had spoken out against the Vietnam War. John Hersey, in addition, had made his statement that he was choosing selections not from his novels but from *Hiroshima* (technically, the passages were from *Hiroshima* and from an introduction to it written by Hersey when he republished it in his volume *Here to Stay*).

Shortly after Mrs. Johnson's return from the Virgin Islands she phoned and asked if I knew exactly what Hersey proposed to read. I had requested that each of the authors confine himself to a total of about ten minutes, and I sent the First Lady the three brief passages Hersey had designated. Two of them concerned Miss Toshiko Sasaki, a clerk at the East Asia Tin Works in Hiroshima, and they were descriptive—the mangling of her body at the time of the bombing and, a month later, her first sight of the ruins of the city as she was being moved from one hospital to another. The third selection gave statistics about the destructive power of existing and potential nuclear weapons.

The next day Mrs. Johnson asked me to lunch with her and a few members of her staff for some "final planning" of the festival.

The lunch was set in the charming Queen's Room of the White House, and the First Lady began the discussion in her most gracious way. But I was soon uncomfortable. Quickly it became clear that the purpose of the session was not planning but the deplanning of John Hersey. I was the more uncomfortable because Mrs. Johnson made it explicit that she was speaking for her husband, and I thought that in a matter as sensitive as this the President should speak for himself.

Mrs. Johnson read from one of Hersey's statistical passages: "'President Truman, announcing the Hiroshima bombing, told the world that the force of the atomic explosion that day was equivalent to that of some twenty thousand tons of TNT.'" The First Lady laid the paper aside and said with a frown, "The President is very close to President Truman. He can't have people coming to the White House and talking about President Truman's brandishing atomic bombs."

I realized that Mrs. Johnson was trying to be indirect, but I simply did not understand what she was driving at and I said so. She became direct indeed. "The President is being criticized as a bloody warmonger. He can't have writers coming here and denouncing him, in his own house, as a man who wants to use nuclear bombs."

I tried to straighten things out. "Mrs. Johnson, may I have the passage you were referring to?" She handed me the paper and I read aloud the whole section. "Now, nothing in this states or implies in any way that President Truman and President Johnson do not abhor the use of atomic bombs. We all know that every decent man loathes the thought of being responsible for nuclear holocaust. What Hersey is saying is something very different. Asked to read from his work, he has chosen selections that talk about the great moral problem of our age—nuclear war. He is doing it in a context which expresses his opinion that the Vietnam War, utterly contrary to President Johnson's wishes, might turn into nuclear war, just as President Truman, against his own personal feelings and because of his conception of the national good, felt it necessary to give the order to drop an atomic bomb."

"It's all disgusting," Mrs. Abell interrupted. "What right does some writer have to tell the President to come and listen to him so that he can make headlines denouncing the President's foreign policy?"

"Gall, incredible gall," Mrs. Keehn said. "Next he'll be telling the President what to eat."

I ignored that. "Bess, I'm sure you misunderstand this. Hersey did not seek out the situation. He was telephoned by a reporter and asked whether he was going to withdraw, like Robert Lowell. He answered that although he agreed with Lowell's opposition to the war, he believed the correct thing to do was to go to the White House and express his criticisms and worries by the choice of what he read. That is all Hersey could say because that is what he happens to think. As for telling the President to come and listen to him, he certainly did not do that. He said he hoped the President would be there, which is surely quite different."

I turned to Mrs. Johnson. "And if I may say so, I too hope the President will be there. As you know, the festival schedule calls for the President to appear only at the dinner and evening session—a fact, incidentally, of which Hersey is unaware. But if the President chose to come to the readings, walked up to men like Hersey and Bellow and spoke with his natural self, perhaps invited them into his office for a talk about his foreign policy, he would appear a mighty big man to a group in which a change of impression about him could make a huge difference. What he would be saying, and saying in a highly effective way is, 'I really care about, I really want to understand, I really want to consider the criticisms of responsible, thoughtful men who are so troubled and who I know are as much dedicated to their country as I am.' "

Mrs. Johnson's face hardened. "The President and I do not want this man to come here and read this."

I decided not to take the remark as an order, and to appeal to the practical. "Mrs. Johnson, if I phoned Hersey and asked him not to read from *Hiroshima,* the odds are ninety-nine to one that he would immediately withdraw from the festival."

"Good!" Barbara Keehn said.

"Of course," Bess Abell added, "I simply don't understand all this fuss over some silly writer."

I'm sure my face hardened too. "Hersey is not 'some silly writer.' He is a distinguished writer. What's more, he is a distinguished American, having given a great deal of himself to his community. On both counts he deserves our respect, not aspersions. But the fuss is not over Hersey, whatever his qualities. It is, if you will pardon the blunt word, over principle. An author was asked to come to the First House of the United States in the name of the President of the United States to read from his writings. He accepted. The President and the White House are symbols of freedom. It is not freedom to tell this author what he can and cannot read."

For such a discussion, the scene was bizarre—four highly political women and a professor in a room of exquisitely feminine décor, around a table of delicately prepared tearoom salad. No one

was eating much. Mrs. Carpenter had said little so far, but her
few comments had made clear her absolute loyalty to Mrs. Johnson
and her personal agreement with the position of the President and
the First Lady. But Liz Carpenter has the kind of mind that looks
for a way out and the kind that understands nuances; she had
always been extremely friendly to me and my work. "Eric," she said
now, "isn't it true that Hersey is known mostly as a novelist?
Couldn't you tell him that we want to honor him for his main field
and ask him to read from one of his novels?"

I hesitated before answering. Out of a desire to solve an impasse and out of friendliness toward me, Liz Carpenter was obviously offering a compromise. Shouldn't I go along with her?
During the discussion, which had now run well over an hour,
disturbing thoughts had gone through my mind. Was I playing the
Boy Scout liberal, indulging my own kind of self-righteousness,
lecturing people about principle, insisting on a situation that upset
a President with grave problems on his desk? Was I really achieving what I wanted to do, help him as much as possible? I hesitated,
but I simply could not accept Liz Carpenter's suggestion; it was
another, if more tactful way of telling Hersey that he was not to
read from *Hiroshima*. That *did* involve a principle, a very basic
one, and I was sure it would not help the President. It would only
lead, I had no doubt, to Hersey's withdrawal and to an uproar that
presented President Johnson in an extremely unfortunate light.

I sighed and said, "Liz, you're right in one sense. Although
Hiroshima is a well-known book, Hersey's chief distinction rests
on his novels. It is also true that I invited him and Bellow as
novelists, novelists of different types. But all that really isn't the
point. I did not tell Hersey he could read only from his novels. I
invited him to read from his writings, choosing as he pleased. For
me to call now and suggest that he read from *A Bell for Adano* or
The Wall would be as obvious as a brick through the window. It
would be clear that the White House did not want him to choose
anything that had implications for what is really on his mind—
Vietnam. I'm afraid there is no other word. It would be White
House censorship."

Mrs. Johnson flushed. "Censorship is a harsh word—"

"This is all ridiculous," Bess Abell cut in. "This festival has
caused enough trouble already—"

The First Lady interrupted firmly. She was angry and she was
taking charge. "The President and I," she said slowly, "do not want
this man to come here and read these passages. The question is
how best to handle the situation." She looked at me coldly. "Don't

you know some mutual friend of Hersey and yourself who could handle this tactfully?"

"Yes, I do. Alfred Knopf publishes Hersey's books and mine, and is a personal friend of both of us. But it is my strong opinion that if I asked Knopf to intervene in the way that you want him to, he would say no."

I glanced at my watch. It was two-thirty, and I was scheduled to introduce Secretary Rusk to a group across town at three o'clock. I told Mrs. Johnson of the appointment and asked if she wanted me to cancel it. Still seeking a way out, Liz Carpenter jumped at the opportunity for a breather. "Yes, maybe we ought to settle this later. I also have to take care of some people."

But I did not want to let the matter ride. I was tired of the problem and my instinct was that the quicker it was settled, the better. The picture of the First Lady as the daughter of Minnie Patillo and Aunt Effie, the coed asking that dates take her to Chekhov and O'Neill, came into my head. I turned to her in an effort to reach that part of Lady Bird Johnson. Later, when I tried to make notes about what I had said, I found I had forgotten most of the words. I must have spoken in a torrent for two or three minutes. The gist of it was, Let's drop trying to find a way around this. I can certainly understand how the President feels. He has the world on his shoulders. He is putting through the kind of domestic program the liberal intellectuals and artists have always wanted. He is doing it by ideals, hard work and skill. But many intellectuals and artists keep throwing Kennedy in his face, keep calling him a Texas ignoramus, keep acting as if he has no motives beyond the nearest vote. He embarks on a war that he is convinced is necessary for the national good, and many of them assail it. He approves a festival of the arts, which is not his dish to begin with. Some refuse to come, and a novelist says he is going to read about atomic bombs. It all seems to him a concerted effort to harass him and to demean him and to embarrass his war leadership. But these were not Hersey's motives. There are many different worlds of the arts and he comes from the great tradition—the tradition of humanity. He represents the kind of liberalism which has created the environment that makes the President's domestic successes possible. He is not against Lyndon Johnson the human being; he is not against *any* human being. He is simply worried about Lyndon Johnson's foreign policy.

Don't let the President put himself in the position of appearing to conform to his enemies' picture of him. Let Hersey read from *Hiroshima*. People will say, Now there's an open White

House, and go on with other matters. Tell Hersey he cannot read from *Hiroshima,* and people will say Lyndon Johnson is a man who simply cannot take it—and, worse, a man who is insincere about one of his favorite words, "freedom."

Mrs. Johnson made no effort to interrupt, but when I stopped I learned immediately that I had not been talking to the daughter of Minnie and Effie Patillo, or to the devotee of Chekhov and O'Neill, but to Mrs. Lyndon Johnson. Once again, this time very slowly and very firmly, she stated, "The President and I do not want this man to read these passages in the White House."

So it was an order, unavoidably so. I said the only thing there was to say: "Mrs. Johnson, with the greatest respect for the President and the First Lady, I must refuse to call Hersey. I don't think it is the right thing to do and as a person who is trying to contribute what I can to the Administration, I also think that it would harm rather than help the President. I am sorry, very sorry, that I feel forced to say this because my respect for you personally—and if you will permit me, my affection—goes far beyond my respect for you as the First Lady of our country."

Not knowing what else to do and suddenly feeling very hungry, I took a piece of tomato from the exquisite salad and ate it. Everyone said mechanical good-byes and I hurried to the waiting White House car.

As I rode across Washington, the inevitable questions went through my mind. Would the White House ask someone else to approach Hersey? Would the President now definitely refuse to come to the festival?

It was Tuesday, six days before the festival on the coming Monday. Word came from Marvin Watson that President Johnson was leaving for Texas at the weekend and would "probably stay there until the middle of next week." I knew it was useless— worse than useless—for me to intervene further with the President or Mrs. Johnson. I was now a copiously certified, card-carrying "these people." Later that day I went to an old Texas friend of President Johnson's who had shown a warm interest in the festival. My point·was the same weary one: the President simply had to attend. It was not a matter of the success of the festival, or what President Johnson thought of intellectuals and artists, or vice versa; it was a matter of what an important segment of opinion, here and abroad, would think of the President.

The old Texas friend agreed readily enough with the point, but sighed deeply. "This is one job I do not cherish. I'll talk to Marvin first." He reached Marvin Watson just after the aide had emerged from a session with LBJ and in the course of the conversation he mentioned "the influence of the intellectual community." Watson's face reddened. "F - - k the intellectual community." The old Texas friend did not go higher.

An order came from the President: the festival was to be blacked out. No reporters, photographers or television people except those already invited as guests were to be present. A television network was planning a one-hour special on the festival; preparation on this was halted. President Johnson was also doing all he could to dissociate himself from the festival. Formal news releases were to be sent out not by his Press Secretary but from the news office of the First Lady. For one of the few times in the Johnson years, a White House project was publicly identified with someone other than the President or First Lady. The identification was no compliment to me.

LBJ went further. A group of last-minute invitations were ready to be telegrammed; he ordered an FBI check of everyone on the list—not the routine inquiry to identify potential physical danger to the President and his family, but one that looked into beliefs and associations. Marvin Watson was to make the judgments. The FBI hastily made the inquiries, and Watson telephoned me with the names of six people who were to be removed from the invitation list.

It was another old story. To a person of Watson's habits of thinking, a man who at some point in his life had been a member of a group including Communists was not fit for the President's house; furthermore, he was likely to criticize Lyndon Johnson. All the people under Watson's interdiction fell within this category, and no good purpose is served by mentioning any of the names now except perhaps one. It is indicative of what the Watson type of approach can produce, and of the kind of atmosphere that was developing in the White House, that one of the excommunicates was the late Newbold Morris, who had been invited to the festival as president of the New York City Center for Drama and Music, and who, in addition to the organizational affiliation that caught Watson's eye, was a Republican and an Episcopal vestryman, a member of the law firm of Lovejoy, Morris, Wasson and Huppuch, a director of the New York Savings Bank, Continental Can, and U.S. Steel, an official of the New York City Civilian Defense, the national Police Athletic League, and the League for the Preservation of Antiquities, and a recipient of the French Legion of Honor from the hand of Charles de Gaulle.

With no taste left for this kind of battling, I went to Watson.

I did not talk the principles of the issue—his mind simply did not run in that direction—but practicality. Four of his six people were artists with works in the festival exhibitions. How would he explain publicly a failure to invite them?

That would be awkward, he agreed. But after all, did I want subversion in the White House?

I took a grip on my impatience and declared the obvious. In the circles in which these people moved and at the time they joined the particular organizations, none of this meant subversiveness. "It was just humanitarianism. They were simply the most zealous Great Society people of that day," I found myself saying. I felt condescending and silly and depressed at talking this way to an aide of the President. But Marvin Watson was Marvin Watson, still the intelligent, honest, decent human being who talked and acted the Rotarian because of his tightly circumscribed background and his concern to do the best for his friend Lyndon Johnson.

Watson genuinely listened to what I was saying. "Well, what about these people and Vietnam?" he asked.

I looked down the list. "Two of them, I'm sure, are against the President's policy. The rest I don't know about. But come on, Marvin, we can't start that up again. The White House will be full of people who are opposed to the war."

"You know, if I showed these reports to the President, he'd cut off even more names."

"I don't doubt that, in his present mood. But one of the ways we can help him is to protect him from his present mood."

The lights on Watson's phone console were blinking. He was a fantastically busy man, and he too wanted to be rid of the problem. "Suppose we invited these six people but held up their telegrams of invitation until, say, June the twelfth [two days before the festival]?"

I laughed and so did Watson. "I bet they'll come anyway," I said.

"Yes, dammit," he replied, "they will." (Four out of the six did.)

The day before the festival, Sunday, was at hand. Mrs. Abell was in charge of the logistics of social and ceremonial events at the White House, and in the case of complicated programs she customarily held a rehearsal. Most of the Sunday was given to a trial run of the festival and the writers' session came late in the afternoon. Mark Van Doren, who was to chair the event, had made no public comment on the Lowell issue and he had not communicated with me about it. No one in the White House had seen what he planned to say. Now, while Bess Abell held a stop-watch, he began making his introductory remarks.

A tall, slim man of seventy-one, with an arresting serenity of face, Van Doren read from his manuscript with measured empha-sis. Most of his remarks concerned Robert Lowell. He praised the man and his poetry, and discussed and supported the right of literary dissent. Then he spoke ambiguously of Lowell's with-drawal. It was not clear whether he was agreeing with Lowell's position or, without expressing an attitude pro or con, wished to state his respect for Lowell's stand. Moreover, though his remarks were to be the opening statement at the festival by a guest, they included no word of appreciation for the sponsorship of it by the President and First Lady.

As Van Doren finished, Bess Abell was at my side, steering me to a corner so that she could not be overheard by the non-White House people who were present. She was so angry her finger wagged in my face. "I've had enough. That man is not going to use the White House as a soapbox, and you are not going to continue to get away with defending such things. The President has told me to watch over this crazy festival. Either you do some-thing about Van Doren or I will. And if you don't do something fast I'm getting on the phone to Texas and telling the President about this latest mess, and you know what will happen to you then."

I flared back. "Don't you threaten me. You know damn well that if I were just trying to please the President and to hold on to my job here, I would not have been saying and doing the things I have. I suggest that you think more about what's involved and less about running to Papa."

So much for my anger. I did not doubt that one way or another, Bess Abell intended to try to stop Van Doren from talking about Lowell, and I was just as sure that if the matter were referred to President Johnson he would back her.

I calmed down and turned to my last weapon. "Bess, the Presi-dent may very well have told you to keep an eye on the festival. He told me to run it. As long as I'm in charge, I am against any re-strictions on these writers. If anyone—I mean *anyone*—in the White House attempts to impose them, I will immediately resign from the staff with a public statement."

Bess Abell said nothing for a long few seconds. "Then you won't talk to Van Doren?"

"I didn't say that. While Van Doren was reading I was thinking that probably it would be helpful if he and I sat down together and talked. I'm not at all sure that his remarks convey the impression that he intends, or that they say everything he wants to say. Obviously he has written them under various pressures, some of which the White House has been doing its damnedest to create. But I am not going to tell Mark Van Doren what he should or should not say."

I asked Van Doren to come to my office so that we could talk privately. I did not have to explain why I wanted to confer; he was a troubled man. He spoke of the number of people, some of whom he respected highly, who had urged him to withdraw from the festival, and of his own ambivalent feelings. He asserted, sadly but firmly, that he felt he must make clear to the audience that he was not appearing in repudiation of Robert Lowell.

I told Van Doren that I happened to disagree with Lowell's argument for withdrawal, but of course that was not the reason I had asked to speak with him. I thought he ought to know—in confidence—that the President and Mrs. Johnson were bitter at what they considered the use of the festival to harass the President. He would understand, I was sure, if I did not think it appropriate for me to say whether I agreed with their attitude. I wanted him to be aware of it and also to know that this festival, a minor episode, had taken a turn which could have serious effects on something in which he and I were equally interested—the development of a healthy and fruitful intercourse between the White House and intellectual and artistic groups. I chose my words carefully as I added, "In the light of these circumstances, I wonder whether your present statement is just the one you want to make —as a matter of fact, whether it makes clear what you really want to say and says everything you would like to include."

Van Doren stirred irritably. "I am not going to come down here and repudiate Lowell—"

"I was not referring to that. What I do have in mind is that your statement, which is to be the opening one of the festival, concerns Lowell almost entirely, does not make clear whether you think intellectuals and artists should boycott presidential ceremonial functions when they disagree with certain presidential policies, and does not mention the fact that a President of the United States has chosen—whatever his alleged motives—to undertake an unprecedented salute to the arts and to the people encouraging them."

Van Doren and I were now in rapport. "What I had uppermost in my mind," he said, "was this Lowell matter."

"I'm sure you did, and that's why I asked to speak with you. And what I am asking now is whether, in the light of our conversation, you would like to take another look at your statement."

Van Doren again came to the nub of the situation. "The White House is not saying I cannot discuss Lowell?"

"Speaking for the White House—and I will take the responsibility of speaking for it in this matter—I am saying the reverse. I'm saying that you have every right and a warm welcome to speak as you please. That means, very specifically, that you are welcome, if such is your choice, to read your present statement down to the last comma."

Van Doren replied that he would go back to his hotel, think things over and telephone me. Within an hour he called to say that he had decided to prepare a different statement, and he read the new form to me. It treated the Lowell issue much more briefly, stated clearly what he wanted to say on the subject, and included an expression of pleasure in the festival and of appreciation to the President and the First Lady for sponsoring it. The main body of his text ran as follows:

"It is well known to most of you, I take it, that a fifth writer was invited to be here, and that he accepted the invitation; but that after further thought he decided not to come. It seems proper now to note with regret the absence of Robert Lowell, who assumed that he could not 'enjoy public celebration wtihout making subtle public commitments.' He may or may not have been correct in this assumption; nor do I commit any of the writers present here to agreement or disagreement with it. I have been troubled as to whether I should speak of it at all; I do so now, after several previous attempts, merely as honoring the scruple of a fine poet who, in his own terms, was 'conscience-bound' to stay away.

"However that may be, we are met here, as I have said, as guests of the President and Mrs. Johnson and we wish in advance to thank them profoundly for their magnificent and gracious hospitality. The honor they are doing the arts today is what in our own fashion we propose to celebrate. Let us get on, then, with the principal purpose of the day—a White House Festival of the Arts in which we are all proud and happy to participate."

About half an hour later John Hersey telephoned. He was staying with Mark Van Doren in Washington, Hersey told me, and the two men had been talking. He had decided to call because he thought I ought to know that before leaving home he had prepared a brief statement with which he intended to preface his readings from *Hiroshima,* and he wanted me to hear it. This full text was: "I read these passages on behalf of the great number of citizens who have become alarmed in recent weeks by the sight of fire begetting fire. Let these words be a reminder. The step from one degree of violence to the next is imperceptibly taken and cannot easily be taken back. The end point of these little steps is horror and oblivion.

"We cannot for a moment forget the truly terminal dangers, in these times, of miscalculation, of arrogance, of accident, of reliance not on moral strength but on mere military power. Wars have a way of getting out of hand."

Hersey then went on to say that naturally he knew of President Johnson's reaction to his statement that he planned to read from *Hiroshima* and he wondered how such a preamble would be received. He and I both laughed. Of course what was on his mind was whether, under the circumstances, he should retain the prefatory remarks. I could only comment that in Van Doren's case there was the question of whether his words conveyed what he wanted to say. This was not true of Hersey's preface; he either did or did not want to read it. Again in confidence, I repeated what I had said to Van Doren, concerning both the President's attitude and my complete readiness to back whatever decision Hersey made. Hersey said he would let me know about the introductory statement in the morning.

That Sunday evening, festival eve, was not festive. After speaking with Hersey, I had a bite of food with Saul Bellow, who was in a decidedly unsettled mood. Now that he was actually in Washington, Bellow wondered whether, feeling as he did about President Johnson's foreign policy, he really should have come to the festival. He was also upset by what he called "pressure from the New York crowd," letters, phone calls and telegrams from intellectuals and artists demanding that he withdraw from the festival. As Bellow described it, this was not the kind of pressure—the concerned comments of friends—which Van Doren had described. It was vitriolic denunciation, charges of turncoating for publicity and preferment, even hints of literary blackmail. Bellow's report was not the first I had heard. The novelist Ralph Ellison, who was coming to the festival as a member of the National Council on the Arts, had spoken of the same treatment, and the Special Assistant for the Arts Roger Stevens said he had indications of a "real campaign." It was Stevens' impression that Robert Silvers was the center of the activity, but Silvers has denied that he made any moves connected with the festival after joining with Kunitz in acquiring signatures for their telegram. Whatever the source, the effort was known in the White House, and gave a weapon to all those who were only too eager to insist that intellectuals and artists are malicious children.

The next morning Hersey came to my office with his decision. Ordinarily he is a pleasant, relaxed individual, but he was not relaxed now. He had given careful thought to the matter of the prefatory statement, Hersey said, and he had decided to read it. He sincerely regretted that the preface, particularly when added to the *Hiroshima* readings, would probably contribute to the development of a situation he did not like, but in good conscience, he felt he must go ahead.

Hersey asked if President Johnson would be present at his reading. I replied that Mrs. Johnson had indicated that she would go to all festival events, but almost certainly the President would not attend the readings. I stressed that this had no connection with his attitude toward Hersey, and that from the beginning President Johnson had been scheduled to appear only in the evening. (And inwardly I flinched because even now, on the morning of the festival, there was still no definite word that LBJ would appear at all.) I am not sure whether Hersey was displeased or relieved but we shook hands in an atmosphere, I believe, of understanding of each other's roles and with more than a touch of, It's a hell of a world.

Monday, June 14, was a fine summer day in Washington, cloudless and windless. Early in the morning I went into the White House by the East Gate, in order to enter as the festival guests would do. Workmen were still busy with finishing touches, but nevertheless the brilliance of the art burst upon the viewer. Harry Lowe, the exhibit expert of the National Collection of Fine Arts in Washington, is a man with a magic touch. In the lobby, as a signature to the whole day, he had placed José de Rivera's "Homage to the World of Minkowski," its chrome, nickel and stainless-steel circles winding off in charming grace. The adjoining corridor, the long narrow hall of the East Wing, had seemed to me a death trap for paintings. Lowe interspersed the paintings with small sculptures that gave just enough interruption to avoid a cluttered effect. He blended traditional, abstract, and pop and op painting in a way that made the corridor a blaze of color and design while, as you approached the individual work, its characteristics disentangled themselves clearly.

J. Carter Brown, the youthful and talented Assistant Director of the National Gallery of Art in Washington, supervised the placement of most of the sculpture. He turned the Jacqueline Kennedy Garden just off the East Wing into a piquance of small sculpture. His triumph was the sweep of the South Lawn. There, usually on rises of ground, he arranged the huge works of sculpture—among others, the abstract bronze of Jacques Lipchitz's "Mother and Child," the half-classical, half-mocking "Ancestor" of Seymour Lipton, and the welded chrome plate of automobile bumpers and grille of Jason Seley's "Masculine Presence." At the head of the South Lawn, near the White House entrance, Brown placed Alexander Calder's "Whale II," done in black sheet metal, and far down the lawn, about three city blocks away, David Smith's "Lectern Sentinel," constructed from highly polished stainless steel. The Calder and the Smith saluted each other. On the festival night, with the sculpture floodlit, you came out of the White House to see the squat power of the "Whale" and then the eye went off into the distance to the 101-foot "Lectern Sentinel," glittering against the multicolored White House fountain and, farther back, the Washington Monument.

I must also record, for I daresay a somewhat reluctant history, my two contributions to the arrangement of the South Lawn exhibition. President Johnson, if he were going to return from Texas, would land by helicopter near the South Lawn entrance to the White House. I wondered out loud whether Seley's "Masculine Presence" would not look especially striking on a hillock some three to four hundred yards away and Brown, to my relief, accepted the suggestion. He might as well know now my real interest in the placement. Having tried for days to get the President to come to the festival, I did not want him to arrive, take a look at Seley's auto bumpers and grille and forthwith go away. And then there was a fire box, a sturdy short pole with a green steel rectangular structure on top, some one hundred yards down the other side of the lawn. Reporters can be frolicsome about modern sculpture, and I envisaged the story about the newsman who went over to examine this *objet d'art,* asked for the name of its creator, and discovered that it was the Washington Department of Engineering, Water Operations Division. In this instance I told Brown what was on my mind, and suggested that some shrubbery be placed around the box. J. Carter Brown is not only an able but a good-humored young man. Grimacing only slightly, he ordered the plants. "This is what happens when originally civilized professors come to Washington," he said, and probably he was right.

Mrs. Johnson, looking as pleasant as if she were delighted with everything, opened the festival with cordial remarks. As the First Lady spoke, I received word that President Johnson intended to make his scheduled appearance in the evening.

At the opening event, the readings, Mark Van Doren's introductory words were received, as is often the case with chairmen, in silence. Saul Bellow read from *Herzog* without additional comment, and received appropriate applause. Catherine Drinker Bowen had chosen passages from her biography of Justice

Oliver Wendell Holmes, *Yankee from Olympus*. Miss Bowen is usually a somewhat reserved lady but this day the occasion took hold of her. She read with such zest and her selections contained so much wry humor that she brought down the house.

One passage concerned a White House dinner party shortly after the new Supreme Court Justice and his wife came to settle in Washington. President Theodore Roosevelt fell into conversation with Mrs. Fannie Dixwell Holmes. Had she met many people since she arrived? TR inquired politely.

Quite a few wives had called on her, Mrs. Holmes said. There was a "veiled note" in her voice and the President looked up sharply. "You found the ladies pleasant?"

"Washington," Fannie Dixwell Holmes replied blandly, "is full of famous men and the women they married when they were young."

For Washingtonians, Fannie Holmes's remark was a well-remembered part of the festival.

John Hersey took the podium, pale and serious. He read his prefatory statement and the selections from *Hiroshima* with slow emphasis, occasionally lifting his eyes to look straight at Mrs. Johnson, who sat in the front row. When he finished, there were a few seconds of silence, then vigorous applause. The First Lady, who clapped for all other readings, sat motionless.

Phyllis McGinley was present as the mistress of light verse, and she had decided to add the blithesome note. An attractive suburbanite, her right arm broken in a skiing accident and now in a gay silk sling, she chose as her chief reading her poem "In Praise of Diversity," and added a new verse:

> "And while the pot of culture's
> bubblesome,
> Praise poets even when
> they're troublesome."

The audience chuckled.

The festival wound on. At lunch in the lushly beautiful garden court of the National Gallery of Art, George Kennan delivered his thoughtful address on "The Arts and American Society." Back in the White House, Marian Anderson, stately in her tall black turban, presided over an all-American musical program ranging from Leonard Bernstein's *Candide* to the Louisville Symphony Orchestra playing recent compositions of Ned Rorem and Robert Whitney. The East Room had been transformed into a small theater to present segments of Frank Gilroy's *The Subject Was Roses*, Tennessee Williams' *The Glass Menagerie*, Arthur Miller's *Death of a Salesman* and Millard Lampell's tart political lampoon, *Hard Travelin'*, which was playing at Washington's Arena Theatre and had been selected to represent the local theater. The daytime program closed with Charlton Heston, recently returned from participating in civil rights demonstrations, reading the narration for a forty-minute film put together from five outstanding American movies produced since World War II.

For the most part, the guests simply enjoyed themselves. Many of them were art devotees who had little in common except that fact. Some were conservative Republicans who completely separated their dislike for Lyndon Johnson and his policies from their pleasure in his sponsorship of the festival. A banker, asked about the Vietnam War, replied, "His whole foreign policy is dreadful; he ought to stop giving our money away—isn't that an interesting Noguchi over there?"

Some of the men and women present because of their achievements in the arts or as critics had a similar attitude. Painters as different in their general thinking as Peter Hurd and Robert Motherwell thought the issue raised by Robert Lowell, to use Motherwell's word, "preposterous." The sculptor Dimitri Hadzi, who was in Paris when he received his invitation, flew back at his own expense—without knowing that his "Helmet V" had been chosen for exhibition—specifically to protest Lowell's "nonsensical" letter. Others agreed with Mildred Dunnock's remark: "I have my political opinions and I express them elsewhere. The whole fuss is as silly as people who said I was a socialist because I played in *Death of a Salesman*."

But for many, perhaps a majority of the intellectuals, artists and critics, the salient personality of the White House Festival of the Arts was the man who was not there. They did not really agree with Robert Lowell—after all, they had come—but his letter continued to have its effects, touching off a variety of opinions and emotions, some significant and relevant, others merely snide. Contributing to these attitudes was the note that is often heard in the arts community—the yearning for popular recognition and yet the dread of being considered popular. The White House was permeated with a kind of schizophrenia. One painter was observed smiling happily as he overheard his work being praised by a manufacturer who sat on the board of a Southern museum and then remarked to a member of my staff, "I couldn't care less what these culture morons think." A member of Duke Ellington's orchestra, having toured the South Lawn, offered his diagnosis: "Man, the trouble with these cats is that they wanna be here and they don't wanna be here."

Some felt no confusion at all. Saul Maloff, an editor of *Newsweek* for books and cultural matters who had been invited before President Johnson's crackdown on the press, arrived with a conviction that the festival was a war plot, and a "middlebrow mess" to boot. At the end of the readings in the morning Maloff came upon Bellow near the stairs leading to the East Room. He hurried to the attack. "How could you stand up there and read from your book after what that man has done in Vietnam?"

Embarrassed, Bellow replied, as he had previously stated publicly, that he considered the festival a ceremonial occasion and that he chose to make plain his views on foreign policy elsewhere.

Maloff did not stop. He spoke of "turncoats" and said, "We made you and we can break you." Bellow edged away.

And there was Dwight Macdonald. A heavy, quick-moving man with a bearded, interesting face and a clever tongue, Macdonald can be quite engaging. He was not engaging at the festival; the spokesman of the tasteful life was a crashing bore. The day before, still exercised about the festival, Macdonald had discussed it with a friend who had a suggestion. Why not distribute a pro-Lowell petition at the festival? Macdonald was delighted with the idea and drew one up: "We should like to make it clear that in accepting the President's kind invitation to attend the White House Arts Festival, we do not mean either to repudiate the courageous position taken by Robert Lowell, or to endorse the Administration's foreign policy. We quite share Mr. Lowell's dismay at our country's recent actions in Vietnam and the Dominican Republic."

The next morning, boarding the New York–Washington air shuttle, Macdonald ran into an acquaintance, Thomas B. Hess, executive editor of *Art News*, who had been added to the guest list at the last moment at the instigation of Marvin Watson. (Watson called me to say, "There are five people the President wants invited," which was White Housese for "There are five people with plenty of power or money behind them—and this time don't argue.") Hess thought the petition was a great idea. As soon as he and Macdonald alighted from the shuttle, they started buttonholing White House guests for signatures. They began in the taxicab taking them and others to the White House and continued between each session of the festival. After a while Hess stopped. "Dwight sure is running around," he remarked, and turned to other pursuits.

In addition to himself and Hess, Macdonald acquired six signatures: the sculptors Herbert Ferber, Isamu Noguchi and Peter Voulkos; the painter Willem de Kooning; Sam Hunter, the director of the Brandeis University Museum; and Reed Whittemore of the Carleton College English department, at the time serving as consultant on poetry to the Library of Congress. A ninth person signed and then asked that his name be removed.

Guest after guest turned Macdonald down, but the repeated rebuffs seemed to spur him on; he kept seeking signatures until late in the evening. At one point, a reporter listened to Macdonald approaching a guest, then asked him, "Aren't you in a strange position? First, when you weren't invited, you signed a telegram stating you would refuse to come to the festival. Then you were invited and you accepted. Now, having accepted, you use the invitation to tell your host what you think of him and to try to turn his party into a mass meeting. If it is all so loathsome to you, why didn't you just stay away?"

"I am here," Macdonald replied, "because of an assignment to write an article about the festival."

During the cocktail period Macdonald went up to Charlton Heston, who was standing in the Rose Garden adjoining the President's office. When the actor declined to sign, Macdonald let him know that he considered him a lowbrow creature of Hollywood. Heston retorted that he had marched in civil rights demonstrations, at risk to his movie career, and asked Macdonald where he had been on those occasions. "But that really isn't the point," Heston went on. "Having convictions doesn't mean that you have to lack elementary manners. Are you really accustomed to signing petitions against your host in his home?" For three to four minutes the two men argued toe to toe, Macdonald's voice rising to a shout. Then Heston, recovering his control, walked away.

In the early afternoon Maloff had returned to New York, but Macdonald remained to show his contempt in all possible ways. During the dinner, he sneered at the exhibits and attacked the President personally in a voice that carried across tables and made other guests squirm. His furious activity left his sports coat wilted, his shirt damp, his face dripping perspiration, his shirt and undershirt pulled out with round pink belly showing, and he made no attempt to repair himself in the break provided before dinner.

Macdonald and Maloff found one further way to express their disdain for Lyndon Johnson's festival. Apparently it was the kind of event that could be reported without concern for facts. Although I was publicly identified as in charge of the festival, neither man sought any information from me or my staff. Maloff wrote an article for *Newsweek;* Macdonald, a long piece for the *New York Review of Books.* Both contained flat misstatements of fact, and were based on misleading generalizations.

President Johnson, having decided to appear at the festival, had also decided to make a further gesture. He found a reason to call to his office Senator Fulbright, the Rhodes Scholar and critic of the Vietnam War who was rapidly becoming a hero to "these people." After the conference the President took the senator for a walk around the White House grounds and had a photograph made with the two of them studying Calder's "Whale." The expression on Lyndon Johnson's face was somewhat enigmatic. But anyhow there it was, the picture in all the afternoon papers, President Johnson and the Rhodes Scholar Vietnam critic taking an interest in culture together.

When LBJ returned to his office he learned of Hersey's prefatory statement and of Macdonald's activities. Once more the word came down: he was not going to appear at the festival. This time I started to think about a substitute who might make his absence less glaring—perhaps Chief Justice Earl Warren, whom I had seen looking with intense interest at Louise Nevelson's sculpture, "Royal Game I," and who was skillful at the few appropriate remarks. Then I brushed aside the thought; the Chief Justice could not put himself in such a position. Now Lyndon Johnson either would or would not attend, and the chips would have to fall where they might.

An hour before the President was scheduled to appear I received the firm assurance that he would in fact show up. He stood in the reception line, his face hard as caliche soil. After a few handshakes he left and let the First Lady do the rest of the greeting. He did not join in the buffet supper. Returning to make his remarks which opened the South Lawn performances, he omitted his customary pleasantries and ad-libbed into the prepared text the gratuitous phrases: "You have been asked to come not because you are the greatest artists of the land, although in the judgment of those who made up this guest list you may be. . . ." The speech over, he did not mingle with the guests in his customary way; he strode brusquely to his office.

The White House Festival of the Arts was closing. The American ballet company, the Robert Joffrey group, went on and the swirling blue and yellow gown of the ballerina, Lisa Bradley, broke into the shafts of light. Then came the final section, led by the superb musician whose father had at one time been a butler in the White House, Edward K. Ellington as the official invitation read.

Duke Ellington began with *Impressions of the Far East,* which he had written with the memorable Billy Strayhorn.

Midway through the *Impressions,* I walked back to my office, located just off the South Lawn. In the White House I had developed the habit of taking ten-minute cat naps which I found wonderfully refreshing. I kicked off my shoes and put my head down, but things kept going through my mind. From the remarks made to me, I knew what most of the critics were going to write. The experts we had consulted had not failed us. The reviews would say that the White House had offered a salute to the American arts which made no compromise with quality or conventionality. Some of the general press would go on to stress, as the *New York Times* did, that "by tolerating dissent within its own precincts, the White House raised its own and the nation's stature. For here was proof that democracy could practice what it preached in its most distinguished citadel."

I felt proud. As for the little band who had worked with me, I was bursting with pride in them. We had insisted upon quality and integrity. This was not difficult for me; I could always return to my professorship and writing. They had their futures very much at stake, and two of them were directly dependent upon the White House for their livelihoods. Yet they had gone straight down the line with me, working their ten to twelve hours a day with enormous good cheer and never, directly or indirectly, making a single move to dissociate themselves from the storm.

I felt pride, but puzzlement too. When the troubles came, I had steadfastly and sincerely maintained that the festival was a salute to the arts and nothing more, and that Lowell was wrong in his statement that he could not appear without at least a "subtle commitment" to Administration policy. Now, having gone through this experience and learned what one political leader actually expected from his ceremonial guests, I wondered. On the other hand, could the intellectual and artistic communities seriously expect to be encouraged and supported by government while some of their leaders engaged in open contempt for the head of the government and others, although preserving respect, refused even a ceremonial invitation from him? The question was no mere philosophical talking point. With the establishment of the national councils on the arts and the humanities, the U.S. government was embarking on its first program of financial support for these groups. Were the only ground rules to be a countervailing play of hostility?

I had seen a President reacting with arrogant know-nothingism, and influential figures in the cultural world reacting with an equally arrogant know-it-allness. Lyndon Johnson was obviously a special case, and so were the Macdonalds and the Maloffs. Most Americans, intellectuals, artists or politicians, are bored by such boorishness. But had we reached a point in the United States where one section of the population, filled with a sense of elitism and snobbery about its ability to take action, was in hopeless confrontation with another segment, equally filled with its own elitism and snobbery about its cultural superiority?

Above all, there was the immediate situation. The President of the United States had embarked on a program of major domestic changes and was taking the nation into a grave war. He needed all the help he could get, particularly from the country's better-educated citizenry. He needed this help especially in the form of criticism and urgings for restraint, the kind that would have come to him if he had looked into the face of John Hersey when he spoke his haunting statement that wars have a way of getting out of hand. He would also benefit richly from genuine interaction with gifted and skeptical Metroamerica. At the same time Metroamericans—intellectuals and artists or Metroamericans in general —needed some sense that just because they had read Macdonald in the *New York Review of Books* and could discuss Calder's "Whale" knowledgeably, they had not attained final omniscience in public policy, foreign or domestic.

Judged by these criteria, the White House Festival of the Arts had been an unmitigated disaster. Almost everything that happened after Lowell's letter and President Johnson's reaction to it had added bricks to a wall between the President and these groups. Mercifully, much of the story was unknown. But enough had become public to make the wall seem as impassable as the barbed concrete between East and West Berlin.

My cat nap was not working; I could not get to sleep. Duke Ellington was into his last selection, *Black, Brown, and Beige,* and the jazz drifted into my office. I walked back to the South Lawn, glanced up at the family section of the White House. Obviously President Johnson was not coming down, as he often did, to say good-night to these guests. I looked off to the Roger Smith, which now seemed to be glittering in the floodlights in a mocking jousting with the President's quarters.

Standing there, I suddenly realized that there were tears in my eyes. This is the silliest thing yet, I told myself; I really must be tired.

I wiped my eyes, walked into the crowd, found my staff. Others from the guests accumulated and we went off for a gay, a very gay drink.

CHAPTER 17

Time to Leave

Once the White House Festival of the Arts was over, naturally my thoughts turned to resigning. My personal urge to get away was strong; obviously my relationship to President Johnson was seriously damaged; and apart from any other consideration, I had been developing sizable doubts about the whole conception of the position of White House "intellectual-in-residence."

Under that title, I had been doing a variety of tasks, some of which were similar to those carried out by aides whom no one would have thought of calling an "intellectual," and others of which could have been executed with at least equal competence by a man unaccoutered by a Ph.D., a professorship or any other mark of intellectualism. Yet from the beginning, I had been considered—inside the White House and particularly outside it—different to a degree because in some sense I was supposed to "represent" the intellectual community. It was this function of the "intellectual-in-residence" about which I was growing increasingly skeptical.

The post was certainly new. My fellow historian, Arthur Schlesinger, Jr., working under President Kennedy and also engaged in a variety of duties, had been the first to be thought of in this way; I was the second. So recently created, the position has never really been thought through. The White House staff is a group appointed to help the President to be the best of himself and to get a mountain of work done. It is not—or at least should not be—a representative body, a kind of little parliament serving particular constituencies. Intellectuals may have more to contribute to public affairs than plumbers, zinc executives or representatives of the D.A.R.; nevertheless, they are still only one of the infinitely varied complex of American groups, with their own parochialisms and self-interests.

Conceptually justified or not, the post caters to some of the less noble instincts of both Chief Executives and intellectuals. Presidents are men who are good enough politicians to be elected President; for the foreseeable future the political climate of the United States is likely to be such that the temptation exists for a Chief Executive to do enough about intellectuals to attract them and little enough so as not to offend the much larger part of the population which takes a dim view of intellectuals as policymakers. The position of White House intellectual-in-residence serves admirably for this purpose. The President installs a properly certified person to assert his interest in the opinions of the intellectual community; then, for the benefit of the rest of the country, he occasionally lets it be known that the man is kept in proper rein, leaving at least one incumbent wondering just how much he was mere front and how much the President considered him a genuinely needed staff member. I have never discussed the post with Arthur Schlesinger, and obviously President Kennedy had an attitude toward intellectuals sharply contrasting with President Johnson's and Schlesinger's role in the JFK White House was different from mine in the LBJ organization. Yet when questioned by the reporter William S. White, who was bearish about intellectuals in government, President Kennedy felt it politic to remark, "Arthur has nothing to do with making policy. He works over there"—indicating the East Wing of the White House—"and he is a good writer. Period." President Johnson was much more prone to spread this kind of word. When asked about my activities, by reporters or White House visitors, he sometimes pointedly commented that he had named me a member of the staff "to please the intellectuals."

On the obverse side of the coin, the intellectual-in-residence position is an encouragement to intellectuals to forget that they are, among other things, merely another pressure group. I don't know an intellectual who would not be outraged, for example, at the thought of the steel industry's going to Marvin Watson, and because he came from a steel firm, urging him to try to influence the President in a direction which that industry desired. Yet during my White House period, many intellectuals acted precisely in this manner toward me. Especially when organized in professional associations, they thought nothing of denouncing lobbyists in one breath, and in another, lobbying furiously for a policy which benefited their group in a material way or represented a program of ideas which they had adopted and expected me to endorse automatically as "one of us."

In the day-by-day workings of the White House, the marking

out of one man as the staff intellectual makes for all kinds of sticky situations. Like almost anyone from the mainstream of American life, a President is likely to have a confused conception of the make-up of a professional intellectual, assuming that he is useful in one area and useless in another in ways that bear little relation to reality. The problem had its special nuances with Lyndon Johnson, but it is certainly not likely to be confined to him. I would have been a good deal more sure that President Johnson was right about the fields in which he thought my opinion worthless if he had not considered it of value in others where I knew it mattered little or not at all.

Designating one man also creates a personnel problem. However you define an intellectual, in the new America the word carries prestige in the eyes of many. Consequently some White House staff members inevitably seek to cut down the intellectual-in-residence. In the case of other aides—and some Presidents—the word will always convey the opposite of prestige, and this too can have its effects. The intellectual-in-residence who succeeded me in the Johnson Administration felt called upon to open his tenure with hairy-chested press statements brandishing phrases about a group of intellectuals like the "artsy-craftsy set" and "high-class illiterates," and describing himself as an "unabashed veteran cold warrior."

Educated Americans have generally applauded the idea of a White House intellectual-in-residence, and understandably so. They want the President of the United States to have the contribution of the intellectual at his best—the informed, analytical, skeptical, questing approach about which men like Tom Wicker have spoken. The growing question in my mind was how much the particular device of a White House intellectual-in-residence contributed toward that laudable aim—whether, in fact, it might not be working in the opposite direction. I was becoming convinced that the goal would have to be pursued by the much more difficult process of seeking to surround the President with as many men as possible, in standard staff posts, professional intellectuals or not, who brought to their daily tasks the better qualities of American intellectualism.

Eager to leave the staff for so many reasons, I knew that I should not resign immediately after the festival. No matter what I said, the action inevitably would be interpreted as a break with President Johnson over the event, and insofar as my resignation had any influence at all, it would injure the purposes I had sought to achieve by the festival and my other activities. I was also in the middle of minor projects which needed cleaning up, and I wanted to do some final plugging away at President Johnson on points that I considered anything but minor.

On his part, the President was making it clear that while I was a grievous sinner and could never again be fully accepted back in the church, some degree of absolution was not out of the question. With LBJ's feudal conception of his staff, he never really liked anybody to resign; he took it as something of a personal affront. He was always edgy about possible political consequences, however small. And after his anger subsided, sentiment and a touch of self-doubt edged him toward reconciliation.

The day after the festival of the arts, Lady Bird Johnson, performing her usual smoothing-over role, telephoned to "congratulate" me on the event, maintaining her complete loyalty to her husband by speaking of the "difficulties created for the President" but tactfully brushing them aside and finding many things to praise. The next week President Johnson sent word that he had been carefully reading the comments in the press on the festival and wanted recommendations from me about such an occasion in the future. That was carrying reconciliation a bit far. I had a profound conviction that one festival of the arts was enough for the Johnson Administration—I have a feeling it will be the first and last festival of the arts in any Administration—and I did about the President's request what I assumed he wanted me to do, which was to note it and to forget it. Soon he found an occasion to call me over to the Oval Office and have a photograph taken of the two of us, which he sent to me with a generous inscription.

I swung into my cleanup, leaving suspended the decision of just when I would resign.

The bicentennial of the American Revolution was at hand (important events connected with the Revolution began in the 1760's), and the approach of the anniversary called to mind the Civil War Centennial which the United States had suffered from 1961 to 1965. This remarkable commemoration had managed almost totally to conceal the point of the Civil War and its significance for the 1960's. For the most part it was devoted to re-enactments of battles for the tourists, "Dixie" and "Battle Hymn of the Republic" oratory, and a flood of publications most of which were a competition in inconsequentiality. (The University of Kentucky Press won grateful applause by announcing that it would observe the last year of the centennial by publishing nothing about the Civil War.) All of this was tawdry enough. But botching the bicentennial of the American Revolution mattered a good deal more.

Seventeen seventy-six was not only a grand moment in the history of the American people. During the centuries that followed, the Declaration of Independence was carried in the pockets and in the hearts of men and women in many parts of the world who persisted in believing that each human being has a right to life, liberty and the pursuit of happiness, alienable by no man or no governmental mechanism. This influence was never greater than in the post-World War II era. As one of the many American professors and writers who made trips to other continents trying to explain America, I had a strong personal sense of the international heritage of the American Revolution. Audience after audience, particularly in the underdeveloped areas, was almost ready to forgive us our foreign policies, our Coca-Cola, even our junketeering congressmen, because we had produced Thomas Jefferson.

During my White House work, this awareness heightened. At one ceremony, when I was receiving a gift for the President from a group of Asian intellectuals, I asked whether I might be of assistance in planning their stay in Washington. The elderly leader replied, "The first form of the Declaration of Independence—am I right in my impression that it is here in the capital?" He seemed a little embarrassed for a moment, and then not embarrassed at all. "You see, I carried a copy of it in Hindi on my first march with Gandhi to the sea." Busy or not, I escorted the group to the National Archives, where the original of the Declaration of Independence is displayed. It was good to stand with them in its presence.

To permit the American Revolution Bicentennial to turn into more antiquarianism and commercialism would not only miss an opportunity, as the Civil War Centennial had done, to say things worth saying to the American public; in this instance, the United States would be making a show of itself with many people around the world. Yet interest in the bicentennial was mounting and judging from the communications coming to my desk, we were about to re-enact, and perhaps to out-re-enact, the Civil War Centennial. Well-known corporations sought a White House letter that would permit them to "co-ordinate" advertising campaigns with the bicentennial. Patriotic units were on the move. With the irony of which only they are capable, they wanted to make sure that the celebration of a revolution would be an assault on dissidence. Bills establishing an American Revolution Bicentennial Commission were being readied for Congress, a few enlightened, others dreadful.

Clearly it was desirable to have presidential leadership in

getting Congress to set up without much delay the kind of commission which would understand the essential meaning of the Revolution. Such a body could not, and certainly should not, control all activities connected with the anniversary, but it could serve as a guiding spirit, get a number of the right kind of projects under way and discourage some of the more horrendous possibilities. In September 1965 I sent a memo to President Johnson outlining some of my thoughts about the bicentennial and recommending that he send to the Hill a message calling for the establishment of a commission and an Administration bill to that effect.

For a man in the mood of cleanup, I was getting myself into the most drawn-out procedure I experienced in the White House, although it was not unrelieved by moments of comic opera. Of course a presidential message to commemorate a national historic event, like a salute to motherhood or to the glories of the pecan crop, is as routine as raising the flag over the White House, and I assumed that whatever President Johnson thought of my ideas concerning the bicentennial, he would promptly okay the recommendation in principle. But he took no action. I kept trying, and still nothing happened. He was not against sending the message and the bill; he simply was not interested in doing it. Some of the reasons were simple enough. The pressure was coming from me, which at this stage was scarcely a radiant recommendation, and I had discussed the bicentennial in a way which no doubt called up for him visions of more White House-sponsored activities by people who did not appreciate Lyndon Johnson. The President also was hearing a bit of political static. Boston and Philadelphia each wanted to be the center of the major bicentennial events; influential interests in the two cities were talking world fairs and other large-scale commercial projects, and jockeying against each other.

Yet neither of these facts was as important or as interesting as other considerations in explaining the LBJ lethargy about this small matter. Lyndon Johnson was a President with a full emotional sense of American history, even if he knew little of it, and he delighted in associating himself with it. But he responded to the history of his America, and this had little connection with the thirteen colonies up in the East which happened, while Texas was still part of Mexico, to get into a hassle with the King of England.

As for the international significance of the Revolution, no President has shown a greater zeal to transfer abroad what he considers the lessons of the American experience. But again this zeal had its LBJ flavor. The worldwide heritage of the American Revolution consists essentially of an ideological conception, a shimmering and exciting one. To Lyndon Johnson no ideological conception, however shimmering, was exciting. What he wanted to present to the world was the American example of how ordinary men, by hard work, an exploitation of technology, and responsive political leadership, can turn grudging soil and rampant rivers into a comfortable way of life. The American Revolution simply did not take hold of his mind, and its anniversary was pushed aside for more important matters and for more appealing small ones.

Finally, after five months, the President gave me an unenthusiastic okay to go ahead. I took as a basis for the Administration legislation a good bill already introduced in Congress by two Republicans, Charles McC. Mathias of Maryland and F. Bradford Morse of Massachusetts, and the principal changes I made were directed toward trying to protect the nature of the observance. By custom, a number of government officials had to be designated members of the commission. Busy men, most of them were likely to take the assignment as a formality. Inevitably a group of patriotic nabobs and politically balanced appointees would also end up on the board. I enlarged the total number of general presidential appointees so as to open the way for more members who would be genuinely interested in the work and who understood the potentialities of the anniversary. I also wrote into the measure the directive: "In all planning, the commission shall give a special emphasis to the ideas associated with the Revolution, which have been so important in the development of the United States and in world affairs. . . ." That sentence had an amusing time of it. Somebody in the White House—I don't know who, but it was not the President—took the lines out of the bill three times. I put them back three times, and mainly by chance they were still there when the measure went to Congress on March 10, 1966.

The Senate passed the bill routinely. By the time it reached the House of Representatives, summer was approaching and it would be appropriate to have congressional action completed so that President Johnson could sign the legislation on July 4. But the measure had to go through the House Committee on the Judiciary, and that group, locked in debate over the open-housing provision of the 1966 civil rights legislation, showed no signs of being ready to act on anything else before July 4. I turned to a former student of mine who was on the staff of the committee and to Harold Barefoot Sanders, Jr., one of those men President Johnson kept pulling out of his bottomless bag of friends.

Somewhere in the past a Sanders had been enough of an Indian to be named "Barefoot." The present bearer of the delightful name—everyone called him "Barefoot"—was Dallas-born, the freckle champion of the 1936 State Fair, a successful young lawyer in Sanders and Sanders and a Texan drawn to politics as naturally as a down-easter takes to lobster, now nominally Assistant Deputy Attorney General and, day and night, a politico maneuvering on the Hill for Lyndon Johnson. Sanders was well aware how little White House steam was behind the bicentennial bill but affable as always and with his own touch of interest in history, he joined with my friend on the committee staff in a resourceful bit of committee interrupting.

It was at this point that the effects of President Johnson's lack of interest in the measure showed. Important Republicans on the Judiciary Committee were querulous about the introduction of an Administration-sponsored bicentennial bill, and congressmen from both parties were feeling pressures from Philadelphia and Boston which made them churlish about the whole measure. Others complained about the $200,000 appropriation in the bill to pay for the first years of planning by the commission. Some of these critics were economy-minded; some talked of the "Civil War Centennial mess," and asked why money should be paid to repeat it. The attitude of the President made any firm line impossible. Soon I learned that the committee was readying the bill for House passage with the entire appropriation removed. The United States government was about to proclaim its pride in its glorious Revolution, a pride so great that it was not ready to pay a penny to express it.

Strange little bill—it was moving into its final bizarre stage. I intervened again, but the indifference within the White House continued and this time no one could help. The bill went through its final formalities and was sent on the courier plane to Texas, where the President was spending his July 4 holiday. On July 5 I picked up my Washington *Post* and was puzzled to see no report of the signing. When I phoned the ranch I learned that LBJ had kept muttering about "this damn thing" and pushing it aside but finally, shortly before midnight, had signed the legislation. Then "somehow" the Press Office had not released the information.

I asked that my call be transferred to the man who was in Texas acting as Press Secretary, Robert H. Fleming. He sounded completely in the dark and agreed that one way or another the Press Office had to state that the President had signed a bill; he also agreed, grimly, that the reporters would have a great time with a story of a July 4 signing printed on July 6—particularly when the bill concerned the American Revolution and when Washington knew that a House committee had interrupted work on important legislation to make it possible for the President to sign it on July 4. I said I would try to think of something and call back.

Colonial American history is no forte of mine, but I thought I vaguely remembered that a few days after the Declaration of Independence was adopted, Philadelphia held some kind of ceremony. Checking, I discovered that on July 5 and 6, 1776, copies of the Declaration were prepared to be dispatched to the states and the document was first publicly proclaimed in Philadelphia on July 8. The original LBJ statement prepared for release at the time of the signing of the bicentennial bill began: "One hundred and ninety years ago today. . . ." Now I changed "today" to "this week," and inserted the sentences: "The Declaration of Independence was adopted on July 4, 1776. On July 8 the Liberty Bell in Philadelphia, proclaiming 'liberty throughout all the land unto all the inhabitants thereof,' summoned the people to listen to the first public reading of the document. In this historic tradition I have signed the American Revolution Bicentennial Bill on July 4 and am releasing it to the Nation on July 8."

And thus liberty throughout all the land unto all the inhabitants thereof was proclaimed in 1966.

The bicentennial and a few other minor projects for the President, tasks for Mrs. Johnson—but after the festival of the arts, in late 1965 and in 1966, these were not my preoccupation. I was trying to get across to President Johnson certain points that I considered vital and which seemed to me most effectively said to him from within the White House. All circumstances considered, I thought it best to make the effort mainly through memos.

As President Johnson escalated American participation in the Vietnam War, I was growing increasingly opposed to his policy and uncomfortable with it on many grounds, including the moral. But my memos concerning foreign policy did not argue the war itself; he would have stopped reading after the first sentence. I sought to help create some willingness on his part to listen to what responsible critics of the war were saying; to encourage him to state to the nation that he was ready to do this; and to attract his attention to a number of problems that were not directly a part of the war but were intimately involved with it.

During this period President Johnson kept brandishing public opinion polls and asserting that the country was overwhelmingly behind the war. If he had a problem, he continued to say privately, it was the hawks, not the doves, whom he dismissed as a band of "rattlebrains." I thought it would be helpful for a loyal aide to say bluntly to the President—what he certainly knew but did not seem to be admitting even to himself—that the dove group increasingly included "a broad cross section—professional people, businessmen, civil rights leaders, women, etc., and it includes many young voters." As tactfully as I could, I tried to cast doubt on a literal reading of the polls. "Much of this dove or semi-dove element, I am convinced, does not consist of people who are outright opponents of the Administration Vietnam policy. As we all know, the polls measure support for a public policy, but they do not necessarily capture other feelings which go along with the support or nuances of attitude that are contained within the support.

"When most intelligent, balanced Americans are asked, 'Do you in general approve of the President's Vietnam policy?' they are inclined to say yes. They respect their President and want to back him. They assume that he has more information, and has given more attention and thought to the problem, than they have. They are reluctant to go along with the irresponsible statements that have marked some of the attack on Administration policy. But within this support there seems to be a degree of uneasiness, of concern and misgivings. A number of supporters as well as opponents are touched with a malaise about the conflict—a vague and confused but potent wondering whether something is not wrong, whether this is really proper business for Americans, whether some means should not be found soon to remove the United States from the fighting."

As opposition to the Vietnam War increased, one segment of American public opinion followed the traditional pattern by its attitude toward the anti-war group. War opponents were being venomously assailed; completely loyal dissidents were denounced as pro-Communist. The White House was silent. After all, Lyndon Johnson himself, with his view of the Presidency in relation to foreign policy, was inclined to believe that enemies of the Vietnam War were enemies of their country. I pressed on President Johnson's attention the fact that a new phrase was being applied to his Administration, "'liberal McCarthyism.' Many of the people using the phrase are simply opponents of your Vietnam policy. . . . On the other hand, the phrase is also used by thoughtful, patriotic people who have been strong supporters of your Administration in general and of your Vietnam policy in particular."

This memo went on to urge that the President should take an appropriate opportunity to "make clear—in a ringing way—that the Administration distinguishes between legitimate argument over policy, which it respects, and illegal draft dodging or incitement to draft dodging," and to caution the country "against sliding into the easy practice of denouncing ideas and activities which we do not like, and which Communists happen to support, as necessarily pro-Communist. . . . The statement could frankly discuss how, in a democracy, honest opposition in foreign policy is inevitably used by the enemy but that this is no reason to try to stifle such dissent." I concluded with practical reasons for making such a statement but "above all, I urge it because I think it is the right thing to do within the American tradition. . . . The statement would surely add a proud page to the history of your Administration—and to the history of responsible freedom in Western civilization."

During these months I was simultaneously making an effort to inject into the President's thinking more awareness of how easy it was for a leader like himself, devoted to domestic social legislation, to turn into a war chief who was a captive or an accomplice of conservative or reactionary forces. Here I turned to the historical parallels which experience had taught me sometimes catalyzed the thinking of Lyndon Johnson. "President Wilson, on the evening before he called for entrance into World War I, made some relevant remarks to a friend, the newspaperman Frank Cobb. Later Cobb paraphrased the President: 'When a war got going, it was just war and there weren't two kinds of it. It required illiberalism at home to reinforce the men at the front. We couldn't fight Germany and maintain the ideas of Government that all thinking men shared. He said we would try it, but it would be too much for us.'

" 'To fight,' Cobb remembered President Wilson's words, 'you must be brutal and ruthless, and the spirit of ruthless brutality will enter into the very fiber of our national life infecting Congress, the policeman on the beat, the man in the street. Conformity would be the only virtue, and every man who refused to conform would have to pay the penalty.' " *

My memo went on: "Wilson was talking about total, not limited war, and he exaggerated what would happen. But his core point—that war helps to produce a reaction against progressivism

For those who would persuade Presidents by history, it is interesting, not to say chastening, to note that I turned out to be using material which may well be fiction. Since the 1920's the Wilson quotation had been assumed in professional historical circles to be as sound as the Washington Monument. The year after I sent this memo to President Johnson, a Brandeis University professor of history, Jerold S. Auerbach, published a deft piece of historical detective work in the Journal of American History (December 1967). Auerbach made a plausible case that the quotation was actually the later invention of the anti-war authors of What Price Glory?, Maxwell Anderson and Laurence Stallings.

—has been proved correct in connection with every major modern war of the United States. The Civil War was followed by Grantism; World War I, by Harding; World War II, by the 80th Congress; and the Korean War, by Eisenhowerism." FDR had been "sharply aware" of this recurring pattern. "As a result of the World War I experience, he tried to conduct World War II in a way that would avoid . . . creating an atmosphere conducive to standpattism; offending a significant section of the liberal element . . . to the point that they would be permanently alienated from the Administration; and building excessive hopes which would produce acute disillusionment after the war."

Applying the parallel to the Vietnam War, I urged that President Johnson take all possible steps to see to it that his leadership remained liberal and that it continued to appeal to the mass of liberals. This meant, at the least, paying attention to the fact that the war critics included "many of the people who have enthusiastically supported your domestic policies. . . . There is a corollary key fact. In the case of all modern American wars, as the fighting has gone on, conservatives, not to speak of reactionaries, have tended to become the all-out, most emotional supporters of the wars, and have sought to use the fact of war to curtail domestic progressivism and to create a general atmosphere of standpattism or reaction. This trend is certainly evident at present. . . . The all-out supporters of Administration Vietnam policy include many people who have been and will be strong enemies of your general policies."

Specifically I suggested that the President put increasing emphasis on a foreign policy which was concerned not simply with Vietnam but with a "whole global effort of the Administration to build a world in which peace is possible, through techniques that are primarily nonmilitary"; press forward vigorously with existing Administration domestic programs and with plans to face further domestic problems, letting the public know at least the broad outlines of these coming moves; and avoid sharp "criticism of critics of the Administration Vietnam policy, particularly any statements that can be construed as implying that the critics are not good Americans.

"The firm intentions of the Administration in Southeast Asia can be made plain to Hanoi without such statements. They anger many general friends of the Administration and, if carried far enough, could result in permanent alienation.

"Wilson lambasted his critics and ended up with deep antagonism from a number of his former enthusiasts and a lashing in history on this point. Lincoln and FDR usually treated their critics in a relaxed, almost whimsical way, and came off much better, in their own time and in history."

Throughout these memos, and particularly in those written in 1966, I kept returning to what seemed to me of cardinal importance—trying, amid the savagely mounting war, to keep at least a part of President Johnson's mind on domestic problems and on them in a way that went beyond consensus as the ratification of yesterday. My most extensive effort along this line pointed out that the two previous highly productive Administrations of the twentieth century—those of Woodrow Wilson and FDR—both began by taking care of unfinished business and putting through legislation toward which public opinion had long been moving and which was wanted, or at least accepted, by a broad cross section. Then the Presidents moved to face new problems in new ways, and in doing this they "could no longer depend on a consensus. While maintaining as much general support as possible, they had to build special rapport with the most dynamic element in the society—the one particularly influential by virtue of rapidly growing numbers, general drive and role in determining national attitudes. . . .

"The initial stage of the Johnson Administration . . . [was] characterized by the brilliant use of consensus politics to enact programs like civil rights, aid to education and Medicare. The historical parallel suggests that a second stage is at hand," and clearly the dynamic class of the 1960's consisted of "a group which might be called the Metroamericans." Here I characterized the Metroamericans as I have done in this book, and argued: "In American history we have had only three periods when new classes of great dynamism have taken center stage—the eighteenth and nineteenth centuries, the era of the frontier man; the earlier twentieth century, the period of the urban man; and now, the Metroamerican. The Metroamericans are, consequently, a phenomenon of major importance, . . . and in my opinion they call for a carefully prepared response by the Administration."

That response, I suggested, was a matter both of tone and of substance. The tone of White House leadership was sensitive territory, as it would be in the case of any human being occupying the Oval Office, and I simply touched upon it. "As you know," there were White House moments that "went over particularly well with the Metroamericans." One instance I cited was his 1965 press conference when, asked about his anti-civil rights votes in the Senate, he had said, A President is different from a senator from Texas and, besides, times change and we all learn. Another was the television special, *The Hill Country,* when the interviewer Ray Scherer remarked, "Those cattle all look very trusting at you" and you replied, "They are young and innocent, Ray." The memo commented, "Bantering, a sense of the complexity of things, a tone of fluidity and flexibility . . . seem to make the Administration stance most appealing to the Metroamerican and bring him the greatest sense of identity with it."

The main thrust of my effort was to get President Johnson to consider the possibility of making the 1967 State of the Union message a declaration of the "second stage" of the Administration in domestic affairs. The message "would open with a broad perspective, pointing out how the Eighty-ninth Congress had brought the nation up to date in many respects by cleaning up a lot of important unfinished business. It would then paint, in equally broad strokes, the new economic and social pattern and problems of the United States." Specific, innovative, non-consensus recommendations would follow, with heaviest emphasis on the metropolitan areas. The key proposal I suggested was the same one I had brought up at the beginning of the Johnson Administration, when a group of us had assembled to discuss the first LBJ State of the Union message. The longer I worked at the White House, the more convinced I became that a degree of decentralization was desirable in order to revitalize local governments, and that a new non-federal governmental instrumentality was the prerequisite to broad progress in the urban field.

"For a long time," this memo of 1966 stated, "most experts in metropolitan affairs have been agreeing that the present governmental structure makes it extremely difficult, if not impossible, really to cope with metropolitan problems. The American governmental tradition is that, when a new governmental tool is needed, it is created not by substitution for present forms but by inserting a new instrumentality which helps organize existing power into a more effective combination. The Federal Reserve Act, with its establishment of a national board but the preservation of broad regional autonomy, is a brilliant instance of this. The rise of various 'authorities,' turnpike, port, etc.—with their power extending over several states but still constructed in a way that gives recognition to each state's interests—is an instance still closer to the metropolitan problem. My suggestion is that the State of the Union message propose a new governmental instrument called the Metropolitan Authority.

"Sketched in the broadest outline, the Authority would be permissive [to render it constitutional]. A metropolitan area, speaking through the state legislatures involved, would have to request the establishment of an Authority. It would consist of representatives of each state involved, named by the Governors; of the counties involved, named by a convention of the counties assembled in each state for this purpose; and of the incorporated towns and cities, named by a similar convention.

"The Authority would do overall planning for the area; recommend programs and—if they were approved by all the legislatures involved—carry them out; eliminate duplication and confusion in federal and state funds flowing into the area under existing programs; and in general serve as a co-ordinator, innovator, and activator for the whole metropolitan area.

"This Authority would not supersede local or state governments or the functions of the Federal Government with respect to the area. It would be an added instrument, doing things that the existing governments cannot do."

Snatches of points and phrases from these memos—the barest snatches—showed up in various White House statements or actions, enough to indicate that President Johnson was reading them and little enough to make it plain that he was rejecting the letter or spirit of their basic points.

Only one memo produced substantial action. In the Spring of 1966, the White House began talking about the coming congressional election, and I was puzzled by the general air of confidence. President Johnson seemed ready for a khaki election—in which he would thunder, Are you for or against our fighting men in Vietnam?—and he appeared to have little doubt that the outcome would be favorable. I was struck by a conversation with Cliff Carter, still the LBJ man at the Democratic National Committee, who said he had been studying polls and political conditions in the doubtful districts and "things look fine."

By coincidence, just at this time Irving Dilliard, the former chief editorial writer for the St. Louis *Post-Dispatch* and a seasoned political observer, wrote me his own misgivings about the coming election. Nineteen sixty-six, Dilliard commented, reminded him of 1942. As late as September the Gallup poll had predicted Democratic gains in the House; on the Sunday before the election, it indicated that the Democrats would do well generally. Having traveled around the country in 1942, Dilliard was highly skeptical, and he wrote an article for the *New Republic* citing the circumstances that might be operating powerfully against the Democrats. The *New Republic* editor Bruce Bliven was so dubious about Dilliard's interpretation that he prefaced the analysis with a firm if pleasant dissenting note. Once the article was published, Dilliard told me, "Secretary Ickes wrote me a letter saying that he agreed with me completely, that he had been trying to get the White House staff, the Cabinet and FDR himself to listen to him [Ickes] on the subject of the November dangers. He said no one would pay him any serious attention, that all cited the Democratic gains forecast by the Gallup poll." On election day 1942, the Democrats came within 14 votes of losing control of the House; the Republicans gained nine Senate seats. The results represented the most sweeping congressional losses by a party controlling the White House since the wartime election of 1918.

In a memo dated May 12, 1966, I used the Dilliard experience as a springboard and called the attention of President Johnson to the similarities between the congressional campaigns of 1942 and 1966. In both cases the election was in an off year, which so frequently has favored the outs; a Democratic President, two years before, had won a decisive victory, carrying into the House of Representatives a large number of vulnerable first-termers; the Administration had entered a war, with all the crisscross of emotions that engenders, and discontent over the administration of the draft was spreading; inflation was nagging the public mind; racial unrest, among both whites and Negroes, existed in Northern urban centers. "If the parallel holds up, the congressional election of 1966 could be a serious problem."

To counteract the possible Republican tide, I suggested that President Johnson undertake a long swing around the country. He would carefully avoid turning the campaign into "a contest in which the chief appeal is, If you support your country and your fighting men abroad, vote for Administration-approved candidates. This—with its inevitable interpretation to mean that other voters do not support their country and its fighting men—can only exacerbate feelings. There are further dangers. . . . The only time in modern American history when a President went far in this direction was during World War I. Shortly before the congressional election of 1918, President Wilson declared: 'If you have approved of my leadership and wish me to continue to be your unembarrassed spokesman in affairs at home and abroad, I earnestly beg that you will express yourself unmistakably to that effect by returning a Democratic majority to both the Senate and House of Representatives.' The Republicans swept the election and took control of both houses away from the Democrats. Although other factors were present, the nature of Wilson's appeal is generally considered a major cause of the debacle. The damage to the President's prestige was severe and irreparable.

"The Administration could also lose by winning a Democratic

Congress on the basis of such a campaign. In view of the apparent growing correlation between general conservatism and highly emotional support of the Vietnam policy, the appeal to these feelings could result in a Democratic Congress which nevertheless contained an unnecessarily large faction hostile to the Administration's general purposes."

Above all, I sought to have the President face more squarely and speak to the nation about the home-front problems which were worrying Americans in 1966—much the same ones as in 1942. I ticked them off, and in each case tried to make suggestions for specific moves. Particularly stressed were the unrest over the race issue and over the inequities of the draft. In white-Negro relations, there was no longer a Goldwater menace to nullify Negro grievances and white backlash; what was needed was a major speech recognizing that the country had reached a "post-civil rights legislation stage, in which the basic constitutional rights of all our people have been asserted and the new need is for each American, acting as a free individual, to get down to the patient, rewarding business of educating himself and exerting himself to take advantage of the opportunities being flung open for everyone. It would speak of common responsibilities as well as common rights, of obligations as well as opportunities. It would hold out as the vista of the new era of race relations an America in which— through civil rights laws and the Negro's own efforts—civil rights laws were no longer necessary."

On the subject of selective service, I emphasized to the President—what I hardly needed to point out to him—"the widespread feeling that the draft simply is not fair." The functioning of the selective service system was complex, and some of the criticism of it was unjustified. In 1966, two thirds of the men in the armed forces came from the middle classes or farther up the economic ladder. Yet the large critical section of the public was also right in its feeling that selective service was selecting, in a disproportionate way, from the disadvantaged.

About two million young men were annually reaching draft age, and only a percentage of these were needed for the armed forces at any given time. The question was, Who should serve when all did not have to? The eligibility and deferment provisions of the existing legislation combined to operate in such a way that the man whose education stopped at elementary or high school was much more likely to be drafted than the one who was able to go to college or beyond. The bias in favor of the nice young man who really should not have his life disrupted was accentuated by the composition of the local draft boards making the case-by-case decisions. They were a composite, almost a caricature, of respectability—and of a respectability with the attitudes of an older generation. Seventy percent of the members were in white-collar occupations; 20 percent, professional men. The average age was fifty-eight, with one-fifth over seventy (four hundred of the draft board members were over eighty, and twelve between ninety and ninety-nine). The representation of Negroes on the draft boards: about 1.3 percent.

The workings of the selective service system had been studied by a number of congressional and Pentagon committees, which put forth a variety of recommendations. But little had been changed, and Representative Alvin E. O'Konski, an eleventh-termer from Wisconsin and a member of the House Armed Forces Committee, was able to say, with the agreement of a considerable part of the public, "Your status in society in my district is now determined by what your draft status is. If you are 1-A, you are a nobody. . . . If you are not 1-A, you have status. . . . That system nauseates me. . . . This is a poor man's war."

The selective service act was to expire on June 30, 1967, and if the White House did not take action, the existing legislation was almost certain to be substantially re-enacted. My memo suggested to President Johnson that he announce that the Administration was preparing recommendations for a new national service law, and that toward this end he was naming a blue-ribbon commission on selective service with a broad mandate. It would consist of men who commanded national respect; would be empowered to examine how the draft was and was not operating "fairly and in the best national interest," and to make specific proposals for change; and would be instructed to report promptly.

On May 16, 1966, President Johnson's reply to the memo came in the form of an instruction to draft the speech on the Negro question (he did not use this), and to proceed with recommending personnel for a commission on selective service and with drawing up points for the announcement of it. He planned to include the whole program, including the members of the commission, in a speech scheduled to be delivered four days later at the thirtieth anniversary rally of the United Automobile Workers in Long Beach, California.

On May 18 Secretary of Defense McNamara flew to Montreal to deliver an address before the American Society of Newspaper Editors. It was quite a speech. For weeks the Secretary had been expressing in private a restlessness with the American frame of mind about world affairs and now he repeated, somewhat circumspectly, his misgivings. Following the kind of thinking which in time would be a factor in his leaving the Defense Department for the World Bank, McNamara spoke out against the tendency to assume that "military hardware" was the prime ingredient for national security. This simply was not the case. "The United States has no mandate from on high to police the world. . . . no charter to rescue floundering regimes, who have brought violence on themselves by deliberately refusing to meet the legitimate expectations of their citizenry." At the heart of American security was "the character of its relationships with the world." This meant "realistic" efforts to seek an accommodation with Communist Russia and China, emphasis on collective peace-keeping measures and above all facing the fact that "security is [economic and social] development. . . . The irreducible fact remains that our security is related directly to the security of the newly developing world." In a few sentences near the end of the speech, and in its same spirit, the Secretary spoke of the "inequity" of the draft. "It seems to me," he said in a paragraph that stopped just short of a policy recommendation, "that we could move toward remedying that inequity" by requiring every young person in the United States to give two years to national service in the form either of military service or of "development" work at home or abroad.

The McNamara speech created an uproar in Washington. Bill Moyers told the press that the White House had seen a rough form of it and approved it completely. He and other aides spread the word: there was nothing new in the address, it was well within established lines of Administration policy. They produced sentences from speeches of President Johnson which, so they said, expressed thinking along the same lines.

Moyers telephoned me to call off all activities connected with the selective service project. The President was angry at McNamara; the Secretary had gone off "on his own," and in his remarks about re-examining the draft he had "pulled the rug out from under things." President Johnson was not flying to Long Beach but would merely speak to the UAW convention by phone. The announcement of the draft commission would have to wait, "if it ever comes off now."

I replied that I did not see why the McNamara speech precluded the presidential announcement. Why not make them complement each other, as showing how the whole Administration was moving to rethink selective service? But I knew that I was wasting my words. Once again Lyndon Johnson was not going to be deprived of the slightest element of surprise or be upstaged in any way—particularly by a man who, however close his ties to LBJ, remained an intimate friend of the Kennedys and was talking about the draft in a way that smacked of the speeches being made by Senator Edward M. Kennedy.

After enough time had elapsed for interest in the McNamara speech to die down, on July 2, President Johnson announced a National Advisory Commission on Selective Service. I am not at all sure why he finally went ahead with the project. It had obvious political advantages but its recommendations also could cut both ways with the voters. My impression is that one important element in his decision was his sense of personal responsibility for the men of the armed forces—they were part of his feudal responsibility too—and his equally strong feeling that he wanted no American governmental institution discriminating against the poor.

Certainly Lyndon Johnson established a strong commission. Its chairman could tell the press that in private conversation with the President, he had been given the broadest of mandates. The order in the instructions to the group was revealing. First came "fairness to all citizens," and then "military manpower requirements." Though the board contained the usual quota of politically balanced people, it was headed by the able and independent-minded Burke Marshall, former Assistant Attorney General in charge of the Civil Rights Division under both Presidents Kennedy and Johnson, and now a vice-president and general counsel of IBM. Its twenty members included such thoughtful critics of the draft as the president of Yale, Kingman Brewster, Jr., who had publicly called the existing system "anti-democratic" and "most objectionable," and spoken of "the endless catacombs of education" where men meandered for years while avoiding the draft.

Meeting in workmanlike conference rooms in the Executive Office Building or at the State Department, the commission spent about a hundred hours in hard study and intensive discussion, basing its considerations on memoranda from the relevant Cabinet officers, all fifty governors, and mayors, manpower experts and major interested organizations, including those of students. It did not adopt a system with an alternative between military and humanitarian service. Though the Peace Corps and similar activities could bring hardship and danger, most of the commission were not persuaded that noncombat social service was really as onerous as potential combat service. They also feared that the proposal was unconstitutional and that such social service would become—or at least be known as—a sanctuary from the draft.

The commission's recommendations, for the most part adopted unanimously, represented a radical reorganization of selective service. Draftees would be chosen by a more nationalized system which would clearly end up in taking considerable discretion away from local draft boards and in placing a much greater representation of younger men and the disadvantaged in the groups making the individual decisions. The basic principle would be a lottery among the nineteen-year-olds, before they had established themselves in draft havens and at an age when they were most useful to the military. Except for medical and dental students and certain scientific categories, graduate school deferments were eliminated. The most difficult question for the commission concerned undergraduate deferments. Kingman Brewster was the chief spokesman for a group, including Chairman Burke Marshall, who wanted to eliminate the practice. George Reedy, the President's former Press Secretary and at this time president of the Struthers Wells Development Corporation, was the most vigorous advocate of deferring undergraduates until they had received their degrees, and then placing them in the lottery with the nineteen-year-olds. By a narrow vote, the commission recommended ending undergraduate deferments.

President Johnson received the Marshall report with publicly expressed admiration, and on March 7, 1967, he sent to Congress a message embodying its major recommendations except the elimination of undergraduate deferments. The commission, he stated, had differed sharply on this point and he invited congressional and public discussion before a decision was made. The President knew what the decision would be and he agreed with it. Persuasive arguments could be offered for continuing the undergraduate deferments. The flow of educated men was important to the nation and although the A.B. candidate received a four-year respite from military service, he could be drafted when he received his degree. In terms of military manpower needs, the college officer-training programs—kept filled by the stimulus of the on-coming draft—had been providing almost four out of five second lieutenants and ensigns for the armed forces. It was the addition of graduate school deferments that had permitted so many of the better-educated to escape service altogether. Arguments aside, Congress almost certainly would never end undergraduate deferments except at a time of mass mobilization. Hundreds of thousands of middle- and upper-middle-class parents, many of them constituents to whom a congressman would listen with special attention, intended to keep their sons in college and out of Vietnam as long as possible. Despite the committee vote, for all practical purposes undergraduate deferments were part of the Administration program.

The Senate was ready to go along with major parts of this

legislation, but in the House the bill ran into the massive road-block of L. Mendel Rivers of South Carolina, chairman of the House Armed Services Committee. Rivers was an acolyte of the old-style military brass and in general suspicious of any idea conceived since John Calhoun. He and his chief ally on the Armed Services Committee, Representative F. Edward Hébert of Louisiana, had thousands of wool-hat constituents who were sure that a draft lottery was immoral ("It sounds like shooting craps with men's lives," as Rivers explained). Backed by a coalition of Southern Democrats and conservative Republicans, Rivers rammed his own draft measure through his committee and the House. It was a re-enactment of the old system, with a few details added that probably accentuated the tendencies of the existing law.

In the House-Senate conference, Senator Edward Kennedy put up a strong fight to save fundamentals of the Administration program. President Johnson did not. The deadline of June 30, 1967, when draft legislation had to be enacted, was approaching; the President was embroiled in a Middle Eastern crisis; he doubted that he could beat Rivers on this bill; and by this time, his congressional power weakened, Lyndon Johnson was husbanding his political capital with extreme care. When Senator Kennedy telephoned the White House, he heard little encouragement. On June 30, President Johnson signed into law what was basically the Rivers bill, and Burke Marshall commented, "In my judgment the new bill makes the system worse than it was before."

Yet all was not lost. The President's commission had clearly and authoritatively injected into public discussion fundamental considerations concerning selective service which seemed to be having a permeative effect. The panel also gave President Johnson a guide for the executive powers which he possessed regardless of legislation. On February 16, 1968, acting through the National Security Council, he put into effect one of the major commission recommendations by ending most graduate school deferments. From time to time, as at a White House meeting of state draft directors on May 4, 1967, he got in some missionary work. The President "suggested" to the state directors that they note the commission criticism of the make-up of local draft boards because "every principle of fairness, every tenet of our democratic faith, requires us to make our institutions representative of the people with whom they deal." By 1968 the director of the selective service system, General Lewis B. Hershey, was reporting that the percentage of Negroes on draft boards, the 1.3 in 1966, had increased to 3.8. There was still a long way to go—Negroes made up about 11 percent of the population, and Alabama and Mississippi still had not a single black man on the boards—but, as Hershey said, "something is happening."

Historians of the future, I believe, will find in the summer and fall of 1966 a dividing line in the Johnson Administration. The first years were those of the ebullient leader—taking a nation through a difficult transition, steering through Congress a domestic program which met the wishes and needs of a genuine consensus, enjoying thoroughly the sheer activity and clamor of power. Then, in 1966, came the completion of his basic legislative program and the full furies of the Vietnam War. These created a new Johnson Administration and brought to the fore a different Lyndon Johnson.

Without the war, it is doubtful how much the President would have embarked on a second stage of non-consensus policies. This was not the man; he was not inclined to get ahead of the crowd and run the risk of turning around and finding no cheering following. Yet he was also perpetually restless, excited by his urges to bring more opportunity to the mass of the population, driven on by his determination to leave his mark broad and plain on everyday American living. There was always the chance that he would have broken loose. The war, preoccupying him, inexorably eating into the funds he thought it feasible to ask of Congress, was throwing the balance of his thinking and emotions to relative inaction in domestic affairs. And whatever the changes in Lyndon Johnson, the congressional election of November 1966 created the kind of Congress which was ready to see to it that he would do little adventuring in the domestic field.

The Vietnam War was not only preoccupying President Johnson; it was dominating him. He felt—and his critics were telling him so day after day—that it was *his* war, *his* big decisions about it and *his* next moves in it that would largely determine his place in history. He was going to carry off this war, come what may, and he would let nothing else take center stage, however briefly. The President planned a campaign swing in 1966, and he spoke of emphasizing domestic concerns in his speeches. He cancelled the trip only in part because when the time came, he was convinced that he would be associated with a defeated cause. Also of importance was the fact that he found it difficult to get interested in anything not directly connected with the war.

Occasionally in 1966 he made public statements endorsing criticism in foreign affairs. Yet the declarations carried little conviction; they were transparently tactics of the moment. Lyndon Johnson's far deeper feeling—that dissent against a Chief Executive's foreign policy was tantamount to un-Americanism—was reasserting itself in greatly heightened form. He was no longer patiently seeking some degree of consensus in foreign policy; he was bursting to flay his critics publicly. On May 18, 1966, the President took off for an appearance at a Chicago Democratic fundraising dinner, and observers on the plane were startled by his mood. His conversation was volcanic; he kept writing stronger phrases into the draft of his speech. He delivered it in a slow, flat *Götterdämmerung* voice, denouncing war critics as "Nervous Nellies" ready to "turn on their own leaders, and on their country, and on our own fighting men." He proposed a "measuring stick" for a man who made statements about the Vietnam War: "Is he helping the cause of his country or is he advancing the cause of himself?"

In a macabre way the White House Festival of the Arts, intrinsically so minor an event, kept having an effect that was anything but minor. The episode simmered on in Lyndon Johnson's mind, becoming another justification for vehemence against opponents of the war. "These people," invited to the President's house, had insulted the President; they were "bastards" and since they were bastards, what they believed was bastardly and contaminated everyone who believed as they did.

By the summer and fall of 1966 the domestic reformer of the Great Society days had become a war chief, finding more and more congeniality with conservatives, even avoiding the phrase "Great Society" in his speeches. The ebullient leader given to moments of testiness and rage was now, day after day, bitter, truculent, peevish—and suspicious of the fundamental good sense and integrity of anyone who did not endorse the Vietnam War.

This Lyndon Johnson was not only depressing; at times he could be downright frightening. As 1966 went on, on one occasion a Cabinet member and three White House aides, including myself, sat talking with President Johnson. At first LBJ rambled on pleasantly with political anecdotes, sipping a Dr. Pepper while all of us munched on potato chips. Then one of the stories introduced the name of a liberal senator who opposed the Vietnam War. The President stopped munching and his face hardened. "These men," he sneered, "knee-jerk liberals," "crackpots," such "troublemakers that they force politicians to the right." He mentioned his friend Governor John Connally of Texas as an instance; Connally had begun as a "progressive" governor but "they hacked away and hacked away, criticizing everything he did, until he had to move to the right to get some support." Liberals were always going off "half-cocked." One of the "gut reasons" for the liberal opposition to the

Vietnam War was that they had "just plain been taken in."

Warming to his theme, President Johnson pounded knees, mine and others. "Liberal critics! It's the Russians who are behind the whole thing." He extolled the FBI and the CIA; they kept him informed about what was "really going on." It was the Russians who stirred up the whole agitation for a suspension of the bombing of North Vietnam. He knew better, but he suspended the bombing to show the nation how foolish such a move was. The Russians were in constant touch with anti-war senators—and he named names. These senators ate lunch and went to parties at the Soviet embassy; children of their staff people dated Russians. "The Russians think up things for the senators to say. I often know before they do what their speeches are going to say."

I was staggered. Did President Johnson really believe that his critics were Soviet puppets? Was he thinking in such Joseph McCarthyite terms that he found it impossible to understand why many Americans, in or out of the Senate, were so concerned over his Vietnam policy? Or was he letting off steam, as he sometimes did, enjoying shocking his listeners and testing how much he could get away with? But when he went on in the same vein in a grimly serious tone, I became convinced that he did indeed mean what he was saying, at least in part.

It was obvious that the three other men were not going to challenge him. One White House aide sat slumped in his chair looking embarrassed; the other was so casual that it was apparent he had been through this before. The Cabinet officer swayed back and forth in the resigned manner of a man who accepted the fact that such was the price of his office.

I did not want it on my conscience that I too had sat silent while a President of the United States talked such dangerous nonsense. LBJ was now at the point where he was stating that during a Senate hearing on Vietnam a member of the Soviet embassy had delivered a message of instructions to one of the committee members. I interrupted, "Mr. President—" But as always it was difficult to cut into one of these monologues. Finally I made my way in: "Mr. President, you *know* that what you are saying simply is not accurate."

The President looked at me in a curious way. I have often recalled that look, and I still wonder what it meant. He continued for a few minutes on the same theme, then shifted to other matters. He and I went back to the potato chips, with one of us not too much interested in them.

The attitude of the Oval Office permeated everything, even the ceremony for my old friends, the Presidential Scholars. The occasion for the third year of the program was to be held in June 1966, and Marvin Watson's office called to say that the mother and father of one Scholar, a brilliant seventeen-year-old girl, "absolutely should not be invited." The parents were "radical" opponents of the Vietnam War and the father had been cited by the House Un-American Activities Committee.

That day Watson was with President Johnson for hours. Trying in vain to reach him on the phone, I took up the issue with him on paper in the pragmatic terms which previously had ended these matters. The parents and the Scholar were "known opponents of the President's Vietnam policy. They also appear to be people who are quite likely to go to the newspapers. If Mr. and Mrs. _____ do not receive their formal invitation and receive it soon . . . there is a strong likelihood that they will go to the newspapers and state that they are not invited because of their opposition to the President's policy on Vietnam. This . . . would certainly put the President in an embarrassing position."

After Watson left the President, he called and we sat down together. This time the pragmatic appeal was not working well. "Since that bunch of nuts for the festival of the arts," Watson told me, President Johnson had ordered the continuance of full FBI clearance and the approval by the President—meaning Watson— of all White House guests. The girl was "bad enough"—she had attended anti-war and anti-draft demonstrations but he was not going to approve her "crummy parents" too. "I haven't told the President about this," Watson added. "He would ban the girl too."

Neither of us had much relish for the discussion that followed. It was an old and hopeless clash, now greatly exacerbated. I tried to keep it on the simple point of how the President would explain a refusal to invite the parents, especially just as a congressional campaign was getting under way. But in the new LBJ White House, any give-and-take on such an issue was gone. "I'll take the issue of being pro-American into any congressional district," Watson replied coldly.

With equal coldness, I'm sure, I replied, "And how are you going to support your charge of un-Americanism—by telling the country that you used the FBI against a bright seventeen-year-old and her parents, when she is coming to be awarded a medal she won in what the President has proclaimed to be a free intellectual competition?"

It was no debating skill of mine that settled the issue; patently, banning the parents would have brought unfavorable publicity. Grudgingly agreeing to invite them, Watson made plain the rules in the future. President Johnson, he said, did not want "this kind of situation." In the White House, all of us were accustomed to saying "the President wants"—which often meant what we wanted and maybe what the President wanted—but this time I did not doubt that what Watson was saying represented LBJ's instructions. In the future, before a Presidential Scholar was named, he and his family were to be given an FBI check. Then the President, i.e., Watson, would decide whether he was to be designated. Presidential Scholars were to be chosen on the basis of their intellectual attainment *and* on whether their attitudes pleased Lyndon Johnson's representative.

For me, there was a special poignance in this incident. I remembered the honest delight with which Lyndon Johnson— years and years ago, it seemed—had received the suggestion that he, the former schoolteacher, "the education President," should encourage "the really bright kids, no matter who they are," as he had put it, "the most precious resource of the nation, the brain-power of its youth," as the official announcement had declared. Now it had come to this.

It was time, high time, for me to leave.

Not sure about the form a resignation should take, I went to Robert E. Kintner, the former president of NBC, who had joined the White House staff to serve as a kind of administrative co-ordinator in certain areas. A long-time friend of the President's with no ambitions within the White House, Kintner, I felt, would give me answers I could trust. To my relief he said that he would not ask me why I was resigning; that was a matter between President Johnson and myself. He told me that the President liked to receive a letter of resignation about three weeks before it was to take effect and that he would want it kept absolutely secret. I should even avoid letting my secretaries know, and should write the letter in longhand.

More of the frenetic secrecy of the LBJ White House—but by now I was inured to it. I planned to return to Princeton for the opening of the fall semester of the university, and on August 23, 1966, I wrote in longhand a brief letter of resignation. It stated simply that after thirty-three months of White House service I thought it best to return to my regular life; that I deeply appreciated the privilege I had been given of serving the President and the First Lady of the United States; and that of course I extended my best wishes for the success of the Administration and my personal best wishes to the President, Mrs. Johnson and the girls. I put the letter in an envelope marked "Personal" and delivered it myself to the office of Juanita Roberts, the President's personal secretary. Without inquiring about its contents, Mrs. Roberts said that she would see to it that the letter was placed directly in the hands of the President and that he would no doubt read it that afternoon.

I heard nothing until seven days later, when I received a letter not from the President but from Mrs. Johnson. It was gracious and exceedingly generous in its praise of my work, and it was signed "Fondly."

That day a White House aide extremely close to LBJ spoke to me about my resignation and asked, "What would you like to have?" I replied that I did not want another government post but was planning to return to Princeton. I added that what I would really appreciate was a letter from President Johnson formally accepting the resignation and a statement from the Press Office that I was leaving, to end the secrecy and allow me to make future plans openly.

The next day I received a letter from the President which was dated the day before Mrs. Johnson's. It was a "deep regrets" letter, complimentary to me in general and thanking me for the "special mark" I had left on "many of the programs which have come into being" and for the "valuable" service I had given "so unstintingly and unselfishly."

So far, so good. But the days went by and there was no sign that my resignation would be made public. This was not surprising; months before, President Johnson had adopted the practice of saying nothing about the departure of White House people. One of his oldest friends had been leaving and needed public clarification of his status so as to announce his new job. When he went to the President, he was told only, Leak it to the press. I went to the aide who had asked me whether I wanted another government position, and inquired, Do you think the President is going to make my resignation public? The answer was a firm no.

I did not want to leave the White House furtively, like some figure in disgrace. Quite ready to stand behind what I had done and tried to do. I saw no reason why I should not be permitted to resign with dignity. I also wanted the resignation known so that I would be freed of White House inhibitions and could make a particular public comment which I believed might be of some usefulness. And I had a further concern. As the Foreword to this volume states, I had reached the decision to write a book about President Johnson and his Administration. I had no apologies for this; it would be, I hoped, a responsible, objective volume, of some value in understanding the America of the 1960's and one of its Presidents. But I knew only too well that Lyndon Johnson held in anathema any writing involving him which he did not control. There were the two alternatives. I could leave the White House saying nothing about my intention to write the book, permitting it to leak out as such matters inevitably do and letting President Johnson express his anger then, amid a situation that smacked of my having resigned under false pretenses. Or I could state my intention as I left. I much preferred the second alternative. After the years of sticky secretiveness, I wanted the fresh air of doing what you thought you ought to do, simply and straightforwardly.

More time went by and still the Press Office made no statement of my resignation. Twice I picked up the phone to arrange an appointment with President Johnson at which I would request that my resignation be released; twice I put down the phone. I did not want to be placed in the position where I would be spoken to in a way which put me under heavy moral pressure to remain bound into the LBJ organization.

There was always the "backgrounder," that technique by which a man talks to the press with the understanding that what he says will be attributed not to him but to informed sources. Almost every official in Washington deplores the backgrounder, and almost every one uses it; in certain circumstances, it seems to be the only way to get information circulated without giving it the inappropriate authority or the bad taste of direct quotation. At my request a newspaper friend arranged a backgrounder with a small group of his colleagues at a hotel. I told the reporters that I had resigned, and in the course of the conversation I made the comments that I had wanted to state: it seemed to me that President Johnson's relations with the intellectual community, and educated Americans generally, had deteriorated woefully, and that some of the fault was attributable both ways. I hoped the public remarks might possibly— barely possibly—lead both sides to a bit of self-examination. When asked the inevitable question whether I planned to write a book about President Johnson and his Administration I said yes, I did.

The backgrounder was on the night of September 6 and the President learned of it the next day. The stories appeared in the morning papers of September 8, and that afternoon Bill Moyers took the initiative in bringing up the subject at his press briefing. Now, finally, the White House announced my resignation. Then Moyers went on the attack. His purpose was unmistakable: to undercut the projected book. He presented me as a man who had done little in the White House and who knew little of any consequence about the LBJ Presidency. He had statistics—exactly how many days I had worked for the White House, and they were interesting statistics. As a Special Consultant I was paid by the day. For most of my White House period I functioned under an arrangement limiting the days for which I would be paid—for nineteen of the thirty-three months, the limitation was two days a week. Of course one does not work in the White House for money, and I had been in my office for whatever time the tasks required, which even when I tapered off after the festival of the arts continued to be at least five days a week. Moyers' figures, presented without explanation, were the number of days for which I had been paid.

As part of his denigration, he stressed a point that must have reminded the First Lady once again what it was like to be Mrs. Lyndon Johnson. After all, Moyers told the press, "Goldman has spent most of his time working directly with Mrs. Johnson and Mrs. Carpenter in the East Wing." To emphasize this further, he stated that it was Mrs. Carpenter who informed the President that I was resigning. When a reporter inquired, "Why would Mrs. Carpenter have to convey the word from a presidential appointee?" Moyers replied, "You will have to ask Mr. Goldman that." The reporter did not bother.

The line had been set and out from the West Wing, in statements from unnamed White House aides, came the further undercutting of the book. Anything I might say should be disregarded because I was an "abrasive" personality, a person of "academic pomposity," a do-nothing "peripheral figure" who would simply be writing as a sorehead.

By now the phone calls and mail were deluging my office. I was the first—and as it turned out the only—LBJ White House aide to leave amid indications that all was not sweetness and light, and the undisguised Moyers tactic had simply heightened the news interest. To all the urgings of reporters for statements or interviews, to the flood of radio and television invitations, to the request for articles that had high price tags attached to them, I made the same reply: "No comment." I have no taste for martyrdom and I was seething. But whatever my personal feelings, I had too much respect for the Office of the President of the United States to engage in public brawling with President Johnson or his spokesman. As a practical matter, I had no desire to inflame the President further and subject myself to more demeanings. And I was very tired, and eager to get away from the LBJ White House.

After lunch on September 15, the formal resignation date I had suggested to President Johnson, I made my departure from my office—it was not without emotion—and I was hardly in my apartment when my secretary called. Just after I left, she told me,

Moyers had come to the office, saying that he wanted to talk to me. The desire was not mutual and I started to pack.

Moyers phoned my apartment and repeated that he would like to see me. It was not a "trivial matter"; he was calling me without the President's knowledge and would appreciate it if I did not mention the call to the press. With no graciousness whatsoever, I suggested that if it was all so secret, why didn't he come over to my place? No, it wasn't secret, but do come to the White House for a talk.

Moyers was often pale and tense; that day he seemed to me unusually so. His greeting was elaborately cordial. I did not respond in kind. Nothing in all his three years in the White House, Moyers told me, had so "distressed" him as what had happened in my case. He had the greatest respect for me—

I cut in to say, Bill, I think you must know how I feel about this. No doubt you acted on the President's instructions, but you chose to do what you did. And you can hardly expect me to be concerned about your resulting distress.

I was puzzled. Was this one more of Lyndon Johnson's involved human jigsaws, publicly going after a man and still seeking to retain a controlling relationship with him?

When the President heard of the backgrounder, Moyers went on, he was angry, and justifiably so. I should not have used the device; he himself had never done so.

At my incredulous look—naturally and understandably the backgrounder was a frequent Moyers procedure—he became more emphatic. If I had just left matters alone, the President would have announced my resignation and everything would have been fine.

I had every reason to believe, I replied, that the President had no intention of announcing my resignation. And I had every right, I added, to get it announced.

As Moyers drifted away from this subject and concentrated on a different one, my puzzlement disappeared. President Johnson may or may not have known about this meeting; be that as it may, it was being used mainly to serve Bill Moyers, not Lyndon Johnson. Riding a high wave of press coverage as the conscience of the Administration, the fine young man who stood for ideals in the roughhouse LBJ operation, Moyers had not liked the reaction to his attack on me. Too many reporters had referred to it as a hatchet job. He did not want to be thought of as a hatchet man, and now he was busy straightening things out, especially for a book that he knew would be written.

The real reason for the President's anger, Moyers continued, was my statement that I planned to write the book. President Johnson had been scheduled to meet with some reporters after he learned this, and he had intended to denounce me personally. He was going to make quite a statement—Moyers tapped a drawer of his desk—"I have it right here." But Moyers had dissuaded him and the President then told him to handle the matter at his regular press briefing. President Johnson had instructed, Don't attack him personally, but take care of the book.

I did not restrain the observation that Moyers had tried hard to fulfill at least part of the instruction.

Moyers continued at considerable length about his "distress." He had not wanted to speak as he had at the press conference; he respected me too much for that. In general he had been protecting me, he wanted me to know. A leading newspaper had asked Richard Goodwin to write an article about me and Goodwin intended to write a slashing attack. Moyers had intervened and dissuaded him.

I did not express appreciation. So far as I was concerned, I replied, Goodwin was entirely free to write what he pleased.

As Moyers related this, his face wore his most earnest expression. A few days later I checked with the editor of the appropriate section of the newspaper mentioned, a man who was an acquaintance of mine and for whom I had written an occasional article before my White House days. To my direct question, the editor replied with equal directness: neither he nor any of his subordinates had asked Goodwin or anyone else to write an article about me, much less an attack. He added, "We don't run that kind of paper."

Moyers spoke still further about his distress. It was all a result of "a failure of communications" within the White House, and he was going to see that such a thing did not happen again.

I had enough. I told Moyers that I would be glad if this incident contributed to better communications within the White House; certainly they could be improved. But in the meantime, since he said that President Johnson felt he had been treated badly by me, I would like to discuss the situation with him face to face. He had always had my absolute loyalty and best efforts, whatever their inadequacies, toward the success of his Administration. I had done nothing for which I had any apologies, and nothing intended to show lack of respect for him or to impede his Administration. Under the circumstances I would like to have a direct talk with him.

Obviously, I added, there was no point in my phoning the President for an appointment in his present mood. I asked Moyers whether he would tell President Johnson that I had requested an appointment. I also asked that he inform me of the answer, regardless of whether it was yes or no. As I rose to leave, I again stressed that I was requesting to be informed, no matter what the answer. Moyers assured me that I would hear from him. I received no call.

I left Moyers' office on a gray September day and headed for the Northwest Gate of the White House, the same gate through which I had first entered some two years and nine months before. On that occasion the guard had gone through the elaborate procedure of identifying me. The man on duty knew me now and gave me the proper restrained greeting for a person in bad favor. As I walked down Pennsylvania Avenue, a jumble of emotions took over.

I was hurt, angry, happy, depressed and relieved. I was proud of what my office had stood for and what we had been able to accomplish, and I berated myself for not having done the job better. I turned and looked at the White House, as lovely as ever in the chill September mist, and my mind went to the man in the Oval Office, no doubt at this moment restlessly doing things, endless things, with all his magnificent attributes and all his colossal faults. My thoughts went to the book. What was it that I really wanted to say in this book, which I had such a powerful urge to write? To narrate certain events, to portray character, to examine motivations, to analyze from the point of view of a historian— all of these, to be sure, but they did not really seem the point. The theme that had long been taking hold of my mind now reasserted itself in much clearer form. I knew that above all what I wanted to do was try to get down on paper not Lyndon Johnson the good or bad President or human being, but Lyndon Johnson the tragic figure.

CHAPTER 18

Tragic Figure

The rest of 1966, then 1967, and into 1968—the Johnson Presidency was more of the same, only more so.

The Vietnam War slogged on, increasingly taking mastery over Lyndon Johnson and most phases of his Administration. President Johnson became more and more the war chief, not the domestic leader. The key anti-poverty program kept running into serious difficulties, as any such drive inevitably would. Even this effort, once so central to LBJ's interests and emotions, was finding no strong friend in the Oval Office.

Slowly changes came in the men around the President, and for the most part they told the same story. The two most important departures from the Cabinet were Secretary of Health, Education and Welfare John Gardner and Secretary of Defense Robert McNamara—Gardner, the symbol of LBJ's old relish for social improvement, leaving in discouragement, McNamara "the perfesser type," finding the World Bank and its development work more congenial than guns, ever more guns. The peculiar rigors of life on the LBJ White House staff went on taking their toll. By mid-1966 most of the old faces had disappeared from the White House Mess—McGeorge Bundy, Horace Busby, Richard Goodwin, George Reedy, Jack Valenti and then, at the end of 1966, Bill Moyers. This meant that Joseph Califano moved into Moyers' place as the chief figure on the staff. But it also signified that Moyers, whose interests and ambitions had been shifting toward foreign affairs, had increasingly little desire to stay associated with an international policy the heart of which was the Vietnam War. He left the White House for a number of reasons but one of them was this feeling, the better side of him, asserting itself. And now in the office of the chief White House specialist on foreign policy was Special Assistant for National Security Affairs Walt W. Rostow, a fervid, almost an exuberant hawk since the far, far JFK days.

Month by month President Johnson's control over Congress weakened. The attrition he had predicted was in full operation; of equal importance, President Johnson the war leader was much less in a position to halt the conservative swing. Even before the disastrous congressional election of 1966, the second, 1966 session of the Eighty-ninth Congress had proved a caricature of the majestic drive of social legislation in 1965. The Administration won approval for a few significant bills, including the Truth-in-Packaging Act, the measure creating a Transportation Department in the Cabinet, the first auto safety regulations, and authorization for a pioneering demonstration-cities program. Generally, it asked for little and got less.

The House and Senate created by the election of 1966—the Ninetieth Congress—fully lived up to expectations. President Johnson showed a flash of his old wizardry in bringing a semblance of home rule to Washington, D.C., now two-thirds Negro. Throughout the post-World War II period, Presidents had tried to get such legislation past the Southerners and their G.O.P. allies in the House of Representatives. This time LBJ turned the trick by acting under the powers given to him by the Federal Reorganization Act of 1949, a move which does not require congressional approval but can be vetoed. He devised a form of home rule so additionally baited with delicacies for various congressional blocs that he split the opposition coalition and prevented the House from voting it down. The Administration also managed to squeeze through Congress the Public Television Act, Truth-in-Lending, the actual appropriation for the demonstration-cities program, a law banning discrimination in 80 percent of the nation's housing, and restrictions on interstate traffic in firearms. But during the Ninetieth Congress the White House was asking for still less and less and getting a steadily lowered percentage.

The two "must" items in the 1968 Administration program were a 10 percent tax surcharge and a crime-control bill; these were obtained only at a heavy price. The Crime Control Act gave much-needed aid to local law enforcement agencies, but it also authorized wiretapping on an alarmingly broad basis and included a provision designed to counteract Supreme Court decisions strengthening the rights of defendants in criminal cases. President Johnson achieved his tax surcharge only by bowing publicly to Congressman Wilbur Mills's demand for a $6 billion slash in federal expenditures, a blow at the whole Great Society edifice constructed in 1965.

The assaults on Lyndon Johnson mounted, unprecedented in their extent, their personal venom and the variety of people engaging in them. These days were not 1964 and 1965; in March 1968 LBJ's general approval rating in the Gallup poll plummeted to 36 percent—the lowest since Harry Truman's nadir of 32 percent. The only type of event that seemed to help President Johnson in the public opinion surveys was a hint of peace. He grew more and more bitter, especially at critics of the Vietnam War. He devoured memos given him by aides describing the name-calling directed at other war Presidents. Increasingly he was seeing himself as the lonely, traduced figure limned against history, resolutely doing right, grimly awaiting the verdict of the future.

As early as August 1966, at lunch with his old friend Merriman Smith, the senior White House correspondent of United Press International, President Johnson warned not to take it for granted that he would run again. He pointedly extolled the delights of life at the ranch and his eagerness to teach young people at the University of Texas. Beginning in late 1966, and then more and more frequently, his conversation included phrases like "in the time left to me" and "there is so much to do and so little time." He toured his ranch, paused at a great tree, remarked disconsolately, "This is the tree I expect to be buried under. When my grandchildren see this tree, I want them to think of me as the man who saved Asia and Vietnam, and who did something for the Negroes of this country." To a visitor at the White House, he told of his yearning to be "like an animal in the forest, to go to sleep under a tree, eat when I feel like it, read a bit, and after a while, do whatever I want to do." In January 1968 President Johnson put the blunt question to Horace Busby: "What do you think I ought to do?" He showed no surprise or annoyance at Busby's answer that he thought the President should withdraw.

On March 31, 1968, I and the millions of others sat at our television sets for a speech of President Johnson's that he had labeled as especially important. I had not seen LBJ on television for quite a while and I was shocked. My mind went back over the changes in his appearance and manner during his five years in the White House. There were the days immediately after the assassination— the rangy, rugged figure, every antenna alert, trailed by edgy aides, looking around him with those hard, piercing eyes, always as if he were sniffing out friend and foe, always as if he were remembering that a smile or a handshake might be needed here or there. Although becoming the President in manner and appearance, he still seemed a bit the Texas senator playing another role, a touch flamboyant in dress, a trifle overzealous in being friendly, a little awkward in the aura of the Oval Office.

I remembered the tremendous successes of the Spring of 1964, especially the settlement of the rail dispute, when the huge shoulders were back, the big head high. He had thoroughly settled into his Office, was handsomely presidential in clothing, more reserved in manner, emanating a confident, almost cocky air. A friend remarked, "He really seems like the President of the United States these days," and I agreed. Curiously enough, the face of the rough-and-ready Texas President was taking on some of the lines of his hero, the New York patrician FDR.

Now, in March of 1968 an old, weary, battered man was on the television screen. The face was deeply lined and sagging; the drawl occasionally cracked and wavered. His manner gave no intimation of FDR, and little of the LBJ of 1964. Rather, it suggested a lecturish, querulous schoolmaster.

President Johnson talked for thirty-five minutes, then paused— he had not lost his pleasure in surprises—looked over to Lady Bird Johnson who was seated nearby, and said, "I shall not seek, and I will not accept, the nomination of my party for another term as your President."

He gave his reason. "For 37 years in the service of our nation, first as a Congressman, as a Senator and as Vice-President, and now as your President, I have put the unity of the people first. . . . In these times, as in times before, it is true that a house divided against itself . . . is a house that cannot stand.

"There is division in the American house now. There is divisiveness among us all tonight. And holding the trust that is mine, as President of all the people, I cannot disregard the peril. . . . [this brings to] the progress of the American people and the hope and the prospect of peace for all peoples." President Johnson did not mention another reason that was in every viewer's mind: almost certainly he could not have won the election of 1968.

The nominating conventions assembled and again, during the Democratic gathering at Chicago, it was Lyndon Johnson's birthday. This time his closest friends advised him he had better stay away lest he be humiliated by the delegates of his own party. The campaign wound on its desultory way; his chosen successor, Hubert Humphrey, however sorely pressed, still called little on Lyndon Johnson. Instead, Humphrey was trying desperately to shake off his heaviest weight—his close association with the Johnson Administration and the Vietnam War. When the votes were counted, there was President Johnson greeting President-elect Nixon at the White House, his smile not concealing the fact that the nation had ended, directly and indirectly, the LBJ era.

Shortly after LBJ's withdrawal, a different kind of news had come from the expiring Administration. President Johnson had ordered each Executive department and some subordinate agencies to prepare a history of all the major decisions made by their divisions. The documents were to be submitted while he was still in the White House, by November 1, 1968, and then deposited in the Lyndon B. Johnson Library in Austin. Most of the news reports concerned the reactions of the officials who received the order, which ranged from "unbelievable, simply unbelievable" to "Can you imagine any bureaucrat turning in a report which reflected badly on the White House while the boss is still sitting there?" and "I have a feeling we are manufacturing a kept history."

Once again my mind went back, this time to 1966 when Mrs. Johnson asked me to go with her to Austin to assist with the first plans for the Johnson Library. A number of discussions were held, often including William W. Heath, from Normangee, Texas, cattle, sheep and goat rancher, state politico, director of the Braniff Airways, Dilliard Department Stores and the Capital National Bank, chairman of the Board of Regents of the University of Texas, and an LBJ friend of many years. (In 1967 President Johnson named Heath ambassador to Sweden, to the anguish of the Swedes and with the resultant production of some of the more uproarious stories in the long history of blunderbuss American diplomacy.)

In Austin in 1966, I had an intimation of what was coming when we carefully reconnoitered locations to make sure that the Lyndon B. Johnson Library would be placed in just the right position on just the right hill to command the whole sweep down to the central University of Texas building. In the conversations it became unmistakably clear that LBJ had not the slightest conception that in order to have value, research must be removed from the control of interested parties. Plainly he intended to keep an unsleeping eye on everything studied, thought about, discussed or written in his library. I was so disturbed by the attitude and felt so strong a sense of responsibility to the President and to scholarship to prevent him from making the basic mistake of proceeding on any such assumption that I argued the point vigorously— enough so that, happily, I was soon removed from any association with the project. But I was on the assignment long enough to have driven into my mind, as nothing else could, Lyndon Johnson's fierce concern with posterity. He had conquered poverty, Texas and the United States Senate, made his way to the White House, outscored FDR in a presidential election, gentled Congress, straddled Asia and now, by the charred cannons of the Alamo, he would conquer history.

It will be quite a feat, if he is able to pull it off. Meanwhile, just where do the five years of the Johnson Administration leave Lyndon Johnson before that judgment of history with which he is so concerned—before a history unassisted by his supervision? The cardinal rule of any sensible historian is to remember that he is a historian, not History, and that no powers of divination have been bestowed upon him by his profession or even by his abounding faith in his own judgment. Yet I think it can be suggested, with the proper tentativeness and with perhaps improper emphasis, that after the furies of the 1960's are laid to rest, Lyndon Johnson may well rank a good deal above where the national mood of the 1960's would place him, closer to the verdict of the Lyndon Johnson Library than of the Gallup poll.

Certainly in past instances the public esteem of a President during his tenure in office has borne no particular relationship to later judgment. In 1962 Arthur M. Schlesinger, Sr., asked seventy-five well-known scholars of American history to rate the Presidents up to JFK. The preponderant opinion called five Chief Executives "great" in this order: Abraham Lincoln, George Washington, Franklin Roosevelt, Woodrow Wilson and Thomas Jefferson. Again in order, it placed in the "near-great" category Andrew Jackson, Theodore Roosevelt, James Polk, Harry Truman, John Adams and Grover Cleveland. The historians categorized as failures Ulysses Grant and Warren Harding. Popular sentiment in 1962 probably would have gone along with most of these judgments. Of the eleven men called "great" or "near-great," six—Jefferson, Jackson, Lincoln, TR, FDR and Harry Truman—were the subject of widespread and sustained abuse during their incumbencies. One, Woodrow Wilson, was sharply repudiated, first by the Senate and then by the voters, and lived out his final days behind drawn shades, in fretful dependence on a future verdict. The most modern instance, Harry Truman, a man reviled during much of his Presidency, went through an almost identical withdrawal ceremony just sixteen years before Lyndon Johnson. Then, while still living, he emerged a favorite of the historians and something of a folk hero. The two Chief Executives deemed failures by a later generation, Ulysses Grant and Warren Harding, were enormously popular during their Presidencies. It is rarely remembered that when the Harding funeral train crossed the United States, it called forth a grief, respect and affection fully equal to, if not exceeding—even allowing for the differences in the eras—the public reaction to the death of Abraham Lincoln.

The question of a President's just place in history is complicated not only by shifts in opinion as time passes but by the inherent difficulties of the assessment process. Arthur Schlesinger, Sr., included among the men to whom he sent his 1962 questionnaire a sometime historian, President John Kennedy. The President was interested and started to fill out the ballot. Then he stopped. "How the hell can you tell?" he remarked. "Only the President himself can know what his real pressures and his real alternatives are. If you don't know that, how can you judge performance?" On other occasions, he commented that some of his predecessors were given credit for doing things to which they had no practical alternative. Historian-President John Kennedy's ultimate test seemed to be concrete achievements. It was an intriguing commentary on the problem of judging Presidents from a Chief Executive who, at least in domestic affairs during his short tenure, was far more notable as an opinion-builder than as an achiever of specific legislation.

Of course if Lyndon Johnson represented posterity, two of the basic questions he would ask of his Administration would be, Did the President serve as a President of national unity? Did he help bring the South back into the Union? No doubt his answer to both would be an affirmative so ringing it could be heard down any corridor of time. It should be noted that while President Johnson stated that he was withdrawing because of serious division in the United States, he did not blame himself for the split. The full context of the renunciation speech makes it plain that he was talking about the division brought about by other people, and a short while later he came close to declaring publicly that he had played no part in creating the rancorous atmosphere. It may be doubted that posterity will go along with this judgment.

The future will probably be much more ready to agree with President Johnson's self-assessment on the question about the South. Unquestionably, in 1968 that region was closer to the mainstream of American life than it had been for decades. In considerable measure this resulted from long-running trends. Yet the fact that it was a Southern President who put through the tough civil rights laws made an enormous amount of difference. So too did Lyndon Johnson's skillful exploitation of this fact, the general thrust of his domestic policies, and his persistent, patient message to the South—delivered publicly and still more often privately— to let up on "nigra, nigra" and concentrate on economic and social advancement.

Central to any long-range judgment of the Johnson Administration is the President's decision to commit large-scale American combat forces in the Vietnam War. I happen to be among those who became convinced that the action was a grave mistake, unnecessary for the national security, inconsistent with a mature American foreign policy, disruptive of our world leadership, destructive of urgently needed domestic programs, and dubious in terms both of the American tradition and of Judeo-Christian morality. If this assessment—which seems to approximate that of much of educated America in late 1968—holds, the Vietnam War will certainly prove a heavy drag on the LBJ reputation.

Just how heavy is quite a different matter. Other Presidents called great or near-great today made moves in foreign policy which are now generally considered serious errors—whether Theodore Roosevelt's imperialist gasconading in Latin America and Asia, Woodrow Wilson's Sunday-schoolish peacemaking after World War I or John Kennedy's bloody fiasco at the Bay of Pigs. But in the passage of time, the specific was submerged in the general memory of the man. If President Johnson or his successor brings the Vietnam War to an end without much further damage, in time a kindly haze may obscure the pointless clomp of American soldiers across a defenseless civilization, even napalm and what amounts to an American defeat.

This is more possible because the future might emphasize a consideration which President Johnson stressed in private and intimated in public. In a sense, he inherited the Vietnam commitment. Three previous Chief Executives—of different parties and foreign policy attitudes—had increased the American noncombat involvement in the area. At least two of these Presidents believed that preventing South Vietnam from falling under Communist rule was important to the national security of the United States. None faced a situation in which he had to decide whether the area was important enough to enter the fighting war. Lyndon Johnson was the Chief Executive who had to make that choice. Another generation may decide that he made an error prepared for by his predecessors and one which any one of them might have committed.

And always there is the possibility which many anti-LBJ commentators of the 1960's simply refused to entertain. The Vietnam intervention might *not* have been a mistake; President Johnson may have a point when he says, Let the future decide. He intervened militarily in South Vietnam because he believed that move was the only alternative to a major threat to the security of the United States. Without America in the fighting, South Vietnam would have come under Communist control, he was convinced;

this would be followed by a gradual fall of most of Asia to Communism, the domination of that continent by a hostile and potentially powerful China and—because China had not been warned off—by ultimate war between it and the United States. If a President other than Lyndon Johnson should accept a compromise Vietnam peace which was followed by such a chain of developments, Lyndon Johnson would be more than forgiven: he would emerge a figure of Churchillian stature, a wise, courageous voice crying out in a crowd of timid and myopic men.

The President's place in the long sweep of American domestic affairs can be assessed with much more assurance. Three times in the twentieth century the United States has faced the harsh facts of an industrializing, urbanizing civilization—at the beginning of the century, under Theodore Roosevelt and Woodrow Wilson; after the crash of 1929, under Franklin Roosevelt; and then, slowly, in the period following World War II.

The 1930's were *sui generis*. The urgency was unique; so too was the public mood. The situations in the early 1900's and after World War II were much more alike. In both instances, there was little sense that the country was falling apart. National opinion, jabbed by a zealous left and troubled by the arguments of a dogged right, was slowly forming around the proposition that the general population was being given too little access to economic and social opportunity. More laws were needed; the President ought to lead Congress in getting them.

At the start of the century Theodore Roosevelt bounded into the White House, caught up the strands of dissidence, wove them into an attractive pattern. America of the early 1900's did not easily dismiss an agitator who bore one of the nation's most aristocratic names, who could charm a Sunday school class or lead a regiment, turn out historical essays or lasso a steer, and who, in addition, happened to be President of the United States. "Teddy," the journalist William Allen White observed, "was reform in a derby, the gayest, cockiest, most fashionable derby you ever saw." TR moved few bills through Congress but he prepared the way for Woodrow Wilson who, without derby or gaiety, had the roused public opinion, the votes in Congress, and the Covenanter certitudes to grind the bills through the House and the Senate.

After World War II, the process began all over again. New needs—whether money for schools or action on urban transportation or justice for Negroes—were pressing. The opinion kept building, the opposition kept fighting, and another generation of leaders prepared the way for another wave of action. Harry Truman, his expletives and vetoes poised, fought off a Congress that yearned to turn back. Dwight Eisenhower, before he drifted into his second somnolent term, led the Republican party into some accommodation with the day. John Kennedy appeared, a second Theodore Roosevelt, associating social change with vigor and glamour and the mischievous cocked eye, legislating little but educating many. Then Lyndon Johnson, the cloakroom operator, re-enacted the presbyter-professor Woodrow Wilson. He too seized the moment to execute the decades' needs—seized it so firmly and wrung it so hard that he built a monument to himself in that 1965 Congress which wrote into law almost everything which the public had decided was long past due.

And all the while, breaking out now and again, however explained or explained away, came the voice which spoke of something far removed from cloakroom chicanery, one which caught the age-old American insistence that somehow, by some effort of hard-headedness and decency, ordinary men and women can live with greater comfort and joy and walk in the tonic air of self-respect. The voice was there when Lyndon Johnson, told by a visitor that he was rushing Congress, replied, "An old man on the Hill said to me a long time ago that there are Administrations that do and some that don't. This one is gonna do";

when, breaking away from legalisms about SEATO and talk of military hardware and of South Vietnamese democracy, he snapped, "If we sit here just enjoying our material resources, if we are content to become fat and flabby at fifty, the time will not be far away when we will be hearing a knock on our door in the middle of the night, and we will be hearing voices clamoring for freedom and independence and food and shelter. . . . Somehow, some way, the Lord in His Heaven will see that they are provided";

when he signed a later, truncated education appropriation, a mist across his cratered face, and muttered, "Not enough, not nearly enough. But I'm proud, damn proud, to have got it started. Education—that's what's needed and that's what every kid ought to get, as much of it as he can take, right up to his neck";

when he told six hundred corporation executives, "I have thought a great deal the last few days—I missed being an elevator boy by just about that much, when my mother reached up and made me go back to school after laying out for two years. . . . When you're dealing with these [Negro] people, in your company, or in your firm, or in your business, just remember they're some daughter's father, or some boy's mother, or someone's sister, or somebody's brother that you are dealing with. And except for the

grace of God, it might be you. . . . And think how you would like
to be treated if you lived in a land where you could not go to school
with your fellow Americans, where you could not work along the
side of them, where you could travel from Texas to Washington,
across many states and not be able to go to the bathroom without
hiding in a thicket or dodging behind a culvert. Ask yourself how
you would feel";

and when President Lyndon Johnson, speaking to a White
House Conference on Natural Beauty, shoved aside his prepared
text and spoke his memories of "a boy that walked through the
sand, hot sand, up to see my grandfather—a child of five or six. I
would cross the dusty field and walk along the banks of the river.

"My granddaddy would ask me questions. He would say, 'How
many ponies do you have? How many chickens do you have? How
many cows are down there at your little place? Tell me about the
state of your crops; when are you going to start picking your
cotton?'

"I would stand there and wiggle my toes in the sand with my
finger in my mouth. And if I knew the answers and answered all
of his questions correctly, Grandpa would take me in and open a
black mahogany desk he had and reach in and get an apple. And
I would walk satisfied, and quite proudly, back across the fields
along the banks of the river. If I failed, the walk seemed endless—
if I hadn't known the answers.

"And those hills, and those fields, and the river were the only
world that I really had in those years. So I did not know how
much more beautiful it was than that of many other boys, for I
could imagine nothing else from sky to sky. Yet the sight and the
feel of that country somehow or other burned itself into my
mind.

"We were not a wealthy family, but this was my rich inheritance. All my life I have drawn strength, and something more,
from those Texas hills. Sometimes, in the highest councils of the
Nation, in this house, I sit back and I can almost feel that rough,
unyielding, stocky clay soil between my toes, and it stirs memories
that often give me comfort and sometimes give me a pretty firm
purpose.

"But not all the boys in America had the privilege to grow up
in a wide and open country. We can give them something, and
we are going to. We can let each of them feel a little of what the
first settlers must have felt, as they stood there before the majesty
of our great land."

History has been generous, and should be, to Presidents who

have talked like that and taken action to turn the talk into laws. Probably history will be generous—and it should be—to Lyndon Johnson.

Probably—but all this is in the murky realm of speculation. There remains a hard, clear fact. Lyndon Johnson entered the White House unhailed, and functioned in it unloved. Only once did warmth and a degree of affection go out to him—when he told the country he was leaving the Presidency.

What went wrong? Obviously LBJ was an able, hard-working President, eager to serve the interests of the American people, more than eager to win their camaraderie. He tried desperately hard, and he delivered in important respects. In the anti-LBJ atmosphere of the 1960's, it is only fair to call the roll. Lyndon Johnson did take over the Presidency at a moment of national emotional disarray and conduct a skillful transition. He did win the election in his own name and win it by a huge majority. He did put through Congress a powerhouse program of legislation, almost all of which was widely applauded. He did run an Administration which functioned without major corruption and in many key posts, was manned by officials of unusually high caliber. Time after time, Americans have judged their Chief Executives primarily by one criterion: What happened to bread-and-butter living during the Administrations? LBJ presided over an America that—without a single break of as much as a month—was the most generally prosperous nation in all of man's five thousand years of recorded history.

What went so wrong? White House aides kept telling President Johnson that the whole source of the public's disaffection was his courageous stand on Vietnam. Well before I resigned, I became accustomed to the litany. Any war creates frustration and resentments, and discontent is always directed at the leader. Abraham Lincoln himself was assailed with unbridled vehemence. Modern limited wars, with their especially frustrating quality, exacerbate these public feelings.

All this was consoling to the President, but three stubborn facts remained. There was that "image crisis" of 1965 when, at the height of LBJ's success and before foreign policy issues were central, the widespread distaste was plain. Moreover, American wars have not usually rendered Chief Executives unpopular in their own time. On the contrary, as Commander in Chief the President has generally proved a rallying point for support and enthusiasm. Finally, important elements in the disaffection appeared to have little to do with Vietnam. Many Americans were snappish about Lyndon Johnson not so much because they were positive he was wrong on Vietnam but because they believed he was the kind of man who was quite capable of making a bad mistake in foreign or any other kind of policy, and having made it, of not admitting it or moving to correct it.

During the campaign of 1964, when the evidence indicated both that President Johnson would win easily and that the trend was as much anti-Goldwater as pro-Johnson, the President would remark querulously to visitors, "Why don't people like me?" One guest, too old to be concerned about preferment by the White House and enough of a Washington character to get away with irreverence, answered the question. He said, "Because, Mr. President, you are not a very likable man." Bald as it is, this was a major part of Lyndon Johnson's problem with the American people. The fact that he was not a very likable man could not be concealed from the public despite all the arduous efforts of his friends and aides, myself included, who wanted so much to believe otherwise and who did their damndest to present him in a way that would convince themselves and the country.

Lyndon Johnson may have risen from Johnson City to being the head of a family he cherished, a multimillionaire and the leader of the free world, but he had not risen above something nagging within him. All the way to the top, and especially at the top, he was combatively, cumulatively insecure. Having started out as a mama's boy, overloved, overprotected and overpraised, he was thoroughly unprepared for a world that did not view him in such a glow. In his youth he was keenly sensitive to the fact that the Johnsons were not among the lead families of the area. He was gawky and rough-hewn; for the most part, he was not too successful with the kind of girl he thought it important to be successful with. Maturing in the environment he did, it took him a long time to realize the high value of one resource he had in abundance, brains, and by then the asset was denigrated by the low status of his schooling (a social chasm existed between Southwest Texas State Teachers College and the University of Texas). And, almost as soon as his career was really under way, he had to function in large measure not amid the comforting ways of Texas but in the sharply different atmosphere of Washington.

After considerable and fascinated study of that special American genus, the Texan, I have come to the conclusion that products of the state generally take one of three marked attitudes toward this background. They honestly believe that Texas represents a civilization not hitherto approached by mortal man. They are ashamed of Texas—or of what many people think of it—and try every device to disassociate themselves from it. Or, taking delight and pride in some aspects of Texas life—and there is much to delight in and be proud of—yet sensitive to the attitude toward the state, they are the more belligerently Texan the more they try to escape their origin. Lyndon Johnson, as a secretary to a congressman or as President of the United States, was clearly of the third group and the fact did not add to the serenity with which he viewed people and policies.

Of course LBJ's genes dictated that he would have had many of his important personal characteristics if he were a graceful product of a wealthy Brahmin family. But a sense of insecurity was woven so thoroughly into the man by external circumstances that it brought to a high state of development his innate tendencies. Facing a world that he thought looked down on him, he sought constantly to prove, to himself and to it, that he could beat it. Dubious whether people liked him, he pleaded, clawed and maneuvered to have them love him. Desperately seeking the bolstering of loyalty—from friends, aides and the public—he pushed his demand for loyalty to the point where it meant obeisance. So anxious to hold on to the loyalty, he was ready to give anything— his own driving efforts, sentiment, preferment for their wishes— anything except what they wanted and what his lurking suspicion of them held back, the gift of his genuine self.

Always fighting off the devils of insecurity, Lyndon Johnson was vain, not proud; boomerish, not confident; for the most part, grandiose, not grand, in conceiving his programs, and grandiloquent, not eloquent, in expressing them. Gnawed by his inner needs, he turned his marriage with a woman he deeply loved into a near-tyranny; a congressional career shot through with instincts for the national good into a feral pursuit of personal domination; a Presidency marked by a broad streak of idealism into what so often appeared to be an exercise in self-interest.

Self-interest—here is the only-too-well-recognized part of the LBJ story. As a student of history, I have read a great deal about men in political or nonpolitical life who are said to have been motivated not by dedication to ideas, passion for ideals, emotional responses to human situations but merely by self-aggrandizement. I have never really believed the analyses. I think over the array of people I have known well, many of whom are not particularly noble, and they have never seemed totally dominated by self-interest. Neither was Lyndon Johnson—and perhaps Lyndon Johnson especially was not.

But President Johnson, lashed by his insecurity, fought his better angels harder than any man I have ever known. It was a hostile world out there, far removed from Mother and Texas and his trusted buddies; you had to keep handling it. Most of the time he appeared afraid to rely on anything except the doctrine that life and politics and government are simply a conflict and confluence between the self-interest of various people and groups. He seemed driven to function as Machiavelli in a Stetson, part of which posture was to keep assuring everyone that rugged he-men in Stetsons would never be Machiavellis. So lacking in confidence, so defensive and wary, those eyes always searching around the room or across the country, he was determined that nobody or no circumstance would get the better of him by playing to his strong personal ideals and emotions. This attitude led to increasing justification for, and ever more extended practice of, his natural bent toward exorbitant secretiveness, labyrinthine maneuverings, a sanctimonious glossing over of reality, the plain withholding of truth which had no need of being withheld and the plain distortion of truth which, at least in part, was much better stated and done with.

The American public delights in ferreting out the shortcomings of its Chief Executives. All the time the men were in the Oval Office, a nation of President-watchers knew that Franklin Roosevelt was an incorrigible political gamesman; that Harry Truman could sound like the village calliope; that Dwight Eisenhower often tried to grin away massive problems; that John Kennedy had some of the frailties as well as the assets of the charmer. But if the American public is endlessly critical, it has also shown itself remarkably indulgent, provided that the virtues of the President appear to outweigh his defects. In this balance, the critical weight is the judgment that at bottom the President is a "good man," fundamentally decent, putting the welfare of the nation first in all of his really important considerations. Most Americans have believed this to be true of every President from the thirties through 1963. It was Lyndon Johnson's basic difficulty that he did not leave such an impression.

His background of the Texas wheeler-dealers, his long years as a congressional manipulator and the association with Bobby Baker, his family's accumulation of considerable wealth based on a government-regulated television station, his very appearance and mannerisms which easily suggested the riverboat gambler— all had prepared the public for skepticism of his basic motives as soon as he entered the White House. After that nothing happened to change the attitude. Even the two achievements that President Johnson considered irreproachable brought him no surcease from suspicion.

He felt that he had incontestably established his right to the national leadership by his landslide victory in the election of 1964. Millions felt that he had incontestably established that he was ready to double-talk about anything, including taking the country into a major war, in order to protect votes. He believed that the great success of his legislative program after the election earned him the confidence and admiration of the nation. The great success of that drive was, among other things, his great undoing. It brought to full development that central irony of his career. The conspicuousness of his political skills, combined with the general impression left by the man, made more people more sure that he did everything only by political legerdemain and only for personal political advantage. It was within this context that the charge of credibility gap cut so deeply. Other modern Chief Executives—widely popular ones like Theodore and Franklin Roosevelt, Dwight Eisenhower and John Kennedy—had been known to play fast and loose with facts. President Johnson not only played faster and looser; he did it amid a widespread conviction that self-serving deceit was a part of his essential make-up.

This distrust militated powerfully against the whole presidential leadership of Lyndon Johnson. It went beyond stripping him of much of the credit for his domestic legislative achievements. With the credit blunted, it dulled public interest in helping him make the laws work. "Why don't people, especially young people," President Johnson complained, "really jump into the poverty program, roll up their sleeves and get it roaring, like we did back in the New Deal." None of the men in the room with the President had the heart to tell him.

In foreign policy, the pervasive suspicion meant that LBJ was given little benefit of the doubt. Worried citizens, facing World War I, World War II or the Korean War, were inclined to hesitate before opposing the President. He was a good man doing his best, with greater knowledge of the situation than themselves; the odds were that he was right. Few worried citizens hesitated to oppose Lyndon Johnson's Vietnam policy, and once in opposition, their attacks came with special virulence. During my White House period, I was naturally in communication with endless critics of the war. With a handful of exceptions, all assumed—usually having granted somewhat grudgingly that Lyndon Johnson really cared whether men were dying—that his moves for peace would be shaped by his reading of his own political interests.

The friend who had once said of President Johnson, "he's a sonofabitch, a great sonofabitch," got to talking about the President again near the end of the Administration. He repeated the phrase, then shook his head sadly. "And the funny thing is, it's never dawned on him that people don't like sonsofbitches even when they are great."

There was President Lyndon Johnson, the human being, and then there was President Lyndon Johnson, the maker of and symbol of certain national policies.

Those policies were coming from a man of exceedingly high intelligence. Many times when I have remarked this, during and after my White House days, people have looked at me as if I were a sycophant of the President or as if, during my association with him, I had taken leave of my good sense. Of course they were thinking of intelligence in terms of a well-educated mind or, I'm afraid, being stuffy and parochial and finding it impossible to associate brains with a man who looked like a polished cowboy and who drawled out so much buncombe and bawdiness. They were decidedly wrong. After years of meeting first-rate minds in and out of universities, I am sure I have never met a more intelligent person than Lyndon Johnson—intelligent in terms of sheer IQ, a clear, swift, penetrating mind, with an abundance of its own type of imagination and subtleties.

The point is that little had happened to fill or to stretch this mind. The high school Lyndon Johnson attended, Johnson City High School, was so bad it lacked accreditation even by the lax standards of its region. Southwest Texas State Teachers College taught a watery pedantry. Bright, restless students like young Johnson could only gravitate toward Professor H. M. Greene, a lovable maverick who, woefully unprepared for professing anything, at least had the instinct to get his students tangled in arguments on whatever subject matter was at hand and to live a laughing offbeat existence far from the campus as a quite conscious assertion that life ought to be lively.

Little in this education suggested to Lyndon Johnson that once out of college, he ought to read books, travel, seek out interesting minds, try to keep up with new trends, shake himself out of Johnson City and into the later twentieth century. Uncomfortable in the bigger world, engrossed in his political career, he had no personal urge to do these things. The powerful mind was feeding on small fare. The grown man came to the White House with a grab bag of facts and nonfacts, conceptions and misconceptions, ways of thinking and ways to avoid thought which had been gathered largely from his early crabbed environment.

During LBJ's Presidency discussions of his intellectual background, like those of his intelligence, frequently turned into sessions of hooting and sneering. No doubt the hoots and sneers served the purpose of self-congratulation for those who felt the need. More important was the fact that the inadequacies of the LBJ preparation hurt not only him but the American people during the long thirty years when he was becoming an increasingly potent force in determining what happened in the nation. The United States paid heavily for its failure to provide a genuine education—a rich body of facts, rigorous demands on the thinking process, a stimulus to mental adventuring after the school days were over—for one of its brightest students. I have found relatively little recognition amid the hooting and sneering that the same process goes on today, in schools often called good or better than good and yet just as inadequate in key respects for the needs of the 1960's and no doubt embracing some of the children of the hooters and sneerers themselves.

Be that as it may, it was President Johnson's severely limited preparation, compounded by his imperious, volcanic personality, which brought many of the most jarring moments of his White House. The President was not really a McCarthyite; he was much too clear-headed for that. But when senators presumed to give him a hard time about the Vietnam War, he angrily reached into the only intellectual stock he had, the folklore of his area, and hit them with its hoary doctrine of radical Easterners. He was not even really anti-intellectual. He was much too curious, and all the while he blasted intellectuals, he continued to look up to men of the books and kept trying to find ones who did not annoy him too much. Lyndon Johnson simply had no equipment which would permit him to understand intellectuals. One of his friends, discussing with me his anger against John Hersey at the time of the White House Festival of the Arts, remarked, "The President just doesn't get Hersey. In his picture of things, when a man does something, he does it for a practical purpose. Hersey is causing him trouble; therefore Hersey is doing it to hurt him politically and to sell his own books. Nobody ever introduced him to Hersey's world, where people do things just because they think they should do them."

Above all, it was the LBJ mental matrix which explains why, in his basic policy attitudes, he was a passé President all the while he crowded the daily television screens. A man out of the Jim Ferguson and Huey Long traditions, he was easily able to move into New Dealism and to take over much of the tone of the 1930's, but for the most part he stopped there. The United States did not stop at all. Nations change not at a steady pace but in slow swings or in rampant rushes, and America had been rampaging between the 1930's and the 1960's. The alterations were so swift and so deep that the country was changing right out from under President Lyndon Johnson.

Like a good 1930's man, he expressed his authentic thinking during the campaign of 1964 when he would shout, "Remember Molly and the children," or "We Americans don't want much. We want decent food, housing and clothing." In the 1960's there were still plenty of Mollys with plenty of troubles. But the essential mass problem had shifted; it was less food, housing and clothing than how to live with a weirdly uneasy general affluence—one that was marked by a maldistribution no longer accepted by a significant section of the population and by a race revolt that was only in part economic. Like FDR, President Johnson might think of domestic policy in terms of satisfying the needs of the grand political coalition which dominated the period before World War II—labor, the farmers, the cities, the minorities and the youthful voters. Now much of labor sounded like threatened burghers and the farm vote was disappearing into technology. The uplifted white minorities had been lifted to a condition where their concern was less social legislation than status trauma. The cities meant more and more the Negroes; the Negroes were wondering how much they wanted to do with any white leadership. The youthful, whether moving left, right or careering down the middle, were inclined to think of bread-and-butter liberalism as quaint if not downright camp.

Among all age groups, the idealism which had helped sweep along the FDR program, and which LBJ kept trying to touch, was turning to a far more demanding program. That talk of quality in American life, in addition to material quantity, had substance. The emerging reformism sought not simply better pay for teachers and more school buildings but a drastically altered educational atmosphere and curriculum; not simply Medicare for the grandparents but aid for the aged fitted into a whole social welfare structure that found a way of asserting human dignity. A new era, a new pattern of social and political forces, a new agenda— President Johnson, acting upon the kind of consensus domestic policy that would merely codify and expand the 1930's, was about as contemporary as padded shoulders, a night at the radio and Clark Gable.

Again in the mood of the New Deal period, the President assumed that foreign policy was something you had, like measles, and got over with as quickly as possible. Suddenly forced to confront the world, he grasped into the past and laid hold of an attic doctrine which included even apostrophes to the flag and international deeds of derring-do. At the farthest stretch of his modernity, he reached thinking that was basically of a Cold War type. In the 1960's, a considerable and influential part of the public simply would not go along with such foreign policy.

They assumed that international affairs were a constant high priority subject. Contemptuous of talk of the flag and derring-do, they were alarmed by what they were sure were outmoded Cold War attitudes of crusading against Communism and of joining with foreign regimes which sought to use military power to stop social change. Out of a sense of guilt over America's past role in world affairs, a sympathy with the aspirations of underdeveloped nations, and fear of nuclear holocaust, they favored accommodation, compromise, political and economic rather than military moves. A Chicago manufacturer caught perfectly the disjunction between President Johnson and this opinion when he wrote me: "The President may be right in going into Vietnam. I can't make up my mind. What really worries me is the kind of thinking that led to his decision." The letter added: "Perhaps it's because I am 37 and he is 57."

The Chicago manufacturer was a Metroamerican. Constantly growing in influence in determining national opinion, Metroamerica was increasingly the focal point of the abrasion between President Johnson and his public. There the uneasiness with him as a human being was greatest; the dissatisfaction with his domestic and foreign policies, the strongest. There, too, was the chief gathering place and the projectory for a disaffection that joined the criticisms of the man and of his programs and added a third—one concerning "style"—which really had little to do with the other two but increased the virulence of both of them.

Some of the attitudes and fashions of Metroamerica were hardly ennobling. They represented little more than the penny-ante snobbery of parochialism, like the Texas lady—I wish I could discover her name, she belongs in a history of the period—who listened to Lyndon Johnson deliver a speech shortly after he entered the White House and commented, "It's good to have a President who speaks without an accent." Many of Metroamerica's standards, parochial or not, were a good deal more praised than practiced. But attitudes and fashions Metroamerica had, and they were applied to Lyndon Johnson with all the rigidity and venom of any newly emerging class.

It is a truism to state that by the 1960's mass communications had largely obliterated local differences in the United States. The statement is fundamentally accurate but in one important respect it is off base. The Metroamerican—whether he lived in New York, Chicago, San Francisco or Houston—tended to take his style of life from the successful classes of the Northeast: to him, everything else was darkest boorishness. Lyndon Johnson used to say in the Senate days, "No Southerner can be elected President." He would have been right if he had said, No Southerner, and particularly no middle-aged Texan from a middle-class background, could win the Presidency in the 1960's and maintain peace with Metroamerica. Mention almost any of the personal habits of Lyndon Johnson—the big white Continental or the sentimentalities—and you bring up something that made Metroamerica snicker.

And always there remained the Kennedys. After his election victory in 1964, President Johnson may have eliminated virtually all references to President Kennedy in his public remarks. He could not eliminate the fact that his predecessor was legend and that the legend was a restive, bitter, yearning element in the whole life of the generation, especially in Metroamerica. Lyndon Johnson had become President by virtue of the death of John Kennedy, and that death continued a major determinant of his Presidency. Not only had the urge to be different from JFK affected what LBJ did and did not do day after day; every difficulty of President Johnson with public opinion was magnified by the Kennedy legend, which made John Kennedy precisely the opposite of all the things that Americans, and especially Metroamericans, thought were wrong with Lyndon Johnson. And throughout the Johnson Administration the JFK legend gradually, but more and more completely, blended with the day-by-day activities of Senator Robert F. Kennedy.

Everything LBJ did, everywhere he turned, there was RFK, pointing up another element in President Johnson's problem with his public. Robert Kennedy was the looks, the voice, the long stabbing finger of the martyred President. He was youthfulness, the North, celebrities, the new-mode family, Hickory Hill always full of interesting people, canoeing into high rapids and then sitting quoting Aeschylus, the Metroamerican's unabashed ambition and the Metroamerican's savor for the throw-away manner. He was post-New Deal politics, talking the quality of American civilization, moving increasingly toward outright opposition to the Vietnam War, centering his domestic legislative program on the cities, probing for a voting coalition based not on the old economic lines but on the new sense of alienation bringing together Negroes, young people, intellectuals and suburbanites who had acquired money at the price of malaise.

Nine weeks after President Johnson's speech of withdrawal, on the night Senator Kennedy scored an important win in his long-shot campaign for the Democratic presidential nomination, more crazed bullets had been fired in Los Angeles. An RFK legend had immediately started forming, an idealization of the younger brother that joined perfectly with the JFK legend. Robert Kennedy, so many were so sure, would certainly have been elected President, ended the war, lifted the Negro, given purpose to youth and to suburbia, brought about an America cleansed and reinvigorated.

The Johnson years were clamped in grim parenthesis of happenstance. Lyndon Johnson came into the White House to the caissons for John Kennedy and he left it to the dirges for Robert Kennedy. He entered and he departed with a Kennedy uppermost in the national thinking and emotions, and perhaps he had not been much elsewhere during his five years in the White House.

In the final months of his Presidency, Lyndon Johnson kept shifting in mood. At times he was bitter and petulant at his repudiation by the nation; at times philosophical, almost serene, confidently awaiting the verdict of the future.

Never was he the mere lame duck. Still stalking, endlessly stalking the Oval Office, he kept doing things, seeking to shore up his domestic achievements and to bring his foreign policy one step further along what he considered a proper path. Strange, complex man in strange, complex circumstances—too astute not to know how seriously things had gone wrong, too limited by background and by self to grasp what had really happened.

No one who worked in Lyndon Johnson's White House can fail to have been moved by the dedication, the abilities and the force he brought to the Presidency of the United States. It was just as difficult not to recall the lines from one of his copybook poems, John Greenleaf Whittier's *Maud Muller:* "For of all sad words of tongue or pen, The saddest are these: 'It might have been!'" The story of Lyndon Johnson's Presidency is a story of tragedy in the ancient haunting sense of the word, the strong man overwhelmed by forces, from within and without.

Hurtled into the leadership of the United States and of the free world in the fiercely demanding 1960's, he was not ready for them. Seriously flawed in personal characteristics, his virtues could not transform him into an engaging public figure. Functioning in the shadow of a relentless legend, he was beset by a host of attitudes which that legend continuously fed.

Lyndon Johnson could win votes, enact laws, maneuver mountains. He could not acquire that something beyond, which cannot be won, enacted or maneuvered but must be freely given. He could not command that respect, affection and rapport which alone permit an American President genuinely to lead. In his periods of triumph and of downsweep, in peace as in war, he stood the tragic figure of an extraordinarily gifted President who was the wrong man from the wrong place at the wrong time under the wrong circumstances.

ACKNOWLEDGMENTS

I would like to express my appreciation to the following for permission to quote from various types of unpublished material written by them: Bruce Catton; David Donald; Robert L. Heilbroner; John Hersey; Edwin H. Land; Elaine A. Leachman; Jack Levine; Robert Lowell; Dwight Macdonald; Donald A. MacGillis; Phyllis McGinley; Lewis Mumford; Norman Podhoretz; David Riesman; Clinton Rossiter; Richard H. Rovere; Francis B. Sayre, Jr.; William G. Sinkford; Barbara W. Tuchman; and Mark Van Doren.

INDEX

A NOTE ABOUT THE AUTHOR

Eric F. Goldman was born in Washington, D.C., in 1915. He was educated in the public schools of Baltimore and at the Johns Hopkins University, from which he received his Ph.D. in history in 1938.

He has taught at Princeton since 1940 and in 1962 was named Rollins Professor of History. The same year, he was also named McCosh Fellow, the highest scholarly award which Princeton confers on a faculty member, and was elected President of the Society of American Historians, an office which he continues to hold. He is especially known for his books on twentieth century American history. *Rendezvous with Destiny: A History of Modern American Reform,* for which he received the Bancroft Prize "for distinguished writing in American history" in 1953, and *The Crucial Decade, America 1945–1955* which was published in 1956 are now both standard works and are widely read in American universities.

From December 1963 until September 1966 Mr. Goldman served as Special Consultant to the President of the United States.

A NOTE ON THE TYPE

The text of this book was set in a typeface called Primer, designed by Rudolph Ruzicka for the Mergenthaler Linotype Company and first made available in 1949. Primer, a modified modern face based on Century broadface, has the virtue of great legibility and was designed especially for today's methods of composition and printing.

Primer is Ruzicka's third typeface. In 1940 he designed Fairfield, and in 1947 Fairfield Medium, both for the Mergenthaler Linotype Company.

Ruzicka was born in Bohemia in 1883 and came to the United States at the age of eleven. He attended public schools in Chicago and later the Chicago Art Institute. During his long career he has been a wood engraver, etcher, cartographer, and book designer. For many years he was associated with Daniel Berkeley Updike and produced the annual keepsakes for The Merrymount Press from 1911 until 1941.

Ruzicka has been honored by many distinguished organizations, and in 1936 he was awarded the gold medal of the American Institute of Graphic Arts. From his home in New Hampshire, Ruzicka continues to be active in the graphic arts.

Composed by Brown Bros. Linotypers, Inc., New York. Printed and bound by The Haddon Craftsmen, Scranton, Pennsylvania.